D1757338

13 MAY 2025

York St John

3 8025 00549262 7

JEWISH THOUGHT
IN DIALOGUE

JUDAISM AND JEWISH LIFE

EDITORIAL BOARD

Geoffrey Alderman (University of Buckingham, Great Britain)
Herbert Basser (Queens University, Canada)
Donatella Ester Di Cesare (Università "La Sapienza," Italy)
Simcha Fishbane (Touro College, New York), Series Editor
Meir Bar Ilan (Bar Ilan University, Israel)
Andreas Nachama (Touro College, Berlin)
Ira Robinson (Concordia University, Montreal)
Nissan Rubin (Bar Ilan University, Israel)
Susan Starr Sered (Suffolk University, Boston)
Reeva Spector Simon (Yeshiva University, New York)

ACADEMIC
STUDIES
PRESS

JEWISH THOUGHT
IN DIALOGUE

Essays on Thinkers, Theologies,
and Moral Theories

DAVID SHATZ

Boston
2009

Library of Congress Cataloging-in-Publication Data

Shatz, David.
    Jewish thought in dialogue : essays on thinkers, theologies, and moral theories /
David Shatz.
        p. cm.
    Includes bibliographical references and index.
    ISBN 978-1-934843-42-0 (hardback)
        1. Jewish philosophy. 2. Jewish law. 3. Jewish ethics. 4. Rabbinical literature —
History and criticism. 5. Bible. O.T. — Criticism, interpretation, etc. 6. Maimonides,
Moses, 1135-1204. 7. Kook, Abraham Isaac, 1865-1935. 8. Soloveitchik, Joseph Dov.
9. Hartman, David. 10. Wurzburger, Walter S. I. Title.
    B755.S457 2009
    181'.06 — dc22
                2009047846

Copyright © 2009 Academic Studies Press
All rights reserved

ISBN 978-1-934843-42-0 (hardback)

Book design by Ivan Grave

On the cover: *Der Samstag (Saturday)*. Germany, c. 1800.
Handcolored engraving. Hebrew Union College, Skirball Museum, Los Angeles.
Based on a painting by Frederich Campe (a fragment).

Published by Academic Studies Press in 2009
28 Montfern Avenue
Brighton, MA 02135, USA
press@academicstudiespress.com
www.academicstudiespress.com

In loving memory of my parents
Meyer and Lillian Shatz
and my in-laws
Rabbi Baruch Meir and Tova Rabinowitz

תהיינה נשמותיהם צרורות בצרור החיים

SOURCES AND CREDITS

"The Bible As a Source of Philosophical Reflection" was originally published in *The Routledge History of Jewish Philosophy,* ed. Daniel Frank and Oliver Leaman (New York and London: Routledge, 1997).

"Maimonides' Moral Theory" was originally published in *The Cambridge Companion to Maimonides,* ed. Kenneth Seeskin (New York: Cambridge University Press, 2005).

"Worship, Corporeality and Human Perfection," was originally published in *The Thought of Moses Maimonides,* ed. Ira Robinson et. al (Lewiston/Queenston/Lampeter: Edwin Mellen Press, 1990). Reprinted by permission of the publisher.

"The Integration of Torah and Culture: Its Scope and Limits in The Thought of Rav Kook," originally appeared in *Hazon Nahum: Studies in Jewish Law, Thought and History Presented to Dr. Norman Lamm on the Occasion of his Seventieth Birthday,* ed. Yaakov Elman and Jeffrey Gurock (New York: The Michael Scharf Publication Trust of the Yeshiva University Press, 1997). Reprinted by permission of the publisher.

"Is Rav Kook A Model of 'Openness'?" was originally published under a different title in *Engaging Modernity,* ed. Moshe Sokol (Lanham, MD: Jason Aronson, an imprint of Rowman & Littlefield, 1997). Reprinted by permission of Rowman & Littlefield.

"Science and Religious Consciousness in the Thought of Rabbi Joseph B. Soloveitchik" was originally published in Hebrew in *Emunah bi-Zemannim Nishtannim,* ed. Avi Sagi (Jerusalem: World Zionist Organization, Department for Torah Education and Culture, 1996). The final section is an abridged version of "The Rav and Torah u-Madda," in *Mentor of Generations: Reflections on Rabbi Joseph B. Soloveitchik,* ed. Zev Eleff (Jersey City, NJ: Ktav Publishing, 2008).

"Divine Intervention and Religious Sensibilities" was originally published in *Divine Intervention and Miracles in Jewish Theology*, ed. Dan Cohn-Sherbok (Lewiston/Queenston/Lampeter: Edwin Mellen Press, 1990). Reprinted by permission of the publisher.

"From Anthropology to Metaphysics" was originally published in *Judaism and Modernity: The Religious Philosophy of David Hartman*, ed. Jonathan W. Malino (Burlington, VT and Hampshire, England: Ashgate, 2004). Reprinted by permission of Jonathan W. Malino.

"Is Matter All That Matters? Judaism, Free Will, and the Genetic and Neuroscientific Revolutions" was originally published in *Judaism, Science and Moral Responsibility*, ed. Yitzhak Berger and David Shatz (Rowman & Littlefield, 2006). Reprinted by permission of the publisher.

"'From the Depths I Have Called to You': Jewish Reflections on September 11th and Contemporary Terrorism" was originally published as a monograph by Yeshiva University in 2002.

"Does Jewish Law Express Jewish Theology?: The Curious Case of Theodicies" is published here for the first time. It is an abridged version of a paper to be published in a forthcoming Festschrift for Saul Berman, *Misphetei Shalom,* ed. Yamin Levy (Ktav Publishing Co.)

"Beyond Obedience: The Ethical Theory of Rabbi Walter Wurzburger," was originally published in *Tradition* (1996). Reprinted by permission of The Rabbinical Council of America.

"As Thyself": The Limits of Altruism in Jewish Ethics" was originally published in *Reverence, Righteousness and Rahamanut: Essays in Memory of Rabbi Dr. Leo Jung*, ed. Jacob J. Schacter (Jason Aronson, an imprint of Rowman & Littlefield), 1992. Reprinted by permission of the publisher.

"Concepts of Autonomy in Jewish Medical Ethics" was originally published in *Jewish Law Annual* 12 (1997). Reprinted by permission of The Institute for Jewish Law at Boston University School of Law.

"The Overexamined Life is Not Worth Living" appeared in *God and the Philosophers: The Reconciliation of Faith and Reason*, ed. Thomas V. Morris (New York: Oxford University Press, 1994). Reprinted by permission of the publisher.

CONTENTS

Introduction xi

ESSAYS IN INTERPRETATION
  The Bible as a Source for Philosophical Reflection 3
  Maimonides' Moral Theory 27
  Worship, Corporeality, and Human Perfection:
    A Reading of *Guide of the Perplexed*, III: 51-54 50
  The Integration of Torah and Culture: Its Scope and Limits
    in the Thought of Rav Kook 93
  Rabbi Abraham Isaac Kook and the Ambiguities of "Openness" 118
  Science and Religious Consciousness in the Thought of Rabbi
    Joseph B. Soloveitchik 138

THEOLOGY, METAPHYSICS AND ETHICS
  Divine Intervention and Religious Sensibilities 179
  From Anthropology to Metaphysics: David Hartman
    on Divine Intervention 209
  Is Matter All That Matters? Judaism, Free Will, and the Genetic
    and Neuroscientific Revolutions 224
  "From The Depths I Have Called To You": Jewish Reflections
    on September 11th and Contemporary Terrorism 257
  Does Jewish Law Express Jewish Philosophy?
    The Curious Case of Theodicies 291
  Beyond Obedience: The Ethical Theory of Rabbi
    Walter Wurzburger 305
  "As Thyself": The Limits of Altruism in Jewish Ethics 326
  Concepts of Autonomy in Jewish Medical Ethics 355

CONCLUDING REFLECTIONS ON RELIGIOUS BELIEF
  The Overexamined Life Is Not Worth Living 387

Index of Biblical and Rabbinic Sources 413
Index of Topics and Names 424

INTRODUCTION

The first time that I delivered a public lecture, I was asked to speak on the topic, "Maimonides: His Life and Thought." A postcard went out to announce the talk, but there was a slight error on the postcard — one word was left out. And so what the card said was, "Dr. David Shatz will speak on His Life and Thought."

This introduction aims to give the speech I didn't give then — more accurately, to convey enough of "my life and thought" so that readers can understand the objectives and orientation of this volume.

––––––––––––

The essays collected here give expression to my long-standing interest in the interaction between Judaism and general culture. A special passion of mine is the relationship between Jewish religious thought, on the one hand, and non-Jewish philosophies of both religious and secular varieties, on the other.[1]

Like the publishing careers of a few other scholars who work in Jewish philosophy, mine has gone through two phases.[2] In the first I devoted my writing to "analytic" philosophy — the dominant Anglo-American mode of philosophizing — where my focus was free will, theory of knowledge, ethics, and philosophy of religion. I pursued these topics with the vocabulary, methods and assumptions of the analytic approach, and with only occasional examinations of historically important figures. In the second phase, represented in these pages, I have published mainly on Jewish thought. I have explored how various Jewish philosophers approached the relationship between Judaism and general culture. And I have aggressively sought to create what today are widely called "conversations" between Judaism and general philosophy, as well as to reflect on conversations of this sort that others have conducted in the past, with stress on theology, science, and ethics. I am of course anything but unique among academics in approaching Jewish philosophy with general philosophy in the background or foreground. Who in academic Jewish philosophy nowadays does not work that way? But my specialization in analytic philosophy may in some places give a distinctive cast to the literature cited, the problems engaged, and the style of argumentation.

However, the book's title, *Jewish Thought in Dialogue*, refers not only to a dialogue between philosophical systems, but also to a dialogue between philosophy (both Jewish and general) and Jewish *law*. Does Jewish law (Halakhah) express a Jewish philosophy? Can our understanding of Halakhah be enhanced by knowing secular ethics, secular law and legal theory? Generally speaking, I submit that the answer to these questions is yes, and a few of the essays deal with issues in this range.[3] Taken together, then, the essays attempt to conduct a three-way discussion between Jewish philosophy, general philosophy, and Jewish law, with different essays involving different participants.

The essays probably make evident that I have grappled largely but not exclusively with Orthodox Jewish thought. Orthodoxy's confrontation with the modern world is especially complex and challenging since the very legitimacy of studying "external" disciplines has been fiercely debated throughout Jewish history.[4] Those in the "ultra-Orthodox" or *haredi* world deny any inherent value to "external" culture, even though many of them believe that Jewish law permits them to pursue secular education for reasons of economic necessity.[5] It is no wonder that historians and sociologists have lavished so much attention on how Orthodoxy engages the modern world. Needless to say, my own perspective is that traditional Jewish self-understanding may be deepened by engaging the surrounding culture. Philosophy provides ideas and categories for rearticulating traditional ideas, such as free will, God's relationship to the world, ethics and theodicy. Such integration can and often does produce intellectual edification and spiritual enrichment. The street is not one-way: Jewish tradition offers to its interlocutors insights into shared questions, though not always identical answers.

Before describing the essays, I offer some words about several distinctions that scholars often make: between "studying" philosophy and "doing" philosophy; between "philosophers" and "thinkers"; and between "philosophers of religion" and "theologians." I believe that these distinctions are tenuous and only mildly helpful in principle, and of diminishing importance sociologically.

First, studying vs. doing. When one studies philosophy, he or she interprets and tries to understand the ideas of others, perhaps (but not necessarily) situating them within a social, historical or biographical context: tracing influences that shaped them, locating views they were combatting, and exploring the ideas' impact on contemporaries or later thinkers. When one *does* philosophy, one *evaluates* the ideas one has studied, seeking to determine their truth or plausibility, and/or tries to fashion one's own position. Thus, for a "doer" the question would be not "What is Gersonides' view?" but "Is Gersonides right?" or "What is the most plausible view of this topic, a topic which happens to have been discussed by Gersonides?"

At times, there have been tensions between those who steep themselves in the history of Jewish philosophy and those who seek to develop original Jewish philosophical ideas.[6] The former might consider the latter ignorant and anachronistic, projecting current problems and solutions onto thinkers from a past universe; while the latter may find the former's historical excavations unhelpful, even pointless, in terms of developing Jewish thought into a living, breathing enterprise that speaks to the contemporary world.[7]

To be sure, this book gestures toward the studying/doing distinction. I dedicate the first section to interpreting texts and thinkers, and the second to assessing and presenting theories. Yet the distinction between studying and doing is not hard and fast. To arrive at a sound interpretation of an author's writings, it is often helpful to reconstruct that author's ideas using what philosophers call "interpretive charity." One construes the ideas in a way that makes them, at least initially, as plausible as possible, and often this will generate compelling conclusions. Interpreting in that way obviously requires assessing positions, a form of "doing." [8] And of course one can scarcely form one's own positions living as an intellectual Robinson Crusoe, sundered from what others have thought. Also, sometimes assessing a single thinker (as I do in two essays in the second half of the book) opens up key issues for those trying to articulate their own ideas. In fact, important contributions to contemporary issues facing Judaism — that is, good samples of "doing" — emanate from scholars whose starting point is interpreting certain thinkers by close attention to texts, sometimes tracing influences, sometimes not.[9]

There is good evidence that old antagonisms between studying and doing have died down, and also that the division is not firm sociologically. Jewish studies departments nowadays include both historically oriented scholars and thinkers seeking to develop their own philosophies, and the groups work cooperatively. More important, many scholars pursue both endeavors. The Academy for Jewish Philosophy, which was founded in the late 1970s so that "individuals actively involved in some form of Jewish religious life who have professional training in philosophy" could "think about contemporary Jewish faith in new ways," has produced a series of stimulating books that illustrate the possibility of using the history of philosophy and the study of contemporary thinkers to fashion understandings of Judaism that speak to modern problems.[10] Many volumes of the Orthodox Forum series also illustrate how fluid the categories of studying and doing are.[11] The weakening of the barrier between studying and doing among specialists in Jewish philosophy reflects a trend in departments of general philosophy. Well known philosophers who engage in "doing" grapple with their discipline's history and see how it can service their present needs without imputing anachronisms. Philosophers who specialize in the history of philosophy frequently link their studies to contemporary problems, albeit some of those problems are of interest only to philosophers.

The second putative dichotomy I mentioned is that between "thinkers" and "philosophers." For those who endorse this distinction, the latter is a badge of honor, a laurel or credential conferred upon those who show a proper level of familiarity with certain vocabularies and methods, or with philosophers who are not "Jewish philosophers." Often, therefore, someone will ask about so-and-so, "Is he/she a *real* philosopher?" But as I see it, the distinction is not of much use, or at least is overrated as a tool for determining who is worth studying. William James defined philosophy as "an unusually stubborn attempt to think things through." As a corollary, I submit that philosophy is not the exclusive province of those who meet the alleged criteria for "philosophers." Plenty of intellectually formidable people have reasoned well about deep problems of existence, including not only individuals who lack academic training but even some who would fiercely resist being labeled philosophers. Mark Steiner, a leading specialist in the philosophy of mathematics and the philosophy of science, and hence someone who unimpeachably is a philosopher by the standard definition, has argued, for example, that Rabbi Israel Salanter, founder of the nineteenth century Musar movement, who styled himself an opponent of philosophy, offers original, cogent contributions to conundra like the explanation of akrasia (weakness of will) and paradoxes involving humility. As Steiner puts it: "[T]o find instances of Jewish philosophy... one must be able to identify philosophical issues and arguments, even if they are labeled as something else entirely, or are subsidiary to some other project."[12] Even the position that philosophy is useless is a philosophical position. In deference to the popularity of the distinction between thinkers and philosophers and to the recognition that a distinction exists even if it is of fairly little significance, I use the term "Jewish thought" in the title of the book. But figures like Nahmanides, or Rabbis Abraham Isaac Kook and Eliyahu Dessler, who ordinarily would not be labeled "philosophers," are in my estimation doing philosophy. Whether the Kabbalistic aspects of R. Kook, which are quite salient, qualify as philosophy is more debatable, but I am willing to say they do. For otherwise Plotinus and Solomon ibn Gabirol were not philosophers. I know that advocates of the philosopher/thinker distinction might warmly embrace that conclusion, but how could asserting what the cosmos is like, teaching an ethic, and making claims about the nature of human beings, not count as philosophy? Some might prefer to study philosophers as opposed to thinkers because they believe, by inductive reasoning from past encounters with philosophers and thinkers, that philosophers are more likely to have insightful ideas. But such a preference , however well or poorly grounded, should not dictate exclusion of "thinkers." Furthermore, sometimes knowing what is wrong with a certain "thinker's" view will facilitate setting up a strong alternative.

Finally, to some scholars "philosophy of religion" and "theology" are antonyms. Those who are commonly called theologians generally operate within the idiom, assumptions and methods of Continental philosophy and often dismiss analytic philosophy as arid and pointless. Returning the favor, analytic philosophers of religion often complain that "theologians" write unintelligibly, supply no arguments, or reason carelessly. This is not the place to discuss the divide in any detail, but I think that the old stereotypes are largely unfair, and that sociologically the divide is smaller than it once was. A significant number of scholars are versed in both Continental and analytic modes of thought.[13]

Armed with the foregoing discussion, I would describe this book as follows. It aims at both studying (interpreting) for the sake of "doing" and doing for the sake of interpreting. I consider figures who by the definition cited earlier are thinkers rather than philosophers, as well as, of course, those who are philosophers by that definition. And my use of general philosophy involves analytic philosophy, even while I recognize that a Continental perspective would enrich and widen certain of the discussions.

I open this collection with "The Bible As a Source of Philosophical Reflection," an essay that I authored with Shalom Carmy. The Bible is not composed as a philosophical book, and its narratives seem generally more interested in psychology, characters, and moral lessons than philosophical perplexities. Furthermore, medieval attempts to read the Bible as primarily a work of philosophy proved futile and misguided. Even so, the narratives, when understood a certain way, not only pose philosophical questions but take positions of interest to philosophers of religion. Among the sample questions we address are whether morality is independent of the divine will, why God allows evil, and how divine plans for history may be assured of realization if free human choices shape the course of events. At the same time, we note that certain conundra that have engaged philosophers are of no interest to the Bible — for example, how divine foreknowledge (as distinct from divine planning) can be reconciled with human free will, and, more significantly, that the Bible's value system as expressed in narratives may contradict that of many philosophers who later grappled with those narratives. For instance they differ about the value of free will. The essay questions certain classic textual supports for particular philosophical positions. Thus the essay disputes Kierkegaard's famous reading of the *akedah* narrative in Gen. 22, and suggests that the stories of Adam's and Cain's sins, as well as the entire book of Genesis, are at least equally good places to look for biblical insight into the relationship between morality and religion. Our observations about continuities and ruptures between the biblical text and later readings of it leave us with questions about the continuity of Jewish thought and the place of the Bible within it. Recent scholarly works, I now note, have brought the topic of Bible and philosophy into increased prominence.[14]

The next two essays move to Maimonides, who always has been and always will be the showcase example of a figure who grapples with tensions between biblical and rabbinic tradition and ideas derived from non-Jewish philosophers. "Maimonides' Moral Theory" analyzes in a synthetic and expository form how Maimonides negotiates between Aristotle's doctrine of the mean and the requirements of Jewish law (which are far more stringent than Aristotle's teachings). It also seeks to determine the places of moral perfection and political leadership in Maimonides' axiology. My next essay addresses several controversial issues in Maimonidean thought by examining a neglected literary peculiarity in the *Guide of the Perplexed*. Maimonides, I argue, jumbled the sequence of his final chapters. Why did he do this? My suggestion is that in these chapters Maimonides might be presenting opposite answers to a question about human corporeality and human potential because he was unsure about which answer is correct. (Understanding how this solves the literary perplexity requires reading the essay.) The article tries to show how this ambiguity about human potential affects the question of whether the philosopher who has attained intellectual perfection must obey the law, i. e. perform the commandments. Overall I seek to "stimulate a reorientation of perspective and emphasis" and create a "new agenda" as regards the key questions we must ask about Maimonides' accounts of the commandments and of human perfection. I am gratified that recent writings by Marvin Fox, Yair Lorberbaum and Kenneth Seeskin support my suggestion that in the case of certain abstruse, rationally irresolvable issues, Maimonides posited competing possibilities without deciding between them. According to Fox, Lorberbaum and Seeskin, this explanation in terms of uncertainty can account for the notorious deliberate contradictions within the work.[15]

I turn next to two towering rabbinic figures of the twentieth century: R. [=Rabbi] Abraham Isaac Kook and R. Joseph B. Soloveitchik. In particular, I focus on their attitudes to general culture, and to an extent modernity itself. Both were major halakhic authorities; both valued general culture and aspects of modernity; and both have attracted the attention of academic scholars, especially in the past two decades. But both challenge interpreters because of ambivalence and tension found in their writings. The interpreter needs both an understanding of why each thinker valued modernity and general culture, and an understanding of the limits that they themselves imposed, explicitly or implicitly.

R. Kook, on the one hand, extols in the loftiest of terms exposure to all forms of culture, and in terms of scope his endorsement goes much beyond the medieval rationalist stress on the religious value of science and philosophy. Yet in some contexts he downgrades secular disciplines. Like other mystical thinkers, he emphasizes an innate religious knowledge, and while he sometimes says that this innate cognition is refined by culture, at other times the cognition appears to stand over against secular disciplines. Perhaps more strikingly and curiously, in some contexts he dismisses claims of modern science. I explain this resistance, ironically, by his embrace of a philosophical viewpoint that was influential in the surrounding culture, namely, nineteenth century progressivism. The idea that truth unfolds gradually (if it is ever fully revealed at all) generates a fallibilist epistemology that diminishes the value of scientific claims at a given time.[16] I also address R. Kook's personal failure to pursue secular studies, arguing that he valued grasping the big picture — the spiritual import of particular philosophies — but devalued details. In addition, he thought that different people may take on different roles in Jewish society. Since the time the essay first appeared, the original manuscripts of R. Kook have been published with the title *Shemonah Kevatzim* (1999). The significance of *Shemonah Kevatzim* for our topic is described briefly in a postscript.[17]

Both R. Kook and R. Soloveitchik are often held up as paradigms for Modern Orthodoxy. In a second essay on R. Kook I explore the extent to which he can properly serve as such a paradigm.[18] Scholars and apologists alike tend to determine a thinker's openness by invoking bottom lines — what did the thinker endorse and reject. I argue that often, when R. Kook arrives at "modern" conclusions, it is by route of un-modern premises, and that un-modern conclusions may flow from "modern" assumptions. This is one of several complexities I discuss about the concept of "openness." The essay has sociological implications for scholars who study the Modern Orthodox community, in particular its recruitment of particular sages as precedents for its outlook. The article raises as well issues about what makes someone an ideological forebear of a movement.

The essay on R. Soloveitchik similarly locates a complicated attitude toward general culture. R. Soloveitchik not only cited science, literature and non-Jewish philosophy extensively, but he adapted ideas from Christian thinkers like Søren Kierkegaard, Max Scheler, and Emil Brunner. In doing so he acted against family tradition and against the position of the vast majority of talmudic giants of the modern period. Yet he supplies no apology or justification.[19] Nowhere in the numerous typologies that fill his writings do we find a type that is exactly what he was.

My essay focuses on science, more precisely how R. Soloveitchik viewed the relationship between scientific study and the religious consciousness of halakhically committed personalities. His first major work, *Halakhic Man* (1944) seems to preclude finding a place for science in the life of the author's halakhic hero.[20] He interprets Maimonides — the prime advocate of using science to advance religious ends — in a way that greatly diminishes the religious role of science in Maimonides' thought.[21] I explain these tendencies in terms of Rabbi Soloveitchik's polemical objectives in the work. A later major work, *U-vikkashtem mi-Sham* (drafted in the late 1940s, but published in 1979), views science as a component of halakhic life. However, R. Soloveitchik there largely ignores two obstacles to integrating science into religious life, obstacles that were placed in his path by a shift from Aristotelian to modern science that he himself elsewhere identifies. One obstacle is the banishment of teleology from science. The other is Kant's positing a barrier between cognizer and the cognized. I consider these problems, and also address R. Soloveitchik's tendency, pointedly noted by Aviezer Ravitzky, to take motifs that Maimonides invokes in discussing the significance of science and transfer them to the study of Halakhah. I suggest an alternative to Ravitzky's explanation of this phenomenon.

In the next part of the essay, I argue that in his 1965 classic, *The Lonely Man of Faith*, R. Soloveitchik celebrates an entirely different aspect of science. He views the scientific enterprise in pragmatic terms and finds in it a new sort of religious significance. Science, along with economics, politics and other cultural activities promote human dignity and responsibility,[22] realize human nature, and better the human condition. I speculate on motivations for the shift just described from the theoretical to the pragmatic aspects of science.

At the very end of the essay, I address the question mentioned earlier — why R. Soloveitchik valued study of the humanities, despite frequent Orthodox opposition to such studies. I offer five possible reasons. Among them is that R. Soloveitchik thought that no justification is required for the study of philosophy and literature, because any resources that could clarify the philosophical and spiritual import of Torah, especially as regards the human condition, are of value. Also, R. Soloveitchik regarded the Jew as belonging to two communities and having two identities — a Jewish one, and a larger human one. Understanding the Jewish religious personality requires understanding the universal religious personality.

From these six interpretive pieces I move to critical and constructive articles that explore issues in metaphysics, theology, religious anthropology, and ethics.

Ever since Immanuel Kant sounded the death knell, or alleged death knell, of metaphysics, many philosophers have shared his despair. Turning away from metaphysics, they focus their energies on phenomenology, that is, descriptions of religious consciousness; on the development of religious anthropologies, that is, religious theories of the human being; and on the study of religious practice. Many philosophers today, some specializing in Continental philosophy and others in analytic philosophy, seek ways of understanding traditional statements about God in a non-metaphysical (or "non-realist") fashion.[23] At the same time, some who focus on phenomenology, anthropology and practice continue to speak of God as a real being, and they provide an interesting focus for reflection on religious values and religious metaphysics. Of particular interest is that some choose a metaphysical outlook by deciding which one would support or encourage their favored anthropology. So, for example, Rav Kook argued that someone who adopts a theistic theology (in which God is separate from the world) becomes depressed and jealous of God; on this score, Rav Kook prefers a pantheistic view, which gladdens the heart.[24]

Two essays explore such attempts to link anthropology to metaphysics, this by considering the question of divine intervention. "Divine Intervention and Religious Sensibilities" considers first the doctrine of occasionalism, the extreme interventionist view that God directly causes everything because only God has causal powers. Occasionalism grows out of the conviction that to attribute causal powers to anything but God is pagan, and it seeks to create a consciousness of that proposed truth. However, I argue that occasionalism — surprisingly — comes at a religious cost. *Inter alia*, it makes belief in free will difficult, exacerbates the problem of evil, and undermines interpersonal obligations.

Hard naturalism, the antithesis of occasionalism, explains all events without invoking divine intervention. For the hard naturalist, there are no miracles. Hard naturalism seeks to create a conviction that events lie in human hands, and it values self-reliance and human initiative. It deprecates, as unhealthy, feelings of dependence and helplessness that it finds in interventionist views. In this way, hard naturalism enhances the prospects of coping theologically with secularization, this by embracing the values of autonomy, independence and self-reliance that power technological advance. Some link these values to human responsibility, for without a stable natural order human beings cannot choose responsibly. Hard naturalists often declare that to free people from dependence on God is also to free them of self-centeredness.

I argue, however, that (a) even robustly interventionist views promote initiative and a sense of control over events, since on robustly interventionist views a person can control his or her welfare through prayer and good deeds; (b) hard naturalism does not dispel self-interest; (c) with regard to religious anthropology, soft naturalist views — views that allow for some divine intervention and miracles within a predominantly naturalist scheme — are as good as hard naturalist ones. At the end of the essay I claim that arguments from anthropology to metaphysics, like the ones explored in this essay, are non *sequiturs*. *Inter alia*, by focusing only on human attitudes they ignore considerations based on divine goodness and justice. Ultimately I declare that only a return to old-style metaphysical argument, based on empirical and philosophical considerations, combined with an appeal to traditional texts, can establish a proper religious metaphysics. Many will view the prospects for arriving at a conclusion dim and the enterprise futile. Others will flatly deny that there are any entities that are not physical. But it should be noted that Christian analytic philosophers have invested enormous energies in time-honored metaphysical questions.

The well-known Israel-based philosopher David Hartman devotes much attention to developing an anthropology based on human adequacy, control and initiative. I discuss his views in the next essay. Contrary to a popular impression, Hartman does not deny divine intervention; rather, he brackets metaphysical questions. His goal is to describe relationships with God that are predicated on the irrelevance of self-centered concerns. He does not declare that an interventionist metaphysics is false, but prefers a naturalist position because emphasizing divine intervention does not promote desirable character traits. Against this, I note that certain undesirable traits can also result from bracketing metaphysics, for example, ingratitude to God or lack of trust. I also note that Freud sees belief in an intervening God as, *pace* Hartman, empowering, and finally I point out that, as an empirical matter, people with an interventionist outlook, far from being centered on themselves, are at the forefront of altruistic social services. Hartman, I say, incorrectly extrapolates from the political quietism that interventionism encourages as regards the creation of a Jewish state, to a general quietism, and he overlooks how an interventionist framework can actually promote even *political* activism. Finally, Hartman's choices of desirable character traits are open to challenge, and perhaps a dialectical approach to anthropological values is better than one that selects one particular set of traits.

In "Is Matter All That Matters?" I engage one of the challenges that contemporary science poses to religion and indeed to the very core of humanity's self-conception. By reducing us to bundles of neurons, materialism, now the leading scientific model of the human being, appears to preclude free will — generally regarded as a fundamental tenet in Judaism and affirmed by many secularists as well. Thus not only religious but also secular people find neuroscience profoundly threatening. By way of response, I explore resources in Jewish tradition that could help create a *modus vivendi* between religion and neuroscience. There are Jewish views that severely limit free will or that stress the biological roots of behavior. Also, some traditional thinkers devalue free will. On top of that, there are Jewish precedents for regarding free will as compatible with determinism. Finally, one may place the rise of the neuroscientific paradigm in a larger historical context and respond on that basis. Some (albeit not all) of the approaches I advance will, I think, be relevant not only to religious people but to secularists as well. Indeed some of the views I cite derive from secular literature but find independently-formed counterparts in Jewish tradition. Despite the resources I propose for *mitigating* the conflicts between materialism and Judaism, I cannot altogether dispose of them.

The next section of the book turns to morality and in particular the relationship between Jewish law and secular or non-Jewish religious moralities (loosely called "secular ethics").

The horror of 9/11 on the one hand drew people to religion as a source of comfort, but on the other created significant challenges for religion. I detail those challenges in the essay: "'From the Depths I Have Called to You'." (The title invokes a verse from Psalms.) Originally published on the first anniversary of 9/11, and therefore displaying emotional tones, the essay examines two themes: (1) how religions breed fanaticism,[25] and (2) how the existence of evil challenges religious belief. With regard to the first topic, religion demands passion from its adherents and can lead therefore to fanaticism by shutting out other considerations, including ethical ones. Several elements in Jewish tradition impose constraints on the expression of religious passion, which serves as a brake on fanaticism. Consider child sacrifice. The practice makes sense religiously — what could show greater devotion to God than an *akedah*? — but the Bible prohibits it. While I do not advance arguments for the objectivity of ethical judgments, I do submit that religious practices like expressing praise and gratitude, or wondering how a good God could allow evil, imply a standard of ethics that is independent of God's will. An independent ethical standard restrains religious violence. However, arguing that religion insists that humans should make ethical judgments (thereby checking fanaticism), accentuates the problem of evil. For the problem of evil unfolds by imposing upon God an independent standard of ethics. I therefore examine an approach, associated with R. Joseph Soloveitchik, that refuses to let philosophical problems inhibit moral action.

This discussion of R. Soloveitchik's views on evil leads into the essay, "Does Jewish Law Express Jewish Philosophy?: The Curious Case of Theodicies." Many authors answer yes to the title question. I try to show, however, that positing an explanation of why a good God allows evil should logically discourage moral action and empathy. Since a theodicy tries to make peace with evil, what sense would it make to fight evil if we accept a theodicy? The requirement of battling evil seems to create a dissonance — a disconnect — between Jewish law and Jewish theology, since Jewish law demands that we fight evil but Jewish theology tells us that evil is justified.[26] I argue that the only theodicy that can repair this disconnect is the "soulmaking theodicy," according to which God allows evil in order that human beings grow in moral character. This theodicy, far from stifling moral action, urges it.

There is another disconnect between law and theology that I consider, and this too leads to a soulmaking theodicy. Jewish law demands that when suffering comes, the sufferer must introspect and repent. This norm is puzzling, since Judaism does not always accept retributivist theories, according to which all suffering is a result of sin. If sin is not the cause of all evils, why should one repent when suffering strikes? I examine various responses to this question and note that some responses seem to reflect a soulmaking theodicy. We see yet again that if one wishes for Jewish law to reflect Jewish theology, one must affirm a soulmaking theodicy. At the end of the paper I turn the argument on its head and ask whether it is always necessary for Jewish theology to fit with Jewish law. Perhaps one should deny the link between law and theology in order to keep options open for a variety of theodicies — in particular, theodicies that are more common in traditional texts than soulmaking theodicies are.

The relationship between Halakhah and morality lies at or near the heart of any Jewish philosophy of Halakhah. "Beyond Obedience" discusses the late R. Walter Wurzburger's views on the subject as articulated in his book *Ethics of Responsibility*. As an Orthodox Jew, R. Wurzburger stresses obedience to law, but, as a Modern Orthodox Jew, he also carves out a place within Halakhah for moral intuitions, particularly in cases where there is no precise precedent for a ruling. Yet in contrast to other theoreticians of Halakhah, R. Wurzburger regards these intuitions as subjective. Jewish law thus contains both a heteronomous and objective component (explicit divine commands) and an autonomous and subjective one. However, R. Wurzburger's view that non-heteronomous judgments are subjective and relative would seem to undermine his own purposes. His aims would be better realized by embracing an objective ethic that supplements technical halakhic rules. Of course, it is not easy to determine objective ethical standards, and many believe it is futile to try. But, as I argue in "From The Depths," religious life demands recognition of an independent ethic, indeed an independent humanly knowable ethic.[27] The essay also touches upon R. Wurzburger's views that Judaism is an ethic of virtue and that it is pluralistic in the sense of balancing conflicting values.

One suggestion I make in "Beyond Obedience" is that Jewish ethics is better compared to other legal systems rather than other ethical systems. Jewish thinkers should take advantage of contemporary secular philosophies of law that help to conceptualize the nature of Halakhah. In recent years, there has been much scholarly literature about how the legal theory of such figures as Ronald Dworkin (the preeminent philosopher of law today) bears on the understanding of Jewish law. Signifying this integration, major law schools regularly provide classes in Jewish law, often taught by philosophers.

"As Thyself: The Limits of Altruism in Jewish Ethics" and "Concepts of Autonomy in Jewish Medical Ethics" are companion pieces. Both fuse halakhic literature with contemporary thinking in applied ethics, in particular medical ethics. "As Thyself" opens with a puzzle posed by the American philosopher Michael Slote: on what basis do secular ethicists permit people to give up their lives for others when they themselves may die as a result, and even (so Slote thinks) when the overall loss of life will be increased by the rescue mission? Still more perplexing, why is such a choice lauded as moral heroism? Within secular principles for evaluating acts, altruistic self-sacrifice often makes no sense — yet it is lauded. In Jewish law, however, while altruistic self-sacrifice — handing over a scarce medical resource, as in a famous case of two travelers (*Bava Metzi'a* 62a) — is sometimes lauded, it is often prohibited altogether or allowed only in restricted cases.[28] Why these differing assessments of altruistic self-sacrifice? It is not enough to say that, in secular ethics, possessors of resources enjoy autonomy, for this would not explain why an altruistic self-sacrifice is thought of as a *higher* choice.

In answering this question, I introduce a topic about which much has been written in recent decades: the difference between an ethic of obligation and an ethic of virtue, or, put otherwise, between act-evaluation and agent-evaluation. I claim that secular ethics is in part an ethics of virtue, and that the virtue of an agent who gives up his or her life for others creates a "halo" around the act itself, thus blurring the logical distinction between assessing acts and assessing agents. Many halakhic analyses of the traveler, by contrast, adjudicate it not by prioritizing the virtues of the actor, but by reference to impartial principles that govern the act itself. One such example I call the "least change principle." By my argument, some rabbinic views about altruistic self-sacrifice are not focused, or not always focused, on virtue. Still, I suggest a few instances in which halakhic decision-makers may take a halo effect into account, in a way that seems linked to virtue ethics. If I am right in my overall thesis, the frequently heard claim that Judaism is an ethics of virtue, while certainly not lacking in supportive illustrations, has to be nuanced and qualified (but not abandoned) in light of these jurisprudential principles.

In "Concepts of Autonomy in Jewish Medical Ethics," I question the widely affirmed claim that Judaism rejects the concept of autonomy in life-and-death decisions. While Judaism certainly denies autonomy in certain cases, it also affirms autonomy in the form of a doctrine that "consent matters." Sometimes people may put themselves at risk, or choose not to extend their lives, in situations where others would not have halakhic license to force them to adopt those courses. And yet, I argue, in Jewish law, autonomy is a *fact* but not a *value*. I look at halakhic analyses of hazardous medical procedures and end-of-life issues to determine when patients have autonomy and why; I also revisit altruistic self-sacrifice, this time with an eye to permissive views.

The paper also argues that, precisely because Judaism does not stress autonomy, therefore in cases where patients are empowered to decide about their lives, Judaism should draw on secular literature that discusses how patients can arrive at better-formed decisions, unencumbered by emotional and other impediments. At the end of the paper, I suggest an understanding of secular ethical thought that highlights another difference between it and Jewish law. In particular, Jewish law makes objective decisions about ranking certain values, while secular ethicists are more liable to see these values as subjective.

Both of these essays on medical ethics call for a rethinking of common stereotypes about Jewish law and its values.

The final essay in the volume was written for a collection of auto-biographical essays by religious philosophers, a book that was designed to show that the term "religious philosopher" is not an oxymoron. Indeed the book, published in 1994, was proof that attitudes in academia to philosophy of religion have changed dramatically over the decades. The article's thesis is epistemological and is stated in its title: "The Over-examined Life is Not Worth Living." I argue that much of what people believe is legitimately shaped by habits, inclinations, role models, and inspiring figures rather than evidence, and that the benefits that accrue from religious life give reason to live it. Although a portion of the material works from within my Modern Orthodox perspective, the approach is easily applied to other religious commitments.

The essays have been revised to clarify claims and arguments and to correct factual errors. In a few places I have made what I think are helpful abridgements. One article, "Is Matter All That Matters?" has been some-what reorganized. It was prohibitive to undertake updating the articles so as to engage literature that has appeared since their original publication. But in a small number of them I have added a brief postscript in the final note. I stand by the core theses and arguments of each article, even while recognizing that some issues demand further reflection. I have not eliminated overlap, since someone reading an essay would find it inconvenient to turn to another essay in order to understand the one he or she is reading. Keeping the overlap also preserves the integrity and coherence of each piece. I have flagged overlaps by means of a note for readers who may otherwise experience a strange sense of déjà vu.

The transliteration scheme should be self-evident, except that I use "h" for both ה and ח. The words "Halakhah," "Midrash" and "Aggadah" are capitalized when I refer to a whole corpus (e. g., "the Halakhah recognizes human weakness"), but I use "halakhah" and "midrash" (i. e., lower case and italics) when referring to a specific law or passage. Finally, except where the original did otherwise, I follow the practice of using the honorific "Rabbi" — abbreviated "R." — for those who in their primary professional roles occupy pulpits or hold faculty or administrative positions in rabbinical schools, or who are widely known as posekim (halakhic decisors). Rabbi Abraham Isaac Kook is so widely known as "Rav Kook" that I often use this designation.

In revising the essays I have profited from the invaluable help of Yoel Finkelman of Bar-Ilan University and ATID, a gifted philosopher, historian, educator and sociologist with superb editorial skills. With remarkable speed and efficiency, Yoel targeted everything from dubious formulations to superfluous commas, and with each piece that he read he put forth penetrating questions and observations. Beyond concrete benefits for the contents of this volume and my thinking generally, I am grateful to have formed such a gratifying friendship. I have met Yoel exactly twice. Rarely have I reaped such rewards by travelling through cyberspace.

Meira Mintz created the index of topics and names, collaborated on the index of sources, and provided editorial assistance.

Looking over the many acknowledgments in the individual essays, I am moved by and deeply appreciate the interest and input of individuals who regularly and helpfully commented on drafts over the years and with whom I bounced around ideas. One clever preface I saw said something to the following effect: I will not engage in the conventional practice of saying that any errors are my responsibility, since I discussed this book with so many people that I don't remember who gave me which idea. Well, I say, there may be some truth in that excuse…but even so, the buck stops with me.

It will come as no surprise to readers of this book that my faculty position is at Yeshiva University, whose mission and motto is *Torah u-Madda*, the integration of Torah and general wisdom. I extend heartfelt gratitude to the leaders of Yeshiva with whom I have worked so closely for so long: Presidents Norman Lamm and Richard M. Joel; Dean Karen Bacon of Stern College for Women, my home base; and Provost Morton Lowengrub. Yeshiva has provided the perfect environment for me to cultivate my interests. The final essay of this book speaks, all too briefly, of how my experience there has impacted my personal and professional life.

I am grateful to colleagues at Yeshiva for advice and counsel on various matters pertaining to this book: David Berger, Dean of the Bernard Revel Graduate School of Jewish Studies; Pearl Berger, Dean of Libraries; Ephraim Kanarfogel, chair of the Rebecca Ivry Department of Jewish Studies; and Jacob Wisse, Director of the Yeshiva University Museum and a professor of art history. Some contacts in Israel, especially Prof. Avigdor Shinan and R. Reuven Ziegler, answered questions about sources. I take this opportunity to express long-standing gratitude to David Berger not only for applying his brilliant critical acumen to drafts of essays and book chapters during the many years in which we have been brothers-in-law, but for answering innumerable queries during that time. Tapping his vast erudition and insight in (*inter alia*) intellectual history, biblical and rabbinic texts, languages, and contemporary Jewry, has had for me — in the words of Bertrand Russell — "all the advantages of theft over honest toil."

Dr. Igor Nemirovsky, Director of Academic Studies Press, and Dr. Simcha Fishbane invited this collection; I am deeply appreciative. Kira Nemirovsky shepherded the book through production in a consistently gracious, accommodating, and skilled manner. I thank her for her work.

It is as appropriate as it is customary for authors to thank spouses for their love, encouragement and support while the book was being prepared. In a volume of collected essays, the thank you must cover decades of such support. And it must cover as well decades of nourishment that led to the author's professional and personal growth. So thank you, Chani, for all that and so much more.

NOTES

1   Virtually every book about Jewish philosophy begins by asking how to define Jewish philosophy, whether it exists, and who counts as a Jewish philosopher. I want to mostly sidestep these questions. Roughly, like others, I consider Jewish philosophy to be an attempt to understand Judaism in philosophical categories and using philosophical arguments. But this formulation invites many questions, not the least of which is how to define Judaism and how to define philosophy, and entering that morass probably means never getting out. Some of my comments below are pertinent, however.

2   In the essay "The Overexamined Life is Not Worth Living," in this volume, I describe this trajectory in greater detail as an initial bifurcation and a later integration.

3   An extended illustration of how philosophical ideas — in this case, political philosophy — can be drawn out of legal texts is the (so far) two volumes of *The Jewish Political Tradition*, ed. Michael Walzer, Menachem Lorberbaum, and Noam J. Zohar (New Haven, CT, 2000 and 2003). (Ari Ackerman and Yair Lorberbaum, respectively, served as co-editors for volumes one and volume two.)

4   See Gerald J. Blidstein, David Berger, Shnayer Z. Leiman, and Aharon Lichtenstein, *Judaism's Encounter with Other Cultures: Rejection or Integration?*, ed. Jacob J. Schacter (Northvale, NJ, 1997).

5   For an assessment of this position from a philosophical standpoint, see my "Practical Endeavor and the Torah u-Madda Debate," *The Torah u-Madda Journal* 3 (1991-1992): 98-149.

6   Actually, framing the distinction as one between examining the history of Jewish philosophy and actively philosophizing is slightly inaccurate, since one can study a contemporary thinker and still be "studying" rather than "doing" philosophy.

7   One can value interpreting philosophers correctly without valuing a study of their antecedents. A rather strident criticism of the study of influences is found in Jonathan Bennett's *A Study of Spinoza's Ethics* (Indianapolis, 1984), 16:

> I am sure to make mistakes because of my inattention to Spinoza's philosophical ancestry; but I will pay that price for the benefits which accrue from putting most of one's energies into philosophically interrogating Spinoza's own text. I am encouraged in this by the massive work [*The*

Philosophy of Spinoza] in which [Harry] Wolfson places Spinoza in a densely described medieval setting: the labour and learning are awesome, but the philosophical profit is almost nil. Such philosophically interesting readings of Spinoza as are contained in Wolfson's two volumes could all have been arrived at without delving into the medieval background.

These are harsh words. Yet even in that context Bennett does not denigrate the importance of fathoming Spinoza's intentions; he merely suggests that finding predecessors "is subject to a law of diminishing returns" (16). It scarcely needs to be noted that, while Bennett may imply otherwise, philosophical value is not the only kind in academic work. The history of ideas has a value of its own, whatever its payoff in creative philosophical thinking.

[8] In the case of Maimonides, "doing" is important for another reason. For many interpreters, a weak argument on Maimonides' part signals elite readers that his stated view is not his real view.

[9] Menachem Kellner's many works on Maimonides are good examples. Through the prism of Maimondes, Kellner addresses such contested contemporary issues as peoplehood and dogma. See his *Science in the Bet Midrash: Studies in Maimonides* (Boston, MA, 2009). See also Kenneth Seeskin, *Maimonides: A Guide to Today's Perplexed* (New York, 1991), which, treating Maimonides as a philosopher of religion and deliberately eschewing historical technicalities, explicates his ideas in a way that makes them resonate for an audience of "today's perplexed." (Seeskin himself also works in the history of philosophy, yet with an eye toward contemporary problems.) It is noteworthy that some well known original thinkers (Emil Fackenheim and R. Abraham Joshua Heschel spring to mind immediately) made the move from scholarly studies of medieval historical figures to articulation of their own philosophies, which became enormously influential. In Israel today, leading interpreters of philosophy have been at the forefront of a larger intellectual dialogue about social issues.

[10] See Norbert Samuelson (ed.), *Studies in Jewish Philosophy: Collected Essays of the Academy for Jewish Philosophy: 1980-1985* (Lanham, MD, 1987), 1. Cf., however, Samuelson, "The Death and Renewal of Jewish Philosophy," *Journal of the American Academy of Religion* 70, 1 (March 2002): 117-34.

[11] Published by Rowman & Littlefield under the general editorship of Rabbi Robert S. Hirt.

[12] Mark Steiner, "Rabbi Israel Salanter As a Jewish Philosopher," *The Torah u-Madda Journal* 9 (2000): 44. Steiner goes on to say that talmudic law is a source for philosophical ideas. On this point, see the first note in my essay, "Does Jewish Law Express Jewish Philosophy?"

[13] For a thoughtful discussion of this issue, see the editor's introduction to Dean Zimmerman (ed.), *Persons: Human and Divine* (New York, 2007), 1-13. I thank Aaron Segal for the reference.

[14] See, for example, Charles Manekin and Robert Eisen (eds.), *Philosophers and The Hebrew Bible* (Berthesda, MD, 2008). Among analytic philosophers, Charlotte Katzoff and Eleonore Stump have been at the forefront. See, for example, Katzoff's essay on Isaac and Stump's essay on Samson in that volume.

[15] See Marvin Fox, *Interpreting Maimonides* (Chicago, 1990); Kenneth Seeskin, *Searching for a Distant God* (New York, 2000), 177-88; Yair Lorberbaum, "On

Contradictions, Rationality, Dialectics, and Esotericism in Maimonides' Guide of the Perplexed," *Review of Metaphysics* 55 (2002): 711-50.

[16] It is not a stretch to call this a postmodern approach, albeit with substantial qualification. See Tamar Ross, "The Cognitive Value of Religious Statements: Rabbi A. I. Kook and Postmodernism," in *Hazon Nahum: Studies in Jewish Law, Thought and History Presented to Dr. Norman Lamm on the Occasion of his Seventieth Birthday*, ed. Yaakov Elman and Jeffrey S. Gurock (New York, 1997), 479-528.

[17] See Jonathan Garb, "'Alien' Culture in the Circle of Rabbi Kook," in *Study and Knowledge in Jewish Thought*, ed. Howard Kreisel (Beer Sheva, Israel, 2006), 253-64.

[18] Many Modern Orthodox Jews argue that R. Abraham Kook's son, R. Zvi Yehudah, distorted his father's teachings by applying a militaristic interpretation, one focused on not surrendering even an inch of land in Israel.

[19] See Yitzchak Twersky, "The Rov," *Tradition* 30, 4 (Summer 1996): 32.

[20] The term "halakhic hero" is featured in chap. 2 of David Hartman, *Love and Terror in the God Encounter: The Theological Legacy of Rabbi Joseph B. Soloveitchik* (Woodstock, VT, 2001).

[21] As I discuss in the essay, *The Halakhic Mind* (written in the 1970s though published in 1986) champions an epistemological pluralism that prima facie segregates a halakhic outlook from a scientific one.

[22] In R. Soloveitchik's thought these do not have the ethical connotation they normally do, but I think it is fair to view science as, on his view, promoting ethical goals.

[23] See, for example, Avi Sagi, *Jewish Religion After Theology* (Boston, MA, 2009), which highlights the thought of Yeshayahu Leibowitz; from Continental standpoints, Mark Wrathall (ed.) *Religion after Metaphysics* (New York, 2003); from analytic standpoints, Peter Byrne, *God and Realism* (Burlington, VT, 2003) and Howard Wettstein "Against Theology" in Manekin and Eisen (eds.), *Philosophers and the Hebrew Bible*.

[24] *Orot ha-Kodesh* (Jerusalem, 1985), II: 395-98. Tamar Ross gives this and other examples from R. Kook in her "The Cognitive Value of Religious Statements."

[25] The past few years have witnessed a spate of atheistic works, many of which use 9/11 to dramatically illustrate why belief in God is a bad thing. The believer's counter, of course, is that secular ideologies like those of Hitler, Mussolini and Stalin bred equal if not greater violence.

[26] This is the question that grew out of my discussion of R. Soloveitchik's views in my "'From the Depths I Have Called to Thee'."

[27] Even if there is an independent ethic, it may not be robust enough or accessible enough to to answer every question one might want answered, or to ground every moral claim one might wish to ground. In this regard the argument is limited. Obviously removing the limitation would require moving into issues I cannot take up here.

[28] In the travelers case, two are traveling and one owns a flask of water. If they split it, both die. If one drinks, he will live while his comrade dies. What should the owner do? Ben Petura says: split the contents; both must die. R. Akiva says the owner keeps it and drinks.

ESSAYS IN
INTERPRETATION

THE BIBLE AS A SOURCE FOR PHILOSOPHICAL REFLECTION*

INTRODUCTION: ISSUES OF METHODOLOGY

Is the Bible a source for philosophical reflection? A natural reaction is that it is. The Bible depicts the character of God, presents an account of creation, posits a metaphysics of divine providence and divine intervention, suggests a basis for morality, discusses many features of human nature, and frequently poses the notorious conundrum of how God can allow evil. Surely, then, it engages questions that lie at the very heart of Jewish philosophy, indeed of religious philosophy in general.

Yet this categorization of the Bible as philosophy must be qualified, as the Bible obviously deviates, in many features, from what philosophers (especially those trained in the analytic tradition) have come to regard as philosophy.

1) The Bible contains, at its very core, a great deal of material that is not necessarily philosophical, such as law, poetry, and narrative.

2) We expect philosophical truth to be formulated in declarative sentences. The Bible yields few propositional nuggets of this kind.[1]

3) Philosophical works try to reach conclusions by means of logical argumentation. The Bible contains little sustained argument of a deductive, inductive, or practical nature, and attempts to impose the structure of rational argument on the biblical text yield meager profit.

4) Philosophers try to avoid contradicting themselves. When contradictions appear, they are either a source of embarrassment or a spur to developing a higher-order dialectic to accommodate the tension between the theses. The Bible, by contrast, often juxtaposes contradictory ideas without explanation or apology; Ecclesiastes is entirely constructed on this principle. The philosophically more sophisticated work of harmonizing the contradictions in the biblical text is left to the exegetical literature.[2]

---

*   Co-authored with Shalom Carmy.

5) Much of what the Bible has to say about subjects of manifest philosophical importance seems primitive to later philosophical sensibilities. For example, the biblical God ostensibly has human form and human emotions; he regrets his actions and changes his mind (e.g. Gen. 6:6; I Sam. 15:11).[3] Miracles are commonplace, and natural events such as earthquakes and winds are often identified as direct divine acts. If Jewish philosophy begins with the Bible, cynics might suggest, it can advance only by casting the Bible behind.

This last problem is at the core of the concerns that Jewish philosophers have often felt about biblical material. Indeed, an acute awareness of the gap between the centrality of biblical teaching in Jewish thought and its apparent philosophical deficiency precipitated much of the subsequent history of Jewish philosophy. Many will derive from that history a pessimism about finding philosophy in the Bible. In particular, the most strenuous attempt to wed the Bible to philosophy — that of medieval thinkers — was of mixed value to biblical theology, as in many cases it arguably forced biblical texts into an artificial model.

Beginning with Philo and continuing on through medieval thinkers like Sa'adyah Ga'on and Maimonides, biblical hermeneutics often rested on the principle that the Bible conveys major philosophical and scientific truths. Biblical discourse, insist medieval rationalists, is not always to be taken literally. Although biblical portrayals of God and of events introduce the masses to basic truths — educating and elevating them — the proper understanding of these texts is available only to those who enter the realm of philosophy and science. Interpreting the text through the prism of reason reveals a philosophically impressive and compelling core.

Thus, for medieval rationalists, the books of the prophets reflect the philosophical and scientific knowledge possessed by their authors, although these individuals are philosophers of a special kind: not only do they perceive intellectual truths, but their faculty of "imagination" presents these truths in figurative terms and concrete images.[4] A salient example of the prophet's activity thus conceived is Ezekiel's detailed vision of the chariot (Ezek. 1:10), which Maimonides treats as a repository of science and metaphysics.[5]

Other examples abound. In their analyses of the book of Job, medieval philosophers sometimes understand each character as espousing a different philosophical position concerning the basis and scope of divine providence.[6] In the Garden of Eden story, man, it is said, represents form, that is, intellect, the essence of a human; woman represents matter. Man sinned as a result of woman's promptings. Hence, the story of Eden captures the human predicament — matter interferes with the proper exercise of intellect and with the realization of the human *telos*.[7]

A telling indicator of the close connection between philosophy and Bible in medieval times is that Maimonides' *Guide of the Perplexed*, the greatest of Jewish philosophical works, is in significant measure an exegesis of the Bible. Gersonides, renowned for his philosophical and scientific achievements, authored a biblical commentary, as did Sa'adyah Ga'on and Abraham ibn Ezra. An entire exegetical tradition, lasting until the end of Jewish life in Spain (Isaac Abarbanel) and even beyond, resorted to medieval philosophy — or rebelled against it.

Opposition to rationalist biblical interpretation came from two directions.[8] Some medieval Jews thought that the Bible must be read with absolute literalness and then taken on faith. If its doctrines, so understood, conflicted with those of philosophy, so much the worse for philosophy. Philosophy would then have been exposed as heresy and falsehood.

In early modern times, a different critical response emerged, one which, in effect, accused Maimonides and other medievals of a colossal anachronism. Spinoza put the charge especially sharply, proclaiming that any and all attributions of philosophical sophistication and truth to the Bible and the prophets were fictions.[9] His subversion of Maimonides' doctrines, however overstated, marked the eclipse of the medieval enterprise. Later efforts to read the Bible through the prism of Kantian or Romantic philosophy could be and were subjected to a hermeneutic of suspicion.

In light of the clear differences outlined between the Bible and works of philosophy — in style, method, and purpose — and in light of the checkered history of attempts to read good philosophy into the Bible, anyone proposing to portray the Bible as a source of philosophical reflection must tread very carefully. Yet, to claim that the religious and moral wisdom of the Bible is philosophically naive is grossly unfair, and not only to believers in divine revelation. An analogy to ancient philosophy is helpful. Recent work in ancient philosophy, including pre-Socratic philosophy, shows that the ancients had a remarkable alertness to contemporary problems along with perspicuous avenues for solution.[10] Differences in terminology ought not blind us to the philosophical character of our predecessors' insights. Philosophy in general has been rediscovering its roots of late, leading to a greater appreciation of centuries past. Although the Bible serves first and foremost as a record of primary religious experience, study of the Bible, in its original context and trailing clouds of exegesis, evokes fruitful lines of theological reflection that repay philosophical attention even today.

The remainder of this essay will strive to illustrate the possibilities for a meaningful encounter between Bible and philosophy, one that will accord the Bible its place among the important sources of Jewish philosophy without exaggerating its analytical character and without blurring the lines between its formulations of certain problems or approaches and the formulations utilized by later philosophers. Needless to say, someone mining for philosophical ore is not likely to treat biblical texts in the same way that scholars in other fields would. Consequently, we have to gloss over and bracket a variety of linguistic, historical, and literary issues that could either complement or undermine our suggestions. "The Torah has seventy faces," but no one can display all of them at once.[11]

The purposes of this essay dictate a focus on familiar biblical sources, texts whose place in the treatment of theological issues has been hallowed by time: the story of Job, the binding of Isaac, the Garden of Eden, and others. We do not seek to uncover neglected corners of the biblical canon with unexpected or oblique implications for Jewish philosophy.[12] We are forced to omit some significant matters that can, and often do, attract reflective philosophical attention, and we devote little room to philosophical issues implicit in the legal material that is so central to the Bible. All that said, the selections should amply demonstrate that narrative and poetry, no less than discursive writing, can express and stimulate philosophical thinking, a point that is surely abundantly evident to students of literature.[13] We note that all ventures at exegesis are condemned to the endless process of trial and error.

DIVINE COMMANDS AND HUMAN MORAL STANDARDS

Is an action right because God commands it, or does God command it because it is right? Is an action wrong because God prohibits it, or does God prohibit it because it is wrong?

These questions, modeled after one posed in Plato's *Euthyphro*, have long stood at the heart of religious reflections on morality. Like their Muslim and Christian counterparts, Jewish philosophers have differed sharply over whether there can be a valid morality independent of God's law.[14]

Biblical teaching on the subject confronts us with contradictions. When patriarchs and prophets ask how God could allow evil, they are judging God's conduct by human moral standards. In Genesis 18, Abraham remonstrates with God not to destroy the innocent of Sodom together with the guilty: "Will you destroy the righteous with the evil.... Far be it from you! Will the judge of all the earth not do justice?" (Gen. 18:23-25). If God's will alone determined right and wrong, Abraham's plea and God's favorable response to it would be senseless. God is expected to be moral by human standards. Yet in chapter 22, the very same Abraham rises early in the morning to carry out God's command to sacrifice his beloved Isaac. No moral scruples are raised either about the apparent command to commit murder or about God's having reneged on his promise to Abraham, "Through Issac you will have seed" (Gen. 21:12). God later commands King Saul to kill all the Amalekites, "man and woman, infant and suckling, ox and sheep, camel and ass" (I Sam. 15:3), and wrenches the kingship from Saul when he does not comply.[15] Midrashic and talmudic interpretations of this episode see Saul as questioning God on moral grounds and trying to be "more righteous than your creator" (Eccl. Rabbah 7:16; see also Yoma 22b). The biblical evidence, then, is confusing and contradictory as to whether there is a standard of ethics outside of God's will and command.[16]

One episode that nonetheless has assumed a pre-eminent place in explorations of this issue is the binding of Isaac (Akedah). In Genesis 22:2, Abraham is commanded by God, "Take your son, your only son, whom you love — Isaac — and go to the land of Moriah, and offer him up there as a burnt offering." In his brilliant "dialectical lyric," Fear and Trembling, the nineteenth-century Danish philosopher Søren Kierkegaard advanced a reading of the Akedah that has dominated interpretations of the episode ever since. Abraham is the "knight of faith," whose greatness consists in obeying God even while he remains conscious of the moral imperative in its full Kantian force and majesty. Abraham was prepared to commit an act whose religious description is "sacrifice," although its ethical description is "murder." This paradoxical "teleological suspension of the ethical" characterizes the religious stage.

Note that Kierkegaard's is not a "divine command" theory of morality in the usual and pure sense; Kierkegaard does not reduce moral prescriptions to divine commands.[17] On the contrary, he recognizes the possibility of conflict between divine commands and morality — and that means that these are distinct.[18]

The Kierkegaardian image of Abraham has affected not only depictions of religious morality but depictions of cognitive faith as well.[19] His interpretation has become so influential that some modern readers may be surprised to learn that, in its time, the reading was novel; until Kierkegaard, the Akedah was not explained in the manner he suggests.[20] Abraham's potential conflict need not be understood as one between obedience to God and adherence to morality. It could be — and was — readily analyzed as a potential conflict between morality, identified with obedience to God, and natural paternal love. The daily and also Rosh Hashanah Musaf liturgy asks God to let his compassion conquer his anger, just as "[Abraham] conquered his compassion to do your will wholeheartedly." Natural feeling for his son, not rational morality, is what made the Akedah difficult. Other readers feature the claim that Abraham was challenged to continue to believe that "Through Isaac you will have seed," despite what God commanded. Some have rejected the very premise that obedience to God overrides conventional morality in the *Akedah* on the grounds that God finally commands Abraham to refrain from the sacrifice.[21]

The problems raised by our brief discussion of *Fear and Trembling* illustrate the pitfalls in extrapolating a modern philosophical doctrine from an ancient and not explicitly philosophical text. One question is whether the modern philosophical theory indeed conforms to what the Bible would have said had it only employed modern formulations. In other words, would Abraham, or the narrator, have chosen the terminology "teleological suspension of the ethical" over the alternatives? Second, assuming that the philosophical theory is congenial to the spirit of the text, is it actually implied by the words of the narrative? Some contemporary approaches deny in toto the pertinence of these questions; we do not.[22]

Another well-known, though we think unduly overshadowed, text for illuminating the problem of religion and morality is the Garden of Eden story. The first instance of a divine command to human beings is: "And from the tree of knowledge of good and evil, do not eat" (Gen. 2:17). Why did God enjoin Adam and Eve from partaking of this tree?

The serpent explains: "For God knows that on the day you eat from [the tree] your eyes will be opened and you will be like gods, knowing good and evil" (3:5). God, insinuates the serpent, is jealously guarding his own prerogatives of knowing the difference between good and evil. We might assume that the serpent is an untrustworthy source of information, and that his rationale is contrived and duplicitous. But the serpent's claim is largely confirmed later in the story: "And the Lord God said, now that man has become like one of us, knowing the difference between good and evil, perhaps now he will stretch out his hand, eat also from the tree of life, and live forever" (3:22).

Thus, the serpent's words contain a large measure of truth. God prohibited the fruit so that humans will not become knowers of good and evil. What does this mean? If "knowledge of good and evil" is the capacity to make moral discriminations, why would God begrudge this to human beings? And in any case, if human beings would become "knowers of good and evil" only after eating the forbidden fruit, how could they sensibly have been issued a command to begin with? If "ought" implies "can," then by commanding humans to refrain from eating, was not God implying that they already had an understanding of good and evil (right and wrong)?

Most classical construals of "knowers of good and evil" — knowers of sexual passion, knowers of sensual temptation, knowers of conventional moral judgments as distinct from knowers of theoretical truths — face a challenge from Genesis 3:22.[23] The contemporary philosopher Michael Wyschogrod has offered a proposal that accounts for 3:22 and also sheds light on the issue of divine command morality. According to Wyschogrod, "knowers of good and evil" means: beings who make autonomous judgments of good and evil grounded in their own criteria of right and wrong.[24] The turning point in human history was "and the woman saw that the tree was good for eating and that it was attractive to the eyes and desirable as a source of wisdom. She took from its fruit and ate; and she also gave it to her man with her and he ate" (Gen. 3:6). The words "and the woman saw that [it] was good"[25] mark the first time that anyone other than God "saw that [it] was good," that is, made value judgments. That God had prohibited the fruit had no motivational impact on the woman; her decision to eat or not to eat was based upon her own criteria and standards. While the introduction of sensuality into her thinking is also a critical part of the verse and has been duly stressed by classical exegetes, the main point for our purposes is that the woman had become an autonomous judger. Suppose Eve had decided to refrain from eating but did so because she found the fruit unattractive. This, too, would have been wrong, for she would have been just as unresponsive to God's command as she was when she decided to eat. The complete lack of rationalization in God's original directive alerts us to the heteronomous character of the command. God gives a command for which he supplies no reason. Humans should not question it but should obey without understanding why.

No wonder that later, when Adam and Eve cover themselves because their nakedness now embarrasses them, and Adam then explains to God that he hid because he was naked, God scolds Adam: "Who told you that you are naked? Did you eat from the tree from which I commanded you not to eat?" (Gen. 3:11). Eating from the tree means becoming an autonomous judger. If Adam judged that nakedness is shameful, he must have eaten the forbidden food.[26]

With this insight, we can understand how a command could have been issued to beings who supposedly could not differentiate right from wrong. Adam and Eve always had the capacity to obey or disobey God's commands. Free choice was theirs, along with recognition of what was right (obedience) and what was wrong (disobedience). In another sense, however, namely, that of autonomously appraising the content of God's commands, they did not "know good and evil" prior to sinning. It is the wrong exercise of freedom that constitutes their sin. Eating from the tree did not cause them to become knowers; rather it *represented* their becoming knowers, that is, judgers of good and evil.

Wyschogrod's explanation of the sin dovetails with a general motif in Genesis, the drawing and preserving of boundaries.[27] In the ordered sequence of chapter 1, where, until the sixth day, God is alone in the world, as it were, the boundaries between created things are clear and distinct. In chapter 2, where the human world and not the natural cosmos becomes the focus, the lines between the days and between parts of creation are obliterated in the narration, anticipating the crossing of lines that will take place in the next chapter. Before sin, only God categorized the created universe and only God originated value judgments of a non-heteronomous nature. When humans sinned by producing their own judgments, God feared that they will now strive to become immortal as well, usurping another prerogative of the divine. The human being is therefore banished from Eden.

If we were to stop here, we would leave with the impression that Genesis does not want humans to make autonomous judgments. But the continuation of the Adam narrative complicates our response and suggests an addendum to Wyschogrod's analysis. In chapter 4, Cain kills Abel; as in the case of Adam and Eve, God seeks out the sinner. This time, as well, He holds the sinner accountable (Gen. 4:10 ff.), but this time the sinner is not accused of disobeying a command — the text mentions no explicit prohibition of murder.[28] Rather, he is held accountable for *not* "knowing," for evading the responsibility of applying his judgment correctly. Cain tries to disclaim responsibility: "I do not know! Am I my brother's keeper?" (Gen. 4:9). To which God retorts, "What have you done? The voice of your brother's blood cries out to me from the earth!" (Gen. 4:10). In the post-expulsion world, God expects humans to make moral judgments of their own; concomitantly, they cannot avoid accountability for the judgments they make.

Within several generations, the world is destroyed because of human oppression; as Nahmanides observes, the sinfulness of social corruption can be grasped independent of revealed divine injunction.[29] The transfer of power to human beings continues in augmented form after the deluge. When the world is recreated by the family of Noah after the flood,[30] human beings are given even more prerogatives than before. They may now eat animals and may now institute capital punishment for the sin of murder (Gen. 9:6). Steadily, their moral prerogatives grow.[31]

True to this expanding autonomy and responsibility, characters in Genesis who evaluate their own or others' actions apply their independent moral reflection. The sons of Jacob kill the Shechemites because they had treated their sister Dinah as a harlot (Gen. 34:31); the same brothers blame themselves for their callous disregard of Joseph's pain when they cast him into a pit (42:21); covenants are made and kept, reflecting the judgment that they are binding. Societies in Genesis are built not on prescriptions imposed from without but on moral thinking. Only at Sinai does God issue a lengthy set of commands (Ex. 19), and questions about how to act will no longer be typically answered by giving human beings autonomy to judge. Yet even after Sinai, God responds to moral give-and-take. For example, when the daughters of Tzelofhad argue that their father's estate ought not to pass from the family simply because he left no sons, God ratifies their claim and permits daughters to inherit in such circumstances (Num. 27:1-11).

Is there, then, a final biblical position on the basis of morality? No single position is reflected in every portion. Before the sin in Eden, human beings are expected to hearken to God's command and not initiate autonomous moral reflection. That expectation is altered after the sin and as a result of the sin. Sinai represents the heteronomous imposition of conduct. But even after Sinai, God is responsive to moral dialectic.

THEODICY

"Is God willing to prevent evil, but not able? Then he is not omnipotent. Is he able, but not willing? Then he is malevolent. Is he able and willing, but ignorant of evil's existence? Then he is not omniscient."[32]

The Bible does not enunciate the problem of evil with David Hume's analytical precision, but it does not shrink from seeking to understand and even challenge the ways of God in the face of apparent injustice. Consternation over evil is a familiar theme in Psalms (e. g., chaps. 73, 74), in the prophetic books of Jeremiah (12:1-2), Isaiah (62-63), and Habakkuk, in Lamentations, in Ecclesiastes, and, of course, in the book of Job.

That the prophets frequently raise the problem of evil has important ramifications. First, it is evident that challenging the justice of God's ways is not blasphemous — if it were, the prophets would not have allowed themselves to engage in it. Abraham even elicits a positive response from God when he argues that to destroy the innocent of Sodom with its wicked, as God seemed ready to do, would be unjust ("Will the judge of all the earth not do justice?" [Gen. 18:25]). Second, despite the celebrated verse in Isaiah, "My thoughts are not your thoughts, nor my ways your ways" (Is. 55:8), which played an important role in Maimonides' doctrine of divine attributes,[33] the problem of evil is not dismissed with the glib assertion that "good" as applied to God does not mean the same as "good" when applied to humans. If such a resolution were valid, authoritative figures in the Bible would not persist in raising the question and leaving it unanswered.[34] Finally, the repeated discussions of the problem throughout the Bible invite another insight, namely, that the biblical writers did not consider the problem of evil as an analytic conundrum, to be solved once and for all, but rather as a mystery perennially tugging at the sensitive theological conscience.[35]

Because the Bible's "problem of evil" is situated within a set of theological presuppositions, it diverges from articulations of the problem that are promulgated by philosophers. In philosophy, the question of evil is usually posed as, "Why is there evil?" The biblical formulation, however, starts with certain background beliefs: that suffering is usually punishment for sin and that God loves Israel. In the Bible, therefore, the problem's formulation is usually narrower: "Why do the righteous suffer while the wicked prosper?" or "How could God allow Israel to suffer and the Temple be destroyed?" In short, "Why do such-and-such evils befall these people or groups?" Another difference between biblical and philosophical formulations is that in the philosophical literature, evil is often thought to disconfirm the *existence* of God, while the Bible does not come anywhere near considering that position. The biblical writers are instead concerned about the threat that evil poses to belief in God's *goodness* or steadfastness.

The most elaborate biblical treatment of evil is, of course, the book of Job. A common approach to biblical theodicy attempts to derive a conclusion from this book as a whole. Leaving aside some stubborn obstacles — most notably that God's wager with the Satan in the narrative prologue (chapters 1-2) is not alluded to in the denouement, and the sudden appearance, and disappearance, of Elihu — let us focus on some key points.

The first is negative. At the end of the work, God chastises the friends "because you did not speak properly to me as did my servant Job" (42:7). In other words, God rejects, in whole or in part, their position. Whatever the differences among the three friends, and whatever development occurs in their respective positions in the course of the dialogue, they are united in the conviction that Job deserves his bad fortune. Whatever the fine points of temperament and argument, they were determined to uphold the traditional theodicy of justified retribution at all cost. Job, by contrast, had stridently and consistently complained that he was a good man and that his actions did not warrant his fate. He had come close to blasphemy. Yet it is Job who must pray on behalf of his friends before *they* can be forgiven. A stronger indictment of the retributivist theodicy could hardly be imagined.

Rabbinic literature was to go beyond the denial of the simple formula that all suffering is punishment for sin by offering a range of explicit alternative explanations of evil.[36] But does the book of Job provide us with any such alternative? Or is its sole conclusion the negative one outlined here?

If Job contains a positive theodicy, it is presumably to be found in God's two speeches (38-41), which lead Job to humility and reconciliation. Alas, the precise philosophical point of these speeches is elusive. Do they contain an argument from the perfect design of the universe, as proposed by Gersonides in his commentary to these chapters? Or is it the dysteleogical features of creation that enable us to perceive the numinousness of the divine other, as was influentially asserted by Rudolf Otto?[37] Are we supposed to identify a discursive solution? Or is the resolution the theophany itself

("I had heard of you by ear, now my eye has seen you" [42:5]), when God accedes to Job's existential plea for his tormentor not to hide His face but rather respond to His creature's anguish?[38]

The idea that Job's *experience* of God is the key to his reconciliation suggests the primacy of the human drama in Job, and this insight leads us to a distinct philosophical appropriation of the book. We discover in Job's ordeal a "theodicy of soul-making." Take the problem of God's wager with the Satan. God's rationale for afflicting Job is theologically problematic, to say the least. Can God justifiably make Job a pawn in order to prove a point? If Job is, at bottom, an exploration of what people make of suffering, then the dispute between God and the Satan becomes less capricious. The Satan suggests that suffering inexorably corrupts; faithfulness is a luxury only the prosperous can afford. God says that suffering can ennoble, and that faithfulness can be forged in the crucible of anguish.

Who is right? Ultimately God's prediction — and Job himself — will be vindicated by the process of suffering. For the voice of God and its aftermath are signs of two things: Job's heightened spiritual perception and his heightened sense of interpersonal responsibility.

Perceiving God out of the whirlwind is a climactic achievement: "And *now* my eye has seen you" (note, however, 5:17). The end result of Job's suffering is that he has the ability to perceive that which previously he could not perceive. Whereas in the prologue Job brought sacrifices for his family alone, he has now broadened his concern — he prays for the friends.[39] Job has grown through crisis. Hence, God was right and the Satan was wrong. We have here a form of soul making theodicy — evil makes people better.[40]

The philosophically reflective student of Job, like the reader of other biblical texts, would be remiss in abandoning the rich detail of the text to philologists and literary scholars. We must not create a false dichotomy between philosophical readings on the one hand and literary or psychological ones on the other. Although, as noted earlier, exegetes such as Maimonides and Gersonides assign specific philosophical positions to the participants in the dialogue, it is surely in keeping with the atmosphere of the debate to emphasize the psychological stance of Job and the other characters. The book of Job is a veritable phenomenology of faith in a state of challenge. It spans moments of commitment (13:15), doubt (23:5), self-pity (19:21), self-confidence (13:18), and defiance (9:22-23).[41] The friends' rhetoric may evolve — and their temper may degenerate — but their faith, in contrast to Job's, is throughout simple and simplistic.

By selecting a single passage we can highlight the lively interaction between philosophical and psychological issues and the suggestiveness of the exegetical tradition, even when the commentators respond to the text in categories alien to its original intellectual setting.

In Job's first answer to Bildad, he addresses God, crying out: "Is it good that you oppress, that you despise the work of your hands, and shine upon wicked thoughts? Are your eyes of flesh? Do you see like man?" (10:3-4). According to Nahmanides, Job here accuses God of an obsessive concern with man's inner thoughts. Is God like a jealous lover who must constantly probe the recesses of the creature's mind and provoke his potential for rebellion? Gersonides, who denied divine foreknowledge of contingents, of free human actions, ascribes his own doctrine to Job. God does not know as man does, that is, he does not know particulars, and he therefore cannot be held responsible for Job's troubles. The Gersonidean Job proclaims his innocence without expressing resentment; the angry tone is not Job's, but rather describes the foul mood which the friends, who have not understood Gersonides, mistakenly ascribe to him. R. Meir Leibush Malbim, the nineteenth-century exegete, adopts the more conventional teaching on foreknowledge. On his reading, Job here advances the classic medieval problem of foreknowledge and freedom: because God is omniscient, and his knowledge is not limited as man's knowledge is, his knowledge determines man's actions, and Job cannot be held responsible for the sins he may have committed.

The philosophical interpretations of Gersonides and Malbim violate our expectations not only because they are based on anachronistic theories but also because they presume a pursuit of metaphysical argument at odds with the existential situation of Job on his dung heap. What happens, however, when we take Job's psychological state in full seriousness?

Remember the context: at the point where we join Job's meditation, his view of the situation has undergone several changes, From the "patient Job" of the prologue, he has moved to the initial curse of chapter 3, a curse that avoids addressing God by focusing instead on his unlucky birthday. In the response to Eliphaz (6-7), Job saw himself as a persecuted figure, misunderstood by his friends and hounded by God. By chapter 9, the logic of the discourse has led Job to see himself as a self divided against itself. His very attempt to exculpate himself becomes a gesture of rebellion that makes him appear all the more guilty: "If I wash with snow water, and purify my hands with lye, then shall you immerse me in the muddy pit, and my very clothes shall detest me" (9:30-31). In short, he is helpless not only because his adversary is powerful but because his adversary condemns him from within, as it were.

Against this background, the argument at the beginning of chapter 10 reflects precisely Job's psychological situation. It is not only that Job's insistence on his innocence does not belong to him, fueling instead the fires of his antagonists who undermine his claim to innocence. Now, he realizes, his very being is not his; he is the handiwork of the same God against

THE BIBLE AS A SOURCE FOR PHILOSOPHICAL REFLECTION

whom he must strive. Job goes on to portray eloquently the experience of creatureliness. All this is reminiscent of Malbim's interpretation, but stripped of the formal philosophical theorizing. The nineteenth-century attempt to read a medieval conundrum into an ancient text helps us, paradoxically, to capture the existential import of the original, the moment we learn to avoid being captured by the formal anachronism.

To return to the main point, Job's religious growth may be taken as the kernel of a compelling explanation of evil. Even so, the text does not seem preoccupied with preaching this or any other insight as a "solution" to a philosophical problem; God, after all, never tells Job the true genesis of his tribulations.[42] Phenomenology, more than theodicy, occupies center stage.

FREE WILL AND DIVINE PROVIDENCE

Philosophers have devoted enormous energy to resolving the seeming contradiction between divine foreknowledge and human free choice. If God knows at a certain time that a person will later do particular acts, how can that person be said to act freely? And if he cannot act freely, how can he be morally responsible for his deeds?

As noted in the previous section, this difficulty is not explicitly encountered in the Bible; indeed, the very notion of foreknowledge is sometimes conspicuously missing. Thus, the Bible speaks of God "regretting" that He had made man, as if He had not foreseen the corruption that brought about the deluge (Gen. 6:6).[43] God tests Abraham and the angel proclaims "Now I know that you are God fearing" (Gen. 22:12), as if Abraham's heart would otherwise have been hidden from its creator.[44] Obvious conflicts between divine providence and human free choice are left unarticulated. God hardens the heart of Pharaoh and of the Amonite king Sihon (Ex. 9:12; 10:20; 11:10; 14:4, 8, 17; Deut. 2:30), without concern that, owing to this divine interference, these individuals ought not to be held responsible for their acts of rebellion. God declares that he will harden Pharaoh's heart "in order to multiply my signs and wonders in the land of Egypt" (Ex. 10:1; 12:9; see also 7:3). Anyone who deems free will a value might well be struck by this invocation of God's greater glory as a reason for depriving someone of free choice. And we must not ignore the implications of legal texts. Thus, God is assigned causal agency in cases of unintentional homicide (Ex. 21: 13);[45] the commandment to build a guardrail around one's rooftop "lest someone fall" (Deut. 22:8) implies that, despite divine foreknowledge, the victim would not have fallen had proper caution been exercised.[46]

Exegetes grapple with the implications of these texts, and their proposals may be judged plausible or strained. What is important for us, however, is that the Bible itself does not directly address the issues.

At the same time, there is a particular type of tension between divine providence and human choice, carrying broad implications for the theology of history, that is often aroused by common reflection on biblical texts and that articulates dilemmas that are often more momentous existentially than the classical ones.[47] In the Bible, God determines the course of history; He elects certain outcomes. Hence, He stage-manages history so as to bring about these results. What responsibility do human beings bear for their actions if the outcome is inevitable? What freedom do they exercise if they are instruments in a divine plan? And does the fact that God wants the result justify the means chosen by humans to achieve it?

These questions come to the surface in the Joseph stories (Gen. 37-50). The brothers of Joseph, jealous of the special treatment he receives from his father Jacob, conspire to throw him into a pit. He is then taken by merchants, who sell him as a slave to Egyptians. Soon, he is thrown into an Egyptian dungeon and incarcerated for two years on a trumped-up charge. By a remarkable sequence of events, Joseph eventually becomes the viceroy of Egypt. His brothers come to Egypt to procure food during a famine. Joseph recognizes them, but they do not recognize him. Joseph proceeds to perpetrate a hoax on them. At last, he reveals his identity.

Interestingly, of all the characters in the story, only one even seems to absolve the brothers of guilt — Joseph himself. He does so three times. "And now, be not saddened or angry that you sold me here [or: caused me to be sold]. For God sent me before you for sustenance" (Gen. 45:5). "You did not send me here; rather God did" (Gen. 45:8). "You thought ill for me; God thought it for good" (Gen. 50:20). Is Joseph's orientation as correct as it is generous?[48]

It is hard to tell. The text plants the question in our minds, but leaves us to our own conclusions. To be sure, a quiet critique of Joseph inheres in the narrative. When Joseph asserts that the purpose of his being brought to Egypt was to save his brothers from the famine, he is being short-sighted and somewhat self-involved. Actually, he has been sent there because Jacob's descendants are destined to be enslaved "in a land not theirs" (Gen. 15:13). Joseph, the great prognosticator, sees into the future, but his lens does not reach far enough. Absorbed with his own place in the here-and-now, he seems oblivious to the persecution that awaits his family. His father Jacob realizes the bitter truth, and does not want to join Joseph in Egypt until God reassures him that He will return to Canaan with Jacob, that is, with his descendants (Gen. 46:3-4).[49] So the text at least mildly suggests the shortcoming of Joseph's reasoning concerning his brothers' actions (by suggesting that he misperceives his place in history). But would Joseph's reasoning have been correct had he focused on the impending enslavement rather than on famine relief? Since the cited texts do not resolve *that* query, our original question returns: if the sequence of events in the Joseph narrative is necessary for the realization of God's plan and God *desires* the Jews to end up in Egypt, would *this* mitigate the brothers' culpability, in spite of their keenly experienced and painfully expressed sense of guilt (42:21; 50:15)?

Joseph's exoneration of his brothers is indeed logically strained.[50] First, their *motive* was plainly nefarious. Second, as commentators note, even if their motivation were to fulfill a divine plan for history, "God has many agents." That is, a divine plan can be realized in several different ways.[51] Hence, the ends justify the means only if the means are also the direct act of God. These considerations render Joseph's assessment open to question.

Nevertheless, Nahmanides, contrary to the position just cited, affirms that if God has pre-ordained a certain end, then human beings are right to act in order to realize this divine end. So, for example, Nahmanides explains why Joseph prolonged his father's grief for over twenty years by failing to communicate with him: the fulfillment of his dreams required that *all* the brothers should bow down to him, and this could not be accomplished until Benjamin would be brought to Egypt through Joseph's subterfuge (commentary to 42:6). Likewise, Nahmanides maintains that the nations that oppressed Israel in the Bible (such as Egypt, Assyria, Babylonia) would have been without culpability — even commended — had they sought thereby to implement divine prophecies and had they not persecuted the Jews more than the prophecies required.[52] Nahmanides' view would, of course, not vindicate Joseph for exonerating his brothers. Nahmanides requires an agent to be conscious of the divine plan and to be motivated by this knowledge. Nevertheless, his thesis is intriguing, even if unconfirmed by biblical material.

The phenomenon of events that are integral to the divine plan but are dependent on human initiative — and sometimes on acts that leave room for moral questioning — appears frequently in the Bible. Rebecca and Jacob deceive Isaac by dressing Jacob as Esau and tricking Isaac into bestowing Esau's apparent blessing upon Jacob. What justified Rebecca in devising the hoax? Perhaps it was the oracle she heard before her twin sons were born: "And the elder [Esau] shall serve the younger [Jacob]" (Gen. 29:29).[53] Her actions sought to bring the prediction to fulfillment. Let us assume this interpretation and inquire how her behavior, as well as Jacob's, is viewed by the narrative.

Often, the Bible neither condones nor approves behavior explicitly; it lets the reader draw his or her own conclusions by subtle literary suggestions. We have already seen how the text imparts a partial censure of Joseph. The Bible also suggests that Jacob suffered in later life measure-for-measure for his involvement in his mother's scheme. His uncle Laban substitutes an older sister (Leah) for the younger sister whom Jacob planned to marry (Rachel), defending his behavior with the cutting words, "In our place, such is not done, to give the younger before the elder" (Gen. 29:26). And the deception perpetrated on Jacob by his sons, including both that of Joseph's brothers and that of Joseph himself, leads him to sum up his years as "few and bad" (Gen. 47:9). As for Rebecca, she sends Jacob away to live with her brother Laban "for a few days," while Esau's fury over the theft cools (Gen. 27:44). But Jacob is forced to remain with Laban for over twenty years and Rebecca never sees her son again.[54] Divine plan or no divine plan, deception is spiritually costly.[55]

In these episodes, the Jacob and Joseph stories, God is rarely acknowledged as the cause of events. From the time that Joseph is incarcerated by Potiphar, the Tetragrammaton, which generally signifies direct divine intervention, is absent; only *Elokim,* indicating God's general providence, appears. Furthermore, Elokim is depicted as the initiator of events only by the characters, not by the biblical narration itself. In the book of Esther, which takes place in exile and during a period when the light of prophecy has become obscured, God absconds completely from the narrative.[56] Yet the light of the events' Author shines through the cracks and crevices of the naturalistic causal network.[57]

Traditional philosophical theories have sought to impose on the Bible a unified theological doctrine, true for all books and circumstances. Our approach recognizes that the biblical metaphysic is as complex as it is enigmatic. Such concepts as providence, history, and responsibility are grasped by human beings in a variety of contexts. Sometimes, God is depicted as in total control of events; sometimes, He appears to relinquish the initiative.

THE ORIGINS OF THE UNIVERSE

We began by asking whether, and in what ways, the Bible can be fruitfully studied as a source of philosophical reflection. Some treatments of the creation story confront us in especially sharp form with the methodological pitfall of taking a book to be something it isn't intended to be. At the same time, they enable us to see why the Bible's *philosophical* trajectory might be of special importance.

Traditionally, Jewish schoolchildren have gained their first insight into the purpose of the Bible (or more specifically, the Torah) from the very first comment of R. Shlomo Yitzhaki (Rashi):

R. Yitzhak said: the Torah should have begun from "This month is for you the first of the months" (Ex. 12:2), for that is the first precept commanded to Israel.[58] And why did it begin with "In the beginning"? Because "He has related the power of His deeds to His people, to give them the inheritance of the nations" (Ps. 111:5). For if the nations of the worlds say to Israel, "You are thieves for having conquered the land of the seven [Canaanite] nations," Israel will say: "All the earth is God's — he created it and gave it to whomever he saw fit."[59]

A striking assumption underlies R. Yitzhak's question in the quoted *midrash*, namely, that cosmogonical and historical narratives are altogether irrelevant to the Torah's purposes; only the laws are pertinent.[60] Although the answer attributed to R. Yitzhak shows that he later modifies this startling assumption[61] — the Torah does more than inculcate laws, it also validates Israel's claim to the land of Israel — Rashi's approach nonetheless tends to minimize the value of any hermeneutic of the Bible that is not centered on its laws. It thereby broaches the possibility that the Bible is not terribly interested in providing accurate cosmogony for its own sake.[62]

Consider next the comment of Nahmanides:

One may question [R. Yitzhak's view as cited by Rashi]. For there is a great necessity to begin the Torah with "In the beginning God created." It is the root of faith; and one who does not believe in it [creation *ex nihilo*] and thinks the world is eternal denies the essential principle [of Judaism] and has no Torah! The answer is that the story of creation is a deep mystery not to be understood from the verses . . . It is for this reason that R. Yitzhak said that it was not necessary for the Torah to begin with the chapter of "In the beginning God created" — what was created on the first day, what was done on the second and other days, as well as an extended account of the creation of Adam and Eve, their sin and punishment, and the story of the Garden of Eden and the expulsion of Adam from it — because all this cannot be understood completely from the verses. All the more, it was not necessary for the story of the generations of the flood and of the dispersion to be written, for there is no great need of these narratives, and for people who believe in the Torah, it would suffice without these verses.[63]

For Nahmanides, unlike Rashi, the inclusion of cosmogony is not puzzling *per se*, as the Bible aims to convey "*ikkarei emunah*," fundamentals of faith. Still, the extensive elaboration of these fundamentals — what was created on each day — is seemingly otiose, and the Torah's narrative is, in any case, too meager to furnish genuine understanding.[64] Nor *prima facie* is there need for the detailed history of the patriarchs that follows. Nahmanides explains the necessity for the ostensibly otiose narrative sections by pointing out the moral lesson they convey to Israel. The stories of Eden, the flood, and the dispersion teach that, "It is proper that when a people continues to sin it should lose its place and another people should come and inherit the land."[65] Like Rashi, Nahmanides adopts a restricted view of the aims of the Torah.

Needless to say, neither Rashi nor Nahmanides questions the historicity of the biblical narrative. On the contrary, to infer the lesson each gleans from the Bible's inclusion of the narrative — the absolute right of the Jews to the land of Israel (Rashi) and the dependence of the Jews' right to the land upon their deeds (Nahmanides) — the narratives must be *true*. For Rashi's lesson to be learned, God must have created the world and granted Israel a particular land; for Nahmanides' to be inferred, there must have been a previous *factual* pattern of sin and expulsion. Nevertheless, approaches like those of Rashi and Nahmanides tend to deter the kind of emphasis on historical and scientific accuracy that would obscure the Torah's larger purposes.

This issue has become particularly acute and sensitive with the emergence of modern cosmology, anthropology, biology, and history. In the twentieth century, R. Abraham Isaac Kook, the first Ashkenazi Chief Rabbi of Palestine and a major theologian, addressed the clash between evolution and creation as well as the contradiction between the scientific assessments of the age of the earth and the biblical chronology, which makes the universe less than six thousand years old. He wrote:

> It makes no difference for us if in truth there was in the world an actual Garden of Eden, during which man delighted in an abundance of physical and spiritual good, or if actual existence began from the bottom upward, from the lowest level of being toward its highest... We only have to know that there is a real possibility that even if man has risen to a high level, and has been deserving of all honors and pleasures, if he corrupts his ways, he can lose all that he has, and bring harm to himself and to his descendants for many generations.[66]

Surely this is not meant to imply that biblical religion, or a theology sensitive to it, is indifferent to matters of historical and scientific fact. The centrality of the creation motif and the history of the Jewish people in the Bible are enough to belie any such notion. Of course, not everyone will draw the line in the same place: thus, for example, there are those who insist that observance of the Sabbath makes sense only on the basis of a literal six-day creation. It should not be difficult, however, to agree on the significance of the Bible's perspective on the fundamental questions of the examined life. Our own attempt in these pages to map a coherent biblical view of morality, of evil, and of human responsibility points to some of the possibilities.

CONCLUSION

Judaism is, of course, not identical with the Bible. Jewish thought must carry on a conversation with Talmud and Midrash, Kabbalah, Jewish philosophy and even legal material from all ages. This quest for integration is often based on the assumption that there is an underlying continuity to Judaism. It also recognizes that unmediated access to the Bible, abstracted from its canonical form and exegetical history, is an unattainable chimera, even though, to the extent possible, the philosopher should be wary of the anachronistic identification of a particular problem or theory with the living data it seeks to capture.[67] The examination of biblical ideas requires the thinker to perceive the continuities between the various biblical statements and later philosophies, even while taking careful note of the ruptures.

The Bible warrants philosophical attention; indeed, as we have seen, it supplies rich resources for philosophical analysis and exegesis. Nonetheless, the Bible is but one element, however central, in constructing a philosophy that does justice to the rich and variegated tapestry of Judaism and Jewish tradition.

NOTES

David Berger, Devorah Steinmetz, and Kenneth Waxman provided useful comments and suggestions on an earlier version of this article.

[1] A single example demonstrates the impossibility of limiting philosophy to conventionally formulated sentences. The book of Jonah concludes on a long rhetorical question: "You were concerned for the gourd on which you did not labor. ...Shall I not be concerned for Nineveh...?" There is no way of turning this interrogation into the indicative mood; yet if this verse is not philosophy, then nothing in the Bible is philosophy!

[2] Modern scholars often account for contradictions by assigning the conflicting materials to distinct traditions and sources, but the Bible has generally been understood as a unified document in Jewish tradition.

[3] Whereas medieval Aristotelian Jewish philosophers denied that God has emotions, mainly because saying otherwise attributes change to God and

change is an imperfection, present day philosophy has less trouble with the doctrine. We nonetheless include the belief in divine emotions among items that seemed primitive to later sensibilities.

4   *Guide of the Perplexed*, trans. Shlomo Pines (Chicago, 1963), I:36-37. References to the *Guide* are by part and chapter(s).

5   *Guide of the Perplexed* III:1-8. Maimonides says, however, in line with his general approach in writing the *Guide*, that to the ordinary reader he will appear in those chapters to be merely translating or summarizing the prophetic text, while the astute reader will penetrate to the real meaning.

6   See Maimonides, *Guide of the Perplexed*, III: 22-23 and Gersonides' commentary to Job.

7   See *Guide of the Perplexed* I:1-2; Lawrence Berman, "Maimonides on the Fall of Man," *AJS Review* 5 (1980): 1-15; Sara Klein-Braslavy, *Perush ha-Rambam la-Sippurim al Adam be-Parashat Bereshit* (Jerusalem, 1986).

8   A third negative reaction should be mentioned, that of kabbalists. Like the philosophers, and unlike either of the two views we will describe, kabbalists posited a deeper, esoteric level of meaning to the biblical text. However, they rejected the particular contents that rationalists claimed were found in those esoteric layers and replaced them with a different set of meanings.

9   Spinoza, *Theological-Political Treatise*, chs. I and II. (In the translation by R. H. M. Elwes [New York, 1951], 3-42.)

10 See, for example, Jonathan Barnes, *The Pre-Socratic Philosophers* (London, 1982).

11 That we do not here address diachronic questions within the Bible should not be taken to gainsay or even downplay their importance for theology and for elucidating the intellectual history of many concepts in biblical literature.

12 For example, David's consecutive inquiries about Saul's intentions and about the subsequent behavior of the men of Keilah in the event that Saul goes there (I Sam. 23:10-12) suggested to later philosophers the problem of whether middle knowledge is possible (that is, knowledge of how a free creature would act in all possible situations, including purely hypothetical ones). (See Robert Merrihew Adams "Middle Knowledge and the Problem of Evil," in *The Virtue of Faith* [New York, 1987], 77-93.) But such questions are distant from the Bible's agenda.

13 The same, we think, is true of legal material, particularly when it is situated in a narrative context, but we will not illustrate that point here.

14 For Christian responses, see Janine Marie Idziak (ed.), *Divine Command Morality* (Toronto, 1979).

15 Biblical interpreters have sometimes defined the episode differently, seeing it as a clash between king and prophet over whether the prophet is the sole arbiter of the divine intent.

16 See Louis Jacobs, "The Relationship Between Religion and Ethics in Jewish Thought," in *Contemporary Jewish Ethics*, ed. Menachem Kellner (New York, 1978), 41-57, Sid Z. Leiman, "Critique of Louis Jacobs," ibid., 58-60, and Aharon Lichtenstein, "Does Jewish Tradition Recognize an Ethic Independent of Halakha?," ibid., 102-23, for further analysis of the sources.

[17] Kenneth Seeskin, *Jewish Philosophy in a Secular Age* (Albany, 1990), chapter 5.

[18] Kierkegaard is generally taken to define the ethical stage in a Kantian manner (see, for example, Ronald Green, *Kierkegaard and Kant* [Albany, 1992]). Jerome Gellman, *The Fear, the Trembling and the Fire* (Washington, DC, 1994) opts for a Hegelian provenance of the ethical. More radically, he construes obedience to God as a label for authentic individual self-expression. For a creative reading of the story as *favoring* Abraham's making independent moral judgments, see Lippman Bodoff "The Real Test of the *Akedah:* Blind Obedience vs. Moral Choice," *Judaism* 42 (1993): 71-92. See also "'From the Depths I Have Called to You'," in this volume.

It is possible that Kierkegaard is not claiming that the religious choice is superior to the moral one, but rather that the difference between the two must be appreciated and the religious must never be confused with the moral — and that the religious choice inspires his admiration.

[19] See, for example, Isaiah Leibowitz, *Al Olam u-Melo'o* (Jerusalem, 1987). This is despite Leibowitz's distaste for Kierkegaard's "Christian bellyaching."

[20] See Ronald Green, *Religion and Moral Reason* (New York, 1988), chaps. 4-5.

[21] Milton Steinberg, *Anatomy of Faith* (New York, 1960), 147; cf. Jacobs, "The Relationship Between Religion and Ethics in Jewish Thought," 53-54. At the same time, R. Joseph B. Soloveitchik has pointed to kindred situations in the Bible where no angel appears to stay the upraised slaughtering knife. R. Joseph B. Soloveitchik, "*Ha-Yehudi Mashul le-Sefer Torah*," trans. from Yiddish by Shalom Carmy, in *Beit Yosef Shaul* 4 (1994): 68-100.

[22] Compare the discussion of Phyllis Trible's analysis of Gen. 22 in Carmy, "A Room with a View;" see also Louis Jacobs, "The Problem of the *Akedah* in Jewish Thought," in *Kierkegaard's Fear and Trembling: Critical Appraisals*, ed. Robert L. Perkins (Birmingham, Alabama, 1981), 1-9.

[23] Cf. Maimonides, *Guide of the Perplexed*, I:2; Nahmanides, commentary to Gen. 2:9; and other sources quoted in Nehama Leibowitz, *Studies in Bereshit (Genesis) in the Context of Ancient and Modern Jewish Bible Commentary*, 4th ed., trans. Aryeh Newman (Jerusalem, 1981), 17-37. For an assortment of Jewish and Christian discussions of this chapter, including references to a similar analysis of good and evil by Karl Barth, see *A Walk in the Garden: Biblical, Iconographical, and Literary Images of Eden*, ed. Paul Morris and Deborah Sawyer (Ithaca, 1992).

[24] See Michael Wyschogrod, "Sin and Atonement in Judaism," in *The Human Condition in the Jewish and Christian Traditions*, ed. Frederick Greenspahn (New York, 1986), 103-26.

[25] Or not good: see Gen. 2:18 , "It is not good for the man to be alone."

[26] Wyschogrod does not directly explain *why* they were now embarrassed by nakedness; precisely at this point, his approach should be combined with the traditional exegesis that relates the "knowledge of good and evil" to sexual arousal. But such a synthesis will not be sought here.

[27] See David Sykes, *Patterns in Genesis*, Ph.D. dissertation (Yeshiva University, 1985).

28 The Rabbis (*Sanhedrin* 56b) derived an Adamic prohibition of murder from Gen. 2:16-17, but God does not invoke a command when he confronts Cain, only when He confronts Adam.

29 See his comment to Gen. 6:2.

30 On the theme of re-creation, see Michael Fishbane, *Text and Texture* (New York, 1979), 30-39.

31 For further development, see Devora Steinmetz, "The Vineyard, Farm, and Garden: The Drunkenness of Noah in the Context of the Primeval History," *Journal of Biblical Literature* 113, 2 (1994): 193-207.

32 David Hume, *Dialogues Concerning Natural Religion*, X. (We have added the sentence about omniscience.)

33 *Guide of the Perplexed* III:20.

34 See Jerome Gellman, "The Meta-philosophy of Religious Language," *Noûs* 2 (1977): 151-61.

35 See Joseph Albo, *Sefer ha-Ikkarim* IV: 14, 15.

36 See Ephraim Urbach, *The Sages: Their Concepts and Beliefs*, trans. by Israel Abrahams (Cambridge, MA, 1987), 420-61; Yaakov Elman, "The Suffering of the Righteous in Palestinian and Babylonian Sources," *Jewish Quarterly Review* 80 (1990): 315-39 and "Righteousness as its Own Reward: An Inquiry into the Theologies of the Stam," *Proceedings of the American Academy for Jewish Research* 57 (1990-91): 35-68; Robert Goldenberg, "Early Rabbinic Explanations of the Destruction of Jerusalem, " *Journal of Jewish Studies* 33 (1982): 517-25.

37 Rudolf Otto, *The Idea of the Holy*, trans. by John W. Harvey (Oxford, 1950), 77-81.

38 See, for example, *The Dimensions of Job*, ed. Nahum Glatzer (New York, 1969).

39 R. Joseph B. Soloveitchik, "The Lonely Man of Faith," *Tradition* 7, 2 (1965): 37-38.

40 Some also find the soul-making theodicy in remarks of Elihu (33:16-20).

41 Seeskin, *Jewish Philosophy*, 173.

42 See Saadiah Gaon, *The Book of Theodicy* (Commentary on the Book of Job), trans. Lenn Evan Goodman (New Haven, 1988), chap. 38.

43 Rashi, following the rabbis in the Midrash, holds that the divine pathos, like the human, adopts, as it were, the emotions appropriate to the present tense; when a child is born, one rejoices, though knowing all too well that the road from birth leads to death. See also R. Hayyim ibn Atar's *Or ha-Hayyim*, ad loc.

44 This verse is, in fact, cited by Gersonides to support his limitation of divine foreknowledge; see his commentary to Gen. 22. Also see Albo, *The Book of Roots*, V:13; Leibowitz, *Studies*, 188-93; Seymour Feldman, "The Binding of Isaac: A Test Case of Divine Foreknowledge," in *Divine Omniscience and Omnipotence in Medieval Philosophy*, ed. Tamar Rudavsky (Dordrecht, 1985), 105-33; Jeremy Cohen, "Philosophical Exegesis in Historical Perspective: The Case of the Binding of Isaac," ibid., 135-42.

45 See Rashi, who takes this to imply that God "arranges" the accident to punish both the victim and the perpetrator for previous offenses.

46 See ibn Ezra, ad loc.

47 See also Robert Alter, *The Art of Biblical Narrative* (New York, 1981), 33-35.

48   To be sure, Joseph may not be exonerating them but rather telling them not to feel badly, since their acts resulted in good. It will be fruitful, however, to work with the stronger reading.

49   Joseph's later request for the Israelites to take his remains with them when they finally leave Egypt (Gen. 50:24) reflects Jacob's eventual influence upon him (note Jacob's request at 47:29).

50   According to some readings of Amos 2:6, the prophet there condemned the brothers' actions.

51   See, for example, Isaac Abravanel's comment to Gen. 37:1; see also Maimonides, *Mishneh Torah, Hilkhot Teshuvah*, 6:5; Nachum Rabinovitch, "The One and The Many: Early Stochastic Reasoning in Philosophy," *Annals of Science* 34:4 (1977): 331-44.

52   See commentary to Gen. 15:14 and *Or ha-Hayyim* ad loc. Note Nahmanides' exploitation of typology as a tool of exegesis in Genesis (see 12:7, *inter alia*).

53   A different interpretation would highlight the ambiguity of the Hebrew — either "elder" or "younger" could be taken as the subject and the other phrase as the object; see Umberto Cassuto, *The Documentary Hypothesis and the Composition of the Pentateuch: Eight Lectures,* trans. Israel Abrahams (Jerusalem, 1961), 86-87.

54   Kenneth Waxman pointed this out.

55   See Leibowitz, *Studies*, 264-79 on Jacob's deception. Late medieval thinkers such as R. Isaac Arama (*Akedat Yitzhak* 1:28) rejected Nahmanides' approach to the Joseph story because they objected to the implication that the divine end justifies unacceptable human means. Walter Wurzburger, "Yavneh Studies in *Vayechi*," in *Yavneh Studies in Parashat ha-Shavua: Bereshit,* ed. Joel B. Wolowelsky, (New York, 1969), 40-42, develops the view that Joseph subscribed to Nahmanides' thesis, but was wrong to do so.

56   Scholars have noted numerous literary parallels between the Joseph and Esther narratives. There may be other explanations of why the divine name is absent from these stories, but finding a common reason seems to us methodologically preferable in light of the other parallels between the stories.

57   One other issue that these episodes raise is the contingency of Jewish history. Believers in the Bible's accuracy are accustomed to think that Jewish history would not be Jewish history had, say, the theft of the blessing, or Joseph's sojourn in Egypt, never occurred. But if, *pace* Nahmanides, we impute blame even to people who try to fulfill the divine plan, this may imply that only certain end results are ordained, not the means; agents are culpable because they did not have to be the ones to bring the ordained result about. Hence, Jewish history does carry an element of contingency. R. Joseph Soloveitchik's lectures on the Bible frequently dramatize the question of alternative outcomes: what if certain meritorious acts had not been performed, and what if certain temptations had been resisted? (See especially J. B. Soloveitchik, *Divrei Hashkafah*, trans. Moshe Krone [Jerusalem, 1992].) He thus combines Nahmanides' consciousness of the large-scale repercussions of acts recorded in the Bible with an existentialist emphasis on the burden of individual choice.

58   The rabbis of the Talmud regard Ex. 12:2 as the commandment to sanctify each new moon.

59   See Tanhuma (Buber), 11.

60   Jon D. Levenson, *Sinai and Zion: An Entry into the Jewish Bible* (New York, 1985), has emphasized that the classic Christian works on Old Testament theology, such as those of Eichrodt and von Rad, are virtually oblivious to the centrality of law in the Bible.

61   Rashi's super-commentaries, for example, those of R. Eliyahu Mizrachi and Maharal, offer detailed analysis of the difference between the implied position of the question and that of the conclusion.

62   Rashi's grandson, Rashbam, goes even farther. In his view, the story of creation is included in order to establish the seven-day week culminating in the Sabbath (see Sara Kamin, "Rashbam's Conception of the Creation in Light of the Intellectual Currents of his Time," in *Scripta Hierosolymitana 31: Studies in Bible*, ed. S. Japhet [1986], 91-132). Remarkably, the sectarian pseudepigraphic book of Jubilees, dated to the second century B.C.E, opens with Moses on Sinai, and reviews creation as a backdrop to the revelation of the law, thus providing, as it were, an alternative version of the Torah that comes close to the spirit behind R. Yitzhak's question.

63   Commentary to Gen. 1:1, following closely the translation of Charles D. Chavel in Nahmanides, *Commentary on the Torah* (New York, 1971).

64   One way to put Nahmanides' thesis is this: the Bible conveys metaphysical *truth*, but is not devoted to metaphysical *enlightenment*. The enlightenment is esoteric, accessible only to kabbalists; for the ordinary reader of the Bible, the fundamentals of faith suffice.

65   Nahmanides, *Commentary on the Torah*, 19.

66   R. Abraham Isaac Kook, *Iggerot ha-Reayah* I (Jerusalem, 1985), #134 (as translated in Tzvi Feldman, *Rav A. Y. Kook: Selected Letters*, [Ma'aleh Adumim, 1986], 12). Note also R. Kook's additional reference to talmudic remarks on "confused dates" in prophetic texts (cited in Carmy, "A Room with a View"). A zesty formulation of the point is found in J.H. Hertz, *The Pentateuch and Haftorahs: Hebrew Text, English Translation, and Commentary* (New York, 1941), I: 195: "And fully to grasp the eternal power and infinite beauty of these words 'And God created man in his own image' — we need but compare them with the genealogy of man, condensed from the pages of one of the leading biologists of the age (Haeckel): 'Monera begat Amoeba, Amoeba begat Synamoebae, Synamoebae begat Ciliated Larva...' Let anyone who is disturbed by the fact that Scripture does not include the latest scientific doctrine try to imagine such information proved in a Biblical chapter." A contemporary philosopher, Peter van Inwagen, a committed Christian, has likewise emphasized, in a colorful way, the moral and spiritual value of the creation stories and the relative unimportance of its scientific implications. See his "Genesis and Evolution," in *God, Knowledge & Mystery* (Ithaca, NY, 1995), 128-62, esp. 128-44.

67   See Carmy, "A Room with a View."

MAIMONIDES' MORAL THEORY

INTRODUCTION: THE STATUS OF MORALITY IN MAIMONIDEAN THOUGHT

What sort of life constitutes the highest perfection for a human being? For Maimonides, as for Aristotle,[1] the answer is not moral excellence, but rather intellectual perfection, that is, "the conception of the intelligibles [eternal truths], which teach true opinions concerning the divine things" (*GP* III:54:692).[2] Attaining this perfection leads to immortality.[3] Morality, by contrast, is "a preparation for something else" (viz., the life of contemplation) "and not an end in itself" (*GP* III:54:635). "To [the] ultimate perfection there do not belong either actions or moral qualities" (*GP* III:27:511). The assertion that intellectual perfection is ultimate is already in Maimonides' early work, *The Commentary to the Mishnah*: one must "set his sight on a single goal: the perception of God...I mean, knowledge of Him, in so far as that lies within man's power."[4]

Moral perfection cannot be supreme, Maimonides argues, for the highest perfection cannot involve, as part of its essence, anyone else besides the person who is questing for perfection. The ultimate perfection must be achievable even by a solitary individual with no social connections. Since moral habits are only dispositions to be useful to other people, "It [moral perfection] is an instrument for someone else" (III:54: 635; see also I:34). Just as God's perfection does not depend on anything outside Himself, so too the perfected person is a self-sufficient agent and his ultimate perfection does not require others for its attainment.

Maimonides alludes to yet another reason why moral virtues cannot be part of the ultimate perfection. In the course of asserting that the ultimate perfection consists only of intellection, he states that the ultimate perfection "consists only of opinions toward which speculation has led and that investigation has rendered compulsory" (III:27:511). Unlike scientific and metaphysical truths, moral claims cannot be supported by a demonstration that renders them "compulsory." At one point Maimonides chastises Jewish thinkers (most likely Sa'adyah Ga'on) who accepted the terms of the Mutakallimun and referred to Torah laws against stealing, killing, and the like as "rational" laws (EC, chap. 6). His objection, one surmises, is that while these laws serve a purpose, and are rational in that sense of being purposive, they are not rational in the way that demonstrated beliefs in geometry, mathematics, science or metaphysics are.

At least some of morality, in fact, consists only of commonly accepted opinions. Consider Maimonides' reading of the narrative of Adam and Eve in the Garden of Eden (GP 1:2). Adam, he says, originally possessed demonstrative knowledge — knowledge of *emet ve-sheker*, the true and the false. But by his sin he fell into an inferior state in which he came to be, as the Bible puts it, "a knower of good and evil," that is, one who exercises moral judgment. Such judgments are inferior to judgments of science and metaphysics for two reasons. The first is that they are not demonstrable in the sense of being deducible from self-evident premises. Similarly, *Guide* II:33 characterizes the final eight commandments of the Decalogue thus: "They belong to the class of generally accepted opinions and those adopted in virtue of tradition, not to the class of the intellecta" (364). While one or two passages suggest that ethics is grasped by the intellect, the predominant Maimonidean view is decidedly otherwise.[5]

The second reason for the inferiority of moral cognition is that the very possibility of moral judgment depends on the shameful fact that human beings are creatures of passion, possessing acquisitive desires and lusts, as a result of being composed of matter as well as form (intellect). It is no surprise that the fall of humankind occurs when moral judgment is introduced into a world that previously had witnessed only intellection directed at "the true and the false." As a further indication of morality's relatively low status, we should note that whereas Maimonides' philosophic sources saw moral knowledge as a function of "the practical intellect," and whereas he recognizes a practical function of the rational faculty, Maimonides never uses the term "practical intellect" nor the term "practical rational faculty." In this way, Howard Kreisel suggests, Maimonides assures that only the theoretical intellect is recognized as intellect, and that the only function of the rational faculty that truly matters is the theoretical.[6]

There can be little quarrel, then, that neither the practice of morality nor moral theorizing could rank as high for Maimonides as pondering science and metaphysics. That having been said, it would be a colossal mistake to ignore what Maimonides does say about ethics. His writings contain extensive discussions of proper *de'ot*, or ethical characteristics, of the processes of ridding oneself of bad ethical traits and acquiring good ones, and of the attempt to "quell the impulses" of matter which distract people from intellectual pursuits and impede cognition of what is not physical. The quelling of such impulses is associated with the attainment of holiness (*Guide* III:8, III:33). Morality is a preparation for contemplation and constitutes no trivial task; how one conducts that preparation is a topic to which Maimonides devotes considerable attention.

Furthermore, although there is a certain sort of morality that precedes and is prerequisite for the *vita contemplativa*, there is another sort of morality that is a *consequence* of intellectual perfection and represents an "overflow" or "emanation" from intellectual achievement. This morality, we shall see, is quite different from morality as we have considered it so far. Let us call the morality needed for intellectual perfection propadeutic morality, and the morality that results from intellectual perfection consequent morality. In what follows we shall explore the two dimensions of morality, propadeutic and consequent, and compare and contrast them.

The crucial texts for the discussion that follows are Maimonides' introduction to his commentary to the moralistic tractate *Avot*, an introduction widely known as *Eight Chapters* (*EC*), the section of the *Mishneh Torah* known as *Hilkhot De'ot* (*Laws of Character Traits*), and *Guide of the Perplexed*, especially I:54 and III:54.[7]

PROPADEUTIC MORALITY IN THE LEGAL WRITINGS

Virtue ethics

Contemporary philosophers distinguish between virtue-centered ethical theories and action-centered ones. In an ethics of virtue the focus is not on the rightness and wrongness of actions, but on the goodness or badness of certain character traits. Virtue ethics examines the psychological characteristics of good and bad people, identifying traits like compassion, humility, gentleness, temperance and courage, which are regarded as virtues, and traits like callousness, arrogance, meanness, intemperance, and cowardice, which are regarded as vices. Actions are important only insofar as they are conducive or inimical to the production of virtuous or vicious characteristics, or insofar as they are the effect of virtuous or vicious traits.

As an adherent of and authority on Jewish law, Maimonides obviously had to devote the lion's share of his attention to questions about how to act. His legal code *Mishneh Torah* accordingly offers myriad rulings about the rightness or wrongness of certain actions as judged by Jewish law.

But as a philosopher he also exhibits a conspicuous concern with virtues and vices, psychological dispositions as distinct from the actions they produce and those by which they are produced. Thus, for instance, in his discussion of repentance, he stresses that repentance is not only for sinful deeds but also for bad character traits.[8] On some occasions he interprets a rabbinic statement about a sinful act as referring to vice.[9] Again, as Herbert Davidson points out, in his *Eight Chapters* Maimonides reserves the terms virtuous and vicious for character traits rather than actions.[10] With Aristotle, Maimonides distinguishes two kinds of virtues and vices: moral and intellectual. Many actions prescribed by the law are important as instruments or means. They build virtue.

There is some conflict in Maimonides' writings as to whether the instrumental value of ethical action and of virtue is that they conduce to individual development or instead to communal order, in which case they are not necessary for an individual living in isolation. In *Mishneh Torah, Hilkhot Yesodei ha-Torah* 4:12-13, the aim of the law is said to be both that it gives composure to the mind and that it contributes to social order. But in *Guide* III:27:510 we read that one of the aims of the law, "welfare of the body," refers to "the acquisition by every individual of moral qualities that are useful for life in society so that the affairs of the city may be ordered." Also in this vein is a passage in II:40:382, which speaks of the ruler's aim of "the well ordering of the community." Other passages, too, such as those quoted earlier from III:54, suggest that the value served by moral virtue is served only in social contexts — if you suppose an individual is "alone, acting on no one," moral virtues are "in vain and without employment and unheeded" and "do not perfect the individual in anything" (I:54:635). Still other passages, however, focus on the role of morality in individual perfection: "it being impossible to achieve true, rational acts — I mean perfect rationality — unless it be by a man thoroughly trained with respect to his morals and endowed with the qualities of tranquility and quiet" (I:34:77). In *EC* 4 specific commandments are related to the acquisition of virtuous qualities. Just why in some passages but not in others Maimonides sees virtue as serving social order rather than individual development is not clear, but this need not detain us at this point.[11] The important point is that moral virtues are instruments.

Moral instruction as therapy for the soul

A core idea in *EC*, where Maimonides treats what I have called propadeutic morality, is that "the improvement of moral habits is the same as the cure of the soul and its powers" (EC, 1). Using an analogy commonplace in Greek thought, he maintains that, just as a doctor who cures bodies needs to know the body he is curing, what the parts of the body are, and what things make the body sick or healthy, so too one who treats the soul — the "wise man" — "needs to know the soul in its entirety and its parts, as well as what makes it sick and what makes it healthy." The Rabbis, in Maimonides' loose paraphrase of a talmudic passage (*Avodah Zarah* 22a), stated that "piety serves to bring about the holy spirit." Hence following a proper cure and regimen for defects of the soul makes knowledge of God possible (to the extent humans may know Him) and even brings about prophecy; contrariwise, moral vices are "veils" (EC 7) that may prevent prophecy.[12]

The example of medicine supplies more than an analogy to what must be done for the sick soul. Health of the body contributes substantively to health of the soul, indeed plays a large role with respect to the development of morality. Virtue and vice have a basis in bodily temperament. But the analogy to medicine is more central to Maimonides' discussion than is the substantive connection between somatic medicine and soul-healing. The health of the body involves maintaining an equilibrium. Just so, the mean is the standard for health of the soul. Virtue lies in the mean between two extremes of temperament.

Here we encounter Maimonides' presentation of the well known Aristotelian doctrine of the mean.[13]

> Good actions are those balanced in the mean between two extremes, both of which are bad; one of them is an excess and the other a deficiency. The virtues are states of the soul and settled dispositions in the mean between two bad states [of the soul], one of which is excessive and the other deficient (*EC* 4).[14]

Thus the virtuous state of the soul that produces "moderation" in action is a mean between lust at one extreme and total insensibility to pleasure on the other, both of which are "completely bad." Liberality is the mean between miserliness and extravagance, courage the mean between rashness and cowardice, wit the mean between buffoonery and dullness, humility the mean between haughtiness and abasement, generosity the mean between prodigality and stinginess.[15] In each case, one of the two extremes is worse than the other (miserliness and cowardice being worse than the opposite extreme), whereas the mean is the ideal.

A person does not possess virtue or vice at the beginning of life, and the soul's dispositions cannot be acquired or changed in one swoop. The agent must repeatedly perform actions that will inculcate a specific trait and must do so over a long period of time. Furthermore, the acquisition of a virtuous trait may well require the person to perform acts that deviate from the mean.

Such deviation may be a form of either (a) corrective therapy which moves one's characteristics on to to the mean, or (b) preventive therapy which sustains one on the mean. Suppose a person tends to the extreme of miserliness. He must correct this by going to the other extreme and performing acts of extreme generosity, so that his character will end up in the middle between the extremes, that is, at the mean. Once cured, he can be encouraged to perform actions at the mean between extravagance and miserliness. Looking again at the analogy to medicine, when a body is out of equilibrium, "we look to which side it inclines in becoming unbalanced and then oppose it with its contrary until it returns to equilibrium" (*EC*, 4). A person might also incline away from the mean in one direction as preventive therapy, i. e. to prevent his going to the opposite extreme. This concept was illustrated by Aristotle using an analogy: one can straighten a bent twig by bending it in an opposite direction.[16]

Maimonides agrees with Aristotle on another significant point. One extreme, he holds, is more opposed to the mean than the other.[17] Put another way, the virtue is closer to one vice (the less bad one) than to the other. Cowardice is more opposed to bravery than is rashness, intemperance more opposed to temperance than is insensibility. In these cases the extreme to which we are more naturally drawn is more opposed to the intermediate condition (the mean). It is easier to move an extravagant person toward liberality than a miserly person, and easier to move an insensible person toward temperance than a lustful person. But it is not only the need to counteract a natural tendency that accounts for one extreme being worse than the other: one extreme is inherently worse.

The notion of therapy for the soul — corrective or preventive — enables Maimonides to develop in *Eight Chapters* the concept of the *fadil,* what his medieval Hebrew translators termed the *hasid* and English translators render as "pious man" or "virtuous man."[18] The *hasid* intentionally deviates from the mean, inclining in his acts toward the less bad of two extremes, in order to avoid the worse extreme of the pair. People of this type would "incline from moderation a little toward insensibility to pleasure, from courage a little toward rashness, from generosity a little toward prodigality, from humility toward abasement, and likewise with the rest." Some of them would fast, rise at night, abstain from eating meat and drinking wine, keep away from women, wear garments of wool and hair, dwell on mountains, and seclude themselves in desolate places with an eye to medical treatment. Yet only those who suffer from an ailment should behave in extreme ways; people who do not suffer illnesses of the soul will be harmed by extreme behavior. Were it not for the necessity of therapy, ascetic behavior would be reprehensible.

This point is illustrated by Maimonides' treatment of the Nazirite (Num. 6), someone who vows not to partake of meat and wine. Acccording to *Hilkhot De'ot* 3:1 and EC 4, the Nazirite is a sinner, and for this reason the Torah requires that, with the aid of the priest, he must secure atonement for his sin. A person whose soul is not diseased should not go toward any extreme; doing so will make his soul sick, just as a healthy person becomes sick when he takes medicine. Unfortunately, those who observed the pious people did not realize that the modes of conduct practiced by hasidim are not good for all people, and they became sick by emulating their actions.[19]

So much for the broad contours of Maimonides' discussion in *EC* and *Hilkhot De'ot*. At this point I would like to address several major issues that Maimonides' "propadeutic" moral theory confronts.[20]

The doctrine of the mean, biblical law, and rabbinic tradition

As noted earlier, Maimonides' ethical theory is heavily influenced by Aristotle's *Nicomachean Ethics*. In particular, the theory of the mean, the distinction between intellectual and moral virtue, the five-part nature of the soul, the strategy of therapeutic deviations from the mean, the notion that one extreme is worse than the other — these are all Aristotelian teachings. Herbert Davidson has further called attention to similarities between Maimonides' *Eight Chapters* and the Islamic philosopher Alfarabi's *Fusul al-Madani* (*Aphorisms of the Statesman*). Maimonides tells us he will cite extensively from other sources without attribution, justifying this practice by indicating that he sees no point in saying "so-and-so said." Alfarabi clearly is prominent among his unnamed sources.[21]

At the same time as he cites philosophers, however, Maimonides seeks to incorporate teachings of the Bible and of the Rabbis of the Talmud and Midrash. What we have in his writings, therefore, is a reading of biblical law and rabbinic tradition through Aristotelian and Farabian eyes — and a reading of Aristotle and Alfarabi through the prism of biblical and rabbinic tradition. The philosophic tradition itself is modified by Maimonides via teachings of the Rabbis and via some ideas that are integral to Maimonides' philosophy.

I shall focus here on the several instances in which Maimonides prescribes deviation from the mean. This point is best grasped by noting Aristotle (and Alfarabi's) distinction between the arithmetic mean, which is always fixed, and the relative mean, which "increases and decreases at different times and with reference of the things to which it is related."[22] To some extent Aristotle allowed for deviations from the mean. With regard to some emotions (spite, shamefulness, envy) and some actions (adultery, theft, murder), it is not the excess of these things that is bad, but the emotions or acts themselves.[23] And we have already discussed therapeutic deviation and the slight deviation away from the worse extreme. But the deviations Maimonides allows go beyond this.

Let us begin with *Hilkhot De'ot* 2:3: "In the case of some character traits, a man is forbidden to accustom himself to the mean. Rather, he should move to the other extreme." One such trait is humility, the other is anger.

Humility: "The good way is not that a man be merely humble, but that he have a lowly spirit" (*Hilkhot De'ot* 2:3). In support, Maimonides quotes R. Levitas in *Avot* 4:4: "Have a very, very lowly spirit."

The significance of this seeming departure from the mean is best seen by means of a contrast to Aristotle. Aristotle favors the proud man, whom he defines as a person who deems himself worthy of great things and indeed is worthy of them. The proud man represents the mean between extremes. At one extreme is the vain man, who deems himself worthy of great things but is not worthy of them. At the other is the humble man, who is worthy of great things but deems himself worthy to a degree less than his true worth. The proud man is both proud of his virtue, and worthy of it; thus, he expects others to honor him for his virtue. The humble man does not accept the honor to which he is entitled. The humble man, says Aristotle, is ignorant of himself.[24]

For Aristotle pride is "the crown of the virtues"[25] (he refers here to moral as opposed to intellectual virtues) and the "prize" for (moral) virtue.[26] According to Daniel Frank, the fact that Maimonides demands not merely humility but extreme humility reflects his belief that "to take an interest in worldly honor is to forget God, to live as if God did not exist. It is to place the mundane above the divine."[27] As Maimonides states in the name of the Rabbis, "Whoever is haughty is as if he denies God" (*Sotah* 4b). So while Aristotle values honor, Maimonides, with his theocentric perspective, disdains it.

The exceedingly humble Maimonidean man accepts insult to a remarkable degree. Maimonides tells a story (which originates as a Sufi tale) about a man who was asked "On what day of your life did you have the most joy?" The man describes a day on which he was traveling on a ship whose passengers included merchants and wealthy men. He was in the lowest part of the ship, wearing tattered garments, and while lying down was urinated upon by one of the men on board. "My soul was not pained at all by his deed, nor was I in the least agitated. Then I greatly rejoiced that I had reached the point where the contempt of that base man did not pain me, and I paid no heed to him."[28]

Is this approach compatible with the approach of the mean? That depends on whether Maimonides' prescription of extreme humility is merely therapeutically useful or instead good in itself. In both *EC* 4 and *Hilkhot De'ot* 2:2, extreme humility is given as an example of the therapeutic mean; and from the commentary to *Avot* 4:4 we get the same impression. God, furthermore, is called *anav* (humble), not exceedingly humble, so *imitatio Dei* would demand only ordinary humility. At the same time it must be conceded that Maimonides's wording in *Hilkhot De'ot* 2:3 is a universal prescription — "A man is forbidden…to accustom himself to the mean," suggesting that ordinary humility is simply unacceptable. The context and flavor of the Sufi tale suggests that it is not to be explained by therapy but by some real sense that the behavior of the offending individual and the general situation of the victim are not causes for pain; there is no reason to care about others so as to be insulted.[29] The various texts of *Hilkhot De'ot* are confusing in that, as Howard Kreisel cleverly puts it, "the person who is extremely humble possesses a trait which is not good (1:1, 1:3), is a righteous person who acts beyond the strict letter of the Law (1:5), while acting in a way mandated by the Law (2:3)."[30] These contradictions demand interpreters' attention, but we can say with some confidence that the extreme humility of *Hilkhot De'ot* 2:3 seems related to the requirement of theocentrism.

Anger: A second trait with respect to which Maimonides counsels extreme behavior is anger. In contrast to chapter 1, where he prescribed the mean, in chapter 2 of *Hilkhot De'ot* Maimonides writes, "It is proper for a man to move away from it to the other extreme and to teach himself not to become angry, even over something it is proper to be angry about" (*Hilkhot De'ot* 2:3). A person may feign anger in order to admonish others, "but his mind shall be tranquil within himself, like a man who feigns anger but is not angry." In this instance, too, Maimonides cites rabbinic sources, for example, "Anyone who is angry — it is as if he worships idols" (*Shabbat* 115b). Adapting *Yoma* 23a, he continues: "The way of the just men is to be insulted but not to insult; they hear themselves reviled and do not reply; they act out of love and rejoice in afflictions. Scripture says about them: 'And those who love Him are like the sun rising in its power' (Judges 5:31)."

Here again a contrast to Aristotle is helpful.[31] Aristotle saw irascibility and inirascibility (feeling no anger at all) as the extremes between which lie the mean of good-temperedness. So, while inirascibility is a vice for Aristotle, it is a virtue for Maimonides. For Aristotle, the virtue is good temperedness, that is, feeling anger as appropriate when insulted and acting on it. Feigning anger is no part of the virtue for Aristotle, since Aristotle's virtuous man exhibits a harmony between inner feeling and outer act.[32] For Maimonides it is otherwise. Notice that the traits of inirascibility and extreme humility are related, in that both reflect a lack of concern for honor. Likewise for Aristotle, good temperedness and pride are related in that both reflect a concern for honor.

It has been argued that for Maimonides the ideal of *imitatio Dei* demands a lack of any emotion whatsoever, since God has no emotional states; and that this is why in *Hilkhot De'ot* he favors inirascibility.[33] Against this explanation I note that in *Hilkhot De'ot* Maimonides does not counsel passionlessness generally, but only lack of anger. More likely, therefore, his point in *Hilkhot De'ot* is only about anger, and he is not saying that other of God's "attributes of action" should be imitated in action only and not in feeling. Still, anger is for Maimonides the paradigm of a bodily based emotion (I:54, III:8).[34] Another important element in Maimonides' condemnation of anger is that, like arrogance, anger reflects failure to make God central in one's life. Caring about honor and insult are antithetical to a God-centered life.[35]

The Law: A larger problem with the claim that Maimonides harmonized Torah and philosophic ethics is that Torah law seems to diverge from philosophic ethics[36] by mandating many actions that are not on the mean. Initially it may be tempting to think of Torah law as identical with the prescriptions of *phronesis* (practical wisdom), and to think of divine commandments as a shortcut to the results *phronesis* would yield if exercised. By observing Torah law, one would think, one obviates the need for *phronesis* and can move that much more quickly to theoretical pursuits. One achieves virtue by obeying the law, and one incurs vice by disobeying it. However this seemingly attractive picture does not fit the facts.

To take one example, the law does not prescribe how much to eat. Rather, it produces virtues that with the exercise of *phronesis* will result in a person's choosing the right amount to eat. Thus practical judgment is still necessary, which indicates that the law is not a full substitute for, that is, not a full functional equivalent of, *phronesis*.[37]

More importantly, the Torah mandates acts that simple adherence to the mean does not. It proscribes certain foods or food mixtures (meat and milk) and forbids certain specific sexual acts that ordinary ethics does not. The Torah commands leaving a corner in the field for the poor, giving tithes, releasing the poor from their debts in the sabbatical and jubilee years, giving charity adequate to providing what someone lacks, returning a stray animal or any lost object to its owner, and other deeds that require action in excess of the mean. Some required acts, such as relieving an enemy's animal of its burden, and the prohibition against taking revenge, reflect the curbing of anger we have already seen Maimonides describe.

Torah law also requires rising before the elderly and honoring and fearing parents. Based on talmudic teaching, one's duty to fear parents applies even if parents take their child's purse full of gold and cast it into the sea (*Mishneh Torah, Hilkhot Mamrim* 6:7). The biblical duty to rescue someone in danger likewise goes beyond the mean's requirements. In addition, the virtuous man eschews all idle talk (*Avot* 1:16).[38] The duty to rebuke a sinner is quite different from these duties in the trait it promotes — it is mandated to remove shyness. But this conduct too goes to excess (impudence). It is true, as Maimonides notes, that the Torah does not prohibit all food and drink or intercourse and does not mandate giving all one's wealth to the poor or to the Temple. The Laws incline one away from the mean without legislating the extreme. Still, the legislated behaviors are decidedly not at the mean.

Given these Torah-legislated deviations from the mean, must Maimonides give up asserting a convergence between philosophic ethics and Torah? Again we must consider that most people tend toward excess in one direction and Torah law is therefore preventive therapy. One of a pair of extremes is more opposed to the mean than the other; often we have a natural tendency toward one excess rather than another, a tendency that needs correction by the Law, which moves us in the other direction. While the *behavior* of the observant Jew is not on the mean, the *character trait* is, since Torah law corrects natural tendencies. On this reading, the Torah is in harmony with philosophy even though the philosophers do not themselves adopt the precepts of the Torah.

The previous explanation of why the Torah law deviates from the mean is not wholly satisfactory. Many observers of the Law may have a tendency not toward stinginess but toward generosity. It is not clear why they should obey the Torah's laws, insofar as such obedience will keep them from the mean and only performing actions that are closer to stinginess will put their traits at the mean. Perhaps this is the problem Maimonides has in mind in *Guide* III:34, when he states that some people may be harmed by the Law, but must nonetheless obey it because, unlike medicine, law is not calibrated and adapted to the individual. By observing Torah law, someone whose natural tendency is toward generosity or humility may go to that pole in a manner that is truly excessive. Nonetheless, he must obey.

Speaking more broadly, vice and virtue are not coextensive with obedience and disobedience relative to the law.[39] Obedience to the law is conducive to virtue and disobedience is inimical to the development of virtue — but this suggests that obedience has instrumental value only. Furthermore, on rare occasions disobedience of a command may be needed to acquire moral virtue. According to one scholar, Maimonides thinks the Rabbis would allow deviations from the Law in such cases, where one can then better engage in finding philosophic truth (notwithstanding III:34).[40]

The Nazirite: As noted earlier, in *Hilkhot De'ot* and *EC* Maimonides portrays the Nazirite as a sinner. But elsewhere in the *Mishneh Torah* (Hilkot Nezirut 10:14), he restricts his condemnation to those who undertake a Nazirite vow frivolously. Someone who makes the vow in sanctity has acted in a fine and praiseworthy fashion and ranks even above the prophets — this apparently despite the deviation from the mean his vow entails. There is no evidence that this praise is restricted to Nazirite vows that are undertaken as corrective or preventive therapy.[41]

Other extreme behavior: Mortification of the body is required for Torah study,[42] and Maimonides declares that one may abstain from marriage if his soul is so passionately committed to Torah.[43] He says this despite Rabbinic condemnation of Ben Azzai for failing to marry. These are definite ascetic strains in Maimonides' legal writings, strains that appear with greater clarity in the *Guide*. They are difficult to reconcile with the mean.[44]

The *Guide* leans strongly in the direction of asceticism. It is true that even in the *Guide*, Maimonides invokes the theme of balance, suggesting the ideal of the mean. He asserts, for example, as in *EC*, that when the Torah states that God has given "just statutes and judgments" (Deuteronomy 4:8), "just" means "equibalanced", and "The Law of the Lord is perfect" (Psalms 19:8) refers to its equibalance and wisdom. In the Law "there is no burden and excess — such as monastic life — nor a deficiency necessarily leading to greed and being engrossed in the indulgence of appetites" (II:39:380). This passage refers to acts; *Guide* III:39:554 speaks of "moderate moral qualities that form a part of the righteous statutes and judgments."

Yet we are told that a prophet will abolish his desire for "bestial things," which include eating, drinking, sexual intercourse, and in general the sense of touch (II:36: 371),[45] that people of science and the prophets will renounce and have contempt for bodily pleasures (II:40:384), that the sense of touch is "our greatest shame" (III:8:433), that "It behooves him who prefers to be a human being, to endeavor to diminish all the impulses of matter" such as eating, drinking, copulation, and anger (3:8:434), that one of the Law's intentions is "renouncing and avoiding sexual intercourse and causing it to be as infrequent as possible" (III:33:533), and that the Nazirite is worthy of praise (III:33, III:48). Clearly the middle way has been rejected except for the ordinary run of individuals, even though one cannot represent an intelligible if he is hungry or thirsty (III:27:511).[46]

We can surmise that the problem with asceticism arises when it is pursued by those who are unprepared for it and still have sensual urges. People who have overcome these urges are at a higher level, and for them asceticism is the proper course. As one scholar has written, "For those who live the life of the intellect, the doctrine of the mean does not provide the path most suitable to follow."[47]

Hakham vs. hasid: In *Hilkhot De'ot* 1:4-5, after telling us that anyone whose traits all lie on the mean is called "wise" (*hakham*) and that "the wise men of old" acted according to the middle way, Maimonides presents a second type, the "pious man," or *hasid*:

> Whoever is exceedingly scrupulous with himself and moves toward one side or the other, away from the character trait in the mean, is called a pious man. ...The pious men of old used to direct their character traits from the middle way toward [one of the two] extremes: some character traits toward the last extreme, and some toward the first extreme. This is the meaning of "inside the line of the law" [*lifnim mi-shurat ha-din*]. We are commanded to walk in these middle ways, which are the good and right ways. As it is said, "And you shall walk in His ways" [Deut. 28:9].

Recalling chapter 4 of *EC*, we are likely to think that the *hasid* of this passage engages in extreme behavior as a means of curing himself from a vice. If so, the *hakham* represents the ideal (behavior on the mean) while the *hasid* represents either the ill person in search of a cure, or a person in search of preventive therapy, or one who wishes to prevent himself from going to the worse of two extremes.

If the *hasid* engages in therapy — as opposed to being different from the *hasid* in *EC* — this induces the judgment that *hakham* is higher than the *hasid*, since the former needs no cure. This judgment is reinforced by the consideration that the *hakham* is the one who walks in God's middle ways, and that in Maimonides' citation of a *midrash* on *imitatio Dei* in the paragraph following the one I quoted, he omits the *midrash*'s attribution to God of the quality of *hesed*, lovingkindness. Why after all would God need therapy? At the same time, the phrase *lifnim mi-shurat ha-din*, assigned to the *hasid*'s behavior, normally signifies an especially positive valuation — supererogation — and it is odd to see it here associated with a lower kind of conduct, namely piety. In addition, there is no denying that in places Maimonides assigns great value to the *hasid*. He quotes a Rabbinic statement that *hasidut* is a rung below prophecy (*EC*, introduction). In several other places, in sources ranging from the *Guide* to *The Epistle to the Jews of Yemen*, *fadil* or *hasid* is his favored term for a person of excellence. In the *Guide*, furthermore, God is said to practice *hesed*, lovingkindness (III:53, 54). In *Mishneh Torah, Hilkot Melakhim* 8:11, *hakham* and *hasid* appear in a context that suggests a *hasid* of the non-Jewish nations is higher than a non-Jewish *hakham*. Space does not permit a full evaluation of these conflicting bodies of evidence on the relative values of *hakham* and *hasid*.[48]

The hasid vs. the continent man: In chapter 6 of *EC*,[49] Maimonides presents a contrast between two personality types. One is the *hasid*, the other the continent man. The *hasid* "follows in his action what his desire and the state of his soul arouse him to do; he does good things while craving and strongly desiring them." The continent man "does good things while craving and strongly desiring to perform bad actions. He struggles against his craving and opposes by his action what his [appetitive] power, his desire, and the state of his soul arouse him to do." Maimonides asks which of these types ranks higher. The philosophers along with King Solomon rank the *hasid* higher than the continent man, while the Rabbis appear to rank the continent man higher. For example, Rabban Shimon ben Gamliel says: "Let a man not say 'I do not want to eat meat with milk, I do not want to wear mixed fabric [the prohibited mixture of wool and linen], I do not want to have illicit sexual relations' but [let him say] 'I want to, but what shall I do — my Father in heaven has forbidden me'" (*Sifra, Kedoshim* 10:11). Likewise the Rabbis declare that "Whoever is greater than his friend has a greater [evil] impulse than he" (*Sukkah* 52a) and "The reward is according to the pain" (*Avot* 5:23).

Seeking to reconcile the respective views of the philosophers and the Rabbis, Maimonides writes that the two groups are speaking about different sorts of actions. The philosophers refer to things generally accepted by people as bad: murder, theft, robbery, fraud, harming an innocent man, repaying a benefactor with evil, degrading parents, and the like. A person who desires to do any of these things has a defective soul, according to both the philosophers and the Rabbis. But when the Rabbis ranked the continent man above the *hasid*, they had in mind "the traditional laws...because if it were not for the Law, they would not be bad at all. Therefore they said that a man needs to let his soul remain attracted to them and not place any obstacle before them other than the Law." "Traditional laws" include prohibitions against consuming meat and milk, engaging in an illicit union, and wearing wool and linen.

This view of the "traditional laws" invites the question of why those deeds were prohibited in the first place. Maimonides gave us the answer in *EC* chapter 4. With regard to the prohibition of forbidden foods and a range of laws, "the purpose of all this is that we move very far away from the extreme of lust and go a little from the mean toward insensibility to pleasure so that the state of moderation be firmly established within our souls." The reasoning is exactly the same as applies to tithes, giving of harvest, the law of forgotten sheaves, the law of the Sabbatical and Jubilee year, and charity sufficient for what the needy lack. These laws move us toward prodigality so we may move far away from stinginess. In all such cases, were it not for the Law, there would not have been anything wrong with doing other than what the Law prescribes. The Torah is interested in inculcating the virtues firmly, and for this it must incline us toward liberality and insensibility. For all that, it is surprising that Maimonides does not say that the goal of such prohibitions is eventually to extirpate the passion. Shouldn't the person eventually lose the desire for the forbidden sexual relations? In the *Guide*, as we noted, we find hints of an ascetic morality that eradicates desire.[50]

ETHICS IN THE *GUIDE*

The Morality that Flows from Human Perfection

When Aristotle assigns supreme value to contemplative activity as distinct from the moral life, the theoretical life is not held to involve any specific practical activity of a moral or political sort. This does not mean that the moral life involves no exercise of reason at all; but the type of reasoning involved in becoming morally virtuous is practical rather than theoretical. Theoretical activity implies no moral or political conduct, even if Aristotle concedes that moral virtue leads to a "secondary" sort of happiness and that some worldly goods are necessary for human life.[51]

One of the reasons Aristotle gives for the supremacy of theoretical activity is that it is godlike. Contemplation is a form of *imitatio Dei*. Aristotle's God is removed from human affairs, and His only "activity" amounts to "thought thinking itself" in a changeless, removed way.[52] In fact Aristotle states that the gods "will appear ridiculous" if they engage in acts of justice.[53]

The idea of *imitatio Dei* is salient in the *Guide*. "The end of the universe is...a seeking to be like unto His perfection as far as in its capacity" (I:69:170); *imitatio Dei* characterizes the final perfection of all existent things. Given this principle, Maimonides could have seen intellection on the part of humans as a mode of *imitatio Dei*, just as Aristotle did. But given his "negative theology" which places God beyond human concepts, he could not brook an explicit comparison between human and divine intellection. In I:1:23, he first makes the comparison, then withdraws it.[54] Although he could not use Aristotle's *imitatio Dei* argument as an explicit comparison between human and divine intellection, however, he did find a different use for *imitatio Dei* in the *Guide*, as we shall now see.

Maimonides differs from Aristotle in at least two respects. (1) For him theoretical activity does result in a particular sort of conduct; (2) This conduct, not the theoretical activity, is what constitutes *imitatio Dei*. Imitation of God's actions is the only sort of imitation open to humans. They cannot know what God is like in himself so as to imitate the divine essence.

Let us approach the issues via the *Guide*'s final chapter (III:54). Maimonides canvasses four perfections: perfection of possessions, perfection of body, perfection of moral virtues, and theoretical perfection. As we have seen, the last of these is the true human end because it is self-sufficient, involving no one else. Whatever value moral perfection possesses is instrumental. Given the fact that intellectual perfection has been portrayed as the goal and morality as the means, it is baffling to encounter the passage that concludes the *Guide*:

> It is clear that the perfection of man that may truly be gloried in is the one acquired by him who has achieved, in a measure corresponding to his capacity, apprehension of Him, may He be exalted, and who knows His providence extending over His creatures as manifested in the act of bringing them into being and in their governance as is. The way of life of such an individual, after he has achieved this apprehension, will always have in view lovingkindness, righteousness and judgment, through assimilation to His actions... (*Guide* III:54: 638).

Maimonides locates this view in a text from Jeremiah 9:22-23, where the prophet states:

> Thus saith the Lord: Let not the wise man glory in his wisdom, neither let the mighty man glory in his might, let not the rich man glory in his riches; but let him that glorieth glory in this, that he understandeth and knoweth me. For I am the Lord, who exercises loving-kindness, judgment, and righteousness [*hesed, mishpat* and *tzedakah*] in the earth, for in these things I delight, saith the Lord...

Hokhmah can refer to moral achievement, even though the word has other senses (III:54:632). In Maimonides' reading, "the wise man" referred to is a *hakham* in the *moral* sense of the term. Hence the wise man has the third kind of perfection in Mamonides' hierarchy. The mighty man is one possessing perfection of the body (perfection two), and the rich man is one having bodily possessions (perfection one). One who "understandeth and knoweth me" has the fourth perfection. But the Lord also performs "loving-kindness, judgment, and righteousness in the earth." So too, must the person who has achieved intellectual perfection. Acts of that kind should come from him. Aristotle's claim that the highest perfection can be seen as *imitatio Dei* now appears, but it seems to support the claim that moral activity is the highest perfection as opposed to contemplation.

Several reactions to this ostensible shift have appeared in the literature.[55] In a 1979 paper, Shlomo Pines took the position that Maimonides does perform an about-face. According to Pines, Maimonides holds that human beings cannot know metaphysics nor even celestial physics. Because of these limits, Maimonides retracts the claim that intellectual perfection is the highest perfection. Nevertheless, human beings can know the actions of

God and His attributes of action, as is clear from I:54. Acccording to Pines: "The only positive knowledge of which man is capable is knowledge of the attributes of action, and this leads and ought to lead to a sort of practical activity which is the highest perfection of man. The practical way of life, the *bios praktikos*, is superior to the theoretical."[56]

Pines is right that the activities of the individual who is described at the end of III:54 are an imitation of God's actions. He is also right that actions and virtues that result from scientific knowledge are not the same as actions and virtues that result from *phronesis* and that constitute the third level of perfection.[57] But Pines' allegation of an about-face is highly problematic. After all, Maimonides proclaims clearly that intellectual perfection, not practical activity, is highest, and gives an argument against interpersonal activity being highest (viz., the perfect individual must not be dependent upon others for his perfection). Only a highly esotericist reading of III:54 would permit us to say that Maimonides maintains the exact opposite of what he says, and while such esotericism may appeal to Pines, we would be wise to seek another explanation of the ostensible shift.

A far more compelling idea is that Maimonides distinguishes between "the perfection of man that may be truly gloried in" and "the way of life of such an individual" who has achieved that perfection. The way of life is not the perfection itself; the way of life is rather a consequence of — an emanation or overflow from — the perfection. By achieving intellectual perfection, the perfect individual engages in a life of *imitatio Dei* with respect to the Deity's actions. This individual acts toward people as God acts toward the world, that is, exercising the same attributes. For this reason Maimonides spells out what loving-kindness, judgment, and righteousness entail (III:53); these are what the intellectually perfect individual practices because of the overflow from the intellect.[58] Proof that the actions toward others do not constitute the perfection itself is Maimonides' statement at II:11:275:

> Know that in the case of every being that causes a certain good thing to overflow from it according to this order of rank, the existence, the purpose, and the end of the being conferring the benefits, do not consist in conferring the benefits on the recipient. For pure absurdity would follow from this assumption. For the end is nobler than the things that subsist for the sake of the end.

There is some question as to whether the effect of the overflow from theoretical perfection is political activity or ethical activity done in a particular way.[59] In the former interpretation, stress is placed on the perfect individual *qua* ruler, and the interpretation is that the law given by the perfect lawgiver will manifest *hesed*, *mishpat* and *tzedakah*.[60] According to the other interpretation, it is ethical activity of a distinctive kind: just as God acts without emotion, so the perfect individual acts without emotion. In support of the first reading, note that all references to *imitatio Dei* that are clear as to whether Maimonides is referring to moral activity or instead political activity, designate political activity (I:24:54, I:38:87, I:54).[61] The political reading gains support in particular from the correlation Maimonides asserts between III:54 and I:54. In I:54, Maimonides describes how Moses came to know God's attributes of action because he needed to know how to govern the people (a practical end). It is worth noting, however, that either way, practical wisdom is needed for the theoretical knowledge that generates the overflow. As Ehud Benor argues, one has to know what character traits have to be exercised to bring about the particular effects we see in nature. Practical excellence thus precedes theoretical perfection, and it is an overflow from it as well.[62]

On either the political or the ethical interpretation, the "consequent morality" is radically different from the propaedeutic morality. It results not from *phronesis* but from scientific knowledge. In addition, actions now seem more important than the psychological disposition. Recall that propaedeutic morality focused on a person's psychological dispositions, traits of personality that involve psychological states like compassion, courage, and the like. The mean was a particular psychological disposition. So although in *Hilkhot De'ot* Maimonides stated that action on the mean, the propaedeutic morality, was a type of *imitatio Dei*, there is a disanalogy between the virtuous person and the God whom he imitates. The human being has psychological dispositions toward certain states; God has no psychological states at all. He acts in certain ways, but feels nothing. To truly counsel *imitatio Dei*, Maimonides ought to say that the person who engages in *imitatio Dei* has no psychological states at all. In the *Guide* he makes this point explicitly with regard to a ruler-prophet:

> It behooves the governor of a city, if he is a prophet, to acquire similarity to these attributes, so that these actions may proceed from him according to a determined measure and according to the deserts of the people who are affected by them and not merely because of his following a passion. He should not let loose the reins of anger nor let passion gain mastery over him, for all passions are evil; but, on the contrary, he should guard against them as far as this lies within the capacity of man. (I:54:126)

Thus, the ruler should do what is fitting and not administer benefits and adversities out of compassion, anger and hatred. The process that produces actions of loving-kindness, judgment, and righteousness referred to in the passage is not of the sort undergone by the morally virtuous person. Those actions are not produced by "aptitudes of the soul" or psychological dispositions.

To account for the difference between Maimonides' treatment of psychological dispositions in his legal writings and his account in the *Guide*, Herbert Davidson maintains that Maimonides simply changed his mind and eventually came to demand the extirpation of psychological traits rather than their cultivation.[63] Theoretically one could view the legal writings' account as referring to propaedeutic morality and the *Guide*'s as referring to consequent morality, and insist that there is no formal contradiction between the psychological states required by one and the absence of such states in the other. But the lack of reference in the legal writings to anything resembling the "consequent" morality is striking and would suggest that Maimonides came to the idea of emotionless perfection late in his career. At the same time, we must recall that the identification of irascibility as an ideal with respect to anger anticipates the generalized passionlessness of the individual in the *Guide* who imitates God.

Questions remain about the "overflow" from intellectual perfection. Does the person who receives the overflow consciously aim at *imitatio Dei,* or is *imitatio Dei* automatic and unavoidable? Is there an element of the irrational in the desire to return from the cave and lead others?[64] Does God have a "motive" for His overflow? Why does Maimonides imply that political activity is a "descent" when he unpacks the message of Jacob's ladder (I:15)? Questions such as these are stimulated by the reading we have given the closing lines of III:54.[65]

SUMMATION

Despite his stress on intellectual perfection, Maimonides devoted much attention to developing a theory of ethics and a practical regimen of therapy for moral illnesses. While he champions the doctrine of the mean, he recognizes several important deviations from it. He also develops the notion of a morality that flows from intellectual perfection and which contrasts with the propaedeutic morality set out in the legal writings.[66]

NOTES

I thank Charles Raffel and Kenneth Seeskin for comments on an earlier version of this paper.

[1]   See *Nicomachean Ethics*, X: 7.

[2]   *GP* refers to Maimonides, *Guide of the Perplexed*, trans. Shlomo Pines (Chicago and London: University of Chicago Press, 1963). References will be to part, chapter,

and page number. References to *Eight Chapters* (*EC*), Maimonides' introduction to his commentary on *Avot*, are by chapter, and references to *Hilkhot De'ot*, along with other subsections of *Mishneh Torah*, are by chapter and *halakhah* number.

3   See, for example, *Mishneh Torah, Hilkhot Teshuvah* 8, and *Guide* III:54:635. ("Therefore you ought to desire to achieve this thing, which will remain permanently with you"; "it gives [the individual] permanent perdurance.")

4   The quotation is from *EC* 5, translated in Raymond L. Weiss with Charles Butterworth, *Ethical Writings of Maimonides* (New York: Dover Books, 1975), 75.

5   For a contrary passage, see *Guide* III:8:432: "The corruption of the intellect and of the body is shunned by the intellect." For a treatment of this passage see Howard Kreisel, *Maimonides' Political Thought* (Albany, NY, 1999), 89-91. Presumably the intellect also determines that the mean is the standard of virtue and that intellectual perfection is the highest.

6   See Kreisel, *Maimonides' Political Thought*, 63-92; Raymond L. Weiss, *Maimonides' Ethics* (Chicago, 1991), 30-31. On the story of Adam and Eve's sin, see also Lawrence V. Berman, "Maimonides on the Fall of Man," *AJS Review* 5 (1980): 1-16 and Marvin Fox, *Interpreting Maimonides* (Chicago, 1990), 152-98.

7   The terms morality and ethics will here be used interchangeably. It is important to realize, however, that morality is more than governing oneself according to right norms of interpersonal conduct. It also involves, as just indicated, the governing of one's impulses.

8   *Mishneh Torah, Hilkhot Teshuvah* 7:3.

9   See Lawrence J. Kaplan, "An Introduction to Maimonides' 'Eight Chapters'," *Edah Journal* 2 (2002), unpaginated available online at http://www.edah.org/backend/JournalArticle/kaplan2_2.pdf (accessed Sept 7, 2008).

10   Herbert Davidson, "Maimonides' *Shemonah Perakim* and Alfarabi's *Fusul al-Madani*," *Proceedings of the American Academy for Jewish Research* 31 (1963): 33-50.

11   See, however, Kreisel, *Maimonides' Political Thought*, 159-88, who suggests that in contexts where Maimonides wants to express the supremacy of intellectual perfection, he makes the aim of ethics to be (mere) social order.

12   In *Eight Chapters*, Maimonides embeds his discussion in a theory of the soul. The soul has five parts: rational, appetitive, sentient, imaginative and nutritive. The therapy for the sick soul is directed specifically at two parts, the sentient and the appetitive. It is true that the soul's rational part may bring about good or bad conduct insofar as the agent may hold true or false opinions about what is good and bad. But — and here Maimonides sounds somewhat like David Hume, the eighteenth century Scottish philosopher — thought does not act. The healthy soul will have correct opinions about what is good conduct and what is bad; but in addition to holding correct opinions, it must govern itself to act in a good rather than bad way. And this is where therapy is required.

13   Scholarship on Aristotle suggests that his doctrine of the mean is far more complex than the simplified picture conveyed by my summary of Maimonides. See for example J.O. Urmson, "Aristotle's Doctrine of the Mean," in *Essays on Aristotle's Ethics*, ed. Amelie Oksenberg Rorty (Berkeley, CA, 1980), 157-70. However, it is not clear that Maimonides understood the doctrine of the mean as Aristotle did, and for that reason I work with the simplified formulation.

14 In Weiss and Butterworth, *Ethical Writings of Maimonides*, 67.

15 Liberality refers to spending on oneself, generosity to spending for others.

16 *Nicomachean Ethics* 1109b5-8.

17 See Ibid., 1109a2-13.

18 See *EC* 4; commentary to *Avot* 5:7; *Hilkhot De'ot* 1:5-6.

19 Cf., however, *Hilkhot Nezirut* 10:14, discussed below. The seemingly polar contrast between this text on one hand and *De'ot* 3:1 and *EC* 4 on the other has elicited scholarly attention.

20 At no point in *EC* does Maimonides refer to the concept *imitatio Dei* that is found in later writings, *Mishneh Torah* and *The Guide of the Perplexed*. As we shall see this concept seems to have undergone an evolution in his various works.

21 See Davidson, "Maimonides' *Shemonah Perakim*."

22 *Nicomachean Ethics* 1106a28-b7.

23 Ibid., II:6 (1107a8-15).

24 Ibid., 1125a22.

25 Ibid., 1124a1-4.

26 Ibid., 1123b35.

27 See Daniel Frank, "Humility As a Virtue: A Maimonidean Critique of Aristotle's Ethics," in *Moses Maimonides and His Time*, ed. Eric L. Ormsby (Washington, D.C., 1989), 89-99.

28 Following the translation in Weiss, *Maimonides' Ethics*, 40-41. Weiss notes that this passage appears in the *Commentary to the Mishnah* as a description of the pious person's conduct and in a responsum as the conduct of a philosopher.

29 Certain positions in the community — community leader, judge — require humility rather than extreme humility, a view which poses certain complications given that Moses, the greatest leader, is described by the Bible as "very humble." (See Weiss, *Maimonides' Ethics*, 108-10.) But the apparent situation is clear enough: there is a departure here from the mean, based on a rabbinic teaching.

30 Kreisel, *Maimonides' Political Thought*, 161.

31 See Daniel Frank, "Anger As a Vice: A Maimonidean Critique of Aristotle's Ethics," *History of Philosophy Quarterly* 7 (1990): 269-81.

32 Ibid.

33 Ibid.

34 I thank Josef Stern for this observation.

35 We need to ask again, as we did in the case of extreme humility, how *Hilkhot De'ot* 2:3 is to be reconciled with texts in chapter 1. I have no answer to this time-worn question.

36 Philosophic ethics is a term used in the *Letter on Management of Health*, as noted by Weiss.

37 See Kaplan, "Introduction," and Weiss, *Maimonides' Ethics*, 76.

38 See Weiss, *Maimonides' Ethics*, 62-81, for further discussion of such examples.

³⁹ See Kaplan "Introduction." Cf. Marvin Fox's view that the rule of the Torah is the rule of the mean, in his *Interpreting Maimonides*, 93-123.

⁴⁰ See Kaplan, "Introduction." Maimonides' reference in *EC* 5 to a "transgression for the sake of heaven" is a piece of the argument.

⁴¹ A similar contradiction attends Maimonides' statements about the general issue of making vows to refrain from certain enjoyments; contrast *Hilkhot De'ot* 3:1 and *Hilkhot Shevu'ot* 13:23.

⁴² *Hilkhot Talmud Torah* 3:12.

⁴³ *Hilkhot Ishut* 15:3

⁴⁴ His suggestion in *Hilkhot De'ot* 1:4 that one should desire only that which one cannot live without is ascetic-sounding as well.

⁴⁵ The prophet does not repudiate what is useful for the body, however.

⁴⁶ My presentation of the evidence is indebted to Herbert Davidson, "The Middle Way in Maimonides' Ethics," *Proceedings of the American Academy for Jewish Research* 54(1987): 47-50, and Kreisel, *Maimonides' Political Thought*, 175-82.

⁴⁷ Kreisel *Maimonides' Political Thought*, 182.

⁴⁸ Relevant literature includes: David Hartman, *Maimonides: Torah and Philosophic Quest* (Philadelphia: Jewish Publication Society, 1976), 88-97; Baruch Asher [Barry] Kogan, "*Ha-Rambam al Musag ha-Ide'al ha-Enoshi: Hasid o Hakham?*" *Mehqarei Yerushalayim be-Mahshevet Yisrael* 9 (1990): 177-91; Kreisel, *Maimonides' Political Thought*, 179-80; Norman Lamm,"*He-hakham ve-he-Hasid be-Mishnat ha-Rambam*," in *Sefer Zikkaron li-Shemuel Belkin*, ed. Moshe Carmilly and Hayyim Leaf (New York, 1981), 11-28; Steven S. Schwarzschild, "Moral Radicalism and 'Middlingness' in The Ethics of Maimonides," *Studies in Medieval Culture* 11 (1977): 65-94; Isadore Twersky, *Introduction to the Code of Maimonides (Mishneh Torah)* (New Haven, CT: Yale University Press, 1980), 459-68.

⁴⁹ See Weiss and Butterworth, *Ethical Writings*, 78-80.

⁵⁰ More on this below. Moses was an ascetic — see *Hilkhot Yesodei ha-Torah* 7:6.

⁵¹ *Nicomachean Ethics* X:8. This and the next paragraphs follow fairly closely the translation in Daniel Frank, "The End of the Guide: Maimonides on the Best Life for Man," *Judaism* 34 (1985): 485-95.

⁵² See *Metaphysics* XII:9.

⁵³ NE X:8, trans. by Frank, "The End of the Guide," 487.

⁵⁴ See also Kenneth Seeskin, *Searching for a Distant God: The Legacy of Maimonides* (New York: Oxford University Press, 2000), ch. 5.

⁵⁵ Hermann Cohen took Maimonides as affirming the supremacy of ethical action. See his "Characteristik der Ethik Maimunis," *Jüdische Schriften* (Berlin, 1924), 221-89.

⁵⁶ Shlomo Pines, "The Limitations of Human Knowledge According to Alfarabi, ibn Bajja, and Maimonides," in *Studies in Medieval Jewish History and Literature, Vol. 1*, ed. Isadore Twersky (Cambridge, MA: Harvard University Press, 1979), 100.

⁵⁷ See also Alexander Altmann, "Maimonides' Four Perfections," *Israel Oriental Society* 2 (1972): 15-24.

[58] This interpretation is offered by Warren Zev Harvey in his "Maimonides on Human Perfection, Awe, and Politics," in *The Thought of Moses Maimonides*, ed. Ira Robinson, Lawrence Kaplan, and Julian Bauer (Lewistown, NY, 1990), 1-15; David Shatz, "Worship, Corporeality and Human Perfection: A Reading of *Guide* III:54," in this volume; Kreisel, *Maimonides' Political Thought*, 125-58.

[59] The thesis that people should stay in solitude (III:51:621) can be relegated to those on the ascent to intellectual perfection.

[60] See Eliezer Goldman, "'Ha-Avodah ha-Meyuhedet be-Massigei ha-Amittot': He'arot *Parshaniyyot le-Moreh Nevukhim Helek* 3 *Perakim* 51-54," *Bar-IlanAnnual* 6 (1968): 287-313.

[61] See Kreisel, *Maimonides' Political Thought*, 306, n. 24.

[62] Ehud Benor, *Worship of the Heart: A Study in Maimonides' Philosophy of Religion* (Albany, NY, 1995), 37-61, esp. 56-58.

[63] Davidson, "The Middle Way in Maimonides' Ethics," 72.

[64] See Kreisel, *Maimonides' Political Thought*, 134-36, regarding the prophet's "internal feeling of compulsion to perfect others."

[65] Once the *Guide*'s final passages are to mean that intellectual perfection is supreme, there is but one passage I know that seems to support the assertion that ultimate perfection is practical, not theoretical. It comes in Maimonides' discussion of *imitatio Dei* in I:54 and is cited by Pines in support of his view that the final perfection is practical: "For the utmost virtue of man is to become like unto Him, may He Be Exalted, as far as he is able; which means that we should make our actions like unto His" (I:54:128). However in this passage "virtue" may refer to ethical virtue, not perfection (Davidson, "Maimonides on Metaphysical Knowledge," *Maimonidean Studies* 3 [1992-93]: 86). If it were taken to refer to perfection, it would create enormous textual difficulties due to the contrast with III:54. So reading "virtue" in a restrictive way seems preferable.

[66] Postscript (2009): I encourage readers to look at the innovative alternative approach to *Hilkhot De'ot* 1-2 found in Bernard Septimus, "Literary Structure and Ethical Theory in *Sefer ha-Madda*," in *Maimonides After 800 Years: Essays on Maimonides and His Influence*, ed. Jay M. Harris (Cambridge, MA, 2007), 307-25.

WORSHIP, CORPOREALITY, AND HUMAN PERFECTION:
A Reading of *Guide of the Perplexed*, III: 51-54

Interpreters through the ages have explored a rich variety of philosophical, historical, and literary aspects of Maimonides' discussion of human
perfection in part III, chapters 51-54 of the *Guide*. The very first sentences of
those climactic sections, however, contain a remark that has not been given
the attention and interpretive weight it deserves. In the opening lines of
III:51, Maimonides provides the following characterization of the ideas he is
about to present:

> This chapter that we bring now does not include additional matter
> over and above what is comprised in the other chapters of this Treatise.
> It is only a kind of conclusion (III:51:618).[1]

Maimonides applies the description "[kind of] conclusion" specifically
to "this chapter," i.e., chapter 51.[2] Yet part III of the *Guide* contains three
chapters *after* this conclusion. It what sense, then, is III:51 the conclusion of
the *Guide*? Why isn't III:54 given that designation?[3]

I submit that Maimonides' use of the term "conclusion" for III:51,
as distinct from III:54, is perfectly apt: III:51, and not III:54, is the real end
of the *Guide*. If we examine closely the content of these chapters, we find
that III:51 and III:54 are markedly different from each other. III:54 presents
a highly simplistic and misleading picture of Maimonides' views on
human perfection; III:51, on the other hand, is fraught with complexities,
tensions, ambiguities, and uncertainties that better reflect Maimonides'
thinking. These complexities, tensions, ambiguities, and uncertainties have
been present in the *Guide* all along, in "the other chapters of this Treatise";
however, they come to a head when Maimonides articulates his account of
human perfection.

In what follows I (1) lay out the evidence for taking the treatment in
III:51 to be more advanced and sophisticated than that in III:54; (2) construct
an explanation of why Maimonides jumbled the sequence of his final

chapters; and (3) explain the significance of my interpretation for our understanding of human perfection in the thought of Maimonides.

I

In what way is III:54 simplistic and misleading? I begin with two impressions conveyed by III:54 that are contradicted by statements in III:51: (1) That intellectual apprehension is the end of a human being; (2) that performance of the commandments plays no role in the life of an individual who has achieved intellectual apprehension, since the commandments are but preparation for intellectual perfection. As we shall see, the contrast between III:51 and III:54 on these issues is but a symptom of a deeper difference between the chapters.

1. *The human telos*

Upon careful reading, it becomes plain that the stage of human development that Maimonides describes in III:54 *precedes* the stage of human development that he describes in III:51. In III:54, Maimonides describes four kinds of human perfection: the perfection of possessions, the perfection of bodily constitution and shape, the perfection of moral virtues, and the perfection consisting in the acquisition of rational virtues ("I refer to the conception of intelligibles, which teach true opinions concerning the divine things," 635). The last of these four perfections is described as "the ultimate end." Later in that chapter Maimonides expands his characterization of what is known by those who attain true perfection, so that it now includes apprehension of God's *providence*: "The perfection of man that may truly be gloried in is the one acquired by him who has achieved, in a measure corresponding to his capacity, apprehension of Him, may He be exalted, and who knows His providence extending over His creatures as manifested in the act of bringing them into being and in their governance as it is" (III:54:638).

The argument given in this chapter for the supremacy of intellectual perfection is that by achieving intellectual perfection one realizes his true self.

> This [i.e., intellectual perfection] is in true reality the ultimate end; this is what gives the individual true perfection, a perfection belonging to him alone; and it gives him permanent perdurance; through it man is man (III:54:635).

The lineage of this argument extends back to Book X of Aristotle's *Nichomachean Ethics*. Intellectual perfection constitutes *eudaemonia* because the human being's "true self" is intellectual.[4]

Now, in III:51, Maimonides speaks of a class of people who, "after having attained perfection in the divine science, turn wholly toward God,...renounce what is other than He, and direct all the acts of their intellect toward an examination of the beings with a view to drawing from them proof with regard to Him, so as to know His governance of them in whatever way it is possible" (III:51:620). Thus far, the stage under discussion (identified as "the rank of the prophets," as distinct from "the men of science") seems identical with "the perfection of man that may truly be gloried in" as depicted in the lines we quoted from III:54. But it is not. III:54 makes no reference to "turning wholly toward God," "renouncing what is other than He," and "directing *all* acts of the intellect toward an examination of the beings." Apprehension, not concentration, is the focus of the closing lines of III:54; and the "fourth perfection" as defined earlier in that chapter makes no mention of anything beyond "conception of the intelligibles" and "true opinions concerning the divine things."

The significance of this omission becomes clear as we read on in III:51. For Maimonides goes on to describe a stage *beyond* apprehension: the stage of worship. At this level, one not only apprehends, but, in addition, concentrates — as totally, exclusively, and continuously as possible — on the object of apprehension. It is eminently clear that worship is the *next* goal of one who has achieved apprehension:

> If, however, you have apprehended God and His acts in accordance with what is required by the intellect, you should afterwards engage in totally devoting yourself to Him, endeavor to come closer to Him, and strengthen the bond between you and Him — that is, the intellect (III:51:620).
>
> The Torah has made it clear that this last worship...can only be engaged in after apprehension has been achieved...after love comes this worship...after apprehension, total devotion to Him and the employment of intellectual thought in constantly loving Him should be aimed at (III:51:621).
>
> Know that even if you were the man who knew most the true reality of the divine science...you would cut that bond existing between you and God if you would empty your thought of God and busy yourself in eating the necessary or in occupying yourself with the necessary (Ibid.).

Here we have a portrait of "the worship peculiar to those who have apprehended the true realities" (620), a worship engaged in "after he has obtained an apprehension of what He is" (618), a worship neglect of which can lead to a severance of the bond between the individual and God. In sum, worship, the subject of III:51, comes *after* intellectual apprehension, the subject of III:54.[5] In fact, Maimonides, in III:51, *contradicts* his portrayal of perfection as given in III:54, for he writes that this worship "is the end of man" (618). Providence is enjoyed to the fullest extent only by those who have achieved this later stage, a sure mark of its supremacy (III:51:622-26).

Thus, an examination of the contents of III:51 makes clear why it, and not chapter 54, represents the "conclusion" of Maimonides' *Guide*. Insofar as III:54 makes no explicit mention of worship, it not only presents a misleading picture of what human perfection is, but also (given the difficulties an individual encounters in trying to sustain the state of worship) encourages an overly generous estimate of the prospects for attaining human perfection. My point here is not a purely literary or structural one about the sequence in which the *Guide's* chapters should be read. Rather, my thesis is that we cannot construct an accurate theory of what human perfection is for Maimonides and of whether it is attainable unless we start with the recognition that III:54 is not Maimonides' last word on the subject.

I acknowledge one respect in which III:54 appears to go *beyond* III:51. After describing "the perfection of man that may truly be gloried in," Maimonides writes that

> The way of life of such an individual, after he has achieved this apprehension, will always have in view loving-kindness, righteousness, and judgment, through assimilation to His actions, may He be exalted, just as we have explained several times in this Treatise (III:54:638).

It is generally agreed that Maimonides refers here to political activities — governance of the people — and possibly to the activity of legislation. The perfect individual apprehends God's attributes as manifested in "His actions," i.e., nature, and uses those attributes as a model for his own activity.[6] Should we say, then, that III:54, since it includes reference to political activity, tells us more about human perfection than III:51, and that III:51 contains the simplistic formulation, not III:54? No. For there *is* a passage in III:51 which makes reference to political activity, specifically that of Moses and the Patriarchs, the end of whose efforts was "to bring into being a religious community that would know and worship God" (624). The full interpretation and significance of the this passage will be explored later, but its existence refutes the assertion that III:54 is more advanced than III:51 by virtue of referring to political activity.[7]

Let us now turn to another respect in which the account of III:54 is inaccurate and misleading.

2. *The place of the commandments in the human ideal*

III:51-54 is preceded by a long section on the purposes of the commandments (*ta'amei ha-mitzvot*) which begins at III:25 and extends through III:49. The relationship between this section and sections that precede and follow it — respectively, the chapters on evil and providence (III:8-25) and on human perfection (III:51-54) — richly deserves study. For the moment, I should like to argue that III:54 presents ideas, themes, and even terminology that belong not to the immediately preceding chapters but to the section on *ta'amei ha-mitzvot*; most strikingly, the key idea conveyed in III:54 concerning the aim of the commandments is inconsistent with the key idea concerning that subject in III:51.

The first chapter in the *ta'amei ha-mitzvot* section (III:25)[8] begins by delineating four kinds of actions: (1) vain (an end is aimed at, but not achieved); (2) futile (no end is aimed at); (3) frivolous (an end is aimed at, but a low end); (4) good or excellent. A good or excellent action is one that not only aims at an end but aims at an end that is noble; furthermore, it achieves that end. Maimonides maintains that all of God's actions are good or excellent; and the chapters on the commandments are designed to verify this claim with respect to a specific class of divine acts, namely, acts of divine legislation. Accordingly, Maimonides (a) argues that all commandments have reasons and purpose, and (b) identifies the specific intellectual and political benefits at which Torah legislation aims.

"The Law as a whole," Maimonides writes in III:27, "aims at two things: the welfare of the soul and the welfare of the body" (III:27:510). The Law helps people attain welfare of the soul because it prescribes certain opinions to the multitude, and, furthermore, observance of the commandments inculcates correct opinions in them. The Law also helps its followers achieve welfare of the body (the body politic) in that it brings about abolition of wrongdoing and fosters the "the acquisition by every human individual of moral qualities that are useful for life in society so that the affairs of the city may be ordered" (III:27:510).

"Welfare of the soul" and "welfare of the body" do not exhaust the aims of the Law as depicted in III:27-28. Maimonides also speaks of "perfection" of the soul and "perfection" of the body.[9]

Perfection of the body, unlike *welfare* of the body, refers to "being healthy and in the very best bodily state"; perfection of this type (in contrast to welfare of the body) is in the first instance a benefit to the individual, though the only means of securing this benefit, the only means of obtaining "food," "shelter," and "bathing," is through political association. Again, *welfare* of the soul, as we have already noted, is a category that pertains to the multitude; the term refers to their acquisition of true opinions. *Perfection* of the soul, however, refers to the (individual's) ultimate perfection, which is "to have an intellect in actu" (III:27, 511). This perfection consists "only of [having] opinions towards which speculation has led and that investigation has rendered compulsory" (Ibid.).[10]

Clearly, perfection of the soul is achieved by the elite few, and although it is "the ultimate perfection" (511), it is not achieved directly by the Law (512). The Law provides directly for welfare — but not for perfection; it directs attention to theoretical opinions "in a summary fashion," but does not "direct attention toward them in detail" (III:27, 512).

When Maimonides enunciates "causes of the Law" in these chapters, he is not formulating reasons that are intended to motivate people to perform the commandments, or which motivated them to do so in biblical times. Nothing in the concept "welfare of the soul" precludes an individual's attaining "welfare of the soul" even if he or she does not know that the Law is aiming at that end.[11] Maimonides' concern is not with identifying motives of the *performer*, but with identifying motives of the *legislator*.[12] In fact, by demonstrating how wisdom is manifest in the commandments, he is showing that the Law is divine. As Warren Harvey has emphasized, the divine law is identified as divine, or *proved* to be divine, by its ends and utility.[13] As Maimonides explains in II:40:

> It is part of the wisdom of the deity with regard to the permanence of this species of which He willed the existence, that He put into its nature that individuals belonging to it should have the faculty of ruling. Among them [is]...the prophet or the bringers of the nomos...If you find a Law all of whose ordinances are due to attention being paid...to the soundness of the circumstances pertaining to the body and also to the soundness of belief...you must you must know that this guidance comes from Him, may He exalted, and that the Law is divine (II:40:384).

III:25-49, then, establishes the divinity of the Law, by the special criteria of "divinity" defined in II:39-40.

Now, the relevance of III:25-49 to our question — the relationship between III:51 and III:54 — is this. At first glance, Maimonides' discussion of the commandments appears to terminate after III:49. Chapter 50 deals with a different though loosely related subject (biblical narratives),[14] and Chapter 51 begins with Maimonides' insistence that, "This chapter...does not include additional matter over and above what is comprised in the other chapters of this Treatise" (III:51, 619). Notwithstanding this insistence, we *are* presented with "additional matter" in III:51, specfically a *new* explanation of the aim of the commandments which contrasts, in particular, with the explanations given in III:25-49. This new and different explanation is responsive to the peculiar goals of the worshipper who is described in III:51. III:54, on the other hand, reverts back to the older conception of III:25-49 — ignoring altogether the account of III:51.

What is the new conception proposed in III:51?

> Know that all the practices of the worship, such as reading the Torah, prayer, and the performance of the other commandments have only the end of training you to occupy yourself with His commandments, may He be exalted, rather than with matters pertaining to this world (III:51:622).

The same basic idea (with additional motifs) is encountered in III:52:

> For it is by all the particulars of the actions [prescribed by the Law] and through their repetition that some excellent men obtained such training that they achieve human perfection so that they fear and are in dread and in awe of God, may He be exalted, and know who it is that is with them and as a result act subsequently as they ought to.

The actions prescribed by the Law bring about fear of God. Love of God is achieved through the opinions taught by the Law (III:52: 629-30).[15] According to these passages, the purpose of the Law is to provide "training," that is, a regimen through which the philosopher empties himself of other thoughts and concentrates exclusively (or as nearly exclusively as possible) on God; the commandments create a consciousness of "who it is that is with" him.[16] This conception is not found in III:25-49.[17] Thus, it appears that we are dealing with two neatly segregated discussions, one in III:25-49, the other in III:51-52; and so there appears to be a discrepancy between these two contiguous portions of the *Guide*.[18]

Before seeing how *ta'amei ha-mitzvot* are treated in III:54, it is important to appreciate that the two accounts of *mitzvot* (III:25-49; III:51) are consistent with each other. The accounts are consistent because the account in III:51 sets down an *additional* dimension of the commandments, one that is the exclusive reserve of the philosopher who aspires to love. In III:52, Maimonides speaks only of *"some* excellent men" who "achieve human perfection" through the particulars of the actions prescribed by the Law (III:52, 628-29). The philosopher who aspires to love or who develops fear utilizes the commandments in a *special* way, as a regimen for concentrating on all he knows, for occupying himself with God rather than with "matters pertaining to this world" ("buying and selling," "the building of your habitation"). Through such concentration he achieves "nearness to God and being in His presence." The fact that the commandments serve this purpose for the exceptional individual does not preclude their serving other, more preliminary purposes for the multitude, nor their having served those same purposes for the philosopher-worshipper at an earlier stage of his development, when he was not yet a philosopher. In III:25-49, Maimonides is explaining the Law as it pertains to the community, the multitude; in III:51, the Law as it pertains to exceptional individuals. The Law can obviously operate on multiple levels, corresponding to the multiple stages of human development.[19]

It is possible that, in making this shift, Maimonides is implicitly responding to two arguments for antinomianism that grow out of his discussion in III:25-49. First, the philosopher has *already* acquired correct opinions and has *already* perfected the moral habits. For him, the Law no longer achieves the ends of "welfare of the soul" and "welfare of the body" set down in III:27. As for "perfection" of the soul, that is achieved through philosophical speculation, independently of any specific performances. If the Law is to be saved from falling into disuse *for the philosopher*, it must serve some other set of ends. What it serves is a new, higher telos: the commandments assist him in directing his thought to God.[20]

Second, the shift to the training conception of III:51 may be viewed as a response to another antinomian implication of the reasons stated in III:25-49. Idolatrous practices are no longer extant; hence, the many commandments whose aim it is to efface idolatry no longer achieve their aim — they become pointless. We may sharpen the difficulty as follows. To fulfill the human telos, a person must understand the natural order. However, God's legislation of the commandments is connected with the natural order.[21] Hence, to understand the natural order (and thereby fulfill the human telos) one must understand the reasons for the *mitzvot*. But anyone who understands those reasons will also realize that God's legislation of the commandments is conditioned by the historical circumstances in which the commandments were legislated. Such a person, assuming he is living in post-biblical times, will ineluctably abandon the Law because the Law is irrelevant to him. Achievement of the human telos, then, results in abandonment of the Law.[22]

By developing his conception of the commandments as training, Maimonides is able to respond to this argument. He can now maintain that the commandments retain their value for the philosopher long after the benefits they provided for the masses in biblical times are no longer needed. As Warren Harvey put it,[23] III:25-49 is concerned with what the commandments meant "then"; III:51 tells us what the commandments mean now.[24]

A third, and simpler, explanation of the shift in III:51 is possible. We have already seen that, in III:25-49, Maimonides is concerned not with motives of the performer, but with motives of the legislator. Now in III:51, Maimonides' mandate to the philosopher is to concentrate only on God, at least to the extent that this is humanly possible. For one who devotes himself exclusively to intellection, however, performance of a bodily activity (a commandment) without proper attention to God can result in a break in concentration. The training conception is introduced because only that conception guarantees that the worshipper will not fail to focus on God while performing the commandment:

> If, however, you pray merely by moving your lips while facing a wall, and at the same time thinking about your buying and selling; or if you read the Torah with your tongue while your heart is set upon the building of your habitation and does not consider what you read; and similarly in all cases in which you perform a commandment merely with your limbs — as if you were digging a hole in the ground, or hewing wood in the forest — without reflecting either upon the meaning of that action or upon Him from whom the commandment proceeds or upon the end of the action, you should not think that you have achieved the end (III:51:622).

The requirement that Maimonides introduces here is *reflection*. To achieve "the end" — constant occupation with God — you must focus upon "the end of the action." I take this last term to refer to the end of focusing on God, as distinct from the ends set out in III:25-49. On either reading of the phrase, however, the doer of the action must be aware of the end of the action; hence, the "end" in this passage is one that motivates an individual to perform the action. Maimonides has altered the *contents* of the reason for the Law (for the philosopher, the commandments serve a purpose distinct from inculcation of actual opinions, abolition of wrongdoing, and so forth), because he must alter the *type* of reason in question. It must be a reason that is a motive for the performer *and* incorporates reference to God.[25]

So, a genuine shift takes place in III:51 with respect to *ta'amei ha-mitzvot*, yet it is a shift which Maimonides not only can make with consistency, but is, furthermore, impelled to make. If we now turn to III:54, though, we find there the very approach to the commandments which Maimonides had abandoned in III:51 in the case of the philosopher![26] For the utility of the commandments in fostering moral virtue and preparing one for intellectual protection — a motif of III:27 — looms prominent in III:54 though it is absent from III:51:

The third species...is the perfection of the moral virtues. Most of the commandments serve no other end than the attainment of this species of protection. But this species of perfection is likewise a preparation for something else and not an end in itself (III:54:635).

[A]ll the actions prescribed by the Law—I refer to the various species of worship and also the moral habits that are useful to all people in their mutual dealings—that all this is not to be compared with this ultimate end [intellectual perfection] and does not equal it, being but preparations made for the sake of this end (III:54: 636).

The difficulty is plain. By now, the conception of *mitzvot* advanced in these lines has been superseded by the explanation given in III:51—that the philosopher uses the commandments as a regimen by which he occupies himself exclusively with God. Even after the commandments have aided the individual in achieving intellectual perfection and are no longer needed for *that* purpose, they serve as a means of training the individual to concentrate his attention on God. The conception in III:54 harks back to III:27-28, and it represents a striking retrograde step. It is, furthermore, a step which carries antinomian implications.

The reason for the retrogression should by now be obvious. III:54 conceptually precedes III:51. The commandments cannot be conceived in III:54 as furnishing a regimen for concentration on God, for this conception of their purpose is appropriate only for people who are on the level of worship described in III:51. That level, which demands total concentration on God, has not yet been achieved in III:54.

In light of the fact that III:54 appropriates the conception of *ta'amei ha-mitzvot* given in III:25-49 rather than the conception given in III:51, it is intriguing that III:54 also contains other literary and conceptual links to III:25-49. For example, after describing four kinds of human acts in III:25 (vain; futile; frivolous; good or excellent), Maimonides ends with a discussion of divine wisdom as manifest in the divine acts. Thus, the chapter exemplifies the following pattern: four kinds of human acts, then divine wisdom. Then, in III:54, Maimonides again begins with a fourfold classification: he describes four sorts of human wisdom. The end of the chapter discusses divine acts. Thus the chapter exemplifies a reversal of the pattern in III:25: four kinds of human wisdom, then divine acts. To take another example of a literary connection between III:25-49 and III:54, Maimonides distinguishes between "the rational matter of the Law" that is received through tradition and is not demonstrated (to be sure, the reader may at first find that description oxymoronic — rational matter that is not demonstrated), and wisdom, through which the rational matter received from the Law is demonstrated. "And this should be the order observed:

the opinions in question should first be known as being received through tradition; then they should be demonstrated" (633-34).[27] This distinction parallels that drawn in III:27-28 between welfare of the soul and perfection of the soul.[28]

Apart from these intriguing literary ties, we may note a conceptual connection between III:54 and III:25-49. Maimonides' argument for the goodness or excellence of the Law (in III:25-49) contains a significant lacuna that is filled by III:54. Maimonides has asserted and then shown that the Law aims at certain ends. However, there is a difference between (1) showing that the Law achieves certain ends, and (2) providing a reasoned argument for the conclusion that those ends are noble. Legislation that aims at welfare of the soul and welfare of the body and that has, as its ultimate aim, perfection of the soul and perfection of the body — such legislation is certainly not futile; it is purposive. But is that legislation good or excellent? That depends on whether the aims achieved are noble. And until chapter 54, Maimonides provides no *argument* for the contention that these ends are noble; instead we have encountered only assertion or presupposition. Hence, until chapter 54, where Maimonides argues for the supremacy of intellectual perfection and assesses the merits of alternative conceptions of perfection, Maimonides has not demonstrated his thesis that Torah legislation is good or excellent.[29]

III:54 supplies the missing argument. Perfection of the soul was said to be an aim of the Law; now intellectual perfection is *shown to be* a noble end. Furthermore, if perfection of the soul or intellectual perfection is a noble end, so is anything that leads to perfection of the soul. Welfare of the soul (acquisition of correct opinions) is necessary for perfection of the soul; welfare of the body and perfection of the body are likewise propaedeutic to intellectual attainment. Thus, in III:54, Maimonides finally completes the argument for the thesis he set out in III:25. And so, we may say that chapter 54, which bears literary connections to chapter 25, also completes the argument for the thesis stated in III:25.[30]

There is also a more straightforward connection between III:54 and the *ta'amei ha-mitzvot* section. As already noted, the individual described at the end of III:54 who imitates God's actions in nature may be the transmitter of the legislation. It has been argued that certain specific categories of explanation given for the commandments in III:25-49 exemplify the divine attributes.[31] If this interpretation is correct, the end of III:54 circles back to III:25-49. In light of the other connections we noted between III:54 and earlier chapters, this more familiar observation must be seen as part of a larger, more comprehensive pattern.

It is difficult to know with certainty whether these literary symmetries and conceptual ties between III:25 and III:54 are intended by Maimonides. Nevertheless, we cannot dismiss the possibility that Maimonides deliberately spiced III:54 with themes and terminology from III:25-49 in order to let the astute reader know that the chapter "belongs" in that section — and hence before III:51. My case, however, need not rest on establishing this possibility. Rather, I have shown that III:54 leaves the casual reader with two mistaken impressions: that intellectual apprehension is the end of man, and that the commandments play no role in the life of the one who has achieved intellectual perfection. The first impression is dispelled in III:51 through Maimonides' assertions that worship (together with love and fear of God) is the end of man; the second, through the "training" conception of the commandments. Clearly, III:54 is not an accurate indication of Maimonides' views.

The task before us now is clear. We need to explain why Maimonides jumbles the sequence of chapters, putting his real "conclusion" before the end of the book.

II

Before proceeding, a word of clarification. I have been speaking as if III:51 is the last word of the *Guide* on human perfection. It would have been more accurate to say "III:51-52, " for III:52 continues III:51. Chapter 52 begins with a variation on the palace metaphor and proceeds to emphasize love and fear of God. Maimonides labels III:51 the "conclusion" only to signal that III:54 is not deserving of that designation.

Chapter 53, which explicates the attributes of *hesed, mishpat,* and *zedakah,* is clearly a prelude to the concluding portion of III:54, which states that the actions of the perfect individual will imitate these divine characteristics. I have already explained that the end of III:54 must be integrated into the brief discussion of political activity in III:51 (623-24). Indeed, an additional reason for thinking that III:54's first part (on the four perfections) is out of place is that III:53 belongs immediately before the section on *imitatio Dei* at the end of III:54; the section on the four perfections interrupts the flow from 53 into the final part of 54. In sum, here is the juxtaposition: III:51-52 on the one hand, III:53-54 on the other.

III

Why did Maimonides jumble the sequence of his final chapters, so as to make it appear that III:54 gives his final view on human perfection? The most plausible answer, I believe, is that he wished to conceal complexities, tensions, and uncertainties in his thinking. These are totally absent from III:54; they find subtle expression, however, in III:51.[32]

What are these complexities, tensions, ambiguities, and uncertainties that emerge in III:51, but whose significance is veiled by III:54? Basically, what III:51 suggests is that the argument used in III:54 to generate the thesis that the fourth perfection is supreme — namely, the argument that man's "true self" is intellectual — is highly simplistic in Maimonides's own mind.

> This [i.e., intellectual perfection] is in true reality the ultimate end, this is what gives the individual true perfection, a perfection belonging to him alone; and it gives him permanent perdurance; through it man is man (III:54:635).[33]

The deepest differences between III:51 and III:54 are related to the following question: can a human being transcend corporeal limitations and realize a purely intellectual "true self," as III:54 suggests? Or is corporeality a constant, ineliminable impediment to realizing a purely intellectual self?

The most obvious loci for an intellectualist, *anti*corporeal conception of the human being are the first and last chapters of the *Guide*.[34] According to I:1:

> The term "image" is applied to the natural form, I mean to the notion in virtue of which a thing is constituted as a substance and becomes what it is. It is the true reality of the thing insofar as the latter is that particular being. In man that notion is that from which human apprehension derives. It is on account of this intellectual apprehension that it is said of man, "In the image of God created He him" (I:1:22).
> Now man possesses as his proprium something in him that is very strange as it is not found in anything else that exists under the sphere of the moon, namely, intellectual apprehension. In the exercise of this, no sense, no part of the body, none of the extremities are used; and therefore this apprehension was likened unto the apprehension of the deity, which does not require an instrument, although in reality it is not like the other apprehension, but only appears so to the first stirrings of opinion (I:1:23).

Again, in III:54 Maimonides insists on the supremacy of intellectual perfection by deploying the true self argument.

What is striking about the chapters which contain these passages is that they include no acknowledgment of the arduous nature of intellectual attainment, and in particular no acknowledgment of the impediments that matter puts in the path of those who seek this goal. Nor do they attend to the difficulties incurred by one who is attempting to *sustain* intellectual focus and see the light of the truth on a *continuing* basis, not merely in brief flashes. These difficulties are noted in Maimonides' introduction (7), but the closest Maimonides comes to stating them in I:1, 2 and III:54 is when he says that Adam was punished for indulging his imagination and senses by being deprived of intellectual apprehension (I:2:25) and when, in III:54, he admonishes a reader over whom corporeal faculties have gained dominion (III:54, 635-36). The possibility of apprehending briefly and then losing what one has attained is at one point almost denied: "Therefore you ought to desire to achieve this thing [intellectual apprehension], which will remain permanently with you" (III:54, 635). Maimonides presents the prospect for realizing and sustaining an intellectual self as a realizable, almost easy task.

Yet, in some places, Maimonides seems to regard matter as an inherent, insurmountable aspect of human beings. Statements along these lines arise in contexts that address epistemological issues. In I:49, Maimonides acknowledges that "it is very difficult for man to apprehend, except after strenuous training, that which is pure of matter and absolutely devoid of corporeality" (I:49:109). Very difficult — but is it impossible? At least one passage suggests so.

> Matter is a strong veil preventing the apprehension of that which is separate from matter as it truly is...Hence, whenever our intellect aspires to apprehend the deity or one of the intellects, there subsists this great veil interposed between the two...The apprehension of His true reality is impossible for us because of the dark matter that encompasses us and not Him, may He be exalted; for He, may He be exalted, is not a body (III:9:437-38).

That a person's corporeal nature makes human knowledge of "His true reality" and knowledge of *any* beings that are "separate from matter" "impossible," has been emphasized by Shlomo Pines in an article[35] that has stimulated numerous other scholars to clarify and rethink Maimonides' epistemology, psychology and metaphysics.[36] Pines severely restricts the metaphysical knowledge that is accessible to man according to Maimonides and draws, from this interpretation, the conclusion that political, not theoretical, activity is the highest perfection of a human being. For Pines, the "great veil" is not to be lifted; escape from corporeality is impossible. Pines perhaps does not do justice to contrary evidence.[37] Nevertheless, the corporeal picture of human beings emerges forcefully in III:8-12. Perhaps it is too much to say that Maimonides definitely thought that human beings cannot transcend corporeal limitations. We must say, nonetheless, that he was uncertain whether they can, and that this uncertainty accounts for divergent statements he issues on the subject.

Interestingly, of all the lexicographical chapters in the *Guide*, only one begins with the words, "the equivocality of the term..." That chapter is devoted to the term "Adam."[38] Besides referring to the first man, "Adam" may refer either to the species or to the multitude (I:14). The three texts cited by Maimonides to illustrate the former use of the term include "My spirit shall not abide in man" (Gen. 6:3), and "That man hath no preeminence over the beast" (Eccl. 3:19), both of which are pejorative to the "species" and express pessimism about its religious capacities. The third text (Eccl. 3:21) at best suspends judgment about whether the destiny of the human spirit differs from that of the animals. Thus, among the three definitions of "Adam" are two that affirm the existence of an elite group of humans (since "Adamites" denotes the multitude in the third definition, and "Adam" the first man in the first sense), but also one that groups human beings with animals. Here, too, we find uncertainty and ambiguity about the nature and potentialities of human beings.

What does III:51 suggest concerning Maimonides' assessment of human potentialities? Which conception does he adopt there? By way of background, we should note that, for Maimonides, commandments are necessary because of human corporeality. "All man's acts of disobedience and sins are consequent upon his matter and not upon his form, whereas all his virtues are consequent upon his form...A man committing an act of disobedience does it only...because of the accidents consequent upon his matter" (III:8:431, 434). "The commandments and prohibitions are only intended to quell the impulses of matter" (III:8:433). Maimonides implies that, if God were to change the nature of human beings, there would be no need for "commandments and prohibitions, rewards and punishments," and hence "sending of prophets and all giving of a Law would have been useless" (III:32:529). Since the aspect of man's nature that produces disobedience is his materiality (III:8), it seems fair to say that "commandments and prohibitions" are necessitated by human corporeality. Similarly, we read: "For all the hindrances keeping man from his ultimate perfection, every deficiency affecting him and every disobedience, comes to him from his matter alone" (Introduction, 13). We may safely assume that the commandments lead a person to perfection by overcoming limitations and deficiencies that are due to matter. Hence only an individual who has not transcended corporeality will have need for the commandments.[39]

Now, let us look at Maimonides' trainee. He must perform the commandments. He, therefore, has not transcended corporeality, has not actualized a non-corporeal self. In III:54, which seems to assert that realization of the intellectual self is possible through intellectual apprehension, we might infer that commandments are not necessary for those who have attained intellectual perfection.[40] In III:51, where we learn that commandments *are* necessary for the trainee, we must conclude that the trainee has *not* escaped corporeality. (Notice that, as we saw earlier, the trainee *has* attained the level of intellectual perfection described in III:54; he is now seeking to go further, to achieve the level of worship.) The differing values placed on performance of the commandments in III:51 and III:54 reflect differing assessments of the prospects for freeing oneself from corporeal limitations. According to III:51, and contrary to III:54, intellectual knowledge alone does not permit one to achieve such a rank.

Without referring to the fact that the philosopher of III:51 is a creature limited by corporeality, it is difficult to see why Maimonides insists on performance of the commandments by the philosopher in III:51. Earlier I said he introduced the trainee conception partly because the conception of *ta'amei ha-mitzvot* in III:25-49 led to antinomianism. But what of it? What philosophic consideration restrains Maimonides from taking an antinomian step, which seems anyway legitimized by his formulation in III:54 (the commandments are "but preparations" for the fourth perfection)? It is his recognition that even the philosopher has not gone beyond the need for commandments.

This interpretation receives support from III:52. In III:52, the actions prescribed by the Law not only serve as a regimen to enhance focusing on God and God alone, but also to bring it about that some excellent men "fear, and are in dread and awe of God, and know who it is that is with them and as a result subsequently act as they ought to" (III:52:630). Earlier in the chapter Maimonides speaks of "perfect men" achieving humility, awe, reverence, fear, and shame. Shame is associated with the sense of touch and materiality (III:8:433), and an immediately succeeding line refers to speech and sexual conduct, which are likewise implicated in Maimonides' discussion of matter in III:8:435. Fear of God would seem to arise out of recognition of one's peculiar status as matter joined with intellect.[41] It is specifically the *actions* prescribed by the Law — associated with corporeality — that instill fear, while the *opinions* instill love. Through acquiring truth, one attains love; knowledge of the truth, in turn, then instills fear. (This sequence, love followed by fear, is reminiscent of *Mishneh Torah, Hilkhot Yesodei ha-Torah* 2:2.) Thus, in III:52 knowledge and then concentration leads to a recognition of corporeality — an implication altogether absent from III:54.

Hence, the continuing need of the philosopher to observe the commandments (in III:51) signals that the concept of the true self in III:54 is a naïve one. III:51 reveals a human being as an essentially corporeal creature even after he has attained the "fourth perfection." Perhaps not wishing to make this implication plain, Maimonides made it appear that chapter 54's optimistic portrait of human potentialities is the *Guide*'s last word on the subject.

IV

It may easily be argued that this "corporealist" reading of III:51 is highly partial and selective. For, if we merely read on in III:51, we amass strong evidence that some exceptional human beings can transcend corporeality. Maimonides' description of Moses and the Patriarchs appears to tell us precisely that. I want to address this claim by subjecting the rest of III:51 to a close reading. That reading will suggest a deliberate and sustained conflict in Maimonides' thought when he assesses the lives of Moses and the Patriarchs.

As set out in III:51, Maimonides' mandate to the philosopher is not only to acquire knowledge, but also to concentrate exclusively on what he knows to the extent that this is possible.[42] It would seem, however, that, for one who devotes himself exclusively to intellection, concentration on any sort of bodily activity is an impediment — it interferes with intellection. In most cases performing commandments involves bodily activity. Hence, one problem with performing the commandments when one has achieved the higher level is the possibility of losing intellectual focus through concentration on physical action. Not only does performing a commandment while thinking about worldly things break the attention of the would-be worshipper, but even performing a physical act required by the Law seemingly requires a break in attention, since one must focus on one's movements.

Maimonides takes stock of this difficulty in III:51. The commandments "have only the end of training you to occupy yourself with His command-ments...rather than with matters pertaining to this world" (III:51:622). By placing himself in the right motivational state, the performer will be able to execute bodily movements without abandoning his intellectual focus. Far from impeding intellectual concentration, the commandments promote it, provided that they are executed with the right measure and mode of reflection.

> If, however, you pray merely by moving your lips while facing a wall, and at the same time thinking about your buying and selling; or if you read the Torah with your tongue while your heart is set upon the building of your habitation and does not consider what you read; and similarly in all cases in which you perform a commandment merely with your limbs — as if you were digging a hole in the ground,

or hewing wood in the forest—without reflecting either upon the meaning of that action or upon Him from whom the commandment proceeds or upon the end of the action, you should not think that you have achieved the end (Ibid.).

One who is concentrating exclusively on God will not perform commandments "with the limbs only."

After implicitly resolving the problem of diverted concentration as it pertains to acts of worship, Maimonides raises a parallel question about the political activities and daily life of Moses and the Patriarchs. These men achieved the "union with God — I mean apprehension of Him in love of Him...Also the providence of God watching over them and over their posterity was great" (III:51:624). Yet they engaged in practical pursuits:

Withal they were occupied with governing people, increasing their fortune, and endeavoring to acquire property.

How shall we explain this paradox?

Now this is to my mind a proof that they performed these actions with their limbs only while their intellects were constantly in His presence (III:51:625).

Thus Moses and the Patriarchs exemplify Maimonides' depiction of a special sort of person, one who attains a rank that Maimonides suggests even he cannot be guided to attain.[43] This is a rank of

a human individual who, through this apprehension of the true realities and his joy in what he has apprehended, achieves a state in which he talks with people and is occupied with his bodily necessities while his intellect is wholly turned toward Him...while outwardly he is with people (III:51:623).

This phenomenon — the existence of special individuals who (in contrast to the trainee) perform physical or political activities "with their limbs only, while their intellects are constantly in His presence" — can be understood against the backdrop of I:72. There Maimonides writes that "the relation obtaining between God, may He be exalted, and the world" may be compared to "that obtaining between the acquired intellect and man; this intellect is not a faculty in the body but is truly separate from the organic body and overflows toward it" (193). Now the acquired intellect is just "the perfect intellect *in actu*."[44]

What the passage suggests, therefore, is that the perfect intellect "overflows" toward the body and determines human actions.[45] If we put this idea of I:72 together with the notion that Moses and the Patriarchs did certain things with their limbs only, we come up with the following possibility for explaining how they did these actions: the actions in question were done with the limbs only because these actions, *like all human actions done by those whose intellects are perfected*, were merely an overflow from the acquired intellect, and this overflow operates through a causality that more closely resembles mechanical causality than it does intentional human action, i.e., action that results from the exercise of practical reason.[46]

This understanding of the Moses/Patriarchs phenomenon dissolves an otherwise puzzling contradiction. Maimonides states:

> In all these actions their end was to come near to Him...For the end of their efforts was to bring into being a religious community that would know and worship God...Thus it has become clear to you that the end of all their efforts was to spread the doctrine of [God's unity] and to guide people to love Him (III:51:624).

Now one would think that, if the end of their activity of governance was "to bring into being a religious community that would know and worship God...to spread the doctrine of the unity of [God's name] and to guide people to love Him," then the one activity that would decidedly *not* be performed "with the limbs only" would be governing the people. And yet, Maimonides explicitly lumps "governing people" together with "increasing fortune," "tending cattle, doing agricultural work, and governing the household" and "endeavoring to acquire property," as actions they performed "with their limbs only."

A possible explanation of this fact is that *all* physical activities done by one who has achieved the highest level are done with the limbs only since these activities are the result of the overflow from the intellect. It has already been observed by others[47] that, at the end of the *Guide*, Maimonides distinguishes between (1) "the perfection of man that may truly be gloried in," which consists in apprehending God and His providence over his creatures, and (2) "the way of life of such an individual," which "will always have in view lovingkindness, righteousness, and judgment, through assimilation to His actions." "The way of life" probably refers to political governance.[48] Based on a principle Maimonides advocates in II:11 ("Know that in the case of every being that causes a certain good thing to overflow from it according to this order of rank, the existence, the purpose, and the end of the being conferring the benefits, do not consist in conferring the benefits on the recipient. For pure absurdity necessarily would follow from this assumption [II:11, 275]"), we may say that the actions referred to are not part of the *essence* of human perfection but rather part of the *overflow*.[49] And based on III:51 (the "limbs only" passage), we might take a further step: action resulting from this overflow does not represent anything like ordinary deliberative behavior, because the explanation of it is so different from the explanation of ordinary deliberative behavior. Indeed, as noted earlier, there is nothing special about the fact that political governance was carried out by Moses and the Patriarchs with the limbs only. *Any* bodily activity performed by them had to be performed with the limbs only.[50]

The section on Moses and the Patriarchs, as just interpreted, has an obvious bearing on Maimonides' conception of the human self. If the philosopher's continuing need for the commandments and his need to focus on God through bodily activity is a mark of his corporeality, the phenomenon of Moses and the Patriarchs, who performed bodily actions with their limbs only, would appear to confirm that rare human beings *can* transcend corporeal limitations. The true self of an individual who is on the level of Moses and the Patriarchs is purely intellectual. Because their "true selves" were intellectual, *any* bodily activity they would execute could be performed with the limbs only. For the body is merely a corporeal entity, and not part of the essential person.

The passage immediately after the one on Moses and the Patriarchs augments the case for this claim about human potentialities. Here Maimonides interrupts the flow of exposition in order to divulge an "extraordinary speculation" that "has occurred to me just now" (624). The speculation is that providence operates over an individual according to the degree to which he is occupied with divine matters without distraction.

> If the man's thought is free from distraction, if he apprehends Him, may He be exalted, in the right way and rejoices in what he apprehends, that individual can never be afflicted with evil of any kind. For he is with God and God is with him (625).

Apart from the literary peculiarity of Maimonides' discussion — a chapter of which he expressly attests that it contains nothing new is also one in which Maimonides remarks that an idea has just occurred to him[51] — commentators suggest that this conception of providence contradicts the naturalistic account of providence developed by Maimonides in earlier chapters. In earlier chapters, Maimonides had maintained that a person who has developed his intellect may enjoy providence in two ways:

> (1) He may utilize his (practical or scientific) knowledge to protect himself from potential harms; (2) he may utilize his (philosophic)

insight that material goods and evils are insignificant as compared to intellectual goods, in order to remain untroubled through periods of adversity.

In both cases, providence is "operating" in an entirely naturalistic manner. Yet, in III:51, Maimonides writes of the individual who is exclusively occupied with God that "no evil at all will befall him" (626), neither floods nor pestilence nor wars nor any physical calamity.

If you should happen to pass... a widely extended field of battle... even if one thousand were killed to your left and ten thousand to your right, no evil at all will befall you (627).

Samuel ibn Tibbon sought to explain why the philosopher enjoys this extravagant degree of protection. It seems difficult to explain, save by shifting from a naturalistic theory to a supernatural one, in which God must directly protect the individual from harm. Thus, the naturalist theory of III:11-12, 17-23 seems to give way to, and be contradicted by, a supernatural theory in III:51.[52]

Of the solutions proposed to Samuel's query, the most compelling appears to be that offered by Moses Narboni.[53] Narboni, in effect, italicizes the word "him": "no evil will befall *him*." If the individual's "true self" — his true form — is the intellect, then, indeed, neither floods nor pestilence nor war can affect *him*; only the material body is affected, while the intellect, the real person, emerges unscathed. To be sure, the protection of the true self is limited to those moments at which the individual's intellectual potentialities are being actualized. Still, at those moments, if only at those moments, the individual becomes one with the separate intellect and thus separate from matter.[54]

While Narboni's interpretation does not exclude the operation of the other types of naturalistic protection identified by Samuel ibn Tibbon (Shem Tov lists all these forms of protection in his construal of Maimonides), the interpretation does force us to say that III:51 anticipates, or, rather, presupposes, the view that man's "true self" is intellectual — a view that will not explicitly be forwarded until III:54.[55] The same view may underlie Maimonides' statement at the end of III:51 that Moses, Aaron, and Miriam achieved salvation from death because they were in a state of passionate love when their bodily faculties were extinguished.[56] And that same view may be invoked to explain why Moses and the Patriarchs must be said to have acted with their limbs only. The limbs are not part of their essential being. The proximity of the two paragraphs; the strong suggestion that the Moses/Patriarchs passage inspired the doctrine about providence; the explicit "proof" that Moses and the Patriarchs must have acted with their limbs only *because* they enjoyed providence — all these render it virtually certain that the two passages are tightly connected and mutually dependent.

The foregoing represents a rather strong case in support of the claim that, for Maimonides in III:51, rare human individuals can actualize a purely intellectual self, just as claimed in III:54. This of course runs contrary to what I argued in the previous section. However, the issue cannot be settled so simply. Reading the Moses/Patriarchs and providence passages as we have leaves us with nagging questions. For example, if, as per Narboni, the "true self" argument of III:54 is needed to explain the phenomena described in III:51, why wasn't that argument introduced in III:51 instead of three chapters later?[57] In addition, the true self argument of III:54 was applied to someone who possesses the fourth perfection; and the fourth perfection is achieved through intellectual knowledge alone. The trainee of III:51, therefore, *by the definition of the fourth perfection given in III:54*, has *already* actualized his true self through knowledge and should not be subject any longer to corporeal limitations; yet he *is* still subject to these limitations and would have to attain the level of Moses and the Patriarchs to transcend them.

In addition to these considerations, some of the evidence in III:51-52 suggests that the portrait of Moses and the Patriarchs, as well as of the man of providence, is presented by Maimonides only as a possibility, not an actuality. He himself may have been uncertain about whether the possibility could be and was actualized; and he presents us, in III:51-52, with ingredients of a competing picture, a picture in which no human individual can transcend all corporeal limitations.

First, Maimonides thinks that one cannot be *guided* to attain the rank of Moses and the Patriarchs.

> This rank is not a rank that, with a view to the attainment of which, someone like myself may aspire for guidance [Pines records two alternative meanings: to be guided, and to guide others]. But one may aspire to attain that rank which was mentioned before this one through the training that we described (III:51:624).

In contemporary philosophical parlance, the Moses/Patriarchs phenomenon is a "nomological dangler": Maimonides has no way of explaining *how* it can evolve within his own theories. The level of Moses and the Patriarchs is not continuous with that of the trainee. To concentrate on God, the trainee must occupy himself with and focus on bodily activities, i.e., the *mitzvot*; and when performing mundane tasks he is to focus on worldly activities, apparently to the neglect of concentration on God (III:51, 613). As I will later show (see appendix below), Maimonides does not even intend the training he prescribes to serve as training for the level of Moses and the Patriarchs, but only, on the contrary, to serve as training for the ability to meditate properly when *not* engaged in bodily activities. How anyone living in the way prescribed for the trainee could *develop* into a Moses is a puzzle Maimonides cannot resolve, and that anyone can enjoy the degree of providence he describes is "an extraordinary speculation" that would not have occurred to him were it not for the existence of Moses and the Patriarchs and his construal of their significance. Lacking a theory to explain how one could *become* a Moses, Maimonides lacks a theory to explain how Moses could be as he appears. Doubts about the ability to *guide* one to this level easily generate doubts about the ability to *attain* the level.

Second, we read in III:51, 627 that "In the measure in which the faculties of the body are weakened and the fire of the desires is quenched, the intellect is strengthened, its lights achieve a wider extension, its apprehension is purified, and it rejoices in what it apprehends." Apprehension and love wax as bodily capacities wane in old age. This passage yields a powerful argument for the possibility of *immortality* — survival of the soul *after* death — in Maimonides' thought. But its implications for the possibility of transcending corporeality *while* soul and body are one — in other words, the possibility of achieving worship in the here and now — are pessimistic. The fullest flowering of the intellect must await the extinction of desire. If even the Active Intellect "sometimes gets an impediment that hinders its act" (I:68:166), the prospects of a corporeal creature remaining in a state of unimpeded intellectual activity would appear to be dim indeed. If the passage on old age is to be read as I have just suggested, III:51 contains a counterpoint to the optimistic picture of human possibilities painted in the passage on Moses and the Patriarchs and the passage on providence. This illustrates my claim that III:51 recapitulates the tensions in Maimonides' conception of the person that have run through the *Guide* all along.

Third, the passage on Moses and the Patriarchs, in which Maimonides describes the special sort of individual who can do physical activities while concentrating on God and who enjoys the fullest extent of providence, does not make that sort of individual appear *too* rare. Not only Moses, but Abraham; not only Abraham, but also Isaac and Jacob, are said to have attained this exalted level (III:51: 623-24).[58] Maimonides here abandons the idea that Moses was singular, an idea that is found in scattered places in the *Guide* and even earlier in III:51:620. Any claims for the uniqueness or near uniqueness of Moses are undermined still more at the end of the chapter, when Aaron and Miriam suddenly surface as individuals who achieved passionate love and secured salvation from death. They seem to rank even above the Patriarchs.[59] By conceding that Moses was not singular, and that even individuals whose achievements as prophets and leaders are surpassed by those of Moses can appropriately be grouped with him, Maimonides is perhaps subtly suggesting that even Moses did not achieve perfection.

Fourth, III:52, I said earlier, caps the discussion initiated in III:51 and is, in my view, the last word of the *Guide*. Here, Maimonides emphasizes man's *lesser* status. "The one who has apprehended the true realities" seeks to liberate himself from all materiality, and not merely to actualize a potential for moral conduct or to actualize the potential of the rational faculty (which, unlike the acquired intellect, resides in matter; see I:72). *Fear results from the realization that this escape is not possible.*

Here, in III:52, we find a counterpoint to III:51:624-26, illustrating the tension I have been highlighting. In fact, even *within* III:52, one finds both acknowledgment of corporeality (as we have just seen) and contrasting sentences about "the bond between us and him." Maimonides begins the chapter by stating that one is not to "sit, move, and occupy himself when he is alone in the house, as he sits, and occupies himself when he is in the presence of a great king" (III:52:629). We know from the lexicographical chapters that such verbs may be used for both corporeal and noncorporeal beings; in context the ambiguity is most appropriate. It accentuates the tension between the two conceptions.

Fifth, skepticism about the Moses example is warranted even as regards *apprehension*. As Pines points out, Maimonides gives expression to two contradictory interpretations of "my face shall not be seen" (Ex. 33:23). His official, stated view in I:38 is that Moses apprehended "*all* things created by me," which would include the separate intellects. But in I:37 he quotes an interpretation of Onkelos to the effect that human beings can know only "things endowed with matter and form." Pines argues that Onkelos's interpretation is the one Maimonides believes (since he had no other reason to cite it) and that the statement in I:38 is made for political reasons.[60] Josef Stern, on the other hand, has argued, more convincingly, that Maimonides is presenting contradictory alternatives between which he cannot adjudicate given his own epistemological theory. In other words, Maimonides himself suspends judgment.[61] Limitations to human knowledge are also conceded in I:21, 31, 32, 54 and in III:9, without Moses appearing to be an exception. A similar agnostic attitude may characterize III:51: Maimonides lays out for us two conflicting pictures.

The situation is analogous to one we encounter when we try to assess the place of matter in Maimonides' metaphysics. As Alfred Ivry has shown,[62] Maimonides on the one hand accepted the Aristotelian definition of substance as including matter and thus saw matter as a necessary part of being — a substratum for form and individual existence, as well as a principle of change and potentiality. On the other hand, he was attracted to certain aspects of the rival Neoplatonic approach, for example, its negative *evaluation* of matter and its view of matter as privation. The conflict that characterizes the evidence in the *Guide* concerning the nature of human beings and the scope of human potentialities mirrors the conflict that characterizes Maimonides' understanding of the place of matter in the world. Multiple approaches to human beings have been said to account for the several and diverse theories of providence found in part III of the *Guide*.[63]

Maimonides tells us in I:17 that philosophers and learned men, in discussing the topic of matter and form, used only riddles, figurative language, and similes. It would be surprising if Maimonides furnished us with a ready, clear statement on the subject of matter and form as those concepts serve to elucidate his conception of the human being. A deliberate ambiguity in III:51-52, a presentation of conflicting pictures, would fit in perfectly with Maimonides' views on the need for care in exposition.

Thus, III:51-52 brings to a head the clash between two pictures of human beings that has been waged in "the other chapters of this Treatise." Maimonides leaves us with a fourfold knot of problems whose resolution depends upon which view of human beings emerges triumphant. These problems are (1) the possibility of knowing immaterial beings; (2) the possibility of enjoying providence to the fullest degree; (3) the possibility of transcending the need for commandments; (4) the possibility of anyone living in the style ascribed to Moses and the Patriarchs. The absence of any explicit assertion of the "true self" argument in III:51 may be due to Maimonides' uncertainty about the possibility of this true self being actualized. III:51 is the *Guide*'s real conclusion; but Maimonides chose to end with a formulation (III:54) that is blissfully free of tensions.

One other consequence of our discussion should be noted. Pines believes that, because theoretical perfection is impossible for human beings, and the only positive knowledge of God of which man is capable is knowledge of the attributes of action, *therefore* the life of practical, political activity, in which one imitates God's attributes of *hesed*, *mishpat*, and *tzedakah*, is the highest perfection of a human being.[64] But, if the individual described at the very end of III:54 who imitates God's attributes of action is identified with or is exemplified by Moses (as is suggested by I:54), *and* we take III:51 as articulating the *nature* of Mosaic governance, then political activity *as defined by Maimonides* is dependent upon theoretical perfection. Any political activity not achieved by escaping corporeality will be different from the political activity of the ideal Moses of III:51. Even in interpreting III:54 itself, we must hold that only the individual for whom political activity represents an "overflow" of his perfection satisfies the description of the ideal personality, for only such an individual rises to the level of Moses and the Patriarchs and rules as they are said to have ruled in III:51 — with the limbs only. Thus, if a human being is precluded from attaining theoretical perfection because matter is an ineliminable impediment, he cannot attain practical perfection as Maimonides defines it; at best he can attain practical perfection in some other sense. The two perfections, theoretical and practical, would appear to stand or fall together.

This consequence follows provided that we take the Moses passage in III:51 and the passage on *imitatio Dei* in III:54 to be describing the same phenomenon. From the connection between I:54 and III:54, however, it would seem that knowledge of God's actions, i.e., knowledge of nature, even without positive knowledge of immaterial beings, can generate (overflow into) a distinctive political way of life modeled on imitation of God's attributes as manifested in nature. III:54 nowhere states explicitly that political activity is not ideal unless it satisfies the account given of Moses and the Patriarchs in III:51; the account in III:51, on the other hand, makes no reference to *imitatio Dei*. Thus, our lack of clarity as to whether Maimonides is describing, in III:51 and III:54, a single type of political activity, or instead two different types, leaves us uncertain as to whether political perfection is dependent on escaping corporeality.

V

My reading of III:51-54 contains several distinct elements, and a reader is not obliged to accept all of these by virtue of having accepted one. A point that I deem beyond controversy is that

(I) III:51 differs from III:54 in its characterization of the human *telos* and in its assessment of the purpose of *mitzvot*.

Also beyond controversy, I think, is that

(II) III:51 describes a stage of human development that comes after the stage described in III:54.

More debatable is whether

(III) The chapters differ in another respect as well: viz., they differ in their assessments of whether human beings can transcend all corporeal limitations and actualize a purely intellectual self.

Lastly, even assuming one grants (I), (II), and (III), there is the question of why Maimonides placed III:54 after III:51. Perhaps

(IV) By placing 54 at the end, Maimonides wishes to conceal the tensions and uncertainties which characterize his real position.

I concede that (IV) is speculative. What is not speculative is that there is a problem about the placement of III:54 and III:51 that must be explained somehow.

The approach to III:51-54 advocated in this paper is significant, I believe, for several reasons.

(1) Scholars who have turned their attention to these final chapters of the *Guide* have tended to rivet their gaze on the question: which is the highest end of a human being, theoretical perfection or practical perfection? Certainly the importance of this issue to our understanding of Maimonides must not be denigrated; and certainly the work that has been produced on this issue is valuable. Nevertheless, focusing exclusively on this question of how to rank the two perfections has led to neglect of other problems with which Maimonides was grappling in these final chapters. Chief among these are problems concerning the nature of a human being, which in turn bear on the prospects for attaining perfection, whether intellectual or practical. Indeed, the salience of these problems throughout the *Guide* needs to be emphasized more than it has been.

(2) Chapters 51-54 have often been treated as a seamless web. The differences between them have been ignored, and as a result Chapter 54 has been taken at face value. I have sought to correct this perspective and to caution against taking chapter 54 superficially.

(3) Some literary features of chapter 51 can now be understood. In particular, Maimonides' insistence that chapter 51 contains nothing new perhaps is meant to divert attention from the significance of the chapter. Interestingly, the heart of the chapter is the segment beginning with "additional matter," viz., the passage on the training conception of the commandments, the passage on Moses and the Patriarchs, and the "extraordinary speculation" about providence which has "occurred to me just now." Attending to this new material helps us define the problematic nature of III:51. To a certain extent, though, Maimonides' remarks about introducing nothing new rings true: the chapter plays out — brings to a climax — themes that have been broached before, indeed have run throughout the *Guide*.

(4) That Maimonides devoted twenty-five chapters to *ta'amei ha-mitzvot* suggests that this topic was central to the philosophic outlook of the *Guide*. This centrality, I believe, traces to Maimonides' view that the commandments represent a way of dealing with human corporeality and the limitations it imposes on human achievement — a problem which, on my reading, is a focal concern of the *Guide*. On my reading, furthermore,

Maimonides' handling of *mitzvot* in III:51-54 provides an interpretive key to the chapters, since the conception of *mitzvot* in III:54 serves as an indication that III:54 precedes III:51.

(5) The place of the commandments in Maimonides' conception of the human ideal has often struck readers of the *Guide* as highly tenuous and problematic. For, first, the notion that "all the actions prescribed by the Law" are "but preparations made for the sake of this end [intellectual perfection]" (III:54:636) ostensibly implies that the commandments are of no value at all for the individual who has achieved the end for which the commandments are designed, and hence that the commandments can have no role in the life of the philosopher. And second, the fact that certain commandments originated in specific historical circumstances would seem to entail that they may be abandoned in changed circumstances.

What has often been overlooked is that the two sources of antinomianism just identified are problems to which Maimonides, as we have seen, presented a reasonably explicit answer in III:51, when he introduced the idea that the commandments train the philosopher to be occupied with God. (III:34 is also of relevance.) Preoccupation with the means/ends argument and the argument from historical origins is unfortunate, because it has crowded out interest in certain other problems that Maimonides cared about and addressed, albeit with characteristic ambiguity. Compounding the error, some readers of the *Guide* work with the pat assumption that Maimonides consistently defended the Law outwardly while rejecting it inwardly, when in truth, it is his *open* declaration that the commandments are but preparations that may be seen from III:51 to be a poor gauge of his real position. In truth, the philosopher, too, must observe the law (III:51:622).

In this paper, then, I have sought to stimulate a reorientation of perspective and emphasis as regards the key questions we must ask about Maimonides' accounts of the commandments, of human perfection and of the figures who seek to create a "religious community that would know and worship God" (III:51, 624). Our discussion has taken us to problems that lie at the deepest levels of Maimonides' psychology and epistemology, and to hard questions about what to make of the peculiar literary features of the *Guide*'s climactic chapters. We are left, at the least, with a new agenda.

APPENDIX

In section IV I called attention to the following question: does the philosopher's concentration on the bodily movements associated with *mitzvot* preclude his concentration on God while he is performing the commandments? Maimonides' implicit reply, I indicated, was no; and that negative answer underlies his entire conception of the commandments (in III:51) as a regimen through which the philosopher trains himself to be occupied with God. More argumentation is needed, however, to support my taking Maimonides at face value when he implies that no conflict is incurred by the philosopher while performing the commandments. Indeed, an interesting line of thought can be wielded against this reading. In this appendix I defend my exoteric reading of the passage against this line of thought.

The problem of diverted concentration that is raised by the examples of Moses and the Patriarchs parallels the problem of diverted concentration that is raised by the example of the philosopher who performs acts prescribed by the Law. In both cases, Maimonides is aware of the possibility that attention to bodily activities will interfere with intellectual concentration. But Maimonides' *solution* to the problem of diverted concentration in the case of Moses and the Patriarchs is the *opposite* of his solution to the problem of diverted concentration that he proposed in the case of the commandments. In the trainee's case, Maimonides had cautioned that, while concentrating on God, one should *not* perform actions (commandments) "only with your limbs." In the Moses passage, by contrast, he holds that, while performing bodily actions — "governing people, increasing fortune, endeavoring to acquire property ... tending cattle, doing agricultural work, governing their household" — Moses and the Patriarchs *did* act "with their limbs only." They *had to*, for otherwise they could not remain constantly in the presence of God. What does Maimonides wish to convey by repeating the phrase ("with the limbs only") that he used in the passage on the commandments? One possibility is that the repetition of the phrase should be taken innocuously, i.e., Maimonides repeats the phrase in order to *contrast* the two situations. Performing the commandments of praying, reciting the *shema* and benedictions, and reading the Torah, readily lead one to concentrate on God, while the mundane activities of Moses and the Patriarchs do not but rather overflow by dint of their concentration. But could he perhaps be intimating, through repetition of the phrase, that the activity of one who performs the commandments as training is more analogous to the activity of Moses and the Patriarchs than appears at first? Might his real view be that the philosopher, too, must split between his mental concentration and his bodily activity when he performs the commandments?

Maimonides' selection of examples — reading the Torah and prayer — might be read in a way that supports a reading of this esoteric kind. As Josef Stern has pointed out,[65] these activities are problematic for the philosopher because they involve the use of anthropomorphic and anthropopathic expressions.[66] Hence, when Maimonides instructs his readers to

> cause your soul, whenever you read or listen to the Torah, to be constantly directed — the whole of you and your thought — toward reflection on what you are listening to or reading (III:51:622).

and to practice the same with regard to discourses of the prophets and benedictions, or when he advises:

> give heed to all that you are reading...aim at meditating on what you are uttering and at considering its meaning (Ibid.)

he cannot possibly mean that you should focus on the anthropomorphic and anthropopathic language and the affirmative attributes. Doing so would lead you down the wrong path, that of "the affections of the imagination" (III:51, 623). Quite the contrary, what the philosopher must do is split his concentration from his action; he must think about philosophic truths, and these are radically different in content from the assertions in verbal prayer. Note that when advising his reader to engage in "intellectual worship" while upon his bed, Maimonides stresses that this worship consists in "nearness to God and being in His presence *in that true reality that I have made known to you* and *not by way of affections of the imagination*" (III:51:623) — not, that is, in the way stimulated by affirmative attributes. On this reading, doing the commandments in the way Maimonides prescribes doesn't merely train you to occupy yourself with God. Rather, it trains you to occupy yourself with God *while engaged in activity that to some extent interferes with exclusive occupation with God*. And in that way performance of the commandments trains the gifted individual to act in a manner more nearly approximating the way of Moses and the Patriarchs, who could remain in God's presence while doing other things, though in fact their rank may not be attainable by others.

The same possibility comes out forcefully in a passage that contains a remarkable ambiguity. Maimonides has allowed one who is free from distraction while performing acts of worship to also occupy his thoughts with worldly things for "many and long stretches of time":

> Thus, I have provided you with many and long stretches of time in which you can think all that needs thinking regarding property, the governance of the household, and the welfare of the body. On the other hand, while performing the actions imposed by the Law, you should occupy yourself *only with what you are doing, as we have explained*. (III:51:623)

79

What are you "doing" when you perform the commandments? Are you "doing" the action — that is the exoteric reading — or are you concentrating on God? With which of these should you "occupy yourself"? What, precisely, has Maimonides "explained"?

According to the esoteric reading, in which Maimonides is encouraging a split between mental focus and bodily movement, Maimonides has chosen the examples of prayer and reading the Torah because in those cases the conflict between concentration on God and concentration on the activity is *maximal*. In fact, since anthropomorphic and anthropopathic concentrations are "affections of the imagination," and imagination is a corporeal faculty, the conflict is one between mind and body. If this reading is correct, then the philosopher is not really concentrating on doing the commandments if he concentrates on God.

However, the selection of examples and the intent of the passage could be explained differently. Reading the Torah and prayer involve minimal bodily movements and maximal possibility of concentrating on God. By choosing these examples, so this reading goes, Maimonides is able to mute the conflict that could arise between the twin demands of occupation with God and concentration on the bodily movements demanded by a particular precept. In short, Maimonides picked examples in which the problem of diverted concentration is *minimal*, not (as in Stern's reading) examples in which the conflict is *maximal*. As for the problems posed by affirmative attributes, the philosopher is to reflect on what those attributes mean within Maimonides' theory of attributes, or on why such attributes are used. Thus the philosopher keeps a distance from the literal meaning of prayers but still uses the texts as an opportunity to reflect on truths pointed to, if only allusively and misleadingly, therein, or on truths which explain why the texts are used. He need not split his thought from his actions. Maimonides saw no conflict between thought and behavior here.

Which reading is correct? There is some reason to support the second, non-esoteric reading. On the first reading (which demands a split between concentration and action during performance of the commandments), the training of which Maimonides speaks is training in the following: doing one thing while concentrating on another. Now, the whole notion of training through the commandments is paradoxical *if* (1) one must not do *mitzvot* with the limbs only; (2) the training is intended to elevate one to the level of Moses and the Patriarchs. How can one train for a level at which one acts with the limbs only, by performing certain activities that must *not* be done with the limbs only? If one is training for the level of Moses and the Patriarchs, then the "diverted concentration" understanding of Maimonides' examples (prayer and Torah reading) is feasible. However,

Maimonides implies quite strongly that one is *not* training for *that* level, but instead for the ability to meditate properly when alone "upon your bed."

> In my opinion this end ["intellectual worship consisting in nearness to God and being in His presence in that true reality that I have made known to you and not by way of the affections of the imagination"] can be achieved by those of the men of knowledge who have rendered their souls worthy of it by training of this kind. (III:51:623)

We also have an explicit statement on 624:

> But one may aspire to attain that rank which was mentioned before [i.e., the rank lower than that of Moses and the Patriarchs] through the training that we have described.

In this passage we have the sense that there is a lack of transition between the lower level and the level of Moses and the Patriarchs. One cannot *be guided to* the rank of Moses and the Patriarchs (624). If by performing the commandments one were doing one thing while concentrating on another, one *would* thereby be guided to the rank of Moses and the Patriarchs, contrary to Maimonides' rejection of this possibility. Since no such guidance is possible, Maimonides' repetition of the "limbs only" phrase is better read as contrasting two levels: a (higher) level at which one *can* concentrate on God while engaged in other things, and a (lower) level at which one can not. The higher level is not continuous with the lower level; rather, attaining it involves a quantum leap.

Even if we reject an esoteric reading which sees prayer and Torah reading as involving a split between thought and action, a modified esoteric reading may yet be proposed. Granted that Maimonides did not intend the examples of prayer and Torah reading to epitomize cases of conflict between mind and body, his selection of examples, one may nonetheless say, is calculated to conceal the problem that arises when we try to extend the training model to other commandments. The examples he chooses are too convenient; they make it too easy for him to illustrate his claim that performance of the commandments does not interfere with intellectual concentration. When it comes to *other* commandments, the way in which we are to apply this approach is not clear. Maimonides' catch-all phrase "and the performance of the other commandments," masks the fact that his "new" explanation of the commandments works only for a select few of them.[67] For instance, social laws seem to have no place in the training conception, though they are prominent in III:54.[68]

Interestingly, although Maimonides' examples — prayer, Torah reading, benedictions — are taken from the commandments in the *Mishneh Torah*'s Book of Love that he itemized in III:44,[69] Maimonides does not here refer to the most physical of the commandments mentioned in III:44, to wit, phylacteries, *mezuzah*, and acquiring a Torah. Also intriguing is the fact that Avicenna, who arguably influenced Maimonides' conception of prayer in III:51, declares that "all the other ordinances of the religion are explicable along the lines" which he sketched for prayer, but then writes: "We would have desired to expound each act of worship separately: but it was impossible for us to enter upon matters which may not fitly be communicated to every man."[70] Avicenna's reluctance to explicitly extend his model to other practices might encourage the notion that, for Maimonides, the performance of the other commandments cannot be explicated along the same lines as his primary examples; at the level of worship, performance of the *other* commandments would interfere with attainment of the human telos.

I do not find this argument on behalf of an esoteric, antinomian reading of the "training" conception persuasive. It is true that, in III:51, Maimonides picks examples that best fit the conception, just as in III:54 he picks examples (social laws) that best illustrate the propaedeutic conception he advocates there. However, this does not mean that he thought the conception in III:51 cannot be applied to any commandments but those in his examples. In other passages in which love and fear are said to be the end of the commandments, no examples are given at all (III:24:501). As for the Avicenna reference, Maimonides may be following Avicenna's lead (of not discussing other precepts), but not because other commandments do not fit his model. Perhaps he is wary of people applying the model incorrectly and paying insufficient heed to the details of the actions. No such danger exists in the cases of prayer and Torah reading.

It would be instructive to compare Maimonides' discussion here with discussions by Jewish writers in the Neoplatonic and Sufi tradition, such as Bahya ibn Pakuda. Like Maimonides, Bahya argues vigorously for the supremacy of interior religious attitudes — love, awe, cognition — over external performances. At the same time, he recognizes that most duties prescribed by Jewish law are external in character, and attempts to specify the proper attitude with which these commandments should be performed.[71] Maimonides was addressing the same problem, but unlike Bahya refrained from specifying appropriate interior attitudes for *all* external performances. Bahya's own attempt[72] to furnish proper motivations for such acts as taking a *lulav* and wearing *tzitzit* illustrates the point that interior attitudes might be defined so broadly as to lose their connection to the *particular* actions that supposedly must be performed with those attitudes.

I see no reason, at any rate, to doubt that Maimonides wanted his trainee to perform *all* commandments in the manner he suggests, that is, with a unity between mental focus and bodily act. We saw earlier that Maimonides' repetition of the "limbs only" phrase may be taken either as (1) accentuating the contrast between, on the one hand, the individual engaged in "training" through the commandments, and, on the other, Moses and the Patriarchs; or as (2) *blurring* that contrast — the trainee is more like them than appears, because he, too, must split himself between mental focus and bodily action. I have argued against this second possibility. Indeed, if, in accordance with the possibility I raise in the text, Maimonides could not adequately understand how the Moses/Patriarchs phenomenon is possible, then perhaps any similarity between the trainee and them works in the opposite way: they, like the trainee, do not fully divert their attention from their physical movements.

Though I do not accept an esoteric reading of Maimonides' remarks on using commandments as the regimen for concentrating on God, it must be admitted that the problem of how the philosopher can concentrate on God *through* prayer and Torah reading, practices which utilize anthropomorphic and anthropopathic conceptions, is an interesting one. In my view Maimonides' reference to activities which utilize these conceptions serve as yet another signal that the trainee has not transcended corporeality and therefore has continued need for *mitzvot*. What he *can* achieve, in a constructive way, through these conceptions is, however, not clear from Maimonides' account.[73]

NOTES

Both the general direction of this essay and numerous points of detail have been sharpened thanks to comments by David Berger, Warren Zev Harvey, Lawrence Kaplan, Barry Kogan, Charles Raffel, and Josef Stern. I also benefited greatly from discussion with Robert Brody, Yehuda Gellman, Steven Harvey, Arthur Hyman, Alfred Ivry, Sidney Morgenbesser, Aviezer Ravitzky, and David Sykes.

[1]   Page references to the *Guide* are to the translation by Shlomo Pines (Chicago, 1963) and appear in the following format: part:chapter:page.

[2]   I will henceforth drop the qualification "kind of" in citing this passage.

[3]   Struck by the oddity of having three chapters come after a conclusion, Shlomo Pines has written that the designation of III:51 as "conclusion" "may, but does not necessarily, mean" that at first Maimonides intended III:51 to be the concluding chapter, but later changed his mind and added 52, 53 and 54. See Pines, "The Philosophical Purport of Maimonides' Halachic Works and the Purport of the *Guide of the Perplexed*," in *Maimonides and Philosophy*, ed. Shlomo Pines and

Yirmiyahu Yovel, (Dordrecht, Boston, Lancaster, 1986), 9. Unfortunately, the suggestion that these chapters were introduced as an afterthought is not at all plausible. The chapters include such important themes as fear of God (52), the divine attributes manifested in nature (*hesed, mishpat, zedakah*) (53), the four perfections (54), and the imitation of God (end of 54). Furthermore, the passage on *imitato dei* in III:54 rounds out a discussion provided in I:54, as pointed out in Pines, "Translator's introduction," cxxi-cxxii, his "The Limitations of Human Knowledge According to Al-Farabi, Ibn Bajja and Maimonides," in *Studies in Medieval Jewish History and Literature*, ed. Isadore Twersky (Cambridge, MA, 1979), 82-109, esp. 98-100, and also in Eliezer Goldman, "The Worship Peculiar to Those Who Have Apprehended the True Realities" (Heb.), *Annual of Bar-Ilan Studies in Judaica and the Humanities* VI (1968), 287-313. The notion that Maimonides thought of these themes only after having set down in writing the themes of III:51 strains credulity. Pines himself uses very guarded language in broaching the possibility of a change of mind, and we would be wise to look for other explanations.

Steven Harvey, in "Maimonides in the Sultan's Palace," in *Perspectives on Maimonides*, ed. Joel L. Kraemer (London, 1996) pointed out that "*al-khatima*," translated as "conclusion," can also mean "seal," and that "in *heikhalot* writing seals are what the adept need to journey safely and successfully through the heavenly palaces." Maimonides "would then be saying that III:51 is the decisive clue to understanding his treatise." I certainly will agree that III:51 is the "conclusion" in this sense, but hope to show why it is the "conclusion" of the *Guide* in the straightforward sense as well.

4   For a classic discussion of III:54 and its relationship to Ibn Bajja's treatment, see Alexander Altmann, "Maimonides' Four Perfections," *Essays in Jewish Intellectual History* (Hanover, New Hampshire, 1981), 65-76. Cf. Goldman, "Worship," 294 ff., who sees significant originality, at least in emphasis, in Maimonides' treatment.

5   There is one passage in III:13:451-52 that might be taken to indicate that worship precedes or is a means to perfection. Speaking of the views that "the final end of man is, as has been said, to worship God," Maimonides notes that "a question remains to be asked regarding the final end of this worship." The answer considered is that worship is a means to perfection. In that context, however, it is not clear either that the worship alluded to is that mentioned in III:51 or that the perfection referred to is purely intellectual, as opposed to being a state of perfection that is constituted by the state of worship.

6   Pines, "Translator's introduction," cxxi-cxxii; Goldman, "Worship," 306 ff. Cf. Miriam Galston, "Philosopher King vs. Prophet," *Israel Oriental Studies* 8 (1978): 204-18.

7   Maimonides says he has explained the political activity based on *imitatio Dei* "several times in this Treatise." The passage in Moses and the Patriarchs in III:51 has as much claim to be among those chapters as does any other passage in the *Guide* with the exception of I:54, in which the *imitatio Dei* motif is explicit. The absence of this motif in III:51 will be touched on later.

8   Until III:25, Maimonides has devoted only two other chapters to *ta'amei ha-mitzvot*: II: 39-40. These chapters contain the only cross reference in the *Guide* to the *ta'amei ha-mitzvot* section. Their relevance to us will become clear later.

9   While generally ignored, the distinction between welfare and perfection is noted by Miriam Galston, "The Purpose of the Law According to Maimonides," *Jewish Quarterly Review* 69 (1978): 27-51, and by Warren Zev Harvey, "Political Philosophy and Halakhah in Maimonides" (Heb.), *Iyyun* 29 (1980): 198-212.

10   Maimonides also speaks of another class of opinions: those opinions belief in which is politically necessary — but (so he implies) need not be true (III:28, 513-14). Transmission of these opinions, evidently, falls under welfare of the body.

11   The process by which the Law inculcates correct opinions is analogous to teleological processes in nature that "benefit" things that are not capable of cognizing and appreciating the processes. See, for instance, III:25:503-4.

       Two additional points support the idea that consciousness of God's ends is not necessary for the Law to achieve its ends as set out in III:25-49. First, in the case of some commandments, specifically those of the "second intention" (sacrifices, for example), it seems likely that in idolatrous times Jews were not motivated by the reasons that Maimonides gives. It is evident, from a passage in III:32:526, that people in idolatrous times were not even told of the reason for sacrifices. Second, even if people *had* been told the reasons for certain commandments — that they instill correct opinions or abolish reciprocal wrongdoing — they would not necessarily have been *motivated* by the ends. On the contrary, Maimonides believes that the masses are motivated by material rewards and punishments. See, e.g., *Guide* III:32:529, where the use of material rewards and punishments is explained in terms of the frailties of human nature. The implication is that rewards and punishments (or promises and threats) are needed to motivate obedience, and motivation does not come through knowledge of the "reasons" Maimonides specifies. Also note I:36:84: "For the multitude grasp only the actions of worship, not their meanings." Shem Tov, in his commentary to III:51, correctly sees that in III:25-49, "*mitzvot* do not require *kavvanah*."

12   This terminology was suggested by Lawrence Kaplan. The same distinction, with different terminology, is central in Stern, "The Idea of a *Hoq*." Much of this section is indebted to Stern's acute and sensitive analysis.

13   "Political Philosophy and Halakhah."

14   Stern, "Idea of a *Hoq*," 130, note 44, suggests that Maimonides interpolates this chapter precisely to conceal the contradiction between III:25-49 and III:51.

15   Goldman, "Worship," 290-91, effectively dispels the impression, created by this passage, that fear of God relates only to actions and has nothing to do with opinions. See below, section IV.

16   The conception, endorsed by Maimonides, that prayer is a means of "training" oneself to be occupied with God is found in Avicenna's treatise on prayer, to which Steven Harvey has referred me. As we shall later see, however, Maimonides' development of the conception contains significant twists.

17   I am overstating matters. Yehudah Gellman has pointed out to me that the approach of III:51 is not new, having been foreshadowed in III:44. There Maimonides lists certain commandments whose end is "the constant commemoration of God, the love of Him and the fear of Him, the obligatory observance of the commandments in general, and the bringing about of such

belief as is necessary for everyone professing the Law." His list includes prayers, recital of the Shema and reading of the Torah — the commandments showcased in III:51 — as well as priestly blessings (he referred to benedictions in III:51). (The list also includes laws concerning phylacteries and *mezuzot*.) Nonetheless, I claim that III:51's approach is new, for in III:51 we find the idea that "the performance of the other commandments" (622) is to be understood along the same line as were the commandments from the *Mishneh Torah's* Book of Love that were discussed in III:44. Interestingly, Maimonides concludes III:44 with these words: "All these are actions that bring about useful opinions. This is clear and manifest and does not require another discourse, for that would be nothing but repetition" (574). Even if Maimonides is here telling us that III:51's approach to the commandments is "nothing but repetition" and "includes nothing new," the fact he provided the "repetition" in III:51 needs explanation. The explanation, I think, is that in III:51 he is setting the approach of III:44 into a larger context (worship) and extending it to other commandments. For further discussion, see the Appendix below.

18 The shift just described is pointed out by Yonah ben-Sasson, "A Study of the Doctrine of *Ta'amei ha-Mitzvot* in Maimonides' *Guide*" (Heb.), *Tarbiz* 29 (1960): 268-81; Goldman, "Worship," 292-93; David Hartman, *Maimonides: Torah and Philosophic Quest* (Philadelphia, 1976), chs. 4-5, and *A Living Covenant* (New York, 1985), ch. 5; Yeshayahu Leibowitz, *Emunato shel ha-Rambam* (Jerusalem, 1980); Josef Stern, "The Idea of a *Hoq*." See also James H. Lehmann, "The Relationship of Love and Fear in the Writings of Maimonides," *Yavneh Review* 8 (1973): 7-24. Several of these writers characterize the shift as one from an anthropocentric to a theocentric explanation of the commandments, or from self-interested to disinterested worship. I am not happy with this formulation, partly because the argument given in III:54:635 for the supremacy of intellectual perfection is boldly anthropocentric and self-interested, and partly because the aims of the Law set out in III:27-49 are not base or self-centered. See Hartman's critique of Yeshayahu Leibowitz on this point in *A Living Covenant*, 117-24.

19 Maimonides has in fact foreshadowed part of his new account in III:27, when he indicated that the Law aims not only at *welfare* of the soul but also *perfection* of the soul. Though the element of concentration and training is not emphasized there, the connection between commandments and philosophic knowledge is.

20 See Goldman, "Worship," 290. Maimonides does not use the term "worship" to refer to performances of the commandments until III:51. However, it is hard to know the precise significance of the term's not appearing earlier, for it appears in III:54 even though III:54 is not referring to the training conception of the commandments but instead, as I shall presently argue, endorses the conception found in III:25-49.

21 See Stern, "Idea of a *Hoq*," for an explanation of this remark. Note II:40:382: "the Law, although it is not natural, enters into what is natural."

22 I borrow this formulation of the argument from Stern, "The Idea of a *Hoq*," 123-24.

23 In discussion at the 1985 conference at which this paper was delivered.

[24] A similar reading is advocated by Josef Stern: "Knowing that content of the earlier chapters…the philosopher will 'possess' the 'premises' from which he can now draw the 'conclusion' [III:51 is said by Maimonides to by a "only a kind of conclusion"] that for him the commandments only serve the end of 'training' Maimonides proposes here" (Stern, "The Idea of a *Hoq*," 124). Of course, on this reading, one must still uncover reasons for the *masses* to observe the commandments!

As Stern points out, (116-119 and 129, note 36), the *Guide* contains other elements that combat the antinomian argument. The Law must be independent of time and place (III:34), and hence even prescriptions that are historically conditioned must continue in force. To be sure, it is not clear what issue Maimonides is addressing in III:34, and it is also unclear from his wording (535, line 4-5) whether the claim of eternality (*a parte post*) applies to all laws or only those of the first intention (see Gerald Blidstein, "Maimonides on 'Oral Law'," in *Jewish Law Annual*, ed. B. Jackson, vol. I [Leiden, 1978], 108-22, 117-21). Nevertheless, the fact that III:34 may contain a response to the antinomian threats, coupled with the fact that the philosopher would have ready access to this response, suggests that the shift to a new line of explanation in III:51 is not necessitated by the antinomian threat. On the other hand, it seems rather weak to say to the philosopher, "Observe these practices because they once served a purpose for a different kind of society, and Law by nature must be eternal." He is likely to want an explanation that links up with his present interests. Thus, even if the antinomian threat could be met, a new motivation must be supplied for the philosopher.

[25] Contrary to my reading, Hartman argues that "reflecting upon the end of the action" means: reflecting upon the utility of the action as defined in III:25-49. The philosopher, on Hartman's understanding, realizes what God has done for the community of Israel by legislating the commandments, and this is a component of his love of God. See *A Living Covenant*, 117 ff. Hartman's reading does have certain advantages. First, on my reading, there is no discernible distinction between "reflecting upon the end of the action" and "reflecting upon Him from whom the commandments proceeds," since on my reading the end of the action *is* "reflecting upon Him from whom the commandments proceeds." On Hartman's reading, the distinction between the two is clear (though on neither reading do we have a good idea of what "the meaning of the action" refers to). Second, nowhere else in the *Guide* do we find a statement enjoining the philosopher to reflect upon the ends in III:25-49. (The statement "marvel exceedingly at the wisdom of His commandments, just as you should marvel at the wisdom manifested in the things he had made," III:49:605, is not an imperative to study and know the reasons, but to react to knowledge of them.) Since, however, understanding those reasons is part of what is required to understand the natural order — the *mitzvot*, as Stern emphasizes, being part of that order — we would expect a clear statement by Maimonides to the effect that the philosopher ought to reflect upon the reasons in III:25-49. The mere fact Maimonides devotes so much of the *Guide* to spelling out those reasons for his reader suggests that knowledge of them is crucial for further religious and intellectual development. Hartman's reading gives us the imperative we expect, namely: reflect on the teleology of *mitzvot* set out in III:25-49.

     Despite these considerations, it strikes me as significant that on Hartman's reading the term "the end" shifts its meaning within the sentence. If we assume that it is preferable to hold the referent of the phrase constant, then, since the second occurrence of the phrase clearly refers to focusing on God, the first must too. Whether this consideration should outweigh those I adduced for Hartman's reading is, I suspect, a subjective matter.

26   While I focus here on the "preparation" conception in III:54, describing the shifts as we have — two neatly segregated treatments — oversimplifies matters in other ways. Maimonides' two treatments of the commandments are not neatly segregated. His explanation in terms of love and fear is not confined to the final chapters of the *Guide*: it also appears, if briefly, in III:24:501, which is not part of the *ta'amei ha-mitzvot* section, but instead (as Lawrence Kaplan observed) parallels III:52. This passage is significant, I think, because it implies that *all* commandments, and not merely those specifically mentioned in III:51 (such as prayer and Torah reading), aim at love and fear. In III:29:518, we again encounter a conception like that in III:51-52, but there Maimonides emphasizes not love and fear *per se* but the *opinion* that God is the one "who ought to be worshipped and loved and feared." Cf. Ben-Sasson, "A Study."

27   Cf. *Guide* I:33-34.

28   However, two differences should be noted. First, one who achieves welfare of the soul need not be aware that the beliefs he has acquired are found in the tradition; and second, one who achieves perfection of the soul need not have started by setting for himself the project of proving beliefs X, Y, Z that he knows are found in the tradition.

29   It is true that I:1 anticipates the true self argument that is used in III:54. However, not only is that chapter spatially distant from III:25-49, it is not directly concerned with the nature of perfection. Therefore, it is plausible to hold that III:54 is needed to complete the argument of III:25-49.

30   It is true that III:54 is concerned with what a *person* should pursue, whereas Maimonides' proof that intellectual perfection is a good end would show that *God* had acted in "good or excellent" fashion in legislating the commandments. But both conclusions — that a person ought to pursue intellectual perfection, and that God's legislation is good or excellent — may be established from the same set of premises.

31   See Goldman, "Worship," 306ff. For example, laws of the second intention (e.g., sacrifices) are needed because of deficiencies in human beings that are due to their corporeal nature. Such laws exemplify *mishpat* as characterized in III:53.

32   Historically, III:51 became better known in popular circles than III:54, thanks in part to the power of the palace metaphor and the mystical quality of the chapter. Perhaps Maimonides did not always correctly anticipate what his audience would emphasize in reading him!

33   Both Alexander Altmann, "Maimonides on the Intellect and the Scope of Metaphysics," in Altmann, *Von der mittelalterichen zur modernen Aufklärung: Studien zur judischen Geistesgeschichte* (Tubingen, 1987), 60-129, and Goldman, "Worship," note a paradox here. The immortal soul is one that loses its individuality; yet the activity that leads to immortality is advocated because

it actualizes the true self. Altmann resolves the paradox by inferring that the immortal soul retains a "modicum of individuality" (90).

34 Lawrence Kaplan has pointed out to me that, by ending the *Guide* with III:54, Maimonides creates a symmetry between the first chapter of the work, which presents a portrait of man's essence as intellectual, and the last. The *Guide* has now come full circle. Interestingly, though, I:1, to my mind, is simplistic in just the way that III:54 is.

35 Pines, "The Limitations of Human Knowledge."

36 Altmann's lengthy paper, "Maimonides on the Intellect," originated as a response to Pines, and the University of Maryland devoted a 1987 conference to Pines' thesis. See also Warren Zev Harvey, "Maimonides on Human Perfection, Awe and Politics," in *The Thought of Moses Maimonides*, ed. Ira Robinson, Lawrence J. Kaplan and Julien Bauer (Lewiston, Queenston, Lampeter, 1990), 1-15; Barry S. Kogan, "What Can We Know and When Can We Know It?: Maimonides on the Active Intelligence and Human Cognition," in *Moses Maimonides and His Time*, ed. Eric L. Ormsby (Washington, D.C., 1988), 121-37.

37 Such as that marshaled by Altmann and Kogan (note 36).

38 Noted by Warren Zev Harvey, *Hasdai Crescas's Critique of the Acquired Intellect*, Ph.D. dissertation, Columbia University, 1973, Excursus II.

39 It is true that what matter will propel people to do in one historical period is not necessarily what matter will propel them to do at another. Consequently, even for "corporeal" men, not all the commandments will be necessary if the commandments were to quell only the impulses of matter at a particular time and place. Recall, however, Maimonides' views about the eternity of the Law and its applying equally to all individuals (III:34).

40 Interestingly, whereas "being healthy and in the very best bodily state" is prized at III:27:511, Maimonides, writing in III:54:634-35, tells us of "the perfection of the bodily constitution and shape" that "utility for the soul is absent from this species of perfection." These two appraisals of bodily soundness are not strictly contradictory — III:54 is concerned with strength and proportionality of the limbs rather than health *per se*. By downgrading the body in III:51 more than he does in III:27-28, while preserving the instrumentalist view of the commandments as preparing one for intellectual perfection, Maimonides paves the way for a purely intellectualist conception of self.

41 Throughout this paragraph I am indebted to Goldman, "Worship," 289-93. The use I make of Goldman's observation is very different from the use he makes of it. His article accepts the possibility of transcending corporeality.

42 Several scholars have noted the extensive influence of Sufi terms and themes on Maimonides' discussion. See for instance, Steven Harvey, "Maimonides and the Sultan's Palace."

43 III:51:624. Note, however, the two readings of the text that are cited by Pines in his note 32. I discuss these later. Like the *Guide*, the legal writings contain some indications that Moses could not transcend corporeality (*Shemonah Perakim 7, Hilkhot Yesodei ha-Torah* 1:10), but contrary indications as well (*Introduction to Helek*, seventh principle, and Hilkhot *Yesodei ha-Torah* 7:6). (This has been noted by Howard Kreisel, *Maimonides' Political Thought* [Albany, NY, 1999], 311, n. 59.)

44   Following Altmann, "Maimonides on the Intellect and the Scope of Meta-physics," 80.

45   Ibid.

46   It is puzzling, however (as pointed out by Lawrence Kaplan), that Maimonides states: "These actions were pure worship of great import."

47   See Warren Harvey, "Maimonides on Human Perfection." Barry Kogan has called my attention to the resemblance between this portrait of Moses's activity and the account of the philosopher's actions in *Kuzari* I:1. The philosopher's organs or limbs behave "as if they were the organs of the Active Intellect" (Hirschfeld translation, New York, 1964).

48   See I:54. For defenses of this reading, see Pines, "Translator's introduction," cxxi-cxii and his "The Limitations of Human Knowledge," esp. 98-100; also Goldman, "Worship."

49   Ibn Tibbon's translation blurs the difference between "perfection" and "way of life," reflecting his own reading of Maimonides as not sufficiently intellectualist.

50   My reading clearly implies (or presupposes) that "overflowing" does not involve deliberate activity. That view would need to be tested by an examination of other "overflowings," such as those from the separate intellect toward that which is below them in rank. Cf. *Guide*, II:12:279-80 and II:7:266.

      It is possible that Maimonides' inclusion of "acquiring fortune" implies a critique of the Sufis, for whom poverty was an ideal. On Maimonides' view, one could acquire fortune — or be engaged in any other activity — without leaving God's presence.

51   Cf. III:22-23.

52   See Zvi Diesendruck, "Samuel and Moses ibn Tibbon on Maimonides' Theory of Providence," *Hebrew Union College Annual* XI (1936): 353-62.

53   *Perush Le-Moreh Nevukhim*, ed. J. Goldenthal (Vienna, 1852), 64-65. Narboni's view is accepted by Goldman, "The Worship Peculiar to Those Who Have Apprehended the True Realities," 300 ff. See also Simon Rawidowicz, "Man and God" (Heb.), *Studies in Jewish Thought* (Jerusalem, 1959), 309-14. For a penetrating analysis of the whole issue of providence see Charles M. Raffel, "Providence As Consequent Upon the Intellect: Maimonides' Theory of Providence," *AJS Review* 12 (1987): 25-71.

54   Note, however, that the importance of achieving *conjunction* should not be overstated. See Altmann, "Maimonides on the Intellect."

55   Narboni does not himself cite III:54.

56   See Goldman, "Worship," 293-94.

57   It is conceivable that Maimonides endorsed the argument fully, but wished to keep his "extraordinary speculation" about providence open to the kind of supernatural interpretation that Samuel ibn Tibbon, with puzzlement, raised. The "true self" argument would have exposed the naturalistic character of the theory. Maimonides therefore had a special motivation for postponing reference to it. The presence of the true self argument in I:1, however, casts some doubt about this explanation; the argument is already available to the reader of III:51.

58 I am indebted to Warren Zev Harvey for this observation.

59 "The other prophets and excellent men are beneath this degree; but it holds good for all of them that the apprehension of their intellects becomes stronger at the separation" (III:51: 628).

60 Pines, "Limitations of Human Knowledge," 92. In these paragraphs, I assume that, if matter precludes complete *apprehension*, it also precludes complete concentration and worship. But I concede that this premise needs further explanation.

61 Stern, "Skeptical Themes in the *Guide of the Perplexed*," presented at the Maryland conference (note 36) in May 1987. For a similar approach, applied to other issues, see Sarah Klein-Braslavy, "The Creation of the World and Maimonides' Interpretation of Gen. i-v," in Pines and Yovel (eds.), *Maimonides and Philosophy*, 65-78, as well as the papers by Ivry cited in note 62.

62 Alfred Ivry, "Providence, Divine Omniscience, and Possibility: The Case of Maimonides," in *Divine Omniscience and Omnipotence in Medieval Philosophy*, ed. Tamar Rudavsky (Dordrecht, 1985), 143-59; also see Ivry's "Islamic and Greek Influences on Maimonides' Philosophy," in Pines and Yovel, *Maimonides and Philosophy*, 139-56.

63 See Raffel, "Providence As Consequent Upon the Intellect." According to John Cooper in *Reason and Human Good in Aristotle* (Cambridge, 1977), cited by Raffel, the "true self" issue contains the key to understanding Aristotle's shifting pronouncements on the question of whether moral activity is integral to the good life. The importance of this issue in other writers known to Maimonides would strengthen the case for reading Maimonides as concerned with the same issue.

64 "Limitations of Human Knowledge."

65 "Idea of a *Hoq*," 123. My turning Stern's points into the idea that prayer and Torah reading are paradigms of a split between act and concentration is not in his article; I am indebted to him for raising it, in conversation, as an interesting possibility. The problem is by no means contrived; mystics, too, had to maintain esoteric *kavvanot* while paying attention to the ideational content of the liturgy. See Joseph Weiss, "The Kavvanot of Prayer in Early Hasidism," *Journal of Jewish Studies* 9 (1958): 163-65. Cf. Lawrence Kaplan, "Response to Joseph Dan," in *Studies in Jewish Mysticism*, ed. Joseph Dan and Frank Talmage (Cambridge, 1978), 121-28.

66 See I:59.

67 On this reading, Maimonides' injunction not to perform a commandment with your limbs as if you were hewing wood or digging a hole can be understood as follows. It is not that these actions are done absentmindedly; generally they are not. It is rather that they are heavily physical.

68 Cf. Goldman, "Worship," 292-93. The phrase translated by Pines, "Know that all the practices of the worship" is better rendered (as in ibn Tibbon and Kafih) "know that all *these* practices of the worship," which more clearly highlights the fact that "and the performance of the other commandments" is tacked on. Cf., however, note 25. If Hartman's view is correct, the difficulty is alleviated, since one is concentrating on the reasons God gave this specific commandment.

[69]   Cf. note 17.

[70]   *On Prayer*, in Arthur J. Arberry, *Avicenna and Theology* (London, 1951).

[71]   See *Duties of the Heart*, V:3 and X:7.

[72]   See especially V:3.

[73]   Postscript (2009): Since the original 1985 oral presentation of this paper, my suggestion that contradictions in the *Guide* about the prospects for escaping corporeality represent alternatives between which Maimonides cannot choose, a possibility that, as mentioned, others also had raised, has gained plausibility from a new approach to contradictions in the *Guide*. Several scholars have argued, without using this specific example, that contradictions in the *Guide* should be understood as alternatives between which Maimonides does not adjudicate because the power of reason is limited. This approach contrasts with the standard understanding, dating back to the Middle Ages and influentially promulgated in our day by Leo Strauss, that Maimonides believes one of the two contradictory views, to wit, the more radical one, and hides it. See Marvin Fox, *Interpreting Maimonides* (Chicago, 1990); Kenneth Seeskin, *Searching for a Distant God* (New York, 2000), 177-88; Yair Lorberbaum, "On Contradictions, Rationality, Dialectics, and Esotericism in Maimonides' *Guide of the Perplexed*," *Review of Metaphysics* 55 (2002): 711-50. At the same time, my reading of the *Guide* in this essay is an esotericist one, for, on my understanding, Maimonides' message is not stated with clarity and is conveyed by his jumbling of chapters. I read *The Guide* in a less esotericist way today than I did in 1985, but the literary features I examine here really do seem deliberately placed and my explanation I think accounts for them.

THE INTEGRATION OF TORAH
AND CULTURE: Its Scope and Limits
in the Thought of Rav Kook

Time and again in his writings, with characteristic force and eloquence,
R. Abraham Isaac Kook exhorts Jews to open themselves to the realm of
general culture, confronting and engaging the full range of secular teachings
and disciplines. An especially powerful, yet nonetheless representative,
statement of this outlook appears in *Arpelei Tohar*:

> And how shall a person come to an estimate of the divine greatness, in
> such a manner that the essential form of the splendor of the soul will
> not be effaced but will, rather, expand? Through the expansion of his
> scientific powers; through the liberation of his imagination and flights
> of thought; through knowledge of the world and of life; through the
> richness of feeling in all of existence — for the attainment of which,
> he must occupy himself with all scholarly disciplines and all of life's
> teachings, all the ways of different cultures, and the contents of the
> ethical and religious teachings of every nation.[1]

For Rav Kook, it is only through the conjunction of natural piety, on the one
hand, with exploration of secular disciplines on the other that the "secrets
of Torah" — its esoteric stratum, its true meaning — will be brought to light
and elucidated.[2]

In the passage cited, Rav Kook directs his mandate toward the individual.
Elsewhere, he puts forward the same imperative in terms of national rather
than individual goals.[3] Each nation has its distinctive talents, he explains;
but the talent distinctive to the Jews is their capacity to absorb, synthesize
and transform the best elements in surrounding cultures.[4] Israel is, thus,
"the quintessence of all humanity."[5] The mission of the Jews in history is
to exercise their talent for integration and creativity and then to bring to
the outside world the new product they have fashioned. Only in that way
will Israel be able to execute its sacred task: to elevate all of humanity and
all of existence.[6] The renaissance of Jewish life that Rav Kook envisions for
the Holy Land is intimately tied to, indeed, is *constituted by*, their fulfilling

this mission.[7] The terms "Judaism" and "Torah" must themselves come to signify nothing less than this grand synthesis and harmonization.

For Rav Kook, then, religious wholeness can be achieved only through refinement of the rational and moral capacities; refinement of these capacities can be produced only by immersion in general culture; and immersion in culture is religiously significant and valuable only insofar as it results in an integrative and harmonistic worldview.[8]

The persistence and centrality of these themes in the writings of Rav Kook can hardly be gainsaid, and further documentation of their prominence would be an exercise in redundancy. Even so, any serious inquiry into Rav Kook's views on religion and culture must come to grips with some basic facts. Let us, for the moment, shift our attention away from Rav Kook's purely theoretical pronouncements about the value of general culture, acknowledging these to be almost uniformly enthusiastic. Let us focus, instead, on what his call to integration really amounts to in practice. To what extent does the personality and thought of Rav Kook exemplify the ideal of breadth and unification that he champions in his writings? How much of his work and his life exemplifies an effort at achieving a harmonization and synthesis of Judaism with world culture? The answer is: surprisingly little. In the sequel, I hope to explain this assessment — and then furnish an account of it.

UNIFICATION OF THE HOLY AND THE PROFANE: RAV KOOK VS. THE MEDIEVAL SYNTHESIS

What does it mean to integrate *kodesh* and *hol* (the holy and the profane)? The project is often conceived in the following way. *Kodesh* and *hol*, first of all, refer to specific bodies of teaching and doctrine: on the one hand Jewish teachings (*kodesh*), on the other hand, the deliverances of science, history, philosophy, archaeology, and so forth (*hol*). To speak about *ihud* or *ahdut* within the framework of these definitions is to show how science and philosophy, for example, may be used as tools for (1) defending religion and (2) interpreting biblical and rabbinic texts with an eye toward harmonizing them with the secular teachings. Integration, in this conception, requires synthesizing or harmonizing *truth claims* made by Judaism with *truth claims* propounded in secular works. This, of course, is what integration meant in medieval times: it meant constructing proofs for the existence and unity of God; demonstrating the truth of other doctrines, such as creation *ex nihilo* and immortality of the soul; resolving apparent conflicts between Judaism and secular disciplines; and, also, as part of that task of reconcilation, reinterpreting biblical and rabbinic texts in general philosophic categories, particularly when the literal import of those texts was inconsistent with conclusions generated by human reason.

Rav Kook certainly read new meanings into classic texts. And to the extent that Rav Kook's philosophy was influenced by secular currents such as Hegelianism and nineteenth century progressivism and by individual secular thinkers like Bergson and Schelling, his reinterpretations of biblical and aggadic motifs in part derive, ultimately, from secular teachings and concepts. Indeed, his thought has been described as "an interpretation of Judaism in terms of the evolutionary concepts of the nineteenth century."[9] Nevertheless, there are important differences between Rav Kook's project and that of the medievals.

Most important is the fact that the sense of *ihud kodesh ve-hol* that dominates in Rav Kook has relatively little to do with issues about truth claims. The key to grasping what Rav Kook does mean by *ihud* or *ahdut* is that *kodesh*, in his conception, does not refer to *disciplines* of *kodesh*, to *limmudei kodesh*. Nor does *hol* refer to *limmudei hol*, the *teachings*, or *contents*, of particular disciplines. Instead, *hol* refers to the entire range of events or facts in the world at large: *that* certain movements have developed, *that* certain theories have sprung up, and the like. Thus, in one context, *hol* may refer to the rise of the secular Zionist movement, in another, to the fact that evolutionary theory has been articulated — as distinct from referring to the *content* of the theory, the propositions it asserts. And what is *kodesh*? *Kodesh* is a controlling vision, a subjective perception through which one is to view these events or facts. This controlling vision is monistic and harmonistic. The phrase *hokhmat ha-kodesh* refers not to the wisdom or discipline through which one apprehends an entity called the holy, but to the wisdom or discipline through which one develops a (subjective) apprehension of all things *as* holy, as fitting into a teleological scheme or design. All events, all movements, all theories, all social trends, are interpreted in light of this apprehension, this vision, even — especially! — when those phenomena, viewed in isolation, carry no overt and evident religious significance. *Kodesh* is the "form" (*tzurah*) which shapes and structures the "matter" (*homer*) of *hol*, investing it with value. To unify *kodesh* and *hol* in this sense is to develop a certain reading of history (including intellectual history) and contemporary events, a reading that fits phenomena and events into a larger (and dialectical) picture of human progress. Once attained, this vision stimulates the individual or group to act in a way that will, if only gradually, promote a yet richer vision and a fuller actualization of it in empirical, historical reality. Integration thus demands both a certain type of apprehension and a program of action.[10]

Kodesh, the controlling vision, thus apprehends and interprets *hol*. Yet Rav Kook states that the relationship is reciprocal: *hol* nurtures *kodesh* as well.[11] How does this other half of the process take place? Not by *"hol"'*s delivering specific truth claims. Instead, culture stimulates, develops and improves certain *faculties* that are needed to apprehend the whole; the faculty that penetrates *kodesh* — i.e., through which one sees all things as holy — results from the integration of *all* human faculties.[12] Thus, one needs to possess the monistic and harmonistic vision to be aroused to use one's faculties; refinement of the faculties, in turn, enhances and clarifies the vision. To unify *kodesh* and *hol* is "to view the *hol* through the looking glass of *kodesh*."[13]

That Rav Kook's emphasis is on the development of faculties rather than the apprehension of truth is borne out by the very passage from *Arpelei Tohar* that I quoted at the beginning of this essay. A person "comes to an estimate of the divine greatness" through the "expansion of his scientific *powers*," and "the liberation of his *imagination*." Maturation of the faculties is achieved by "occupying himself with all scholarly disciplines" and "all teachings of every nation." "Knowledge of the world and of life" — even if it refers to knowledge of truth-claims — is at best *one* of the prerequisites. Thus, culture is valuable because it promotes maturation of the *faculties*, the realization of *all* the powers of a human being — of which the power of cognizing truth claims is but one.

The consequences of Rav Kook's emphasis on the development of faculties rather than the formation of accurate belief are important. By stressing that the value of cultural activities lies in the role they play in refining and stimulating human faculties, Rav Kook escapes the narrow view that these activities are religiously important only when they deliver truths. This feature of his approach makes significant room for activities that the medieval conception does not justify — on the one hand, aesthetic pursuits,[14] and, on the other hand, technological advances and political developments, whose fruits are not so much cognitive (i.e., theoretical) as pragmatic.[15] Rav Kook's approach allows for a *comprehensive* positive evaluation of cultural products. He responds to "modernity" in a full sense of the term.

The aim of exposure to culture, we said, is to develop human faculties. Unfortunately, Rav Kook is glaringly imprecise about which elements in a culture accomplish this most effectively, and he offers precious few exact details of the process of development. Plainly he needs to draw lines between the permissible and the prohibited. If every viewpoint may play a role in the dialectical unfolding and expansion of human consciousness, if no cultural phenomenon, no matter how ostensibly deplorable, is without value, then Rav Kook would have to find value even in pornography.[16] Rav Kook's reply to this difficulty is probably that yes, everything has value, but, no, not everything should be tolerated. This formulation invites us to explore the limits of tolerance in Rav Kook's thought, but I must set aside that topic for now.[17] What is clear is that Rav Kook made an important contribution by construing modernity and its challenges more broadly than medieval thinkers did (vis-à-vis the "modernity" of their time).

If we return now to the medieval synthesis, we see clearly other differences between it and Rav Kook's call for integration — differences that revolve mostly around the notion of reinterpretation. (a) Rav Kook's focus was not the reinterpretation of *texts*; it was, instead, the interpretation of *views* and *events* in the world at large. (b) Rav Kook's "rereading" of texts, where it does take place, has a voluntary, optional character to it that medieval rereadings do not have. Medieval thinkers were *forced* into reconstruing classic texts that came into clash with philosophy or science, because reinterpretation was for them a *project* that had to be carried out in systematic fashion. But for Rav Kook, reinterpretations are utilized more as literary devices that contribute rhetorical and literary force. (c) We cannot know for certain whether Rav Kook introduced reinterpretations because he was trying to accommodate secular teachings, or instead, because he had found these ideas in Jewish (specifically, kabbalistic) sources. This question is open to varying answers.[18]

What of the other objective of the medieval program, viz., defending religion by means of philosophic or scientific arguments? Rav Kook engaged in no such enterprise. There is no attempt, certainly no sustained attempt, to draw on the tools of science and philosophy so as to show or argue for the truth of religious convictions. Rather, Rav Kook cites certain features of scientific thought that are suggestive of the accuracy of his holistic and optimistic vision. That the sciences drive toward increasing generality and comprehensiveness, for example, reflects for him a *cosmic* drive toward cognizing reality under conceptualizations that reflect greater and greater generality and wholeness.[19] The evolutionary trend in science, as noted, fits kabbalistic teaching beautifully, as it bolsters a sense of interconnectedness and feeds human optimism.[20] Such connections between scientific theories and kabbalistic truths have primarily heuristic, illustrative, or rhetorical value, as distinct from probative force. In fact, Rav Kook may not have even believed evolutionary teaching as scientists understand it, as distinct from appreciating its aptness as metaphor.[21] Most importantly: when Rav Kook "evaluates" modern theories such as evolution, he reflects the post-Kantian emphasis on phenomenology and religious consciousness, as distinct from philosophical proof. What he proffers is an assessment of their psychological and sociological impact — not a rigor-obsessed appraisal of their epistemological merit.[22] Similarly, it is difficult to imagine him toiling to construct a new version of the ontological, cosmological, or teleological argument. His focus is not on proof but on insight into consciousness.

Rav Kook was advocating more than *openness* to culture — openness is one thing, integration another. But he conceives the project of integration in such a way that its focus is not the harmonization of conflicting truth claims, but rather the infusion of spirituality into the interpretation of ideas and world events.

INTEGRATION AND RAV KOOK'S EPISTEMOLOGY OF RELIGION

Obviously Rav Kook cannot and does not ignore truth claims entirely.[23] But what *does* happen when he considers them? Even in those contexts, we sometimes find Rav Kook embracing a position that approximates fideism rather than executing a true harmonization. Important strands in his thought, specifically in his epistemology, serve to restrain and limit the project of integrating secular and religious teachings. They infuse his approach to conflicts of truth claims with a conservative character and direction.

Rav Kook's epistemology is rife with ambiguity. For instance, he distinguishes between two possible sources of religious knowledge and feeling. On the one side stands the innate cognitive and affective equipment of a human being; on the other stands rational thought. While the distinction is fairly constant in his writings, he is not clear on either the nature of the interplay between these two factors, or their relative values in a religious epistemology. In some contexts, he takes rational thought, along with moral refinement and other aspects of cultural development, to be necessary for religious cognition. But in other contexts, his religious epistemology is quite self-consciously at odds with a rationalist perspective.

As an example of the former orientation, consider the following passage in the essay "The Significance of the Revival" ("*Erekh ha-Tehiyah*"): "Cleaving to God is the most natural yearning of a human being...Just as we must live, be nourished, and grow, so must we cleave to God."[24] Now, although cleaving to God is a natural aspiration, Rav Kook affirms very clearly that the natural striving of a person must develop "in an intellectual and emotional form." Thus, while a human being yearns for God owing to his innate constitution, this innate longing needs to be cultivated and refined by intellectual and emotional growth.

This portrait of culture's role — in which culture works to improve an existing religious impulse, cognition or longing — emerges in other passages as well. Rav Kook writes, for example, that, although any spiritual ascent must be built upon a foundation of natural feeling and reason,[25] a religious feeling that is wholly natural (*tiv'i*), i.e., that is not cultivated and refined by exposure to secular disciplines and on which the light of rational refinement has not shone — such an impulse is baneful, and will give rise to distorted forms of religiosity, specifically, to idolatry.[26] *In potentia*, the *tiv'i* contains all knowledge, but it cannot generate proper religiosity if left in a raw state. Rational and moral refinement is needed to purify the innate longing and cognition. Absent the right raw materials, rational and moral development could not generate religious enthusiasm. Absent rational and moral refinement, however, the natural strivings of human beings would prove destructive.[27]

In similar fashion, Rav Kook explains that Abraham's route to belief in God, described in the Midrash as a process of inference based on the ordered character of existence, served only to purify his innate, already existing cognition.[28] In *Orot ha-Emunah* Rav Kook also suggests that other sciences only bring out that which is already in the soul,[29] a view that reminds us of the Platonic teaching that experience merely triggers, and in that way actualizes, knowledge that is possessed innately.[30] Other sciences are needed to "expand" the "inner point (*ha-nekudah ha-penimit*) of the sense of faith and the natural, clear fear of heaven [piety]."[31] Here is the same motif: culture and experience refine that religious knowledge and orientation which a person possesses as his innate endowment.

In another passage Rav Kook is explicit about the superior value of refining an antecedent inward cognition: "Whatever is learned is absorbed from the outside, and is inferior in character to that which is contemplated within the soul."[32] At first, Rav Kook here seems to be negating his emphasis on rational and moral refinement; but, he proceeds to say, "All that is acquired by study is only a profound strategy as to how to draw on what is hidden in the heart, in the depths of the soul, one's inner understanding, from the knowledge within."[33]

Rav Kook's acceptance of a contrast between a natural love for God and one that arises as a response to experience is also crystal clear in his comments on *Shir ha-Shirim*.[34] It stands at the very center of his analysis. However, the opening passage of that essay, while continuing the contrast, suggests a perspective different from the one I have described thus far.

> There is a love for God, Blessed Be He, that derives from creation and its splendor, [from] the lovingkindness of God that fills the world and the good He bestows upon His creatures. And there is a love that is felt within the soul, that derives from the very exalted rank [or nature] of the soul to love the wholly good. This latter love is fundamental, and is more precious than any love that arises out of considerations of [external] reality.[35]

The terms of the contrast between the two types of love are not set out precisely; but it is certainly possible to read the passage in a way that assigns a higher value to uncultivated, innate feeling than do the passages we have considered until now. What we need to know is: Is the love that is "felt within the soul" a love that is *wholly* innate? Or is it, rather, a love that, like Abraham's knowledge of God, is innate but *in addition* is nurtured by "considerations of external reality" at a subsequent stage? Is Rav Kook contrasting a love that is *wholly* innate with a love that is *wholly* acquired? Or is he contrasting a love that is partly innate and partly acquired (that is, a love that is innate but is then cultivated and refined through thought and culture) with a love that arises *exclusively* from "considerations of [external] reality"? The question is crucial: for if raw, uncultivated feeling *is* here being assigned a higher value than in the other passages we considered ("this latter love...is more precious than any love that arises out of considerations of external reality"), it is conceivable that Rav Kook's failure to deploy secular thought in a manner analogous to medieval thinkers owes to his conviction that genuine religious knowledge is innate and natural — as distinct from knowledge in whose formation culture has played a critical role.[36]

Such a notion — of a natural, innate religious attitude needing no refinement — seems in fact explicit in some passages. Reading on in *Orot ha-Emunah*, we encounter a passage that takes an anti-rationalist stance and, indeed, is strikingly reminiscent of Yehudah Halevi, Rav Nahman of Bratzlav, and other Jewish critics of rationalism. This particular passage underscores the value of knowledge that is *not* molded by culture:

> It is specifically in the simple faith in God, which contains no boundary and no clever human rationalizing (*hithakkemut enoshit*), that the supernal light (*or elyon*) and the inner splendor (*ha-ziv ha-penimi*) of the most perfect life are revealed.[37]

I would suggest we formulate Rav Kook's ambiguity about the role of culture in terms of two different images that Rav Kook uses in speaking of culture: *rahavut* (breadth) and *penimiyyut* (interiority, inwardness). The expansive, outward movement toward general culture, represented by *rahavut*, is restrained by a movement inward. Depth, interiority, *penimiyyut* — these are the hallmarks of spiritual cognition. Or, to manipulate the imagery differently, *rahavut* itself is used in two senses. In one, a person becomes broader by going outside himself; in the other, he achieves *rahavut* as his inner being expands.[38] It is interesting to see how Rav Kook manipulates the contrast between inward and outward movements in certain passages. Consider the following, from *Arpelei Tohar*:

A person should always expand his mind ... and from this outstretched, external cognition, he will arrive at an inward cognition (*hakkarah penimit*), which flows from the source of the holy. The secrets of Torah shall [then] be revealed to him.[39]

Here, the inward cognition — *hakkarah penimit* — *results from* an outward movement. This use of *penimiyyut* contrasts with one we encountered earlier, where Rav Kook speaks of secular disciplines working to "expand" a *nekudah penimit*.[40] There, "*penimi*" seems to correspond to "innate"; in the present passage, *penimiyyut* is *acquired*, through "expansion" of the mind. But then again we find this statement: "We do not know God in the world and by means of the world, but from within our inner souls."[41]

More striking still are passages in which Rav Kook speaks about conflicts that might arise between religious teachings and parts of one's culture. We have already seen that Rav Kook does not utilize secular disciplines to argue for the truth of religious teachings. But not only is this constructive integration absent, he has little to say about how harmonization is to be achieved in cases in which the two realms make opposing and contradictory truth claims.[42] He endorses the *vision* of harmony, but evinces no powerful urge to *demonstrate* harmony in a systematic way. At points, his attitude to conflicts borders on indifference, and displays a kind of religious triumphalism:"If modern science will boast that it has been liberated from theology, it must know that, over against this, theology has been liberated from science."[43]

No idea produced by secular inquiry can impugn faith, unless the inquirer is of a flawed or wicked character.[44] It is inappropriate to judge religious doctrines by secular yardsticks.[45] Especially noteworthy is this passage:

Those who possess inward vision (*ha-mistakkelim ha-penimiyyim*) are not oppressed in the course of their thought by the orderly progression of a vision that is directed outward (*ha-histakkelut ha-hitzonah*)...Theirs is a world of certainty, and the contradictions which come from another world [or: and contradictions, which come from another world,] are entirely irrelevant to them.[46]

This passage leaves no room for meaningful harmonization of religious with secular truth claims. As if to underscore and illustrate the thesis that religious knowledge grounded in intuition prevails over philosophical arguments, Rav Kook apprises us that Maimonides' anti-Aristotelian stance on the issue of creation was not the effect of any *philosophical* influence, but the consequence of a special *religious* insight.[47]

How are we to explain this approach to conflicts? What has happened to the ideal of harmonization? A likely explanation, already alluded to, is that the innateness of religious cognition and feeling bridles the effort at harmonization.[48] Rav Kook was original, if not unique, in using the ideas of Kabbalah — which frequently had gone together with hostility toward secular learning — as a means of encouraging a receptive attitude toward general culture. Yet, Rav Kook could not deploy secular knowledge to confirm religious truths, and could not give secular teachings priority over religious ones, without undercutting mystical epistemological assumptions. In cases of conflict, cultural teachings would pale into irrelevance, as they are now pitted against the luminous certitude of innate knowledge. Thus, Rav Kook's mystical epistemology, which emphasized innate endowments and interiority, ultimately dulled the contrast between himself and earlier kabbalists with regard to the value of general culture and its power to reshape religious convictions. Just as *tikkun* — restoration of the shattered harmony in the cosmos — involves a return to the source of all, so is Rav Kook's ideal for the religious personality predicated on a deepening perception on the part of the soul, a return to one's inner being. The reliability and sureness of innate religious perceptions prevents the emergence of what would otherwise be exceedingly natural corollaries of Rav Kook's plea for openness, breadth and harmony. Emphasizing as it does innate cognition, his religious epistemology must assign an inferior place to religious knowledge that is gleaned from *outside* sources.

INTEGRATION, GRADUALISM, AND FALLIBILISM

Another factor that limits and restrains Rav Kook's practical program of harmonization is the *a priori* character of his harmonistic outlook. Given his foundational belief in the harmony of all teachings, no challenge that arises to religion can be ultimate and unmeetable. Why, then, *should* one fear "contradictions which come from another world"? Is not the harmony of everything guaranteed in advance? Human and cosmic progress, to be sure, require *perception* of this harmony, and not merely the *existence* of harmony. But in addressing the issues of challenges to religion, Rav Kook seems to waive this requirement, expressing, instead, his *faith* in the accuracy of the harmonistic outlook.[49]

Now, medieval philosophers also maintained an *a priori* commitment to the harmony of religion and philosophy, yet this did not stand in the way of their seeking reconciliations of specific conflicts. However, if we add one more ingredient to our explanation, we can see why Rav Kook, unlike them, was not perturbed by contradictions. For, whereas some of the forces that restrain the integration of secular and religious teachings in the thought of Rav Kook are drawn, as we have suggested, from Jewish mystical tradition, another is drawn from, or at least related to, secular philosophical currents of the nineteenth century — in particular, nineteenth century progressivism.

For Rav Kook, reconciliation and harmony do not have to be evident in the here and now. The unity of all teachings may not be evident until a later stage in history. Since truth emerges dialectically, we, in our present day, are at a stage in which two opposites are in clash and cannot be resolved in the here and now. If truth evolves gradually, and does so by a dialectical process, then any discipline, at any given time, encapsulates only grains of truth, not the whole truth; we come closer to the (whole) truth only through the continuing collision of partial truths with one another. Narrowness is the very hallmark of secular disciplines: the scientist focuses on isolated things; culture develops isolated faculties.[50] Truth in its wholeness will not emerge from this realm. Because truth emerges only gradually and piecemeal, culture is not yet complete, and we do not know what culture will look like in final form.[51]

Rav Kook thus accepts a moderate form of a doctrine known nowadays as "fallibilism." On the one hand, we know, from monistic assumptions, that none of our theories will turn out false *in toto*. But on the other hand, we also know (from Rav Kook's evolutionary outlook) that none is true *in toto*. Now, if truth exhibits this dynamic, evolving, gradual character, why should Rav Kook feel pressured to incorporate into his world picture the contents of secular disciplines at a given time? After all, we have no reason to take those contents as settled and decisive. Culture moves us *toward* a greater truth, and we should always seek to isolate the kernels of truth in particular theories. But Rav Kook did not have to think, nor could he think given his evolutionary view, that culture at a particular slice of history — let alone one discipline within culture — expresses the totality of truth. The science of his day, therefore, is transient; and if it conflicts with religious tenets, one need not worry all that much about it. This view contrasts sharply with the sanguine outlook that medieval philosophers adopted vis-à-vis their own theories. They took those theories to be fixed, settled, conclusive.[52]

This evolutionary view of truth, which I claim restrains Rav Kook's program of integration, emerges as an element — albeit only as *an* element — in those surprisingly few of his writings that touch on particular conflicts between secular disciplines and Judaism. As cases in point, I would cite his letters to Moshe Seidel on the subject of evolution,[53] his letter to Shmuel Aleksandrov on (*inter alia*) criticism of the Bible's historicity,[54] and an important section of *Eder ha-Yakar*.[55] While some interpreters have stressed the "enlightened" character of Rav Kook's response to cultural challenges, these selections are in fact a curious mix of radical-sounding positions and conservative reactions. In these texts on evolution, we may differentiate at least four strains:

1. A mildly radical position: *Ma'aseh Bereshit* (the creation story) has always been regarded by the Sages as containing *sitrei Torah* (secrets of Torah). If the account in Genesis is to be accepted in its entirety and in a purely literal way, what room remains for secrets? On this view, evolutionary theory may serve to reveal esoteric truths within the biblical account. The biblical account is not false, but it is incomplete, at least at the exoteric level.

2. A more radical position: Even if the biblical accounts are not factually correct in all details, it is their capacity to inspire, to provide moral direction, to impress upon us the nexus between our deeds and our lot, and to inculcate a general belief in God's hegemony over creation, that is important — not their literal accuracy. The prophets spoke as they did in order to communicate to the masses, in fact, to the masses of their time in particular.[56] What makes this suggestion more radical than (1) is that it opens up the possibility that the biblical account of creation is *false*, and its mode of expression historically bound.

3. A conservative stance: Midrashic thought presents us with the idea that God "creates worlds and destroys them."[57] So, paleontological findings that ostensibly support scientists' view of the age of the earth may actually be remains of earlier worlds that God destroyed. On this view, we need not tamper with the traditional account as far as the age of the earth is concerned.[58]

4. A very conservative stance: the biblical account will triumph over all secular views, for scientific accounts will be exposed as "conjectures suspended in thin air";[59] they are "like the withering bud."[60] On this view, we need not tamper with the biblical account at all. Instead, we reject the claims of science.

It is striking how Rav Kook shuttles back and forth among these positions even though their implications are so different from one another's.[61] But for present purposes category (4) is especially important. In contemporary apologetics, it is not uncommon to find writers who on the one hand argue for the legitimacy of reconstruing biblical texts in the face of scientific challenge, but, on the other hand, preface this move with a conservative caveat to the effect that science or scholarship has often turned out to be wrong and may be so yet again. Sometimes, at least, such gestures toward the fallibility of science seem ritualistic and not deeply felt. Not so in the case of Rav Kook: His invocation of fallibilism when discussing such matters as evolution is anything but a gesture. It is true that Rav Kook's monism commits him to relating positively to every development.

But "relating positively" is not equivalent to accepting. On the contrary, Rav Kook's theory of history commits him to questioning the credentials of any given scientific theory. It is no surprise that, as explained earlier, his analyses of changes in scientific theories focus on the psychological repercussions of the old and new theories — the human self-understanding and self-image that they reflect or else engender — as distinct from their epistemological credentials.[62] Awareness of epistemological limitations leads naturally to a phenomenological focus.

Another example of Rav Kook's willingness to discount scientific claims is found in responsa concerning the practice of *metzitzah*, in which the person performing a circumcision sucks the blood out from the site of incision.[63] The Sages in the Talmud (*Shabbat* 133b) required *metzitzah* to protect the infant from health risk. But modern thinkers (whom Rav Kook refers to derisively as "*mithaddeshim*" and "lusters after new things") were now denying the rabbis' contention, even maintaning that *metzitzah* can cause serious infection.[64] One rabbinic scholar had argued for continuing *metzitzah* on the grounds that it is a *mitzvah* in itself, one that stands independently of the assumption that failure to do *metzitzah* is dangerous. Rav Kook finds that this approach concedes too much to the modern critics, and is not the proper way to battle them: "Heaven forbid that we should budge from the words of the Sages." We must not accept the word of modern physicians against that of the rabbis.

Especially striking is the fact Rav Kook refuses to resort here to a conventional method of reconciling rabbinic statements with modern medicine — namely, claiming that "natural phenomena have changed." For Rav Kook this response too concedes too much. It accepts the opinion of contemporary doctors as truth, when in actuality that opinion is accorded by Halakhah merely the status of a *safek* (doubtful proposition). Rav Kook defends this categorization by noting that sometimes some fundamental principle is set down in medicine ("and other branches of wisdom") "and many decide that it is true, and then another generation arrives and determines on the basis of inquiry that everything they said is insubstantial. So what one builds, the other demolishes." At best the opinion of the doctors might reduce the halakhic classification of the level of danger to "*safek sakkanah*" (possible danger), but Rav Kook does not want to go even this far — he does not want to doubt the words of the Sages at all. "For when [doctors] contradict the words of the sages, their reliability is nil, and surely they are mistaken in their judgment."

In these responsa we see, first, Rav Kook's conservatism with regard to conflicts between tradition and modern ideas; and second, an argument against the "modernists" that is grounded in the (proven) fallibility of science over the course of history. If we generalize from his remarks on medicine, then we have a good illustration of how Rav Kook's appreciation of scientific changes and progress led to a conservatism in his thought. (I do not utterly reject the possibility that his arguments are not to be generalized, but the reference to "other branches of wisdom" is noteworthy.)

In this example, unlike the evolution example, there is no ambiguity as to what the tradition is saying. Yet Rav Kook's evolutionary views impact on questions concerning conflicts between religion and science to an extent greater than I have so far indicated. For Rav Kook believes that Judaism itself, and not only culture, possesses a fluid, evolving, gradual character, the result of its possessing a hidden, esoteric stratum which must gradually be brought to the surface. An implication of this view is that, just as we do not know what *culture* will look like in final form, we do not know what *Torah* will look like in final form, when its secrets become revealed. We are exposed only to the "revealed," not the "hidden," meaning of Torah; the esoteric layers will emerge, if at all, only slowly.[65] But given this doubly fallibilistic posture — we do not know what culture will say, *and* we do not know what Torah will be seen to have been saying — we are obviously in a poor position to distinguish between conflicts that are real and abiding, and conflicts that arise only as a result of our poor understanding and limited vision. A truly consistent approach on the part of Rav Kook might even entail denying that we ever know the tradition's precise point-of-view on a matter. To put it in a manner that is only slightly hyperbolic, what should surprise us is not the fact that Rav Kook does not extensively harmonize Torah and science where they conflict, but quite the opposite: that he is often certain of what the Torah position is such that he can characterize it as superior.[66] It was Rav Kook, after all, who emphasized the poverty of all attempts to capture the supernal reality: "Relative to the supernal divine truth, there is no difference between formulated faith and heresy."[67]

The fallibility of science also flows from another idea, this one drawn from mystical tradition. In one essay, Rav Kook states that rational analysis and philosophy can discover only the externals, the shadows.[68] For Plato, we may recall, knowledge gleaned by the senses is an inferior type because the external physical world is not ultimately the "real" world. For Rav Kook, similarly, rational analysis and philosophy are epistemologically inferior to mystical knowledge because the world they study is ontologically inferior. The fallibility of science is a corollary of this line of thinking.[69]

The fact that Rav Kook did not address at real length specific conflicts between the truth claims of Judaism and those of culture, and, more so, the fact that certain elements in his philosophy tend to shrink the very significance of concrete harmonization in his eyes, diminishes his contribution to and impact on contemporary discussions of Orthodox Jewish confrontation with modernity. Religious Jews who are troubled by modern thought are generally troubled by its clash with truth claims made by Judaism; moreover, they tend to take the deliverances of science, history and other disciplines to be epistemologically firm, and consequently remain unmoved by appeals to the fallibilistic character of these disciplines. To the extent that Rav Kook, even while extolling the unification of *kodesh* and *hol*, does not engage in harmonizing truth claims, and to the extent that he takes the teachings of contemporary science to be fallible — to that extent, the relevance of his vision to contemporary discussions would seem to wane. At the same time, his view that science is fallible and that scientific theories keep replacing one another in every domain captures a trend that many philosophers have pointed to, albeit they, unlike him, do not necessarily imply that these continual changes mark a steady progress toward greater or more encompassing truth.[70]

If conflicts appear to arise between Rav Kook's enthusiastic calls for integrating religion and culture and the limited extent to which he carried out a program of integration with regard to truth claims, these conflicts are ostensible only. They arise out of a superficial understanding of the objectives of integration as he defined them, along with an underappreciation of how his epistemology, especially its stress on innate cognition and its endorsement of a nineteenth century progressivist outlook, limited the extent to which he could achieve anything like the medieval synthesis.

THE RAV AND HIS TEACHING

We have another area to explore: the extent of Rav Kook's own personal involvement with general culture. Rav Kook did not fashion for himself expertise in a secular discipline, as Maimonides fashioned for himself expertise in philosophy and medicine, or Rabbi Joseph B. Soloveitchik in philosophy and literature. He gleaned his secular knowledge in a relatively casual and unsystematic way: from reading periodicals, studying selected digests, and conversing with individuals who were more at home in secular thought than he was. He does not seem to have responded to his own call for breadth.[71] Can an explanation of this discrepancy be found within the dynamics of his thought?[72]

A revealing passage is found in *Ikkevei ha-Tzon*:

> While it is impossible for every student of Torah to become a certified scholar in all branches of science, it is possible for him to be a man who knows the overall situation of the sciences of the world and their influence on life, in order that he recognize the overall style of

the spiritual character in his generation, so that he will know how to sustain and improve it.[73]

We need search no further for an apt characterization of the nature and degree of Rav Kook's own involvement with secular works and ideas. While not versed in the fine details of areas to which he was exposed, he did have an extraordinary sense of the *geist,* and with it a firm overall grasp of the overall contours and thrust of major schools of thought. In that way, he became equipped to shed light on the religious predicament that was his real concern. He could grasp the whole without mastering all the parts.[74]

It is instructive to contrast the passage just quoted from *Ikkevei ha-Tzon* with a passage that deals with halakhic scholarship. Rav Kook remarks that the more light is found in the originating principle of a particular domain, the more salient and illuminating the details of that domain appear. Consequently, dialectic and exactitude in halakhic scholarship,while they must be accompanied by a broad vision, will have results that are robust, since the source of such activity is especially luminous.[75] Likewise, Rav Kook interprets the Talmudic dictum, "sage is superior to prophet"(*Bava Batra* 12a) to imply that, in the period in which the two have become separated, those who deal in the minutiae of the law surpass those whose strength lies in their perception only of the whole.[76] Details are of prime significance, then, in legal study. But as we have seen in the passage quoted from *Ikkevei ha-Tzon,* details of secular subjects are not the primary thing.[77] This attitude makes sense in light of our earlier exposition of what *ihud kodesh ve-hol* mean in Rav Kook's thought. For if, as we said, to unify *kodesh* and *hol* is to allot a place for particular secular theories or movements within a larger picture, why should one need to penetrate all details of those theories? It should suffice to recognize their overall spirit, style and import.

Rav Kook also seems to have distinguished secular and religious domains of study with reference to the category of creativity. In a speech at the dedication of the Hebrew University, Rav Kook described the function of the Jews in the world as *hakhnasah ve-hotza'ah* — absorbing values from the outside, transforming them by integration with the religious outlook, and, finally, bringing this product to the outside world.[78] Jews, he tells us elsewhere, are not merely *metzayyerim* (depicters, in this case of ideas) but rather *yotzerim* (creators).[79] Now, this understanding of the Jewish mission does not generate a demand that Jews be creative *within* the realm of secular disciplines; their creativity lies, rather, in the process of infusing these disciplines with religious significance. Consistent with this approach, page after page of Rav Kook's work in Halakhah and Aggadah testifies to an extraordinary pursuit of novelty; but, again consistent with the approach, he was not creative in secular areas.[80]

Hence, with respect to (1) the need to explore details and (2) the need to be creative, Rav Kook does not demand in secular disciplines what he demands in *limmudei kodesh* (religious studies). The style in which he cultivated his own secular knowledge merely reflects these limitations. He was suspicious of secular inquiries taken in isolation; in the Hebrew University address, he places "fear" at the center of his reaction to the founding of a university — fear that the secular realm will stand alone, without Torah. An institution of this kind, he says in effect, can work for the good only if accompanied by vibrant yeshivot. This sounds a bit like dedicating a science museum by saying "we need an art gallery."[81]

We should bear one other fact in mind when we ponder the limited nature of Rav Kook's study of secular works. Rav Kook did not pave a royal road to spirituality. Much of what he says by way of criticizing parochial educational positions is fundamentally a plea for tolerance of an educational model that prizes breadth. It is not an argument that this model is ideal and requisite for every individual. Some students, he laments, have gone astray because they have been forced into educational models that are not suited for their temperaments.[82] Education must be tailored to individual proclivities and talents. "The Holy One, Blessed be He, performed an act of *tzedakah*" by not placing all talents "in one place, in one person, in one nation, in one land, in one generation."[83] Not all people are equally motivated and equally equipped to pursue just any educational program. Maimonides's injunction, "It is not proper to stroll in *pardes* [esoteric study] unless one has filled himself with meat and bread [legal studies],"[84] is interpreted by Rav Kook as follows: one *need* not study *pardes* before pursuing legal study, but *may* if that suits him.[85]

Thus, what you study must conform to your person; as there are different characteristics of the soul, so are there different courses of study. Rav Kook's own distribution of time and energy over the various subjects that fascinated him may simply have reflected a particular cast of mind and preference — a particular assessment of self. Similarly, for different students, he encouraged different courses of study.[86]

This individualization of advice makes sense in terms of a distinction I drew at the outset of this essay between two kinds of grounds for encouraging cultural pursuits. Rav Kook offers both an individualistic and a national rationale for such pursuits. It may be that to the extent he thought in terms of integration as a *national* goal, he was not prepared to recommend one course for all people. We must distinguish between a renaissance of Jewish life that involves integration on the national level, from a renaissance that demands integration within the person of each individual from within the nation.

The conclusion we should draw is that the limited extent of Rav Kook's personal study of secular subjects is compatible with the principles of his philosophy. There is a coherent fit between the man and his teaching.[87]

CONCLUSION

The approach to culture that Rav Kook adopted was complex, nuanced and somewhat paradoxical. On the one hand, his epistemological assumptions, both those drawn from the notion of innate knowledge in mystical thought and those inspired by or related to ideas of nineteenth century philosophy, tended to suppress the reemergence of the medieval project of proving religious truths by philosophical argument and reconciling specific conflicts between religious dicta and secular theories. Indeed, truth claims and the evaluation of truth claims were not Rav Kook's main concern. On the other hand, his monistic vision forced him to respond to an extraordinary range of cultural developments — intellectual, moral, socio-political, aesthetic — and to confer value on cultural activities for which earlier "open-minded" Jewish philosophies found no ready place. The result is a view that is at once far more closed and far more open than the medieval response to the confrontation between religion and culture.[88]

NOTES

I am indebted to Shalom Carmy, Yaakov Elman, Jerome Gellman, Mark Gottlieb, and Tamar Ross for their comments on this essay.

1   *Arpelei Tohar* (Jerusalem, [HaRav Zvi Yehuda HaCohen Institute], 1983), 46.

2   Ibid., 79.

3   See his Hebrew University address (n. 78 below). See also *Orot ha-Emunah* (Jerusalem, 1984), 57, where the individual and nationalistic formulations are clearly differentiated.

4   See *Orot* (Jerusalem, 1985), 129-30, 138; *Olat Re'iyah* (Jerusalem, 1984), I: 376-77. As an aside, I would point out that Rav Kook's own thought reflects the very ability he describes — to absorb elements from others and transmute them in a novel way.

5   *Orot*, 130.

6   See the references in notes 3 and 5 , and cf. *Orot ha-Teshuvah* (Jerusalem, 1985), 5:8, p. 19, and *Olat Re'iyah* I: 386-87. Although the primary influence behind Rav Kook's teaching about the role of the Jewish people may be R. Nachman Krochmal (see *Moreh Nevukhei ha-Zeman*, in *Kitvei Rabbi Nahman Krochmal*, ed. Simon Ravidowicz [Waltham, MA, 1961], esp. *Sha'ar 7*, 34-39), it is also

instructive to compare and contrast Rav Kook's views (and for that matter Krochmal's) with those of Yehudah Halevi in the *Kuzari*. Like Halevi, Rav Kook maintains that the Jews have a distinctive, innate, talent. But he discards Halevi's thesis that whatever is valuable in the scientific or philosophic achievements of the non-Jewish world was taken from the Jews. On the contrary: the Jews took such material from non-Jews, precisely because of their distinctive gift for appropriating elements of *other* cultures.

7   The concept that Jews are to serve as a "light unto the nations" has frequently been invoked by anti-Zionists, who argued that the Jewish people would best fulfill their mission by remaining in the Diaspora. Rav Kook appropriates the *or la-ammim* concept, but turns it into a rationale *for* Zionism, by insisting that Jews cannot attain a proper perception except in the Holy Land.

8   For an appreciation of the richness and complexity of this theme of integration, see: Shalom Carmy, "Rav Kook's Theory of Knowledge," *Tradition* 15, 1-2 (Spring-Summer, 1975): 193-203; Norman Lamm, "Two Versions of Synthesis," *Faith and Doubt* (2nd ed., New York, 1986), 69-81, *Torah U-Madda: The Encounter of Religious Learning and Worldly Knowledge in Jewish Tradition* (Northvale, New Jersey, 1990), 127-37, and "Harmonism, Novelty, and the Sacred in the Teachings of Rav Kook," in *Abraham Isaac Kook and Jewish Spirituality*, ed. Lawrence J. Kaplan and David Shatz (New York, 1995), 159-77; Shalom Rosenberg, "*Torah u-Madda be-Haguto shel HaRav Kook*," *Mahalkhim* 6 (1974-1975): 35-49; David Shapiro, "The World Outlook of Rav Kook," in *Samuel K. Mirsky Memorial Volume: Studies in Jewish Law, Philosophy, and Literature*, ed. Gersion Appel (New York, 1970), 75-100, reprinted in *Essays on the Thought and Philosophy of Rav Kook*, ed. Ezra Gellman (New York, 1991); Zvi Yaron, *The Philosophy of Rav Kook*, trans. Avner Tomaschoff (Jerusalem, 1991), esp. 107-30, 167-230. The core of my own analysis in what follows is similar to the one presented by Yaron, but the details are developed differently.

9   Eliezer Goldman, "Responses to Modernity in Orthodox Jewish Thought," *Studies in Contemporary Jewry* 2 (1986): 64. See 63-65, 67-71.

10   The account of integration I have just developed can best be seen in the selection "*Nedar ba-Kodesh*," in *Ma'amarei ha-Reayah* (Jerusalem, 1984), 399-417. I am indebted to a paper by Eliezer Goldman, "Rav Kook and the Secular," delivered at a conference on Rav Kook at City University of New York in 1986. See also Yosef ben-Shlomo, *Poetry of Being*, trans. Shmuel Himelstein (Tel Aviv, 1990), chap. 7-9.

It is often said that for Rav Kook, everything is holy, and there is no *hol* altogether. That interpretation cannot survive a reading of "*Nedar ba-Kodesh*," where Rav Kook, even while declaring that there is no *absolute hol*, insists on a differentiation of *kodesh* and *hol*. What is true, however, is that *hol* is the not-yet-*kodesh*. It becomes *kodesh* when it is viewed a certain way — and perhaps, as well, when it is put through the dialectical grinder of history. I think there is a problem here for Rav Kook, since certain unenlightened forms of Torah Judaism fall short of true *kodesh* and likewise have to be viewed through a controlling vision and likewise need to be worked out in history. Surely they are not *ipso facto hol*! Rav Kook himself recognized the need to differentiate narrow forms of Judaism from *kodesh*. See for example, *Orot*, 72, at the end of section 18.

11   "*Nedar ba-Kodesh*," 406. See also *Orot ha-Kodesh* I:145: "The holy must be established on the foundation of the profane," and I:64: "The heavenly *kodesh* is

blessed according to the value of the underlying foundation of *hol*, to which it relates in its purity."

12   See the section "Hokhmat ha-Kodesh," in *Orot ha-Kodesh*, I:1-158, but esp. pp. 1-18.

13   *Orot ha-Kodesh*, I:143.

14   See *Arpelei Tohar*, 9, 42; *Iggerot ha-Reayah* I: #158. See Yehuda Gellman, "Aesthetics in the Thought of Rav Kook" (Heb.), in *The World of Rav Kook's Thought*, ed. Benjamin Ish-Shalom and Shalom Rosenberg, (New York, 1991), 195-206.

15   See *Orot ha-Kodesh* I:278; II:563. On Rav Kook's approach to technology and scientific advance generally, see Tamar Ross, "Immortality, Law and Human Perception," in Kaplan and Shatz, ed. *Abraham Isaac Kook and Jewish Spirituality*, 237-53.

16   For some comments on such problems of line drawing, see Yaron, 183-87.

17   See, however, Shalom Carmy, "Dialectic, Doubters, and a Self-Erasing Letter: Rav Kook and the Ethics of Belief," and Benjamin Ish-Shalom, "Tolerance and Its Theoretical Basis in the Teaching of Rav Kook," both in Kaplan and Shatz, *Abraham Isaac Kook and Jewish Spirituality*, 205-36 and 178-204, respectively; Tamar Ross, "Between Metaphysical and Liberal Pluralism: A Reappraisal of Rabbi A. I. Kook's Espousal of Toleration," *AJS Review* 21, 1 (1996): 61-110.

18   Whereas Goldman, in a passage already cited, traces Rav Kook's progressivist outlook to secular currents, Shalom Rosenberg has emphasized that Rav Kook's progressivism was inspired principally by Kabbalah and that he related his views to those of secular writers only after forming them under Jewish influence. See his "*Ha-Reayah ve-ha-Tannin ha-Ivver*," in *Be-Oro*, ed. Chaim Chamiel (Jerusalem, 1986), 317-18. Contrast with Rosenberg the views of Eliezer Goldman, "*Tziyyonut Hilonit, Te'udat Yisrael, ve-Takhlit ha-Torah*," *Daat* 11 (1982-1983): 103-26; next contrast with both of these the approach of Benjamim Ish-Shalom, in *Ha-Rav Kuk: Bein Rationalizm le-Mystikah* (Tel Aviv, 1990), 19-23, translated by Ora Wiskind-Elper as *Rav Avraham Itzhak HaCohen Kook: Between Rationalism and Mysticism* (Albany, NY, 1990). On the connection between the theme of progress and development within Kabbalah in general and its role in Rav Kook's thought in particular, see Ehud Luz, "*Halakhah va-Aggadah be-Mishnato shel ha-Rav Kook*," *AJS Review* 11 (1986): Hebrew section, 4-6.

19   See *Orot*, 129-30, for example, where the tendency of science to subsume phenomena under increasingly general theories is said to be attended by increments in certainty and absoluteness.

20   See *Orot ha-Kodesh*, II: 537: "The doctrine of evolution fits kabbalistic teaching more than does any other. ... How can one despair at a time when everything is developing and ascending?"

21   On evolutionary theory, see below.

22   See especially his discussion of scientific change in *Orot ha-Kodesh*, II:538-42. For an extensive and illuminating study of the centrality of psychological impact as a criterion in Rav Kook's evaluation of views, see Tamar Ross, "The Cognitive Value of Religious Truth Statements: Rabbi A. I. Kook and Postmodernism," in *Hazon Nahum: Studies in Jewish Law, Thought, and History*

Presented to Dr. Norman Lamm on the Occasion of his Seventieth Birthday, ed. Yaakov Elman and Jeffery S. Gurock (New York, 1997), 479-528. Also note the remarks by Aviezer Ravitzky in the symposium in *The World of Rav Kook's Thought*, 454-61. See also Ravitzky, "Rav Avraham Yitzchak Kook and Modern Consciousness," *Jewish Action* 57, 1 (1996): 28-30.

[23] For analysis of a context in which truth does matter to Rav Kook, see Shalom Carmy, "Dialectic, Doubters, and a Self-Erasing Letter," in Kaplan and Shatz, *Rabbi Abraham Issac Kook and Jewish Spirituality*, 205-36.

[24] *Orot*, 135.

[25] *Orot ha-Kodesh*, I:64.

[26] "*Derekh ha-Tehiyyah*," *Ma'amarei ha-Reayah*, 1-9; cf., e.g. *Eder ha-Yakar* (Jerusalem, 1985), 34-35; *Arpelei Tohar*, 79.

[27] Rav Kook is to this extent an exception to an otherwise tempting and plausible generalization about religious thinkers. One might expect that scientific and philosophical reasoning would cease to play a positive role in the religious life of a thinker who does not believe that such reasoning can demonstrate the truth of religion. But in Rav Kook, a strong role is assigned to reason even though rationalism (as soon we shall see) is rejected. Another example of a thinker who combines a fideist outlook on basic religious issues with a positive evaluation of the role of reason in religious life is Rabbi Joseph B. Soloveitchik. See his *The Lonely Man of Faith* (New York, 1992). Note especially the fideist character of his remarks on pp. 1-7 and the note on pp. 51-52.

[28] *Orot ha-Emunah*, 83-84.

[29] Ibid., 65-66.

[30] See, e.g. Plato's *Meno*.

[31] *Orot ha-Emunah*, 65.

[32] *Orot ha-Kodesh*, I:178. A few of my translations are adapted from *Abraham Isaac Kook*, trans. Ben Zion Bokser (New York, 1978).

[33] Ibid.

[34] *Olat Re'iyah*, II:1-3.

[35] Ibid. II:1. For an analysis and translation of Rav Kook's introduction to his commentary on *Song of Songs*, see Daniel Landes, "Aesthetics as Mysticism: Rav Kook's introduction to Song of Songs," *Gesher* 9 (1985): 50-58, and Moshe Sokolow, "Rav Kook on Shir ha-Shirim: A Study of Aesthetics and Allegory," *Texts and Topics in Jewish Studies*, no. 7 (1989) (published by the Torah Education and Culture department of the World Zionist Organization). These translations have aided me in preparing my own.

[36] Eliezer Goldman has brought out another aspect of the contrast between inner and outerly-derived knowledge, namely, its connection to Kant. See his "Rav Kook's Relation to European Thought," in *The World of Rav Kook's Thought*, ed. Ish-Shalom and Rosenberg, 139-48.

[37] *Orot ha-Emunah*, 73. In correspondence, Yehuda Gellman suggested to me that to laud simple faith is not necessarily to embrace an anti-intellectual position. Rather, simple faith might be the end result of a lengthy and arduous intellectual process: simple faith is something that some have at the start but others must

work for. (In kabbalistic terms, simple belief is reached at the level of Keter.) So construed, Rav Kook's position would resemble that of Rav Nahman of Bratzlav as portrayed by Arthur Green in *Tormented Master: A Life of Rabbi Nahman of Bratzlav* (New York, 1981), 285-336. I have chosen to interpret "simple faith" more simply.

38 See the poem,"*Merhavim, Merhavim*," *Sinai* 17, 1 (1945): 13-15.

39 *Arpelei Tohar*, 127.

40 *Orot ha-Emunah*, 65-66.

41 *Iggerot ha-Reayah* I: #44, p. 45.

42 I discuss some of these below, in the section on fallibilism. Note also his claim that *kodesh* and *hol* have to be cultivated separately. See *Orot ha-Kodesh* I:15 (the spatial separation of plants aids their growth; unity results only from separation); and ibid, I: 145 (the stronger the profane, the more significant the holy).

43 *Arpelei Tohar*, 40.

44 *Eder ha-Yakar*, 52.

45 Note the lecture on biblical criticism quoted by Yaron, 227, n. 74. Rav Kook is also reported by Yaron to have offered a more direct reply to biblical criticism (viz., that even works written by a single author may display differences in style and approach).

46 *Orot ha-Kodesh*, I: 208. See also *Arpelei Tohar*, 55.

47 *Orot ha-Emunah*, 60.

48 Since I am about to seek an explanation of tensions or discrepant statements in Rav Kook's writings, a word is in order concerning the proper methodology for handling such tensions.

Any attempt to so much as identify tensions, let alone resolve them, is strewn with obstacles. First, we do not have anything near the entire corpus, oral or written; second, Rav Kook did not as a rule edit his writings, preferring spontaneity and freshness (see Yaron, ch. 1); third, notoriously, his writings have been edited and amended by others; fourth, Rav Kook maintains that he is unwilling and unable to express the whole truth; fifth, as Eliezer Goldman has pointed out, Rav Kook's published writings are put together from manuscripts composed at different periods. *Orot ha-Kodesh*, for example, takes in eight manuscripts covering a period of sixteen years. A chronological ordering is a scholarly desideratum if lines of development are to be identified; "the blurring of the chronological dimension" is a serious flaw in Rav Kook scholarship, even though Rav Kook's spontaneous way of writing may result in synchronic as well as diachronic discrepancies. (See Goldman, "*Tziyyonut Hilonit*," 103-104.) What I propose in the rest of the paper, therefore, is not a definitive resolution of the tensions in Rav Kook, but a framework that should prove useful in identifying certain themes in his outlook. In the absence of a definite theory of how his views developed chronologically, this conservative tack is probably the best to take.

For a different approach to conflicting statements in Rav Kook, see Yonah ben-Sasson, "*Mishnat he-Hagut shel ha-Reayah Kuk ve-ha-RYd [Rav Yosef Dov] Soloveitchik*," *Be-Oro*, ed. C. Hamiel, 403-18. Ben-Sasson highlights several tensions between general theoretical principles articulated by Rav Kook and stands he takes on specific practical issues. Cf. my "Is Rav Kook a Model for Modern Orthodox Openness," in this volume.

[49] Rav Kook sometimes sees the emergence of a dialectical opposite to a given approach and the subsequent harmonization of opposites, as a series of developments guided by providence and not consciously brought about by human beings.

[50] *Orot ha-Kodesh*, 1-3.

[51] "*Ha-Torah ve-ha-Tarbut ha-Enoshit*," *Ma'amarei ha-Reayah*, 101-4. I do not mean to suggest that the progressive dialectical unfolding of truth will *ever* end according to Rav Kook.

[52] Some of the material in this section overlaps with material in "Is Rav Kook a Model of 'Openness'," in this volume.

[53] *Iggerot ha-Reayah* I: #91, #134 (pp. 105-7 and 163-64, respectively). See also *Iggerot* II: #478, pp. 118-20. A fine translation of thirty-nine of Rav Kook's letters, including those I refer to in this context, is Tzvi Feldman, *Rav A. Y. Kook: Selected Letters* (Maaleh Adumim, 1986).

[54] Ibid., I: #44, pp. 48-49.

[55] *Eder ha-Yakar*, 34-62.

[56] Ibid., 37-38.

[57] *Genesis Rabbah* 7:3.

[58] This argument does not address the problems posed by evolutionary accounts of the origin of species. Cf. R. Israel Lipschitz (author of *Tiferet Yisrael*), "*Derush Or ha-Hayyim*," trans. Yaakov Elman, in Aryeh Kaplan, *Immortality, Resurrection, and the Age of the Universe: A Kabbalistic View* (Hoboken, NJ, 1993), 110-22.

[59] *Eder ha-Yakar*, 38, 42.

[60] *Iggerot ha-Reayah* I: #91, pp. 105-6.

[61] Aviezer Ravitzky noted in a lecture that immediately after declaring that is irrelevant whether the world began with a golden age or instead evolved gradually from lowly beginnings (since what is important is the moral lesson, that sin causes us loss), Rav Kook goes on to say that this lesson emerges from "the *fact* that" Adam, the first man, was expelled from Eden. See *Iggerot* I: #134, pp. 163-64. For further analysis of the letters on evolution, see Shalom Rosenberg, "Introduction to the Thought of Rav Kook," in *The World of Rav Kook's Thought*, ed. Ish-Shalom and Rosenberg, 88-97.

[62] *Orot ha-Kodesh*, II: 538ff. Also see note 20 above.

[63] See *Da'at Kohen* (Jerusalem, 1969), #140-42. For additional sources on *metzitzah*, see *Tov Ro'i al Masekhet Shabbat*, ed. Binyamin Elon (Jerusalem, 5747), 78, 126-28.

[64] For the history of this issue and a survey of rabbinic opinions, see Israel G. Hyman, "The Halakhic Issues of Metzitzah," *Proceedings of the Association of Orthodox Jewish Scientists* 8-9 (1987): 17-44; Jacob Katz, *Ha-halakhah be-Metzar: Mikhsholim al Derekh ha-Ortodoksiah be-Hithabutah* (Jerusalem, 1992), 150-84.

[65] Cf. "*Ha-Torah ve-ha-Tarbut ha-Enoshit*," *Ma'amarei ha-Reiyah*, 101. The issue of a "changing Torah" is explored along different lines in *Iggerot ha-Re'iyah* I: #140, pp. 173-78 and *Orot ha-Kodesh*, IV: 516-17.

66 These positions are especially clear with regard to moral issues. See Carmy, "Dialectic, Doubters, and a Self-Erasing Letter."

67 *Orot ha-Emunah*, 23-24. My translation of *"ha-emunah ha-metzuyeret"* as "formulated faith" borrows from Tamar Ross's translation of this expression as "formulated religion."

68 *"Derekh ha-Tehiyyah," Ma'amarei ha-Reayah*, 1-9.

69 Note, however, that full knowledge of God is equally unattainable.

70 See, for example, Thomas Kuhn, *The Structure of Scientific Revolutions* (Chicago, 1970).

71 See Eliezer Schweid, *Ha-Yahadut ve-ha-Tarbut ha-Hilonit* (Jerusalem, 1980-1981), 114. Eliezer Goldman has shown that Rav Kook acquired knowledge of philosophy, particularly of Solomon Maimon and Schelling, mainly from a book on modern philosophy by Fabius Mises (Leipzig, 1887). See Goldman, "Rav Kook's Relation to European Thought," *The World of Rav Kook's Thought*, ed. Ish-Shalom and Rosenberg, 139-48.

72 For an eloquent statement affirming the *unity* of "the man and his thought," see R. Shlomo Y. Zevin, *Ishim ve-Shittot* (Jerusalem, 1958), 231-33.

73 *Ikkevei ha-Tzon* (in *Eder ha-Yakar ve-Ikkevei ha-Tzon*), 129.

74 A good example, as we have seen, is *Orot ha-Kodesh* II: 538-42.

75 *Orot ha-Torah* (Jerusalem, 1985), chaps. 2-5 and chap. 6, sect. 1. But cf. 3:8 on scientific knowledge.

76 *Orot*, 120-21.

77 But cf. *Orot ha-Torah*, 8:6 (end), where Rav Kook argues that detail is important in halakhic scholarship by drawing an analogy to geography and other subjects. I doubt that this reflects more than a convenient analogy to explain the need for halakhic detail; it is not a reflection of a deep commitment to detailed study of secular subjects.

78 This speech is printed, together with an English translation in *Hagigat ha-Petihah* (Jerusalem, 1925) and in *Torah U'Mada Reader* (Experimental Edition), ed. Shalom Carmy (New York, n.d) and in Hebrew alone, in *Hazon ha-Geulah* (Jerusalem, 1942) and *Ma'amarei ha-Reayah*, pp. 306-8. The term *"hakhnasah ve-hotza'ah"* (literally, bringing in and taking out) is borrowed from the laws concerning transport of objects on the Sabbath.

79 *Orot ha-Kodesh*, III: 67-68.

80 Rav Kook began his address at the opening of his yeshiva, Merkaz ha-Rav, with a plea for the vigorous production of works of halakhah and aggadah: "I call you to a life of creativity (*yetzirah*)." In context, *"yetzirah"* seems to refer not just to productivity but to creativity. See *"Hartza'at ha-Rav,"* included in certain editions of *Orot ha-Torah*.

81 See also *Iggerot ha-Reayah* II: #570.

82 *Orot ha-Torah*, 9:6.

83 *Orot*, 152.

84 Maimonides, *Mishneh Torah*, *Hilkhot Yesodei ha-Torah* 4:13.

85 *Orot ha-Torah*, 9:12.

[86]   Contrast, for example, his advice to Seidel in *Iggerot ha-Reayah* I: #108, pp. 131-32, with his advice to his son Tzvi Yehudah in I: #40, pp. 37-38.

[87]   There are other facets of Rav Kook's life and thought that bring out clearly the qualified nature of his openness to culture. For instance, he seems to counsel this openness only for the Holy Land, where the monistic vision is clear and pure; his program is not intended for the Diaspora. Even in Israel, his yeshivah did not include a secular component in its curriculum. See Justin Harley Lewis, *Vision of Redemption: The Educational Philosophy of Rabbi Abraham Isaac Kuk in Historical Perspective* (New Haven, 1979), 58-60.

[88]   Postscript (2009): Since the time this essay first appeared, R. Kook's original manuscripts have been published with the title *Shemonah Kevatzim* (1999). These at once clarify the picture and make matters confusing. In some passages in those manuscripts, Rav Kook portrays general culture as "alien" to the national spirit. See Jonathan Garb, "'Alien' Culture in the Circle of Rabbi Kook," in *Study and Knowledge in Jewish Thought*, ed. Howard Kreisel (Beer Sheva, Israel, 2006), 253-264. Garb also cites the attitudes of Rav Kook's followers as evidence of his negative approach. The recent discoveries do not nullify the strains I examine in the article, but they suggest an additional source of negativity toward culture in Rav Kook's thought. The insularity generated by his nationalism conflicts with passages that see the integration of cultures as the special talent of the Jewish people.

RABBI ABRAHAM ISAAC KOOK
AND THE AMBIGUITIES OF "OPENNESS"

When scholars seek to locate rabbinic thinkers who are "open to modernity," they often execute their search by applying a simple "bottom line" algorithm for determining openness. Thus, since Rabbi Abraham Isaac Kook (1865-1935) is ardently Zionist, extols the spiritual fruits of a comprehensive exposure to general culture, pleads for breadth and balance in yeshiva curricula, rails against narrow legalism, advocates tolerance of the irreligious, waxes positive about other religions, credits even heresy with divine origins, suggests a non-literal understanding of the biblical story of creation that is compatible with evolution, situates the Tanakh in a historical context and explains the emergence of movements in Judaism in terms of historical forces (usually, the force of other ideas) — ergo, he is, many declare, "open." In fact, even for Modern Orthodox groups, who value modernity,[1] the real question about Rav Kook would seem to be not, "Is he open?" but, rather, "Is he *too* open?"

I suggest in this essay, however, that we need to scrutinize bottom lines carefully. My aim, indeed, is to move away from bottom-line criteria of classification toward more complex and, I think, more useful taxonomies. These deliberations should offer us a better vantage point from which to evaluate the legacy of particular rabbinic figures. Our positioning of Rav Kook, I suggest, is strongly affected by such a reorientation.

I

For one seeking a religious model for his or her own belief and practice — with regard to Rav Kook, it is easiest to consider the Modern Orthodox Jew — the most obvious danger with bottom-line classifications is that one may be choosing bottom lines selectively. But what is meant by selectivity? We can distinguish three types.

The first involves accepting views of a thinker in one area while rejecting his views in another. Within limits, selectivity or eclecticism of this kind may be defensible practices when forming a religious outlook, even when the individuals seeking the Weltanschauung argue for their views by invoking authorities. Moreover, a reflexive Kookian analysis, i.e., an application of Rav Kook's theory to Rav Kook's own viewpoint, would show that one looking for a religious model can be selective in using Rav Kook even according to the master himself. If no single theory can express the whole truth and all theories are adulterated with error, then even Rav Kook must be articulating but a partial truth; his theory, too, is infected with elements that we might want to reject.[2] Hence one might plausibly advance the following distinction: selectivity is objectionable in the enterprise of *interpreting* or *representing,* but, even so, is defensible in the course of finding a pedigree for an ideology — especially an ideology that is (partly) grounded in Rav Kook.[3]

A second form of selectivity is selective *citation.* Here the danger is that we might misrepresent a thinker's bottom line on particular issues. This danger is realized when people ignore some of Rav Kook's harsher words and deeds in his dealings with secularists and misconstrue his doctrine of tolerance.[4] Fear of misrepresentation is especially warranted in the case of Rav Kook, as it is easy to overlook the fact that vigorous endorsements he gives to position X may be part of a dialectic. Elsewhere or even mid-speech, what the Talmud calls *tokh kedi dibbur,* he abruptly shifts the other way. Such shifts reflect, variously, an appreciation of the manifold and variegated nature of reality, dislike for fixity, a penchant for spontaneous, unedited flights of thought, love of balance, diplomacy, and maybe inconsistency of the prosaic kind. Whereas with some thinkers (Maimonides, for example), competing portrayals turn on tight analyses of ambiguous individual passages, in Rav Kook it is less a question of identifiable ambiguities and more a question of finding, for every quotation, an equal and opposite one.[5] Again, it is easy to forget that a chronological editorial arrangement of his writings, in particular *Orot ha-Kodesh,* as distinct from the topical organization of the published texts by Rav Kook that we generally use, would be needed in order to straighten us out on what he believed and when.[6] More frequently lamented are the facts that we have so little of the total corpus in hand, and that we cannot always trust the texts we have. For all these reasons, selecting individual quotations is a path strewn with methodological pitfalls.

There is, however, a third type of selectivity besides selection of topics and selection of passages; and it is this type of selectivity to which scholars must be especially alert in deciding whether and to what extent Rav Kook was open to modernity, and whether his thought can ground either the outlook of Modern Orthodoxy or that of its critics. In citing a bottom line, even one that reflects a stable, clear position, self-described followers may be detaching a position from its moorings. By doing so, they falsify the intent and the thought processes of the forebear they claim to have discovered; and they invite as well a pair of crucial questions: may one accept the thinker's larger assumptions and framework, and whether, if not, one can still plausibly and with full integrity trace one's intellectual pedigree to him.

I shall give several examples of this kind of selectivity. As the examples all make clear, the point is dual-edged. On the one hand, Rav Kook's modernity and his serviceability for Modern Orthodoxy are highly debatable, in spite of vigorous endorsements he gives to bottom lines congenial to Modern Orthodoxy. And yet, at the same time, words and rulings that could be cited as proof of his *anti*-modernity and of his serviceability for Modern Orthodoxy's *opponents* might derive from "modern" premises and methods. My aim in presenting this is partly taxonomic, that is, to enrich our understanding of how to classify Rav Kook, and partly normative — to caution, in general, against determining affinity to a thinker's outlook on the basis of bottom lines alone.[7]

II

What would contemporary Modern Orthodoxy look like if it strictly followed Rav Kook's model? Benjamin Ish-Shalom rules out "strictly following Rav Kook," for "reality changes constantly." For instance, circa 1920, Rav Kook opposed granting voting rights to women, a denial which could not be part of ideological and halakhic reality for contemporary Modern Orthodox Jews.[8] Yet, Ish-Shalom still sees a significant role for Rav Kook in defining Modern Orthodoxy. He explains that this role would not be in "a set formula, but rather flux and ongoing development, born of dialectical tension between conservatism and openness." Ish-Shalom concludes with a call to "carry on and build our own model of Orthodox Judaism," an effort which Rav Kook would have looked upon with favor.[9]

I concur that "strictly" following Rav Kook will not yield a viewpoint widely palatable to Modern Orthodoxy. However, the case should not rest on bottom-line details like the women's rights issue. After all, the women's issue arose for Rav Kook only shortly after "modernity" itself conferred these rights; who knows whether he would have said the same thing a few decades later?

I am not sure how to translate into concrete terms Ish-Shalom's suggestion that dialectical tension between conservatism and openness be part of a Modern Orthodoxy that follows Rav Kook, and dialectical tension is not in line with the kind of "integration" or "synthesis" between Judaism and modernity that many Modern Orthodox Jews commonly think must be pursued. I proffer this not as a normative claim, namely, that dialectical thinking is not adequate or appropriate, but rather as an observation about the difficulties that Rav Kook's underlying premises and methods are likely to encounter among the Modern Orthodox. Since dialectical tension is also central in the thought of R. Joseph B. Soloveitchik — who is more influential within American Modern Orthodoxy than is Rav Kook — the general neglect of dialectical thinking is striking; Modern Orthodox Jews, apparently prefer logical harmony to dialectical swings. As we shall see, Rav Kook, like R. Soloveitchik, is fundamentally indifferent to the enterprise of reconciling conflicting truth claims of science or scholarship and religion.[10] I wonder whether that commonality might reflect their shared enchantment with dialectical thinking, inasmuch as such thinking will tend to disparage the value of attempts at concrete harmonization.

There is a more basic problem with Modern Orthodoxy's appropriating Rav Kook wholesale. Here I would appeal not to departures made at the bottom line but to a different theme — the need to connect a view to its origins. To buy into the whole of Rav Kook's philosophy entails more than being open to general culture, secular Zionism, and so on. It entails, also, grounding one's openness to modernity in the sources that grounded *his* openness: (a) Kabbalah and (b) the evolutionary, progressivist philosophy espoused in the nineteenth century.[11] Modern Orthodoxy would probably not be comfortable resting its case on either foundation. Most Modern Orthodox Jews would probably want to salvage the bottom line in Rav Kook — his Zionism, his openness to modernity in the generic sense — while remaining diplomatically nebulous about the persuasiveness of his premises.[12]

Nineteenth century progressivism was refuted by history a few years after Rav Kook's passing in 1935.[13] As for Kabbalah, one senses that it is an unlikely candidate to serve as Modern Orthodoxy's most comprehensive assumption. Modern Orthodoxy reflects a rationalistic mindset. Therefore, those most enamored of Kabbalah and Hasidism are perhaps least likely to translate kabbalistic motifs into a version of Modern Orthodoxy. R. Norman Lamm's proposal that Orthodox Jews utilize mystical ideas to validate *Torah u-Madda* (the ideal of combining Torah and general studies) is a bold effort to alter the existing pattern, but this interesting line of thought has not exerted much influence.[14] Mystical doctrine and Modern Orthodoxy seems an unlikely union.[15]

Moving now from psychological and sociological obstacles to logical difficulties, those who would appropriate Rav Kook wholesale confront as well a tension not adequately acknowledged by Rav Kook. If no single branch of Judaism can contain the whole truth, is it not inappropriate to isolate one particular stream within Judaism (Kabbalah) and one particular theory in the modern world (progressivism) and grant them hegemony over Orthodox thinking? Also, isn't one particular value (balance) being absolutized? While I can anticipate certain responses to this standard philosophical maneuver (known as the "self-refutation" of a position), all in all, a fiercely loyal Kookian outlook is not a plausible translation of what Modern Orthodoxy stands for in the minds of its adherents, however avid and passionate those exposed to Rav Kook become about imbibing his thought.

Of course, modern-day followers might look for mini-arguments in Rav Kook's work that are free of kabbalistic or evolutionary presuppositions (if "arguments" is the right word). Apart from the fact that this focus on smaller "arguments" violates Rav Kook's strictures against seeing only the parts and not the whole — we've agreed to tolerate that — are we really ready to accept the mini-"arguments"? To cite a specific example, one I hesitate to raise only because it is hackneyed. Rav Kook viewed secular Israelis tolerantly on the grounds that their outlook is nurtured, subconciously, by religious strivings. But this charitable piece of psychology misrepresents the nature of secularism and ignores, especially, the gulf between turn-of-the-century socialist Zionism and contemporary manifestations of secularism in Dizengoff Square.[16] Making a false (and possibly merely projective) presumption about the mindset of secularists is a dangerous way to do ideology, especially in light of Modern Orthodoxy's passionate insistence on understanding the world around it.

Naturally, I do not deny that, on some issues, Modern Orthodoxy will be irresistibly drawn to analogues of Rav Kook's mini-arguments. For example, Rav Kook's rousing, rhythmic depiction of how the soul expands through immersion in culture, through exposure to experience in all its variety and richness, parallels the position of Modern Orthodox theoreticians that exposure to general culture refines one's spiritual sensibilities.[17] The core idea that a full Jewish life requires Israel is compelling even in the absence of mystical motifs about the union of body and soul.[18] So, too, the concept of *Keneset Yisrael* has seldom received more eloquent articulation. Nobody can gainsay the extraordinary power of Rav Kook's vision and spirit. Yet we must make a distinction. Rav Kook opens up possibilities, expands horizons, deepens experience, enables one to view the world differently and stimulates love of both the Land and its people. Yet for all that, wholesale, strict Kookianism is a daunting option for Modern Orthodoxy, which wants

Kookian bottom lines and the overall spirit, but not necessarily what Rav Kook uses to justify all this. This might be a problematic procedure for those who want to claim him as a model and authority on the issues they care most deeply about.

III

As we have seen, some of the selectivity involved in the case of Rav Kook will consist in severing some conceptual connections — his congenial bottom lines may have been produced by methods and assumptions that the Modern Orthodox appropriator might not wish to make central. Now we shall turn to the opposite phenomenon: in some cases, Rav Kook adopts bottom lines that Modern Orthodox Jews may find uncongenial, or, better put, not what they expect of "modern" rabbis, but he does so by means of premises or methods that they might want to endorse. Accepting the "congenial" premises or methods, they may remain unhappy about the "uncongenial" bottom line.

The first of my two examples of this pattern has to do with Halakhah. Time and again Rav Kook called for the fusion of Aggadah with Halakhah, arguing that the spirit of *nevu'ah* (prophecy) exemplified by such a fusion must now be recaptured as part of our national revival.[19] Now there are obvious examples in Rav Kook of how values and vision can inform a halakhic analysis; among those that spring to mind are his use of the *hetter mekhirah*, a permission to execute a formalistic sale of the Land of Israel to a gentile in order to circumvent many of the laws of the sabbatical year (*shemittah*), and his declaration that a democratically elected Jewish government in Israel would enjoy the halakhic status of king and hence be legally empowered to rule.[20] Nevertheless, some writers have shown that a tendency to stringency also exists in Rav Kook's halakhic decisions — even those that treat agricultural issues, even those that deal with *shemittah* in particular, and even those that deal with irreligious Jews.[21] While stringency per se is not a sensible criterion of modernity or anti-modernity,[22] it is surprising that on matters central to national life, like milking on Shabbat and autopsies, Rav Kook was more stringent than other rabbis. Why did his own "Aggadah" (by which I here mean his overall religious worldview) apparently exert little influence upon his own Halakhah? Is it that, when all is said and done, Rav Kook, contrary to his own avowed principles, did not infuse his halakhic decisions with the spirit of prophecy?

Some people might experience no difficulty in answering this question in the affirmative. After all, they might insist, the procedures of *pesak* are purely formal and legalistic. They are not suffused with ideological objectives. And so, the argument will go, Rav Kook's stringencies come as no enigma; he was just reading his sources and taking them where he thought they led — the method of a "pure" halakhist. We cannot rule this option out, but consider the magnitude of the anomaly which this rejection agrees to tolerate. Here we have a thinker who openly and repeatedly revealed a conception of Halakhah that is not purely formalistic, who called for an approach to Halakhah that would be infused with a prophetic spirit, and who, on such matters as *shemittah*, appealed to a sense of moment as part of his rationale. Yet on other matters, this same thinker, we are told, utterly detached law from outlook in his decision-making and instead used thoroughly conventional methods in *pesak*. This representation fosters a charge of hypocrisy and, for that reason, strains credulity.

Some interpreters, willing to concede that the anomaly is an anomaly and that it bears explanation, might argue that precisely because of the volatile nature of Rav Kook's theology, he has to be stringent in halakhic matters lest the result be antinomianism, if not anarchy, on a large scale.[23] I am not confident about this analysis either, partly because Rav Kook was not consistently stringent in matters of law — which he should have been were he seeking to keep a lid on his halakhic rulings — and partly because a still more interesting hypothesis is available.[24]

Let us examine an explanation suggested by Michael Nehorai. He argues that Rav Kook, precisely *because* he was caught up in a messianic vision, tended to issue rulings that were appropriate for an ideal polity but not for the empirical reality of his time. Rav Kook felt, Nehorai claims, that to decide leniently on national issues is to give normative status to contemporary outlooks which in truth are but part of a dialectical preparation for the impending ideal Jewish society. Openness to Aggadah and to messianic thinking therefore yielded conservatism rather than innovation; other decisors, less rooted in ideal visions and more rooted in harsher actualities, tended to leniency. Nehorai maintains that deep philosophical commitments about gender differences led to Rav Kook's stance regarding women's rights as well, so that even this conservative stance reflected his ideal of an Aggadah-permeated Halakhah.

I do not know whether Nehorai is right; and even if fundamentally his thesis is sound, he may push it too far. But Rav Kook's comparative stringency is a fact, and *if* Nehorai is right, an important lesson follows. Focusing on bottom lines is misleading not only because bottom-line endorsements may come from larger, highly debatable assumptions, as we have seen previously; but also because stringent bottom lines on "national" matters (as catalogued by Nehorai) may come from staunchly pro-Zionist perches in worldview (in this case, a belief that the redemption is in progress and that our vision and values should affect halakhic rulings about the Land of Israel). That stringencies can reflect ideology no less than leniencies is not news; but that stringency on questions essential to national life can come from a Zionistic ideological stance is surprising until further reflection explains how this is so. Rav Kook was congenial to Zionism *despite* his stringencies. To be selective here, to accept the vision but reject the rulings, we need to break a link he forged (if Nehorai is right).[25]

In saying that, on Nehorai's analysis, Rav Kook is starting from a position that is congenial to Modern Orthodoxy, I do not mean to say that a messianic form of Zionism is a necessary component of Modern Orthodoxy. On the contrary, the Modern Orthodox are often wary of extreme messianic versions of Zionism. The Zionism of R. Yitzhak Yaakov Reines — founder of the religious-Zionist Mizrahi party! — and also the Zionism of R. Soloveitchik illustrate that religious Zionism need not be messianic; also, Gush Emunim's (a prominent religious settler movement) messianism is no mark of its modernity.[26] At the same time, many Modern Orthodox Jews would like to preserve *some* form of Messianism in their Zionism, and "followers" of Rav Kook especially so. Further, even in the case of non-messianic variants of religious Zionism, religious Zionists will emphasize, as Rav Kook did, the sense of historical moment, thereby distinguishing themselves from anti-Zionists who gainsay the providential character, or at least the positive providential character, of the establishment of the State. What Nehorai points us to is the *possibility* that a sense of moment, which inheres in Rav Kook's notion of the spirit of *nevuah*, will generate stringent positions on national matters. The expected link between bottom lines and ideology has been severed in Rav Kook's writings — again, assuming, with Nehorai, that his body of halakhic rulings does exemplify the fusion of *nevuah* and Halakhah for which he vigorously called.

IV

Another example of how bottom lines can mislead is found in Rav Kook's attitude to scientific theories.[27] Rav Kook insisted on the value of modern ideas and on the need to integrate them into one's total worldview. But it is not clear what his openness and call to "integration" amounts to when it comes to science.

Illustrative of the problem is Rav Kook's reaction to evolution. While his two letters to Moshe Seidel on the subject are popularly regarded as samples of how evolution can be reconciled with Torah by boldly giving up literalism, closer reading reveals these texts to be a confusing — or perhaps dialectical? — mix of conservatism and radicalism.[28] On the one hand we find the bold claim that the biblical account is open to reinterpretation and the still bolder suggestion that the moral message of the Torah is what counts, not its cognitive import. On the other hand we find disparaging references to the status of scientific theories. They are transient, *ke-tzitz novel* ("like the withering bud"), since science itself is likely to overturn its own theories in time.[29] This attitude contrasts vividly with Rav Kook's famous remark that evolution fits kabbalistic ideas better than does any other theory.[30]

Rav Kook reflects similar ambivalence about science in a practical halakhic context as well. The responsum concerns the practice of sucking out blood from the wound created during circumcision, a practice known as *metzitzah*. The Sages held that this procedure has hygienic value and that foregoing it poses a danger; the scientific community denied this, maintaining on the contrary that *metzitzah* can cause serious infection.[31] Like other rabbinic authorities of the time, Rav Kook was presented with a query: should *metzitzah* be mandated in spite of the mounting claims from science that the Sages were wrong about its hygienic value? In response, Rav Kook, instead of seeking to integrate science and Torah, rejects any harmonizing solutions. He chides one rabbi for suggesting that *metzitzah* is a *mitzvah* that is independent of the hygienic considerations; this response concedes too much to the critics, he avers, insofar as it grants the correctness of the scientific community's claims. Nor is Rav Kook prepared to do away with *metzitzah* on the grounds that *nishtannu ha-teva'im* (nature has changed), for this approach would be appropriate, he maintains, only on the assumption that the position of contemporary doctors is to be taken as certain truth. Instead, he argues vociferously that history reveals medicine and science to be mutable and fallible, and he firmly rejects scientific claims that contravene those of the Sages. He suggests that the medical information has

> the status only of a *safek* [doubtful proposition]. For they themselves cannot possibly hold their statements to be certainties, as sometimes one and even many set down a fundamental principle in medicine (and so too in other branches of wisdom), and many decide it to be true, yet afterwards another generation arrives and determines on the basis of inquiry that all their assertions are insubstantial. So what one builds, the other demolishes. Their words, then, are only asserted as *asmakhta* or *umdana* [mere probabilities and surmise].[32]

Although one could claim that Rav Kook is here concerned only with halakhic definitions of proof, *safek*, and *ne'emanut ha-rofe'im* (the reliability of doctors), the rhetoric in this passage seems to operate not on a legal plane alone but on the level of general epistemology. Extrapolating, with some hesitation, to a vexed current issue, we may project that Rav Kook might have rejected the use of blood testing to (negatively) determine paternity.[33] By way of contrast, the later Chief Rabbi R. Isaac Halevi Herzog challenged R. Ben-Zion Uziel on this matter: "How can there be a question of the credibility of the doctors in a matter which has been clearly accepted by all the giants of medicine throughout the entire world?"[34]

As in the examples of halakhic rulings I discussed earlier, it appears initially that Rav Kook, in the case of *metzitzah,* took a stringent bottom line that was not as liberal as those of other rabbinic authorities; he seems less open to modernity than commonly thought. But here again we must inquire into *why* Rav Kook took conservative stances. Was it his traditionalism alone? Was he all talk and no action on the need to integrate general culture into a religious worldview? [35] These diagnoses might be correct, but another possibility is at hand, one which keeps Rav Kook's teaching better aligned with his general principles.

Rav Kook endorses two ideas: that all ideas have value; and that truth (if can we call it that) is constantly evolving. Rav Kook's refusal to accept the claims of science as determinative makes perfect sense in light of this evolutionary outlook. If you think that we are only *progressing toward* truth and do not yet possess it, it follows that at any given slice of time your culture has only a piece of the truth. Eventually your view will be overthrown.[36] There is really no reason, Rav Kook could say, why Orthodoxy has to accept individual secular theories; it may be a mark of greater cultural and intellectual sophistication to recognize the limitations of our *present* knowledge and to take notice of the ever fluctuating state of scientific opinion. Rav Kook's attitude contrasts sharply with that of medieval thinkers, who took their own theories to be fixed, settled and conclusive — and consequently felt great pressure to integrate specific truth claims from those theories into their corpus of belief.[37]

Rav Kook did not view *ihud kodesh ve-hol*, the uniting of the sacred with the secular, as Modern Orthodox Jews often do, as the reconciliation of conflicting truth claims; rather, he construed *ihud kodesh ve-hol* as the viewing of all events, ideas and movements as part of a progressive revelation of the Divine.[38] In addition, he subordinated epistemological questions about what to believe in the realm of science to questions about the psychological roots and impact of modern theories.[39] Both tendencies, I submit, are marks of sophistication and perspective. Rabbinic authorities who lack a broader epistemological framework and who are less sensitive to psychological categories would not always be as "unmodern" as Rav Kook was in his bottom lines. Thus, Rav Kook was not less open to modernity if he rejected aspects of it, or if he belittled the very importance of reconciling

127

conflicting truth claims. His encounters with thinkers like Spinoza, Bergson, Kant, Darwin and Schopenhauer are models of *critical engagement*. Worth inheres in all ideas, but that dictates no specific consequences about what we must believe. Relating positively to modern ideas is not synonymous with accepting them.[40]

In my experience, religious Jews who are troubled by modern thought are generally troubled by clashes between its truth claims and those of Judaism. Many of these people assume that particular disciplines deliver claims that every rational person has to accept, and that acceptance of secular bottom lines is a condition of true openness. What Rav Kook points to is a version of Modern Orthodoxy that will or at least can be conservative in its bottom lines but is bold — and modern — in the route it takes to those bottom lines.[41] This type of Modern Orthodoxy will look unfamiliar to many Modern Orthodox Jews. It is prepared to reject modern values and cognitive claims; it does so, however, partly on the grounds that modern methods themselves show that the bottom lines in particular disciplines can never be supported adequately. Such reasoning is used at times in "non-modern" circles, but there it gets demoted to the status of an *ad hominem* argument, one raised only to reject Modern Orthodoxy on its own terms,[42] rather than being appreciated as an outgrowth of sincerely accepted methods. The reasoning also crops up in Modern Orthodox apologetics, but it usually seems ritualistic and not deeply felt. For Rav Kook, the fallibility of secular disciplines is a matter of deep conviction grounded in critical thought. With adjustments in formulation, Rav Kook's conclusion will have a thoroughly contemporary ring to it, for it resembles the views of contemporary historians and philosophers like Thomas Kuhn, Alasdair MacIntyre and Richard Rorty. There are also affinities with the cognitive pluralism advocated by Rav Soloveitchik in *The Halakhic Mind*.[43] Call this, if you will, postmodern Orthodoxy.[44]

One would need to tread cautiously before developing this form of Orthodoxy. The historicism it entails has religiously problematic elements for the Orthodox. Also, we must remember that if the clash of ideas is to bring truth by generating ever more comprehensive theories, people will have to pitch claims, make assertions and hold beliefs, for otherwise there will be no combatants in the "war of ideas," the *milhemet ha-de'ot*.[45] Once that point is recognized and appreciated, contradictions between different areas take on importance again. Still, I think we have in Rav Kook an interesting example of how bottom lines quite different from those associated with Modern Orthodoxy can issue from a romance with contemporary intellectual currents. Here, too, Rav Kook's bottom line is less "modern" that some modernists would like, but ultimately might be more steeped in modernity. Just as in the case of his Halakhah, I conceded the possibility that his philosophy did not penetrate into his decisions, likewise I concede the *possibility* that Rav Kook was just being a "traditionalist" when he assailed the credentials of science. But, again as in the case of Halakhah, his own writings, in this instance those that call for integration of culture and Torah, make so prosaic an assessment unsatisfying and stimulate us to seek alternative explanations.

V

I turn to a final question: how significant is it that Rav Kook was influenced by non-Jewish ideas? To what extent is this influence a sign of "openness to modernity"?

There is no escaping that Rav Kook was enamored of nineteenth century progressivism and that it formed a crux of his philosophy. But his own self-perception on this matter is strikingly different from the perspective of academic scholars. In one of his letters, Rav Kook asserts that his thoughts derived only "from the tents of Shem, the well of Torah."[46] This passage seems to cut against Ish-Shalom's reading of Rav Kook, according to which Rav Kook was in fact greatly influenced by philosophical currents. Ish-Shalom writes that "Rav Kook himself was apparently not conscious of the influence of European philosophy on him"[47] just as Rav Kook misidentified other influences.[48] With regard to another quotation — "Not to Kant will we return, but to the Red Sea, to Sinai, and to Jerusalem, to Abraham, to Moses, to David, to R. Akiva, to R. Shimon bar Yochai"[49] — a similar reply suggests itself: the influence of non-Jewish culture on Rav Kook was not conscious.

While audience and context may have a lot to do with explaining statements in the letters,[50] we should be wary of the view that Rav Kook willfully misled his correspondents about his own positions; and so I, like Ish-Shalom, take the letters at face value. Now, we might interpret phrases like "the tents of Shem" with a breadth of spirit — anything drawn from anywhere is, in Rav Kook's thought, an aspect of Torah. Surely, however, such an interpretation makes Rav Kook's words grossly misleading to his addressee. Hence it seems wiser to admit that Rav Kook reacted negatively to a characterization of himself as a scion of philosophers. And indeed, he did not study philosophy extensively.[51]

Two questions now arise: (1) Did Rav Kook derive such core principles as progressivism from non-Jewish sources or instead from Kabbalah? (2) If he was unaware of non-Jewish influences on him and wrongly made a point of denying them, does this detract from Rav Kook's suitability as a model for Modern Orthodoxy?

Taking question two first, clearly a thinker's self-perception affects where we situate him on the spectrum of openness.[52] With respect to our other question — where Rav Kook's progressivist philosophy came from — scholars differ. A particularly extreme formulation of progressivist philosophy's influence on Rav Kook is that of Eliezer Goldman. Goldman describes Rav Kook's view as "an interpretation of the life of Judaism in terms of the evolutionary concepts of the nineteenth century."[53] Drawing on a sequential analysis of Rav Kook's writings, Goldman argues that only *after* developing his core progressivist ideas in early writings (under the influence of Moses Hess in particular) did Rav Kook come to frame these ideas in the idiom of Kabbalah's stress on the divine character of the cosmos and to appreciate that its doctrine of progressive restoration fit nineteenth century thought beautifully. Rav Kook took advantage of this congeniality to produce a Jewishly packaged version of a secular worldview that he had accepted antecedently and independently. Similar points apply to the development of his (Kantian) epistemology. Hence, the kabbalistic framework, for Goldman, has but the status of an *asmakhta*, a prooftext that is used more as a literary prop than as genuine evidence.[54] Goldman refers us to a statement by Rav Kook to the effect that some ideas, though universal, are altered according to a nation's style. "And sometimes there are found valiant men, wise of heart, who know how to filter and purify the inner content... to present it as well in the unique pure Israelite style."[55] Given Goldman's reconstruction, modern currents were the original germinators of Rav Kook's thought.

However, one could view Rav Kook's philosophy entirely differently, as a development of kabbalistic ideas from within.[56] Ish-Shalom is more moderate than either Goldman or this opposite view. He writes only that, although "many of the linguistic building blocks fundamental to Rav Kook's oeuvre" derive from "Bible, *midrash*, [Jewish] philosophy, and Kabbalah," "his central views and his understanding of the nature of reality, and of human essence and destiny were undeniably chiseled and developed in the quarry of the ideological and social revolutions of his own era."[57] Here, then, and again later,[58] Ish-Shalom emphasizes that the *problems* Rav Kook considered were specifically those raised by the modern era. By framing matters this way Ish-Shalom remains more or less noncommittal on the question of whether Rav Kook developed his interpretation of Jewish materials after, before, or simultaneous with his internalization of nineteenth century thought.[59] He also remains noncommittal about the exact substantive influence. In his book, Ish-Shalom explicitly rejects two extremes — *both* an approach that sees Rav Kook's roots as lying solely in Kabbalah and one that insists on the priority of philosophy as an influence — and cautions against being overly specific about tracing influences.[60] The existence of influence is clear; but the lines of influence, the precise intellectual biography, the exact chronological ordering of Jewish and non-Jewish ideas, defy simple characterization.

Shall we define "open to modernity" in terms of the problems that a thinker addresses? The idiom in which he casts his response? The existence of external influence? Awareness of such influence? I hope that these remarks bring out the usefulness of Rav Kook as a vehicle for exploring these questions.

VI

There may be no way to identify the "real" Rav Kook. Our problems are not exhausted by the difficulty of knowing his bottom lines nor even by the difficulties inherent in the very premise that he took definite positions. Rather, we have uncertainties and hesitations about delineating his thought processes. His premises and his bottom lines do not go together naturally. We have here a fascinating example of how premises suitable for Modern Orthodoxy can be turned against bottom lines likely to be favored by the movement, and of how congenial bottom lines can emerge from starting points that the movement is likely to be wary of or even find discomfiting. To the extent that Rav Kook's views and tendencies can be rendered cohesive in the manner I have suggested in this essay, he eludes classification. The labels "modern" and "antimodern" are too dichotomous to capture the complexities of his thought. And to the extent that we cannot be certain of the validity of any particular reconstructions of his thought processes, we are all the more befuddled over which labels to apply.

Philosophically reflective Modern Orthodox Jews face hard choices in either appropriating Rav Kook or rejecting him. *Caveat emptor*, because you may be buying into more than you bargained for. Yet rejecters among the Modern Orthodox, too, should beware: for such curiosities as his refusal to accord certainty to contemporary science might reflect a more sophisticated form of openness to modernity than that exemplified by authorities who, though more congenial at the bottom line, are less philosophically informed and inspired.

But then again, if Rav Kook was plainly and simply a "traditionalist," then we have nothing remarkable here at all. Nothing, that is, besides a truly dramatic gulf between the theoretical pronouncements and actual practice of a major rabbinic figure.[61]

NOTES

1.   They value modernity mainly in the sense of embracing general culture, affirming the positive religious significance of the State of Israel, endorsing inclusive attitudes toward the non-Orthodox and non-Jews, and seeking new roles for women.

2.   These remarks contrast with those of Benjamin Ish-Shalom, "Rabbi A.I. Kook as an Authoritative Figure for Modern Orthodoxy," in *Engaging Modernity*, ed. Moshe Sokol (Northvale, NJ, 1997), 72. Whereas Ish-Shalom takes the dialectical character of Rav Kook's thought to militate against selectivity, I emphasize that Rav Kook himself used selectivity in reacting to other views.

3.   For this reason we should not repeat uncritically the familiar lament that Rav Kook's disciples falsify his legacy by isolating parts of it for partisan and tendentious purposes. Anyone who would utilize my suggested response (that Rav Kook himself used selectivity), however, would have to temper his self-depiction as a disciple. Hence, it is fair to say that those who most need the defense are least likely to use it. In equal fairness, however, selective focus is not the monopoly of one group. The full scope of the charge of selectivity and partisanship has been elegantly formulated by Hillel Goldberg; see his "Review of Israeli Intellectual Life," *Tradition* 18, 1 (Summer 1979): 122-23.

   It would be interesting to explore how the notion of authority in developing a *hashkafah* (religious worldview) can be understood from the perspective of Rav Kook's mandate of eclecticism, or of any authoritative figure's *permission* to be eclectic.

4.   See, for example, "*Al Bamoteinu ha-Halalim*," *Ma'amarei ha-Reayah*, (Jerusalem, 1988), part I, 89-93. Rav Kook hesitated to eulogize two irreligious guards who died in defense of the Galil; also note what he writes of Ben Yehudah: "When desiccated leaves such as these fall from trees, they do not result in a great loss to the vineyard of *Kelal Yisrael*" (*Iggerot ha-Reayah* II [Jerusalem, 1985], #18, p. 16). Both examples are cited by Michael Nehorai in "Halakhah, Metahalakhah, and the Redemption of Israel: Remarks on the Rabbinic Rulings of Rabbi Kook," in *Rabbi Abraham Isaac Kook and Jewish Spirituality*, ed. Lawrence Kaplan and David Shatz (New York, 1995), 126-27.

5.   For example, see the assemblage of passages about secular studies in Zvi Yaron, *Mishnato shel ha-Rav Kook* (Jerusalem, 1974), 167-230.

6.   On this point see Eliezer Goldman, "*Tziyyonut Hilonit, Te'udat Yisrael, ve-Takhlit ha-Torah*," *Daat* 11 (Summer 1982-83): 103-26. However, as David Berger pointed out to me, the usefulness of this procedure is partially offset by the dialectical character of Rav Kook's thought that I spoke of earlier.

7.   In what follows, I argue for a de facto claim (that Modern Orthodoxy will not accept Rav Kook's premises wholesale) but imply as well two de jure claims. The first de jure claim is that it is wrong to determine modernity or anti-modernity on the basis of bottom lines alone. The second is that, to some degree, it is improper for someone who cites a particular thinker as an authority for his or her own views to invoke the thinker's bottom line without accepting the premises that led up to it. In conversation, R. Nathaniel Helfgot raised important challenges to the second de jure claim, instancing, *inter alia*, Modern Orthodox attitudes to

Maimonides' neo-Platonized Aristotelianism. Clearly, some degree of "selectivity of the third kind" is appropriate. However, I would argue that Rav Kook's commitment to Kabbalah, which is where my emphasis lies, is analogous not to Maimonides' neo-Platonized Aristotelianism but to his commitment to reason. Someone who claimed to be a Maimonidean but rejected reason or did not allow it to "do work" in his system would be liable to criticism. And analogously, someone who claimed to be a follower of Rav Kook but did not endorse Kabbalah or use it to generate positions would be engaging in a suspect procedure.

8   See the communication on women's suffrage, "Al Behirat Nasahim," in *Ma'amerei ha-Reayah*, part I, 189-94.

9   Ish-Shalom, "Rabbi A. I. Kook as an Authoritative Figure," 77-78.

10 With regard to R. Soloveitchik, see especially *The Lonely Man of Faith* (New York, 1992), 1-9. With regard to Rav Kook, see further in this essay.

11 Here we should note the *contrast* between Rabbis Kook and Soloveitchik. Rav Kook spells out reasons for integrating cultural achievements into Torah life. In R. Soloveitchik's work, we find explicit justification for the pursuit of science and technology, but not for other aspects of culture. See the essay on R. Soloveitchik in this volume, which finds resources for such a justification.

12 At one point Ish-Shalom notes that a post-Kantian stance could be used to legitimate differing metaphysical theories, ideologies and religions. However I do not think this stance will generate enough of Rav Kook's teaching to serve as well as Kabbalah and progressivism. See Ish-Shalom, "Rabbi A. I. Kook as an Authoritative Figure," 74.

13 It is true that Rav Kook clung to his principles even through World War I, which he viewed in apocalyptic terms (*Orot*, [Jerusalem, 1985], 13-16). However, I once heard Eliezer Goldman remark (I do not know whether he published this) that World War I was a turning point in Rav Kook's attitudes — he became soured on general culture thereafter.

14 Lamm, *Torah u-Madda: The Encounter of Religious Learning and Wordly Knowledge in Jewish Tradition* (Northvale, NJ, 1990), chaps. 10, 11.

15 I offer two qualifications of the argument in this paragraph. First, sophisticated Modern Orthodox Jews will appreciate that *madda* itself generates a critique of a narrow empiricism, paving the way to a pivotal thesis in Rav Kook's thought, that reality escapes our empirical, conceptual and linguistic nets. Second, Rav Kook seems far more interested in psychological dimensions of mysticism than theosophic ones. Aviezer Ravitzky has written: "Rav Kook deals even with theological questions like pantheism and monotheism and with modern scientific developments primarily in terms of the human consciousness that these engender." The quotation is from a section titled "Symposium" in *The World of Rav Kook's Thought*, ed. Binyamin Ish-Shalom and Shalom Rosenberg (New York, 1991), 458. But neither of these points changes the basic picture.

16 For a reply, see Tamar Ross, "What Would HaRav Kuk Have to Say About the State of Israel Today?," in Kaplan and Shatz, 301-307. (She is the source of my Dizengoff imagery.)

17 See, e. g., Rav Kook, *Arpelei Tohar* (Jerusalem, 1983), 47; R. Lichtenstein, "Torah and General Culture: Confluence and Conflict," in Gerald J. Blidstein, David

Berger, Shnayer Z. Leiman, and Aharon Lichtenstein, *Judaism's Encounter with Other Cultures: Rejection or Integration*, ed. Jacob J. Schacter (Northvale, NJ, 1997), 220-92.

18 Such motifs appear in *"Orot ha-Tehiyyah"* in *Orot* (Jerusalem, 1985), 48-88.

19 See for example, *Iggerot* I (Jerusalem 1985), #103, esp. 124.

20 For a powerful statement of how religious outlook influences halakhic decision-making about *shemittah*, see *Iggerot* I: #311. The example of kingship comes from *Mishpat Kohen* (Jerusalem, 1985), #143.

21 See Nehorai, "Halakhah, Metahalakhah," and also his "Rav Reines and Rav Kook: Two Approaches to Zionism," in *The World of Rav Kook's Thought*, 255-67. He cites R. Aharon Szelensky, *Likkutei Batar Likkutei*, (Jerusalem, 1973), 6-11. (For example, "I am unaware of almost any great rabbi in recent times who was more stringent" [6].) Halakhic questions discussed by Nehorai include milking on Shabbat, conversion, autopsies, and more. For a different approach to disparities between Rav Kook's broad statements and his specific positions, see Yonah Ben Sasson, *"Mishnat he-Hagut shel ha-Reayah ve-ha-RYD Soloveitchik,"* in *Be-Oro*, ed. C. Chamiel (Jerusalem, 1986), 403-18. Also see Binyamin Ish-Shalom, *Ha-Rav Kuk: Bein Ratzionalizm le-Mystikah* (Tel-Aviv 1990), 190-92. An English version of this book was published by SUNY Press in 1993 under the title *Rav Avraham Itzhak HaCohen Kook: Between Rationalism and Mysticism* (Albany, NY, 1993). Finally, see the preceding essay in this volume.

22 See R. Walter Wurzburger's reflections in "Rav Soloveitchik as a *Posek* of Postmodern Orthodoxy," in *Engaging Modernity*, 119-36.

23 Ish-Shalom identifies anarchy as a consequence of Rav Kook's view that all ideas have legitimacy and value, and he suggests that Halakhah serves as a check on anarchy. See Ish-Shalom, "Kook as an Authoritative Figure," 70-71.

24 I would add another possibility: that within a monistic outlook, precedent is an important value. For in his address to his yeshivah (*"Hartza'at ha-Rav,"* in certain editions of *Orot ha-Torah*), Rav Kook stakes out a rationale for his proposed commentary on Talmud — the commentary will link later rulings to their source. He bemoans the disengagement of one from the other, in a way that calls to mind his theme of cosmic separation. Conservatism, I suggest, is a result of such thinking.

25 Nehorai's thesis raises one other issue — whether making Messianism "concrete" is really a departure from Rav Kook. On Nehorai's view, Rav Kook did exactly that. Cf. Ish-Shalom, "Rabbi A. I. Kook as an Authoritative Figure," 71-73, and his *Ha-Rav Kuk*, 261-62.

26 For a penetrating classification of Orthodox Zionist and anti-Zionist positions, see Aviezer Ravitzky, *Messianism, Zionism and Jewish Religious Radicalism* (Chicago, 1991), chap. 1. On R. Soloveitchik's Zionism, see Wurzburger, "Soloveitchik as a *Posek*," 125-28 and Blidstein, "On The Jewish People," 27-33.

27 This section overlaps with some material in "The Integration of Torah and Culture: Its Scope and Limits in the Thought of Rav Kook," in this volume.

28 *Iggerot* I: #91, #134.

29 *Iggerot* I: #91, p. 106.

[30] See *Orot ha-Kodesh* (Jerusalem, 1985), II:537; *Eder ha-Yakar* (Jerusalem, 1985), 37ff.

[31] For a brief history of this issue and a survey of rabbinic opinions, see Israel G. Hyman, "The Halakhic Issues of Mezizah," *Proceedings of the Association of Orthodox Jewish Scientists* 8-9 (1987): 17-44.

[32] *Mishpat Kohen* (Jerusalem, 1985), #140; see also #142; also see *Tov Ro'i al Masekhet Shabbat*, ed. B. Elon (Jerusalem, 1987), 78, and Elon's notes *ad loc*. (My thanks to Shalom Carmy for this reference.)

[33] The reasons for "hesitation" include: (1) the scientific evidence may be weightier here than in the case of *metzitzah*. (2) There is no explicit ruling on paternity tests in classical rabbinic sources, but there is on *metzitzah*; the problem with using the paternity testing arises from the statement in *Niddah* 31a that blood comes from the mother — which is arguably an "aggadic" statement. It should be noted, however, that Rav Kook's view of science-Torah conflicts in the responsum on *metzitzah* does not draw distinctions of the type just drawn.

One could also argue that Rav Kook would be *more* open to evolution than to narrower claims about the hygienic value of *metzizah* or the reliability of blood testing, because evolution carries such broad symbolic status for him. There is truth in this, but notice what is now being said. (A) The more straightforwardly a claim can be tested by experiment and observation, the more fallible it is, while the more it utilizes theoretical reasoning, the more secure it is; and (B) the acceptability of a physical theory is determined by its correspondence to Kabbalah. If the aim of asserting (A) and (B) is to show that Rav Kook was not unmodern in rejecting science, that is hardly the way to achieve that end. (For a brief survey of positions regarding science-Torah conflicts in halakhic contexts, see R. Yaakov Neuberger, "Halakhah and Scientific Method," *Torah u-Madda Journal* 3 [1992]: 82-89.)

[34] R. Herzog, in a letter originally published in Dov Frimer, "Kevi'at Abbahut al Yedei Sugei Dam (Be-ma'arekhet ABO)," *Assia* 9, 3 (February 1983): 49-50, then translated by Frimer in his "Jewish Law and Science in the Writings of Rabbi Isaac Halevy Herzog," *The Halakhic Thought of R. Isaac Herzog, Jewish Law Association Studies* V, ed. Bernard S. Jackson (Atlanta, Georgia, 1991), 42-44.

[35] It is also possible that the demotion of science is inevitable in a system focused on the trans-empirical.

[36] See also *Iggerot* II: #478, p. 119, which I quote now in the translation of Tzvi Feldman: "And if we find in the Torah certain things which other people think were based on the widely accepted opinions of the distant past but are incompatible with the scientific knowledge of today, indeed, we do not know at all if today's research is absolute truth, and even if it is true, certainly there is also some important and sacred objective for which certain matters [in the Torah] needed to be presented in the commonly accepted description and not the exact one." See *Rav A. Y. Kook: Selected Letters*, trans Tzvi Feldman (Maaleh Adumim, 1986), 17-18.

[37] Rav Kook also indicates that Torah, too, unfolds gradually, which makes it especially hard to identify *genuine* conflicts.

[38] See especially *"Nedar ba-Kodesh,"* Ma'amarei ha-Reayah, 399-417.

39 See *Orot ha-Kodesh* II: 538-42, along with Ravitzky's comments in the symposium in *The World of Rav Kook's Thought*, 458.

40 Indeed, according to many Modern Orthodox thinkers, trenchant criticism of modernity can (and should) be part of Modern Orthodoxy. See R. Jonathan Sacks, *Arguments for the Sake of Heaven* (London, 1990); as well as his "Torah Umadda: The Unwritten Chapter," *L'Eylah* 30 (September 1990): 10-15.

41 See also Shalom Carmy, "The Nature of Inquiry: A Common Sense Perspective," *Torah u-Madda Journal* 3 (1992): 42-44.

42 In talmudic parlance, a *"le-shittatekha"* ("on your view") argument.

43 *The Halakhic Mind* (Philadelphia, 1986).

44 In his "Rav Soloveitchik as a *Posek*," Walter Wurzburger has made a similar point with respect to R. Soloveitchik's views of critical scholarship; and indeed the two of us arrived independently at the same phrase, "post-modern Orthodoxy." Students of the Orthodox scene need to rethink the "modern/unmodern" taxonomy in light of post-of modernism. For example, some opponents of evolutionary theory who are not "Modern Orthodox" are quite enamored of Thomas Kuhn's *The Structure of Scientific Revolutions* (Chicago, 1961), which they cite to deflate exaggerated conceptions of scientific rationality and objectivity.

45 Ish-Shalom notes this in "Tolerance and Its Theoretical Basis in the Teaching of Rav Kook," in Kaplan and Shatz, 178-204.

46 *Iggerot* II: #493, p. 132.

47 *Ha-Rav Kuk*, 268, n. 29.

48 Ibid., 24-26.

49 *Iggerot* I: #44, p. 47.

50 See Ish-Shalom, *Ha-Rav Kuk*, 22 and 267 n. 17.

51 See Eliezer Schweid, *Ha-Yahadut ve-ha-Tarbut ha-Hilonit* (Jerusalem, 1980-1981), 114. Eliezer Goldman has shown that Rav Kook acquired knowledge of philosophy, particularly of Solomon Maimon and Schelling, mainly from a book on modern philosophy by Fabius Mises (Leipzig, 1887). See Goldman, "Rav Kook's Relation to European Thought," *The World of Rav Kook's Thought*, ed. Ish-Shalom and Rosenberg, 139-48.

52 There are certainly cases where the roots of a thinker's most comprehensive assumptions are transparent to him. But the eminent nineteenth century rabbinic figure R. Samson Raphael Hirsch was influenced by Hegelianism and romanticism; and yet he avers time and again that Judaism must be reconstructed from within, and wields this constraint as a critical yardstick to discredit Maimonides' philosophy, as in his *Nineteen Letters*, letter 18. Again, those who align themselves with Modern Orthodoxy sometimes argue, with cutting irony, that external disciplines and *zeitgeist*s may have exerted influence even on thinkers who opposed secular studies, reflecting a pedigree that is "tainted" on their own terms. If this perception is accurate, this strengthens the point that influence is a possibility even when vehement denials would issue from the thinker being studied. Such discrepancies between the perception of a historian of ideas and the perception of the subject himself of course call out for explanation.

[53] Goldman, "Responses to Modernity in Orthodox Jewish Thought," *Studies in Contemporary Jewry* 2 (1986): 64.

[54] Ibid. See also Goldman, *"Tziyyonut Hilonit, Te'udat Yisrael, ve-Takhlit ha-Torah,"* and his article, "Rav Kook's Relation to European Thought," in Ish-Shalom and Rosenberg, 139-48.

[55] *Ikkevei ha-Tzon* (Jerusalem, 1975), 122-23, as translated in Goldman, "Rav Kook's Relation to European Thought," 140. One might distinguish between Rav Kook's evolutionary outlook, which may have come from progressivism, and his view that all things have value, whose origin is more arguably Jewish (kabbalistic). But I will not pursue this line.

[56] Cf. Shalom Rosenberg, *"Ha-Re'ayah ve-ha-Tannin ha-Ivver,"* in *Be-oro*, 317-18.

[57] "Rabbi A. I. Kook as an Authority Figure," 61. See also *Ha-Rav Kuk, passim.*

[58] Ibid., 74.

[59] In *Ha-Rav Kuk*, 21, Ish-Shalom cites a comment of Rav Zvi Yehudah Kook to the effect that two selections on theology in *Ikkevei ha-Tzon* were based on a published lecture by Hermann Cohen.

[60] See *Ha-Rav Kuk*, chap. 1. Ish-Shalom's book came under attack in Israel even for its relatively moderate view of how philosophy influenced Rav Kook. R. Yehuda Filber assailed the book for (*inter alia*) its portrayal of Rav Kook's attitude to philosophy, citing various passages in which Rav Kook seems hostile to non-Jewish ideas. Cf. Yehuda Gellman's discussion of this controversy in his review of Ish-Shalom's book in *Jewish Action* 51, 3 (Summer 1991): 74-76.

[61] Postscript (2009): A highly illuminating book by Avinoam Rosenak analyzes the relationship between Rav Kook's thought and his halakhic rulings, and sheds light on other matters considered here and in the previous essay, such as contradictions in Rav Kook's *oeuvre*. See Rosenak, *Ha-Halakhah ha-Nevu'it: Ha-Pilosofyah shel ha-Halakhah be-Mishnat ha-Reayah Kook* (Jerusalem, 2007). See also the reference to *Shemonah Kevatzim* in my postscript to the preceding essay.

SCIENCE AND RELIGIOUS CONSCIOUSNESS IN THE THOUGHT OF RABBI JOSEPH B. SOLOVEITCHIK

In every one of his major philosophical works as well as several of his public lectures and popular essays, R. Joseph B. Soloveitchik refers heavily to modern science as he develops his various analyses of religious life and experience.[1] Generally speaking, R. Soloveitchik's references to science reflect a complicated dialectical mix: favor balanced with criticism, enthusiasm tempered by recognition of cognitive limits and moral or spiritual shortcomings. Yet notwithstanding the regularity with which this dialectic appears, a reader who closely examines R. Soloveitchik's *oeuvre* with an eye toward defining the exact place of science in religious consciousness cannot help being struck by sharp distinctions among the works.

Indeed, I hope to show that R. Soloveitchik's thought concerning the role of science in religious life evolved over a twenty-year period. That period begins with the publication of *Ish ha-Halakhah* in 1944, includes the completion of *The Halakhic Mind* in that same year and the writing of an early draft of "*U-Bikkashtem mi-Sham*" in the late 1940s, and concludes with the appearance of "Confrontation" and *The Lonely Man of Faith* in the mid 1960s. I refer here to an analytical evolution — that is, an evolution in the ideas that are articulated and presented — but, as I will explain at the end of the essay, not necessarily a "biographical" evolution in R. Soloveitchik's thinking.

R. Soloveitchik vigorously and firmly rejects any attempt to completely translate faith commitment into cultural categories.[2] Nonetheless, he did not embrace the view of thinkers like Søren Kierkegaard and Yeshayahu Leibowitz that cultural categories are altogether irrelevant to religious commitment. Rather, R. Soloveitchik is rooted at least partly in the tradition of medieval rationalism, which made the pursuit of general wisdom, in particular science and metaphysics, part and parcel of such commitment. As we explore R. Soloveitchik's writings on science, we will indeed see him laboring to appropriate this medieval tradition — but only in a manner that matches his own principles and objectives. That struggle often brings forth surprising uses of medieval rationalism.

1. THE STUDY OF SCIENCE IN *HALAKHIC MAN*

Our topic bears upon a larger question, namely whether R. Soloveitchik was an adherent of the ideology known as "*Torah u-Madda*," which asserts that Torah should be combined with general wisdom.[3] From one point of view, it is difficult to grasp the question. R. Soloveitchik's life was an open book. Surely it is not credible that a person would pursue a doctorate in philosophy (in radical departure from family precedent), cultivate for decades an impressive sophistication in Western culture, allocate time and energy for substantial philosophical writing, and yet all the while *not* be committed to an ideology that licenses and encourages such endeavors.[4]

Yet even while this argument shows that R. Soloveitchik lived a life of *Torah u-Madda* and valued general wisdom highly, it does not tell us about the content of R. Soloveitchik's thought. The fact that R. Soloveitchik lived his life a certain way and that his writings recruit categories, arguments, sources and vocabulary from Western philosophy does not guarantee that the philosophy itself tries to show, let alone that it successfully shows, that such knowledge should play a role in religious life and has religious value. On the contrary, in several of his writings R. Soloveitchik wanted to carve out a place for Torah study and halakhic practice in the philosophy of religion, in order to make intelligible to scholars a category of religious orientation that had eluded their taxonomies.[5] In other words, his stress in these writings was on validating the place of Halakhah within a philosophical outlook, not on clearing a place for science and culture in a traditionalist outlook.

A case in point is *Halakhic Man*. This work is halakhocentric and *excludes* non-halakhic pursuits from the lives of its religious heroes. This, we shall see, is a consequence of the work's objectives.

Early in *Halakhic Man*, R. Soloveitchik offers a preliminary contrast between cognitive man and *homo religiosus*. To sharpen his portrait of *homo religiosus*, he introduces Maimonides' teachings on the attributes of God. R. Soloveitchik tries to show that two opposite strands in Maimonides' philosophy are complementary: on the one hand, the doctrine of negative attributes "which denies all possibility of knowing God," and on the other hand, Maimonides' view that knowledge of God is the first of the 613 *mitzvot*, the "guiding criteria for man, [and] his ultimate end" (11).

A standard resolution of this Maimonidean tension is that knowledge of God may be acquired through knowledge of the "attributes of action," which come to be known through science.[6] Such knowledge exhausts our knowledge of God completely — but it is adequate for fulfilling the commandment to know God. Hence the contradiction is dissolved: God's actions are knowable, allowing us to achieve knowledge of God,while His essence remains utterly unknown and unknowable.

This answer does not satisfy R. Soloveitchik. Perhaps he is concerned that restricting knowledge of God to knowledge of science eliminates the quest for transcendence that he views as central to *homo religiosus*. Hence, R. Soloveitchik argues that knowledge of affirmative attributes, which is gained through scientific study, *leads to* knowledge of negative attributes. That is to say, precisely because God transcends the concepts that we use to describe His creation, knowledge of the attributes of God that do characterize creation, i.e. knowledge of nature, will aid us in apprehending what God is not. "The entire phenomenon of negative cognition is only possible against the backdrop of affirmative cognition" (11). This negative cognition is attained by *homo religiosus*, who seeks it as part of his quest for the transcendent. Cognitive man, in contrast, is persuaded that scientific categories exhaust reality.

According to this conception, studying science plays a beneficial role in religious consciousness. Not only does it disclose the attributes of action, but it impresses upon us how different God is from that which is cognitively accessible to us. Scientific knowledge inculcates within *homo religiosus* the "negative way." Science is thus a source of a twofold religious knowledge, affirmative and negative.[7]

R. Soloveitchik's suggestion beautifully connects two seemingly polar doctrines in Maimonides' thought, not only reconciling them but showing how one generates the other. Regardless of whether one follows R. Soloveitchik's interpretation of Maimonides, however,[8] one fact is glaring about the place of the passages about attributes in the work as a whole. This praiseworthy dimension of *homo religiosus* — that by means of science he understands what categories God transcends, that he masters scientific categories but resolutely refuses to *exhaustively* describe reality through them, as cognitive man does — vanishes from the remainder of the essay. The very idea that science may be used for the purpose of theology, to attain knowledge of God, is missing from the subsequent characterization of halakhic man, even though the latter is supposed to represent a fusion of *homo religiosus* and cognitive man. This omission becomes understandable in light of how the portrait of *homo religiosus* itself changes as the essay proceeds. Early on, *homo religiosus* was said to focus on this world, on scientific study, and from there move to the realm of the transcendent. Later that rootedness in the world is ignored. *Homo religiosus* becomes one who achieves transcendence by fleeing this world. Halakhic man resembles *homo religiosus* only in that both seek transcendence. Halakhic man achieves transcendence not by studying science, as *homo religiosus* did before his flight, but by attaining *kedushah* (holiness) through bringing the divine norm into this world (40). The disappearance of the scientific dimension of *homo religiosus*, then, signals that scientific study is not part of halakhic man's life either.

Let me pre-empt a misunderstanding. In *Halakhic Man*, R. Soloveitchik appreciates science and values it highly. He bestows high praise upon cognitive man and extensively compares halakhic man to cognitive man. Again, he refers to science as "the crowning achievement of civilization" (19), and declares that "religion should ally itself with the forces of clear logical cognition, as uniquely exemplified in the scientific method" (141, n. 4). Nevertheless, none of these elements of the essay indicate that R. Soloveitchik assigns religious value to scientific study in the life of halakhic man. Rather, the formal, abstract, freely-created conceptualizations of the mathematician, geometrician and scientist serve strictly as models for and formal parallels to the formal, abstract, freely-created conceptualizations of halakhic man.[9] The required "logical cognition" is halakhic reasoning. It is the *cognitive orientation* of the scientist that halakhic man imitates; he does not master the substance of the scientist's knowledge. R. Soloveitchik is not creating a place for the study of science in the halakhist's life, but only for the rigor, objectivity, creativity, freedom and idealization characteristic of the scientific enterprise.[10]

The purposes of the essay *Halakhic Man*, I submit, necessitate that things be this way, that halakhic man *not* master scientific knowledge. For *Halakhic Man* may be viewed, as others have suggested, as a response to the *Haskalah* or, perhaps more accurately given when R. Soloveitchik wrote, liberal Judaism. (Alternatively, it may show how halakhic men combated the Haskalah in their time and place.) Against critics who saw *yeshivah* study as pointless, empty, stifling and irrelevant, R. Soloveitchik penned a philosophical eulogy for his father and his world and advanced a vigorous defense of Torah study and the Lithuanian ideal.[11] As Eliezer Schweid summarizes the point, "Torah study does not stifle, nor darken, nor enclose the student within narrow confines."[12] Halakhic man finds the four cubits of the Halakhah entirely sufficient for his spiritual needs, discovering therein rigor, freedom, individuality and creativity. Nothing of conceivable value — in particular, no *modern* value — is missing. Ironically, by affirming modern values like creativity and freedom, R. Soloveitchik is able to turn matters around and show modernists how halakhic heroes embody those values.[13] How could the study of anything outside the realm of Torah have significance for halakhic man? What more could he want?[14]

The theme that a life of halakhic study and practice is self-sufficient is made evident by R. Soloveitchik's careful and at times surprising construction and wording of particular passages. For example, R. Soloveitchik explains that although halakhic man achieves "a powerful, exalted [religious] experience," this achievement "only occurs after he has acquired knowledge of the a priori,

141

ideal Halakhah and its reflected image in the real world." Halakhic man's religious experience is heightened, not diminished, by the fact that it comes pursuant to "rigorous criticism and profound penetrating reflection" (83). To explain how intellection can impact on experience, R. Soloveitchik compares the halakhist to the physicist. The latter begins by manipulating mathematical quantities, but eventually he is "swept to heights of rapture in the act of cognizing the world" (83).

> From the midst of the order and lawfulness we hear a new song, the song of the creature to the Creator, the song of the cosmos to its Maker...Not only the qualitative world bursts forth in song, but so does the quantitative world. From the very midst of the law there arises a cosmos more splendid and beautiful than all the works of Leonardo da Vinci and Michelangelo (84).

A more stirring articulation of how the study of science brings one to religious enthusiasm would be difficult to come by. But does R. Soloveitchik then infer that halakhic man studies science? No. Instead we read, "So is it with halakhic man. His religious experience is mature and ripe when he cognizes the world through the prism of the Halakhah" (84). The greatness of halakhic study is not that it *includes* scientific study, but that as a subject for cognitive engagement, halakhic study is *as good as* scientific study. Halakhic man's inspiration comes not from study of nature, but from study of Torah. It would simply be impossible for R. Soloveitchik to establish parity between Halakhah and science were he to insist that halakhic man studies science too. It is the *parallel* between science and Halakhah that he wants to advance; a substantive overlap would be contrary to his purpose.[15]

R. Soloveitchik's preference for parallelism over substantive overlap is also evident when he cites a remark attributed to the Gaon of Vilna. He quotes the remark in an unusual formulation: "To the degree that a man is lacking in the wisdom of mathematics he will lack one hundredfold in the wisdom of the Torah" (57).[16] R. Soloveitchik comments: "This statement is not just a pretty rhetorical conceit, testifying to the broad mindedness of the Gaon, but a firmly established truth of halakhic epistemology" (57). But what is this "truth"? Not, it turns out, the truth of mathematics *per se*; rather, the "truth" refers to the propensity of the Halakhah to translate "the qualitative features of religious subjectivity...into firm and well-established quantitites." Once more: parallel, not overlap.

The tendency we have noted to keep science out of halakhic man's life is surprising in light of the strong association between R. Soloveitchik and Maimonides. According to Maimonides, the Halakhah itself requires a Jew to occupy himself with theology. Knowledge of God is the first commandment, and the Jew is commanded to both love and fear God.[17] In the Maimonidean scheme, all these commandments can be fulfilled only through studying science and philosophy. Hence, if we follow Maimonides, the scientific activity of *homo religiosus*, linked as it is to theology, need not and should not disappear from the life of halakhic man. For even if study of science does not enter the four cubits of the Halakhah through the front door, as part of the very spirit and motivation of halakhic man, it could easily enter through the back door, as a fulfillment of a specific halakhic requirement. Yet we find no such assertion in *Halakhic Man*. R. Soloveitchik's uses of Maimonides in "Part Two" of *Halakhic Man* to develop his own conceptions of providence and prophecy seem artificial.[18] In Maimonides' opinion, these elevated states require scientific and philosophical knowledge, something halakhic man does not possess. When R. Soloveitchik explains how one achieves providence and prophecy, he makes the attainment depend on creativity, a concept that Maimonides does not mention.[19]

The specific people whom R. Soloveitchik seems to regard as halakhic men[20] — with the exception of Maimonides and the Gaon of Vilna — did not study science. Moreover, the very idea that one needs to turn to secular disciplines in order to live the life of a halakhic man threatens the thesis that immersion in Halakhah is self-sufficient for ensuring freedom, creativity and individuality. R. Soloveitchik thus suppresses a major motif of Maimonidean thought. The omission can be explained only in light of the objectives of R. Soloveitchik's essay, which can aptly and without a negative connotation be characterized as polemical.[21]

The argument that an existence focused exclusively on Halakhah is self-sufficient fits nicely with another work that was written the same year that *Halakhic Man* was published (1944), namely *The Halakhic Mind* (published in 1986). In that essay, R. Soloveitchik presses his own vast knowledge of science and philosophy into the service of cognitive pluralism, and then utilizes that pluralism to carve out a place for the cognitive autonomy of religion. Here again R. Soloveitchik seems committed to isolating the religious person from secular disciplines. What use is cognitive autonomy if simultaneously one must engage the very disciplines from which one has gained independence?[22] Since *The Halakhic Mind* argues for the autonomy of religion, and regards Halakhah as the highest form of objectification in religion (85), it is plausible that in the mid-1940s R. Soloveitchik consistently advocated the idea that Halakhah is self-sufficient for the Jewish religious consciousness.

Let us sum up. In the two works he wrote or published in 1944 — *Halakhic Man* and *The Halakhic Mind* — R. Soloveitchik, with the exception of one passage (*Halakhic Man*, 63-64), does not assign the study of science a *substantive* role in the life of halakhic man. Rather, R. Soloveitchik invokes science for one of two purposes:

(1) *Analogical*: By drawing parallels to scientific activity, R. Soloveitchik illuminates certain aspects of halakhic thinking. We encounter this use of scientific knowledge in *Halakhic Man*.

(2) *Critical*: By showing that science has no monopoly on objectivity and truth, he carves out a place for Halakhah as a valid cognitive enterprise. We encounter this appraisal of scientific knowledge in *The Halakhic Mind*.

In these earlier writings, then, science — more accurately, epistemology of science — is part of a second-order, "meta-level" reflection on the nature and legitimacy of halakhic life. It is not part of the halakhic life itself.[23]

All that said, we cannot help but accentuate the ostensible inconsistency between the theses of *Halakhic Man* and *The Halakhic Mind* on the one hand and R. Soloveitchik's career on the other. He apparently saw religious value in doing phenomenology (studying religious consciousness). Thus the outlook of halakhic man is not that of R. Soloveitchik himself. (This calls to mind a by-now popular quip that a halakhic man would never have written the essay *Halakhic Man*.[24]) On the contrary, R. Soloveitchik *describes* the mindset of halakhic man, but does not fully *identify* with it. For polemical reasons — to silence liberal approaches — he aims to capture "the image of his father" (to cite the rabbinic phrase he invokes in the opening epigraph about the biblical Joseph), but he does not identify with the portrait. His failure to argue for the religious value of scientific study need not reflect his own posture at the time he wrote the essay. R. Soloveitchik is describing a way of life that was not his own.

This suggestion is cogent, but we confront a difficulty. We said that *The Halakhic Man* contains an overarching argument that Halakhah supplies freedom, creativity, rigor and objectivity. If so, why would R. Soloveitchik have thought that one must look elsewhere for a fuller spirituality? Consider also that *The Halakhic Mind*, we said, aims to establish cognitive pluralism. Its overall thrust is to segregate Halakhah from scientific endeavors. So, if R. Soloveitchik's arguments succeed, he has no reason for pursuing science rather than content himself with halakhic study as a means of satisfying spiritual needs. The very effectiveness of his defense would intensify the question of why as a halakhic personality he engaged in secular pursuits.

2. SCIENCE AND THE RELIGIOUS ODYSSEY OF "U-BIKKASHTEM MI-SHAM"

At the time that he wrote *Halakhic Man*, R. Soloveitchik had already conceived of another essay (titled "*Ish ha-Elokim*," i.e. the man of God) that would characterize the religious personality of "the man of God." There are characteristics and activities that are necessary to a full religious experience but were left muted or undeveloped in *Halakhic Man*. Specifically, R. Soloveitchik had not adequately explained at least two aspects of halakhically committed individuals: how they relate to God, and how they attain the halakhically mandated states of love and fear of God. (Halakhic man is either a portion of the *ish ha-Elokim*, or a different, less variegated personality.[25]) Together with these contrasts, R. Soloveitchik's depiction of the relationship between science and halakhic life changes in "*U-Bikkashtem mi-Sham*."

"*U-Bikkashtem mi-Sham*," a revised and retitled version of "*Ish ha-Elokim*," was published in the periodical *Hadarom* in 1978 but was drafted not long after *Halakhic Man* was composed. The essay emphasizes two related dialectical movements. First, the dialectic between the "natural consciousness," on the one hand, and the "revelational consciousness" on the other; second, a parallel dialectic between freedom (which is experienced initially in the natural consciousness) and necessity (which is experienced through submission to revelation in the revelational consciousness). In "*U-Bikkashtem mi-Sham*", in other words, revelation and necessity are both prominent elements of religious existence. The essay's dialectical emphasis contrasts with *Halakhic Man*'s nearly one-sided focus on halakhic man's creativity and freedom. In addition, whereas *Halakhic Man* drew heavily on Maimonides — modified, of course, according to R. Soloveitchik's unique interpretation — "*U-Bikkashtem mi-Sham*" occasionally turns to the existential, non-rational dimensions of a human being's encounter with God, invoking Yehudah Halevi's name at certain junctures.[26] Hence, the reader might expect that the essay reduce rather than expand the role of science in religious life. Yet in "*U-Bikkashtem mi-Sham*" R. Soloveitchik forcefully and explicitly embraces scientific knowledge as a constituent of religious life.

Scientific knowledge — along with other cultural endeavors — is an aspect of the "natural consciousness," which represents the first phase of the religious odyssey charted by the essay. At first the human being tries to encounter God through "the cosmic drama" (7), among other phenomena.[27] Eventually the natural consciousness proves inadequate by itself, and needs to be supplemented by the revelational consciousness. Neither the study of science nor even the exercise of an immediate, non-scientific intuition into nature will take the human being far enough toward an encounter with and knowledge of God, and the natural consciousness can even generate pantheism (24).[28]

Moreover, sin prevents the human being from finding God through the cosmos. Consequently, seeking God through the study of science — and culture generally — is but an early stage on the road to the later, higher attainments: *imitatio Dei* and (ultimately) "cleaving to God" (*devekut*). The natural consciousness will not lead even to love of God, let alone to *imitatio Dei* and cleaving to God, unless it is fused with submission to "the divine, halakhic, moral law." According to the Jewish view, the human being cannot be redeemed from his pollution and contamination, or find his happiness and purpose, by coming close to God through creation alone. Another sort of approach is necessary (22-23). "He who relies only on the cosmological approach will end up ruined and faithless. ... Seeking God only within existence...does not bring man closer to God" (25).

As the essay proceeds to describe further stages — *imitatio Dei* and *devekut*, cleaving to God — some cultural endeavors simply drop out of the odyssey, since they failed to lead to an encounter with God. Yet it would be a mistake to think that scientific study, too, is merely a preliminary to a later stage in which such study is transcended and therefore discarded. Rather, the study of science, unlike other cultural endeavors, continues to play a role at higher stages of religious existence.

> All the prophets called upon us to observe creation (19).
> As science progresses, so does man's knowledge of God as His Creator, as the One who endows man with reason (43-44).
> Man is commanded not only to believe in God, but also to know God, as Maimonides formulated the first commandment The meaning of "knowledge" is knowing God by knowing His works — the works of creation (41).
> If he lacks natural consciousness and experience...then he is liable to abandon practical action and the real world (56-57).
> Our sages distinguished two aspects of the fulfillment of the commandment to love God, whose purpose and essence is cleaving to Him: (1) contemplating the acts of creation; and (2) contemplating the word of God, which appears in its objective form as the various branches of the Halakhah (106).

Theoretically it is possible to insist that each of the above passages refers to an early stage of religious experience; all but the last quotation, after all, are from contexts that precede the section on *devekut* (cleaving). But it would be implausible to understand the quotations that way. To begin with, the final quotation is from a section describing *devekut*. Moreover the quotations suggest an *ongoing* effort to encounter God through a study of the created world. Now, as we shall soon see, there is some question as to whether the absolutely final stage of the final stage, i.e. the last and crowning part of *devekut* itself, requires any cultural component at all. The absolutely final stage might be construed as embracing pure halakhic study, uncontaminated by the study of anything else. But up until that point, the religious hero of "*U-Bikkashtem mi-Sham*" has a continuing involvement with science. Since both God and human beings know the cosmos, and since the knower becomes identical with the object of knowledge, it follows that God and the cognizing human are to a degree one. The two become unified with the same object, and thereby become unified with each other.

Thus, in "*U-Bikkashtem mi-Sham*" R. Soloveitchik did not elect to stay with the purely formal, structural parallel between halakhic man and cognitive man that he accepts in *Halakhic Man*. Rather, he chose, in "*U-Bikkashtem mi-Sham*," to link the actual study of science to the life of the halakhic master. He posits a religious figure with greater breadth of interest than halakhic man and a greater range of religious experience.[29] This move brings R. Soloveitchik closer to Maimonides. Whereas, as we said, R. Soloveitchik's uses of Maimonides in Part Two of *Halakhic Man* to develop his own conceptions of providence and prophecy seem artificial and un-Maimonidean, "*U-Bikkashtem mi-Sham*"'s open embrace of scientific study and cultural endeavors fits with Maimonides' stance.[30]

3. MEDIEVAL AND MODERN SCIENCE

Is R. Soloveitchik's attempt in "*U-Bikkashtem mi-Sham*" to integrate scientific study into the religious ideal successful? And how closely does it match the medieval approach? In approaching these questions, we need to appreciate the dramatic contrasts between the medieval Aristotelianism of Maimonides — whom R. Soloveitchik quotes to ground his explanation of *devekut* — and the modern science of R. Soloveitchik himself. These contrasts place obstacles before R. Soloveitchik's attempt in "*U-Bikkashtem mi-Sham*" to appropriate classic Maimonidean ideas and to include scientific study within the activities of his religious heroes. The two obstacles we will examine, drawing on the approach of Aviezer Ravitzky, may be identified as the problem of a-teleology and the problem of realism.[31]

A. *The problem of a-teleology*

Post-Aristotelian science does away with teleological explanations in favor of mechanistic ones. Nature, for modern science, is devoid of purpose. Yet Maimonides' concepts of love and fear of God are grounded in teleological assumptions. In the *Mishneh Torah*, Maimonides explicitly says that love and fear arise "when a person contemplates His great and wondrous works and creatures and from them obtains a glimpse of His wisdom which is incomparable and infinite."[32] The wisdom in nature,

147

rather than its lawfulness and regularity, stimulates love and fear. This wisdom seems clearly related to teleology.[33] In the absence of teleology, Maimonidean love of God is not possible.

In order to predicate love of God on the study of nature while adopting an a-teleological view of nature, one will have to take the ontological dependency of the world on God, its contingency, as an adequate basis for love, regardless of the world's specific character. Any cosmos of any character — whether teleological or not — would stimulate this type of love of God. R. Soloveitchik comes very close to taking such a position. [34]

The teleological character of nature is also essential to grasping what Maimonides means by *imitatio Dei*. The thirteen attributes of action that were revealed to Moses reflect God's governance of nature, His "actions" (*Guide* III:54). Nature has a moral character. R. Soloveitchik clearly asserts that "The fact of existence is the embodiment of the moral will" (131). "In creating the world, the Creator fulfilled the supreme moral purpose" (131). "Prophecy, which revealed God's acts to humans, sees the entire world as the embodiment of the Hidden Intellect within the Supreme Will, as the uncovering of the divine apprehension-volition, which is totally moral and purposeful" (187, n. 16).[35]

Value, nature and purpose are clearly connected in R. Soloveitchik's mind. But when scientific conceptions do not entail teleology, it becomes difficult to draw the connections that R. Soloveitchik suggests here.

By way of reply, we might distinguish between two theses about teleology:

(1) Thesis one: *science* utilizes final causes when explaining phenomena,

(2) Thesis two: *nature* is teleological.

According to R. Soloveitchik, I believe, thesis one is false, but R. Soloveitchik may posit that thesis two is true. That is, even though modern science does without final causes, other modes of examining nature might detect purposefulness. Could a religious thinker like R. Soloveitchik deny teleology altogether? Indeed, in his writings, R. Soloveitchik asserts that nature *is* teleological.[36] However, he claims that people perceive its purposive character only when they move beyond science, when they have an immediate, non-rational encounter with the "qualitative" aspects of the world that science does not capture. Teleology can be ascribed to nature, but only if we exit the scientific framework:

> Only outside of formal symbolic cognition, with its free structures of thought, can the secret be revealed . . . Reason cannot govern an absolute, non-contingent realm, a realm which cannot be symbolized by the free creations of contingent understanding (13-14).
> There are hints in the world that turn man's mind toward Heaven (14).

Man finds his God in the splendor and glory of the world, the abundance of radiances, the myriads of captivating sights, motion and action, power, the static and the dynamic, the greatness and might in the cosmic drama (32).

The "qualitative" character of nature enables a religious perception of it. Hence, the non-scientific — or, if you prefer, the pre-scientific or trans-scientific — admiration of nature promotes proper religious attitudes, but scientific study of nature does not.[37] Teleology cannot serve as a basis for scientific analysis, as it did according Maimonides. But R. Soloveitchik seems to urge the religious person to find teleology not in the study of science, but in the lush and variegated qualitative universe that is not captured in scientific thought.[38] In the absence of teleology *within* science, it remains unclear how the study of science will promote love of God or *hiddamut* (imitating Him). [39]

B. *The Problem of Realism*

Since Kant, it is generally accepted that science cannot describe things as they are in themselves. Science consists of human constructions, the creation of formal parallels to the world as it appears to us through our senses. The gap between cognition and reality cannot be bridged. Idealism, such as the outlook of the Marburg school, sought to remove the gap by denying the existence of a reality beyond thought. But R. Soloveitchik, notwithstanding occasional gestures in its direction, rejected idealism.[40] Thus, if knowledge of nature is not necessarily knowledge of reality, how can knowledge of nature be religiously valuable? How can one achieve "knowing God by knowing His works — the works of creation" (41) under these conditions? How can God's actions in nature serve as a moral blueprint, if we apprehend those actions only in our own confining conceptual prisons and distorting prisms? It is one thing to posit knowledge of nature as a religious imperative in an Aristotelian epistemology; it is another to do so in a post-Kantian framework.

This problem is especially acute given R. Soloveitchik's account of the climactic stage of *devekut*: "The secret of cleaving to God involves the principle of the identity of the knower and the known" (94). To achieve *devekut*, one must identify with God's thought, will and action. But one cannot realize the cognitive element (*mahashavah*) in the equation of the knower and the object of knowledge when a barrier separates the knower from the known. How can R. Soloveitchik allow the equation to apply to human cognition?

There would seem to be two responses to this difficulty.

(A) The first is to construe the task of cognition (knowledge of God through knowledge of nature) as an imperative to engage in a certain kind of *process* rather than to emerge with a specific content. If six physicists create six different and conflicting theories, all of them fulfill the commandment of knowing God because all of them have exercised their scientific intellects. Such an approach would fit well with R. Soloveitchik's pronounced preference for phenomenology over truth claims. Unfortunately, although this approach might handle the general problem of why cognitive barriers do not prevent knowledge of God through nature, it is not adequate to solve the problem posed by the principle of the identity of the knower and the object of knowledge. For on the present hypothesis, none of the physicists in our example have merged with the object of knowledge in the way R. Soloveitchik describes, namely, by matching God's knowledge.

(B) In a characteristically profound and penetrating article, Aviezer Ravitzky has suggested another approach. Ravitzky believes that R. Soloveitchik was in fact sensitive to the problem of realism, but that he responded to this problem by placing halakhic cognition rather than scientific cognition at the highest rung of achievement. In other words, a denial of realism is part of R. Soloveitchik's own argument; it provided him with an epistemological basis for prioritizing Halakhah over science. The modern critique of knowledge, which threatens the claim that we cognize the physical world, does not apply to halakhic cognition. The potential gap between cognition and reality is forever doomed to hinder the identification of the knower with the object of knowledge in the realm of science, but not so in the area of Halakhah. In Ravitzky's words:

> It is there, and only there, that the theoretical and abstract character of the spiritual endeavor does not remove cognition from true reality, from the absolute. Unlike natural science, halakhic creativity "suits," so to speak, by its very nature, the idealistic approach. Because, in the realm of the halakhah, we are — to begin with — dealing with nothing but the infinite Divine intellect and the finite human intellect, and there is no need to seek a correlation to any concrete reality; Talmud Torah, unlike the science of the cosmos, is not derived from any reality. It imposes its rule upon reality. One cannot know the world as it is, but one can know it as it ought to be.[41]

Stressing "the priority of halakhah" nicely illustrates a pattern that Ravitzky identifies in R. Soloveitchik's use of Maimonides:

> A close study of Soloveitchik's words will reveal an interesting fact, a subtle but far-reaching transition in the original doctrine. Whenever the author presents and explains Maimonides' own position, serving as a loyal interpreter of the philosophy of the *Guide of the Perplexed*, the object of knowledge referred to is *the world*, the

cosmos. … On the other hand, when the author goes on to develop his own independent thought, expounding his personal "neo-Maimonideanism," the object of knowledge referred to becomes the *halakhah*, the study of Torah (163).

Ravitzky concedes, I think, that R. Soloveitchik does not overtly present the anti-realist argument that Ravitzky suggests. Remarkably, though, R. Soloveitchik's discussion proceeds as if scientific cognition were not in fact riddled by the problems Kant had identified. Throughout the section of *"U-Bikkashtem mi-Sham"* that elaborates on the principle of the identity of the knower with the known, R. Soloveitchik takes knowledge of the natural world to be unproblematic, omitting any reference to the Kantian problem. "Man apprehends the world" states R. Soloveitchik, as if such apprehension were completely attainable (103). A statement such as, "The world is the object of both God's knowledge and human knowledge" (102), entails that human cognition, like God's, successfully apprehends aspects of the world. Although R. Soloveitchik draws some distinctions between human and divine cognition, he does not propose a distinction from the standpoint of content. He does not say that there is a veil that separates reality-as-it-appears-to-man from reality-as-it-appears-to-God.[42]

Because in this context R. Soloveitchik seems unconcerned with the Kantian/neo-Kantian barrier between the phenomenal world and the world as it truly is, it is difficult to maintain that R. Soloveitchik's shift to Halakhah as the primary object shared by human and divine cognition is motivated by an awareness of the barrier. An additional indication of his lack of concern is the following statement:

> The objective Halakhah is enclosed within the realm of the actual. Its object is the world that encompasses us completely. It approaches this world with a normative yardstick. Yet, in order to formulate the norm in halakhic terms, objective Halakhah requires a clear acquaintance with the object. Without such knowledge, it is totally impossible to discuss the world from a halakhic standpoint. There is therefore an intimate connection between the objective, normative Halakhah and the scientific cognition of the free, creative intellect… Efforts are made in the halakhic consciousness to penetrate the secrets of the scientific world (120).[43]

Halakhah does not simply impose a norm upon reality; it first studies the reality and only then applies the norm to it. Given the statement just quoted, erecting epistemic barriers to cognition of the world would undermine the project of Halakhah. Yet nowhere in this passage is there any indication that science cannot achieve "clear acquaintance with the object"(120).

On the contrary, R. Soloveitchik asserts that many halakhic topics require "a mathematical and conceptual grasp of space" (120); concepts of causality; and psychological or epistemological propositions. While R. Soloveitchik is surely aware of the neo-Kantian problem, that awareness does not enter his discussion of *devekut*. [44]

Thus, any shift that R. Soloveitchik may make from the cosmos to Halakhah is not motivated by the existence of Kantian barriers. Other explanations of a shift to Halakhah are available, assuming the shift is genuine. Let me briefly present them.

As Ravitzky observes, R. Soloveitchik's approach is partly motivated by his traditionalist outlook: not simply his veneration of halakhic study, but also his regard for the precedent of R. Hayyim of Volozhin, who also views Torah study through the lens of the principle of the identity of the knower and the object of knowledge. Two other, more significant factors are worthy of note, however. Both relate to internal structural features of *"U-Bikkashtem mi-Sham."* First, the divine activity embraces knowledge, will and action, and in the case of God these elements are a single unity. Full *devekut* entails that a human being, like God, actualizes the equation of knowledge, will and action: "Man must imitate his Creator not only regarding the identity of the knower with the known, but also in the identity of thought, will, and action. Without fulfilling this equation, man cannot succeed in cleaving to God" (103). Only halakhic study, not scientific cognition, transcends the realm of knowledge and permits the wondrous "identification of wills" (and identification of actions) as well (150).[45]

Second, only Halakhah fuses the natural consciousness and revelational consciousness:

> The halakhic ideal is embodied in its striving for joint revelational and intellectual activity. Halakhic man grasps supra-rational topics and discusses them in an objective, rational manner...This is a strange phenomenon: on the one hand the Torah embodies a supra-cognitive, supra-ontological revelational vision, yet on the other hand it is grasped by the human mind and constricts itself into the ontological realm (119).
>
> [The spiritual consciousness] combines the natural human aspiration for God with revelational faith (107).

R. Soloveitchik's elevation of halakhic cognition over scientific cognition, it seems, is due to the fact that examining the word of God, unlike examining creation, recapitulates the central dialectic of the essay, that between natural consciousness and revelational consciousness. No secular object of study would achieve that.

Three additional points are in order.

(I) R. Soloveitchik's shift to Halakhah as the focus of *devekut* will not solve the problem of the Kantian barrier to knowledge. Like scientific cognition, halakhic cognition also includes barriers between the knower and the object of knowledge. It is difficult to maintain that in the case of Halakhah, "There is no thing-in-itself beyond it: the novellae of the Talmud scholar are the very truth of the Torah."[46] For R. Soloveitchik adopts the notion that Halakhah is in the first instance a result of revelation and not human creativity.[47] In addition, surely there are better and worse constructions in Halakhah. In order to successfully maintain that we can penetrate to halakhic essences, R. Soloveitchik would need to create a theory of halakhic truth that would explain how simultaneously one could regard all *hiddushim* (novel interpretations) as "truth" and yet also rank some methodologies, analyses and analogies as better and more persuasive than others.[48]

(II) R. Soloveitchik's enlistment of the principle of the identity of the knower with the known to assign religious significance to scientific knowledge is problematic on several counts. Although his use of this principle as a paradigm for Torah study is not unprecedented (as we said, R. Hayyim of Volozhin and others advocated it), R. Soloveitchik's attempt to draw on the principle is unexpected and curious. However common the principle was in medieval and kabbalistic thought, the equation is obscure and not adequately justified in the modern epistemologies on which R. Soloveitchik builds. Further, his attempt to compare human cognition to divine cognition with regard to the identity of the knower and the object of knowledge relies on *Guide of the Perplexed* I:68, where Maimonides openly invites this parallel. R. Soloveitchik therefore has to derogate passages in the *Mishneh Torah*, (*Hilkhot Yesodei ha-Torah* 2:10; *Hilkhot Teshuvah* 5:5), where Maimonides distinguishes between divine and human cognition by saying that in the case of divine cognition the knower is identical with the object of knowledge while in human cognition that equation does not hold.[49] Since interpreters have noted that *Guide* I:68 does not cohere with Maimonides' insistence elsewhere in the *Guide* that God's knowledge is unlike ours, to utilize *Guide* I:68 as the very foundation of a depiction of *devekut* requires elevating an aberrant text to the level of a central and dominant Maimonidean position.[50]

(III) Despite R. Soloveitchik's elevation of halakhic knowledge over scientific knowledge when he describes *devekut*, I believe that in his opinion knowledge of science is necessary even at the absolute end of the final stage. For if one knows only Halakhah then one's cleaving is less complete than if one also shares in God's knowledge of science and the world.

To sum up this discussion of "*U-Bikkashtem mi-Sham*," the problems of a-teleology and of realism challenge the essay's attempt to carve out a place for science in religious life beyond that found in the first phase of the individual's religious odyssey. R. Soloveitchik can deal with the first, but largely ignores the second. He highlights halakhic cognition not because scientific knowledge is impossible due to a Kantian barrier, but because halakhic cognition best encapsulates certain themes of the essay. And there is good reason to think that one cleaves to God not only via halakhic cognition but also via scientific cognition.

We turn finally to *Lonely Man of Faith*, which suggests a final model of how science can enter religious life, a model that differs from that offered in the earlier works. Indeed, this new approach overcomes some of the problems we have discussed.

5. *LONELY MAN OF FAITH*: A NEW CONCEPTION OF SCIENCE

Lonely Man of Faith, in the words of Gerald Blidstein, "endows Western technology with the fullest acknowledgment Judaism could offer."[51] To be sure, halakhists had often mandated the use of medical treatment and had often urged working for a living, implying an endorsement of practical endeavors. But the authorities of the tradition did not typically extend this orientation of "We do not rely upon miracles" (*Pesahim* 64b and elsewhere) to mandate scientific *research*, the project of discovering *new* ways of harnessing nature for human benefit. "We do not rely on miracles" in its traditional usage, merely prescribes using whatever means of practical aid are available to a person at a given time. R. Soloveitchik's contribution is to expand the scope of practical initiative required by Halakhah so that it now encompasses research endeavors.[52]

This is a vigorous expansion indeed. Observe, for example, how his famous dialectic between "majesty and humility," which parallels the dialectic between Adam the first and Adam the second, unfolds. One might expect that "humility," the counterweight to the orientation of Adam the first, would place limits on technological endeavors. This is not the case. Instead, in "Majesty and Humility" and "Catharsis," humility is exemplified by altogether different gestures: the mind's surrendering to laws that seem irrational (*hukkim*); a person's observing *mitzvot* even when it is emotionally difficult to do so; and a person's restraining the sexual drive.[53] Humility is manifested, then, not *within* the technological context but outside of it. Hence, when R. Soloveitchik cautions against an excess of "majesty" and mandates the other pole of the dialectic, humility, that is not a plea to curtail technological labors. On the contrary, the diatribe one so often hears against technology today — that it has become arrogant and therefore we ought to draw bounds beyond which technology must not tread — finds no parallel in R. Soloveitchik's discussion.[54]

Lonely Man of Faith and "Confrontation" mark a critical turn in R. Soloveitchik's orientation toward science. Here he breaks from both medieval Jewish philosophical accounts of how science contributes to religious life, and from his own earlier conceptions. I shall identify three areas of difference.

1. *Theoretical/practical*: In *Halakhic Man* R. Soloveitchik had emphasized the independence of both science and Halakhah from the real world, since neither the mathematician-scientist nor the halakhist is deeply bothered when their a priori models fail to correspond to the real world (25). In line with this emphasis, the main religious value R. Soloveitchik assigns to science in *Halakhic Man* (in the life of the scientist, that is) comes from theoretical study, but the theme of technology is absent. In "*U-Bikkashtem mi-Sham*," the value of theoretical study again predominates, while practical technological achievements and medical advances are invoked only as secondary themes (e.g., "*U-Bikkashtem mi-Sham*," 56). (It is possible that those passages in "*U-Bikkashtem mi-Sham*" that refer to technology were written after the ideas of *Lonely Man of Faith* were published or conceived.)

This preference for theoretical science over practical technology changes in "Confrontation" and *Lonely Man of Faith*. In the 1960s, R. Soloveitchik emphasized the practical side of science, describing its theoretical side only secondarily.

> God, in imparting the blessing to Adam the first and giving him the mandate to subdue nature, directed Adam's attention to the functional and practical aspects of his intellect through which man is able to gain control of nature. Other intellectual inquiries, such as the metaphysical or axiologico-qualitative, no matter how incisive and penetrating, have never granted man dominion over his environment... Adam the first is interested in just a single aspect of reality and asks one question only — "How does the cosmos function?" ... In fact, even this "how" question with which Adam the first is preoccupied is limited in scope. He is concerned not with the question *per se*, but with its practical implications. (12-13)[55]

Adam the first learns what he needs to know for his technological endeavors. Scholars have noted that both cognitive man and Adam the first exemplify creativity, but the two figures differ significantly in their respective approaches to science. One has a theoretical orientation, the other a practical one.

Emphasizing the practical orientation of Adam the first limits *Lonely Man of Faith*'s advocacy of the pursuit of secular studies, since the essay seems to defend only those fields of study that have practical application. Admittedly, early in the essay R. Soloveitchik describes Adam the first as not only "a creative theoretician" but also "creative aesthete" (18). In this context, he expands Adam the first's efforts from technology and medicine to the fashioning of norms and the creation of pleasurable things. Yet even here R. Soloveitchik emphasizes the functional and practical. "His mind is questing not for the true, but for the pleasant and functional" (19). Herein lies a significant departure from medieval syntheses of Torah and culture. Consider: could Maimonides ever have appraised secular wisdom as something other than "questing for the true"?

What induced R. Soloveitchik to change his emphasis from the theoretical aspects of science to its practical applications? Yonah Ben-Sasson has speculated that *Lonely Man of Faith* reflects the "instrumentalist" or pragmatist view of scientific theories then influential in American philosophy.[56] R. Soloveitchik's move toward the practical may also be linked to his intensified allegiance to Mizrachi. In his lectures on Zionism (1962-1967), he occasionally refers to the fact that the construction of the Zionist polity requires extensive involvement in technology, economics and secular disciplines.[57] The timing of *Lonely Man of Faith* might also be relevant. The essay was written during the heady fervor of the new space age, and at a time when illness had struck the Soloveitchik family — and it highlights precisely these areas of transportation and medicine.

Whatever its origins in R. Soloveitchik's thought, the instrumentalist account of science helps address an issue that was conspicuously missing from the earlier writings. Conflicts between science and Torah are often the basis for religious objection to the study of science. Science may lead to love of God, the argument goes, but it may also lead to an opposite result, namely heresy. Any attempt to make the study of science a religious ideal is most plausible when scientific truths accord with those asserted by Torah. But modern science does not accord with Torah, so its value to the religious life is highly suspect. An instrumentalist approach to science does not necessarily see science as submitting a "true" picture of reality. Hence the cognitive conflict between science and religion is alleviated.[58] Perhaps that is one reason why in *Lonely Man of Faith* R. Soloveitchik declares that he is not concerned with "the confrontation" of the "Biblical doctrine of creation vis-à-vis the scientific story of evolution...the mechanistic interpretation of the human mind with the Biblical spiritual concept of man" and other "theoretical oppositions and dichotomies" (7).[59]

2. *Individual/community*: In the earlier works, R. Soloveitchik had emphasized the impact of scientific activity (i.e. study) on the individual's

religious consciousness. In several ways, the essays of the 1960s portray science (i.e. technology) as a communal endeavor. To begin with, Adam the first's attempts "to harness and dominate the elemental natural forces" (15) cannot succeed without the contribution of others.

> Whenever Adam the first wants to work, to produce, and to succeed in his undertakings, he must unite with others...Distribution of labor, the coordinated efforts of the many, the accumulated experiences of the multitude, the cooperative spirit of countless individuals, raise man above the primitive level of a natural existence and grant him limited dominion over his environment. What we call civilization is the sum total of a community effort through the millennia." (30, 32)[60]

Furthermore, R. Soloveitchik sees "the social contract," which is inherent in Adam the first's community, as the product of "biological, instinctual pressures...to come together in [the] face of opposition" (29) — a position that calls to mind *Kol Dodi Dofek*'s description of "camp" (*mahaneh*) as opposed to "congregation" (*edah*).[61] In these respects, Adam the first's majestic community differs from the covenantal faith community.[62] By the very nature of his goals, Adam the first requires a communal context. "Dignity as a behavioral category can find realization only in the outward gesture...Dignity can only be predicated of *kerygmatic* man, who has the capability of establishing lines of communication...Dignity is linked with fame" (26).

R. Soloveitchik's emphasis on the communal aspects of science differs dramatically from the approach of medieval thinkers. When they spoke of the place of science in religious life, they referred primarily to the pursuit of science *by an individual*. In *Lonely Man of Faith*, however, R. Soloveitchik does not contend that each and every religious personality ought to strive to integrate within himself both religious and scientific activities. It is true that he tells us that "No matter how far-reaching the cleavage [between Adam the first and Adam the second], each of us must willy-nilly identify himself with the whole of an all-inclusive human personality, charged with responsibility as both a majestic and a covenantal being" (85). Nevertheless, he expressly points out that "This essay refers to Adam the first as a type representing the collective human technological genius, and not to individual members of the human race" (17). Although one might claim that R. Soloveitchik is only pointing out that scientific achievements are a collective effort, he may also be implying that the mandate to human beings to be both Adam the first and Adam the second does not require *each individual* to be a scientist. It requires each person to share in humanity's exemplification of Adam the first, to appreciate that Adam the first is a piece of an overall religious conception. Each of us, both Jew and non-Jew, "belongs to both communities" in the sense that we are members of a human race that integrates and ought to integrate these very outlooks and activities. As R. Soloveitchik says elsewhere: "Like other people, the Jew has more than one identity. He is part of a larger family of mankind, but he also has a Jewish identity which separates him from others."[63] It is in this light that we might understand R. Soloveitchik's statement that, "I hardly believe that any responsible man of faith..., who is verily interested in the destiny of his community and wants to see it thriving and vibrant, would recommend now the philosophy of *contemptus saeculi*" (85-86). I would suggest that R. Soloveitchik is not advocating that every individual be a scientist, but rather that no individual harbor contempt for the scientific enterprise.[64]

3. *Cognitive/ethical*: In these later writings, R. Soloveitchik emphasizes the ethical thrust of science rather than its cognitive thrust. He moved from stressing the role that science plays in the growth of the individual to stressing the role that it plays in the life of the community — as a solution to social ills. Through the development of science, human beings attain dignity and elevate themselves above the brute; and they expand the scope of their responsibility.

> Man of old who could not fight disease and succumbed in multitudes to yellow fever or any other plague with degrading helplessness could not lay claim to dignity. Only the man who builds hospitals, discovers therapeutic techniques, and saves lives is blessed with dignity...The brute is helpless, and, therefore, not dignified. Civilized man has gained limited control of nature and has become, in certain respects, her master, and with his mastery he has attained dignity as well. His mastery has made it possible for him to act in accordance with his responsibility. Hence, Adam the first is aggressive, bold, and victory-minded...He engages in creative work trying to imitate his maker (17-18).

Here, as in previous writings, the Rav applies the principle of *imitatio Dei* to the construction of scientific theories, not to their application. Yet it is clear that, when Adam the first engages in applying science, then whatever his motivation — that is, regardless of whether he aims at ethical and religious goals — he is *de facto* fulfilling ethical demands. "Victory... is an ethical goal."[65]

In stressing the impact of science on the community rather than the individual, R. Soloveitchik broke ranks with his medieval predecessors. This is not to say that Maimonides did not advocate "technology"; he did advocate at least its medieval equivalent. In all areas of life, but most noticeably the medical and the political, Maimonides stood for a naturalist outlook that counsels pragmatism and the exercise of practical wisdom.[66] For example, he berated those who claim that since people must place their trust in God, they must also resist the use of medicines.[67] In viewing the pragmatic use of science as an imperative, Maimonides and R. Soloveitchik are similar. Nevertheless, there are instructive differences between them in this area.

Whereas Maimonides emphasizes using inquiry to further one's *own* ends — for example, to promote one's *own* health — R. Soloveitchik underlines the role of inquiry in enabling human beings to carry out their responsibilities *to others*. In addition, Maimonides embedded his pragmatism in the context of a teleological outlook, while R. Soloveitchik did not. For Maimonides, our intellectual abilities reflect the teleological structure of nature, a structure that in turn reflects divine wisdom and "general providence." God wants people to relate to Him *by* exploiting the teleology in nature, *by* manipulating the provisions for human benefit found within it.[68] R. Soloveitchik refers to teleology in *Lonely Man of Faith* only in the context of Adam the second (see 21-22, 29, 47-49, 81-84) in accord with a pattern we discussed earlier of finding teleology outside of science rather than within it. The universe of Adam the first is not teleological.

This absence of teleology, as well as R. Soloveitchik's embrace of an instrumentalist conception of science, creates problems, I believe, in the worldview of Adam the first. For we are not offered any theory of *why* technology succeeds for Adam the first. How and why do the formal, abstract theories that science proposes as parallels to the qualitative world succeed so dramatically in improving the world? Especially puzzling is that the theories on which technology is based omit an integral part of experience, the qualitative; they merely "duplicate" the qualitative world. "To be precise, his [Adam the first's] question is related not to the genuine functioning of the cosmos in itself but to the possibility of reproducing the dynamics of the cosmos by employing quantified-mathematized media which man evolves through postulation and creative thinking" (13).

R. Soloveitchik's only comment on the question of how science succeeds is that Adam the first "constructs his own world and in *mysterious fashion* succeeds in controlling his environment through manipulating his own mathematical constructs and creations" (18, emphasis mine). An admission of mystery is of course no answer. Plainly, an instrumentalist conception is less equipped to account for the remarkable practical success of science than is a realist account. Belief in teleology (especially when coupled with scientific realism but not only then) could remove the mystery. If nature is teleological and is designed to be "user-friendly," as Maimonides supposes, then God has created a world that can be bettered through technology. God gives us both the mandate to "fill the earth and subdue it," as well as the means to fulfill that mandate. Likewise, the motif of *imitatio Dei*, that our technological creativity imitates God's creative activity, is enriched by the idea that nature is teleological. For our actions, just like God's original creation, produce objects that can benefit us.[69]

A final point. *Lonely Man of Faith* draws upon certain concepts from two decades earlier. But the very motifs that formerly had been used to praise the Halakhah and to argue for dedication to it are now invoked as reasons to engage in technology and research. Through science and technology, human beings fulfill the mandate to be creative, and they elevate themselves above the brute. Arguably, science in *Lonely Man of Faith*, like Halakhah in *Halakhic Man*, is democratic.[70] This transfer of motifs from Torah study to science may be one reason why the motif of Torah study is virtually absent from *Lonely Man of Faith*.[71] In *Halakhic Man*, which presents the talmudist as a synthesis of two other types, R. Soloveitchik can attribute to the talmudist the characteristics of those constituent types. Thus, the talmudist can be viewed as a creative personality just as cognitive man is. But in *Lonely Man of Faith*, the talmudist would have to be Adam the second, the religious type. Yet Adam the second cannot be the talmudist depicted in *Halakhic Man*, for he would then have to share some of the defining characteristics of Adam the first.[72]

6. SUMMATION CONCERNING SCIENCE

In this essay I have argued that R. Soloveitchik's thinking about the place of science in religious life underwent an evolution. The first essay we considered, *Halakhic Man*, claims that halakhic men need nothing for their spirituality besides Halakhah, and R. Soloveitchik appears to make a studious, persistent effort to exclude science from halakhic man's religious foci even when it would have been quite natural and smooth to include it. His novel treatment of Maimonides in the work obscures the fact that providence and prophecy are for Maimonides linked to scientific cognition. The exclusion of science from halakhic man's life, we said, does not necessarily represent R. Soloveitchik's own view; it is an approach he attributes to others, namely, halakhic men, who receive full spiritual satisfaction from halakhic life. Nonetheless, insofar as *Halakhic Man* conveys the idea that freedom and other values can be attained by halakhic study alone, the work leaves us in the dark as to how R. Soloveitchik himself views the role of science. What does it contribute to the halakhic personality's life that he cannot achieve without it? Why would one assign religious value to it? *The Halakhic Mind* goes even further, suggesting that science and Halakhah can exist as two equally valid realms.

In *"U-Bikkashtem mi-Sham,"* R. Soloveitchik refers to scientific study in the course of mapping an early stage of a religious odyssey. Unlike other cultural endeavors, apparently, it is an ingredient in the final stage of the religious odyssey, namely *devekut*. But it is not clear whether in the final stage of that final stage knowledge of science is required. One could read the work as Aviezer Ravitzky does, as transferring motifs from Maimonides' views of science and applying them to halakhic study *instead of* scientific study. I suggested that the transfer does occur, but for reasons different from those Ravitzky mentions. Still, scientific cognition would appear to enhance cleaving by dint of the principle of equation of the knower with the known, regardless of whether R. Soloveitchik stresses this. He seems to ignore the problems that Kantian epistemology poses to his scheme.

Finally, in later works such as *Lonely Man of Faith*, R. Soloveitchik held that the principal religious value of science lies neither in cognition nor in creativity, but rather in its effect on the life of the community and its ethical contribution.

As I stated at the outset, my claim about evolutionary development refers to an analytical evolution, not a biographical one. I have laid out the *works* in a developmental frame. I am not asserting that R. Soloveitchik's *personal thought* evolved as well. Readers can speculate endlessly as to why the works differ from one another. The seemingly obvious hypothesis that R. Soloveitchik actually changed his mind is but one hypothesis among several. One can argue, for example, that at the time he wrote *Halakhic Man*, R. Soloveitchik had already conceived *"U-Bikkashtem mi-Sham"* as an essential sequel that would unveil aspects of the religious personality beyond those set out in *Halakhic Man*.[73] One might argue that at the time he drafted *"U-Bikkashtem mi-Sham,"* R. Soloveitchik already had conceived of the key motif of *Lonely Man of Faith* — that technological advance fulfills a divine mandate — but put it aside for later use. One could also contend that R. Soloveitchik thought that the essays are mutually compatible and even complementary. Or one could claim that R. Soloveitchik regarded each of his treatments as equally valid, however different they may be from one another. That is the way he often looked at a talmudic topic or a Maimonidean halakhic decision: one way one year, another way another year, and a third way the next year. R. Soloveitchik may have felt that religious life may or must be viewed from a variety of angles and perspectives.[74] What we construe as inconsistencies he may have construed as multiple valid positions. Finally, one could argue that R. Soloveitchik's decision to publish two essays of the 1940s, *"U-Bikkashtem mi-Sham"* and *The Halakhic Mind*, long after *Lonely Man* came to light, is a sign that he reverted back to the older position, retracing his steps. The fact that these diverse suggestions are available renders the claim that R. Soloveitchik underwent a biographical change of mind highly speculative.

7. CONCLUDING THOUGHTS: THE PLACE OF THE HUMANITIES IN RELIGIOUS LIFE

Let me return, in closing, to an issue with which I began this essay: what was R. Soloveitchik's overall position on the ideology of *Torah u-Madda*? *Lonely Man of Faith* emphasizes the functional aspects of science, and with respect to *Torah u-Madda*, the pragmatic pursuit of medicine, politics, law, economics and aesthetics (*Lonely Man of Faith*, 18) is one thing, the study of the humanities another.[75] As Gerald Blidstein submits, *Lonely Man of Faith* does not provide a rationale for the "philosophical or literary achievements of Western culture."[76] Similarly, R. Soloveitchik's son-in-law, the late Yitzhak (Isadore) Twersky, notes that in R. Soloveitchik's writing, "there is no attempt to argue and demonstrate the importance of general learning as an abstract proposition just as there is no attempt to defend or glorify western culture."[77] To put it in terms that permeate R. Soloveitchik's and his ancestors' talmudic analyses: While the "*gavra*" (person) of R. Soloveitchik evinced an abiding interest in world culture and made that interest plain in his writings, the "*heftza*" (object) of thought that R. Soloveitchik produced in the 1960s delivers something less than an articulate justification for all-embracing cultural pursuits.[78]

In closing, therefore, we might ask ourselves what value R. Soloveitchik assigned to his own second-order, meta-reflections on religious life, which drew heavily on philosophy, literature, and the humanities generally. What legitimates — or mandates — the use of such sources from a religious standpoint?

Although my focus in this paper is science, the question is an important one, and I propose several answers based on various hints in R. Soloveitchik's writings.

First, in a powerful homiletical exposition, R. Soloveitchik comments on two explanations that Rashi gives of the verse "And the Lord God created Adam from the dust of the earth" (Gen. 2:7).[79] The first explanation says that He took the dust from all over the universe; the second, that He took it from the eventual spot of the altar. R. Soloveitchik says that these two explanations represent two aspects of a human being — on the one hand, the human being is cosmic, on the other he is rooted to a single spot, a home. R. Soloveitchik itemizes the human being's cosmic interests, both intellectual and experiential. Now, in *The Lonely Man of Faith* R. Soloveitchik takes human nature, which is after all created by God, to in some way validate activities of human beings that express that nature. The human being's cosmic interests would (using his homiletic message) validate R. Soloveitchik's own quest for broad horizons. Indeed, the homiletic teaching to which I refer depicts a person who is not only cosmic, who not only roams the universe driven by intellectual and experiential curiosity, but who also then returns to his spot of origin. In R. Soloveitchik's case the return is to the world of Brisk, the world of Torah, the world of faith, the world of covenant. It is tempting to take this image of the dual personality, who is both cosmic and rooted, as an expression of R. Soloveitchik's thinking about general culture and to consider it an apt portrait of the man.

Second, just as R. Soloveitchik maintained that the Jew possesses a dual identity as a member of both a Jewish and human community, he believed (I propose) that a Jewish religious personality partakes of a universal religious personality. Studying that universal personality, as non-Jewish phenomenological explorations of religion do, enhances understanding of the Jewish religious personality.[80]

Third, R. Soloveitchik believed that philosophy is part of religious experience. He complains that his students are religiously immature.[81] Why? Because they are lacking in religious experience. Experience and philosophy go hand in hand in the Rav's thought. Philosophy is a means of deepening one's understanding of what one is doing as a believer, as an observer of commandments, and as one immersed in Torah study, whether as teacher or disciple. Because R. Soloveitchik's emphasis in doing philosophy was phenomenological, therefore if one studies philosophy (whether Jewish or general), one's religious experience and sensitivity to religion's inner core are heightened. The Rav always held that Judaism has two components — intellectual and experiential. Philosophy was not only — and in some sense not even primarily — part of the intellectual component; it was also part of the experiential one.

Fourth, it is important not only to have experience, but to communicate it to secular people in language that they understand. "Since majestic man is in need of a transcendental experience in order to strengthen his cultural edifice, it is the duty of the Man of Faith to provide him with some component parts of this experience."[82] The Rav may have very well seen that, too, as part of his mandate when he took on the substantial commitment to translate "faith" into the cultural vernacular.[83] If nothing else, the act of translation will aid the translator in the act of self-understanding.

A fifth answer relates to an intriguing tendency in R. Soloveitchik's writing. He often refers to his understanding of Jewish ideas as what "the Halakhah" says. R. Soloveitchik was convinced that "out of the sources of Halakhah a new world view awaits formulation" (*Halakhic Mind*, 102), and that the Halakhah is the only authentic source of Jewish philosophy.[84] If we take this idea with the literalness with which R. Soloveitchik seems to intend it, we are forced to conclude that, however far afield R. Soloveitchik's discussion may roam, however much Western science, philosophy and literature may inform and shape his discussion, he always seeks to return to the Halakhah as the ultimate source of his ideas.

Now no doubt the supposition that the philosophical content of R. Soloveitchik's writing arises organically and naturally from "the Halakhah" is too simple. A more plausible representation is that certain ideas are shown by R. Soloveitchik to *cohere* with "the Halakhah" — and "cohere with" is hardly the same as "derive from." Still, it is altogether possible that in R. Soloveitchik's self-perception, the magnificent philosophical castles that he built are *not* best characterized as "second-order reflections on religious life." They are instead first-order religious activities: *divrei Torah*, efforts at halakhic interpretation — which I think really means the interpretation of the entire Jewish tradition, including Bible, law, philosophy, mysticism, and so forth. Any tools needed for halakhic interpretation (especially in this expanded sense) would be automatically legitimate.

Twersky captures this line of thought:

> One utilizes contemporary philosophical terminology and phenomenology...but one's goal is the same as that of the great thinkers of previous generations: to penetrate to the inner core of Torah, to expound its essential beliefs,... to understand the dynamics of Torah *she-be-al peh* and hence to deepen one's comprehension and intensify one's experience. This endeavor is not extraneous to Torah, not independent of halacha, but is an integral, indispensable part of it.[85]

In other words: R. Soloveitchik was unapologetic because he thought that *madda* sources are ways of understanding and elucidating what lies in Torah itself. They are tools — not only for, say, understanding the laws of sowing diverse seeds (as he states in *Halakhic Man*[86]), but for formulating a worldview. So, if Martin Buber's philosophy of "I and Thou" would create a framework within which the Rav could explicate the notion of community, then he applied it. If in *Halakhic Man* he credited some of his discussions about *teshuvah* (repentance) and time to the philosopher Max Scheler, it is because he thought Max Scheler could help him understand *gemarot* and Maimonides.[87] If in his *teshuvah* lectures he quoted William James, it was because he felt that the sublime experience of sensing God's presence, the "reality of the unseen" in James's words, was a critical element missing in the religious experience of contemporary Orthodoxy.[88] There is nothing to say beyond that — study of general culture requires no (further) justification because it provides a deeper grasp of Judaism.[89]

To appreciate the reasoning here, try the following experiment. Take an essay by R. Soloveitchik. Expunge all of the places where is drawing upon secular studies. Slice out mercilessly the parts that reflect Scheler, Emil Brunner, Søren Kierkegaard, Buber, Karl Barth, Hermann Cohen — the whole lot of them. Then see what is left. No notion of dialectic, no comparison between halakhic man and scientific man, no "I-Thou" vs. "I-It," no sense of "the absurd," no relation between *teshuvah* and time. Compare this expunged version to the original. Which is better, more powerful, more incisive? Would R. Soloveitchik have stood out to the same degree as a major thinker were he to have buried these ideas? The questions are of course rhetorical. The humanities enhance Jewish philosophical thinking, and this is justification enough. Further — and admittedly this is my own speculative construction of an argument he might have endorsed — it is a very short step from saying that secular studies have value to him because they enhance his understanding of the Torah's worldview, to saying that they have value in themselves. For truth and insight are good things to have, things God would want people to own no matter what their religious orientation. One might even say: It is because they have independent value that they can be of value to the interpretation of Jewish tradition.[90]

It should be evident, then, that R. Soloveitchik's works supply enough themes to help us appreciate the value of humanities in his worldview. Taking those together with rationales we have seen for scientific labors, we have, I think, a good sense of why R. Soloveitchik valued the modern world.

NOTES

I am indebted to Shalom Carmy, Avi Sagi, and Moshe Sokol for comments on an earlier version of this essay.

[1]   Among major works I include "*Ish ha-Halakhah*," "*U-Bikkashtem mi-Sham*," *The Halakhic Mind*, "Confrontation" and *Lonely Man of Faith*. Relevant "public lectures and popular essays" include, for example, "*Mah Dodekh mi-Dod*," in *Divrei Hagut ve-Ha'arakhah* (Jerusalem, 1982), 57-97; "Majesty and Humility," *Tradition* 17, 2 (Spring 1978): 25-37; "Prayer as Dialogue," as adapted by Abraham R. Besdin in *Reflections of The Rav* (Jerusalem, 1979), 71-88. Although other Orthodox rabbinic figures of recent times (for example, R. Samson Raphael Hirsch, R. Moshe Amiel and R. Yitzchak Yaakov Reines) drew upon analogies to science to clarify either the nature of *mitzvot* or the activity of halakhists, none treated the subject with the erudition, sophistication and richness of application that R. Soloveitchik's work exhibits. See Eliezer Schweid, *Bein Ortodoksiah le-Humanizm* (Jerusalem, 1978), 38-42; Lawrence Kaplan, "Rabbi Joseph Soloveitchik's Philosophy of Halakhah," *Jewish Law Annual* 8 (1988): 189-91.

Page references to the works of R. Soloveitchik will be given as follows. In the case of *Ish ha-Halakhah*, which was originally published in *Talpiot* 1 (1944):

651-735, references will be to Lawrence Kaplan's translation, *Halakhic Man* (Philadelphia, 1983). References to *"U-Bikkashtem mi-Sham"* will be to Naomi Goldblum's translation, *And From There You Shall Seek* (New York, 2009). For *The Lonely Man of Faith,* which was originally published in *Tradition 7, 2* (Summer, 1965): 5-67, references will be to the Doubleday edition (New York, 1992). *The Halakhic Mind* has been printed only once (New York, 1986). Publishing information for other works will be given ad loc. I refer to *Ísh ha-Halakhah* by its English name and *U-Bikkashtem mi-Sham* by its Hebrew name because the former but not the latter is most widely known by the English title.

2   See especially "Lonely Man of Faith," 55-57; also *"U-Bikkashtem mi-Sham," passim.*

3   Typically, advocates of Torah u-Madda assign *religious* value to the study of *madda.* An adherent of Torah u-Madda, however, might acknowledge multiple sources of value and assign *non-religious* value to study of general wisdom. In this approach, the crucial obligation of the religious person is not to shun the secular but rather not to blur boundaries, that is, to understand what is religious and what is not. Leibowitz can I think be read this way. Mainstream Torah u-Madda, however, assigns *religious* worth to *madda,* and by asking how science functions in halakhic life I am asking what religious value it has, if any, in a certain form of religious life.

4   Remarkably, some have questioned — particularly after his passing in 1993 — whether R. Soloveitchik had a positive attitude towards general studies. I am not idiosyncratic in thinking that such questioning comes from those who themselves oppose studying *madda* and are fashioning their master in their own image. R. Soloveitchik's grandson, R. Mosheh Lichtenstein, trenchantly remarked that the question about the Rav's attitude to secular studies could easily be settled by putting his library on display. R. Soloveitchik's speeches also include some very strong statements about the importance of secular culture generally. For example, in an address delivered to parents of the Maimonides School in Boston in 1971 (a school he founded in the late 1930s), and published by the school in a compilation called "Legacy," he stated,

> What do we at the Maimonides school believe?...We believe that the Jewish child is capable of carrying a double load, the universal secular and the specific Judaic. We believe...that the child is able to study and comprehend two systems of knowledge and to excel in both. Some people deny it.
> The Jewish child, they say, has to choose between being a literate Jew and a literate human being. Literacy in both realms [they say] is an absurdity. We reject this philosophy of doom. We say the Jewish child is teachable and educable in both fields and at the same time. Not only literacy, but even scholarship in both is attainable.

It is crucial to note, however, that we have only an assertion that Torah u-Madda (or synthesis) is doable — not an explanation of why the doable should be done. Again, in a discourse delivered for Yeshiva University Rabbinic Alumni on February 19, 1955, R. Soloveitchik invokes the image of Elkanah, the father of the prophet Samuel, who came from Ramatayim Tzofim — two peaks facing each other, separated by an abyss. The Rav suggests that these two *ramot,* or peaks, represent Torah and general knowledge. Many have refused to build a bridge between these two peaks, lest they plummet into the abyss below. Yet efforts should continue. "We must build both — we have no other *etzah*...no other solution." Judaism must reach the broad sectors of American Jewry. Refusal to live on both peaks will turn us into a sect and lock us into "*dalet amot* of *batlanus*" — four ells of irrelevancy. Apart from appealing to the damage of sectarianism, though, the Ramatayim Tzofim lecture does not explain *why* it is so important to be on both peaks. In short, however clear the *whether* is, the *why* is so far murky. It is worth asking this question, and I hope this essay will shed light on it. (I thank Dr. Arnold Lustiger and Rabbi Dr. Aharon Rakeffet-Rothkoff for elucidating the contents of the Yiddish tape. A Hebrew version of the 1955 *shiur* appears in the compilation *Ha-Adam ve-Olamo* [Jerusalem, 1978], 73-83.)

5   See especially *Halakhic Man*, 1; 146, n. 18; 137.

6   Based on *Guide of the Perplexed* I:54, III:54. On negative attributes, see I: 50-60, esp. I:58.

7   R. Soloveitchik distinguishes between "the process of cognition" and "the goal and final aim" (12). The "process" is thoroughly focused on the affirmative; its "goal" is negation. The commandments of love and fear of God refer specifically to affirmative knowledge, he explains.

8   For an assessment of R. Soloveitchik's discussion, see Zev Harvey, "*He'arot al ha-Rav Soloveitchik ve-ha-Pilosofyah ha-Rambamit*," in *Emunah bi-Zemannim Mishtannim: Al Mishnato Shel ha-Rav Y.D. Soloveitchik*, ed. Avi Sagi (Jerusalem, 1996), 95-107. The "attributes of action" that scientific study yields are summarized by moral terms such as "merciful" and "compassionate" and so on, and Maimonides does not suggest that these are the subjects of negative theology (see *The Guide of the Perplexed* I:58).

9   There are other similarities. For example, both Halakhah and science are also idealized — neither the halakhist nor the scientist is perturbed if his constructs do not find instantiation in the empirical world (*Halakhic Man*, 24-25).

10   Elsewhere, ("*Mah Dodekh mi-Dod*," 75ff.) R. Soloveitchik retains the analogy between the halakhist and the scientist but alters one of its terms. The activity of the halakhist is now characterized as the imposition of freely created abstract categories on halakhic *texts*, rather than on the empirical world. This shift of course affects the claim of idealization discussed in the previous note, since the halakhist's construction must match the data of text. See Kaplan, "Philosophy of Halakhah."

11   See for example Schweid, 38-42; David Singer and Moshe Sokol, "Joseph Soloveitchik: Lonely Man of Faith," *Modern Judaism* 2 (1982): 232-39. As evidence that R. Soloveitchik was responding to attacks on halakhic men, see the final lines of *Halakhic Man*; cf. *And From There You Shall Seek*, 107-110, where R. Soloveitchik argues that "unlimited innovation" in Halakhah refutes those who claim that "Halakhah has become fossilized" (108). According to Rav Yosef Dov, were it not for R. Hayyim Soloveitchik, who instituted "a complete revolution in halakhic thinking and cognition," then "Torah would have been forgotten from Israel and we would be unable to spread it at this time" ("*Mah Dodekh mi-Dod*," 70-71). This remark suggests a competition for souls between R. Hayyim Soloveitchik and the *maskilim* (followers of the Jewish enlightenment). Norman Solomon notes that the very word "*hakirah*" used to describe the analytical distinctions of Brisk was also used by the *maskilim* to

describe their own explorations into secular disciplines. See his *The Analytic Movement: Hayyim Soloveitchik and His Circle* (Atlanta, 1993), 119-20. Also note R. Isser Yehudah Unterman, "Torah Mehazzeret al Akhsanyah Shelah," *Sefer ha-Yovel le-Rav Shimon Shkop* (Vilna, 1937), 12-20. Also see "The First Jewish Grandfather," in *Man of Faith in the Modern World: Reflections of the Rav, Vol. 2*, adapted by Abraham R. Besdin (Hoboken, NJ, 1989), 22-23. Some have noted that *Ish ha-Halakhah* appeared at the very time that the world of the European yeshivah was being destroyed in the Holocaust. This adds poignancy for the reader, though it is difficult to know how much the Holocaust, which is to be sure alluded to, stimulated R. Soloveitchik to write it.

12   Schweid, 37. My formulation in this paragraph emphasizes the talmudist of the study hall rather than the halakhic decisor. On this distinction as it pertains to interpreting *Halakhic Man*, see Avi Sagi, "R. Soloveitchik and Prof. Yeshayahu Leibowitz as Theoreticians of the Halakhah" [Hebrew], *Da'at* 29 (1992): 131-48.

13   The term "halakhic hero" is featured in chapter 2 of David Hartman, *Love and Terror in the God Encounter: The Theological Legacy of Rabbi Joseph B. Soloveitchik* (Woodstock, VT, 2001).

14   Some passages in the essay imply that anything other than the study of Talmud is objectionable, at least in certain contexts. See, for example, the critique of recitation of Psalms or of liturgical poems (*piyyutim*) (*Halakhic Man*, 87, cf. 58).

15   Halakhic man feels antagonism toward the *pure* scientist owing to the latter's preoccupation with a domain that contains no dimension of transcendence. If *homo religiosus* goes too far in seeking to escape this world and comes in for more criticism than does cognitive man, both are nonetheless deficient.

16   What is unusual here, and apparently inaccurate, is the reference to mathematics. As quoted by R. Barukh of Shklov (*Sefer Uklidus* [The Hague, 1780], introduction), the Gaon of Vilna is alleged to have spoken of "other wisdoms," not mathematics alone. R. Soloveitchik's formulation in terms of mathematics serves his own purposes very well, as we shall see momentarily.

17   See *Hilkhot Yesodei ha-Torah* 1:6, 2:2. R. Soloveitchik softened the notion that knowledge of God requires scientific knowledge when he interpreted *Hilkhot Yesodei ha-Torah* 1:1 and 1:5. He maintains that for Maimonides, "This knowledge is not based on logical inference, but is, rather, immediate" (*And From There You Shall Seek*, 158, n. 4). See also *Lonely Man of Faith*, 51-52, n. 2. For yet another treatment of Maimonides' ostensible appeal to proofs, see *Soloveitchik on Repentance: The Thoughts and Oral Discourses of Rabbi Joseph B. Soloveitchik*, ed. Pinchas H. Peli (New York, 1984), 129-34. Whether R. Soloveitchik adequately explains why Maimonides constructs philosophical proofs is debatable, given the notion that knowledge of God is immediate. It seems that scientific knowledge contributes to knowledge of God for Maimonides, even if non-scientific, intuitive knowledge does so as well. Yet, what is that contribution?

18   The treatment of repentance faces far fewer problems and is more convincing than R. Soloveitchik's treatment in these pages of Maimonides on providence and prophecy. Cf. *Guide of the Perplexed* II: 32-40 and III: 17-23, 51.

19   There are several problems with R. Soloveitchik's reading of Maimonides: (1) R. Soloveitchik, not Maimonides, emphasizes creativity as the critical

ingredient of repentance, providence and prophecy. Indeed, as Harvey points out, imagination, for Maimonides, is the nemesis of intellect, and imagination would seem to be free, while grasp of a demonstration would appear to be coercive. (2) Within Maimonides' theory, we can explain in a natural manner how the protection of the individual is "consequent upon the intellect," and upon knowledge of science and philosophy in particular. The scientifically informed individual knows how to best protect himself from the workings of nature. The philosophically educated individual will, like Job, come to deal with material adversities by devaluing material goods and evils. Furthermore, the individual who concentrates upon philosophical and scientific knowledge will achieve a partial conjunction with the Active Intellect. R. Soloveitchik's emphasis on providence as creativity does not explain how the person who enjoys providence is protected. This may be precisely why R. Soloveitchik refers to providence as "a concrete commandment, an obligation incumbent upon man" (*Halakhic Man*, 128) — as a norm rather than (merely) a descriptive category. (3) It is possible that, according to Maimonides, intellectual perfection leads to loss of individuality. R. Soloveitchik views the intellectual process as leading to individuality. (4) If providence is attained by exercising creativity, why cannot a scientist attain providence according to R. Soloveitchik? It is true that R. Soloveitchik imposes ethical and religious requirements too, but why are these imposed?

20   I must bracket here one contradiction in *Halakhic Man*. R. Soloveitchik implies that halakhic man is not exemplified in reality, and yet he singles out actual people with the implication that they are halakhic men.

21   In the interests of balance and accuracy, we must note a brief section that, contrary to the essay's general thrust, introduces the substantive study of science into halakhic man's existence. R. Soloveitchik explains that study is necessary for practice (63). So, for example, halakhic man must study botany so that he can determine laws pertaining to agriculture. Here the halakhist's "ontological" inquiry is conducted only for the purpose of a normative inquiry. R. Soloveitchik then suggests another connection between the ontological and the normative. The verse, "The heavens declare the glory of God, and the firmament reciteth His handiwork" (Psalms 19:2) is glossed by him as follows: "What is the tale of the heavens, if not the proclamation of the norm?" (64). How does nature entail the norm? R. Soloveitchik responds by invoking the principle of "*imitatio Dei.*" This principle, R. Soloveitchik explains, is to be understood along the lines sketched by Maimonides in *Guide* III:54: "Cognition of the attributes of action is the source of ethical life. In order to implement the ethical ideal, we must fix upon the whole of being and cognize it" (64). From the passage it seems that R. Soloveitchik will "allow" halakhic man to study reality *if*, but *only if*, this ontological inquiry is directed toward a normative end.

At first glance the cited passage forces us to revise our earlier portrait, for it indicates that science plays a substantive role in religious life. However, the passage is so problematic that one can reasonably regard it as a short-lived departure from the essay's main theses. If God has *revealed* the thirteen divine attributes, why would one have to study the cosmos to learn them? For Maimonides, at least, one's study of the sciences has inherent value because it produces knowledge of what the attributes are. But in the case of R. Soloveitchik the knowledge can come through study of revelation. In addition, the thesis that the norm is derived from study of the cosmos contradicts R. Soloveitchik's earlier insistence that the categories wielded by halakhic man are *a priori* and that the real is subjugated to this ideal. Because of these difficulties, I am inclined not to alter my general understanding of the place of science in the life of halakhic man on the basis of a single citation. R. Soloveitchik himself abruptly drops the whole matter!

I have taken most of the points in this note from Aviezer Ravitzky, "Rabbi J. B. Soloveitchik on Human Knowledge: Between Maimonidean and neo-Kantian Philosophy," *Modern Judaism* 6, 2 (1986): 157-88.

22   The impression that science is separated from religion is reinforced by R. Soloveitchik's closing attack on medieval Jewish philosophy. He claims that the medieval writings reflect non-Jewish rather than Jewish concepts. Only the sources of Halakhah will provide an authentic Jewish worldview.

My remarks about *The Halakhic Mind* do not negate R. Jonathan Sacks' suggestion that *The Halakhic Mind* is a prologue to *Halakhic Man* and "*U-Bikkashtem mi-Sham.*" *Halakhic Mind* paves the way to a reconstruction of the halakhic personality in which the other works engage, a reconstruction that emerges "out of the sources of Halakhah," as the end of *The Halakhic Mind* insists. See Sacks, "Rabbi J. B. Soloveitchik's Early Epistemology: A Review of *The Halakhic Mind*," *Tradition* 23, 3 (Spring 1988): 75-87.

23   To be sure, the passage I cited from p. 84 shows how science can inspire religious enthusiasm and wonder. But, as already noted, R. Soloveitchik does not say that it inspires enthusiasm in halakhic man or that halakhic man should seek out such moments of enthusiasm and wonder.

24   See R. Jonathan Sacks, "Rabbi J. B. Soloveitchik's Early Epistemology: A Review of *The Halakhic Mind*," *Tradition* 23, 3 (Spring 1988): 86, n. 10.

25   See the references to the "man of God" in the closing sections of *Halakhic Man*. *Halakhic Man*, *The Halakhic Mind*, and "*U-Bikkashtem mi-Sham*" appear to be part of a single intellectual program, but the precise relationships are unclear. For fuller discussion, see my and Reuven Ziegler's introduction to *And From There You Shall Seek*, xi-xii, xxxv-xxxvii. I thank Shalom Carmy for some pertinent observations.

26   See, for example, 24, 135-136, 162 n. 10, 164 n. 10, 169-72 n. 11.

27   This attempt to describe a religious odyssey is not a description of how actual people arrive at God. A better way to regard the "odyssey," I think, is as a rationale for revelational religion.

28   The natural consciousness also generates immorality (162-63) and faces other problems, but I focus here on the cognitive limitations of science and study of nature as a means for encountering God.

29   The accounts of halakhic cognition in "*U-Bikkashtem mi-Sham*" and *Halakhic Man* are quite similar, except that in "*U-Bikkashtem mi-Sham*" R. Soloveitchik relates it to the individual's quest for *devekut*. The portrait of halakhic cognition that concludes "*U-Bikkashtem mi-Sham*" bears a powerful resemblance to the concluding sections of *Halakhic Man*. R. Soloveitchik characterizes that cognition as he had characterized prophecy in *Halakhic Man*: as a union of the knower with the object of knowledge. He no longer applies this description to prophecy, perhaps because in *Halakhic Man* he had stressed that prophecy

cannot determine Halakhah, as Halakhah is decided by the intellect. His seeming equation of prophecy with halakhic and intellectual activity at the end of *Halakhic Man* contradicts this principle, and R. Soloveitchik may have been striving to eliminate the inconsistency when he altered his concept of a prophet. (My former student Dr. Aviva Krauss pointed out that the portrayal of the prophet in *Halakhic Man* is not fully consistent.)

30   R. Soloveitchik's posture toward Maimonides in halakhic contexts differs from his posture toward Maimonides in philosophical contexts. In the realm of Halakhah, Rav Yosef Dov, like his grandfather and father before him, always heroically attempted to question, clarify, reconstruct — and ultimately vindicate — Maimonides. (See the warm vignette in *And From There You Shall Seek*, 143-46.) R. Soloveitchik certainly perceived himself as Maimonides' faithful interpreter and as his vigorous defender.

In the realm of philosophy, R. Soloveitchik's relationship with Maimonides is more complex and tensile. The gap between Maimonides and R. Soloveitchik is often as wide as that between medieval Aristotelianism and modern neo-Kantianism, or that between medieval rationalism and modern existentialism. He sometimes criticizes and rejects Maimonides, as in the final section of *The Halakhic Mind*. Still, citations from Maimonides lace both *Halakhic Man* and "*U-Bikkashtem mi-Sham*," and some of the passages "defend" Maimonides (for example, "*U-Bikkashtem mi-Sham*," n. 2). At times he seems to uncritically equate Maimonides' teachings with those of "Judaism" (or, as R. Soloveitchik often prefers to call Judaism, "the Halakhah").

31   Ravitzky, "Rabbi J. B. Soloveitchik on Human Knowledge."

32   *Hilkhot Yesodei ha-Torah* 2:2, in Mishneh Torah, trans. Moses Hyamson (New York, 1981).

33   Maimonides also indicates that attempts to "know His governance of them in whatever way it is possible" can lead to love of God (*Guide of the Perplexed*, trans. Shlomo Pines [Chicago and London, 1963], III:51, p. 620). I believe that this progression too involves recognition of teleology. For an account of Maimonides that places teleology at the center of Maimonides' view of religious attitudes, see Jerome Gellman, "Radical Responsibility in Maimonides' Thought," *The Thought of Moses Maimonides*, ed. I. Robinson, L. Kaplan, and J. Bauer (Lewiston, NY, 1991), 249-65.

34   Perhaps R. Soloveitchik's use of the phrase "Everything is a wondrous miracle" (21) is meant to connote exactly this, that any existence of any character is wondrous. See also p. 129: "If there is a world, if anything at all is real...then there is a God" (12). Also see pp. 157-58, n. 3 which deals with the demolition of the cosmological proofs and theological proofs after Newton and Galileo.

35   Hermann Cohen had ignored this link between the natural order and the ethical norm when he interpreted Maimonides' concept of *imitatio Dei*, this in accord with Cohen's wish to keep a rigid separation between ethics and nature.

36   *Halakhic Man*, 64; "*U-Bikkashtem mi-Sham*," 13-14; *Lonely Man of Faith*, 21-22, 29, 47-49, 81-84.

37   Cf. *Soloveitchik On Repentance*, 129-134, 180-182. In these sections R. Soloveitchik distinguishes between a scientific approach to natural phenomena and an immediate, extra-scientific experience of nature.

Ravitzky suggests a different approach to the matter of teleology. He explains that R. Soloveitchik indeed links love of God and *imitatio Dei* to teleology, but not to the teleology of individual laws of nature and natural objects. Instead, the linkage is to the teleology of the cosmos as a whole. The contrast with Maimonides is rather striking. Maimonides refused to assign a purpose to the cosmos as a whole (*Guide* III:13), but specified the teleology of individual laws of nature and in parts of natural objects. Also, whereas Maimonides develops a parallel between the teleology of nature and the teleology of the Torah's laws (*Guide* III:25-26), R. Soloveitchik replaces it with a parallel between the very existence of nature and the very existence of Torah. For Maimonides, the criterion of whether a law is divine is the teleology of its specific laws — their ability to promote both true opinion and social order (*Guide* II:39-40, III:25-29). R. Soloveitchik, in contrast, fights fiercely against any attempt to uncover the telos of any given *mitzvah*. He allows only (a) *ta'amei ha-mitzvot* (reasons for the commandments) in the sense of specifying general principles or particular laws from which a particular law may be deduced, or (b) articulations of subjective human response and reflection upon *mitzvot*. (See "May We Interpret *Hukkim*?" *Man of Faith in the Modern World*, 91-99.) Maimonides' standard for divinity — teleology (see *Guide* III:39-40) — would be the last one R. Soloveitchik would consider! But, even according to Ravitzky, our earlier question returns in a new formulation: if teleology will be located in the very existence of the cosmos, why would science be needed to find that teleology? A bit of metaphysical reflection will suffice instead.

38   One can also argue that recognizing teleology in science is not tantamount to fathoming God's purposes. But I leave this complication aside.

39   This reflection may exaggerate the extent of teleology in Maimonides' thought. On this subject, see Shlomo Pines, "Translator's Introduction," in *Guide of the Perplexed*, lxx, lxxi, n. 29; Eliezer Goldman, "*Al Takhlit ha-Metzi'ut be-Moreh Nevukhim*," in *Sefer Yeshayahu Leibowitz*, ed. Asa Kasher and Yaakov Levinger (Tel Aviv, 1977), 164-91. In this context I should note that *hesed* as defined by Maimonides in *Guide* III:53 would apply to a universe of any character. In addition, R. Soloveitchik at times indicates that even a mechanistic science can serve as the basis for a transcendental experience (136-37, 155). I have focused in this section on what I think are the dominant tendencies in each thinker.

40   On R. Soloveitchik's relationship to idealism, see Ravitzky, esp. sections II-IV. Ravitzky argues convincingly that R. Soloveitchik's recognition of a non-rational element in existence points to a realist position. See *Halakhic Man*, 144 n. 10 and 146 n. 18. See also Reinier Munk, "Soloveitchik on Cohen," in *Torah and Wisdom, Kabbalah and Halakhah: Essays in Honor of Arthur Hyman*, ed. Ruth Link-Salinger (New York, 1992), 147-65.

41   Ravitzky, 169-70.

42   Cf. *Reflections of The Rav*, 71-72, 162. As Ravitzky notes, the passages reflect the influence of Solomon Maimon, but R. Soloveitchik was not an idealist, whereas Maimon was.

43   Cf. Ravitzky, 184, n. 53.

44   Perhaps one will reply that all scientific cognition is really cognition that has the human mind as its object, as idealism would have it, and that the knowledge

needed to apply halakhic concepts is knowledge of the mind's conceptions. If that is R. Soloveitchik's intention, it is not made clear.

45 Apparently, even if norms can be derived from nature (see 131-33), a human being who cognizes only the cosmos does not fully share in the divine activity and does not achieve *devekut*, even if he seeks to derive norms from that knowledge. Only the halakhist, who merges with God's will, can achieve *devekut*.

46 Ravitzky, 171.

47 See Sagi, 133-34, which is based on *Halakhic Man*, 153, n. 80.

48 A similar challenge confronts the idealist interpreter of science. Idealists handle the difficulty by differentiating between the finite and infinite intellect. In infinite cognition nothing is external to the knower. In finite cognition we project the existence of a thing-in-itself (see Ravitzky 162-63). It is not clear if such a strategy will work easily in the case of Halakhah.

49 See also the end of *Guide* I:1.

50 Ravitzky suggests an alternative account of how R. Soloveitchik relates to *Guide* I:68 (Ravitzky, 161-62). Maimonides intends only a formal parallel between human and divine cognition, but R. Soloveitchik extends Maimonides' assertion of a formal parallel to a material one. The resulting divergence between R. Soloveitchik and Maimonides makes R. Soloveitchik's use of Maimonides problematic.

51 Gerald Blidstein, "On the Jewish People in the Writings of Rabbi Joseph B. Soloveitchik," *Tradition* 24, 3 (Spring 1989): 24.

52 Indeed, R. Soloveitchik blurs the very distinction I am making. (See his argument in the note on 87-90.) From the fact that Halakhah encourages medical treatment and the seeking of medical care, R. Soloveitchik *deduces* that according to "the Halakhah, God wants man to fight evil bravely and to mobilize all his intellectual and technological ingenuity in order to defeat it." R. Soloveitchik seems correct to view technology and research as an extension of the Halakhah's attitude toward medical care. My point is that rabbinic authorities not friendly to modernity might well resist the extension by means of a technical distinction.

53 See his examples of "self-defeat" in "Majesty and Humility," 34-37 and in "Catharsis," *Tradition* 17, 2 (Spring 1978): 38-54, esp. 44ff.

54 Cf. *The Rav Speaks: Five Addresses on Israel, History, and the Jewish People* (New York: Toras HoRav Foundation and Judaica Press, 2002), 69-70.

55 *Lonely Man of Faith*, 12-14. See also "Imitating God," in *Reflections of The Rav*, 26-27 and "Mt. Sinai — Their Finest Hour," 97; "*Keneset Yisrael be-Sod ha-Yetzirah ve-ha-Tikkunim*," in *Yemei Zikkaron*, trans. Moshe Kroneh (Jerusalem, 1986), 87-88: "It is the task of man to improve his environmental conditions."

56 Yonah Ben-Sasson, "*Mishnat he-Hagut shel ha-Reayah Kuk ve-ha RYD Solo-veitchik*," *Be-Oro*, ed. Chaim Hamiel (Jerusalem, 1986), 421. R. Soloveitchik refers to pragmatism in note 4 of *Halakhic Man*, but presumably it took time for him to abandon the European conception of science and embrace the American conception.

57   See for example, "And Joseph Dreamt a Dream," in *The Rav Speaks*, 25-33; and *Reflections of The Rav*, 26.

58   See Jonathan Sacks, "Alienation and Faith," *Tradition* 13, 4 and 14, 1 (Spring-Summer 1973): 152-53: "If we as Jews adopt it [the instrumentalist view], it becomes clear that the use of scientific hypotheses does not represent the adoption of any alternative world view... Only under an essentialist construction of the scientist's search for the truth could we maintain the semblance of an incompatibility between the task of creation and the work of redemption." A contrary argument would be that the success of science in practical affairs is best explained by an essentialist conception.

A non-instrumentalist, neo-Kantian conception of science also makes science less threatening to religious belief than a view that takes science to penetrate reality as it is. But insofar as a religious person advocates studying science because of its cognitive value, i.e. because it leads to knowledge of the cosmos, the capacity of science to generate false conceptions presents a powerful problem. By contrast, insofar as one advocates studying science because of its instrumental value, cognitive conflicts are a less serious problem.

59   But cf. "The World Is Not Forsaken," *Reflections of The Rav*, 34; "The Symbolism of Blue and White," in *Man of Faith in the Modern World*, 30-31.

60   Cf. the more qualified passage in *R. Soloveitchik Speaks*, 78.

61   See the translation of *Kol Dodi Dofek* by Lawrence Kaplan: *Fate and Destiny* (Hoboken, NJ, 2000), 57-60. The distinction between camp and congregation is paralleled by several other distinctions in *Kol Dodi Dofek*.

62   Note also "As A Bridegroom With His Bride," *Man of Faith in the Modern World*, 56-65, p. 62.

63   "A Stranger and A Resident," in *Reflections of the Rav*, 169-77. See also "Confrontation."

64   Of course there is an asymmetry here — R. Soloveitchik wants each individual, not only humanity as a whole, to exemplify Adam the second.

65   "Majesty and Humility," 33-34. Cf. *The Lonely Man of Faith* (New York, 1992), 95-96. Let me frame the rationale for scientific study in a more informal way. The Jew has a dual role, expressed by Abraham: *ger* and *toshav* — a stranger and yet a citizen. (See Gen. 23:4.) As human beings, as part of the human community, as *toshavim* or citizens, Jews face certain problems in common with everyone else — disease, poverty, social disorder. These problems confront people regardless of religious or ethnic identity; they arise not because of the Jew's identity as a Jew, but because of his or her identity as human. Adam the First is not a Jew, and he has no religion yet. He belongs only to the human community. But his work of harnessing nature to try to satisfy human needs and solve everyday problems of living is for the Rav a divinely sanctioned endeavor (whatever Adam the First's motives). Here is an elegant paraphrase of R. Soloveitchik's view by Shubert Spero:

> Since man is a moral agent, has been given responsibility to help others, to conserve value, to preserve life, to eradicate evil, he is morally obliged to seek the power and the knowledge, the means and instrumentation to achieve all this. If new sources of energy can eradicate poverty, if knowledge

of genetic engineering promises to prevent certain diseases, then man is obligated to seek out this knowledge. As G-d is creative, so man is creative. ("Towards a Philosophy of Modern Orthodoxy," *Modern Judaism* 6 [1986]: 83). And it is not simply the physical sciences that enable people to live with dignity, but also economics, political science and social science generally. We are obligated to better this world by marshalling all the secular resources at our disposal. The value of secular culture in these areas is not a *hora'at sha'ah*, a temporary measure introduced because of a special exigency. It is built into the very nature of the world, a place that is full of suffering, full of evil, full of need. Technology, economics, political science and social science are not accommodations to the times. They are warriors in a battle that Halakhah mandates and are part and parcel of the human condition since Creation. The mandate is in the Bible itself: "*ve-khivshuha*, conquer it [the earth]" (Gen. 1:28). For uses of the *ger ve-toshav* imagery, see *Reflections of the Rav: Lessons in Jewish Thought adapted from Lectures of Rabbi Joseph B. Soloveitchik by Abraham R. Besdin"* (Jerusalem, 1979), 169-77; *The Rav Speaks: Five Addresses on Israel, History, and the Jewish People* (New York, 2002), 73-80. "Confrontation," *Tradition* 6, 2 (Spring-Summer 1964): 5-29, develops the same theme using the image of the patriarch Jacob.

66 See Bernard Septimus, "Biblical Religion and Political Rationality in Simone Luzzatto, Maimonides and Spinoza," in *Jewish Thought in the Seventeenth Century*, ed. Isadore Twersky and Bernard Septimus (Cambridge, MA, 1987), 399-434; Gellman, "Radical Responsibility in Maimonides' Thought;" and my "Practical Endeavor and the Torah u-Madda Debate," *The Torah u-Madda Journal* 3 (1991-1992): 98-149. See also this volume, pp. 190-96.

67 See *Commentary on the Mishnah, Pesahim* 4:9.

68 For this account of Maimonides' pragmatism, see Gellman and Septimus. See also "Divine Intervention and Religious Sensibilities," in this volume.

69 R. Soloveitchik also raises arguments that run in a different direction: from fact to norm. "Man reaching for the distant stars is acting in harmony with his nature which was created, willed and directed by his Maker" (20). Adam the first is part of our nature; therefore we ought to actualize that nature.

70 See *Halakhic Man*, 45-46, and then the association of technology with the masses in *"U-Bikkashtem mi-Sham"*: "The masses see nothing but its technological conquests. The essence of creation in all its purity is hidden from the many" (57). My analogy is not perfect. The masses are not scientists, but the applications of science are democratic. In the case of Halakhah, democracy means that all may and should study and practice Halakhah.

71 Singer and Sokol, 157, suggest that the talmudist lacks adequate emotion to serve as the focal type in the covenantal community of Adam the second.

72 Cf., however, *Reflections of The Rav*, 26-27, where R. Soloveitchik demands both material and spiritual creativity. My remarks on *Lonely Man of Faith* need not mean that R. Soloveitchik had abandoned his earlier view that Halakhah is a means to achieve these ends of creativity, *imitatio Dei*, elevation above the brute, and democratization. His audience in the 1960s was more concerned with the subject of faith in an age of scientific advance than with the nature of Halakhah. Hence, R. Soloveitchik may have drawn on motifs he had already

developed in order to treat this new topic. (Here, though, it is good to recall that *"U-Bikkashtem mi-Sham"* was published later than *Lonely Man of Faith*, suggesting that he retained the latter's motifs.)

73   See the concluding sections of *Halakhic Man*.

74   Both the beginning of *Lonely Man of Faith* (9) and the end of *Halakhic Man* (137) highlight the subjectivity of the ideas contained in the works. It is within the spirit of those remarks for R. Soloveitchik himself to view matters in different ways at different times.

75   The term "secular disciplines" is a misnomer but is used here as a concession to popular usage; "general wisdom" is a better term. Clearly Barth and Kierkegaard were not secular!

76   Blidstein, "On the Jewish People...," 24. See, however, note 90 below.

77   Yitzhak Twersky, "The Rov," *Tradition* 30, 4 (Summer 1996): 29. Note again that although *"U-Bikkashtem mi-Sham"* provides a place for the full range of cultural endeavors during the early stages of the religious odyssey, they drop out in his depictions of higher stages.

78   Blidstein, "On the Jewish People...," 24.

79   See "Majesty and Humility," 27-31.

80   The existence of the universal religious personality was impressed upon me by Yehuda Seif in his senior thesis at Columbia University.

81   Aaron Rakeffet-Rothkoff, *The Rav: The World of Rabbi Joseph B. Soloveitchik* (Jersey City, NJ: Ktav, 1999), 238-41.

82   *Lonely Man*, 97-98.

83   *Lonely Man*, 93-102.

84   On the importance of this theme in R. Soloveitchik's writings, see Marvin Fox, "The Unity and Structure of Rabbi Joseph B. Soloveitchik's Thought," *Tradition* 24, 2 (Winter 1989): 44-65.

85   Twersky, 28-29.

86   *Halakhic Man*, 63.

87   See *Halakhic Man*, 110-17 and 161, notes 125 and 127

88   See *Before Hashem You Shall be Purified: Rabbi Joseph B. Soloveitchik on the Days of Awe*, summarized and annotated by Arnold Lustiger (Edison, NJ, 1998), 135 and 139 n. iv.

89   See also Twersky, 29-31.

90   Indeed, contrary to a common assumption that the study of science is easier to justify in a religious framework than is study of the humanities, Gerald Blidstein points out, as one possibility, that the Rav may see technology as *more* in need of justification than the humanities; in fact, the humanities may require none. After all, despite the challenges and risks they pose, philosophy and literature — in contradistinction to science — address the all-important *spiritual* dimension of the human being. See Blidstein, *"Am Yisrael be-Haguto shel ha-Rav Soloveitchik,"* in Sagi (ed.), *Emunah bi-Zemannim Mishtannim*, 151-52. This article is a translation, revised and expanded, of Blidstein's "On the Jewish People...," and the earlier English version does not include the point I am citing.

THEOLOGY, METAPHYSICS AND ETHICS

DIVINE INTERVENTION
AND RELIGIOUS SENSIBILITIES

1. INTRODUCTION: ON THE MOTIVATIONS
FOR RELIGIOUS NATURALISM

During the Middle Ages, several prominent Jewish philosophers embraced a naturalistic metaphysics that severely restricted — or virtually eliminated — instances of direct divine intervention in the universe. Maimonides, on a prevalent albeit contested interpretation, is the most illustrious example of this tendency. Prophecy, in Maimonides' view, is the outcome of a natural process, one which involves the self-initiated development of moral character, intellect and imagination. Providence, too, is a natural outgrowth of accomplishment: reward and punishment represent not divine incursions into the natural order, but rather benefits or adversities that flow *naturally* from human deeds, or, more precisely, from human intellectual efforts and achievements. Finally, stories of miracles that are recorded in the Bible are to be understood either as reports of dreams and visions or else as descriptions of events which, though unusual, can be explained in terms of natural laws and were programmed into nature at its original creation.[1] In short, concepts central to an interventionist metaphysics were reconstrued by Maimonides, and others in the Aristotelian tradition, in a naturalistic fashion. Indeed, Maimonides construed prophetic locutions of the form "God does X" as statements of the form, "within the natural order ordained by God, X occurs."[2]

Why did philosophers like Maimonides apparently opt for this naturalistic, or largely naturalistic, version of theism?[3] Most accounts trace the acceptance of the naturalistic outlook to the power of the Aristotelian framework that held sway at the time and that posits an inviolable natural order. On such accounts, medieval antagonism to interventionist views results purely from certain philosophic methods and theories — as distinct from, say, religious or ethical considerations that might motivate such views.[4] On the contrary, from a religious standpoint naturalism would seem to be heretical or quasi-heretical. To religious critics, it represents an accommodation to secular methods (albeit in the guise of a religious imperative to interpret traditional texts in the light of reason) as opposed to a faithful and proud representation of truly religious teachings, both biblical and rabbinic, concerning God's role in the universe.[5]

In recent years, however, a significant body of writing has presented an alternative or additional understanding of the motivations for naturalism. Specifically, it has been argued that interventionist and naturalistic outlooks can be compared by examining the religious sensibilities each view creates. Each correlates with different sets of character traits and different religious attitudes. They are powered by different norms and different core conceptions of God. A preference for certain character traits, certain norms, certain religious attitudes, or certain conceptions of God can dictate the adoption of one metaphysic over the other. What this new approach avers, in effect, is that, from a *moral* or *religious* point of view, and not just a scientific and philosophical one, naturalism — contrary to standard assumptions — is superior to interventionism.[6]

Some quick examples of this strategy will suffice to clarify it. Interventionism, it is said, creates an undesirable mindset of human dependence and helplessness. It sees religious activities as designed to get God to satisfy human needs in miraculous fashion, in a way that is not available through the resources provided by nature. Thereby, interventionism encourages preoccupation with self-interest. Further, because interventionism stresses directly conferred reward and punishment, it creates a deplorable pattern of action based on ulterior motives, "*lo lishmah*" in rabbinic terminology. Also, the belief that God intervenes in human affairs tends to diminish worshippers' responsibilities for concrete, pragmatic action and initiative, in defiance of Jewish norms that require people to utilize the natural order in such pursuits as medical treatment, economic effort, war and general security. ("We do not rely on miracles" is a well established principle of Halakhah.[7])

Naturalism, in contradistinction to all this, is said to encourage disinterested rather than self-interested worship; to create a sense of adequacy, a feeling of control over one's destiny; to imbue a stark, firm sense of responsibility for taking practical initiative. Finally, in the extreme opinion of one prominent Israeli philosopher, the late Yeshayahu Leibowitz, naturalism clears the way for a foundation to halakhic commitment that is wholly deontological — rather than predicated on self-interest, community interest or any other teleological rationale. As he puts it, interventionism portrays God serving (i.e., benefiting) humans; naturalism emphasizes humans serving (i.e., worshipping) God. Interventionism stresses that religion confers benefits; naturalism, that it makes demands. "A utilitarian conception of religion," writes Leibowitz in a passage not all naturalists will agree with, "depletes religion of all *religious* import."[8]

Interventionist and naturalist approaches likewise differ in their core conceptions of God. Interventionism celebrates brute divine power manifest through miracles, at the cost of implying that God had originally created a flawed universe that requires his miraculous intervention. Naturalism, by contrast, celebrates the divine wisdom manifest in the original creation.[9] Some have argued that if — as interventionists typically hold — God only *sometimes* intervenes to save or help individuals of merit, but does not always or frequently do so, this intensifies the problem of evil. For, having committed Himself not to let nature determine all events, God then becomes responsible for all those evils He does *not* prevent. Deny intervention altogether, and you have a better theodicy.[10]

In sum, despite intramural differences, naturalists assert that the cluster of attitudes, character traits, norms and depictions of God engendered by naturalism are preferable from a religious standpoint to those stimulated by interventionism. Granted, much traditional teaching conveys interventionism, but naturalists could claim, with Maimonides, that religion needs to cater to unsophisticated understandings. The masses of people cannot appreciate lofty ideals like disinterested worship. Furthermore, it is possible to reinterpret practices such as petitionary prayer that ostensibly make sense only on interventionist assumptions. For example, petitionary prayer helps the believer to introspect, to scrutinize his or her behavior, to empathize with the community or to recognize his or her dependence on God's natural order. Alternatively, though this is less likely, a naturalist could adopt a deontological approach like Leibowitz's that regards prayer as a commandment alone, devoid of connection to concrete human interests.[11]

Contemporary naturalistic Jewish theologians need not and should not argue that the connections between naturalism and religious sensibilities actually *influenced* or motivated the Aristotelian philosophers to adopt their naturalistic outlooks. Such a historical claim would be highly implausible. Nevertheless, one might reasonably enough suppose that Jewish Aristotelians regarded disinterested worship, a stress on practical initiative and so forth as salutary and appealing.

The historical etiology of naturalism aside, attempts to link the question of naturalism versus interventionism to issues about attitudes, character, norms, and the nature of God are of great import to the contemporary Jewish theologian. This is so for three reasons.

First, it is desirable or at last enticing for a theologian to have his or her metaphysic grow not simply out of a quest for scientific respectability — which is a secular concern, after all — but, as well, out of a quest to maximize the coherence and systematicity of one's religious outlook. To be sure, some theological views, Maimonides' among them, locate religious significance in the very exercise of reason. On such views, a quest for scientific respectability and rationality itself boasts a religious foundation. Nevertheless, the desire for coherence can nourish a religious sensibility even if one does not accept Maimonides' attribution of immense religious value to rational thought per se.

Second, in the climate now prevailing in the "analytic" approach to the philosophy of religion, settling disputes between naturalism and interventionism on religious grounds could prove more compelling than trying to settle the disputes on straight philosophical or scientific grounds. For, despite David Hume's notorious indictment of belief in miracles,[12] philosophers of religion often argue that scientific methods cannot rule out the occurrence of miracles and of divine responses to prayer unless we already assume in question-begging fashion that all events have a natural explanation.[13] We cannot know whether or not science comprehensively explains all events, and debates about Hume always seem to reach a dead end. Fascinatingly, even so extreme a version of interventionism as occasionalism — the view that objects in nature have no causal powers and that God is the cause of all seemingly natural events — is compatible with all the observational data that could be adduced for a non-occasionalist view.[14] A contemporary analytic philosopher goes still further: he suggests that occasionalism explains the existence of scientific regularities in a clearer fashion than other views could ever hope to, particularly if one takes seriously the position of "antirealism" that has emerged in recent philosophy of science.[15] Given that it is difficult to refute interventionism on purely philosophical grounds, naturalists will welcome a shift of focus from metaphysical to ethical and religious considerations.

A third attraction of such a shift is that it enhances the prospects of coping theologically with secularization. The modern scientific attempt to explain the universe in purely natural categories is linked to the celebration of autonomy, independence and self-reliance as paramount values. As R. Walter Wurzburger explains:

> The secularization of modern culture has brought about the emphasis upon the utilization of our rational faculties, human resources and energies to fashion instruments to improve the condition of humanity. In contrast with the mentality prevailing during the pre-modern 'age of faith' which placed exclusive reliance upon God and denigrated the efficacy of human action since human fate was completely in His hands, the modern mind emphasizes man's capacity to help determine the human condition.[16]

Religious people thus get caught in a dilemma. On the one hand, they enjoy the benefits of scientific inquiry, appreciate the urgency of trying to improve human life through such inquiry, and want this aspect of secularization to continue. On the other hand, such an appreciation of science and technology appears to conflict with the attitude of dependency and quietism seemingly championed in Jewish tradition. A modern theologian could mitigate this conflict by adopting the naturalism championed by medieval Jewish thinkers and its subsequent emphasis on self-reliance and human initiative (even if the medievals were motivated by metaphysics, and not by the attraction of self-reliance and practical initiative). The medieval theories would give an imprimatur not only to a naturalistic understanding of the universe, but also to the values to which such an understanding is wedded. Modern values and religious values will converge.

In what follows, therefore, I should like to explore in detail some of the religious and ethical import of naturalism and interventionism. To do so, we will need to look at three metaphysical theories: occasionalism; soft naturalism, which posits a natural order but allows for *some* divine intervention; and hard naturalism, which denies intervention. In section 2, I argue that occasionalism (extreme interventionism) is *religiously* problematic. Hence, I claim that some version of naturalism is religiously preferable to extreme interventionism. In the rest of the essay, I argue that attempts to establish "hard" naturalism by reference to the religious sensibilities such a view creates are flawed in several ways. The upshot is that debates between hard naturalism and soft naturalism will have to be waged by other means.

2. IS MORE INTERVENTION BETTER?
RELIGIOUS DRAWBACKS OF OCCASIONALISM

In this section I should like to validate one fundamental insight of contemporary naturalists: namely, that the overall religiosity of a theologian's metaphysics is not necessarily enhanced by multiplying instances of divine intervention. I realize that occasionalism exerts little attraction for most of my readers, but understanding its problems will prove important.

Occasionalists see God as the only causal force in the world. No substance other than God has any causal powers, active or passive.[17] This position was held by, *inter alia*, some Islamic philosophers and by the early modern philosophers Nicolas Malebranche and George Berkeley. In Jewish thought the occasionalist position is expressed in some biblical and talmudic passages and is common in Hasidic philosophy, but is presented in an especially clear and encompassing fashion by Rabbi Eliyahu Dessler (d. 1953), a leading Musar figure first in England and then in Bnei Brak, Israel. He explains that,

> There is no essential difference between the natural and the
> miraculous. Everything that occurs is a miracle. The world has no

other cause but the will of God...We call God's act a "miracle" when
He wills an occurrence which is novel and unfamiliar to us... We call
God's acts "nature" when He wills that certain events should occur in
a recognizable pattern with which we become familiar.[18]

How do occasionalists argue for their position? Often they do so by
highlighting the contingent character of what we ordinarily term causal
relationships. We do not perceive any logical connection between any two
events we designate as cause and effect. Hence, there are no causal powers
in nature, and only God exercises causal power. What the ordinary person
calls "causes" and theistic naturalists call "secondary causes" are really
just *occasional* causes, i.e. events that merely precede some event that God
directly produces, and are correlated with that latter type of event, but
which we perceive (wrongly) as the true causes of the later events.

The doctrine that causal relationships are contingent was made famous
by David Hume, but he was no occasionalist (some even doubt he was
a theist). There are purely philosophical problems with the occasionalist
argument from the contingency of causal relationships. In particular, if
we use this argument, should we not tar divine and natural causes with
the same brush? Should we not conclude that there are no causal powers,
period, because there are no logical connections between *any* two events?
The occasionalist argument for the denial of causal powers can be used
to generate an argument for divine inefficacy, and hence it does not seem
promising to use it as the linchpin of a theistic worldview.[19]

However, it seems likely that religious occasionalism is motivated at the
deepest level not by philosophical reflection but by religious sensibilities.
Religious occasionalists, both non-Jewish and Jewish, condemn any grant of
causal power to nature as a form of "idolatry" or "paganism."[20] The initial
impression, then, is that occasionalism is a "remarkably devout theory of
divine causation."[21] And indeed it is. Yet, occasionalism entails a religious cost.

(a) *Free choice*: Religious occasionalists need to recognize at least one
category of events not caused by God: human free choices. They cannot
simply acknowledge human choices to be the sole exception to the principle
that God is the only cause of events in the universe, since any exceptions
undercut the general principles that motivated the occasionalist position
originally. Interestingly, Maimonides, in one of his broadsides against
Islamic occasionalism, rejects it strictly on the grounds that it negates human
free will, without considering the possibility that human free will could be
the one place where God allows for other causes.[22] Maimonides may have
sniffed the ad hoc character of such a dichotomy.

(b) *Evil*: Every theistic system has to face the question of why there is
evil. But rejecting occasionalism allows many evils to be the products of

natural processes, and theodicy becomes a matter of explaining why God *passively allows* these evils to occur, why He does not step in to thwart evil. But for occasionalists the problem is worse. It is not just why God allows evils: it is why He *directly produces* them — sometimes even assisting the wicked to carry out their intentions. God, not humans, produces earthquakes and disease, brings enemy missiles on Israel, turns weapons of destruction against Jews throughout history. Unless we challenge the premise that producing evil is morally worse than not intervening to stop an evil in progress — a challenge that seems ad hoc and unpromising — it will become more difficult to justify God's ways in an occasionalist framework than a non-occasionalist one.[23]

(c) *Divine concern with the trivial*: Imagine how an occasionalist would describe an athletic event: God causes the quarterback's arm to rise and personally throws the football fifty yards in the air. God swings Babe Ruth's bat and personally escorts the ball into the stands. These descriptions will strike many as odd, more so than saying that God is the cause of a certain forest fire. Another issue to wonder about here is whether God cares about whether a batter singles on each particular at bat, or a player successfully kicks a field goal in a given situation, or someone gets a particular rebound in basketball or a particular team wins a particular game. When athletes kneel in prayer and ask God for victory, or thank Him after a triumph, can we readily accept that God was really arranging for their team to win? True enough, one person's *reductio ad absurdum* is another's *hakhi nami*.[24] But those who find counterintuitive the occasionalist view that God arranges the outcome of even the most meaningless ball games, will reasonably reject it as contrary to their religious sensibilities. Occasionalists could not even argue, as they do in explaining why there seem to be regular sequences, that God has to produce such events in order to preserve the illusion of a regular natural order (see below). For athletic events hardly display so much causal regularity as to make credible the idea that God has to choose the particular effects He in fact creates just in order to preserve the illusion of regularity.

(d) *The value of temptation*: Occasionalists confront two more questions: (1) Why do there *seem* to be regular sequences of events in nature. (2) Why must human beings (as Jewish law insists) labor to produce results?

R. Dessler responds to question (1) as follows:

[Nature] is merely an illusion which gives man a choice to exercise his free will: to err, or to choose the truth.[25]

God creates the illusion of causal relationships by creating regular sequences of experiences, and He does so in order to test our faith. Will we continue to recognize His providence?

Regarding question (2) — why do we need to labor at all — R. Dessler responds along related lines:

> We have to engage in worldly endeavors for one reason only: to learn to see God's providence even in the world of mundane activity. We have to stand the test and realize that nature has no power.[26]
> We have to do enough to ensure that the divine bounty which comes down to us from the Lord could possibly be attributed to some other cause.[27]

One could challenge these answers, since they seem inconsistent with injunctions not to place temptations before others and not to court temptation in other areas. God, in the occasionalist view, tempts us to sin by creating regular sequences of events; and we should tempt ourselves to sin by engaging in practical labor. Even if God has the prerogative to tempt, what allows us to tempt ourselves?

(e) *Bittahon (trust) vs. interpersonal responsibility*: An occasionalist axiology, such as R. Dessler's, sees *bittahon*, trust, as the prime virtue. That virtue entails both a cognitive recognition that God is the sole cause of things, and also an affective attitude of trust that He will tend to our needs. On the practical level, this stress on *bittahon* shrinks human initiative and opposes the modern ethos of human self-sufficiency.

This appears to be a better accounting of *bittahon* than any naturalistic theory could offer. Did not the prophet declare, "Blessed is the person who trusts in the Lord, and the Lord will be his security" (Jer 17:7)? That faith in God can itself trigger divine protection is an idea that not only is frequently found in the Bible but was emphasized even by medieval rationalists like Bahya ibn Pakuda.[28] Yet, while the Jewish tradition values *bittahon*, the occasionalist's glorification of *bittahon* leads to a challenge — one that R. Dessler recognizes. If we are aware that all depends on God, and therefore cut back on practical initiative, perhaps we should also decrease our practical efforts to help others. In R. Dessler's words:

> If physical endeavor has no real value, and I follow this principle in my own life, why do I have to exert myself so much in physical endeavor on behalf of my neighbor? Why should I not apply trust in God to his concerns, too?

Here is his reply:

> We read:"'Cast your burden upon the Lord and He will sustain you" (Eccl. 11:1). That is, so far as *your* burden — your own affairs — are concerned it is God's will that you should leave these to Him. ... But when we are dealing with other people's needs, He has referred

them to us and wants us to make every effort to provide for them, so that we should perfect ourselves in the quality of lovingkindness. If we were to use the quality of trust and faith instead, we should have no opportunity for doing *hesed*. It is our command therefore to work for others in exactly the same way as the one who lacks trust works for himself. It remains true, however, that we must bear in mind that here, too, everything is in the hands of the Lord.[29]

Clearly R. Dessler concedes that there are traits other than *bittahon* which we must exercise, and among these is *hesed* (lovingkindness). *Bittahon* is called for when we deal with our own needs, *hesed* when we deal with our comrade's.[30] Interpersonal relations call for an attitude sharply different from the trust that controls self-directed activity. But can't acts of *hesed* at times be detrimental to spiritual health because they harm *bittahon*? A person may find that repeated acts of *hesed* weaken his *bittahon* by making him too confident in his own power, too disposed to believe in an autonomous system of nature. Should he or she risk further attrition of *bittahon* in order to help others? On an occasionalist view, this ought to be a legitimate concern: it is not clear *why hesed always* trumps *bittahon*. Naturalism, on the other hand, would see no threat here, because naturalism does not see involvement in the natural order as a potential harm to *bittahon*. In this regard the naturalist's view is more persuasive.

There is, to be sure, something attractive about the self/other distinction that R. Dessler tries to uphold. But naturalists could express the self/other distinction in a more consistent fashion. Consider this formulation: "We should not strive to maximize our own material good but should strive to maximize our neighbor's."[31] In this and other naturalist formulations, the self/other distinction does not see helping others as potentially detrimental to trust in God — as occasionalism seems obliged to do.

(f) *The imperative to help others (continued)*: The imperative to help others is difficult to explain within an occasionalist framework for yet another reason. If God is the only true cause of events (or at least of events other than our choices) then our efforts cause nothing. This gives rise to two problems. (i) Anyone who realizes that nature is an illusion and that human beings cannot really do anything will not even try. Effort makes sense only when one believes that one can bring about a result. (ii) All rewards and punishments are now dependent on effort, not on causation of a result. We will receive credit or blame not for our deeds (we *do* nothing), but for our intentions. But this suggestion would undermine a reasonable moral distinction between X intentionally producing bad or good results and Y implementing X's bad or good intentions. If the human, X, never produces good or bad results, but only God does, this seems to make God, not X, responsible for the bad or good result.[32]

Let us first consider problem (i), that of justifying making an effort. Occasionalists would likely reply that when they "make the effort" to save another, they are not trying to *save* the person, but are really trying to influence *God* to extricate the person. The effort counts as successful if God rescues the person. It is no different from starting off and eventually completing any causal chain in a naturalist framework — only the intermediate links are different. And indeed we can "get" God to do things — prayer and good deeds can influence God. But, it must be asked, is this not an instance of our exercising causal power, something that occasionalists said is impossible?

We turn next to problem (ii), that if God implements X's decision, then God bears much of the responsibility for the result, relieving X of some of the credit or blame. Occasionalists might assert that X still bears full responsibility, no less than if his or her intentions had been linked to their products by natural cause-effect relations rather than divine agency. This reply is weak; occasionalism must throw an unseemly responsibility for human welfare onto God's shoulders. For if God is doing the saving, why should He wait for my effort? Why shouldn't He save the other person if he deserves to be saved? Why is God's decision conditioned by mine?

Presumably the answer is that God would encourage total passivity if He were to save everyone who needs saving regardless of whether humans try to save the people. People would soon catch on! God (continues the occasionalist) therefore stays on the sidelines, as it were, until humans act. But what now becomes of individual *zekhut* (merit)? It could be replied that analogous problems affect praying for someone's welfare or, say, giving charity to a synagogue so God will heal the other person, and that should mitigate the force of the last set of questions. The question, "Why should God make X's fate dependent on whether someone else prays or gives charity on behalf of that person?"[33] seems just as sharp as "Why should God make X's fate dependent on whether someone tries to save X?" But prayer, or charity on behalf of another, are *recognized* exceptions to the quite palatable principle that what God does for person X is solely a function of X's merits and not those of a potential benefactor Y. Occasionalism recognizes so many exceptions to this principle — all situations that require interpersonal aid violate it — that it calls the larger occasionalist position into question.

Naturalism accounts for interpersonal responsibility much more simply. Our actions *genuinely*, without direct divine activity, promote or hinder the welfare of others. Therefore, we cannot thrust responsibility for others' welfare onto God's shoulders. According to this position, God adopts a policy of non-intervention in order to promote human responsibility. Hard naturalists will say "He never violates this policy";

"soft" naturalists will say that He violates it at times. But both types of naturalism greatly reduce divine responsibility for the consequences of human moral indolence.

I have argued that the religious attraction of occasionalism — its seeking to venerate God by making Him the sole cause of all events — must be balanced against other religious considerations. Occasionalism faces significant difficulties involving free choice, evil, divine concern, temptation and interpersonal responsibility. Of course occasionalists may be willing to pay the price. But they should understand why others will not. Naturalism has the potential to escape all of these problems. Let us turn to examine the religious sensibilities it creates.

3. VARIETIES OF NATURALISM

A rejection of occasionalism establishes the need for some form of naturalism, but it does not help adjudicate between two grades of naturalism. "Soft" naturalism allows for the occurrence of natural events and affirms the existence of a natural order that prevails most of the time, but it insists that some or many events can be explained only by direct divine intervention. Miracles occur, including miraculous responses to prayer, miraculous prophecy, and some miraculous reward and punishment. Thus, soft naturalism is itself a kind of interventionism, and whereas I deemed it "naturalist" when the contrast case was occasionalism, in what follows I shall use "interventionism" as a label for soft naturalism.[34] When I speak of soft naturalism in what follows, I shall refer to a view that sees God as a general cause of nature and a sometimes intervener, but not as the direct initiator of all events, nor even of most.

Hard naturalism, on the other hand, either denies phenomena like prophecy, providence and miracles altogether, or construes them in naturalistic categories. Hard naturalists do not deny that the world is dependent on God — they will typically insist that He created it, and/or that He conserves it, and/or that were God not to exist, nothing else would. They do not deny the metaphysical dependence of the world on God. However, hard naturalists hold that God is never a direct cause of specific effects in nature. He does not intervene in the natural order, period.[35]

Now in order to assess the religious impact of naturalism, whether hard or soft, I suggest that we pose the following question: what is the significance of the natural order? What should be the self-perception of a person who is involved in the natural order? Here we can distinguish two views which boast medieval precedent. The first, represented by Maimonides, is that nature represents the locus of divine *providence*. The second, represented by Nahmanides, is that nature is the locus of divine *punishment*. Our focus will be Maimonides, who, for purposes of discussion (that is, setting interpretive issues aside) I shall take to be a hard naturalist.

4. ON THE ATTRACTIONS OF MAIMONIDES

As we have already noted, contemporary thinkers are quite enthusiastic about a Maimonidean framework because of religious and ethical strengths they perceive in it. In a very penetrating essay explaining the "self-perception" created by Maimonides' naturalism, Jerome Gellman makes the following points about what he takes to be Maimonides' position:

> [A] In a world enclosed within its natural boundaries, the fate of a person is entirely up to him. There is no divinely initiated salvation. Our actions always have their natural consequences, and our hopes and wishes can only become true if consistent with the world as we know it. God will not change the natural order to conform to our needs. What becomes of us is basically in our own hands. This self-perception contrasts strongly with the sense of helplessness and waiting for God characteristic of a metaphysic of divine intervention and human depravity.[36]
> [B] The self-perception of weakness or helplessness naturally inclines to the fear-mode of service of God. That is why Maimonides in his writings wants to foster in the reader a sense of radical human responsibility. The reader is made to feel that what becomes of him is basically in his own hands. ... Armed with a sense of self-responsibility, the reader is freed from the motive of seeking self-aid, in order to pursue the goal of love of God — a relationship based on disinterested worship. ... A sense of radical freedom and competence in cognition makes possible a relationship to God not grounded in one's needs for oneself.[37]

This is all put extremely well. Is it really true, however, that a hard naturalist position (attributed here to Maimonides) actually results in these personal sensibilities?

Let us begin with quotation [A], which asserts that an interventionist metaphysic must take our fate out of our hands. This, I believe, is mistaken. An interventionist metaphysic puts our fate very much in our hands. Just think of the Bible's stark claim (Leviticus 26): "If you walk in my statutes..." you will be healthy, victorious, secure, and spared all suffering; "If you reject my statutes..." you will suffer greatly. There is nothing in this formula that takes the fate of people out of their hands. Quite the opposite![38]

What, then, is the hard naturalist's point? Perhaps it is this. *In the world as we experience it*, a person's future cannot be reliably predicted from the person's religious deeds, let alone predicted to conform exactly to the pattern promised by the Bible. By contrast, a person's future *can* be reliably predicted from the steps one takes to protect oneself within the natural order. Therefore, naturalism gives a person greater control over his or her fate.

One difficulty for this naturalist argument is that its contrast between the surety of the natural order and the unreliability of the alleged religious-moral order sorely needs qualification. Neither proper exercise nor proper diet nor any other set of practical steps *guarantees* a beneficial outcome in terms of personal health. Illness often arises unpredictably. Also, much of what we do is contingent on the behavior of others, and the unexpected often happens when we make predictions about other people's choices. (This is true even if one believes human choices are determined.) Finally, being able to foretell the future by a Laplacean predictor[39] is not the same as having the future in your hands. Heredity is an important predictor of many diseases, but it does not yield control to the individual; often its effects cannot be guarded against.

Now a hard naturalist could still say that predicting a person's future on the basis of a stable natural order is a more reliable enterprise than constructing the prediction on the basis of his or her religious deeds, and confers more control of destiny on the individual. But if this is the point, then it is misleading to say that naturalism per se places a person's future in his or her hands, while interventionism does not. Interventionism could promote that same feeling of control *if tight connections between deeds and rewards/punishments were to obtain in the actual world*. The argument against interventionism, therefore, must not be that interventionism necessarily implies that my future is not up to me, but rather that, as a description of how the world works, interventionism seems false. Hence the argument in [A] is not really based on the sensibilities created by naturalism and interventionism as such, but on an independent rejection of interventionism's claims.[40]

Hard naturalists might reply as follows. The pressures that force us to deny a strict nexus between one's religious deeds and one's material welfare come from within religion and not from without. That is to say, there are good *religious* reasons for there being no obvious connection between deeds and rewards. "A world which is to be a moral order," writes F. R. Tennant, "must be a physical order characterized by law or regularity...Law-abidingness is an essential condition of the world being a theatre of moral life." Or, as C. S. Lewis put it, "The very conception of a common, and therefore, stable world demands that [miracles] be extremely rare."[41] Religious sensibilities themselves explain why interventionism cannot be right.

This is true. But does the fact that a stable natural order is needed for moral life preclude divine intervention altogether? Certainly not. Soft naturalism (interventionism) could create a mindset much like that created by hard naturalism. For assume that God only rarely intervenes in the natural order, so that there are no sure connections between deed and recompense. Assume further that the push to concede this comes, as the hard naturalist insists, from religious sensibilities and not scientific discovery. Can't God intervene *sometimes* without abrogating a stable natural order? Lewis's words, "The very conception of a common, and therefore, stable world demands that [miracles] be extremely rare" imply exactly this — that God could intervene on rare occasions. No matter how seldom God deems an individual worthy of divine intervention, a person who prays would still be raising the odds that he or she will be saved, just as if he or she were to use a low-risk medical therapy with a small chance of succeeding.[42] A religious advantage of allowing for some divine intervention is that petitionary prayer would then make sense — which it does not in a hard naturalist framework unless one reconstrues the point of petition.[43] Consequently, not only belief in the possibility of divine intervention but also acting on this belief could be integrated into an intelligently planned life in much the same way as "long shots" are in a natural scheme. Only an independent argument against interventionism can show that God's intervention is not even a long shot.[44]

To review, the argument against interventionism found in [A] can be rebutted in two ways. First, we may argue that argument [A] uses a covert premise, namely that the nexus between religious deeds and material welfare does not hold in our world. This assumption may be correct, but its correctness could be known only by scientific and philosophical investigation. *Potentially*, pervasive interventionism can create a stable order. Thus, while the argument in [A] may validly distinguish naturalism from interventionism *given how the world actually is*, Maimonides' criticism of interventionism (as explained by Gellman) is not based on a mindset that interventionism *must* create. Second, if hard naturalists will insist that there are also good *religious* reasons for denying a strict deed/reward nexus, they will not be able to triumph over soft naturalism by means of the argument in [A]. The uncertainty that would infect life if God's interventions are uncertain find a parallel in the uncertainty that prevails in the naturalist's world. So, although there is merit in the Lewis-Tennant suggestion that there are good religious reasons for belief in a stable natural order, such a belief is perfectly compatible with either rare or fairly frequent divine interventions and with such phenomena as miracles and supernaturally endowed prophecy.

Now let us look at quotation [B].

5. MAIMONIDES: NATURE AS PROVIDENCE
AND THE PROBLEM OF SELF-INTEREST

In evaluating [B], we need to ask whether Maimonides' own version of naturalism succeeds in divesting an elite individual of concern for self. I submit that it does not. To explain why, I need to elaborate on Maimonides' view.

A. *Exposition*

For Maimonides, nature, though fixed, has a teleological structure which is of the deepest religious significance. Teleology reflects divine wisdom and divine providence. Consequently, when you utilize knowledge of nature to promote your welfare, you are not abandoning your relationship with God, but, on the contrary, are operating squarely within a providential nexus.[45] You relate to God *by* exploiting the teleology in nature, *by* manipulating nature's provisions for human benefit. Those provisions include both the characteristics of natural objects and human cognitive endowments.[46]

Because taking advantage of knowledge of nature has religious value, Maimonides vehemently assails a popular notion: that seeking medicine and physicians signals a condemnable lack of reliance upon God. On the contrary, he declares, taking medicine is no more audacious than ingesting food or drink, and hence Jews must deal with illness by exercising their capacity to discover and administer cures.[47] Likewise, in a famous letter to rabbis of Southern France concerning astrology, Maimonides explains why the Jews lost the Temple and were exiled from their land. Having become infatuated with the sinful follies of astrology, "They did not occupy themselves with the art of warfare and the conquest of lands."[48] Their failing, in other words, was a lack of pragmatism.

Especially striking is Maimonides' approach to the biblical prohibitions against engaging in magic, divination, soothsaying, sorcery and astrology, as well as to the accompanying imperative, "*tamim tihyeh im Hashem Elokekha*" (Deut. 18:13).[49] Endorsing both talmudic and medieval science,[50] many commentators suggest that the prohibited practices are effective, but the Torah prohibits them so that human beings develop trust in God over and against reliance on other means.[51] Maimonides, in contrast, explains

193

that these practices are foolish and ineffective, and that is precisely why the Torah prohibits them.[52] Torah laws are teleological just as laws of nature are.[53] Maimonides' discussion of *tamim tihyeh* suggests that he regards it as a prescription to be among the "*temimei ha-da'at*," the intellectually perfect, those whose opinions and actions are not adulterated by folly but rather are formed according to sound principles of science and wisdom.[54] Thus, for Maimonides, the contrast that Deut. 18 sets out is this: the Torah represents rational, practical, scientifically-grounded living, while Canaanite practices represent irrationality and futility.[55]

For Maimonides, then, nature is providentially arranged and human beings are equipped with means of understanding its workings and exploiting its structure. Therefore people *must* actively devote themselves to improving their condition by natural means. To wait for divine intervention is to nurture passivity and to fall out of a proper providential relationship; God commands us to engage His providence through self-direction and activism. Maimonides' well known clamor against all forms of predestination[56] is but a piece of his overall view. Belief in providence should galvanize people to execute their responsibilities rather than drive them into a sense that their destinies are outside their personal control.[57]

What now becomes of reward and punishment? Or the virtue of *bittahon*, trust? Regarding reward and punishment, Maimonides, as far as I can see, asserts that the natural order, consistent with its providential character, *is* in fact set up so that there is special providence in addition to general providence. The "righteous" prosper while the "wicked" suffer. *Nature, for Maimonides, is virtue-sensitive.* But his method of assuring this result was to see the exercise of intellect as the highest merit or virtue, and then to show how by that definition of virtue, the virtuous prosper. People with superior knowledge of nature will enjoy providence for three reasons, all of them naturalistic. (1) They will be able to protect themselves from threatening elements in nature; (2) they will deprecate the value of their material condition, and thereby remain untroubled by physical adversity; finally, (3) they can achieve at least partial conjunction with the Active Intellect, which facilitates an escape from corporeality.[58] Almost astonishingly, Maimonides gives a personal "guarantee" that an individual who follows his regimen for bodily health in *Hilkhot De'ot* "will [except for certain cases Maimonides specifies] never fall ill until he grows old and dies."[59] Note, as well, that when, in *The Letter on Astrology*, he says that the Jews lost the Temple because they busied themselves with astrology, he is saying that the exile was a *natural* consequence of their not training in "the art of war and the conquest of lands."[60]

I suggest further that Maimonides' desire for an organic connection between deed and personal welfare sheds light on his insistence that *avodah* (service or worship) must be performed "out of love (*me-ahavah*)," which, for Maimonides, means that "he does the truth because it is truth" (that is, the person does acts based on a perception of their merits).[61] The ideal of doing out of love/ doing *lishmah* strikes me as an especially pure form of the demand that an organic, natural connection exist between deed and reward/ punishment. What tighter connection could obtain between deed and outcome than the deed being its own reward?

What of *bittahon*? In his entire mammoth legal code, the *Mishneh Torah*, Maimonides mentions *bittahon* only twice — and in both instances, the word *bittahon* may refer to a virtue of another sort, namely, a rejection of wealth and property (material goods) as significant values in life.[62] If Maimonides is a naturalist, trust in the classical sense eludes his schema, so perhaps that is why he construes *bittahon* as a willingness to forego *interest in* certain types of ostensible goods.

B. *Implications for the Problem of Self-Interest*

Informed by this exposition, let us return to Gellman's quotation [B]. According to Gellman, Maimonides' naturalism makes possible the negation of self-interest. Clearly, however, Maimonides' prescription of certain medical regimens and his attack on various types of bad science are geared to benefit the individual who follows them, and to benefit him or her *materially*. It is true that material goods are but a propadeutic to higher, intellectual and spiritual goods, but there is nothing in an interventionist metaphysic that precludes an interventionist from regarding material goods in exactly the same way. It is also true that Maimonides' view of "general providence," which stresses the welfare of the species rather than of individuals, means that an individual who contemplates God's providence will to some extent turn his attention from self to species. But the fact remains that Maimonides recognizes individual providence as well, since he believes that, for example, those who develop their intellects will be protected from physical harm. The teleological character of Maimonides' universe ensures that people will be able to relate their actions to their human needs, both material and intellectual. Any desired transition from a self-interested to a disinterested stance is just as difficult to make in a hard naturalist framework as in a soft naturalist one. To purge people of concern for self-interest would require banishing teleology — and Maimonides is not prepared to do that.

Maimonides' view *is* centered on the self. Notice that the nexus he sees between righteousness and reward smacks of a highly individualistic intellectual imperialism — and a tenuous intellectual imperialism at that. After all, great scientists contract cancer and suffer heart attacks, and even great philosophers have difficulty bearing up under physical suffering just by concentrating on restructuring their value system. Were we, however, to restructure Maimonides' view and frame it at the level of the *collective*, it would become more persuasive and make it easier for people to diminish self-interest. Construed collectively, Maimonides' view would posit an intellectual obligation devolving on humanity to improve the human condition through the resources of nature, thereby mandating that the community use scientific inquiry for the benefit of the community. R. Joseph B. Soloveitchik makes this point forcefully,[63] and other writers have also drawn compelling connections between scientific labors and interpersonal responsibility.[64] Such an approach takes account of the fact that the intellectually virtuous individual of the fourteenth century did not have the same range of modalities available for self-protection as we do, which once again points to the interdependence of individual and community, and to the communal nature of scientific advance. Providence would be located in the benefits accruing to the community by the community's intellectual inquiry.

This emphasis does not accord with Maimonidean individualism. *He* is self-oriented, the "communal" thinkers are other-oriented.[65] Hence, we may conclude that Maimonidean naturalism does not lend itself easily to the kind of disengagement from self that is required by disinterested worship; and there is no reason to think that interventionists will have a harder time producing such disengagement. Maimonides did see disinterested worship as an ideal. But he did not chart a clear, smooth transition from earlier stages of development to this highest one in a way not available to soft naturalists.

"All right, then," a hard naturalist may respond, "let's eliminate teleology. Surely if nature is not teleological a person will not expect God to satisfy human needs." Putting aside the bizarre implication that naturalists who don't believe in teleology are not self-interested, the problem with the proffered solution is self-evident. If nature is not teleological and God does not intervene *at all* in the natural order, then there simply is no divine providence in the sense of protection. This seeming *reductio ad absurdum* is in truth embraced by Yeshayahu Leibowitz. The latter is perfectly content to sever religion from any and all human needs, this in the name of valuing only God and not human beings. I think that this conclusion totally overlooks the implications of God's goodness and power and can only appeal to a noncognitivist (someone who does not take religious statements as describing truths about God), which Leibowitz is.

C. Reinterpreting Interventionist Concepts

Soft naturalists may be able to reconstruct traditional concepts in ways that hard naturalists think that only they are capable of doing. A hard naturalist's views of petitionary prayer, for example, could be co-opted by soft naturalists. In this connection, special mention must be made of *bittahon*, trust. If one thinks that instances of divine intervention, whether as responses to prayer or as immediate dispensations of reward and punishment, are rare, one initially will not be able to make sense of *bittahon* as a virtue. How can someone be sure that all will be well for him or her?

There are at least four alternative understandings of *bittahon* which make sense of the virtue. The first defines *bittahon* as a call to restructuring one's values, a move that I have already suggested Maimonides may have made. This definition is available to hard and soft naturalists alike. The second is that *bittahon* is faith in God's *power* to intervene, but not in the certainty of His intervening. This definition is available to both soft and hard naturalists, though it would puzzling if a hard naturalist were to say that God *has* the power but never exercises it. The third is to define *bittahon* as faith not in God's *benevolence*, but in God's *justice*.[66] Assuming that both hard and soft naturalists will want some way of understanding "God is just," this third definition would be available to both.

A fourth suggestion is perhaps the most compelling. *Bittahon*, on this view, should be reconstrued as *commitment*. Rather than view *bittahon* as a call to believe that God will intervene to help us — He may not — let us view *bittahon* as a call to believe in God and to aspire to be close to Him even when He does not intervene to help us.[67] This view is the opposite of the familiar one that ties *bittahon* to self-interest. On the contrary, it severs *bittahon* from self-interest. *Bittahon* does not involve an expectation that our needs will be satisfied, but rather dedication to carry through our commitments even when dark days await us. Thus, a soft naturalist framework also makes room for a disinterested stance.[68]

This brings me to a final and completely general criticism of the attempt to establish naturalism on the basis of the mindset it creates.

5.   FROM MINDSET TO METAPHYSICS

Even if a hard naturalist mindset creates a preferable religious sensibility, that does not generate a good argument for the *truth* of hard naturalism.[69] At best, it creates a good argument for believers not placing interventionism at the forefront of their religious consciousnesses. For a religion might demand that an individual maintain a delicate tension. The person might be required to *believe* that God can and will intervene in the natural order (either to satisfy human needs or to execute justice), but at the same time be required not to let this belief motivate him.[70] If religion demands maintaining this sort of tension, then attempts to establish hard naturalism by appealing to the fact that Judaism demands a noninterventionist mindset would not be persuasive.

Indeed, when hard naturalists appeal to religious sensibilities to support their view, they focus on the human point of view and fail to consider God's point of view. They focus on how humans should think; they do not focus on how God should act. A good God will not stay out of human affairs. He will act to better the world and to create a just order by dispensing reward and punishment. Should God withhold good from people just because if He intervenes in things people might then develop a base motivation? It would be better for God to intervene, while demanding that people not let belief in intervention influence their actions. God may wish to limit such intervention, to be sure, for if it is widespread it will make disinterested worship psychologically impossible, but the crucial responsibility for proper motivation falls on the believer.

To an extent, therefore, religious and ethical arguments for hard naturalism are *non sequiturs*. All that follows from them is something about the proper religious consciousness and mindset, not something about what metaphysical structure the universe has. In certain ways this strategy (of affirming interventionism while demanding that belief in interventionism not influence action) captures the insight of a "*lishmah*" religious ethics even better than hard naturalism does. We are committed to worship God even *if* God does nothing for us; but it does not follow from this commitment that He does nothing for us. Believers can be humble and agnostic with respect to how God relates to the universe, without that uncertainty affecting their commitment.

This idea, that religious belief can be separated from religious motivation, is suggested by a rabbinic source that chides Antigonus of Sokho for preaching in Mishnah *Avot*: "Do not be as servants who serve the master so as to receive reward but as servants who serve the master not in order to receive reward."[71] We are told that two disciples misunderstood Antigonus. They took him to be denying that there is an afterlife in which reward and punishment will be dispensed.[72] Antigonus was right about the motivational ideal, but was wrong to publicize this ideal because people would have difficulty maintaining it while believing in reward and punishment in the hereafter. But for one who can maintain this tension, it seems desirable to do so.

Hard naturalists might object that it is psychologically too demanding to expect people to endorse an interventionist metaphysic but to make decisions using a naturalist one. On their view, even though a good God might want to exercise justice and mercy and therefore intervene in human affairs, God's ultimate decision would be to refrain from intervening in human affairs *because* He does not want to create a wrong mindset. But this understanding of God's behavior is problematic. If God makes hard naturalism true in order to prevent belief in interventionism, then He has badly miscalculated. Despite His nonintervention, after all, interventionists are alive and well.

It is worth noting here a still more extreme antinaturalist point of view advanced by Isaac Abarbanel.[73] Criticizing Maimonides' reading of Antigonus, Abarbanel complains that Maimonides' construal of the ideal of acting "*lishmah*" as "doing the truth because it is the truth"[74] does not represent a Torah belief. The non-Jewish philosophers, he says — no doubt alluding to the opening lines of Aristotle's *Nicomachean Ethics* — had no choice but to assert that some deeds are worth doing for their own sake. They denied providence and denied reward and punishment, and therefore did not find any motivation for acting rightly other than the intrinsic merits of the act. But we who believe in providence, Abarbanel continues, have no need to resort to intrinsic merits of an act as a motivation for acting. Instead, we can and ought to be motivated, without a trace of shame, by hope of reward and fear of punishment.[75] Acting out of self-interest is actually commendable, because it translates our distinctive metaphysical beliefs into a concrete pattern of affect and behavior. For Abarbanel, once belief in intervention loses its vitality and its applicability to decision-making, once its motivational power is suppressed, our acts lose their distinctive religious character and value. Hence the seeming benefits of a *lishmah* orientation — as Maimonides defines it — may not be worth the price they entail. It seems to me that, on Abarbanel's premises, even a stance of worshipping God out of sheer obedience — a divine command notion of *lishmah* — threatens belief in reward and punishment.

To sum up this section, so long as hard naturalists try to establish naturalism *solely* on the basis of religious or ethical considerations, without appealing to epistemological principles that validate a naturalistic world-view, they are open to two charges. First, they have failed to distinguish between what beliefs are true and what beliefs should exercise motivational control. Second, as Abarbanel points out, the mindset which naturalism breeds is attractive *only* if interventionism is false. If interventionism is true, as it may have to be for God to be wholly good and wholly just, then the noninterventionist mindset is *not* proper. Even if we reject Abarbanel's view, we should not argue for hard naturalism solely on the basis of the mindset it creates. Rather, an independent argument is required.

6. CONCLUSION

The prospects of finding a religious or ethical ground for hard naturalism, even one that highlights the teleological character of nature, are far from bright. To be sure, as we have seen, holistic religious considerations persuade us to reject the extreme interventionist view known as occasionalism.

What emerges from that critique is that religion can and ought to allow itself to take the natural order seriously and to encourage human beings to exploit its workings for beneficial purposes. Hence the methodology of using religious sensibilities to evaluate metaphysical views bears some fruit. But we cannot next apply a similar tactic to adjudicate between hard and soft naturalism; or, if we can, the argument may well support soft rather than hard naturalism. (I refer to the argument from God's justice and goodness.) My own suspicion is that the choice between hard and soft naturalism will have to made on the familiar and heavily trod territory of scientific and philosophical reflection, combined with appeals to traditional texts.

NOTES

1   See *Guide of the Perplexed*, II:32-48 (prophecy); III:17-23, 51 (providence); II:29 (miracles). See also commentary to *Avot* 5:6 and *Guide* II:29, which cite rabbinic roots for the view that miracles are part of the natural order. For the purposes of this essay, namely to explore the roots of religious naturalism, it would be counterproductive to explore the distinct possibility that Maimonides' naturalism is less thoroughgoing than this exposition suggests.

2   See *Guide*, II:48. For a broader survey of medieval naturalism see Howard Kreisel, "Miracles in Medieval Jewish Philosophy," *The Jewish Quarterly Review* 75 (October, 1984): 99-133. As Kreisel notes, naturalists sometimes explained miracles by reference to the causal influence exerted over nature by the soul of the exceptional individual. See also Aviezer Ravitsky, "The Anthropological Theory of Miracles in Medieval Jewish Philosophy," in *Studies in Medieval Jewish History and Literature, Volume II*, ed. Isadore Twersky (Cambridge, Mass., 1984), 231-72.

3   I am *not* using the term "naturalism" to denote a rejection of the existence of a transcendent deity, a position adopted by R. Mordecai Kaplan. I am using the term in a way that is compatible with the existence of a traditional theistic God.

4   Ironically, though, much of philosophy was accepted on the basis of a philosophic *tradition* that encompassed certain methods and theories.

5   Indeed one might wonder how religious people embraced such an austere naturalism. Eliezer Goldman makes an important point in this regard:

> That Maimonides could consider his own conception to be an authentic interpretation of the idea of Providence is due to his cosmology. In his world picture, any event occurring in accordance with natural laws could be regarded as resulting from the divine influence mediated by the heavens (the spheres and the intelligences). ...On the modern cosmic model, the world, even when considered to be created, is construed as self-subsistent. The human intellect is unique in the sense that there are no intellects on the cosmic level to mediate between God and the human mind. If man is at all able to confront God, it must be in the immediacy of His presence. ... It follows that, granted the modern world picture, the philosophically concerned religious person confronts a problem of the relation of the wholly transcendent to the created world.

See Goldman, "Responses to Modernity in Orthodox Jewish Thought," *Studies in Contemporary Jewry*, 2 (1986), 57.

6   Eloquent and well developed examples of this approach may be found in: David Hartman, *Maimonides: Torah and Philosophic Quest* (Philadelphia, 1976) and *A Living Covenant* (New York, 1986); Yeshayahu Leibowitz, in many works, including *Yahadut, Am Yehudi, u-Medinat Yisrael* (Tel Aviv, 1975), *Emunah, Historiyah, va-Arakhim* (Jerusalem, 1982), *The Faith of Maimonides*, trans. John Glucker (New York, 1987), *Judaism, Human Values, and the Jewish State*, ed. Eliezer Goldman, trans. E. Goldman, Y. Navon, *et. al.* (Cambridge, MA, 1992); Jerome I. Gellman, "Radical Responsibility in Maimonides' Thought," in *The Thought of Moses Maimonides*, ed. Ira Robinson, Lawrence Kaplan, and Julien Bauer (Lewiston, NY, 1991), 249-65. Gellman has informed me that he intended his article as an interpretation of Maimonides and does not necessarily endorse the argument he presents. The summary that follows is an amalgam of elements found in the cited thinkers and ignores critical differences between them. For example, Leibowitz and Hartman disagree about (a) the religious desirability of submission and obedience and (b) the religious relevance of human needs and values (see Hartman, *Living Covenant*, Chap. 5). The common denominator of the views is that hard naturalism coheres with other religious sensibilities.

7   *Pesahim* 64b; *Yerushalmi Shekalim* 6:3; and elsewhere. Though the dictum "We do not rely on miracles" is subject to dispute in the Talmud, it has been codified as binding in later codes. There are also specific imperatives governing the areas I itemized (medicine, economics, war).

8   Leibowitz, *Judaism, Human Values, and the Jewish State*, 63.

9   As Kenneth Seeskin writes, "A person might argue [as Spinoza did] that so far from constituting proof of God's greatness, such acts [miracles] testify to the opposite: a disorderly world in which there is constant need of makeshift solution" (Seeskin, *Jewish Philosophy in a Secular Age* [Albany, 1990], 76). Compare a computer programmer who can correct bugs in the program as they come up, to one whose *original* program is bug-free.

10   See David Basinger and Randall Basinger, *Philosophy and Miracle: The Contemporary Debate* (Lewiston, NY, 1986), Chap. 5.

11   For criticism of these naturalist understandings of petitionary prayer, see Daniel Cohn-Sherbok, *Jewish Petitionary Prayer: A Theological Exploration* (Lewiston, NY, 1989), chap. 3. Cf. Shalom Carmy, "Destiny, Freedom and the Logic of Petition," *Tradition* 24, 2 (1989): 17-37. For discussion of the problems inherent in Maimonides' view on prayer, see Marvin Fox, *Interpreting Maimonides* (Chicago, 1990), chap. 11, and Ehud Benor, *Worship of the Heart: A Study of Maimonides' Philosophy of Religion* (Albany, NY, 1995).

12   *Enquiry Concerning Human Understanding*, X.

13   See, for example, George N. Schlesinger, *New Perspectives on Old-Time Religion* (Oxford, 1988), 100-19; Richard Swinburne, *The Concept of Miracle* (New York, 1970); Michael Peterson, et al., *Reason and Religious Belief: An Introduction to the Philosophy of Religion* (Oxford, 1991), Chap. 9. For an interesting engagement with Hume from a Jewish perspective, see Seeskin, 71-98. See also Louis Jacobs, *A Jewish Theology* (New York, 1975), Chap. 8.

14 See Alfred J. Freddoso, "Medieval Aristotelianism and the Case Against Secondary Causes in Nature," in *Divine & Human Action: Essays in the Metaphysics of Theism*, ed. Thomas V. Morris (Ithaca, NY, 1988), 74-118, esp. 99-105. George Berkeley's philosophy is in large part an effort to demonstrate the compatibility of occasionalism with observational data.

15 See Freddoso, 112-18. Cf. in the same volume, Philip L. Quinn, "Divine Conservation, Secondary Causes, and Occasionalism," 50-73. Anti-realism is the view that scientific theories do not provide a literally accurate account of the world. Typically anti-realists will see science as (merely) providing instruments for prediction and control. Freddoso refers as well to "explanatory realism," the view that science discovers the real causes of natural phenomena.

16 Walter S. Wurzburger, "Confronting the Challenge of the Values of Modernity," *The Torah u-Madda Journal* 1 (1989): 105-6. Ian Barbour aptly notes that technology "has offered power, control, and the prospect of overcoming our helplessness and dependency" (Barbour, *Religion in An Age of Science*, [New York, 1990], Vol. 1, xiii). See also Goldman, 53.

17 Freddoso arrives at this formulation after pointing out problems with more moderate forms of occasionalism that attribute unexercised causal powers to substances.

18 See his *Mikhtav me-Eliyahu*, ed. Aryeh Carmell and Alter Halperin (Bnai Brak, 1955), I: 178. The English translation is borrowed from A. Carmell's *Strive for Truth* (New York, 1985), II: 236-310. Goldman explains that this ideology represents "a frontal attack upon the modern ethos with its emphasis on foresight, calculation, planning, and domination of nature through knowledge of its workings" (55). It is designed to enhance Torah study by implying that God will tend to personal livelihood and political welfare.

19 Malebranche is aware of this problem and seeks to meet it by saying that "God wills X" logically entails "X happens." See *The Search After Truth* VI:2:3, in Nicolas Malebranche, *Philosophical Selections*, ed. Steven Nadler (Indianapolis, IND, 1992), 94. It is not clear to me whether this rejoinder succeeds.

20 Note Charles J. McCracken's attribution of the following view to Nicolas Malebranche and George Berkeley: "Belief in *nature*, if by that term be meant a realm of entities that produce effects by their own power, is the hallmark of the pagan, and the antithesis of the Christian, view of the world" (*Malebranche and British Philosophy* [Oxford, 1983], 211, cited by Freddoso, 98). See also the analysis of Malebranche given by Louis E. Loeb in his *From Descartes to Hume: Continental Metaphysics and the Development of Modern Philosophy* (Ithaca, NY, 1981), 191-228. Loeb stresses the religious motivations behind many of the philosophical positions taken in the seventeenth and eighteenth centuries.

21 Freddoso, 77.

22 *Shemonah Perakim*, Chap. 8. Cf. Freddoso, 81-82. In "Is Matter All That Matters?," in this volume, I note that some may view affirming free will to be an unseemly diminution of divine control.

23 See Freddoso, 115-16, and his interesting suggestion that for occasionalists there may be no intrinsic goods and evils.

24 "*In hakhi nami*" is a talmudic expression that means, roughly, "just so" — that is, I accept the conclusion of your *reductio ad absurdum*.

25   *Mikhtav*, I: 178; Carmell translation, *Strive for Truth*, II: 240.

26   Ibid., I: 197; Carmell, II: 288.

27   Ibid., I: 188; Carmell, II: 264. Developing the Musar concept of *"hishtaddelut"* (effort), R. Dessler counsels use of minimal practical endeavor. For a midrashic criticism of practical effort, see Gen. Rabbah 89:2.

28   See Bahya's *Hovot ha-Levavot (Duties of the Heart)*, IV. For discussion, see Alexander Altmann, "The Religion of the Thinkers: Free Will and Predestination in Saadia, Bahya and Maimonides," in *Religion in a Religious Age*, ed. S. D. Goitein (Cambridge, MA, 1974), 33-35.

29   *Mikhtav*, I: 194-95; Carmell, *Strive for Truth*, II: 280-81.

30   Nahmanides appears to have a different rationale for administering medical care. If someone consults a doctor, this in itself shows that he is not among the *"adat Hashem"* (congregation of God) who place their welfare in God's hands, and so the doctor need have no compunctions about trying to heal. See his commentary to Lev. 26:11.

31   Admittedly, even this simple thesis is not consonant with Jewish law, for Jewish law generally demands more than minimal efforts at self-preservation and mandates prioritizing self over other in some crucial cases. See my "'As Thyself: The Limits of Altruism in Jewish Ethics," in this volume.

32   This point is related to, but not identical with, the earlier point that in occasionalist theories God directly causes evils.

33   See Cohn-Sherbok, 3-4, 98-102, 154-56. Note H. D. Lewis, *Our Experience of God* (London, 1959), 251, quoted by Cohn-Sherbok: "Ought not God to benefit men according to their needs or merits and not in terms of the rather haphazard and arbitrary condition of being the subject of prayer?" The problem is exacerbated by the fact that it also matters *who* chooses to pray for the party, the prayers of the righteous being of special efficacy.

34   I have deliberately sidestepped distinctions between different categories of intervention — interventions that appear to violate natural law vs. interventions that do not; "violative" interventions that work through the natural order by starting off new natural causal chains vs. "violative" interventions that bypass the natural order entirely, etc. See, however, Cohn-Sherbok, *Jewish Petitionary Prayer*, chap. 5, for some necessary distinctions.

35   Soft naturalists have trouble explaining the "concurrence" of divine and natural causation. See Freddoso, 78 and the references in his note 4.

36   Gellman, "Radical Responsibility," 252.

37   Ibid., 262-63.

38   I grant that the curses of Lev. 26 and Deut. 28 could be read as attributing a strict deed/consequence relationship to the collective rather than to individuals. Still, the theoretical point — that interventionists could assert a strict, regular, stable nexus — remains.

39   A Laplacean predictor, conceived by the French mathematician and astronomer Pierre Laplace (1749-1827), is an intelligence that knows all the laws of nature and all the states of nature at a given time, and deduces therefrom all future states. The predictor is widely used as a picturesque way of describing determinism.

40 Hard naturalists can plausibly argue that natural law has wider scope in Jewish theology than normally thought (see, e. g. Rava's statement about *mazzal* on *Mo'ed Katan* 28a) and that some Sages say that reward for commandments are not given in this world (*Hullin* 142a). But regarding the former text, it will be very difficult for a hard naturalist to maintain that in Jewish tradition there are no interventions; and the view that there is no reward in this world involves the idea that we can control our reward in the next through prayer and good deeds.

41 Tennant, *Philosophical Theology* (Cambridge, 1929), vol. 2, 199-200; Lewis, *The Problem of Pain* (New York, 1962), 34. Both are quoted by Basinger and Basinger, 110-11. Talmudic sources sometimes admit that the reward/punishment nexus does not hold — again, "There is no reward in this world for a commandment" (*Hullin* 142a). See also "'From the Depths I Have Called to You'," part II, in this volume.

42 Maimonides believed, however, that if you follow a particular medical regimen you will not get sick (*Hilkhot De'ot* 4:20).

Sidney Hook, one of the twentieth century's leading critics of supernaturalism, claims that combining medical treatment with praying betrays bad faith, an underlying disbelief in the power of prayer alone. (See Hook, "Naturalism and First Principles," *Philosophy of Religion*, ed. Steven M. Cahn [New York, 1969], 344.) As armchair psychology, the objection is overly cynical. Believers may do both because they think God requires both, and they may do so with great sincerity. Furthermore, it may be asserted that divine causation accompanies the natural variety, so there is no inconsistency in the believer's behavior. Yet Hook seems to be saying this: we would give far more dramatic expression to *bittahon* if, in addition to praying, giving charity, repenting, and studying, we would also cut back on some of our practical endeavor. This is in fact R. Dessler's position. Soft naturalists, who may think that God intervenes only for the most worthy, do not want anyone to be so presumptuous as to assume he or she is worthy of intervention, so they may advise everyone to do what seems to be practically necessary.

43 For such a construal see Benor, *Worship of the Heart*.

44 One point that fortifies this criticism is that in some soft naturalist theories, the reason that some rare people (those who show an exceptionally strong attachment to God) escape natural causality is that they *naturally* escape natural causality. Specifically, within the context of the kabbalistic metaphysics which Nahmanides endorsed, the special providence won by the pious can be explained in terms of law-like cause-effect connections that obtain in the kabbalistic universe. See David Berger, "Miracles and the Natural Order in Nahmanides," in *Rabbi Moses Nahmanides: Explorations in His Religious and Literary Virtuosity*, ed. Isadore Twersky, (Cambridge, MA, 1987), 121. See Meir ibn Gabbai, *Avodat ha-Kodesh* (Warsaw, 1894), II, 17, p. 36b; Isaiah Horowitz, *Shenei Luhot ha-Berit* (Jozewow, 1878), 9b-10a. What we have, then, in the Maimonides-Nahmanides dispute over intervention, is not a disagreement over whether exceptional people are protected from harm in natural or instead miraculous fashion, but one over what are the precise laws and rules of cause and effect that will explain this protection naturally, and what are the precise virtues that are required to secure it. In short, even within a non-scientific system ample room exists for naturalistic explanations of reward and punishment. Take, as another example of naturalist

elbow room, the ways in which doing *mitzvot* secure "rewards" for a person. Like Maimonides, Nahmanides allows that all *mitzvot* have a reason, and, like him, he stresses the fact that certain commandments *naturally* inculcate certain (true) beliefs and certain (positive) character traits. (See, e. g. commentary to Lev. 19:19, Deut. 22:6.) It is true that this is a lower, non-kabbalistic account of *ta'amei ha-mitzvot*, but we have already seen that this sort of naturalism might continue on through the kabbalistic explanation of "reward."

45   See *Guide* II:48; III:25, 32. See also "Worship, Corporeality, and Human Perfection," in this volume.

46   See the comment of Isaac Abarbanel to Deut. 8:17-18 in his *Perush Abarbanel al ha-Torah* (Jerusalem, 1984), 92-93. In the idiom of Deut. 8:17-18, God does not directly produce human success, but gives people powers by which they can achieve.

47   Commentary to the Mishnah, *Pesahim* 4:9. The context is a rabbinic passage commending King Hezekiah for hiding a "book of cures." Maimonides asserts that Hezekiah hid the work because it contained quack medicine; others thought that the cures were effective but were hidden in order that people trust in God instead of doctors. See also *Mishneh Torah, Hilkhot De'ot* 4:20. In the *Pesahim* source, Maimonides points out that one can thank God for providing medicine just as one can thank God for providing food and drink — both reflect providence. "God provides food," for Maimonides, does not mean "God directly provides food"; it means that food has been made available through the mediation of the natural order, of which God is the ultimate cause. See *Guide* II:48. As Gellman points out ("Radical Responsibility," 256), both bread and medicine are products of human labor.

48   *Iggerot ha-Rambam*, ed. Yitzhak Sheilat (Jerusalem, 1988), vol. II, 480. An English translation of this letter by Ralph Lerner is found in *Medieval Political Philosophy*, ed. Ralph Lerner and Muhsin Mahdi (Ithaca, NY, 1963), 227-36. Note also *Guide* III:32, where Maimonides maintains that military training is needed for Jewish conquest.

49   Maimonides takes the word *"me'onen"* in Deut. 18: 10 to refer to an astrologer, taking his cue from R. Akiva's opinion in *Sanhedrin* 65b. See *Hilkhot Avodah Zarah* 11:8. Others, including Nahmanides, follow a different talmudic opinion (Rav in *Pesahim* 113b), according to which astrology is prohibited because of the verse *tamim tihyeh*.

50   Maimonides notwithstanding, rejection of astrology was highly unusual in the Middle Ages.

51   *"Tamim tihyeh"* then means "be perfect in your trust." The most famous construal of the imperative along these lines is that of Nahmanides in his commentaries to Deut. 18: 9, 13. and Lev. 26:11. See also *Torat Hashem Temimah*, in *Kitvei ha-Ramban*, ed. C. Chavel (Jerusalem, 5724), I, 148-50; responsum in Chavel, I, 378-81 (note the delicate balance there between trust and *ein somekhin al ha-nes* in the use of astrology); *Torat ha-Adam*, in Chavel II, 41-48. On these issues see also my "Practical Endeavor and the Torah u-Madda Debate," *The Torah u-Madda Journal* 3 (1991-1992): 98-149. For sources on *tamim tihyeh*, see the materials quoted by R. Yaakov Hillel, *Tamim Tihyeh* (Jerusalem, 1986-87).

52   *Hilkhot Avodah Zarah* 11:16.

53   See esp. *Guide* III:25-31.

54   For this use of *"temimut,"* see, besides *Hilkhot Avodat Kokhavim* 11:16, *Hilkhot Yesodei ha-Torah* 2:2;, where God is described as *"temim de'ot."* Presumably by having wise thoughts we imitate God. Also note Maimonides's understanding of *"ha-tzur tamim pa'alo"* ("The Rock whose work is perfect", Deut. 32:4): God's creation is perfect in the sense that it exemplifies wisdom and purposiveness. See *Guide* III:25, 49 and II:28. Cf. Isadore Twersky, *Introduction to the Code of Maimonides (Mishneh Torah)* (New Haven, 1981), 412, 420, 482.

55   See Bernard Septimus, "Biblical Religion and Political Rationality in Simone Luzatto, Maimonides and Spinoza," in *Jewish Thought in the Seventeenth Century*, ed. Isadore Twersky and Bernard Septimus (Cambridge, MA, 1987), 399-434. Note especially Maimonides' assertion that the Torah "was intended to efface those untrue opinions from the mind *and* to abolish those useless practices which brought about a waste of lives in vain and futile things" (*Guide* III:49; see also III:29). In Septimus's paraphrase of Maimonides' position, "The prophets underscored the practical as well as the spiritual futility of Israel's backsliding into idolatrous superstition" (Septimus, 407).

56   See *Mishneh Torah*, Laws of Repentance, chap. 5; *Shemonah Perakim*, chap. 8. In his *Letter on Astrology*, Maimonides argues that astrology is invalid on the twin grounds that it is scientifically refuted and that it runs counter to religious teachings about free will. Note that there is an impact on the doctrine of *sakhar va-onesh*, reward and punishment. Instead of seeing human destiny as a result of the character of one's deeds, astrology attributes the benefits and adversities of a person's life to factors outside of his or her control. Some Jews who believed in astrology thought that a person can override the constellations. See my discussion of this position in "Is Matter All That Matters?," in this volume.

57   These remarks are not intended to exclude the possibility that Maimonides is a soft determinist (compatibilist), an interpretation defended by Altmann, "Religion of the Thinkers," and by Shlomo Pines, "Abu'l-Bakarat's Poetics and Metaphysics," *Studies in Philosophy, Scripta Hierosolymitana* 6 (1960): 195-98 (Excursus). For criticism of Altmann and Pines, see Jerome Gellman, "Freedom and Determinism in Maimonides' Philosophy," in *Moses Maimonides and His Time*, ed. Eric L. Ormsby (Washington, DC, 1988), 139-50. Ironically, the existence of free will weakens the predictability argument, since our fates are often in others' hands.

58   For discussion of these ways of connecting providence to intellect, see Charles M. Raffel, "Providence as Consequent Upon the Intellect: Maimonides' Theory of Providence," *AJS Review* 12 (1987): 25-71. Scholars debate whether conjunction with the Active Intellect, even partial conjunction, is possible. See my "Worship, Corporeality and Human Perfection," in this volume. Leibowitz attempts to make "special providence" virtually *identical with* worship of God for its own sake. (See especially *Faith of Maimonides*, Chaps. 11-13.) Suffice it to say that, in my opinion, Leibowitz does not fully face up to the implications of Maimonides' teleology.

59   *Hilkhot De'ot* 4:20.

60   See also his naturalistic explanations in *Hilkhot Teshuvah*, chap. 4, of the "twenty-four things that hold back repentance."

61   *Hilkhot Teshuvah* 10:2. See also Commentary to the Mishnah, *Sanhedrin* 10, Introduction to Helek. I interchange *me-ahavah* with *lishmah*.

62   This point was first made by Altmann, "The Religion of the Thinkers," 45, who credits R. Menahem Meier with the discovery. See *Hilkhot Mattenot Aniyyim* 10:19 and *Hilkhot Zekhiyyah u-Mattanah* 12:17.

63   *The Lonely Man of Faith*, originally published in 1965 but reprinted (New York, 1992); "Majesty and Humility," *Tradition* 17:2 (Spring 1978): 25-37; "Confrontation," *Tradition* 6:2 (Summer 1964): 5-29. Illustrative of R. Soloveitchik's communal orientation is the following passage: "Distribution of labor, the coordinated efforts of the many, the accumulated experiences of the multitude, the cooperative spirit of countless individuals, raise man above the primitive level of a natural existence and grant him limited dominion over his environment. What we call civilization is the sum total of a community effort through the millennia" ("Lonely Man of Faith," 32). For more on R. Soloveitchik's communal orientation, see my "Practical Endeavor and the *Torah u-Madda* debate" and "Science and Religious Consciuousness in the Thought of Rabbi Joseph B. Soloveitchik," in this volume.

64   See, for example, David Hartman, *Joy and Responsibility* (Jerusalem, 1978), 60, who argues that secularization and scientific advances expand the domain of human responsibility by putting human fate into humanity's collective hands. For Leibowitz, none of this matters, since no activity aimed at furthering human ends is truly religious.

65   That Maimonides' focus is individual material welfare is further accentuated by his view of how Torah scholars relate to their communities. The Torah scholar must not receive material support from the community for his study, but rather must find his own means of livelihood; and equally, the scholar, while bearing some burdens of taxation, is not obliged to devote efforts to improve the material welfare of the community, but rather is stringently obligated to promote their spiritual and educational welfare. See *Mishneh Torah, Hilkhot Talmud Torah*, esp. 1:2, 9; 2:1; 3:4, 10, 11. Most remarkable is Maimonides's earlier formulation at the end of his introduction to his commentary on the Mishnaic order of *Zera'im*. There Maimonides asserts that God created non-scholars in order that they serve the scholars and settle the world! To the extent that the scholar, in the *Mishneh Torah* formulation, tends to his own material needs but is excused from tending to those of others, he is isolated, disengaged from all but himself with respect to material welfare. This, I submit, reflects a perceived necessity for the scholar to be occupied with material needs of the self rather than those of others, and it represents the halakhic correlate of the well known individualism and self-sufficiency of Maimonides's (and to an extent Aristotle's) philosophical ideals.

66   This suggestion was made by a luminary of the ultra-Orthodox in Israel, R. Avraham Yeshayahu Karelitz (the "Hazon Ish"; d. 1953). *Bittahon* does not require the individual to believe that all will go well. Rather, *bittahon* amounts to "the faith that there is no happenstance (*mikreh*) in the universe, and that everything that happens under the sun is by way of divine decree." See *Emunah u-Bittahon* (Jerusalem, 1953), 16-17. A naturalist would need to define God's justice in order to make this definition helpful.

67   For a beautiful articulation of this viewpoint, see Aharon Lichtenstein, "*Le-berurah shel Middat ha-Bittahon*," *Deot* 52 (1975): 352-55.

68   A different approach to *bittahon* is suggested by R. Soloveitchik, "Lonely Man of Faith," 90:

> The doctrine of faith in God's charity, *bittahon*, is not to be equated with the folly of the mystical doctrine of quietism. ...This kind of repose is wholly contrary to the repose which the Halakhah recommends: the one which follows human effort and remedial action. Man must first use his own skill and try to help himself as much as possible. Then, and only then, may man find repose and quietude and be confident that his effort and action will be crowned with success. The initiative, says the Halakhah, belongs to man; the successful realization, to God.

But if successful realizations belong exclusively to God, then the plans of a nefarious dictator are not themselves sufficient to produce the dictator's desired results. God has to nudge the process along. And so on the cited view (no doubt contrary to R. Soloveitchik's intent) God has to assist the wicked in carrying out their plans, and that becomes part of *bittahon* too.

69   This section overlaps with one in "From Anthropology to Metaphysics: David Hartman on Divine Intervention," in this volume.

70   This is a type of tension we might attribute to Kant. Acts done just to acquire a benefit have no moral worth, but if a desire for benefit does not motivate the act, the act has moral worth even if the person desires the benefit.

71   *Avot* 1:3.

72   *Avot de-Rabbi Natan*, 5:2. Cf. the discussion of Antigonus by Maimonides in introduction to *Helek*. Despite Maimonides' praise of Antigonus's position, in defining *lishmah* and *ahavah* Maimonides himself emphasizes not servant-like obedience to the commandments, but rather reasoned endorsement.

73   *Nahalat Avot* [Abarbanel's commentary to *Avot*], on *Avot* 1:3. Abarbanel suggests that Antigonus was only discouraging people from serving the master to receive "*peras*," a fixed, immediately dispensed reward, but not discouraging them from pursuing "*sakhar*," an ultimate, far-off recompense. This could imply that Abarbanel does not think that the *peras* arrangement even holds. While this nuance affects the precision of my formulation in the text, since Abrananel does not really countenance focusing on material rewards in the here and now and may not believe that the nexus holds, the basic issue he raises — that belief in reward and punishment should dictate the legitimacy of having that belief serve to motivate action — holds just the same. I should also note that Abarbanel obviously does not wish to reject the rabbinic notion that acting *lishmah* is higher than acting *lo lishmah*; rather, he will demarcate *lishmah* and *lo lishmah* differently, so that the critical difference will be between types of rewards.

74   *Hilkhot Teshuvah* 10:2.

75   In this context, however, Abarbanel does not include motivations for developing a particular set of character traits.

FROM ANTHROPOLOGY
TO METAPHYSICS:
David Hartman on Divine Intervention

It is often said that, in post-Kantian religious philosophy, metaphysics and theology are replaced by anthropology. This formulation does not quite capture the most interesting varieties of the post-Kantian turn. For, in the case of some theologians, metaphysics and theology are not so much replaced by anthropology as shaped by it. A thinker might determine what metaphysics to adopt by seeing what metaphysics fits his or her favored anthropology.

Twenty-five years ago David Hartman's book on Maimonides brought this seductive idea onto the landscape of Jewish theology.[1] It was an eye opener to me. Having been trained in analytic philosophy, I was used to philosophers evaluating metaphysical perspectives using the criterion of whether the perspective is logically supported by evidence and reasoning that bore directly upon its truth. Thus a philosopher would make the choice whether to believe in widespread divine intervention on the one hand or a naturalistic framework on the other based on whether the evidence supported belief in a fixed and closed natural order. Hartman broached a different option. Assess metaphysical claims by their psychological impact, by what sort of human being they create. Select the claims that will best produce the kind of personality you think one should be. The value judgment as to what personality is best can be made on the basis of philosophical reasoning accompanied by citations of models suggested by traditional religious texts, albeit, in the case of texts, with the understanding that one was going to choose particular models and reject others. Regarding Maimonides, Hartman's argument was that Maimonides' naturalism, which clearly sought to limit the frequency and scope of direct divine intervention, was linked to his valuing a personality who is autonomous and who, overcoming feelings of dependence, learns not to rely on miraculous intervention but to develop initiative instead. Study nature, use your intellect, provide for yourself, and in this way you can have a meaningful relationship with God — for providence is reflected in the fact that nature, including the human intellect, is structured so as to make possible the improvement of the human condition by rational means.[2]

The specific human characteristics Hartman deems desirable — autonomy, initiative, freedom, responsibility, celebration of finitude and self — are usually assessed as secular, Enlightenment-inspired values. In Hartman's theology, as in parts of R. Joseph B. Soloveitchik's, they are affirmed as religious values. Hartman fully acknowledges that many sources in the tradition highlight submission, terror, human frailty and the like, but he asserts that we should embrace the anthropology of human adequacy virtually without the dialectic of majesty and humility, joy and dread, insisted on by R. Soloveitchik.

In philosophy of religion one finds pragmatic arguments for believing in God, most famously in William James' 1896 essay "The Will to Believe." Belief in God, the pragmatist argues, brings security, meaning, optimism and so on. But philosophers do not frequently invoke pragmatic arguments (under which I include anthropology-driven arguments) for believing this or that view about the extent of God's intervention. On the other hand, some thinkers see anthropological impact as realistically the only way to discriminate among competing metaphysical views, given the ultimate transcendence and unknowability of God in Himself. R. Abraham Isaac Kook, for example, opts for pantheism over theism by arguing that in theism a human being becomes jealous of God.[3] The methodology here is to eschew metaphysical argument and rivet attention on the relationship between mindsets and theology.

In this essay I wish to demonstrate that Hartman, contrary to first impressions, could accept an interventionist viewpoint (a viewpoint according to which God occasionally intervenes in history and performs miracles). For he does not in fact use anthropology to ground metaphysics. Rather he uses anthropology to render metaphysics irrelevant, to make the choice of a metaphysic a matter of indifference to how one experiences the framework of *mitzvah*. After presenting this revised understanding of Hartman's views, I hope to show why his attempt to render interventionist metaphysics irrelevant to the life of *mitzvah* is problematic.

FROM MINDSET TO METAPHYSICS

Suppose that a naturalist mindset creates a religious sensibility that is preferable to one created by interventionist understandings. Does this generate a good argument for the *truth* of naturalism? *Prima facie*, no. Rather, it creates a good argument for believers not placing interventionism at the forefront of their religious consciousness. A religion might expect that an individual maintain a delicate tension. On the one hand, the person might be required to *believe* that God can and will intervene in the natural order (either to satisfy human needs or to execute justice), but at the same time he ought not let this belief motivate him.

To warm up to this distinction between what is true and what should motivate, one should realize that, when thinkers maintain that an anthropology of a certain sort (one valuing autonomy, responsibility, etc.) supports a metaphysics of non-intervention by God, they fixate on the human point of view and fail to consider God's point of view at all. They focus on how humans should think and act, and what sort of metaphysics best undergirds particular ways of acting; they don't focus on how God should act in response to human deeds. A good God, and in particular a God who is truly a partner in the covenant, who seeks to be intimate, will not want to stay out of human affairs. He will want to act so as to aid the other partner and show appreciation. Hartman's own God is in fact a caring God. "Prayer...is part of a total life organized by *mitzvah*. It is part of living with the knowledge that one has particular obligations and that God *is concerned about and responsive to* the human situation."[4] God also would want to create a just order in which evil is punished and goodness rewarded, and to protect those who uphold the covenant, His partners, from oppression at the hands of those who do not. Surely God should not be expected to withhold good from people *just because* if He intervenes in things people might become base and self-interested. What makes more sense is that He would urge people not to let belief in intervention influence their actions — while He continues to intervene. To be sure, God may wish to limit such intervention, for if it is widespread it will make disinterested worship psychologically impossible. But an occasional intervention out of care or a sense of justice is compatible with making the believer responsible for his or her own motivation.

To an extent, therefore, anthropology-based arguments for naturalism (my term here for the view that denies intervention) are *non sequiturs*. All that follows from them is something about a proper religious consciousness and mindset, not anything about a metaphysics of divine intervention. It can obviously be argued, as Hartman does,[5] that goods and evils are not distributed in the world in a way that supports an interventionist metaphysics. But that is beside the present point, since once the objection to interventionism is based on evidence, we are no longer predicating metaphysics on anthropology. The entanglement of metaphysics and anthropology, even for Hartman, has to give way to just the opposite — a recognition that these are two distinct problems, and anthropology has little to contribute to establishing a metaphysics.

Hartman himself recognizes how his anthropology could coexist with an interventionist metaphysics. The recognition does not come because of the *non sequitur* I spoke of, but because of a discomfort with being branded, in effect, a deist or worse. In an essay responding to a critic of *A Living Covenant*, [6] Hartman says it is not that he denies God's intervention in history, but rather that the framework of *mitzvah* does not require belief in divine intervention beyond the miracle of the revelation at Sinai (he acknowledges Sinai as a miracle in *LC*, 235).

- I do not deny God's ability to act unilaterally, but simply *decline to base expectations* upon it.
- Instead of developing a metaphysics about what God can or cannot do, I ask only: can the Sinai covenant retain its vitality if one does not build into that notion the idea of messianic expectation? Can you, despite every adversity and defeat, retain human freedom and human responsibility as permanent features of the covenantal life? ... Can religious passion be nurtured, although one remains fully open to the possibilities of radical tragedy and radical destruction?
- Therefore, I asked, how might Jews celebrate their religious life if they do not rely upon having an escape from this world, if they do not have the certainty of a transformed history, if they do not presuppose the promise of eternal resurrection, of another world to be created in the future in which all the dreams and aspirations that the Jews bring to life will reach their fullest expression? To live religiously without these assumptions is not to claim that the resurrection of the dead is false or that the immortality of the soul is impossible or logically contradictory, nor is it to rule out the possibility of God's unilateral redemptive grace in history. These are metaphysical claims which I clearly stated that I was not making [see below-DS]. I asked only: how would a Judaic religious passion articulate itself if it did not rely upon these belief frameworks to support its religious commitment?
- I do not claim that Jews who believe in a personal God who acts in history become irresponsible. Nor do I believe that deism is necessary for a moral reawakening of human beings. I do not need an impotent God in order to make human beings potent.
- My concern with petitional prayer was not to determine God's ability or inability to answer petitional prayer, but the motive impulse that the worshipper out of love may bring to petitional prayer.

Hartman actually made this point — as he notes in the reply article from which I just quoted — in *A Living Covenant*:

I am not claiming or implying that belief in a future radical transformation of history is naive, childish, escapist or illogical. Far be it from me to deny the ability of God to act in such ways. I am merely claiming that those eschatological beliefs are not constitutive of the Sinai covenant and that, consequently, the covenant can retain its vitality even when those beliefs are not adduced in its support or when they are given demythologizing interpretation (*LC*, 257).

Elsewhere he cautions only against "exaggerated expectations," not against belief in intervention *tout court*.

In essence, Hartman, in the material quoted, is pushing for a tension roughly parallel to the one Kant holds must be maintained in ethics, on some interpretations of Kant. Kant notoriously said that acts of benevolence done purely out of sympathy or just to reap rewards have no moral worth. But, some interpreters suggest, acting in a way that accords with natural sympathies and that reaps rewards is fine, as long as the desire for reward is not operative when one acts. Desiring reward is thus compatible with performing morally worthy acts, so long as the act is not performed out of that desire. In fact, going further, one could allow multiple motives as long as the motive of duty is strong enough to prevail should the other motives oppose it.[7] In religious life, to articulate now the parallel claim of Hartman, one may yearn for an afterlife and messianic redemption and desire reward, but in a covenantal relationship one must not be motivated by these desires when one acts. Everyday acting is determined by Halakhah. Whether God does or does not intervene for human beings is supposed to be *irrelevant* to us; that is not the same as *denying* that God intervenes. We can be humble and agnostic with respect to the question of how God relates to the universe, without that uncertainty affecting our commitment.

Critics who predicate their objections to Hartman on his supposed denial of supernaturalism are misreading him, or at least misreading *A Living Covenant*. He is seeking to bracket the question of intervention, not to deny divine intervention, nor to deny God's role in transforming the world in messianic times. This bracketing resembles, though it is not identical with, that of Maimonides. Maimonides affirmed the afterlife and affirmed the coming of the messiah, but specifically cautions against being motivated by the World to Come, and when it comes to the messiah, his view seems to be that messianic times will be created by human beings doing what they need to do even in non-messianic times — namely, seeking Jewish political autonomy in order to create conditions conducive to acquiring and spreading knowledge.[8]

But now we confront the following question. Once Hartman has conceded that his anthropology can hold even if interventionism is true, there is no anthropology-driven reason to reject an interventionist mindset across the board. On the contrary, Hartman now appears to be free to adopt the traditional view that God intervenes, in cases where this belief will have no harmful effect on mindset.

Consider holidays, a topic about which Hartman says little. Observances of holidays are *mitzvot*; and observing *mitzvot* is the only way the Jew has of acting out his covenantal role. With what mindset should holidays be observed? In traditional Judaism, the holidays commemorate God's saving acts in history — taking us out of Egypt, protecting us in booths during our sojourn in the wilderness. It is one thing to say that our acts do not depend upon future redemption; it is another to celebrate a happy holiday without marking it as a time of *past* redemption. Similarly, it is admissible to make the moment of Sinai more central than the moment of the Exodus, as Hartman does, but this very way of putting things implies that the Exodus is a paradigm of miracle and intervention. So why not celebrate the Exodus as commemorating intervention and have an interventionist mindset at least to that extent?[9] Likewise, one can celebrate the establishment of the state of Israel as an act of providence, in the full-throated manner of R. Joseph B. Soloveitchik,[10] without denying (as R. Soloveitchik does not deny) that human initiative played a role in the State's birth. One could argue in fact that the best religious motivation for observing these holidays is that God intervened, without that somehow challenging or undermining Hartman's larger project. Being grateful to someone who has saved me in the past does not imply that I will sit back and do nothing in the future to help myself, forcing the hand of my past benefactor. And what about gratitude to God for giving the Torah, for issuing "the divine call to understanding the broad range of responsibility" (*LC*, 183)? Hartman describes Sinai as a "miracle" that "marks a shift away from spontaneous divine miracles in history to an immanent structured communal framework that enables an orderly development of history based on the human freedom to act" (*LC*, 236). There seems to be no anthropology-driven reason to mute the miraculous aspect of Shavuot, the anniversary of God's very giving of the *mitzvot*. The Sinai moment that Hartman celebrates does not require us to ignore divine intervention, but rather to acknowledge it. In addition, doesn't gratitude for the Torah — as well as the whole range of gratitude to God — depend upon God's doing for the Jewish people? Ingratitude is surely not a desirable quality; but we risk being guilty of it if we leave in limbo whether God intervenes. Would we not be indecent if we did not believe in and acknowledge those saving acts? Furthermore, while the Jewish calendar is tilted in the direction of celebratory feasts, even those that are observed as commemorative fast days assume that the past has shown a nexus of reward and punishment, and even Hartman sees value in viewing events as not the product of chance (*LC*, 243-47).

Hartman writes in *A Living Covenant* that, "I do not wish to divide my world into two separate realms, one of which is characterized by autonomous action based upon human understanding of the divine norm and the other by anticipation of and dependence upon divine intervention" (232). But a reader may wonder, "Why not?" Moreover the reader may conclude that Hartman has done exactly that by advocating acting as if interventionism is false while suspending belief about whether God intervenes. By taking this stance Hartman appears to ignore the perfectly appropriate recognition of interventions past. Hedging bets cuts both ways. If interventionist consciousness gives rise to undesirable human traits, a naturalist one has moral drawbacks of its own, namely ingratitude.[11]

Let us turn now to a wider discussion of the strategy of affirming interventionism while demanding that belief in interventionism not influence action.[12] The proposal is not (as per naturalism) that we are committed to the covenant even *though* God *does not* intervene to help us; it is, rather, that we are committed to the covenant with God even *if* God does nothing for us. A naturalist might retort that it is psychologically too demanding to expect people to endorse an interventionist metaphysic while making decisions using a naturalist one. The argument would go like this: even though a good God might want to exercise care, justice and mercy and therefore intervene in human affairs, God's ultimate decision would be to refrain from intervening in human affairs *because* He does not want to create a wrong mindset. But a reply is at hand. If God makes naturalism true in order to prevent belief in interventionism, then we must admit that He has badly miscalculated. Despite His supposed nonintervention, after all, interventionists are alive and well. So no good argument is to be found here for a move from anthropology to metaphysics.[13]

It is worth noting here a still more extreme interventionist point of view advanced by Isaac Abarbanel.[14] Criticizing Maimonides's reading of Antigonus, Abarbanel complains that Maimonides' construal of the ideal of "service [of God] out of love" (*avodah me-ahavah*) as "doing the truth because it is the truth"[15] represents a departure from Torah belief. The non-Jewish philosophers, he says — no doubt alluding to the opening lines of Aristotle's *Nicomachean Ethics* — had no choice but to assert that some deeds are worth doing for their own sake. Why? Because, insofar as Gentile philosophers denied providence and denied reward and punishment, they did not find any motivation for acting rightly other than the intrinsic merits of the act. But we who believe in providence, Abarbanel continues, have no need to resort to the intrinsic merits of an act as a motivation for acting. Instead, we can and ought to provide, without a trace of shame, a different motive: hope of reward and fear of punishment.[16] Acting out of ulterior motivation is actually commendable, because it translates our distinctive metaphysical beliefs into a concrete pattern of affect and behavior (cf. *LC*, 194). For Abarbanel, once belief in intervention loses its vitality and its applicability to decision making, once its motivational power is suppressed, one's acts lose their distinctive religious character and value. Hence the seeming benefits of a "love" orientation — as Maimonides defines *avodah me-ahavah* — may not be worth the price they entail. In fact, it seems to me that, on Abarbanel's premises, even a stance of worshipping God out of sheer obedience — a divine command notion of *me-ahavah* (*à la* Yeshayahu Leibowitz) — threatens to annihilate belief in reward and punishment. One's experience of the other partner in the covenant is enhanced, not diminished, by having intervention by the other on one's mind.[17]

Abarbanel aside, if interventionism is true, then an anthropology that distracts one from this belief is *unhealthy* because it leads one away from truth. A mindset which naturalism breeds is attractive *only* if interventionism is false. If interventionism is true — and as I said, it may have to be for God to be wholly good and wholly just — then the noninterventionist mindset is *not* a good one.

I can envisage contexts in which placing an interventionist attitude could theoretically have a harmful effect. As R. Soloveitchik points out, when we carry on the struggle against evil, we must put aside all theodicies. In part, the point is that finding reasons for evils that would justify their existence might diminish the urge to wage battle against them.[18] But even this concern is theoretical — in actual fact, those who believe that there is a justification for evil do not show less concern for their fellow human being.

The choice between a naturalism which denies divine intervention altogether and a naturalism that affirms some intervention should be made on the familiar and heavily trod territory of scientific and philosophical reflection combined with the weight of traditional texts. The attempt to moot the question of whether interventionism is true, to maintain neutrality on this question, risks ingratitude and a failure to recognize (if interventionism is true) the truth about God. It should be understood that my aim, at least in this context, is limited — not to argue against naturalism *per se*, but only to refute anthropological arguments for it.

FREUD VS. HARTMAN

I want next to question the thesis that interventionism reduces human initiative and control. I claim in this section that interventionism *adds* initiatives and means of control, and, in the next, that as an empirical matter the mindset of interventionism has not precluded social action.

The former point is best brought out by a consideration of Sigmund Freud. Hartman cites modern critiques of religion, and mentions in particular Marx (*LC*, 2), for whom religion fostered belief in the inalterability of the *status quo*. But he does not cite Freud. And Freud would seem to provide an interesting foil to Hartman's view of the relationship between interventionist metaphysics and human adequacy. According to Freud (*The Future of an Illusion*), religious ideas are created to protect human beings against the dangers of nature and fate. Children tend to think of their fathers as powerful and as able to protect and provide for them. When the children grow older, they realize that their fathers are not very powerful and that they themselves are unable to control nature so as to be protected from its dangers. They seek a figure to protect them, a (father-) figure who if placated and prayed to can provide for them. That figure is God (or the gods). When later in history the gods themselves came to be thought of as subject to fate, religion instead stressed the gods' role in evening out the evils of civilization. By providing precepts (via promises of reward and threats of punishment) the gods reconcile people to the sacrifices and privations they must endure in civilization for the sake of others. Eventually, just as the child matures and achieves independence from the father, so too the human race will eventually acquire autonomy, exercise reason, and rid itself of the God-figure.

For Freud, then, religion originates not in a sense of dependence but in the drive to control, to master nature. Science does not provide enough of that control. We are fundamentally disadvantaged in our struggles with nature. We lack the intellect and the wherewithal to prevail. Contemplation of nature propels us into hopelessness, despair and a sense of inadequacy. So we invent the figure of God.

The fact that, if Freud is correct, religion is infantile is beside the present point. I cite Freud only as an entry into the point that prayer and observance might be thought of as means of controlling the forces that run the universe. Religious practices are part of a practical strategy, a calculation. Religion affords control through dependence, like finding the right bureaucrat to help you out of a rough situation. You are dependent, and maybe you don't like being dependent. But the strategy of placation and submission is a smart one. Better to be obsequious and succeed than to fail dismally. Ultimately religion, precisely by stressing the human being's dependency upon God, *expands* the arena in which we can experience human adequacy. It is naturalism, not supernaturalism, that gives rise to human inadequacy. Just think of the fatalism that naturalism induces when it makes disease a matter of pure genetics (unaffected by prayer and good deeds) or makes hopes for Israel's future to ride exclusively upon the likelihood, dim by rational calculation, that peace will be achieved in the land. If one objects that such hopes are irrational, one has to base that judgment on evidence for a naturalist outlook, and not on anthropology alone. Notice also that belief in an intervening God expands the *responsibilities* of one human to another — praying for the other becomes part of your duty. So the belief has a healthy outcome from the point of view of responsibility. It is true that human adequacy would here be promoted only by stressing our ultimate dependence on God. Maybe Hartman is seeking a version of adequacy that means "adequate even if there is no God." But (A) Freud is correct that we are somewhat helpless in a non-religious framework; (B) It is hardly a criticism of a religious mindset that it makes humans dependent upon God. (Would not Hartman concede that the Jewish people were dependent during the Exodus and at Sinai?) (C) The bottom line is that belief in intervention promotes adequacy in the sense I outlined.[19]

The virtue of trust deserves mention in this context. It is one thing to say that one ought not trust in God just because one will be rewarded for trusting. It is quite another to say that one ought not trust in God's saving acts in the future at all. If interventionism is true, trust in God's saving power is a virtue, and it enhances the covenantal bond. No one can deny, either, the potential benefits of belief in divine intervention in fostering the arguably healthy human attitude of optimism. Belief that God helps those who help themselves will enable people to pursue their projects with a greater sense of confidence than otherwise; belief that God is just enables people to adjust to tragedies that otherwise might crush their spirits.

In short, Hartman underestimates the way in which an interventionist metaphysics expands the sense of human adequacy, control and responsibility. If there is to be an argument against religion here, it has to be that ultimately religion does not work — the prayers go unanswered, the deeds unrewarded. But to argue this way is no longer to argue on the basis of anthropology. It is rather to engage in metaphysics straight and simple.

INTERVENTIONISM AND SOCIAL ACTION

"Human responsibility for the conditions of life,..." Hartman writes, "was not [in the covenant as he sees it] confined to the religious sphere in the narrow sense, but included mastering sciences and establishing institutional frameworks for alleviating disease, poverty, illiteracy, and other social ills" (*LC*, 227). Hartman believes that noninterventionism (naturalism) stimulates such social action while interventionism diminishes social action. But this is not borne out by the facts.

The militant Orthodox in Israel certainly defy Hartman's stereotype, endorsing as many of them do an activist messianism. As Hartman acknowledges (*LC*, 255), interventionist beliefs in these circles led by a complex process to the justification of brazen (Hartman's word is "imprudent") social action. It should be noted that Nahmanides, who represents for Hartman a passivist type, considers it a *mitzvah* to actively bring about God's plan through practical means even when an act of that type ordinarily would be prohibited (commentary to Gen. 15:14). Let us not forgot either the *haredi* Jews' extensive use of the political system to achieve their practical objectives. And not all examples of social action by interventionists would invite criticism. It is well known that *haredi* social services in both America and Israel are superb. Countless lives are saved by *haredi*-run medical referral services. (Many *rebbe*s specialize in finding the right doctor for patients and arranging the appointment.) Again, countless patients are cheered and furnished food by *bikkur holim* — and the beneficiaries are not only *haredim*. Of course it is a *mitzvah* to aid the sick, but that is exactly the point: you can be an interventionist and not have that compromise your initiative. Why have noninterventionist theologians not mobilized social services programs even remotely resembling those of the *haredim* in efficiency and scope? Are the interventionists really guilty of, to call up a phrase Hartman uses in another context, "self-centered moralism" (*LC*, 196)? Might not a person's sense of autonomy and freedom diminish his or her sense of responsibility for others? The refusal of *haredim* to study in a university for fear of religious attrition or of *bittul Torah* (taking time away from Torah study) must not be mistaken for a passivist approach to social amelioration once wherewithal is available.[20]

I claim, therefore, that the wholesale association of interventionism with passivity and lack of initiative and responsibility is a mistake. The examples Hartman points to of a passivist position in Judaism involve those who considered the founding of the State to be a violation of their messianic vision, and those like Nahmanides who in medieval times considered it impudent to seek medical care (but not, note, to administer it to those who seek it).[21] Regarding the first, opposition to Zionism involved much more than a vision of messianism, most notably a refusal to collaborate with secularists. The messianic argument could be suspected — though I admit the case would need to be made — of being a theological overlay for a position held on other grounds.[22] As for medical treatment, it was easier to oppose intervention when medicine seemed so impotent and uncertain. In modern times one finds virtual unanimity that it is a *mitzvah* to seek medical care, and interventionists go to great lengths to administer proper care; indeed they usually require more by way of aggressive end-of-life treatment than noninterventionists do. Hartman may well object to the notion that, at least in theory, medical care does not require patient consent — a position that violates autonomy — but certainly no one could accuse the position of not being activist in the face of disease.

CONCLUSION

Hartman's theology, we have seen, at first appears to deny divine intervention as a consequence of his favoring a particular anthropology. Closer reading, especially of subsequent clarifications of *A Living Covenant*, suggests that he does not wish to deny intervention, but only to say that the *mitzvah* framework neither requires belief in intervention nor is enhanced by putting interventionism out of consciousness. I have argued that he should have no objection in principle to making interventionism a part of one's mindset when it comes to observing certain *mitzvot*, and that Sinai itself is in his own writing characterized as a miracle. In addition, I have argued that interventionism expands human adequacy, and finally that, as an empirical matter, belief in interventionism does not lead to passivity. Instead, we find interventionists, whether Jews or non-Jews, at the forefront of social services.

I have not quarreled with Hartman's selection of an anthropology, other than to say that he needs more space for gratitude and trust on his list of desirable qualities. I have mainly argued that he can have the anthropology he wants without denying divine intervention, and that belief in interventionism brings other desirable traits as well, such as gratitude. But in the end I do not think he adequately motivates selecting the particular cluster of traits he prefers. He does not give adequate reason, in my opinion, for denying that the ideal personality is one who experiences a range or dialectic of mindsets.[23] Napoleon is reputed to have said: when you pray, pray as if it all depends on God, and when you fight, fight as if it all depends on you. Such an approach fits much of Jewish tradition. If nothing else, an anthropology is stronger if it integrates conflicting Jewish models rather than excludes all but one.[24]

NOTES

[1]   *Maimonides: Torah and Philosophic Quest* (Philadelphia, 1976).

[2]   See also my "Divine Intervention and Religious Sensibilities," in this volume. Whether Hartman's reconstruction correctly captures the trajectory of Maimonides' reasoning is questionable. More plausible is the idea that Maimonides' acceptance of aspects of Neoplatonized Aristotelianism led to

reflection on the kind of human personality this metaphysical view required and an endorsement of that sort of personality. In recent writing Hartman effectively concedes that he is not looking for an exegesis that captures authorial intent. Rather:

> I do not claim that my analyses and interpretations are what the author intended, only that what the author said or wrote makes the interpretation or application plausible.
>
> One could say that the task of Jewish philosophy is not only to present an intellectual history of Jewish ideas and arguments but also to carry the discussion within the tradition further, to recognize and explore what it makes possible, undeterred by the fear that the discussion might go beyond what past participants intended. Talmudic and medieval writers do not, ought not to, control all the implications and consequences of their creative contributions to the tradition (*Israelis and The Jewish Tradition: An Ancient People Debating Its Future* [New Haven, CT, 2000], xiv).

This passage blurs somewhat the difference between admitting that an author may not have intended to say P and admitting that the author may not have accepted Q, which is a consequence or application of P that the author was in no position to foresee. Fundamentally, however, while criticism of a particular representation of Maimonides is in place when a scholarly interpretation is being offered, it is out of place when it comes to building a creative theology out of elements found in the tradition. On this score, Hartman is entitled to rearrange the trajectory of Maimonides' ideas as well as to endorse implications from which Maimonides might have recoiled, so long as he is careful to state what he is and is not claiming.

An interpretation of Maimonides related to but distinct from Hartman's is put forth by Jerome I. Gellman in "Radical Responsibility in Maimonides' Thought," in *The Thought of Moses Maimonides*, ed. Ira Robinson, Lawrence Kaplan and Julien Bauer (Lewiston, NY, 1990), 249-65. The difference between Gellman and Hartman is that Hartman sees Maimonides' naturalizing tendency as also related to the issue of universalism vs. particularism. My interest here is only in other aspects of Hartman's understanding of naturalism.

3   See R. Abraham Isaac Kook, *Orot ha-Kodesh* (Jerusalem, 1985), II: 395-98. On Rav Kook's use of anthropology-based assessments, see Tamar Ross, "The Cognitive Value of Religious Truth Statements: Rabbi A. I. Kook and Post-Modernism," in *Hazon Nahum: Studies in Jewish Law, Thought, and History Presented to Dr. Norman Lamm on the Occasion of His Seventieth Birthday*, ed. Yaakov Elman and Jeffrey S. Gurock (New York, 1997), 479-528.

4   *A Living Covenant: The Innovative Spirit in Traditional Judaism* (New York and London, 1985), 148. (My emphasis.) Henceforth *LC*.

5   *LC*, 267, 318.

6   "A Response to Landes' Review," *Tikkun* 2, 1 (1987): 121-24. The quotations that follow are from pp. 123-24. Daniel Landes' review appeared in *Tikkun*, 1, 2 (1986): 106-11, and he replies to Hartman's reply in 2, 1 (1987): 125-26.

7   See Richard Henson, "What Kant Might Have Said: Moral Worth and the Determination of Dutiful Action," *Philosophical Review* 88 (1979): 39-54;

Barbara Herman, "Acting from the Motive of Duty," *Philosophical Review* 90 (1981): 359-82.

8 Maimonides, *Mishneh Torah, Hilkhot Teshuvah* 10:1; *Hilkhot Melakhim*, chs. 11-12. The former passage is somewhat puzzling since Maimonides' view of the World to Come is such that to be motivated by acquiring it is not objectionable; the world to come is an intellectual existence.

9 At one point (*LC*, 164-65), Hartman criticizes the notion held by Rashi, Rabbenu Jonah, and Meiri that petitional prayer is founded on the memory of the Exodus. But even if petitional prayer is not founded on the Exodus, remembrance of the Exodus is founded on the Exodus, and that is all my argument requires.

10 "*Kol Dodi Dofek*," a 1956 lecture reprinted as *Fate and Destiny*, trans. Lawrence J. Kaplan (Hoboken, NJ, 2000).

11 For a stimulating proposal regarding the role of gratitude in a Maimonidean conception of prayer, see Ehud Benor, *Worship of the Heart: A Study of Maimonides' Philosophy of Religion* (Albany, 1995), esp. 114-28.

12 Some material in the next few paragraphs overlaps with material in "Divine Intervention and Religious Sensibilities," in this volume.

13 That religious belief can be separated from religious motivation is suggested by a rabbinic source that chides Antigonus of Sokho for preaching: "Do not be as servants who serve the master so as to receive reward but as servants who serve the master not in order to receive reward" (*Avot* 1:3). We are told in *Avot de-Rabbi Natan* 5:2 that two disciples misunderstood Antigonus. They took him to be denying that there is an afterlife in which reward and punishment will be dispensed. The thrust of this text is not that Antigonus was wrong as to what the motivational ideal is, but rather that he was wrong to publicize this ideal because people would have difficulty keeping this ideal in equipoise with belief in reward and punishment in the hereafter. But for one who can maintain this tension — why not do so?

Cf. the discussion of Antigonus by Maimonides in his introduction to his commentary to the tenth chapter of Mishnah *Sanhedrin* (*Perek Helek*). Despite Maimonides's praise of Antigonus's position and his implication that this position is correct, Maimonides's own view of serving God out of love is actually different. For Maimonides emphasizes not servant-like obedience to the commandments, but rather reasoned endorsement.

See also my "Divine Intervention and Religious Sensibilities," in this volume.

14 *Nahalat Avot* [commentary to *Ethics of the Fathers*], commenting on *Avot* 1:3.

15 *Hilkhot Teshuvah* 10:2.

16 In this context Abarbanel does distinguish, however, between motivations for developing a particular set of character traits and motivations for doing a particular act. Only the latter requires belief in reward and punishment.

17 Does Abrabanel reject Antigonus, then? No. Abarbanel suggests that Antigonus was only discouraging serving the master to receive "*peras*," a fixed, immediately dispensed reward, but not discouraging them from pursuing "*sakhar*," an ultimate, far-off recompense. This could imply that Abarbanel does not think that the *peras* arrangement even holds. While this nuance affects the precision

of my formulation in the text, since Abrananel does not really countenance focusing on material rewards in the here and now and may not believe that the nexus holds, the basic issue he raises — that belief in reward and punishment should dictate the legitimacy of having that belief serve to motivate action — holds just the same. I should also note that Abarbanel obviously does not wish to reject the rabbinic notion that acting *lishmah* is higher than acting *lo lishmah*; rather, he will demarcate *lishmah* and *lo lishmah* differently, so that the critical difference will be between types of rewards.

[18]   See for example, R. Soloveitchik's "A Halakhic Approach to Suffering," in Rabbi Joseph B. Soloveitchik, *Out of the Whirlwind*, ed. David Shatz, Joel B. Wolowelsky, and Reuven Ziegler (New York, 2003), 86-116. See also *Fate and Destiny*, cited above. Theodicies that explain evil as necessary for free human responses are exceptions to the point that theodicies imply that people should not remove evil. It is precisely free human responses to evil, human efforts to vanquish evil, that justify its existence. See "Does Law Express Jewish Theology? The Curious Case of Theodicies," in this volume.

[19]   I ignore here the other thesis of Freud, that civilization imposes restrictions that religion makes one more liable to accept.

[20]   For further discussion of *haredi* activism, see my "Practical Endeavor and The Torah u-Madda Debate," *The Torah u-Madda Journal* 3 (1991-92), 98-149.

[21]   See Nahmanides' commentary to the Torah, Lev. 26:11.

[22]   See Aviezer Ravitzky, *Messianism, Zionism, and Jewish Religious Radicalism*, trans. Michael Swirsky and Jonathan Chipman (Chicago, 1993), 18-19. Ravitzky explains that the Lubavitcher Rebbe at the turn of the twentieth century, R. Shalom Dov Baer Schneerson, is the figure who thrust the messianic argument against Zionism (that the messiah must be awaited passively) into prominence; prior to him, the emphasis of anti-Zionist rabbis was on the irreligiosity of Zionists.

[23]   Cf. R. Aharon Lichtenstein, "*Le-Berurah shel Middat ha-Bittahon*," *Deot* 52 (1975): 352-55.

[24]   Finally, a general question of methodology. Hartman is explicit that he is selective, seeking to develop one strand in the tradition without gainsaying the existence of others. But what role can *any* parts of tradition really play in the argument if one believes in human adequacy? If Hartman appeals to the tradition as a necessary condition for establishing his position, he runs into the question of why an anthropology that stresses human adequacy should care about what the tradition says. If the tradition made no reference to human adequacy, wouldn't an advocate of adequacy just say flat out that the tradition is wrong?

IS MATTER ALL THAT MATTERS?
Judaism, Free Will, and the Genetic and Neuroscientific Revolutions

Judaism, along with Christianity, has lived through its share of scientific revolutions. The history of responses to the Copernican revolution suggests that religious communities eventually adjust to new scientific theories that threaten traditional conceptions of the universe and humanity's place in it, though the process can take a long time.[1]

In this essay, I will examine the religious implications of a view known as materialism or physicalism, whose influence is spreading rapidly. According to materialism, all things are made exclusively of matter and all facts can be explained by reference to material or physical causes. Can Judaism adjust to this scientific revolution?

THE CURRENT SCIENTIFIC REVOLUTION

Materialism has a long pedigree, extending back to pre-Socratic philosophy. But in our time materialism has matured from an essentially speculative assertion or one that was defended on a priori grounds into a well developed, empirically grounded scientific theory. Not only does the theory muster impressive and ever-growing empirical support, but it may justly be called a central image, a model, a sovereign approach — in Thomas Kuhn's famous phrase, a scientific paradigm.[2]

The materialist revolution is profoundly altering how we conceive of mind and personality. Neuroscientists seem to be successfully mapping a gamut of mental phenomena onto states of the brain — from higher level cognitive functions, to emotions and personality traits, to raw experiences of color, taste, and sound.[3] Moral judgment, economic choices, religious experience, and religious belief are linked to neural excitations.[4] Simultaneously, geneticists have explained how neural pathways are set, and they identify genetic causes of character traits, personality disorders and the like. As gaps in our understanding of the mind get filled in, we become like those who gradually learned the mechanisms behind diseases and earthquakes and had no need for the "God of the gaps." We, it seems, no longer need the soul-of-the-gaps to explain mental phenomena and solve the hoary problem of mind and body.[5] Francis Crick, co-discoverer of the double-helix formation of DNA, articulates what he calls "The Astonishing Hypothesis": "that 'you,' your joys and sorrows, your memories and your ambitions, your sense of identity and free will, are in fact no more than the behavior of a vast assembly of nerve cells and their associated molecules."[6] On the grass-roots level, materialism gains credibility by means of the dramatic applications of science in daily life. In medical ethics, you are your brain — alive if it lives, dead if it's dead. And in his best selling book, *Listening to Prozac,* psychiatrist Peter D. Kramer thoughtfully and eloquently shows how society's extensive use of mood altering drugs has altered people's conceptions of their selves — often they view themselves as purely biological beings.[7]

To be sure, materialism faces difficulties. Consider the materialist view that only material entities can explain mental phenomena — i.e., that physical systems are closed. This view sets limits on *scientific* explanations, but only because scientists have chosen to adopt certain constraints on what they will call "science." Must the constraints apply to explanations *tout court*? Imagine that cosmologists retrieved distant sounds, "*yehi or*" "*totzei ha-aretz nefesh hayyah le-minah*" ("Let there be light," "Let the earth produce living things"), and tiny particles revealed the words, "I am the Lord your God."[8] It would then be clear that God created the universe and the species. One could say this would not be acceptable as a scientific explanation. But why should we care, since we would regard it as the best explanation overall? Furthermore, methodologies other than science may yield truth and correct explanations. We must distinguish belief in science from scientism, the thesis that science is the only path to truth. In addition, materialism, if taken too far, would render knowledge of ethical, aesthetic and mathematical truths impossible (assuming those refer to nonphysical, abstract properties and objects.)[9] And finally, some scientists seek to refute current materialistic theories in genetics and neuroscience.[10] Yet, despite these difficulties, no matter how often presentations of materialism are leavened with caveats about it being a merely a research program or working hypothesis, no matter how often we are reminded that science changes, no matter how recalcitrant the pockets of dissent and resistance may be even within the scientific community, the sense that something true and important has been discovered about human beings is credible and widespread.[11] We ignore it at the cost of an inadequate anthropology and an inadequate understanding of what it could mean for human beings to be created in the image of God.

Can religious people make their peace with materialist assertions? Which religious ideas does materialism threaten? How bad is the damage to a religious outlook, and can it be contained? Are there precedents in Jewish tradition, or ideas in the general philosophical world, that might help here? If a believer goes along with materialists for part of the ride, at what stop must he or she get off the train? Are there even — *mirable dictu* — healthy, positive spiritual messages that religious believers can extract? To ask such questions is not to assume the scientific view as the whole truth, but rather to use a seemingly worst-case scenario as a heuristic device for sorting out what a believer must reject to retain consistency and coherence, and what he or she may accept.

Obviously, a truly cosmic materialism, a metaphysical viewpoint that denies the existence of any entities or causes that are not material, is flatly unacceptable to most adherents of monotheistic religions. God, after all, is a disembodied being. Furthermore, though disembodied, He acts on the physical world. A religious person could accept cosmic materialism as a methodological constraint on scientific inquiry ("In science, qua science, we do not form hypotheses about the non-physical"), but, short of embracing Mordecai Kaplan's naturalism, he or she will most likely reject it as a true description of the cosmos.[12] However, materialism about human beings may be better grounded than cosmic materialism, and even if *cosmic* materialism is not compatible with theism, materialism concerning the mind might be. The question remains: how far can Judaism go in accepting materialism?

In what follows, I focus primarily on the question of how materialism influences our understanding of free will, as opposed to how it affects belief in the soul.

FREE WILL CHALLENGED

Of all the capacities of humans that are affirmed in ordinary discourse but are jeopardized by neuroscience and genetics, free choice is the most significant, and the problems surrounding it are the most difficult. With regard to other phenomena that could be labeled "achievements of the spirit," physicalism does not gainsay these phenomena; it only questions a particular explanation of them. If we identify spirituality with certain capacities — abstract reasoning, moral intuition or spiritual insight — then these capacities might well be included in a physicalist description of the human being.[13] All lie within the scope of the materialist's account. Needless to say, if you take sticks and stones as your model of a physical system, you will have a hard time imagining that a physical system could think, feel, or experience. But this is a patently silly way to conceive of physicalism. Physical systems vary in complexity, and according to physicalists, a sufficiently complex physical system can do an awful lot. There is no a priori way of knowing that a sufficiently evolved and complex brain, possessed of sufficiently complex neural pathways, could not reason abstractly, form moral judgment, or feel, any more than there is an a priori reason that a collection of pieces of metal and wire assembled in the form of a computer could never be smart enough to defeat a chess grand master. This is not to say that, at the end of the day, the materialist explanation of human thought and deed will be successful. But at least materialism, in the cases I mentioned, does not deny the very occurrence of phenomena we deem crucial to human spiritual achievement. Asserting that materialism denies achievements of the spirit is therefore facile.

Not so in the case of free will. Here the materialist denies the very phenomenon, at least as it is conceived by many people. This is because generally free will is thought to involve (whether it *truly* does will be discussed later) a non-material cause, an "agent" or "will" or "self" that controls the physical body. Agents and wills do not fit into a materialist ontology.[14] As a result, scientists who have sought to locate a space for agents, wills, and selves, have met with the charge that, while these entities cannot be ruled out, one who introduces them

> wants to find a non-neural, non-physical basis for free will (some sort of mental conscious control over the brain itself) and he wants to find it doing research predicated on the assumption of neural cause and effect. Such a research agenda, wedded to the a priori goal of defeating mechanism yet rooted in physicalist science, is surely doomed from the outset.[15]

This criticism is, to be sure, ambiguous. Is the critic saying that, as a neuroscientist, bound by certain procedures of the discipline, one must not posit non-physical entities? Or that even in doing metaphysics as opposed to neuroscience, we cannot posit such things? Would the critic concede that the best scientific explanation of a phenomenon need not be the best overall explanation? However these problems are resolved, the critic of free will quoted above certainly emphasizes that, unlike other human achievements, free will is not something a materialist accepts but explains differently from a non-materialist. Rather, free will, at least in the sense of a will that is non-material, is something that the materialist qua scientist denies altogether.

The challenge with regard to free will is obvious and widely known:[16] absent free will, gone are moral responsibility and "reactive attitudes" — feelings like blame, resentment, condemnation, guilt, gratitude, forgiveness, approbation, indignation, and the whole "complicated web of attitudes and feelings which form an essential part of the moral life as we know it."[17]

Faced with this challenge, a religious person may reasonably adopt one of two options. First, he or she may seek precedents in which religious philosophers confronted ostensibly deterministic explanations of human thought and behavior and responded either by accepting them or finding a way to salvage free will in the face of the challenge. Alternatively the religious person could belittle the importance of having free will and thus cut losses. My argument in what follows is that there are a variety of precedents that help reduce the conflict between materialistic science and Judaism. None of these approaches serve fully, but collectively they may make the glass look more full than it does at first glance. There is a surprising degree of consistency between current science and Jewish tradition. But given that belief in some degree of free will dominates Jewish sources, I cannot provide more than a measure of consistency and therefore cannot call myself the harbinger of great news.

Before examining the precedents, one more observation concerning the role of the free will problem in religious life. Neither the Bible nor the Rabbis evince much interest in reconciling free will with divine activity or divine foreknowledge.[18] Jewish philosophical literature, by contrast, contains a vast amount of material on such topics. Curiously, though, while these problems present formidable brain-teasers, for many people they have little existential impact. As a rule, so far as I can tell, people do not bring to these discussions any emotional investment. By contrast, the threat of scientific determinism posed by neurophysiological and genetic theories — these developments genuinely worry people. In fact, the theory of scientific determinism was often presented by philosophers merely as a "what if" possibility — the very possibility of it was thought to be scary.[19] In sharp contrast, no one thinks that the very possibility that God exists is scary because of the problems His existence would pose for free will. Agnostics often endorse the view that divine foreknowledge and human free will are incompatible, but I have yet to find one of them worrying, "Oh no, what if God exists!? Then He knows everything I'll do and my choices aren't free!"[20]

How do we explain the discrepancy between people's indifference to challenges posed by divine knowledge/divine causation and their grave concern regarding scientific determinism? Perhaps the explanation (for theists) is as follows. In the worst case scenario, if we are deprived of free will because we affirm that God has a plan for history, or that God knows what I will do, we are sacrificing free will to affirm another religious principle, namely, divine providence. To give up one religious principle under pressure from another religious principle — and in particular, divine providence — is understandable from a religious perspective and reflects pious motives. By contrast, to embrace scientific determinism and to then surrender free will is to surrender a religious doctrine because of an external body of knowledge, namely science. That step is one that religious people are far less prepared to take.

THE PRECEDENTS

Hasidic Thought: The Question of Arrogance

According to one line of interpretation, some Hasidic thinkers denied almost all human freedom because they held an extreme form of divine providence in which God controls everything, including human action.[21] The only free will we have is the will to acknowledge this truth.[22] Free will, the reasoning goes, would entail human control and human ontological separateness from God. For such deniers of free will, the point is not so much that there is no free action or will but that there is no human agency or action at all. Human will is nothing more than God's will. In fact, for at least some deniers of free will, there would be no value in our being the authors of our acts or maybe even of our motives. There is value only in an awareness of His will and/or our own helplessness, even nothingness.

Of course, scientists could deny free will even in the one sphere that the theory under discussion accepts it: the free will to mentally acknowledge or reject the putative Hasidic metaphysics. But one need not subscribe to the metaphysics of Hasidut to appreciate the issue about piety that it raises. Attempts to place humans above nature, and in particular to preserve a human will that is above physical causation, assert human superiority and distinctiveness. Such attempts could be viewed as religiously objectionable efforts to shift power away from an almighty deity into human hands and to confer upon human beings supra-natural control in the form of free will. "[T]hat many believe that we stand above nature in some essential respect suggests that the Enlightenment was more successful in its glorification of the individual than in its challenge to the supernatural."[23] Whereas Maimonides treated free will as a type of natural cause, nowadays, with nature identified as the material, free will seems supernatural. It should be stressed that many explications of free will view the essence of free will to be control over the world — the ability to make the world conform to what we want.[24] It is religiously healthier, one may argue, to have a worldview that encourages humility, shame, and insignificance.

As we will see later, this insight could be incorporated into a certain providential reading of history. For now, the point is this: even though some religious thinkers may deny free will due to a pietistic motive, whereas contemporary materialists deny free will for different reasons, at the bottom line, rejecting the principle of free will may produce a certain kind of piety, regardless of the motivation for that rejection. Determinism in nature would give expression to the truth that God controls all, and could generate the desired ethic of humility.[25]

Note, as well, that if scientific determinism were accepted, one could construe the realm of nature , including genes and neurons, as an expression of the divine will — the hand of God. In short, for followers of the approach under discussion, there is religious value in denying free will.

Determinism and Medieval Astrology

With the major exception of Maimonides and minor exceptions like R. Isaac Pulgar, medieval Jewish philosophers and scientists conspicuously believed in the truth of astrology.[26] Astrology as embraced by medievals was the functional equivalent of contemporary genetics, though it went far beyond explanations of human actions. The stars set your character and natural tendencies (dispositions), just as in modern times genes are understood to do.

Medievals also believed, however, that people can overcome natural tendencies. Responsibility thus flows from your ability to battle and conquer naturally caused inclinations. We may call this the "override" theory: freedom and responsibility come from the possibility of overriding natural tendencies. R. Abraham ben David (Ravad) asserts "And it is well known that all of man's deeds, great or small, were given by God to the power of the fortunes (be-koah ha-mazzal). God also gave man the intelligence (sekhel) to elude the hand of Fortune, and this is the power given man for good or evil."[27] Similarly, Charles Manekin tells us about Gersonides: "Nowhere does Gersonides say that one freely chooses to be drawn after one's temperament. Rather he says that one's choice itself is 'drawn' after temperament."[28] In other words, a "choice" made by temperament is caused by physical elements, and free will is located only in the power of reason to override temperament. So, in a certain respect, we might feel about genetics and neuroscience, to put it colloquially, "been there, done that." We had a seemingly deterministic theory in earlier times, and the clash with free will was "solved" through the concept of override.

The analogy is needless to say imperfect. Medieval thinkers often assumed that whether or not a person would try to quell his or her natural tendencies would be up to him or her, and not predetermined by anything

230

physical.[29] To be truly analogous to astrology, the genetic/neuroscientific view would have to say (what it does not say) that the choice to override biological dispositions itself is not determined by biology. Hence the override theory seems to provide no full precedent. Even so, the fact that according to a medieval Jewish tradition scientific factors cause human dispositions — that is significant. This is a step, if a small one, toward greater comfort with contemporary science.

The physical roots of sin

We frequently encounter the idea that wrong, sinful acts are traced to the body. Maimonides writes, for instance: "All man's acts of disobedience and sins are consequent upon his matter and not upon his form [viz. the intellect], whereas all his virtues are consequent upon his form."[30] Maimonides, who asserts that astrology is nonsense, nevertheless holds a type of "override" theory, according to which one may override the influence of matter.[31] But one passage is closer to determinism:

> There are, moreover, many people who have received from their first natural disposition a complexion of temperament with which perfection is in no way compatible. Such is the case of one whose heart is naturally exceedingly hot; for one cannot refrain from anger, even by subjecting one's soul to very stringent training…Similarly one can find among people rash and reckless folks whose movements…indicate a corruption of the complexion and a poor quality of temperament…Perfection can never be perceived in such people (*Guide* I:34).[32]

To be sure, in Guide III:8, Maimonides states that, "It is easy…to control suitable matter…[I]f it is unsuitable, it is not impossible for someone trained to quell it."[33] However one resolves the contradiction between the quotations from III:8 and I:34, the key point is that Maimonides, like Jewish believers in astrology,[34] views vice as the outgrowth of physical causes and views virtuous action, where it does take place, as the overriding of matter/ nature through the discipline of Torah. Likewise, Gersonides, who as we saw believes that character traits are caused by astral phenomena but that a person's reason can override astrological causation, concedes by the very statement of this thesis that an act not based on reason is determined by the person's physical makeup.[35] Jewish literature often represents the *yetzer ha-ra* (evil inclination) as a biological urge.[36] It is true that the spirit (or, for Maimonides, form, which denotes intellect) is said to be able to control matter. This suggests that spirit's delinquency is complicit in matter's sin. But the causal antecedents of wrong are still biological. The "spirit's" failure to control the body is like a person's failure to douse a fire with water — the failure isn't a cause of the fire, though the person is responsible for not dousing it. These outlooks, then, view evil as emanating from the biological part of the person. This idea may be meant metaphorically; but if it is religiously acceptable to put it forward as a figure of speech, it should not be objectionable to take it literally when doing so is necessitated by scientific investigation.

R. Joseph Soloveitchik never tired of stressing that Judaism accepts the physical aspect of the human being. The first chapter of Genesis describes man, in R. Soloveitchik's words, as "an integral part of nature...a child of mother Nature, as is the brute and the beast." The Bible accepts "the unity and continuity of organic life, considered an indispensable postulate in all biological sciences...Man and beast share equally in the same biology, physiology and pathology."[37] Needless to say, this acceptance of physicality, of "man-natura," must not eradicate what R. Soloveitchik calls "man-persona," the spiritual being in Genesis 2 who stands apart from and above the rest of nature and upon whose behavior the redemption of physicality depends. In contemporary science, this man-persona turns out to be man-natura in disguise. Still, according to R. Soloveitchik, Judaism sees salient strands of continuity between humans and the physical world. The question is how much of the science of the brain and the genes we can accept, not whether we can accept any. If we accept R. Soloveitchik's contention, which is I think hermeneutically compelling, then to reject all physicalizing of humanity is contrary to tradition.

In essence, then, half the materialist thesis, the idea that "the bad" is biological, is consistent with a prominent theme in traditional thought. And even when it comes to the good, a talmudic model embraced by R. Soloveitchik counsels finding creative, healthy outlets for destructive drives of the *yetzer ha-ra*[38] rather than eradicating them. In some or many cases, biology is redirected, not exterminated.[39]

Devaluation: Nahmanides and Rabbi Dessler

Another way to ease the problems associated with determinism is to diminish the value of free will in a way different from the alleged Hasidic precedent. For Nahmanides, when Adam and Eve became *"yode'ei tov va-ra"* (knowers of good and evil) upon eating of the fruit of the tree (Gen. 3:22), they acquired the capacity to choose either of two alternatives in a situation, the good and the evil (commentary to Gen. 2:9). Prior to sin, they automatically did what was right, just as they automatically breathed and digested. But after the sin, they lost this automatic connection to the right and the good; now doing good became a matter of choice. The loss of innocence, the acquisition of free choice, is a step backward. In messianic times, when God "circumcises your heart and that of your seed" (Deut. 30:6), when the Jewish people repent, they will return, says Nahmanides in his commentary to that verse, to a situation of automatic conformity. For Nahmanides, then, free choice, moral struggle, is not a good; conformity to the good is better, even without choice. Nahmanides accepts that people do act with free will — but his approach might allow believers to live more comfortably with determinism, if that is indeed the outcome of the conflict with physicalism (i.e., if our good deeds turn out to be determined).

The Nahmanidean approach does not sit well with certain other theological ideas. In particular, many explanations of evil argue that free will is so great a good that preserving it provides adequate justification for God's allowing evil. But a theologian is not obliged to accept these theodicies. Moreover, there are considerations that support Nahmanides' devaluation of free choice. For example, the fact that Jewish law permits coercion in the case of certain types of behavior, the fact that the Torah seems untroubled by biblical episodes of God's hardening of hearts (Pharoah's, Sihon's),[40] and indeed the very fact that God uses promises of rewards and threats of punishments to influence behavior — all suggest that conformity to the right sometimes or often counts more than free choice. Our educational techniques contain at least a measure of deterministic influence. In addition, Jews pray each day that God subjugate their wills to Him — "ve-khof et yitzrenu le-hishtabed lakh." Nahmanides's devaluation, then, has something to ratify it.

R. Eliyahu Dessler takes a position superficially resembling that of Nahmanides. R. Dessler believes that to be unfree but to automatically do the good is greater than being free and choosing to do the good. A person's task, therefore, is to transform himself from one who chooses (boher) to one whose actions are necessitated (mukhrah).[41] I say that this opinion "superficially" resembles Nahmanides' because one could argue that in R. Dessler's thought, it is not being a mukhrah per se that is good, but rather turning oneself into a mukhrah by using free choice. Even so, the thought that Nahmanides and R. Dessler have in common — that, abstracted from its connection to the good, free will is not something of value — might lead us to make peace with the loss of free will preached by modern science. One could argue that the value of a free evil choice and that of an unfree evil choice are the same, whereas they would not be equivalent on a view that sees free will per se as a value. Hence, to learn that evil choices are unfree is not to lose something of value, nor is the loss of good free choices bad if the good free choices are replaced by irresistible good choices.[42]

Biological factors that predispose one to altruism or appreciation of the good could be viewed as "automatically" instilling the good in us. To that extent the deterministic situation might be viewed as good, even if not as good as the pre-sin situation in the Garden of Eden.

Restrictivism

Isaac Bashevis Singer said in an interview: "The greatest gift which humanity has received is free choice. It is true that we are limited in our use of free choice. But the little free choice we have is such a great gift and is potentially worth so much that for this itself life is worthwhile living."[43] Let us use the term "restrictivism" to denote the thesis that we have free choice but the extent of choice is quite limited — we have some but little free will.[44] Restrictivists may value free will, but need not.

Restrictivism can marshal a surprising degree of support. In an instructive article published over thirty years ago, Solomon Schimmel catalogued evidence that "Although Maimonides and most other Jewish philosophers vigorously defend the doctrine of free will...in practical terms the doctrine is never carried to its logical conclusions and is considerably circumscribed in several ways."[45] Schimmel mentions, among other evidence, the educational system, which works, at least in part, by reducing choice.

The most famous champion of restrictivism in Jewish sources is R. Dessler. I put aside in this context his devaluation of free will — I am interested in the scope of free will. R. Dessler argues that the vast majority of a person's actions are determined either by environment or by a character shaped by previous choices. A person retains only a *nekuddat ha-behirah*, a point or small area of free will, at which moral struggle takes place.[46] R. Dessler stresses the role of environment in molding character, while contemporary scientists highlight the role of biology, but this does not affect the key point.[47]

R. Dessler's willingness to restrict free will suggests, especially when combined with the sources and points Schimmel cites, that free will is more limited in Judaism than the ordinary person supposes.

Compatibilism

Until now we have been assuming that whether there is free will and moral responsibility, and whether reactive attitudes are defensible, will be determined purely by scientific facts. Implicitly, we have reasoned as follows: if science shows us that thought and behavior are determined, whether by environmental influences or biological ones, then we don't have free will or moral responsibility; if science is unable to do this, then there is at least a possibility of free will and responsibility, and the scientific challenge evaporates. Either way, scientists settle the question by figuring out whether thought and behavior are determined.

But many philosophers dispute the move from "determinism is true" to "there is no free will," "there is no moral responsibility," and "reactive attitudes are not justified". The popular assumption that free will, responsibility, and reactive attitudes are incompatible with determinism is itself merely one view, known as incompatibilism. Other philosophers embrace compatibilism. For compatibilists, determinism is compatible with free will, moral responsibility, and justified reactive attitudes. Some Jewish philosophers were compatibilists.

Compatibilism can be broken down into three sub-theses.

(A) *Indeterminism Excludes Free Will*

Compatibilists reject a position called Libertarianism, which affirms that there is free will and that free will requires rejection of determinism. This compatibilist position argues that the libertarian lacks a plausible model for how free action occurs. Often, libertarians posit a metaphysical "self," "will," or "agent" that guides or makes decisions. This notion of "agent causation" is frequently charged with metaphysical murkiness.

Libertarians sometimes assert that quantum physics reveals indeterminism in nature. Champions of human free will often welcome quantum physics as having shown that determinism is false, thereby salvaging free will. But let us look at the situation more closely. Suppose that someone robs a bank because of a random neuron misfiring in that person's brain. There is no fully deterministic pedigree for the person's act; but the individual is hardly exercising free will, and anyone who held him responsible for the act is simply wrong. Free will is not just a matter of indeterminism; it's a matter also of control, of agency. The person's behavior in my example is not something he *does*; it's something that *happens* to him. Undetermined neural events do not imply that there is free will, but rather that there isn't. Undetermined actions, compatibilists argue, are "arbitrary," "capricious," "random," "uncontrolled," "irrational," "inexplicable," or "matters of pure luck or chance." "Undetermined events in the brain or body...would occur spontaneously and would be more of a nuisance... than an enhancement of freedom or responsibility."[48]

This point quickly leads to a sharpened formulation of what the free will problem really is. Think of the problem as a dilemma, a "*mi-mah nafshakh*" argument. On the one hand, determinism seems incompatible with free will because free will requires being able to do otherwise. On the other hand, indeterminism or chance at the level of brain events would seem to be incompatible with free will as well because it results in chance actions and deprives us of agency. So, whether we are determinists or indeterminists, free will is a chimera, and so, apparently, is moral responsibility.[49] Since indeterminism cannot salvage free will, compatibilism seems to be the more promising path.

(B) *Utilitarian Considerations Suffice For Responsibility and Appropriate Reactive Attitudes*

Incompatibilists argue that if actions are determined, it is impossible to justify punishment. Combatibilists respond that punishment is, in fact, not based on retribution, but instead on social utility, society's need for protection. If this is correct, people can properly be punished for actions even in a deterministic world.[50] Judaism is not short on utilitarian approaches to punishment.[51] My point is not that these utilitarian rationales are correct — only that it is possible that responsibility, punishment and reactive attitudes make sense in a deterministic world, and that whether they do is a philosophical matter rather than a scientific one.

Reactive attitudes may likewise be justified by their utility. Praise and blame function in a utilitarian way to encourage or discourage certain sorts of behavior. Moreover, reactive attitudes need not presuppose indeterminism. We praise people for their intelligence, good looks, and native athletic ability, even though these qualities are genetic and not due to any agency of their own, and the bearers of those properties often deserve no praise for these qualities.[52] And we often praise people as "good people" without having the foggiest idea of how much of their goodness is self-initiated and how much is due to upbringing alone. The same applies to wrong actions. How many of us, when blaming perpetrators of Nazi or other atrocities, really think it relevant, the compatibilists ask, whether an individual butcher and mass murderer was the product of environment, lacking exposure to other value systems? Our judgments are not dependent on whether the actions are determined, nor do we feel they must be.[53]

(C) *Free Will Does Not Require Alternative Possibilities*

Like the divine foreknowledge-human free will argument,[54] the argument that determinism excludes free will, moral responsibility, and reactive attitudes supposes that in order for a person to act freely in a given situation, and/or be responsible and/or deserve the reactive attitudes, the person must possess a two-way power. He or she must be able to do, in the very same circumstances, something other than what he or she in fact does. This thesis is often called the Principle of Alternative Possibilities (PAP), or the Forking Paths principle (borrowing from Jose Luis Borges' story, "The Garden of Forking Paths"). If the Forking Paths Principle is false, if freedom does not require alternative possibilities, then, barring further problems, neither God's foreknowledge nor determination by physical causes will deprive an agent of freedom or responsibility.[55] Freedom would be compatible with foreknowledge and with scientific determinism. The issue at hand, then, is whether the Forking Paths Principle is true; if not, compatibilism is viable.[56]

A case developed by John Locke (which I will adapt in my own way) serves as a counterexample to the Forking Paths Principle.[57] A man is standing in a room and deliberates whether to leave the room. He decides to stay in order to continue an enjoyable conversation. Unbeknowst to him, the room is locked, so he could not leave even if he wanted to. Has he made a free choice? The Forking Paths principle says no; intuition says yes, which suggests that the Forking Paths Principle is false.

Another example of this type: while talking to a relative on the phone, you witness a car theft in progress. You callously decide it's not worth hanging up to call the police. Unbeknownst to you, the police phone line is down. You could not have reached the police even if you had tried. Intuitively we hold you responsible for not contacting the police by phone, and we say that you freely refrained from contacting them. But here, you do not have the power to contact them, so we have a case of free will in which the Forking Paths Principle is not satisfied.[58]

These cases do not seem that powerful as objections. In each instance there is something you did freely, something over which you had a two-way power: namely, deciding to remain in the room, or deciding not to call the police. The fact the room is locked only means you could not have succeeded in leaving the room; you still could have *decided* and *tried* to do so. Likewise you could have still have *decided* and *tried* to call the police, even if the lines are down. So you are responsible for your deciding not to call the police, even if you are not responsible for not reaching them. To attack the Forking Paths Principle, we need not an example in which only one act is possible yet the person is free to decide, but rather, an example in which only one *decision* is possible. The prominent contemporary philosopher Harry Frankfurt produced a family of cases that many philosophers view as a decisive refutation of the Forking Paths Principle. I will not take the space to explain the complex structure of his imaginative examples. The literature on Frankfurt's example is enormous, and the matter remains contested.[59] Issues about compatibilist examples abound: maybe PAP applies to omissions and not acts; maybe it applies to bad actions but not good actions; maybe the person isn't really responsible, etc. I will not go over this literature here.[60] The point is that a denial of PAP and the Forking Paths Principle would refute the argument for the incompatibility of free will and determinism.

There is a second type of counterexample to the Forking Paths Principle. Many of the everyday actions that we regard as free, and assign responsibility for, are determined by people's character and psychological nature. Consider this passage from David Hume's essay, "Of Liberty and Necessity":

Were a man, whom I know to be honest and opulent, and with whom I live in intimate friendship, to come into my house, where I am

> surrounded with my servants, I rest assured, that he is not to stab me before he leaves it, in order to rob me of my silver standish; and I no more suspect this event, than the falling of the house itself which is new, and solidly built and founded.[61]

Hume's point is that in real life we treat people as if their acts are determined. If someone wrongs you, your decision whether to criticize them to their face will depend on how well, based on your experience, they take criticism. If someone is self-absorbed and therefore likely to listen to other people's problems with only half an ear, or if someone is a gossip-monger, you won't choose that person as someone in whom to confide. And, as Hume so pointedly puts it, "A prisoner...discovers the impossibility of his escape, as well when he considers the obstinacy of the jailer, as the walls and bars, with which he is surrounded." As Hume also points out, literary criticism as well as the study of history and politics depend on our ability to identify both general human motivations and motivational patterns in specific people. In Hume's view, although we may talk like libertarians when we delve into philosophy, in everyday life we think like determinists.

R. Soloveitchik made this very same point in a *teshuvah* discourse published under the title "Repentance and Free Choice":

> Free choice does not mean a state of chaotic anarchy, with sudden and frequent changes of mind that have no rational explanation... We usually expect a certain display of consistency in a man's thought and actions; we expect him to embody a certain way of life with its own consistency of character. The law of cause and effect, action and consequence, does prevail in a man's life... The question now is: where does 'free choice' come in?[62]

Some deeds are psychologically impossible — unthinkable[63] — for us or for people we deal with. If you attend a lecture by a renowned rabbinic scholar, you know very well that he will not pull out a machine gun or tell scatological jokes; and if he did, you would not attribute it to free will. If you are offered $5 to torture an innocent child, you will not and cannot comply. You cannot now spread a vicious rumor that your colleague, who you know is morally upright, is a child molester. When we say of someone, "He cannot hurt a fly," we are not saying he lacks free will. When Martin Luther stated, "Here I stand; I can do no other," he did not mean that he is not freely standing up to the Catholic Church and that he bears no responsibility. If George Washington could not tell a lie, this hardly means he lacks free will and gets no credit for confessing to chopping down the cherry tree.[64] There might even be people who have powerful urges to do things, and think they are refraining from doing them as an act of will, when in fact they simply could not go through with the act. For example, people who have suicidal urges may genuinely be incapable of acting on them at a particular time. In all these cases, the person is free even though he or she could not do otherwise.[65] And here is the moral: to act freely or decide freely, one need not be able to do otherwise, decide otherwise, or desire otherwise.

In these cases, it is folly to look for alternative possibilities, i.e. other actions that the person *could* have done.[66] (I call the examples character cases.) After all, what are you looking for? Basically, you want to find a real possibility that the agent would do something that is contrary to all of her values and reasoning. But if this is the desired "alternative," the demand for an alternative possibility amounts to the demand that the person be able to do something insane, like Dostoevsky's Underground Man who believes that to be truly free is to be able to act against all his logic and all his interests. To insist that being able to act insanely is a condition for free will is strange, quite apart from the utter lack of evidence that the people in examples like mine are able to act insanely.[67]

Can a defender of the Forked Path Principle account for the freedom of the agents who lack alternative possibilities in these character cases? One strategy for retaining the principle is that of Aristotle, who maintains that although people with a fixed character who act in character seem to have no real choice in the matter, in fact people choose their characters and are therefore responsible for actions that flow from the characters they have chosen.[68] R. Soloveitchik suggests that

> It lies within man's power to determine the framework of cause and effect within which he lives and acts...Man can be the architect of his own personality; he has the ability to fashion his own character and map out the path he will follow. Indeed, man is capable of determining in advance what his reactions will be to given phenomena and events in the course of his life.[69]

In evaluating this strategy, the first question we face is whether it is true that we choose our characters. Let us bear in mind that educational institutions and home environments use rewards and punishments to mold the character of young children. As Solomon Schimmel puts it, "Rather than cultivating and encouraging the exercise of free-will as some internal operating factor, these techniques tend to preempt freedom by substituting determinants of behavior whose locus is the social environment rather than the individual's will or reason."[70] The notion that teachers should be role models is an instance of trying to influence behavior through means that one presumes can be effective. When a teacher is not providing a good enough role model, we seek a better role model. Our educational and social practice thus belie the idea that character must be the result of choice. R. Shlomo Wolbe goes so far as to state, as "a fundamental principle in the *chinuch* [education] of others and of ourselves," that "one should relate to every person *as if he had no bechira*, and as if he is 'compelled' by his 'nature,' education, habits and emotional needs."[71] It is true that a person could later in life reflect on his or her acquired values and retain or reshape his or her personality as a result of that evaluation. But our intuition that people act freely when they act in character does not depend on whether this evaluation has taken place.

Elsewhere,[72] I have criticized this Aristotelian strategy. I maintained that the fact that a person once chose a certain character does not entail that every choice made thereafter as a result of that choice is a free one. Suppose an addict is overwhelmed by irresistible cravings for drugs, but he brought on those cravings by continually failing to resist earlier desires for drugs. I do not think that the addict now shoots up freely just because of this causal connection. Rather, a more accurate description of his condition would be that right now he acts unfreely, due to earlier free choices. Similarly, suppose you choose to travel through a dangerous area in which muggings are frequent. While there, you are coerced into handing over valuables. Shall we say that you freely surrendered the valuables just because you made a choice that enabled the later situation to arise? Clearly not.[73] It is not true that an act will be considered free now, when there are no alternative possibilities, simply because they resulted from earlier choices that were made when alternatives were genuine. A person can freely sell himself into bondage, but bondage is bondage.

What seems more plausible is that when a person makes choices in the context of alternative possibilities, and those earlier choices cause him to do certain later actions without entertaining alternative possibilities — as in the example of the addict or the mugging victim — the person bears a degree of responsibility for the later act even though it is not free. Someone may chide the addict: "See, I told you! Once you take one drug, you'll have no control later." The friend is producing an effective reason for assigning responsibility. Even here, however, I would claim that the degree of responsibility for the later act is diminished. An epileptic bus driver whose bus crashes because he had a seizure, when he should have foreseen this possibility, is not as responsible as if he had crashed the bus deliberately.

My own view is that the best strategy for a libertarian to adopt in the face of character cases is that of R. Dessler. That is, one could argue that free will is restricted, and that the agents in question do not have it, but then find a theory of responsibility that explains why agents in those cases are responsible for what they do. In another essay I have tried to do precisely this, arguing that a libertarian may coherently assign responsibly even in cases of fixed character.[74] I will not go into the details here, however, since my goal to this point has been merely to show that compatibilism has substantial attractions, not that it is the only theory left standing upright.

I want to say a few words, though, about why developing a compatibilist alternative to libertarianism will be difficult. What is the compatibilist's positive view of free will? If free will does not entail alternative possibilities, as the foregoing examples suggest, what do compatibilists think it entails? Shall we say that acting freely is just a matter of doing what you want to do? No, for if that were all that is involved, we may as well assign responsibility to cats and dogs, who carry out their desires. Furthermore, intuitively we do not regard compulsive behavior (e.g., of kleptomaniacs), or the behavior of people who have become addicts through no choice of their own, or the actions of people suffering from phobias, as free, responsible behavior. But why not? If free action is a matter of acting on desire, why exclude people in the grips of phobias or addictions who act on their desire? What, according to compatibilists, is the difference between free and unfree acting or willing? What makes addicts, phobics, compulsives, and animals different from free and responsible human agents?

Many contemporary philosophers who reject the Forking Paths Principle propose the following theory. Freedom of the will is a matter of conforming the will to the judgments of either (a) reason or intellect, or (b) one's "deep self" (in Hebrew, the *ratzon elyon* as opposed to *ratzon tahton*, the "higher" will as opposed to the "lower").[75] The notion that free will lies in conformity with reason has deep roots in Plato, Aquinas, Spinoza, Kant and others in general Western thought, and is found as well in Maimonides, Ravad, Gersonides and others on the Jewish side. Josef Stern writes that Maimonides's "views both in the legal works and in the *Guide* rest…on one feature traditionally associated with classical compatibilism, in particular the notion of self-determination."[76] Moshe Sokol also regards Maimonides as a compatibilist.[77] On this view, Maimonides is indifferent to determinism vs. indeterminism because his view on free will is consonant with either position.[78] This is a common stance in medieval Jewish philosophy. Charles Manekin informed me (in correspondence) that no Jewish philosopher before Isaac Arama (15th cent.) used the term "free will" or "free choice" (*behirah hofshit*). Those terms, he relates, entered philosophical Hebrew from the Latin. Jewish philosophers in the Middle Ages tended to see reason, not liberty, as the main component of freedom, and only later in history did the requirement of being able to do otherwise become important. In other words, a person with free will is someone who conforms his or her desires to his or her reasoned value judgments — period. No ability to act evilly or insanely is demanded.

In one place, Maimonides seems to develop a notion of a "deep rational self," combining the notions of the centrality of the intellect in freedom with the notion of freedom as conforming to one's true, inner self. In *Hilkhot Gerushin* 2:20, Maimonides discusses a man who refuses to give a *get* (writ of divorce) when *Hazal* required him to do so. *Get* requires *retzon ha-ba'al*, the husband's willingness to effect the divorce, yet a Jewish court can coerce him until he says *"rotzeh ani"* (I want). There are various ways in which this *halakhah* could be explained, but Maimonides proposes that insofar as this man is violating a precept of the Halakhah, he has been attacked and coerced by his evil inclination. By beating him, the court weakens the impulse and allows the true self, the self that represents what the person most values — and is the objectively right thing — to be expressed.[79]

The "reason" and "deep self" conceptions of freedom run into the following major difficulties:[80]

Selfhood: Why is the self identified with intellect, while desires are deemed external to the self? Can we just dismiss Humean and Freudian views of the self, for example?

The first-person perspective: In his defense of a conception of free will that does not include a condition that the agent be able to act otherwise, John Martin Fischer makes the following intriguing concession:

> Moral responsibility is surely only one aspect of a complete understanding of agency. Another dimension of agency pertains to our view of ourselves as practical reasoners. That is, we deliberate about the future... And in this deliberation and practical reasoning, we typically take ourselves to have genuine alternative possibilities... [I]t is not a straightforward task to give a picture of deliberation and practical reasoning according to which we may not have alternative possibilities.[81]

As I read Fischer, he is acknowledging that the denial of the Forking Paths Principle fits a third-person perspective — onlookers ascribe responsibility and freedom even in the absence of forking paths — but not a first-person perspective. It is difficult to argue that determinism precludes deliberation; determinists still speak of self-control, effort, etc.[82] Indeed, as Schimmel points out, just as Jewish thinkers who affirmed free will circumscribed it in practice, psychologists who espouse determinism, including B. F. Skinner, invoke concepts like rational-emotive control of behavior, phenomenological freedom, and delaying gratification.

Akrasia vs. compulsion: The idea that freedom of the will is a matter of conforming will and behavior to value judgments does a nice job of explaining why people who act compulsively, or who have phobias, are unfree: their behavior does not conform to their value judgments. But human beings are notoriously prone to acting against their better judgment even in cases where intuitively their behavior is free and they are responsible for it. Acting against better judgment is known as akrasia. Akrasia is very different from compulsion. Intuitively the difference is this: the akrates is able to act differently, to do the right thing; the compulsive is not. But to say this is to reinstate a version of the very Forking Paths Principle which the "reason view" of free will was meant to supplant.[83]

Evildoers: A particularly difficult corollary of the akrasia problem is that only right-doers, not wrongdoers, are classified as free, and so no evil acts are free. This is a strange result. To cope with it, some philosophers have suggested that freedom involves being able to act rightly. When people act rightly we declare them free even when they are not able to act otherwise. They are, after all, able to act rightly, since they do act rightly. But when they act wrongly and were not able to act rightly, we do not hold them responsible and free.[84] To require that they be able to act rightly, however, is to re-introduce the Forking Paths Principle in modified form, with all the problems that that entails in a deterministic world.

Brainwashing: Another problem with the "reason" view is that it does not properly handle cases of brainwashing. For a person to have free will, it is not enough that the person's actions conform to his or her values; we must ask how he or she acquired those values. If they were implanted by brainwashing, hypnosis and the like, the person did not act freely. The "reason" view does not explain why this is so.

Coercion: If freedom is a matter of acting in accordance with reason, then the paradigm of free action is coerced action. In coercion, you have just one rational choice. Obviously, though, coerced acts should be classified as unfree.

Ostensibly, the smoothest way to deal with these objections is to re-introduce the Forked Path Principle and thereby surrender to incompatibilists. But as we saw, incompatibilism has its own difficulties. Here, then, is the real problem: we don't know what free will is. No matter where you turn to explain what it is, eventually you run into a brick wall — every definition is problematic. But if we don't know what it is, how can we figure out whether we have it in a deterministic world? No wonder the late Harvard philosopher Robert Nozick wrote that the problem of free will is "the most frustrating and unyielding of philosophical problems."[85] It is, in part, that frustrating and unyielding character that leaves us unsure of what direction to take in responding to the challenge of genetics and neuropsychology.

The Historical View

Major revolutions in science in the past six centuries — the Copernican, the Darwinian, and now the neuroscientific — have in one way or another seemed to dethrone human beings from a special place in the universe. In philosophy, David Hume's stress on the instinctual, non-rational or even irrational side of human thought and Immanuel Kant's highlighting of the limitations of human knowledge also tend to humble human beings. Freud, furthermore, made the irrational, instinctual side of human beings a central motif in the explanation of human behavior. Today's enthronement of biology and the denial of free will by many materialists seems to further reduce human power and standing. From a religious perspective, this is ironic. The Enlightenment's confidence in the autonomous powers of the human mind, which undergirds all scientific inquiry and has led to the abandonment of religion, has brought us to a day in which humans, the builders of those sweeping theories, the same human beings who dared to replace God, seem reduced to glorified beasts.

R. Abraham Isaac Kook, who had a penchant for viewing history as a dialectical drama and assessing scientific theories by their spiritual impact rather than the evidence they can marshal,[86] might well have seen the development of contemporary neuroscience as a needed corrective for the world, a dose of humility, a counter to Enlightenment hubris, after which the pendulum will swing back and the physicalist paradigm will be retracted. In this narrative of changing trends in science, humanity can extract from materialism a healthy message for our time and place. Specifically, the moral import of materialism is *yir'ah*, awe, in Maimonides' sense: humanity's awareness of its insignificance (*Hilkhot Yesodei ha-Torah* 2:2) and its shame (*Guide* III:52).[87]

This is not to say that free will, dignity, and *ahavat Hashem* (love of God) have no place. To begin with, *ahavah*, in the classic Maimonidean sense of seeing God's wisdom in nature,[88] might be aroused by the intricacies of the human brain no less than by other marvels in nature. (The reaction might be identical even if one believes that the brain evolved.) More importantly, there could be, for someone following in the footsteps of Rav Kook, a dialectic between what R. Soloveitchik later called humility and majesty.[89] As opposed to R. Soloveitchik's stress on dialectic within an individual's experience, Rav Kook emphasized collective history as the arena of dialectical combat. Were he alive today, Rav Kook might have argued that although there are times when the right message is "majesty," ours is not one of them. The recent surge of quests for spirituality in the thick of a materialist scientific paradigm and, indeed, on the psychiatrist's couch, might have suggested to Rav Kook that the road back to *ahavah* and an uplifted spirit goes by way of the confinement imposed by the materialistic world and the *yir'ah* it produces. We need to choke on materialism before expelling it, so as to appreciate the more liberated life.

Viewed differently, of course, materialism is not humbling; it actually expands human power. If everything is matter and nothing is unembodied spirit, then with sufficient scientific knowledge and technological advancement, humans can control a very broad range of events.[90] If scientific method is the only way of knowing about the world, then science projects an "apparent sense of intellectual dominion."[91] And, there are other religious problems with materialism. Determinism can lead to despair, something that concerned Maimonides greatly in his letter on astrology. Materialism may perhaps be fueling a devaluation of human life and noxious trends in end-of-life issues. Finally, while the irony of brilliant scientists declaring themselves to be clumps of matter may amuse some, none of that provides cause for rejecting the scientists' picture and celebrating human beings in the here and now. And yet: a dialectical reading of history holds some promise for the religious personality.

CONCLUSION

Understanding the human being is a task of great religious importance. To borrow a thought from R. Aharon Lichtenstein, applied by him to study of the humanities, it would be odd for religion to endorse the study of atoms and electrons on the grounds that these are part of the world God created, but then turn a blind eye to the pinnacle of that creation, the human being. (R. Lichtenstein might not agree with my application of his idea.)

Judaism affirms free choice. We have seen, however, that Maimonides, R. Abraham ben David, Nahmanides, R. Eliyahu Dessler, and perhaps some Hasidic thinkers, adopted views that go against simplistic conceptions surrounding this affirmation. Medieval and modern Jewish thought contains a surprising array of physicalistic explanations of human action. In fact, medieval figures also adumbrated certain elements of the compatibilist approach to free will found in philosophical literature today.

In addressing evolution, R. Kook writes that "We should not immediately refute any idea which comes to contradict anything in the Torah, but rather we should build the palace of Torah above it."[92] I take that to mean that if people believe that a particular doctrine of the Torah is true, then other things they accept can only deepen their understanding of that doctrine. If no Darwinist had ever lived, religious intellectual life would now be easier; but it would not be richer, nor closer to the truth. Likewise, if the world had never discovered the complex causes of disease and natural disasters, theology would be much simpler — but not only would we have lesser capacity to heal and alleviate suffering, we would present a skewed picture of how God operates in the world. Teaching the truths unveiled by secular methods, so R. Kook says, enables one's understanding of religious teachings to grow.

For contemporary Jewish philosophers who want to situate themselves within both Jewish tradition and contemporary science and philosophy, the challenge is to utilize religious insights about free will, combine them with the best that scientists, psychiatrists, psychologists and philosophers have to offer, and "build the palace of Torah above it." We cannot do otherwise.

NOTES

I thank Yitzhak Berger, R. Yitzchak Blau, R. Michael Broyde, Shalom Carmy, and R. Dov Linzer, as well as Charles Manekin and Meira Mintz, for valuable communications relevant to this paper.

[1]   On Jewish reactions to the Copernican revolution, see Andre Neher, *Jewish Thought and The Scientific Revolution of the Sixteenth Century: David Gans (1541-1613) and His Times*, trans. David Maisel (New York, 1986); David Berger, "Judaism and General Culture in Medieval and Early Modern Times" (to which I owe many of the references in this note), in Gerald J. Blidstein, David Berger, Shnayer Z. Leiman, and Aharon Lichtenstein, *Judaism's Encounter with Other Cultures: Rejection or Integration?*, ed. Jacob J. Schacter (Northvale, NJ, 1997), 133-35; Hillel Levine, "Paradise Not Surrendered: Jewish Reactions to Copernicus and the Growth of Modern Science," in *Epistemology, Methodology, and the Social Sciences*, ed. R. S. Cohen and M. Wartofsky (Dordrecht, 1983), 203-25; David Ruderman, *Jewish Thought and Scientific Discovery in Early Modern Europe* (New Haven, 1995), 266-68. Tobias Cohen, Yosef Shlomo Delmedigo, David Gans, Tovia Katz, Isaac Lampronti and David Nieto were among Copernicus' rejecters, with Nieto calling the heliocentric theory *piggul* (see Berger, 134-35 and Ruderman, 266-67). Without necessarily accepting the truth of evolutionary theory, some rabbinic figures early on accepted the *compatibility* of evolution with Judaism. These include R. Samson Raphael Hirsch, R. David Zvi Hoffman and R. Abraham Isaac Kook. For sources and analysis, see Geoffrey Cantor and Marc Swetlitz (eds.), *Jewish Tradition and the Challenge of Darwinism* (Chicago, 1996); Shai Cherry, "Creation, Evolution, and Jewish Thought" (Ph. D dissertation, Brandeis University, 2001) and "Three Twentieth-Century Responses to Evolutionary Theory," *Aleph* 3 (2003): 247-90; Raphael Shuchat, "Attitudes Towards Cosmogony and Evolution Among Rabbinic Thinkers in the Nineteenth and Twentieth Centuries: The Resurgence of The Doctrine of the Sabbatical Years," *The Torah u-Madda Journal* 13 (2005): 15-49; Natan Slifkin, *The Challenge of Creation: Judaism's Encounter with Science, Cosmology and Evolution* (2nd ed., New York, 2008). As Shuchat, for example, notes, rabbinic figures in the second half of the twentieth century were more resistant to the compatibility of Darwinism and Judaism and rejected evolutionary theory.

[2]   Kuhn, *The Structure of Scientific Revolutions* (Chicago, 1962).

[3]   R. Joseph B. Soloveitchik and others take the inability of science to capture raw sensory experiences to signal a need for an explanation of the world beyond the physical. See *The Lonely Man of Faith* (New York, 1992), 12-14, 18; *U-Vikkashtem Mi-Sham*, in *Ish ha-Halakhah: Galuy ve-Nistar* (Jerusalem, 1992), 137-41. (In English, see *And From There You Shall Seek*, trans. Naomi Goldblum [New York, 2008], 22-27.) See also Robert Merrihew Adams, "Flavors, Colors, and God," in *The Virtue of Faith and Other Essays in Philosophical Theology* (New York, 1987), 243-62.

4   Cf. Eugene d'Aquila and Andrew Newberg,"The Neuropsychological Basis of Religion: Why God Won't Go Away," *Zygon* 33, 2 (June, 1998): 187-201.

5   Most so called "dualists" today are "property dualists," meaning that they deny that there are non-physical substances but accept that there are non-physical properties like the redness of a mental image or the sharpness of a pain. This is the position presented in, for example, what is in some circles regarded as the strongest case against materialism yet made, David Chalmers's *The Conscious Mind: In Search of a Physical Theory* (New York, 1996). Yet substance dualism — which accepts an immaterial self — is not lacking in support among academic philosophers. See Robert Audi, "Theism and the Mind-Body Problem," *Faith, Freedom and Rationality*, ed. Jeff Jordan and Daniel Howard-Snyder (Landham, MA, 1996) 155-69; J. Foster, *The Immaterial Self* (London, 1991); W. D. Hart, *The Engines of the Soul* (New York, 1988); and Richard Swinburne, *The Evolution of the Soul* (New York, 1997). See also Shubert Spero, "What Is Self-Theory and Does Judaism Need One?," *The Torah u-Madda Journal* 12 (2004):130-57.

6   Crick, *The Astonishing Hypothesis: The Scientific Search for the Soul* (New York, 1994), 3. Likewise, philosopher Daniel Dennett asserts:

> There is only one sort of stuff, namely matter — the physical stuff of physics, chemistry, and physiology — and the mind is somehow nothing but a physical phenomenon. In short, the mind is the brain...We can (in principle!) account for every mental phenomenon using the same physical principles, laws and raw materials that suffice to explain radioactivity, continental drift, photosynthesis, reproduction, nutrition, and growth. (Dennett, *Consciousness Explained* [New York, 1991], 33.)

7   *Listening to Prozac* (New York, 1993). Kramer's point is not entirely new. The effects of older antidepressants as well as of food, drink and exercise can likewise stimulate the biological concept of a person, and we have long known the effect of "bad drugs" (crack, etc.) on the mind. Kramer asserts a difference in rapidity and effectiveness between Prozac and earlier antidepressant interventions that suggests something new occurs with recent "good" drugs.

The culture of pharmacology for the mind breeds other questions. Traditionally, responsibility is tied to the notion that certain behaviors are "owned" by the patient and reflect his or her "true self." Who is the real self when medicine alters mood and behavior? Is the patient accurate in declaring, after a few months on an anti-depressant/anti-anxiety regimen pursuant to thirty horrid years of entirely different moods and behavior, that after those few months on the pill "now I feel like myself"? Or has he or she, during those recent few times, been living as somebody else? Even people who take blood pressure medications or medications that slow heart rate sometimes wonder, when they exercise, "was that me or the medicine that went 5.1 miles an hour at 4% elevation without losing breath?" Athletes who take steroids often are thought to be not "really themselves" when they are capable of hitting baseballs 500 feet; hence the outcry against steroid use in competitive sports. *A fortiori* when the changes are psychological. Should a person get credit for the better behaviors even when there has been no "internal" labor? Is a pharmacological enhancement "external" — like someone pushing a long-since trailing runner over a finish line — or "internal" to the self?

8   Cf. Robert Nozick, *The Examined Life* (New York, 1989), 49-51.

9   See the essays in Howard Robinson (ed.), *Objections to Physicalism* (New York, 1993) and Steven Wagner and Richard Warner (eds.), *Naturalism: A Critical Appraisal* (Notre Dame, IND, 1993). In addition to difficulties in construing ethical facts in a materialist way, there are problems with normative concepts of other kinds, such as rationality. See, e. g., my essay in the Wagner-Warner volume, "Skepticism and Naturalized Epistemology," 117-45. Cosmic materialism, in short, has a lot of explaining to do.

10 Dissenting neuroscientists voice their view in Benjamin Libet, Anthony Freeman and Keith Sutherland (eds.), *The Volitional Brain* (Thorverton, UK, 1999). See also Jeffrey M. Schwartz and Sharon Begley, *The Mind and the Brain: Neuroplasticity and the Power of Mental Force* (New York, 2002). Cf., however, the dissenters from the dissenters, notably Thomas W. Clark, "Fear of Mechanism: A Compatibilist Critique of 'The Volitional Brain'," in Libet et al., 279-93.

11 Few go so far as the philosopher Paul Churchland, however, who believes that ultimately neuroscience will develop to the point where we can discard our everyday talk of beliefs, desires, emotions, motives and the like, a discourse which is highly unregimented, unscientific, and "inaccurate," and speak instead in purely biological terms, explaining human action exclusively in neurological discourse. Churchland's books include *Matter and Consciousness* (Cambridge, MA, 1988) and *The Engine of Reason, The Seat of the Soul* (Cambridge, MA, 1995). See also his wife Patricia Churchland's *Neurophilosophy* (Cambridge, MA, 1986).

12 Similarly, a behaviorist might acknowledge that there are inner mental processes, but claim, as B. F. Skinner did, that since they are unobservable they have no place in science. Again, someone could believe that God creates each species by a special act of creation, but acknowledge that God should not be invoked in a *scientific* explanation, because of constraints on what entities science can allow in. See the debate between Alvin Plantinga and Howard van Till in *Christian Scholars' Review* 21:1 (1991): 8-41. Times have changed in this regard. To handle planetary motions that did not fit his equations perfectly, Isaac Newton posited that God adjusts orbits every once in a while. No scientist today could do that! (A final note: ironically, Mordecai Kaplan, naturalist though he was, insisted on free will.)

13 The same holds of R. Joseph Soloveitchik's list of "man-persona's" qualities (man-persona as opposed to man-natura) — the longing for vastness and boundedness, the sense of loneliness, the ability to discipline the body, and the ability to think in moral terms. The list is from *Family Redeemed*, ed. David Shatz and Joel B. Wolowelsky (New York, 2001).

14 Phenomenologically, when we act, we feel that we are deliberating between alternatives; the deterministic materialist describes what is happening in terms of neurons and posits only one option. These represent two pictures, two typologies, of humanity. Some writers think that the two pictures are viewing the same phenomenon from two different perspectives, each valid in its own right. A recent articulation of this view is Hilary Bok, *Freedom and Responsibility* (Princeton, NJ, 1998). But critics complain that this is not a solution to the problem, but only a restatement of it; for the two perspectives seem incompatible. See Linda Ekstrom, "Introduction," *Agency and Responsibility:*

Essays on the Metaphysics of Freedom (Toscadero, CA, 2001), 4-5. The philosopher Elizabeth Anscombe once wrote of such attempts at reconciliation (e. g., Kant's) that "[they] have always seemed to me either so much gobbledegook, or to make the alleged freedom of action quite unreal." See Anscombe, "Causality and Determination," in *Metaphysics and the Philosophy of Mind: The Collected Papers of Elizabeth Anscombe* (Oxford, 1987), 146.

15 Clark, "Fear of Mechanism," 281. The criticism is directed at Benjamin Libet.

16 The challenge that genetics poses to religion goes beyond the problem of free will and extends to religious teachings about reward and punishment. If your genes determine your liability to cancer or hard arteries, where do your deeds enter the picture?

17 The term "reactive attitudes" was coined by British philosopher P. F. Strawson in a classic and frequently reprinted essay, "Freedom and Resentment," *Proceedings of the British Academy* 48 (1962): 1-25. Responsibility for an act or omission does not entail that the act or omission was done freely. (We can speak of omissions being "done" when they are deliberate, such as deliberately not returning a phone call.) A person who negligently flicks cigarette ash on a patron in the next row of seats in the stadium, is not "freely" doing that because he does not will it. He may even feel badly once it is done, but he is responsible for the negligence.

18 On this point, see Charles Manekin's introduction to *Freedom and Moral Responsibility: Jewish and General Perspectives*, ed. Charles H. Manekin and Menachem M. Kellner (Bethesda, MD, 1997), 8-11. In fact, some interpreters maintain, contrary to popular belief, that, when R. Akiva famously declared *"ha-kol tzafuy ve-ha-reshut netunah"* (all is known and choice is given) (*Avot* 3:15), he is not stating a contradiction but rather affirming an incontestable truism: since God knows what you are doing (as opposed to what you will do), you should exercise your free will responsibly. See R. Ovadayah mi-Bartenura, commentary to *Avot* 3:15; Ephraim Urbach, *The Sages: Their Concepts and Beliefs* (Jerusalem, 1979), 257-58.

19 Despite this disanalogy, John Martin Fischer, in his highly regarded book, *The Metaphysics of Free Will* (Oxford, 1994), seems to equate the two problems and implies that they should be equally worrisome. For more on scary "what if" scenarios, see my "The Metaphysics of Control," *Philosophy and Phenomenological Research* 57 (1997): 955-60.

20 In suggesting that the *problems* of divine foreknowledge and divine planning are irrelevant to this discussion, I am not suggesting that the *literature* on them is irrelevant. On the contrary, the literature contains certain conceptions of free will that make free will compatible with determinism by physical causes. The solution to one proves to be a solution to the other, assuming the solution is correct.

21 I have I mind the Izbicer (R. Mordecai Joseph Leiner) and his disciples — his son Jacob and R. Tzadok ha-Kohen of Lublin. See Jerome I. Gellman, "The Denial of Free Will in Hasidic Thought," in Manekin and Kellner, 111-31. To sin, in this construct, is to think you have a will of your own beyond the will to affirm or reject the truth that God does all. *Ha-kol bi-yedei shamayim hutz mi-yir'at Shamayim,* "All is in the hands of Heaven save for fear of Heaven" (*Berakhot* 33b) means, on this view, that *ha-kol mi-yedei Shamayim,* all is *from* the hands of Heaven, except for your attitude about providence.

22   This argument is also found in the Kalam philosophers whom Sa'adyah sought to refute. R. Shnayer Zalman of Lyadi claimed that even the separate existence of created things is illusory. The doctrine of *tzimtzum* was understood by R. Shnayer Zalman epistemologically rather than ontologically. That is to say: it *appears* to us that the *Ein Sof* has withdrawn from the world, but the truth is that He is in everything; hence the creaturely consciousness of separatedness is only an appearance. In actuality it is only *bittul ha-yesh*, the eradication of any existence but the *Ein Sof*. For R. Shnayer Zalman, free will is no more real than tables and chairs. I stress, though, that I am interested in putting forth possible readings rather than arguing that Hasidic thinkers really did hold the view I am considering.

23   T. W. Clark, "Fear of Mechanism," in Libet, Freeman and Sutherland, *The Volitional Brain*, 280.

24   The subtitle of Fischer's book, *The Metaphysics of Free Will: An Essay on Control*, is indicative.

25   The position that nature represents divine action is held in *Guide of the Perplexed* II:48, where Maimonides equates prophetic statements of the form "God does X" with "X happens in accordance with natural law and the course of nature." It also dovetails with many other attempts in Jewish thought to see nature as reflective of divine activity and providence.

    In a kabbalistic or medieval philosophical framework, to be sure, direct divine activity is always taking place in the form of emanations (or overflow). But according to contemporary scientific materialism, nature has independent existence and runs on its own. One could say, nonetheless — I repeat myself — that the laws of nature that science discovers are patterns of divine agency.

26   See Dov Schwartz, *Astrologiyyah u-Magiyah be-Hagut Yehudit bi-Yemei ha-Beinayim* (Ramat Gan, 1999). In the Talmud, Rava declares: "Length of life, children and sustenance depend not on merits but on *mazzala*" (*Mo'ed Katan* 28a), and there is abundant evidence that talmudic sages believed in astrology. The "override" view I mention is articulated by some commentators on talmudic passages.

27   See also Pinchas H. Peli, *Soloveitchik on Repentance* (Ramsey, NJ, 1984), 173.

28   Manekin, "Freedom Within Reason?," 180. See Gersonides, *Milhamot Hashem* II:2.

29   Override theories need elucidation. Supposing for the moment that physical causation is incompatible with free will, it seems to me that when the agent does not exercise the override, his situation *should not* be described as one of exercising free will. It is true that he/she could have (in the medieval theory) overridden the "natural" (astrological) causes of action. But it hardly follows that the astrologically caused acts were free. If I'm standing at a bus stop and fail to brace myself for a strong wind, and as a result of my unpreparedness I topple onto someone else and injure him, I do not freely will to topple onto the person just because I could have (freely) braced myself. What does follow from my being able to do otherwise is that I am responsible for the results of my negligence (if negligence it indeed was). By analogy, in the case where an act of mine is astrologically caused and I do not override the astrological cause, I do not freely will the act. Manekin's view of Ralbag, furthermore, is that "I cannot just will myself onto the intellect track" (180).

30   *Guide of the Perplexed* III:8, trans. Shlomo Pines (Chicago, 1963), 431, 433.

31   Maimonides writes in *Shemonah Perakim* (chap. 8) that "It is not possible for a person to possess virtue or vice by nature...Still, it is possible to be naturally disposed toward a virtue or a vice, so that it is easier to perform the actions that accord with" a particular virtue or a particular vice. Through training, though, a coward can become brave — sometimes easily. The translation is from *Maimonides' Ethical Writings*, ed. Raymond L. Weiss and Charles Butterworth (New York, 1975), 83-84.

32   *Guide*, p. 77.

33   Ibid., p. 433.

34   See Charles H. Manekin, "Freedom Within Reason?: Gersonides on Human Choice," in Manekin and Kellner, 165-204. Note especially Manekin's statement:

> The power possessed by humans to make opposing choices follows, according to Gersonides, from two facts about their condition: they possess intellect, which motivates them to choose according to reason, and they are corporeal creatures whose material faculties (sense, imagination, etc.) motivate them to choose in opposition to intellect. (177).

Also see p. 180, a passage I cite later in the paper.

35   Manekin's reading of Gersonides leads him to an important revision of the standard view that, according to Gersonides, God cannot know "future contingents." See his "On the Limited-Omniscience Interpretation of Gersonides' Theory of Divine Knowledge," in *Perspectives in Jewish Thought and Mysticism*, ed. Alfred Ivry et al. (Amsterdam, 1998), 135-70.

36   Cf., however, R. Samson Raphael Hirsch's reading of *yetzer mahshevot libbo* in Gen. 6:5 not as instinct or impulse but rather that which the person, the *yotzer*, forms.

37   *Family Redeemed*, 6. See also *The Emergence of Ethical Man*, ed. Michael S. Berger (New York, 2005).

38   See, e.g., *Bereshit Rabbah* 9:7.

39   Maimonides' model, however, unlike R. Soloveitchik's, involves the human being dissociating as much as possible from matter, but not channeling.

40   For discussion of various analyses of these cases and a constructive suggestion, see my "Freedom, Repentance and Hardening of the Hearts: Albo vs. Maimonides," *Faith and Philosophy* 14 (1997): 478-509, abridged in *The Jewish Philosophy Reader*, ed. Daniel H. Frank, Oliver Leaman and Charles H. Manekin (London, 2000), 51-57; "Hierarchical Theories of Freedom and the Hardening of Hearts," *Midwest Studies in Philosophy XXI*, ed. Peter French et al. (Notre Dame, 1997), 202-24.

41   *Mikhtav Me-Eliyahu* I: 116-18. Actually R. Dessler has a still higher stage beyond *mukhrah*. At this stage, there is no subjective feeling of compulsion at all, but rather *avodah me-ahavah*, service out of love. "One cannot speak of compulsion to do something that one loves. At this point the human being becomes truly free, finding no resistance within him to the good which he loves...'No one is free but he who occupies himself with the Torah'...This man of the spirit is the truly liberated man" (*Strive For Truth*, II:63).

42   Similarly, Robert Nozick coins the term "tracking bestness" to refer to the process of doing the right without free choice. "Let us ask which you would

choose for yourself: tracking bestness (without the process) or the process of free will (without tracking bestness). Our difficulty simply in choosing the second indicates the value of the first, of tracking bestness." See Nozick, *Philosophical Explanations* (Cambridge, MA, 1981), 327. Cf. my "Compatibilism, Values, and 'Could Have Done Otherwise'," *Philosophical Topics* 16, 1 (1988): 167-75.

43 Interview by H. Flender in *Writers At Work*, ed. George Plimpton (New York, 1968), cited in Libet, et al, "The Volitional Brain," 57.

44 I take the term from philosopher Peter van Inwagen, "When is the Will Free?," *Philosophical Perspectives* 3 (1989): 399-422.

45 Solomon Schimmel, "Free Will, Guilt and Self-Control in Rabbinic Judaism and Contemporary Psychology," *Judaism* 26 (1977): 425.

46 *Mikhtav*, I:111-18. For similar views in the secular literature, see C. A. Campbell, "Is Free Will A Pseudo-Problem?" *Mind* 60 (1951): 446-65; Peter van Inwagen, "When Is the Will Free?" For more on R. Dessler's views, see Shalom Carmy, "Use It or Lose It: On the Moral Imagination of Free Will," in *Judaism, Science, and Moral Responsibility*, ed. Yitzhak Berger and David Shatz (Lanham, MD, 2006).

47 R. Dessler's view faces at least two problems. First, the view that past choices determine present ones seem to undermine the possibilities of repentance or backsliding. Second, it is not clear to me that one can always retain a morally and religiously significant *nekuddat ha-behirah*. If a person reaches a high level of religious ardor and his only choices are whether to travel to the *bet midrash* by train or bus, this is hardly an important *nekuddat ha-behirah*, and decidedly not what R. Dessler means by the term.

48 The prominent libertarian Robert Kane addresses this problem in *The Significance of Free Will* (New York, 1996) and "Responsibility, Luck and Chance: Reflections on Free Will and Indeterminism," *The Journal of Philosophy* 96 (1999): 217-40. Kane, however, does not believe in a special type of causation usually called "agent causation."

49 In addition, even if there are undetermined neural events that result in actions that can plausibly be called free, we need to know how often these undetermined events occur and to how many people. Suppose scientists discovered that on October 18, 1924, a farmer in Fayetteville, Arkanas arose early and deliberated whether to feed his chickens or go back to sleep. In an undetermined fashion, scientists conclude, he decided to go back to sleep, causing the chickens the pain of hunger. Now, if that were the only case of undetermined behavior in the history of the world, would we say "Hurray! There's free will!"? Hardly. Moreover: Even if we knew there were a large number of undetermined actions in real life, we want to know *what precise choices those involved*. Even if a person's choice to beat his neighbor to death is determined neurologically, the decision whether to use a rock or a baseball bat may not be. But we would hardly find this as "consoling" a thought as the discovery that his choice to beat his neighbor (or not) was not determined. And if your most significant choices in the world were "Strawberry or vanilla?" or "Should I use a fork or a spoon?" or "A machine gun or a bomb?" this would not be, in Daniel Dennett's phrase, "a variety of free will worth wanting." (The term is from Dennett, *Elbow Room: The Varieties of Free Will Worth Wanting* [Cambridge, MA, 1984].) (Some of this note reflects observations I heard long ago from the late Sidney Morgenbesser.)

50 There is a world of literature on utilitarian vs. retributive theories of punishment. For a brief guide to the issues, see Joel Feinberg, "The Classic Debate," in *Philosophy of Law*, ed. Joel Feinberg and Jules Coleman, 7th edition (Belmont, CA, 2004), 799-804. A utilitarian theory of punishment faces problems, since, for one thing, we would not justify "punishing" an innocent person just because people think he is guilty and incarceration would prevent rioting. For another thing, by invoking utility we could punish minor offenses like double-parking with harsh punishments like flogging. But several philosophers have worked out utilitarian theories of punishment and reactive attitudes that overcome standard objections to such approaches. For example: Strawson, "Freedom and Resentment"; Derek Pereboom, *Living Without Free Will* (Cambridge, UK and New York, 2001), chs. 5-7. It is clear that some punishments we do administer cannot easily be justified if we stay within a retributivist straitjacket. Take, for example, cases where the law assigns "strict liability," meaning that for certain types of acts or omissions we do not accept any excuses, even if there was no criminal intent. Legislators might oppose allowing mental illness as an excuse for an action on the grounds that it can be too easily feigned, but those suffering from mental illness do not deserve to be punished.

51 Maimonides, for one, includes elements of a utilitarian theory regarding quantity of punishment. See, for example, Guide III:41. For a lengthy listing of harsh punishments meted out by rabbinic authorities on utilitarian grounds (e.g., killing of *moserim* [informers]), see Aaron Schreiber, *Jewish Law and Decisionmaking* (Philadelphia, 1979), 375-424. Familiar examples include *mishpat ha-melekh* (the king's law) and *makkin ve-oneshin she-lo min ha-din* (a court may inflict harsher measures than the law prescribes).

52 This point is standard. See for example Pereboom, 139-40; Eugene Schlossberger, *Moral Responsibility and Persons* (Philadelphia, 1992), 4-7, 79, 101, 112, 117-18.

53 One might argue that what these examples show is that attributions of moral responsibility are only one type of evaluation; maybe in blaming the perpetrators of atrocities we are evaluating their actions and not *them* — the sins, not the sinners (*Berakhot* 10a). There is something importantly correct in this response. We must be wary of homogenizing assessments of responsibility with assessments of reprehensibility. Likewise, being *admired* for one's goodness is different from being *credited with* one's goodness. We do want to say that some people are not to be blamed for their heinous acts because they are victims of horrible upbringings. My point, however, is not that moral praise and blame definitely are consistent with determinism; it is rather that whether they are is a philosophical question, not a scientific one. On the distinction between moral and non-moral evaluation, see Michael J. Zimmerman, "Responsibility Regarding the Unthinkable," in *Midwest Studies in Philosophy XXI: Moral Concepts*, ed. Peter A. French, Theodore Uehling, Jr., and Howard K. Wettstein (Notre Dame, IN, 1996), 213-14; cf. Robert Merrihew Adams, "Involuntary Sins," *Philosophical Review* 94 (1985): 3-31.

54 In his acclaimed *The Metaphysics of Free Will* (Oxford, 1994), Fischer treats theological determinism and scientific determinism as parallel arguments.

55 Classical compatibilism, the version of compatibilism developed by David Hume, John Stuart Mill and other British philosophers, actually did not reject the Forking Paths Principle so much as reinterpret it. The British compatibilists insisted that

a person acts freely provided that (a) the person does as he desires, because he desires to; (b) if the person were to desire not to do the action, the person would not do it. The problem with this view is that the only person who isn't free is someone who is chained. Counterintuitively, kleptomaniacs, drug addicts, phobics, and the like all turn out to be free using this constraint. Indeed, not only humans but animals could satisfy the conditions of the British compatibilists. For this reason philosophers today opt either for a wholesale rejection of PAP or a different reading of the principle than the classical compatibilists gave it.

56 That determinism cancels alternative possibilities is surprisingly difficult to show, as is clear from Fischer, *Metaphysics of Free Will*. But, in the end, Fischer thinks determinism rules out alternative possibilities. One might think that even if determinism does not rule out alternative possibilities and our actions and thoughts are determined, still determinism excludes free will, moral responsibility, and reactive attitudes. For, if our thoughts and actions are determined, we do not "own" them — they are not ours. But this objection draws on the obscure concept of ownership. I will confine myself here to the Forked Paths Principle.

57 See Locke, *Essay Concerning Human Understanding* II:21:10. Locke's view is that the man who chooses to remain is more fortunate than someone who would want to leave but cannot — but he is not more free.

58 The example is given by Peter van Inwagen, "Ability and Responsibility," *Philosophical Review* 87 (1978): 201-24.

59 See especially Fischer and Mark Ravizza, *Responsibility and Control* (Cambridge, UK and New York, 1998). Frankfurt does not mention a contrast with Locke's view, but I believe that Locke applies the Forked Paths Principle to actions while Frankfurt applies it to decisions.

60 David Widerker has shown that Frankfurt's examples cannot be effective in the case of decisions because those examples presuppose conditions about the scenario that a libertarian defender of PAP would not accept. See, among others of Widerker's papers on the subject, "Libertarianism and Frankfurt's Attack on the Principle of Alternative Possibilities," *Philosophical Review* 104 (1995): 247-61.

61 Hume, *Enquiry Concerning Human Understanding*, VIII.

62 Peli, *Soloveitchik On Repentance*, 172.

63 See Frankfurt "Rationality and the Unthinkable," in his *The Importance of What We Care About* (Cambridge, 1988), 177-90. Cf. Michael Zimmerman, "Responsibility Regarding the Unthinkable."

64 This paragraph amalgamates cases found in: Daniel Dennett, *Elbow Room*, 131-52, Van Inwagen, "When Is the Will Free?," and Susan Wolf, *Freedom Within Reason* (New York, 1990). Mark Twain reportedly quipped: "I am a greater person than George Washington. George Washington could not tell a lie. I can — but I won't."

65 In presenting these examples to people, I have found that they keep responding, "No, you *could* do the other thing, you just *won't*." I do not agree with this. We can *picture* the person doing the act, but that's not the same as saying the person is *able* to perform it. See my "Compatibilism, Values and 'Could Have Done Otherwise'," "Irrestible Goodness and Alternative and Alternative Possibilities," in Manekin and Kellner, and "The Metaphysics of Control."

66   See Wolf, *Freedom Within Reason, passim.*

67   See again Wolf's attack on the idea that freedom requires the ability to act insanely.

68   *Nicomachean Ethics* III:5. See also Robert Kane, "The Dual Regress of Free Will and the Role of Alternative Possibilities," in *Philosophical Perspectives 14: Action and Freedom,* ed. James E. Tomberlin (Boston MA and Oxford UK, 2000): 57-79.

69   Peli, 173.

70   Schimmel, "Free Will," 425. The supportive points that follow are my own.

71   R. Wolbe, *Alei Shur* (Jerusalem, 1986-98), I, p. 156, quoted by Baruch Sorotzkin, "*Bechira*: How Free Is Free Will?," *Jewish Observer* 29, 3 (April 1996): 21, emphasis is Sorotzkin's. For more general criticisms of the Aristotelian position that we choose our characters, see Joshua Dressler, *Understanding Criminal Law* (New York, 1987), 695-96; Michael Moore, "Choice, Character and Excuse," in *Crime, Culpability and Remedy,* ed. Ellen Frankel Paul et al (New York, 1990), 45.

72   "Irresistible Goodness and Alternative Possibilities."

73   Maimonides in *Hilkhot Yesodei ha-Torah* 5:4 states that if a person can escape a hostile ruler and does not, and as a result is coerced into worshipping idols, he is not an *anus* (i.e., he is not acting under duress) but instead an *oved avodah zarah be-mezid* (i.e., he is deliberately committing idolatry). I believe that this ruling is best understood as a ruling about the person's responsibility, not his freedom. For further scrutiny of such situations, see *Teshuvot Tashbetz* I: #63. (I thank R. Dov Linzer for the Tashbetz reference.)

74   "Irresistible Goodness and Alternative Possibilities," in Manekin and Kellner, 63-73.

75   Philosophers who adopt (a) often rationalize (a) in terms of (b), invoking the Platonic-Kantian idea that the true self is the rational self. While I question the thesis, I will work with a version of (a) that accepts this rationale.

76   Stern, "Maimonides' Conceptions of Freedom and the Sense of Shame," in Manekin and Kellner, 231-32.

77   Sokol, "Maimonides on Freedom of Will and Moral Responsibility," *Harvard Theological Review* 91, 1 (1998): 25-39. In particular, Sokol reads Maimonides as endorsing the "sane deep self view" expounded by contemporary philosopher Susan Wolf. Charles Manekin sees an affinity between Gersonides' and Wolf's views. See Manekin, "Freedom with Reason?: Gersonides on Human Choice," in Manekin and Kellner, 165-204. (His title is a play on Wolf's.) My descriptions of medieval compatibilists are inexact since I do not draw their distinction between theoretical and practical intellect, interested as I am only in the general flavor of the theories.

78   See also Stern, "Maimonides' Conceptions of Freedom," 232, n. 25.

79   I won't enter here into the question of whether all Jews, according to Maimonides, have the desire to obey the law as their "deepest self." On one reading of Maimonides's approach to the hardening of Pharaoh's heart (especially the version in *Shemonah Perakim* 8), Maimonides holds that there too Pharaoh's deep self was restored, in which case the key to Pharaoh's freedom is not God's restoring the choice that reason establishes, but merely God's allowing the true

self to have its way. See also Nehama Leibowitz's chapter on this topic in her *Iyyunin be-Sefer Bereshit* (3rd edition, Jerusalem, 1973), 110-17.

80   My criticisms of compatibilism are explained most fully in "Free Will and the Structure of Motivation," *Midwest Studies in Philosophy X*, ed. Peter French et al. (Minneapolis, 1985), 451-85; "Irresistible Goodness and Alternative Possibilities"; "Compatibilism, Values and 'Could Have Done Otherwise',", and "The Metaphysics of Control. " Also see "Hierarchical Theories of Freedom and the Hardening of Hearts."

81   Fischer, *The Metaphysics of Free Will*, 206.

82   Schimmel, 427.

83   See Gary Watson,"Skepticism About Weakness of Will," *The Philosophical Review* 86 (1977): 319-39.

84   See Wolf, *Freedom Within Reason*; Allen Wood, "Kant's Compatibilism," in *Self and Nature in Kant's Philosophy* (Ithaca, NY, 1984), 73-101.

85   *Philosophical Explanations* (Cambridge, MA, 1981), 293.

86   For an elaboration on this remark, see Tamar Ross, "The Cognitive Value of Religious Truth Statements: Rabbi A. I. Kook and Postmodernism," in *Hazon Nahum: Studies in Jewish Law, Thought, and History Presented to Dr. Norman Lamm on the Occasion of His Seventieth Birthday*, ed. Yaakov Elman and Jeffrey S. Gurock (New York, 1997), 529-56, as well as my "The Integration of Torah and Culture: Its Scope and Limits in the Thought of Rav Kook" and "Is Rav Kook a Model of 'Openness?,'" both in this volume.

87   For more on the connections in Maimonides between matter, shame, and *yir'ah*, see Josef Stern, "Maimonides' Conceptions of Freedom and the Sense of Shame," in Manekin and Kellner, 247-66. More generally, see R. Soloveitchik, *Family Redeemed*, 73-85.

88   See Maimonides, *Mishneh Torah, Hilkhot Yesodei ha-Torah* 2:2.

89   "Majesty and Humility," *Tradition* 17, 2 (Spring, 1978): 25-37.

90   On these themes see also John Haught, *Science and Religion: From Conflict to Conversation* (Mahwah, NJ, 1995), 83-84, 93. Cf. however, Freud, *The Future of An Illusion*, trans. James Strachey (New York: W.W. Norton, 1961), which offers a theory of religion predicated on the idea that whereas humans are unable to control nature by natural means, religion claims to give them the ability to control nature by influencing the divine through supplication and other means. See "From Anthropology to Metaphysics," in this volume.

91   Haught, 83.

92   *Iggerot ha-Reayah* I: #134, trans. by Tzvi Feldman in *Rav A. Y. Kook: Selected Letters* (Jerusalem, 1986), 14. This letter admittedly contains a potpourri of strategies, at times conflicting ones, for responding to evolution. See this volume, pp. 103-107 and 125-29.

"FROM THE DEPTHS
I HAVE CALLED TO YOU":
Jewish Reflections on September 11th
and Contemporary Terrorism*

Expounding the Psalmist's words, "From the depths I have called to you, O Lord" (Ps. 130:1), R. Joseph B. Soloveitchik asserts that prayer and turning to God arise specifically "*mi-ma'amakkim*," "from the depths" — that is, from the experience of crisis.[1] True to this insight, in the aftermath of September 11th, 2001, many people here and abroad found comfort and hope in religion. After the tragedy we witnessed a revival of the religious spirit, a "spiritual thunderclap," as *The New York Times* put it. "Stunned Americans," the paper reported, "flocked for prayer and comfort not only to their local house of worship, but also to sports stadiums, public plazas, and convention centers."[2] This turn to God in the wake of assault calls to mind the words of God delivered to Isaiah. The prophet's message is addressed specifically to one who fears attacks by others, who "live[s] all day in constant dread because of the fury of an oppressor who sets out to destroy" (Isaiah 51:13). To such individuals God says: "I am the one who is your consoler (*Anokhi Anokhi hu menahemkhem*)" (Isaiah 51:12). We turn to God, and He to us, when we need comfort and consolation.

The surge of religious devotion, however, was only one side of a complex story. Many thoughtful and sensitive people felt not spiritually aroused, but spiritually challenged. Today, one full year later, those people will look beyond America's pragmatic measures and will be beset by hard, brooding questions that form the eternal problems of faith.

Religion is under siege — not necessarily in the public domain, but in many minds and hearts. The challenges to trust in God are formidable, affecting believers of many persuasions.

First of all, the attacks were undergirded and propelled by religious beliefs. This led many to wonder whether religious convictions *by their very nature* contain the seeds of fanaticism, whether they inevitably and inexorably give rise to the bursting of ethical restraints in the service of

---

*   This essay was published on the first anniversary of 9-11.

a higher cause. Such questioning has led and will continue to lead morally sensitive Christians, Jews and Muslims to ponder dangers that they might feel lurk in their own religions.

Second, the numbing numbers of lives lost, a number made worse still by the fact so many died in the midst of selfless acts of rescue or in a radiant prime, leaving children, spouses, parents, siblings and friends to grieve, makes us wonder about that oldest of theological conundra: how does God allow evil, particularly horrific evil? How does one sustain a commitment to God in the face of such tragedy? True, many of the people who in the aftermath of 9/11 pondered why God allows evil have done so before. They have thought deeply about the many victims of terror in Israel and elsewhere, as well as about the unprecedented destruction that was wrought in Europe six decades ago. But this particular adversity has its own poignancy for Americans. Despite prior attacks on America, such as the 1993 bombing of the World Trade Center, Americans thought this country was different, that it was safe. Now it too is a place where citizens feel vulnerable, fragile and frightened. With the Arab-Israeli conflict escalating at the same time to horrible proportions, the world itself at times seems to lie on the brink of destruction. Americans therefore feel acutely the force of the question, "Where is God?"

There are no quick, definitive answers to challenges so profound. But we must find a *modus vivendi* with them, even an unstable one; we need some starting point for absorbing what we are living through and for girding ourselves for the future. This essay is devoted to mapping out some issues of faith posed by last September 11th and to evaluating possible reactions. The positions are not meant to be novel; more importantly, in no way are they meant to be final. On the contrary, the task of living with faith is arduous and ongoing. R. Soloveitchik denounced the idea that religion is meant to be "an enchanted stream for crushed spirits." It is, rather, "a raging, clamorous torrent of man's consciousness, with all its crises, pangs and torments."[3] If we take seriously this conception of what a faith-full life entails, and if we further understand that religious growth must be ongoing, we cannot see any questions as easy. Answers, while never glib, must be fluid and tentative; they should be tested against reason and our collective religious experience, and most importantly should reflect the intensity and turmoil of our inner struggle.

In what follows, I deal with these two problems of fanaticism and evil. In part I, I explain how the passion that religion demands of its adherents may lead to fanaticism, and will identify some resources that Judaism offers to deal with that danger. In parts II and III, I turn to the problem of evil, and in particular sketch how the approach of R. Soloveitchik to the problem of evil affords a meaningful way of coping with the horrific events we have recently experienced. As we will see, the questions of fanaticism and evil are connected in a striking, ironic way.

I. RELIGION AND FANATICISM

The Importance of Passion

However well-grounded a person's commitment to God is from a purely intellectual standpoint, it cannot be truly religious if it functions in an emotional vacuum. Judah Halevi, the great medieval Spanish poet and thinker, saw clearly that intense passion is crucial to religious life. Halevi's *Kuzari*, in fact, is a famous attack on a certain type of religion. Specifically it criticizes forms of religion in which a believer's convictions are based upon a theoretical argument, rather than on the intense, living experience of God's presence.

A crucial complaint Halevi lodges against philosophically-based religion is that because it is grounded in philosophical or rational proofs, on what we would consider a detached, objective weighing of "the evidence," such a religion can never generate in its adherents the level of passion exemplified by a martyr. He made this point by saying that philosophy could bring a person only to Elokim, the impersonal God of the cosmos, and not to the caring, personal deity denoted by the Tetragrammaton, which we pronounce "Hashem" in ordinary parlance:

> One yearns for Hashem as a matter of love, taste and conviction; whilst attachment to Elokim is the result of speculation [philosophizing]. A feeling of the former kind *invites its votaries to give their life for the love of Him, and to prefer death to His absence.* Speculation, however, makes veneration only a necessity as long as it entails no harm, and bears no pain for its sake. (*Kuzari* 4:16; my emphasis).[4]

Passion for an idea, Halevi suggests, is manifest through willingness to die for it. A purely rational religion cannot bring that passion about. On the contrary, intellectualizing cools the passions.

If, as Halevi says, the possibility of martyrdom is essential to a religion that views God as personal, there arrives the possibility, which Halevi does not address, of fanaticism or "radical religion," which expresses itself in such forms as mass suicides, suicide bombers and other forms of violence. Willingness to die for one's religion does not logically lead to willingness to kill for it; but insofar as both a willingness to die and a willingness to kill reflect religious passion, a slide from one to the other is all too easy.[5]

The centrality of religious passion and its potential connection to immorality is brought out especially vividly, if somewhat radically, by R. Abraham Isaac Kook (1865-1935). As a mystic, R. Kook believed that all existence emanates from a single divine source — all things are holy. For him, therefore, no phenomenon in the world — no thought, no idea, no movement — is entirely without worth, and one must pierce through ugliness and perversity to get at the positive in everything. True to this vision, R. Kook found value even in idolatrous religion: "The source of the idolatrous urge is in holiness (*mekor yitzra da-avodah zarah bi-kedushah hi*)."[6] Idolatrous religion may be morally and intellectually odious,[7] but it involves, among several worthy characteristics,[8] intense passion for the divine. This passion, Rav Kook held, is, in isolation, holy. "In the pollution of idolatry is to be found the greatness of the spirit of faith in all its wildness and grossness, in its hot-bloodedness, and in its horse-like power, in the burning of sons and daughters."[9] "The deep passion of idol worship...is a darkened consequence of the recognition...that the Divine is more precious than anything else, and all that is lovely and beloved is as nothing in comparison to Him."[10] However distorted and perverse this passion, however grotesque its expression, we may learn from it, says Rav Kook; it teaches us something of the quality of heart needed to experience the infinite God. What is needed is not that the quality be eradicated, but that it find its proper expression.[11]

The nineteenth century Danish existentialist philosopher Søren Kierkegaard took the importance of passion in true religion beyond anything entertained by Halevi and R. Kook. For Kierkegaard, a religious commitment must never be confused with, for example, an intellectual one. If you believe in religion because it is "rational" to do so, because the "facts" support it, that is a *secular* gesture, not a religious one. To be religious you would need to go, or at least be prepared to go, contrary to what is intellectually safe and sound. Passion and intensity are measured by the degree to which one is willing to take risks. A man's love for a woman, his passion for her, is measured by how much he is willing to risk and give up for her; so, too, your passion for God is measured by how much you are willing to give up for Him, and *part of the required price is the surrender of intellect and the willingness to act against all odds and all evidence.* Furthermore, just as religious commitment must not be confused with an intellectual one, likewise a religious act must not be confused with a *moral* one. Morality is valuable — on that Kierkegaard is clear. But a religious person, Kierkegaard asserts, is not merely someone who does the moral thing. That makes religion too easy. The religious person is someone who takes, or is at least ready to take, moral risks by going against that which seems obvious to his or her moral conscience.

Kierkegaard elaborated this view in his famous essay *Fear and Trembling*, which focuses on the *akedah*, the Binding of Isaac narrated in chapter 22 of Genesis. If Abraham is commanded to sacrifice his son Isaac, Kierkegaard says, then religious commitment requires that he do it, even though from a moral point of view it constitutes murder. This, to him, is the point of the *akedah*.[12] It is not that ethics has no value for Kierkegaard; on the contrary, it is precisely because morality has value, and Abraham would ordinarily cling to it, that Abraham's religious commitment is significant. To be religious he must override all else that is valuable in his life. Even where religion and morality do not conflict, the religious commitment is adulterated if reason and morality are marshaled to strengthen the commitment in any way. There is nothing religious about rational or moral considerations, Kierkegaard maintains.[13] Rather, to repeat, religious commitment finds its highest, clearest expression in the overriding of other modes of thinking and feeling that we value, when those modes conflict with the religious demand. This is why in a true religious life the ethical might have to be suspended.

When we confront people who in the name of religion aim at randomly killing people who are innocent, we must discern what we are up against. What for the stunned observers is fanaticism, for the perpetrators is religion. To be sure, the perpetrators in this case are not Kierkegaardian philosophers (nor has Kierkegaard's exegetical path historically led to violence, despite its seeming potential to do so). Al Qaeda do not see themselves as overriding morality; in their self-conception, they are fighting the just and moral fight. They see themselves as warring for Allah against wrong ways of life, they deem the innocent victims guilty by complicity, and they explain their actions in terms of "rational" arguments for inflicting violence on foes of true religion, so as to keep the world on the straight path. To this extent their religion is "rational." Nevertheless, as Jerome Gellman incisively remarks, "A belief system can be rational — yet crazy."[14] It can be internally coherent and logical, but crazy nonetheless. It seems to me that in al Qaeda's case and others, the passion generated by religion is what leads to the come-what-may rejection of moral and prudential considerations that otherwise might deter action and that in fact are accepted by moderate Muslims; the passion closes off the extremist from perceiving other dimensions of life that have value, and in this way it permits a suicide bomber to see the world as he does and to translate his conclusions into deeds.[15] Normal standards of decency and, for that matter, self-interest have no hold, not just because they may not be valid for the terrorist, but because even if they were, they would be outside the religious sphere and hence of no real account in the context of religious demands.

In sum, religion celebrates extreme devotion, and seems not satisfied with less. Hence the natural and very intimidating question: is religion — at least when it contains a political component or agenda — too dangerous to human security to be pursued with confidence, commitment and verve? Does the history of religious wars and extremism signal that religion, or religion mixed with politics, is too grave a social threat to be encouraged? Why continue as before with an idea that carries such dangers? Religious "insiders" may see these questions as reflections of the questioners' own spiritual coldness and alienation, their inability to muster in themselves adequate religious feeling. But this perception, even if accurate, surely would not constitute a rebuttal of the objections; it would only be an excuse for avoiding them, a timid flight from a genuine issue. Eugene Korn eloquently puts that issue on the table:

> [T]he very form of human relationship to God requires that a religious person surrender himself to the Divine word, disregarding practical concerns and conventional moral judgments. Yet who is the fanatic if not the unreasonable person who ignores normal considerations and social constraints to pursue an ideal without limit? The religious fanatic is not someone with faulty reasoning. On the contrary, he is the perfectly consistent religious servant, unwilling to allow any personal interest or ethical constraint to interfere with his understanding of the divine command...therefore fanatical extremism is a philosophical difficulty for all theologies and a potential ethical horror for all faith communities.[16]

What shall we say about this challenge?

On Balancing Values

We may begin our reply as follows. Any idea can be taken to extremes. Hence, if we resolved to abandon ideas that individuals or societies might take to extremes, we would have to jettison many of the best and noblest ideas there are. As R. Norman Lamm has written in a different context:

> Any idea contains the risk of distortion; and the nobler the idea, the greater the danger and the uglier the perversion. The concept of government can be reduced to tyranny; must we, therefore, all be anarchists in order to avoid such dangers? Religion can become superstition; democracy, mobocracy; liberty, libertinism; respect, subservience; love, lechery. Shall we abandon the former because they can and often do degenerate into the latter?[17]

Ideologies, secular as well as religious ones, frequently take healthy values to unhealthy extremes. Even having witnessed in our time the degeneration of some of the very ideals R. Lamm identifies, we must surely go along with his conclusion that the ideals are still, for all that, worth holding. Thus, religion can be worth holding even if some religious ideologies take it to an extreme; religious passion can still be worth striving for even if some allow it unbridled reign.

But this reply, as it stands, is not adequate for the case of religion. For let us ask: how can the taking of ideals to extremes be stopped, once they are taken as values?

In R. Lamm's examples, the answer is clear: by placing some competing ideal or ideals against them — law against liberty, self-respect against respect for others, discipline against love. In the case of religion, however, this placement of a competing ideal is *prima facie* inappropriate. After all, tempering the religious ideal would require placing some value against religion, a value, furthermore, that overrides religion in some cases; and surely to allow one's religion to be superseded in this way is to miss the whole point of its being a religious commitment. For religion, we said, is supposed to be overriding; it trumps all rational and moral calculation.

There is a solution to this problem, however. There is a way to have the passion for God tempered by morality and rationality without compromising the religious framework. That way is to embrace morality and rationality *not as external to the religious outlook but as part and parcel of it*. One must allow for religion to balance and integrate competing values *and see them all as part of the religion*.

Such an approach, which is called "dialectical," sees religion as requiring not a single-minded commitment to one of a pair of values — freedom vs. submission, fear vs. love, self-negation vs. self-affirmation, emotion vs. intellect, and so on — but rather a commitment to each of these values and a careful calibration and balancing of them, perhaps an oscillation (or dialectic) between one and another.

Dialectic is a brake on extremism, because it refuses to absolutize. In a dialectical approach one value can be overridden, in some circumstances, by another, and that latter, in other circumstances, by the original one. In our time what we experience is a failure to *balance* passion with restraints born of cool reason and moral sense. The key to defusing fanaticism is to infuse not only reason with passion but also passion with reason, to understand God's will with the aid of general moral judgment, and to view moral and rational judgment not as antithetical to the religion but as part, albeit not the whole, of it.[18]

"It is forbidden," writes Rav Kook, "for the fear of heaven to push aside man's natural morality. There is a sign showing that the fear of heaven is pure, when the natural morality, planted in man's honest nature, ascends through it [the fear of heaven] to higher levels than it would attain without it."[19] Introducing natural morality does not reduce the quality of one's commitment, it enhances it. R. Kook saw the need to integrate passion with intellectual reflection, obedience to God (or fear of heaven) with a natural sense of morality. The avoidance of extremes is in the spirit of Maimonides' famed "middle path" in ethics.[20]

A Kierkegaardian theory of religious commitment, which sets religion against all other human values like morality and rationality, is singularly unattractive. Such a conception would see Jim Jones' cult as more religious than Roman Catholicism just because the latter integrates rationality and "natural law" (a moral standard grasped by reason) into religion. Kierkegaard's approach simply conflates the concept of religion with that of insanity and immorality. Ironically, secular critics of religion view religion much in the way Kierkegaard does: as irrational and immoral. His viewpoint thus plays right into the hands of religion's critics. A dialectical approach that integrates morality into religion justly escapes the critic's barbs.

The Akedah Revisited

Even if religion need not *absolutize* passion, we must face the question as to how far Judaism, our particular religion, goes in advocating passion. The passage just cited from Rav Kook refuses to demand a passion so strong as to disregard morality and forsake moral sanity vis-à-vis the preservation of human life. But what shall we then say about the *akedah*, where Abraham's willingness to sacrifice his son seems so contrary to morality and, in particular, to moral principles about taking life? To answer this question, I propose now to examine an approach Rav Kook developed to the *akedah* narrative. In effect, he converts that narrative from one that epitomizes religious passion to one that calls, on the contrary, for the tempering of passion via moral and intellectual reflection on the value of human life.

As background for explaining Rav Kook's reading, it must be noted that Kierkegaard's interpretation of the narrative as depicting a clash between religion and Abraham's sense of morality, and as identifying religious heroism with the suspension of morality for a higher purpose, is, for all its power and popularity, neither the understanding of the talmudic Sages nor the best literary fit to the text.[21] First of all, from a certain point of view, sacrificing an only child to God could be said to make sense. This is not just because in Abraham's culture, child sacrifice was practiced, making sacrifice "relatively" permissible. Nor is it just that if our possessions are on loan from God, God might want them back. Rather, the point is that to live in the presence of God is to be prepared to part with one's most precious possessions. It therefore may have made sense to Abraham to offer his beloved son to God. Abraham, on this view, would not have seen such a sacrifice as immoral, any more than others in his time and place did.

Instead of viewing God's command as contrary to morality, Abraham may have seen the divine command as a call to suppress fatherly love for the son in whom he had invested all hopes, this for the sake of serving God properly. "He conquered his *rahamim* [compassion]," we say in our prayers, "so as to do your will wholeheartedly."[22] This suggests the suppression of parental feeling. So in the first place, whereas Kierkegaard views the *akedah* as a clash between morality and God's command, it is more compelling to view it as a clash between parental love and God's command.[23] Accordingly its message is not necessarily, or at least not exclusively, that God's commands may at times clash with morality.

A more basic reason for rejecting Kierkegaard's reading is that, even assuming that God's command to Abraham is at odds with rational and moral judgment, at the bottom line, Abraham never kills Isaac. An angel of God comes down and enjoins him from going ahead. "Do not lay your hand upon the child; do nothing to him…" (Gen. 22:12). Yes, Abraham expresses his passion for God by bringing Isaac up to the site of the altar — but ultimately God forbids him to touch his son. Commitment to God may require readiness to do for God what God commands us; but God will not allow child sacrifice. Although such sacrifice makes *religious* sense, it *is* at the end of the day objectionable to God after all, as God *will shape His own demands according to the value of human life*. The *akedah*, thus read, testifies to God's wanting religious acts to be controlled by sanity, moral judgment, and compassion. The consequence is that we, emulating God, won't abandon morality and compassion either; in our lives, we will find a way to have both (along with obedience). Had Kierkegaard assigned the ending of the narrative due weight, he could not have sustained his thesis that religion is contrary to everyday morality. The lesson we draw from the end of the episode is the opposite of Kierkegaard's: the lesson is that "murder is never a legitimate way to worship the God of Israel because true *Avodat Hashem* [service of God] entails valuation together with obedience."[24]

For a powerful rendition of the *akedah*'s significance along these lines, we turn, again, to Rav Kook. Rav Kook understands the *akedah* as extolling "passion without fanaticism":[25]

> The permanent essence of life is expressed only through ethically pleasing behavior. "Its [Torah's] ways are pleasantness, and all its paths are peace" (Proverbs 3:17). That deep addiction to paganism, which to primitive man was the main ideal [of life], overcoming even parental mercy, and making cruelty to sons and daughters an established institution of the worship of [the Canaanite fire god] Molekh, is a nebulous outcome of the realization deep within the recesses of man's heart that the divine is the most precious of all

things...[The *akedah*] showed that fervor and addiction to the divine idea does not necessitate that the perception of the divine should be covered in shameful trappings as those of pagan worship, where the spark of divine goodness loses its way, but it [the same fervor and submission] can also be reached by a pure perception...[W]ithout [the *akedah*], humanity would have continued to relate to the divine either savagely and wildly, through powerfully pulsating emotions, or with a cool disposition and reservedness lacking the characteristics of a profound life...Idolaters used to claim that it was impossible for human culture to exist without this [unbridled passion]...Came "the father of many nations" and taught what had to be taught, so that no matter how low subsequent generations sink, there is room for the penetration of the pure light. And the binding of Isaac is mercifully remembered for his children forever and ever.[26]

In the end, the *akedah* testifies that divine morality cannot contradict natural morality, the human being's innate moral sense. As one observer paraphrases Rav Kook's point: "Man is not forced to choose between the throbbing savagery of pagan enthusiasm and the shallow frigidity of lifeless detachment. Abraham finally expressed his deepest religious striving without having to take the final step of killing his son."[27]

While at certain points Rav Kook's presentation may reflect homiletic excess, his general approach affords a way to think about and teach the *akedah* to our children and also to adults without inviting the charge that Abraham is a child abuser. The usual lesson preached is, "Look how eagerly Abraham went to sacrifice His child because He saw it as a *mitzvah*, so it is permissible and even obligatory to kill children and perhaps other innocents when God beckons." But if that's the lesson, then I daresay that listeners today don't need Genesis 22 to learn it. They can find it in the daily papers. Common sense dictates that which part of the *akedah* narrative should be stressed in *derashot* — the beginning of the chapter, which depicts Abraham's readiness to comply with God's command, or verses 12 and following, which relate his withdrawal of the knife — depends upon circumstances, and on how the *darshan*'s words reverberate and are processed in the immediate community and the larger world. In our time, the ending of the story, not its beginning, is the punchline we need to get across.[28] We must not allow anyone to conflate *akedah* and al Qaeda.

I stress that this is what we, in our time and place, ought to emphasize. I well understand that in other circumstances, for example, one in which society stresses moral conscience so greatly that people have no appreciation of God's commanding authority, but only of their own moral autonomy, a *darshan* might emphasize the beginning of the episode: Abraham's alacrity in rising early to follow God's command, preparing the wood himself, and

266

so on. Indeed, if one means it when one claims to embrace a dialectical approach to religion, one must perceive not only the pole of morality but also that of on occasion surrendering morality, rationality or human emotion to God's command. Certainly R. Soloveitchik, master of dialectic, emphasized this point.[29] It is the greatness of Torah that it has "seventy faces." But no one can display all those faces at once; one must select a message appropriate to the context by perceiving the needs of one's own times.

Recent events should sensitize us to the problem of religion run amok. In our situation, therefore, we must let moral constraints and intuitive moral judgments have their say. We must be judicious in our preaching, knowing when to kindle fires and when to wet them down.[30]

Morality and Religion

It cannot be gainsaid that within Judaism, as within the other major religions, there are strains that stress the supremacy of God's will over moral principles, just as there are strains (like Rav Kook's view) that see God as consistently and necessarily conforming to moral demands. So, on the one hand, we must admit that some strands in Judaism court extremism and reject ordinary moral constraints. On the other hand, to be obsessed with these extremist strands, to see them as exclusive or even dominant, is equally to be in denial.

In the first place, R. Yitzchak Blau has shown in detail that recent writings coming out of militant groups in Israel on topics like war and peace, *kiddush ha-Shem*, and the role of moral judgment in decision-making perpetrate serious distortions and falsifications of traditional texts and concepts. The attempts to justify violence do violence to sacred texts.[31] Moreover, even if we acknowledge with a full throat that we have not escaped laying seeds for bigotry, cruelty, and fanaticism in our long history, we may argue that many or most voices in our tradition call for ordinary moral principles to restrain religious acts. Those calls are as conspicuous as they are forceful.

In the name of triumphing over the forces of evil, God commands His people to destroy the people of Amalek and "the seven nations" (Ex. 17:14-16; Deut. 20: 16-17; 25:17-19). We ought not to suppress this fact, and we ought not let it pass without feeling concern about it. But we are a people whose understanding of the Bible is based on the authoritative traditions of *Hazal* as well as subsequent traditional exegesis, and the history of interpretation of the command to destroy Amalek testifies to Judaism's ultimate stance on the value of innocent life. Our commentators have developed a variety of approaches to the law, the thrust of many of which is that these laws apply only in a highly limited way in concrete situations, and/or that their primary relevance is symbolic.[32] It is clear that the position from which these commentators operate is one that sees the need either to justify the command morally or to limit its application and concretization in the physical world. Without entering into details, suffice it to say that the thrust of this position is to place the commandment to eradicate Amalek within a morally more satisfying framework. Thus Maimonides, reflecting talmudic sources, severely limited the command's practical application, saying that the nation is not to be killed if they make peace with Israel and choose to accept the Noahide laws, and that we cannot identify those who are from Amalekite seed.[33] Moving to another example of troubling behavior in the Bible, Jewish biblical conquerors used what strike us as cruel or barbaric practices. Rav Kook addressed this too. The harsh scale of wars conducted by Jews in biblical times is geared, he said, to an earlier stage in the development of morality. The biblical morality is calibrated to the moral level of people at a particular time, in that since all nations conducted themselves with extreme cruelty in war, the Jewish people would have been destroyed had they rejected the prevailing canons of war.[34] No doubt this approach cries out for more detail. How should we understand this notion of a contextual morality? What are its implications? Should we posit an evolving morality? What are *its* implications?[35] But the general direction of the argument should be clear: interpersonal morality is a value within religious life.

Unfortunately, declarations of distrust of the human moral sense come disturbingly easily to the lips of some religious individuals committed to Halakhah. They belittle natural human moral sensibilities as unreliable and contrast them with the sure, clear dictates of Halakhah. While distrust is in place in certain contexts, wholesale distrust is out of place. To see why, let us briefly think about how different religious life would be if we really denied the claims of natural morality, our own intuitive moral judgments. When we realize the implications, we must conclude, as I remarked earlier, that logic is on the side of those who acknowledge the value of human moral intuitions.

This point can best be illustrated by means of a single verse: "Give thanks to the Lord because He is good (*hodu la-Shem ki tov*)" (Ps. 18:1, 136:1). We thank God for good things He has done and also praise Him for His actions — based on our estimation of what is good. Gottfried von Leibniz made a telling point about the conception of goodness that allows goodness to stimulate praise: "In saying that things are not good by virtue of any rule of goodness but solely by virtue of the will of God, it seems to me that we unknowingly destroy all of God's love and all of His glory. For why praise Him for what He has done, if He would be equally praiseworthy in doing the exact contrary?"[36] The same would apply to thanks: why thank Him for what He has done, if you would thank Him even had He done the contrary? There must be some standard of goodness *besides* "God willed it," or else thanks to God or praise of God *for His works* would make no sense. So much for distrust of human judgments of value.[37]

Consider also the following point about the obligation of "*hodu* (give thanks)." *Hakkarat ha-tov*, gratitude, is a central Jewish teaching. Sa'adyah Ga'on explains, "Reason bids us respond to every benefactor either by returning his kindness if he is need of it, or by offering thanks if he is not in need of recompense."[38] We all believe we must be grateful to God for good things that He does. In other words: "One should thank God" follows logically from "God has done good for us." But how can this inference hold unless we endorse the *moral principle*, "One should be grateful to a benefactor"? R. Yitzhak Hutner, in fact, maintained that the duty to be grateful precedes the revelation at Sinai and exists independently of it.[39] Anyone who thinks that human moral judgment is irremediably flawed (the position adopted by Martin Luther, John Calvin, and others) will have a hard time explaining why we can trust our moral judgment that a person owes gratitude to his or her creator.[40]

There is a larger lesson here. What people really believe about a philosophical question is not what they say about the question when they are asked about it explicitly in a philosophical *shmooze*, but how they think and act when their guard is down and they are living their ordinary religious lives. You may, when asked, insist that human moral judgments have no validity. But when not thinking about the philosophical question, you will find God to be *worthy* of our worship *because* He has done for us X, Y, and Z, in which case you are using your native moral sense.

Other religious gestures and attitudes make no sense if there is no independent ethical standard. Think of the problem of evil, which is so central to religious thinking and pervades biblical and rabbinic thought. Anyone who is troubled by the existence of evil, anyone who asks how God could allow the Temple's destruction or the Holocaust or September 11th, is imposing some external standard of morality on God. Since the prophets wondered how these-or-those evil events can happen, they must be endorsing such a standard.[41] Perhaps you will say by way of retort, "Well, the prophets are not asking how God violates *our* standards, they're asking how He violates His *own*," or "They're asking how God violates His own promises to His people." But if you ask even how God can violate His own standards or how He can break His promises, you are *still* using a standard of ethics that is independent of God's will. For you are endorsing the judgment, "It is wrong for one to violate one's own standards," or the judgment "It is wrong to break promises." Again, it is easy to deny that one is using moral judgment when one thinks about that question outside of a concrete context like the problem of evil. But once we look at our actual reactions and judgments, we see how central such judgments are in religious life. Judaism assigns importance to natural moral intuitions even in the determination of Halakhah. I will not try here to document this last point; others have done that work.[42] Their observations will only reinforce the role that morality plays for Jews.

To summarize: quite apart from mountains of traditional texts that endorse intuitive moral judgments implicitly or explicitly,[43] quite apart from the many interpretations of Scripture and of law that use morality as an interpretive tool to choose between differing interpretations, quite apart from the fact that commentators seek to explain and evaluate the behavior of patriarchs in moral terms that we can accept,[44] quite apart from the moral assumptions made by those authorities who seek to understand problematic biblical commands such as executing the "stubborn and rebellious son" (Deut. 21:18-21) in human moral categories that preclude or severely limit the law's application (*Sanhedrin* 71a), we have seen that the most basic religious attitudes and practices — praising God, worshipping Him, calling Him good, feeling gratitude to Him, wondering how He allows evil — depend upon human beings trusting their own moral judgments, on their having standards that allow them to affirm with surety, "God is worthy of worship," "We ought to praise Him for the good He has done," "We ought to thank Him," and so on. In religious life, you can't escape making moral judgments of your own; religious life requires such judgments on a daily basis. While human moral intuition may on occasion mislead, a complete distrust in it would destroy the basis for many proper attitudes and practices.

The alternative approach, which denies validity to human moral intuition, pictures a God who could theoretically call for the torture of innocent children — and pictures, along with that, a person of faith who wouldn't be bothered by such a command if it were to come to pass. Hence, religious passion must be balanced by moral sense; and when it is, the power of fanaticism is curbed.

In light of the link between martyrdom and religious passion that was brought out by Yehudah Halevi in the quotation we cited earlier, a brief point should be made about Jewish conceptions of martyrdom. A clear distinction exists between the core Jewish concept of martyrdom and the vision that drives suicide bombers to their zealous acts of destruction. The commandment of "sanctifying the Lord's name" (*Kiddush ha-Shem*) requires, in its core, dominant application, that a Jew give up his life, let *himself* be murdered, rather than murder another. This act of "sanctification" does not devalue innocent life — to the contrary, it expresses the value of the innocent life the Jew refuses to take. This is a far cry from urging, as a route to heaven, that people kill themselves in order to bring about the deaths of innocent people. Certainly there is no analogy, for example, between letting oneself be killed to prevent one's own forced violation of the cardinal sins of idolatry, sexual immorality, and murder, and killing someone else for not being part of my religion, for the sake of attaining personal reward in the hereafter. More generally, authorities have held that a Jew is considered to have died *al kiddush ha-Shem* if, like the victims of Nazism, he is killed because he is a Jew. The sanctification is achieved through submission, not aggression.[45] It bears noting that *kiddush ha-Shem*, the same idiom used for martyrdom, also connotes the ideal of ethical behavior. Unethical behavior desecrates God's name. That is really the key point behind mandated martyrdom as well. Furthermore, even when Judaism allows active martyrdom, the circumstances are decidedly different from those in which suicide bombers commit their evil acts.[46]

II. RESPONDING TO RADICAL EVIL

Earlier I wrote that the two questions of fanaticism and evil "are connected in a striking, ironic way." Let me explain.

We have just seen that Judaism accords credibility to human moral judgment. But once a religion does this, once it sees human moral judgment as worthy and reliable, the problem of evil becomes more difficult for that religion to address. In particular, the problem of why God allows evil cannot glibly be dismissed as a symptom of poor human capacities for moral judgment; after all, in our discussion we have invested human moral judgments with credibility and force. Inexorably, therefore, our reflections on the use of human moral judgment in religion lead us to reflect also on whether, post-September 11th in America, or while witnessing the carnage in Israel, we can continue to believe in God's goodness. This is the ironic connection I had in mind between the problem of fanaticism and the problem of evil: solving the problem of fanaticism makes the challenge of evil loom larger and more intimidating. That is to say, the stance I have taken against fanaticism — that religion must allow for moral judgment — exacerbates the problem of evil.

The evil overwhelms us. First there is the sheer loss of life with all that goes with it — the torment of those trapped in the fiery furnace of the World Trade Center, the trauma and pain of the survivors, the anguish of the families, the brutal catalogue of death after death. Second, there is the stark, utter depravity of the perpetrators, their hatred, their callousness, which is evil independent of any deaths and suffering they wrought. Although we know the biblical teaching that "the *yetzer* (inclination) of man is evil from his youth" (Gen. 8:21), our commentators rarely took this to mean that each individual is fundamentally evil.[47] Decent people cannot fathom the kind of malice nor the utter, total indifference to — or, worse, joy over — the evils endured by victims. Can we continue to praise Him, worship Him, thank Him? Our Sages teach: "Just as one must bless [God] over the good, one must bless [God] over the bad" (*Mishnah Berakhot* 9:5). How can a believer do that?

To view these problems as new, or the evils as unprecedented, would be absurd. And so it is natural for believers to turn to time-honored solutions. A classic religious response to questions about evil is to construct a "theodicy," an explanation or justification of God's ways. In a theodicy one attempts to show that evil is somehow necessary logically for a greater good — in other words, that in the big picture, *sub species aeternitatis* (under the aspect of eternity), the evil contributes to a greater good that could not be attained otherwise. To use well-worn analogies, what we call "evil" is like a musical note that is jarring in isolation but contributes vitally to a lovely symphony, or like an ugly paint dab on a canvas that, in combination with others, helps make a painting beautiful.

Often people assume that Judaism knows but one theodicy: that "there is no death without sin, and no suffering without transgression" (*Shabbat* 56a, the view of R. Ammi). This assumption accounts for offensive statements, heard with disturbing frequency after a calamity, by those who claim to know the precise sin for which God brought about this or that tragedy. The Versailles wedding hall in Jerusalem collapsed, we were told by one rabbi, because it was the site of improper dancing; the United States was bombed, some Jews have suggested along with Jerry Falwell (who later retracted), because God is punishing the country for its sexual permissiveness and other sins of excessive liberalism.

In truth, while the approach of "no death without sin, no suffering without transgression" is affirmed by R. Ammi, the Talmud ultimately rejects R. Ammi's view.[48] Rejection of R. Ammi of course in no way entails that in Jewish tradition *no* suffering is punishment for sin, or that *no* death is retribution. That would be flatly inconsistent with tradition and the notion of *hashgahah* or providence. But it is a fallacy, or at least problematic, to infer that *all* suffering and death are retribution.[49] And to assume that one has fathomed God's reasons in a particular case — not only that God is administering punishment, but that He is administering punishment for this or that sin — is, in R. Aharon Lichtenstein's phrase, "the height of arrogance vis-à-vis the *Ribbono Shel Olam*."[50] No wonder the Sages taught (*Bava Mezi'a* 58b), "One must not speak to the sufferer as his companions spoke to Job." The friends had insisted, "Who ever perished, being innocent?" (Job 4:7). Those words are grossly inappropriate, not only in their tactlessness but in their substance.

In fact, putting aside the offensiveness and crassness of the friends' words, the book of Job is cogently read as a *protest* against the view that suffering implies sin. Job's friends, whatever the differences among them, are united in affirming that Job deserves his bad fortune. The friends are determined to uphold the traditional theodicy of justified retribution at all costs: all suffering is due to sins, known or unknown. Job, by contrast, had complained that he was a good man, and that his actions do not warrant his fate. Yet, at the end of the book (42:7), Job's friends need Job to pray on their behalf because (God says), "You (the friends) did not speak to me correctly as did my servant Job." But it was the friends who *defended* God, and Job who spurned their defense! A stronger indictment of the retributivist view could hardly be imagined.[51]

In a series of illuminating studies, Yaakov Elman has shown that the Sages of the Babylonian Talmud realized full well that innocent people suffer, and devised a range of explanations for this phenomenon.[52] These include, *inter alia*, the ideas of sufferings of love,[53] *nissayon* (trial), and vicarious atonement. Jewish exegetes and philosophers developed some of these ideas further, for example by explaining "sufferings as love" as tribulations that righteous people suffer in this world to permit them greater reward in the next. Strikingly, some rabbinic explanations of evil are not so much a theodicy as an explanation that imputes certain outcomes to astrological causes (*mazzala*): witness Rav's dictum that "length of life, children and sustenance depend not on merits but on *mazzala*" (*Mo'ed Katan* 28a).[54] Again, there is the view of R. Jacob that "the reward for a *mitzvah* is not found in this world" (*Kiddushin* 39b). To be sure, there are numerous Jewish texts that prod a sufferer to introspect when evil comes upon him, implying, it seems, that sin must be explained by wrongdoing.[55] However (and this we shall see in more detail later), to say that one ought to use occasions of suffering to reflect on one's deeds and character is not yet to say that one always comes up with the correct explanation of the evil this way. It may be salutary for a person to treat evil *as if* it is due to his or her misdeeds, but this is not the same as saying that one has hit upon the true explanation.

The enterprise of giving theodicies is, as I said, time-honored. I certainly do not want to minimize the cogency of some of the explanations offered by philosophers through the centuries. But nearly *all* theodicies carry a danger, and theodicy-building looms as a potentially inappropriate response to tragedy.[56]

The point is not just the routine one that logical explanations for evil often cannot be psychologically assimilated by the sufferer. Rather, the point is that treating evil as if it were explicable would blunt our moral responses. Imagine for a moment that you accept a particular theodicy — for instance that all suffering is punishment for sin. Suppose I meet a friend who is undergoing a terrible illness and needs my help. No one would deny I am obligated to help. But why should I help? After all, he (presumably) deserves this suffering. Suppose, alternatively, that you accept the thesis that God increases the suffering of the righteous in this world in order to maximize their reward in the next. Or suppose that you think suffering is a way of improving the sufferer. Or suppose you think that the suffering of the righteous atones for the community's sin. No matter what the specific explanation, endorsing that explanation means that the evil is being viewed as something positive, something contributing positively to the totality. Given that fact, it is clear that any theodicy, any attempt to explain why suffering occurs, ought to diminish our perception of the evil as something negative, as something to remove. If translated into action, theodicy would make nonsense out of attempts to fight evil. Theodicies can be not only ineffectual, but even harmful.[57]

R. Soloveitchik on Evil

The underlying problem is this. The objective of a theodicy is to make *peace* with evil. But the objective of ethical action is to make *war* with evil (metaphorically). If we focus too much on the ultimate reasons for evil, we lose our appreciation of its horror. We see it as part of a beautiful, harmonious whole, as conducing to a greater good. All seems right with the world. Clearly, we must not let the aim of theodicy, namely, to render evil palatable, override the aim of ethical response, which treats evil as unacceptable.

R. Soloveitchik expressed this thought in several works, but most fully in an essay titled "A Halakhic Approach to Suffering," delivered as a lecture in 1961 to a conference on mental health.[58] In the lecture, the Rav distinguishes two forms that halakhic creativity can take. One is the "topical" Halakhah, the term deriving from the Greek word *topos*, meaning surface. At the "topical" level, the Halakhah posits formal legal categories and rules that relate to the human mind and will, resulting in action. In its topical mode, Halakhah is a formal cognitive system that is applied in practice.

But there is a second form of halakhic creativity, the "thematic," from the Greek word for root. The thematic Halakhah is addressed to "the axiological gesture," that is, the apprehension of values and metaphysical motifs. The topical Halakhah is understood; the thematic Halakhah is beheld, tasted or confronted.

Thus, on the one hand, Halakhah is "a reasoned, clearly defined, precise system of thought," which is applied via concrete actions (topical); but, on the other hand, Halakhah is "a singular, unreasoned order of experiential themes" (thematic). It may be easiest to think of "thematic Halakhah" as what we commonly call *aggadah* — the non-legal part of Judaism, the part that deals with, *inter alia*, theology. For example, when the topical Halakhah addresses the Sabbath, it formulates legal categories of, and rules about, the prohibited forms of *melakhah* (work) on that day; but the thematic Halakhah treats the Sabbath as a living reality, as a great experience of a sacred, blessed time, a period of *kedushah* (holiness). The Rav maintains that whereas the topical Halakhah deals exclusively with the physical universe, the world known to science and to our senses, the thematic "envelops Being in its majestic totality." The thematic Halakhah enters into the realm of a transcendent reality unfettered by bounds of time and space — the realm of the infinite.

Accordingly, the topical and the thematic Halakhah treat suffering and evil in profoundly different ways. The thematic Halakhah views evil, or rather what we call evil, as something that we can transcend after death, or as something that is swallowed up in the totality of boundless Being.[59] But the topical Halakhah, grounded as it is in the world of the physical, the transient, the here-and-now, could not accept the idea that evil can be explained.

> Thus, the topical Halakhah (the formal legal system) saw death as a dreadful fiend with whom no pact may be reached, no reconciliation is possible...Death appears in all its monstrosity and absurdity, and an encounter with it knocks out the bottom of human existence. If the topical Halakhah concurred with the thematic in its interpretation of death as deliverance, as a victory over nihility, then why mourn and grieve for the departed? Why rend our garments, sit on the floor...[60]

For the topical Halakhah, then, which is practically oriented, there is no metaphysic of suffering, no grand picture that makes evil inconsequential or unreal. Instead there is only an *ethic* of suffering, a way of responding to it. This ethic regards evil as real, as something to which we must never acquiesce. "Man is summoned by God to combat evil, to fight evil, and to try to eliminate it as much as possible." We must marshal for this battle all scientific resources at our disposal. We will lose from time to time, but the war is long, and the time will come when "He will swallow up death forever, and the Lord God will wipe off the tears from all faces" (Isa. 25:8).

Without entering into further detail, suffice it to say that for R. Solo-veitchik we must, in responding to evil, follow the way of the topical Halakhah. R. Soloveitchik summarized this approach in a letter (dated April 15, 1965) to Dr. Dan Vogel, then dean of Stern College for Women, Yeshiva University, in which he summarizes a lecture (albeit one which differs from the one we have considered so far[61]).

> Therefore, Judaism has recommended that the metaphysical inquiry be replaced by the halakhic ethical gesture. Man should not ask: Why

evil? He should rather raise the question: What am I supposed to do if confronted with evil; how should I behave vis-à-vis evil? The latter is a powerful challenge to man and it is the duty of man to meet this challenge boldly and courageously. Suffering, in the opinion of Judaism, must not be purposeless, wasted. Out of suffering must emerge the ethical norm, the call for repentance, for self-elevation. Judaism wants to convert the passional frustrating experience into an integrating, cleansing, and redeeming factor.[62]

We must not let the aim of theodicy override the aim of ethical response. "Response, not explanation, is focal."[63]

Upon hearing the Rav's philosophy of evil expounded, people have sometimes said, "Oh, I see: his point is that we have no answers." No, that is only *part* of the point. The *whole* point is not that we do not know the answers, but that *having an answer* would logically lead to abandoning the fight against evil. We must *act as if* there were no answers in any specific case we encounter — as if suffering is not integral to a higher good. Were we to do otherwise, we could not explain the ethical responsibility of eliminating evil.[64]

Applications

R. Soloveitchik's approach has several crucial applications.[65]

Messianic fervor: Almost immediately after the tragedy of September 11th, 2001, some Jews called attention to a passage in the *Zohar* according to which three walls of Rome and a great building will fall on the 25th of Elul, and the city's leader will die, seventy days before the Messiah comes.[66] Speculation was quickly rife that we were living through the war of Gog and Magog, the apocalypse foretold by Ezekiel (chs. 38-39), a prelude to the Messiah. It is not unusual that when major events transpire in the world, and especially tragedy, believers look for signs that they were foretold by the Bible or by the Sages. Recall, for example, the attention given to the assertions that the assassination of Yitzchak Rabin was encrypted in the Torah portion of *Lekh Lekha* read that week, and that the crash of two Israeli helicopters in 1997, in which 73 soldiers lost their lives, was foretold in a verse in Isaiah. The war between Napoleon and Russia was viewed in its time as the battle between Gog and Magog, as was World War II in 1940. Current readings of history join such earlier ones.[67]

Put aside for now the inconvenient fact that the text of the *Zohar* speaks of the toppling of Rome, identified with Edom, so that in the desired interpretation, the United States — of all countries! — has to stand in for Edom. Such inconvenient details aside, what is the point of such readings?

What exactly is accomplished by saying the events were foretold? R. Yosef Blau has suggested, incisively, that the attempt to find events of our time in biblical predictions (after the fact, notice) is a coping mechanism.

> If the crash of two helicopters...was foreseen by the prophet Yeshayahu, then instead of a problem of how a just G-d could have allowed the tragedy to happen, we have another indication that we are living in an era where prophecies are being fulfilled...Unable to find a rational explanation for all that is occurring, many have turned to messianic speculations. Events are thereby explained in terms of their being fulfillment of prophetic visions or necessary components of the unfolding of the messianic process. Dealing with the complexities and inconsistencies of actual events is no longer necessary...Most of the Jews who repeat these biblical interpretations are not consciously messianic. They are relieved, however, not having to face the difficulties in trying to come to terms with these unexplained tragedies...A play on a verse...adds nothing to our response to the tragedy but can serve to distract us from facing it.[68]

Faced with a bewildering reality and ravaged by seemingly uncontrollable, insane forces, people seek solace in the fact that it was all foretold. For that means it is all fated — and all part of a divine plan. But insofar as such an approach diminishes the horror of evil, insofar as it "proclaims peace when there is no peace" (Jer. 6:14, 8:11), it must be rejected, as R. Blau insists; for it is an instance of minimizing evil in a way that can blind us to its horror and absurdity and dull the urge to ethical action. As such, the Rav's approach precludes it. And well it does: the supposed prophecy never materialized.

Blame: Also in the category of improper responses are responses that blame the victim. Blame American capitalism. Blame the decadent morality wrought by freedom, or America's flouting of precepts of modesty in dress and conduct. What exactly is the thought here? If you can find fault in the victim, the evil becomes at least partly justified; blaming the victim thus minimizes the evil. But if we really believe that this is adequate reason for God to permit the deaths at bin Laden's hands, why not say equally that it was adequate reason for bin Laden to order them?[69] By blaming the victim, we once again obscure the need for ethical response (besides mitigating.the perpetrator's responsibility).

Moral relativism: There is one more approach that would minimize our sense of evil, and that is the position, often promoted in academic circles, known as moral relativism. The latter denies that moral judgments have any universal validity; all such judgments, relativism submits, are culturally and temporally bound. We can speak of acts being evil from this-or-that cultural perspective, but other cultures, this thinking goes, can claim no less validity for their own judgments. So if Osama bin Laden thinks that making war on the United States and bombing the World Trade Center is a correct course, he is right from his perspective.

Relativism, along with various cousins such as "post-modernism," lost some favor after the attacks. Intellectual fashions change in the face of atrocities. Prior to World War II, for example, moral philosophy was dominated by ideas like "ethics is subjective," i. e., that morality is a matter of personal likes and dislikes (a theory that came in a variety of versions). After the Nazi horror, philosophers, understandably realizing the tenacity of the judgment that this was clear, objective evil, sought to reconstruct ethical theory so that it includes an objective component after all. Likewise, before World War II, philosophers of law often espoused the view that law and morality are totally separate; a law can be a law even if it is horrendously immoral. Such a view could easily support those who followed Nazi laws — they were after all just loyal citizens obeying the law. As a result of the experience of the war, some of these erstwhile adherents of positivism defected to the view that at some point a legal system might become so immoral that it loses its status as law.[70] Some observers believe that we will witness a parallel repudiation of post-modernism, and that school of thought indeed has come upon heavy attack for its relativist implications.[71]

Of course, post-modernism seeks to contribute something positive, for by weakening convictions and delegitimizing certitude, it could be a brake on extremism and intolerance. But in point of fact it can have the opposite effect: it can lend succor to dogmatism by allowing people to justify their perspective in their own terms and then walk away from further discussion and debate. Moral judgments do vary wildly depending upon what individual or society is making the judgment. Relativists are right about this. But keeping R. Soloveitchik's approach in mind, we must not let this lessen in our minds the atrocity perpetrated by bin Laden and others like him in recent and ancient history. If you try to rationalize evil away by saying that moral judgments cannot be trusted, you run afoul of the Rav's insistence that evil must be recognized for what it is.

III. CLOSING THOUGHTS: EVIL AND YISHUV HA-DA'AT (COMPOSURE OF THE MIND)

It is fascinating to contrast R. Soloveitchik's perspective with that of Ramban (Moses Nahmanides). Ramban, in his commentary to Job, explicitly encourages and legitimizes the pursuit of theodicy. Having presented a theodicy in the commentary (the details of which need not concern us),

Nahmanides turns to the objection that it is improper to try to fathom God's ways. He replies:

> This [objection] is the claim of fools, despisers of wisdom; for through the above mentioned study [of theodicy], we will benefit ourselves by becoming wise people and knowers of God may He be Blessed, from [contemplation of] His ways and deeds...Likewise, it is the obligation of every creature who serves [God] from love and fear to investigate in order to make [His] justice right and to show the judgment true, according to his ability...in order that his mind become composed [*kedei she-tityashev da'ato*] in this matter, and the verdict of his creator will be true to him...[72]

Absorb the contrast: for Ramban, the pursuit of theodicy is legitimate and encouraged because it affords us "*yishuv ha-da'at*," repose, tranquility, peace of mind, equanimity. For R. Soloveitchik these effects are the mark of complacency, of having made inner peace with evil. And complacency with evil is the very antithesis of what we are called upon to experience.

I suggest, nonetheless, that the question "why?" has a legitimate use even for the Rav. There are times that the question "why?" is not a demand for explanation; it is, rather, an expression of woe over the tragedy, a cry that betokens empathy and love, not theological rumination. Uttered in this spirit, "why?" is of a piece with *hesed*, with benevolent action — it affirms one's grasp of the depths of the evil, which is a prerequisite to meaningful ethical action. The prototype for this "why?" is the biblical lament "Eikhah (how)." Jeremiah in Lamentations is not really expecting an answer to his question. The question is an exclamation, a "*krekhts*," a wail, rather than a query. An answer would not even be an appropriate response, for *Eikhah* is really an attempt to absorb the depth and scope of one's loss.

One year after the September 11th attack, we still ask "why?" and "how?" But it is a "why?" and "how?" that do not await an answer. It is a "why?' and "how?" that makes us reach deeply into ourselves, into reservoirs of generosity and care we never knew we had, a "why?" and "how?" that drives us to action, to sympathy with the victims' families, to multifarious and wide-ranging acts of kindness, to concern for victims of evils anywhere and everywhere. Asking "why?" and "how?" can also give us a more penetrating understanding of religion. Finally, during these *Aseret Yemei Teshuvah* (Ten Days of Repentance), the classic response of introspection could not be more appropriate.

That the destruction of the World Trade Center led to creative ethical responses and to spiritual strengthening does not *justify* the evil of that dark day. Many, if not most, would forego the benefits of moral growth which suffering can breed if that meant foregoing the adversity, just as several sages, when asked "Is suffering welcome to you?" responded, "neither they, nor their reward" (*Berakhot* 5b).[73] Still and all, we can seek to battle evil by containing its effects and on the contrary making great good come out of it. In turn, perceiving acts of human goodness can itself lead the disillusioned back to God.[74] Let us seize this opportunity to develop sensitivities, refine our moral character, and make the world a safer, more comforting place, even while never forgetting the victims of these horrific events. Let us also renew our commitment to forms of religious life that are healthy and morally sound. May God the consoler ultimately "wipe the tears from all faces."[75]

NOTES

This essay was published by Yeshiva University in September 2002 to mark the first anniversary of the attacks of 9-11 and displays emotions bred by the occasion. I extend my profound appreciation to R. Norman Lamm, then President and now Chancellor of Yeshiva University as well as head of the Rabbi Isaac Theological Seminary (*rosh ha-Yeshivah*), for his interest in this project and his copious comments on both an early and a late draft. In addition many people offered valuable comments on an earlier version: David Berger, Pearl Berger, R. Yitzchak Blau, R. Yosef Blau, Shalom Carmy, Bernard Firestone, Dedi Firestone, Meira Gross, R. Dov Linzer, Meira Mintz, Charles Raffel, Atara Segal, Chani Shatz, Michael Shmidman, Joel B. Wolowelsky, and R. Reuven Ziegler. To all of them, my gratitude.

1 See, for example, *Halakhic Man*, trans. Lawrence Kaplan (Philadelphia, 1983), 143 (n. 4); "*Ra'ayonot al ha-Tefillah*," in *Ish ha-Halakhah: Galuy ve-Nistar* (Jerusalem, 1979), 239-71.

2 *The New York Times*, Nov. 26, 2001, A1.

3 *Halakhic Man*, 143.

4 Judah Halevi, *Kuzari*, trans. by Hartwig Hirschfeld (New York, 1964), IV:16, p. 223. Halevi's stress on the nexus between passion and martyrdom has roots in the Sages, who remark on the verse "Love the Lord your God...with all of your soul" that love of God is mandated "even if He takes your soul" (*Sifrei* 32 to Deut. 6:5). Even rationalist philosophers like Maimonides, who did present philosophically-based conceptions of the divine, made love central to religious experience, and believed in the need for a kind of intellectualized passion. Indeed, Maimonides' description of the love of God in his *Mishneh Torah* (*Hilkhot Teshuvah* 10:2, 6), is one of the most passion-centered descriptions of God in our literature, notwithstanding that Maimonides elsewhere has negative things to say about emotion. See also *Guide of the Perplexed* III:51.

5 In a trenchant passage, the character of the Khazar (the king who converts to Judaism) says to the Rabbi that Jews prize humility only because they are powerless, and that "If you had power, you would slay." The Rabbi answers: "You have touched our weak spot." Ibid., I:113–15, pp. 78-79.

6 R. Abraham Isaac Kook, *Arpelei Tohar* (Jerusalem, 1983), 32. A midrash portrays Abraham as worrying, "I have sin on my hands, for I worshipped idols all

those years." In the midrash, God tells him, 'To you is the dew of your youth' (Ps. 110:3) — just as dew rises, so your sins rise up. Just as dew is a sign of blessing for the world, so you are a sign of blessing for the world" (*Gen. Rabbah* 39:8). Rav Kook, as pointed out by Jerome I. Gellman, quotes the midrash as follows: "Just as dew is a sign of blessing to the world, so, too, *those years that you worshipped idols are a sign of blessing to the world*" (*Orot ha-Emunah* [Jerusalem, 1985], 77). Idol worship could contribute to Abraham's spiritual development! See Gellman, *The Fear, The Trembling, and the Fire: Kierkegaard and Hasidic Masters on the Binding of Isaac* (Lanham, MD, 1994), 106.

7   As Eugene Korn notes, Menahem ha-Meiri, in his famous distinction in *Beit ha-Behirah, Avodah Zarah* 20a, between idolatrous and non-idolatrous non-Jewish societies, saw morality as an essential component of non-idolatrous religion and its absence as characteristic of idolatrous ones. See Korn, "*Tselem Elokim* and the Dialectic of Jewish Morality," *Tradition* 31, 2 (Winter 1997): 6. See also Moshe Halbertal, *Between Torah and Wisdom: Rabbi Menachem ha-Meiri and the Maimonidean Halakhists in Provence* (Hebrew) (Jerusalem, 2000).

8   Gellman (p. 106) lists also spiritual novelty, imaginative representations, and infinite commitment to the Divine.

9   *Orot ha-Emunah* (Jerusalem, 1985), 3, as translated by Gellman, 108.

10   *Iggerot Ha-Reayah* II (Jerusalem, 1985), #379, p. 43, as translated in Gellman, 109.

11   A homily of R. Meir Shapira of Lublin is but one illustration that passion is central in traditional rabbinic consciousness. In Genesis 36, Jacob flees Laban's house, and Rachel, who is to travel with Jacob, steals her father's *terafim*, or miniature idols. Laban pursues Jacob hotly and traverses a seven-day distance in three, eventually catching up to Jacob. Jacob says, "What is my transgression and my sin that you have hotly pursued me?" (36:36). The explanation of these words, Rabbi Shapira suggests in the classic style of *derush*, is that after witnessing how Laban's attachment to his idols led him to move so energetically and frenetically as to travel a seven-day course in three days, Jacob felt embarrassed by his comparative lack of zeal for a real God: "What is my transgression and my sin?" — You have shown such dedication to inane idols; what comparable dedication have I shown to the true God? (I thank R. Joseph M. Baumol and R. Norman Lamm for referring me to R. Shapira's homily.)

12   Readings similar to Kierkegaard's are often adopted in Jewish and Christian circles, but I will later argue that the text is better read along different lines.

13   In our time the late Jewish thinker Isaiah (Yeshayahu) Leibowitz has advocated at least this minimal position.

14   Gellman, "In Defense of a Contented Religious Exclusivism," *Religious Studies* 36 (2000): 415.

15   There is a school of thought that seeks to dissociate terrorist acts from religion and to view them as powered by purely political or other motives. I do not know if this view is correct, but believe we are obliged to consider the possibility that terrorism can arise from within the very soil of religion. Professor Mark Lilla writes cogently in a *New York Times* op-ed piece ("Extremism's Theological Roots," October 7, 2001, section 4, p. 13) that "If any religion is to cope with these deviations it must recognize that they do not arise from nowhere but have

roots, however twisted, in the faith itself. Christians who bomb abortion clinics appeal to the Christian Bible and persuade others to join them on Biblical grounds. That Islamic fundamentalism and its militant offshoots appeal to the Koran is therefore not an incidental matter. It means that they have found a way to breed in the religious space opened up by the revelation Islam presupposes. ... Reflections on this matter must begin with the uncomfortable fact that in religion, as in nature, there is no such thing as spontaneous generation." Again, a secular political vision like communism can lead to violence too, but the question is not whether *only* religion leads to extremist acts, but whether religion can lead to such acts. In Israel, suicide bombing clearly serves political goals, whatever next-worldly prizes are thought to await the bomber as a result of certain religious beliefs he or she holds.

[16]   Korn, 7. My analysis differs somewhat from Korn's in that I do not stress obedience so much as the realization of some religious ideal or other, whatever it may be. But, in the present context, the difference does not matter much.

[17]   Norman Lamm, in *The Condition of Jewish Belief*, ed. Milton Himmelfarb (New York, 1966), 125.

[18]   See also Korn, "*Tselem Elokim.*"

[19]   *Orot ha-Kodesh* (Jerusalem, 1985) III, *rosh davar*, p. 27; the translation is by Shalom Carmy and Bernard Casper and is found in *The World of Rav Kook's Thought*, ed. Benjamin Ish-Shalom and Shalom Rosenberg, trans. Shalom Carmy and Bernard Casper (Jerusalem, 1991), 423. (The essay in which their translation appears is R. Yehuda Amital, "The Significance of Rav Kook's Teaching for Our Generation.")

[20]   See for example *Mishneh Torah, Hilkhot De'ot*, chap. 1; I comment on this chapter in "Maimonides' Moral Theory," in this volume. On the ideal of moderation and the danger it produces of losing passion, see Norman Lamm, "Centrist Orthodoxy and Moderationism: Definitions and Desiderata," in his *Seventy Faces: Articles of Faith* (Hoboken, New Jersey, 2002), vol. 1, 54-64. Commenting on the verse, "And God saw that it [the creation] was very good" (Gen. 1:31), R. Meir remarks: "'Very good' [*tov me'od*] — this is death" (Gen. Rabbah 9:5). R. Joseph Engel glosses R. Meir's words as follows: all "*me'od*," all extremes, spell death. See *Otzerot Derush*, 8, p. 45, quoted by Lamm, *Seventy Faces*, 61-62.

[21]   On this point, see, among recent writers, Ronald Green, *Religion and Moral Reason* (New York, 1988), 77-102; Korn, 23-25; Jon D. Levenson, "The Abusers of Abraham," *Judaism* 47, 3 (Summer 1998): 259-77. See also Lippman Bodoff, "The Real Thrust of the Akedah: Blind Obedience vs. Moral Choice," *Judaism* 42, 1 (Winter 1993): 71-92. See also "The Bible As a Source of Philosophical Reflection," in this volume.

[22]   The *selihot* prayers that refer to the *akedah* suggest Abraham and Isaac complied without conflict or ambivalence. In its own way, this could bring up questions of both a psychological and ethical nature.

[23]   R. Soloveitchik, "Majesty and Humility," *Tradition* 17, 2 (Spring 1978): 36.

[24]   Korn, 24.

[25]   The paraphrase is Shalom Carmy's: see his "Paradox, Paradigm, and the Birth of Inwardness: On R. Kook and the Akeda," in *Hazon Nahum: Studies in Jewish Law,*

Thought, and History Presented to Dr. Norman Lamm on the Occasion of His Seventieth Birthday, ed. Yaakov Elman and Jeffrey S. Gurock (New York, 1997), 473-78.

[26] *Iggerot ha-Reayah* II (Jerusalem, 1985), #379; the translation is, with slight modifications, from *Rav A. Y. Kook: Selected Letters*, trans. Tzvi Feldman (Maale Adumim, Israel, 1986), 158-60. Cf. *Olat Reiyah*, I (Jerusalem, 1985), 84-97. See also Gellman, *The Fear, The Trembling, and the Fire*, 104-16.

[27] Carmy, "Paradox," 472-73. It has often been noted that whereas God Himself commands the *akedah*, an angel calls it off. One moral to draw from this is that even though human sacrifice might express religious devotion, it should not be undertaken by Abraham without a specific command of God. This point should prevent us from extrapolating ongoing duties from special, occasion-specific divine commands in the Bible.

[28] Unfortunately, one pernicious effect of Kierkegaard's influence is that modern thinkers portray Abraham simply as a child abuser, someone who took the wrong horn of the dilemma Kierkegaard sets out between morality and religion. For examples, see the writers criticized by Levenson in "The Abusers of Abraham."

[29] See Shalom Carmy, "Pluralism and the Category of the Ethical," *Tradition* 30, 4 (Summer 1996): 145-63. See also the discourse of R. Aharon Lichtenstein, "Being *Frum* and Being Good," in *By His Light: Character and Values in the Service of God* adapted by Rabbi Reuven Ziegler (New York, 2002), 122-25.

[30] This contextual approach accords with that which emerges from Shalom Spiegel's historical study of *midrashim* concerning the *akedah*, *The Last Trial*, trans. Judah Goldin (New York, 1979).

[31] Yitzchak Blau, "Ploughshares Into Swords: Contemporary Religious Zionists and Moral Constraints," *Tradition* 34, 4 (2000): 39-60.

[32] See Avi Sagi, "The Punishment of Amalek in Jewish Tradition: Coping With the Moral Problem," *Harvard Theological Review* 87, 3 (1994): 323-46; Josef Stern, "Maimonides on Amalek, Self-Corrective Mechanisms, and the War Against Idolatry," in *Judaism and Modernity: The Religious Philosophy of David Hartman*, ed. Jonathan W. Malino (Burlington, VT, 2004), 371-410. Cf. R. Aharon Lichtenstein, "*Halakhah va-Halakhim ke-Ushiyyot Musar: Hirhurim Mahshavtiyyim ve-Hinnukhiyyim*," in *Arakhim be-Mivhan Milhamah* (Jerusalem, n.d.), 23-24 and a parallel passage in "Being *Frum* and Being Good," 126-29; R. Ahron Soloveichik, *The Warmth and the Light* (Jerusalem, 1992), 197-210.

[33] *Mishneh Torah, Hilkhot Melakhim*, 6:1, 4; see also *Guide of the Perplexed* III:50.

[34] Rav Kook, *Iggerot ha-Reayah* I (Jerusalem, 1985), #89, p. 100.

[35] See Aharon Lichtenstein, "The Human and Social Factor in Halakhah," *Tradition* 36, 1 (Spring 2002): 14-19.

[36] Leibniz, *Discourse on Metaphysics* (1686), sect. 2, trans. by Roger Ariew and Daniel Garber in *Leibniz: Philosophical Essays* (Indianapolis, 1989). I thank Atara Segal for valuable suggestions that improved my formulations in this and the next paragraph.

[37] Anyone who thinks that God's goodness is totally unrelated to human standards of goodness should ponder this challenging, if strident, statement of the 19th century British thinker John Stuart Mill:

> If, instead of the 'glad tidings' that there exists a Being in whom all the excellences which the human mind can conceive, exist in a degree inconceivable to us, I am informed that the world is ruled by a being whose attributes are infinite, but what they are we cannot learn, nor what are the principles of his government, except that the highest human morality which we are capable of does not sanction them; convince me of it, and I will bear my fate as I may. But when I am told that I must believe this, and at the same time call this being by the names which affirm and express highest human morality, I say in plain terms that I will not. Whatever power such a being may have over me, there is one thing which he shall not do: he shall not compel me to worship him. I will call no being good, who is not what I mean when I apply that epithet to my fellow-creatures; and if such a being can sentence me to hell for not so calling him, to hell I will go.

See Mill, *An Examination of Sir William Hamilton's Philosophy* (4th ed., London, 1865), 127.

38 Sa'adyah Ga'on, *Book of Doctrines and Beliefs*, partially translated by Alexander Altmann in *Three Jewish Philosophers* (New York, 1974), III:2, p. 95.

39 R. Yitzhak Hutner, *Pahad Yitzhak: Rosh Ha-Shanah* (New York, 1974), 121-23. I thank R. Dov Linzer for this reference.

40 See also the vigorous statement by Mill, "Sedgwick's Discourse," *The Collected Works of John Stuart Mill*, (Toronto, 1969), vol. 10, p. 53: "Why should I obey my maker? From gratitude? Then gratitude is itself obligatory, independently of my maker's will. From reverence and love? But why is he a proper object of love and reverence?...Is it because he is just, righteous and merciful? Then these attributes are in themselves good, independently of his pleasures." I thank R. Yitzchak Blau for this reference.

41 Cf., however, the assertion of R. Kalonymus Shapira, rav of the Warsaw ghetto, that the problem of evil disappears — or rather does not even arise — once we realize that goodness and truth are determined by what God lets happen or doesn't let happen. See his *derashah* (5701) in Mordechai Piekarz, *Hasidut Polin bein Shtei Milhamot Olam u-bi-Gezerot* 5700-5705 (Jerusalem, 5750/1990), 68-69. The notion that one should be untroubled by evil has its own costs, as will be clear from the final sections of this paper.

42 The literature is huge; I mention here only two of the best known treatments in English: Aharon Lichtenstein, "Does Jewish Tradition Recognize an Ethic Independent of Halakhah?," reprinted in *Contemporary Jewish Ethics*, ed. Menachem Kellner (New York, 1978), 102-23; Walter Wurzburger, *Ethics of Responsibility* (Philadelphia, 1994). See also, *inter alia*, Korn, 17-22, and Yitzchak Blau, "The Implications of a Jewish Virtue Ethic," *The Torah u-Madda Journal* 9 (2000): 19-41. My essay "Beyond Obedience" in this volume discusses some of these issues.

43 Routine but still cogent biblical examples are Abraham pleading that God not destroy the righteous of Sedom together with the wicked (Gen. 18: 20-33), and God responding to the moral arguments of the daughters of Tzelofhad (Num. 27:1-11), endorsing, ostensibly at least, both their position and their argument. In the book of Genesis, after the sin of Adam and Eve, individuals are largely left on their own to make moral decisions and are held accountable for the

judgments they make. For development of this last point about Genesis, see Shalom Carmy and David Shatz, "The Bible as a Source for Philosophical Reflection," in this volume, pp. 6-11. These Genesis examples, I believe, force us to seek an interpretation of the *akedah* that does not yield the conclusion that ordinary morality is not to be trusted.

44 See David Berger, "On the Morality of the Patriarchs in Jewish Polemic and Exegesis," in *Modern Scholarship in the Study of Torah: Contributions and Limitations*, ed. Shalom Carmy (Northvale, New Jersey, 1996), 131-46.

45 Shortly after the attack of 9/11, R. Yehuda Amital of Yeshivat Har Etzion asserted that Muslim *shahidim* (martyrs) are not surrendering themselves to a principle; they die to achieve the World-to-Come. "Their self-sacrifice is not for the sake of God, but rather for the sake of their own physical desires." While I continue to view suicide bombers as devoted to a deity, the element of self-interest complicates the picture.

46 Let me elaborate. It must be acknowledged that during the Crusades in Ashkenaz, many Jews took their own lives actively to prevent forced conversion. They regarded Christianity as *avodah zarah*, worship of a foreign god, and, further, took the lives of their children rather than allow them to be converted. Since the core instances of *kiddush ha-Shem* mandate only passive submission to death at the hands of others, the halakhic justification for such active taking of one's own or others' life, is not clear, and scholars are divided as to whether the acts can be accorded such justification at all. If these killings for the sake of one's principles are morally troubling, as they are to some observers, if they were performed out of religious passion and not reasoned argument, this may suggest that normative Judaism, on occasion, has crossed moral bounds because of religious enthusiasm, albeit in a way that could *post facto* be backed up by some halakhic argument.

The critics of the Jews' actions during the Crusades argue that there is a large moral distinction between passive martyrdom (allowing oneself to be killed) and active martyrdom (actively taking one's own life). While not questioning the moral propriety of passive martyrdom, they object to active martyrdom. But even so, there is no analogy between killing someone (oneself or a family member) to prevent one's own or another's forced conversion from a religion he or she accepts, and killing someone else for not being part of that religion. Those who kill themselves or others to escape conversion by the sword are hardly comparable on the moral scale to those who seek to convert them that way. Moreover, it must be recalled that the killing is done in response to a difficult, cruel choice forced upon a person by an aggressive attacker. In context, the act takes on an element of spiritual self-defense that gives it a different moral color. This is hardly comparable to instigating a scenario in which one wants to kill. I thank R. Yitzchak Blau for this last point.

R. Blau also noted (in correspondence) that parents have a right to make difficult choices for children as responses to acts of aggression by others. For example, a parent might raise a child to be a rebel in a totalitarian society even if that puts the child at risk. Likewise, a parent might teach a child to prefer death to violating some moral code. While this analogy *per se* does not justify killing a child, it does underscore the importance of context with regard to understanding acts of martyrdom.

"Martyrdom" carries in English an aspect of "testimony" ("martyr" is from the Greek for "witness") and in Hebrew of (publicly) "sanctifying" God's name by refusing to abandon His law under pressure. The martyred Jew sees his own life as less important than higher demands. Symbolic actions of this sort cannot be reduced to considerations of utility and are subject to their own moral principles. For an analysis of martyrdom in terms of symbolic action, albeit from a non-Jewish perspective, see Robert Merrihew Adams, "Symbolic Action," *Midwest Studies in Philosophy XXI: Philosophy of Religion*, ed. Peter A. French, Theodore E. Uehling, Jr. and Howard K. Wettstein (Notre Dame, IN 1997), 1-15.

On the suicides and killings of others engaged in by Jews during the Crusades, see Haym Soloveitchik, "Religious Law and Change: The Medieval Ashkenazic Example," *AJS Review* 12 (1987): 205-21. Cf. Avraham Grossman, "*Shorashav shel Kiddush ha-Shem be-Ashkenaz ha-Kedumah,*" in *Kedushat ha-Hayyim ve-Heruf ha-Nefesh: Kovetz Ma'amarim le-Zikhrono shel Amir Yekutiel*, ed. Isaiah Gafni and Aviezer Ravitsky (Jerusalem, 1993), 99-130; Israel Ta-Shema, "*Hit'abbedut ve-Retzah ha-Zulat al Kiddush ha-Shem: Li-She'alat Mekomah shel ha-Aggadah bi-Masoret ha-Pesikah ha-Ashkenazit,*" in *Yehudim mul ha-Tzelav*, ed. Yom Tov Assis et al (Jerusalem, 2000), 150-56; and David Berger, "Jacob Katz on Jews and Christians in the Middle Ages" in *The Pride of Jacob: Essays on Jacob Katz and His Work*, ed. Jay Harris (Cambridge, MA, 2002), 1-23.

I thank David Berger for comments that enhanced my discussion of martyrdom.

47 See for example the commentaries of Nahmanides and of R. Samson Raphael Hirsch to this verse.

48 The Tosafists (*Shabbat* 56b, s. v. *u-shema mina*) point out that technically the Talmud's refutation — based as it is on a text identifying four individuals who died without sin — proves only that there is death without sin, not that there is suffering without transgression. On one reading of the Tosafists, they are saying that once one half of R. Ammi's statement is rejected, so is the other half. It is as if the Tosafists see R. Ammi's view not as two isolated statements, but as a total package, one overall outlook on the bad things suffered in the world. To refute the part is to refute the whole.

But there is more to the story. The midrash (*Va-Yikra Rabbah* 37:1, *Kohelet Rabbah* 5:4) does not reject R. Ammi's assertion. Further, we could interpret the Tosafists differently, as leaving the proposition about suffering unrefuted. Nahmanides differentiates between death and suffering as regards the Babylonian Talmud's refutation. See *Torat ha-Adam, Sha'ar ha-Gemul*, in *Kitvei Ramban*, trans. Charles B. Chavel (Jerusalem, 1963), 274. (I thank R. Yitzhak Blau for noting this.) Maimonides, *Guide of the Perplexed*, III:17 and III:24, accepts R. Ammi (contrary to the *sugya*'s conclusion). Maimonides' view of providence is unusual, so his acceptance of the statement must be viewed in these terms. Note that the Talmud's disproofs of the "death" part of the statement could be read technically and narrowly as rejecting R. Ammi's view for just the four cases that are cited as refutation. (As regards Nahmanides, it is good to keep in mind that, for Nahmanides, most if not nearly all suffering is the result of God consigning all but exceptionally righteous people to the operations of natural law. See David Berger, "Miracles and the Natural Order in Nahmanides," in *Rabbi Moses Nahmanides [Ramban]: Explorations in His Religious and Literary Virtuosity*," ed. Isadore Twersky [Cambridge, MA, 1983], 107-28, esp. 113-28.)

A particularly powerful story that rests on assuming a retributivist theodicy is in *Mekhilta de-Rabbi Yishmael, Nezikin,* at *Mishpatim* 18. On a communal level, of course, the dominant explanation is, "Because of our sins we were exiled from our land."

At the end of the day, in forming a theology based on traditional texts it does not decisively matter whether certain sources accept R. Ammi. What matters is that other sources propose non-retributivist theodicies.

49   Careful reading of R. Ammi's proof texts show that they prove that evil deeds bring about suffering as a punishment — but not that all suffering is retribution for evil.

50   Aharon Lichtenstein, "The Duties of the Heart and Response to Suffering," in *Jewish Perspectives on the Experience of Suffering,* ed. Shalom Carmy (Northvale, NJ, and Jerusalem, 1999), 46.

51   See also "The Bible As a Source of Philosophical Reflection," in this volume.

52   See, e.g., Elman, "The Contribution of Rabbinic Thought to a Theology of Misfortune," in Carmy (ed.), *Jewish Perspectives on the Experience of Suffering,,* 155-212. He points out that the Jerusalem Talmud by and large does not offer these alternatives.

53   This notion may be understood in various ways, including two broad ones: (a) the righteous suffer more in this world to increase reward in the next; (b) the suffering of the righteous gives them an opportunity to display virtue, independently of any reward they will receive. Regarding (a) (a view later stressed by the Geonim), see *Kiddushin* 39b, *Berakhot* 61b. Cf. Joel B. Wolowelsky, "A Talmudic Discussion on *Yissurin Shel Ahavah,*" *Judaism* 33, 4 (Fall 1984):465-68. See also "Does Jewish Law Express Jewish Theology?," in this volume, which presents other ways of dealing with the concept.

54   In an attempt to reconcile this statement of Rava with the accepted view that "Israel is not subject to *mazzal*" (*Shabbat* 156a-b), the Tosafists and other commentators posit that a person can override the constellations by righteous deeds. However, in the text in *Mo'ed Katan,* Rava came to his view that length of life, children and sustenance depend not on merit but on *mazzal* based on the fact that of two equally meritorious individuals, R. Hisda and Rabbah, one had a life filled with good or happy things and the other one filled with hardship. If good deeds override the constellations, they should have had the same fates. Even Tosafot states only that good deeds "*sometimes* can override *mazzal.*" See also *Tosafot Ha-Rosh, Rosh Ha-Shanah* 18a, s. v. *Rabbah va-Abbayei,* where it appears that *mazzal* can override the merit of Torah study. I thank Yehuda Galinsky for this reference and R. Gedalyah Berger for further discussion of it.

55   See n. 64 below.

56   The next two paragraphs overlap with material in "Does Jewish Law Express Jewish Philosophy?," in this volume.

57   There is at least one exception, and that is the "soulmaking" theodicy. On this view, evil is present because it is logically necessary for the development of such virtues as sympathy, benevolence, courage, and faith. This theodicy makes it easy to see why we should aid the sufferer, since our free benevolent acts

toward the sufferer justify the evil he or she is undergoing. I set this theodicy aside in what follows, but see "Does Jewish Law Express Jewish Philosophy?," in this volume.

58   Published in *The Torah u-Madda Journal* 8 (1998-1999): 3-24 and then in *Out of the Whirlwind: Essays on Suffering, Mourning and the Human Condition*, ed. David Shatz, Joel B. Wolowelsky, and Reuven Ziegler (New York, 2003), 86-115. See also the opening sections of "*Kol Dodi Dofek*," delivered on Yom Ha-Atzmaut (Israel Independence Day), 1956, published in English as *Fate and Destiny*, trans. Lawrence Kaplan (Hoboken, NJ, 2000), 1-17. There are differences between "*Kol Dodi Dofek*" and "A Halakhic Approach to Suffering." See n. 61 below.

59   See also the statement by the school of R. Akiva in *Berakhot* 60b: "Whatever God does is for the good."

60   "A Halakhic Approach to Suffering," *Out of the Whirlwind*, 101.

61   The difference lies in the following statement:

> The gist of my discourse was that Judaism did not approach the problem of evil under the speculative-metaphysical aspect. For such an inquiry would be a futile undertaking. As long as the human mind is unable to embrace creation in its entirety and to gain an insight into the very essence and purposiveness of being as such it would not succeed in its attempt to resolve the dilemma of evil. The latter is interwoven into the very fabric of reality and cannot be understood outside its total ontological configuration. Job was in error because he tried to grasp the nature of evil.

In "A Halakhic Approach to Suffering," R. Soloveitchik did not say that Judaism does not quest for theodicies, but on the contrary identified a tradition of thematic Halakhah. And he did not say that the reason we must act is that we do not know the reason for evil, but rather that, if we had a reason, we would not fight evil. The approach in the letter reflects that of *Kol Dodi Dofek*, not that of "A Halakhic Approach to Suffering."

62   I thank Dr. Dan Vogel for permission to quote the letter. In *Out of the Whirwind*, xxxvi, the editors misidentify the lecture being summarized.

63   Lichtenstein, "The Duties of the Heart," 25. Several talmudic and midrashic sources suggest that there is no answer at all, thereby encouraging the idea that we can only respond to tragedy but not explain it. Samples include *Berakhot* 7a, *Yoma* 69b, *Avot* 4:19 and 5:6, *Menahot* 29b, *Va-Yikra Rabbah* 20. The idea that we must respond creatively to suffering is found as well in an insight offered by R. Samson Raphael Hirsch with regard to a verse in Psalms. "*Keli Keli lammah azavtani*" (Ps. 22:2) normally translated as "my God my God, why have you abandoned me?" R. Hirsch suggests that "*lammah*" means here not "Why?" but "For what purpose? What should I derive from this?" R Norman Lamm cited R. Hirsch's comment in an address at a gathering at Yeshiva University on the afternoon of September 11th, 2001.

64   An obvious question about this view is that it seems to run contrary to various statements by the Rabbis. *Hazal* encourage both individuals and communities to locate the sins which may have been brought on adversity. "If a person sees that tribulations have come upon him, he should search his deeds" (*Berakhot* 5a). Also see *Shabbat* 2:6, *Sotah* 1:7, *Bava Kamma* 38b, *Mekhilta de-Rabbi Yishmael*

at *Mishpatim* 18, and the festivals and High Holiday *musaf* service, "Because of our sins we were exiled from our land." Maimonides is clear that when adversity strikes the community, that is a time for *teshuvah* (repentance) (*Hilkhot Ta'aniyyot*, ch. 1). Regarding communal tragedy, *Hazal* do not present alternative explanations other than retributivist ones, but in the wake of the Holocaust, numerous writers have sought theodicies based upon the notion of *hester panim*, the hiding of God's face. See R. Norman Lamm, *The Face of God: Thoughts on the Holocaust* (New York, 1986)

However, as I remarked earlier, to say that one ought to use occasions of suffering to reflect on one's deeds and character is not yet to say that one always comes up with the correct explanation of the evil this way. It may be salutary for a person to treat evil *as if* it is due to his misdeeds. *Hazal*'s statements that individual suffering should lead to self-examination make eminent sense even if the introspection will not pinpoint the true culprit, and even if there is no culprit sin. Finding fault with myself leads me to improve myself and to strengthen my deeds of repentance, prayer, and charity. The logic of responding this way does not depend on my being able to *explain* evil in this manner. See, again, "Does Jewish Law Express Jewish Philosophy?" in this volume.

Indeed, if every person were to assume that all his or her suffering is punishment for sins, how could this be reconciled with the fact that *Hazal* propose other explanations, besides punishment, or declare that we do not know the reason for certain evils? One way to do justice both to the variety of responses *Hazal* propose *and* the frequent calls to improve one's ways in the face of suffering, is to say that the sufferer must act *as if* the suffering has come because of a flaw. In this way the sufferer develops and grows in spiritual character. R. Soloveitchik's discussion of Job in *Fate and Destiny* ("*Kol Dodi Dofek*"), 11-17, should be understood this way; otherwise "*Kol Dodi Dofek*" would be self-contradictory.

[65]   R. Soloveitchik describes other positive responses to suffering besides benevolent action. For example, he identifies a loneliness that brings one closer to God and a healthy sense of finitude as products of suffering. See the title essay in *Out of the Whirlwind*, 116-50.

[66]   *Zohar, Balak*, 212b.

[67]   R. Menahem Mendel of Rymanov saw the war between Napoleon and Russia as ushering in the end of days and prayed that Napoleon be victorious (*Ateret Menahem*, ed. Avraham Simha Bunam [Lublin, 1910], 38b). Cf., however, R. Naftali Horowitz of Ropshitz, *Ohel Naftali*, ed. Abraham Haim Simhah Bunim (Lemberg, 1912), 13b.

[68]   R. Yosef Blau, "Biblical Prophecy and Israeli Events," *The Commentator* 61, 8 (February 19, 1997): 14.

[69]   Cf. however, Nahmanides' commentary to Gen. 15:14. Nahmanides believes that a perpetrator who in fact is doing God's will can be credited with having fulfilled a *mitzvah*, a commandment, but only provided that the person is motivated by the decree of God. Lacking this motivation, the perpetrator is culpable for the outcome rather than deemed praiseworthy. Cf. R. Isaac Arama, *Akedat Yitzhak* 1:28; and Walter Wurzburger, *Yavneh Studies in Parashat Ha-Shavua: Bereshit*, ed. Joel B. Wolowelsky (New York, 1969), *Va-Yechi*, 40-42, who raise objections to Ramban's justifying of certain deeds on the grounds that the

individual is consciously fulfilling a divine plan. See also "The Bible As a Source of Philosophical Reflection," in this volume, at pp. 15-18.

70 An oft-cited example is Gustav Radbruch, who moved from positivism to a "natural law" theory as a result of the war. Ironically, the German philosopher Martin Heidegger, an ideologue of Nazism, declared: "Do not let principles and 'ideas' be the rules of your existence. The Fuehrer himself, and he alone, is the German reality of today, and of the future, and of its law." After Germany lost World War II, and the French confiscated Heidegger's property because he was a known Nazi, he wrote angrily to the French forces: "What justice there is in treating me in this unheard of way is inconceivable to me." The inconsistency is noted by Eleonore Stump, "The Mirror of Evil," in *God and the Philosophers*, ed. Thomas V. Morris (New York, 1994), 245, n. 7.

71 See the symposium "Can Postmodernists Condemn Terrorism?" in the summer 2002 issue of *The Responsive Community* (www.gwu.edu/~ccps).

72 Nahmanides, *Torat ha-Adam (Sha'ar ha-Gemul)* in *Kitvei ha-Ramban*, vol. 2, ed. Chaim B. Chavel (Jerusalem, 1964), 281.

73 See also Lichtenstein, 46.

74 See Stump, "The Mirror of Evil."

75 Postscript (2009): This essay presumes that religion can cause violence and does so in today's world. Recent (and not so recent) studies give much weight to other causes of fanaticism — social, political, psychological, economic — and sometimes view religion as a veneer that in itself plays little role in the explanation of the violence. In contrast, atheists like Richard Dawkins and Christopher Hitchens maintain that religion has bred violence throughout its history and is culpable again today, and thus attack religion on moral grounds. Their critics respond that the butcheries of Hitler, Stalin, and Mussolini prove that secular ideologies, too, breed moral horrors, and they criticize Dawkins's and Hitchens's attempts to dispel this counter-argument. I obviously lack the expertise to adjudicate the escalating debates about the causes of violence, but were I writing this essay today I would devote some space to the relevant issues. Still, I believe that religion can and sometimes does create violence, that religious people need to acknowledge this potential and reflect deeply on it, and that they should examine how a religion can limit or quash its own potential for fanaticism. (See also note 15.) For Jewish perspectives on violence, see the essays in Roberta Rosenberg Farber and Simcha Fishbane (eds.), *Jewish Studies in Violence* (Lanham, MD, 207).

DOES JEWISH LAW EXPRESS
JEWISH PHILOSOPHY?
The Curious Case of Theodicies

A natural and widely held assumption about Jewish law is that Jewish law expresses a Jewish philosophy. Many *halakhot* reflect theses in metaphysics, theology and anthropology, along with ideas about time, identity, free will and other philosophical concepts. Put another way, part of the philosophy *of* Halakhah is that there is philosophy *in* Halakhah: Jewish law is a repository of Jewish philosophical principles.

In light not only of the prevalence of the view that Halakhah reflects philosophical ideas, but of the range of nice examples that advocates of the thesis have produced, I am not disposed to question its general cogency.[1] However, there is one domain in which Aggadah and Halakhah would appear to conflict. The rest of my essay is devoted to examining that apparent exception.

A PROBLEM WITH THEODICIES

My example of a disconnect between Halakhah and philosophy involves the problem of why a perfect God would allow evil.[2] Offering theodicies is a time-honored enterprise. I certainly do not minimize the attraction of explanations offered by philosophers through the centuries. But nearly all theodicies carry a danger. Indeed, theodicy building looms as a potentially inappropriate response to tragedy.

The point is not just the routine one that logical explanations for evil often cannot be psychologically assimilated by the sufferer.[3] Rather, treating evil as if it were explicable would blunt our moral and halakhically mandated responses — or at least logically should. Imagine for a moment that you accept a particular theodicy — for instance, that all suffering is punishment for sin.[4] Suppose I meet a friend who is undergoing a terrible illness and needs my help. No one would deny that I am obligated to help.

But why should I help? After all, he (presumably) deserves this suffering. Suppose, alternatively, that you accept the thesis that God increases the suffering of the righteous in this world in order to maximize their reward in the next. Or suppose that you think suffering is a way of improving the sufferer. Or suppose you think that the suffering of the righteous atones for the community's sin. No matter what the specific explanation, endorsing that explanation means that the evil is being viewed as something positive, something that contributes a greater good to the totality. Given that fact, it is clear that any theodicy, any attempt to explain why suffering occurs, ought to diminish our perception of evil as something negative, something we must remove. If translated into action, theodicy would make nonsense out of attempts to fight evil. To be sure, on a psychological plane, people who accept theodicies actively seek to fight evil. Their human empathy is strong and naturally leads to moral action. I am speaking, though, of logical fit. Does having a theodicy cohere with moral action and with empathy?[5]

Here is the nub of the matter. The objective of a theodicy is to make our *peace* with evil. But the objective of ethical and halakhically mandated action is to make *war* with evil. If we focus too much on the ultimate reasons for God's allowing evil, we lose our appreciation of its horror. We see it as part of a beautiful, harmonious whole, as leading to a greater good. All seems right with the world. Clearly, though, as moral agents and halakhic agents, we must not let the aim of theodicy, namely, to render evil palatable, override the aim of ethical response, which treats evil as unacceptable. To put it another way, if we were to build a philosophy of evil out of halakhic requirements for responding to suffering, we would not conclude that evil is justified and rationalizable in the larger picture. In the realm of theodicy, then, we confront a seeming disconnect between Halakhah and Jewish philosophy.[6]

RECONNECTING

The key to reconnecting is finding a theodicy according to which the reason for evil is one that encourages moral action. There is one candidate: a soulmaking theodicy.

First some terminology. Free-will theodicies focus on moral evil (evil done by humans to one another) and maintain that moral evil is the result of God granting human beings a greater good, human free will. Advocates of this theodicy maintain that the value of free will exceeds the disvalue of evil. Soulmaking theodicies,[7] while complementing or filling out free-will theodicies, address not only moral evils but also natural evils such as earthquakes, floods, fires, diseases and deaths.[8] These theodicies maintain that such evils exist, or at least many of them, in order to elicit free virtuous human responses like benevolence, empathy, faith and sacrifice. Such responses could not arise in an evil-less universe, and their value exceeds the disvalue of evil.

A soulmaking theodicy would provide a solution to the problem of disconnect. We *do* know the reason for suffering: it is to elicit from us virtuous responses whose value outweighs, or potentially outweighs, the suffering. This provides a tight fit between theodicy and moral action; the theodicy makes sense precisely *because* moral action is required. To be sure, one could assign high value to virtuous responses without saying that the possibility of such responses justifies the evil. Thus we can extol heroic rescue efforts on 9/11 without saying that the rescuers' empathy, sacrifice and benevolence justify the evil. But if we are looking to repair the disconnect, a soulmaking theodicy as a *justification* of the evil seems, all else being equal, to be the right next step. In short, I am suggesting that one who believes that Halakhah reflects Jewish philosophy will have to endorse a soulmaking theodicy.[9]

Whether one embraces a soulmaking theodicy to repair the disconnect will depend, in part, on whether one believes that soulmaking theodicies are found in Jewish tradition. The closest fits I know of are certain understandings of *yissurin shel ahavah*, tribulations of love, a term introduced in *Berakhot* 5a. R. Nissim of Gerona (Ran), Maharal, and R. Ya'akov Yehoshua ben Tzvi Hirsch Falk (*Penei Yehoshua*) suggest that the sufferings of the righteous cleanse them of physicality or distance them from the physical in some way.[10] The cleansing or distancing improves the character of the sufferer, who becomes more spiritual.

These, however, are not soulmaking theodicies in the sense intended by most contemporary philosophers.[11] First, soulmaking theodicies normally justify God's *allowing* suffering, not, as in the suggested precedents, His actively *inflicting* it. Second, soulmaking theodicies are not targeted at the sufferings of the righteous in particular. Rather, the world runs mostly by natural law; neither the righteous nor the wicked are special targets of the Deity. Third, soulmaking theodicies explain that some people suffer so that *others* may grow in character. This element is not part of Ran's, Maharal's and *Penei Yehoshua's* models.[12] Because soulmaking theodicies involve a constriction of providence, they are controversial. A theologian who rejects them on this or other grounds is left with a disconnect.

It might seem as if we can remove the disconnect if we make Jewish philosophy into a phenomenological endeavor. A phenomenologically oriented philosophy attempts to describe religious consciousness rather than to create a metaphysics.[13] Hence, a phenomenological philosophy of suffering would inquire into how humans, both observers and sufferers, react to evil and also how they *should* react (emotionally and behaviorally) according to Halakhah. Theodicies, which respond to the metaphysical question of why God allows suffering, would not be part of this discussion. To some extent, of course, the derivation of the phenomenological philosophy will be trivial or tautological, since the philosophical lesson about behavior and emotion is often identical with the halakhic requirement from which it is said to be derived. But it is abundantly clear from, say, analyses of repentance and prayer found in the writings of R. Joseph Soloveitchik that we can move far beyond such obvious derivations to truly substantive claims, so occasional tautology poses no problem.[14]

It seems to me, however, that even if one conceives of philosophy as phenomenology, a phenomenological philosopher must not deny that evil is justified. And the bare fact that there is a solution logically should stifle action even if a person has no *specific* solution. So even if we conceive of philosophy as phenomenology, the disconnect will remain so long as a philosopher believes that evil has a justification — unless our philosopher adopts a soulmaking theodicy.

ANOTHER DISCONNECT?

Jewish law requires individuals and communities to examine their deeds and repent when suffering comes upon them.[15] This imperative suggests that sin is explained by wrongdoing. Yet the Sages of the Talmud realized full well that innocent people suffer, and they devised a range of explanations for this phenomenon.[16] These include, *inter alia*, the ideas of sufferings of love,[17] *nissayon* (trial), and vicarious atonement. Some rabbinic explanations of evil are not so much theodicies as expressions of despair at finding a theodicy: witness Rav's dictum that "length of life, children and sustenance depend not on merits but on *mazzala*" (astrological influence) (*Moed Katan* 28a).[18] Again, there is the view of R. Jacob that, "The reward for a *mitzvah* is not found in this world" (*Kiddushin* 39b). The Book of Job, furthermore, may be read as a protest against the retributivist theodicy.[19] And when R. Ammi asserts that, "There is no death without sin and no suffering without tribulation," the Babylonian Talmud rejects his position (*Shabbat* 55a-b).[20]

The obvious question is how to reconcile the imperative of introspection and repentance, which suggests a retributivist theodicy, with the existence of the other explanations of evil found in the Talmud and Midrash. Why, if we reject retributivist theodicy, should suffering be the occasion for introspection and repentance?

A common answer is that the imperative to repent and change one's actions as a result of suffering is nothing more than a legally required response. It may be salutary for a person to treat evil *as if* it is due to his misdeeds, without implying that one has hit upon the true explanation.[21] But this does not *answer* the question; it *is* the question. There is a disconnect here, a normative requirement that does not reflect the philosophical position that not all suffering is punishment for sin. This is, we might say, a first-person form of disconnect, a seeming inability to explain why the sufferer should react with introspection and repentance, whereas previously we examined a third-person form of disconnect, a seeming inability to explain why other parties should come to the aid of the suffering person.

We do not understand, then, how the first-person response of intro-spection and repentance is justified. One approach is to see introspection and repentance as predicated on the sheer *possibility* that the suffering in my particular case is punishment for sin. Another is to regard suffering as the occasion for introspection and repentance in the way that birthdays, anniversaries (from weddings to *yahrzeits*), and the reciting of *Yizkor* (the memorial prayer recited on holidays) are means of reflecting upon that which one should be reflecting on always: remembering loved ones, feeling gratitude to God for granting us life, and so on. Similarly, repenting during the High Holiday season involves doing that which one always ought to be doing. The press of life makes it impossible to experience these feelings or do these deeds every single day, let alone every moment, so we create certain dates on the calendar as triggers that create an association and special intensity in our minds. The association is, in some cases and to some extent, artificial. In like manner, it might be said, we use suffering as an occasion to introspect and repent, without endorsing a metaphysical thesis. Here, too, the association is artificial, goes this explanation, but we need occasions like these.

Without dismissing these accounts of the first-person disconnect, I will suggest what strike me as stronger reasons for a believer to introspect and repent in the face of suffering.

1) In some cases, the link between suffering and inner change is quite logical. For example, R. Joseph Soloveitchik says that his bout with cancer in 1959-60 brought him down from "fantastic flights of human foolishness and egocentrism" by freeing him from a "distorted conception" of himself as immortal. Imagining oneself as immortal makes one think that "his desires, dreams, ambitions and visions assume absolute significance." R. Soloveitchik even says that shifting "from the illusion of eternity to the reality of temporality" and accepting defeat makes suffering bearable.[22] Here, the suffering *naturally* produces certain thoughts in the believer that lead to a salutary shift in perception and behavior. In addition, the loneliness brought on by suffering can bring one closer to God.[23]

Another example: empathy. A 1991 film, *The Doctor*, portrayed a rude physician who became a cancer patient himself. The distasteful behavior of the staff and physicians he dealt with made him realize how hurtful and dispiriting his own rudeness was to his patients. Personal suffering often makes a person sensitive to others' pain and needs. Using one's suffering creatively can mean developing empathy for others. For R. Soloveitchik, this is a lesson of the Book of Job, for Job emerges from his ordeal more caring toward those outside his own family circle.[24] Indeed, R. Soloveitchik goes further:

> Whoever permits his legitimate needs to go unsatisfied will never be sympathetic to the crying needs of others. A human morality based on love and friendship, on sharing in the travail of others, cannot be practiced if the person's own need awareness is dull, and he does not know what suffering is.[25]

Elsewhere, he speaks about how mourning sensitizes a person to man and God.[26] The accounts of *yissurin shel ahavah* proferred by Ran, Crescas, Maharal and *Penei Yehoshua* lend themselves to positing a logical or empirical relationship between suffering and repentance/self-improvement.[27]

2) As is well known, R. Soloveitchik argues in *Kol Dodi Dofek*, his address on Israeli Independence Day in 1956, that searching for a cause of sin is living the existence of *goral* (fate), whereas actively responding to the suffering is living the existence of *yi'ud* (destiny).[28] In an existence of *goral*, one views oneself as an object rather than a subject, as the victim of outside forces beyond one's control. In an existence of *yi'ud*, one takes control as a subject. Introspection and repentance are for him a way of escaping subjugation to fate. As Moshe Sokol puts it, active responses to suffering spare us from being "ensnared by a discourse which is antithetical to our essential humanity."[29]

3) R. Soloveitchik wrote: "Suffering, in the opinion of Judaism, must not be purposeless, wasted."[30] In other words, we must observe *bal tashhit* (the prohibition of uselessly wasting things) on the experiential level. Even if God does not inflict suffering for the purpose of punishment, all experiences, R. Soloveitchik submits, are there for us to create purpose, significance and meaning. The essay "Out of the Whirlwind" puts matters more strongly. God addresses the sufferer through his suffering and discloses Himself to a person who finds himself confronting nothingness.[31]

This third account in terms of finding meaning and purpose has limitations, for it stops short of saying why the meaning we create must take a particular form (introspection and repentance).[32] Despite this lacuna, the explanation is compelling, I think, because it is difficult to conceive of what *other* form a proper response — a proper attempt to use the suffering purposefully — would take.[33]

Once we move beyond viewing introspection and repentance purely as norms, we are in a position to offer a theodicy of suffering from a first-person perspective. The reason that God allows (or in some cases inflicts) suffering is to let individuals grow. In short, the believer who embraces a soulmaking theodicy repairs the disconnect.

Let us recapitulate our discussion of the first-person disconnect. Self-examination is mandated specifically during a time of suffering even if the introspection will not pinpoint the true culprit, and even if there is no culprit sin at all. My suffering can lead me to improve myself, to grow and develop in spiritual character, to strengthen my prayer and my charity, to remove my arrogance and sense of being almighty, to empathize, to create meaning in my existence, to move me from a life of fate to a life of destiny. The logic of responding as Halakhah requires does not depend on my being able to explain a *particular* evil as a result of my deficiency. Rather, Halakhah's mandate could be explained by the purpose of God weaving evil into existence — namely, again, soulmaking. The ostensible disconnect between repudiating retributivist theodicies on one hand and responding to evil with self-examination and repentance on the other, thus can be repaired by reference to the soulmaking theodicy.

All that said, it should be acknowledged that sometimes seeing *someone else's* suffering as punishment for his sin will stimulate my own self-examination and repentance. If the orchestrator of a scam that ruins untold numbers of lives meets with a harsh fate, and I see that outcome as the divinely inflicted consequence of sin, I might be inspired to look into and repair my own greed. Thus, sometimes imputing sins to others serves a positive purpose.[34] But such responses to others' suffering comes at a cost. I may make unfair judgments, and those may lead me to presumptuous, distasteful readings of God's mind more than introspection will. Hence, perhaps retributivist understandings of the suffering of others should be shunned despite their occasional utility. In many of these cases, furthermore, I learn a lesson about the consequences of certain behaviors even if I do not regard those consequences as divinely inflicted punishments, but rather as the result of natural processes that operate pursuant to poor judgment and lack of self-control (as in the case of an alcoholic stricken with liver disease).[35]

CONCLUSION

Prima facie, the problem of evil yields a striking counterexample to the claim that Jewish philosophy must grow out of the Halakhah. For an examination of the problem suggests, in effect, that law is not always predicated upon theology. On the contrary — in the case of suffering, the theology renders the law mysterious, and the law may render the theology irrelevant. Even if we refrain from affirming any particular theodicy, and a fortiori if we do proffer a theodicy, it is difficult to see why moral action is required given that *some* theodicy or other is true (even if unknown). The law and the theodicy do not cohere. I called this the third-person form of disconnect. We encountered another disconnect — the first person version — when we considered that self-examination and repentance are the mandated responses to suffering even though the Sages offered theodicies that are not retributivist.

I have suggested that a soulmaking theodicy can repair both disconnects. Someone who rejects the soulmaking theodicy will, I think, have to accept a disconnect between Halakhah and Jewish philosophy.

Is that a bad move? Is it important to preserve a connection in every case? On the one hand, it would seem that, other things being equal, a Judaism whose behavioral code and theology are integrated and har-monized is better than a Judaism with dissonance. Furthermore, the philosophical virtues of soulmaking theodicies are, in my opinion, consi-derable.[36] On the other hand, it seems odd for a Jewish thinker to be forced into a theodicy just by a wish for a complete congruence between law and philosophy, especially when that theodicy is not conspicuous in classic sources.[37] I leave the dilemma unresolved. I believe, however, that I have identified a neglected way to think about both theodicy and the connection between Halakhah and philosophy.

NOTES

R. Yitzchak Blau, Yoel Finkelman, and Aaron Segal provided valuable comments on an earlier version of this essay.

[1]   This thesis in reflected in myriad analyses of particular *halakhot*. As for explicit statements of a connection between Halakhah and Jewish philosophy, Louis Ginzberg goes so far as to say that Halakhah and not Aggadah is the main source for Jewish philosophy. Aggadah, he says, consists of "opinions or views uttered by Jewish sages on the spur of the moment," and so writers who reconstruct post-biblical ethics exclusively on Aggadah "have erected their structures upon shifting sand." Ginzberg adds that there is "a vast array of intellectual products that are temporary, accidental and individual, in which the national soul has but a small share ... It is only in the Halakhah that we find the mind and character of the Jewish people exactly and adequately expressed." See Louis Ginzberg, "Jewish Thought As Reflected in the Halakhah," in his *Students, Scholars and Saints* (New York, 1928), 115-17. Other statements of the Halakhah-theology nexus include R. Joseph B. Soloveitchik, *The Halakhic Mind* (New York: MacMillan, 1986), 101-102 and his *"Avelut Yeshanah* and

Avelut Hadashah: Historical and Individual Mourning," in *Out of the Whirlwind: Essays on Suffering, Mourning and the Human Condition*, ed. David Shatz, Joel B. Wolowelsky, and Reuven Ziegler (New York, 2002), 9-10. He explains that, "There can be no philosophy of science or nature unless one is an expert in the fields of physics, chemistry and biology, the sciences of animate and inanimate objects. So, too, it is impossible for one to philosophize about Judaism and speak about its experiential universe without having the Halakhah at his fingertips." In these passages, R. Soloveitchik seems even to scant Aggadah, though in his writings he draws on Aggadah frequently and to great effect. (For more on R. Soloveitchik, see R. Meir Twersky, "Towards a Philosophy of Halakhah," *Jewish Action* 64, 1 [Fall 2003]: 49-62; R. Shubert Spero, "Rabbi Joseph Dov Soloveitchik and the Philosophy of Halakha," *Tradition* 30, 2 [Winter 1996]: 41-64.) See also R. Nahum (Norman) Lamm, *Halakhot va-Halikhot* (Jerusalem: Mossad HaRav Kook, 1990), 12. "There is no entry into the world of *halikhot* [by which he means Jewish thought] save through the Judaism of Halakhah." The theme is elaborated for five pages more. R. Lamm's book is notable for the intricacy of its halakhic discussion — it is a work of what is generally called *lomdus* (conceptual legal analysis) — and for the range of philosophical ideas it identifies in positions that typically are analyzed in technical, legalistic terms. Approximately half of the book's twenty-seven essays illustrate this motif. Thus, R. Lamm argues that the question of what *kavvanah* (intention) is needed for the prayer "*Barukh shem kevod malkhuto le-olam va-ed*" implicates a debate about acosmism, and he solves a difficulty in Maimonides' writing concerning the topic in Jewish commercial law known as *bereirah* by reference to Rambam's views on free will and divine foreknowledge. In his English writings on halakhic topics, R. Lamm relates *halakhot* about self-incrimination to theories of death wish, laws about privacy to a theory of personality, and questions about ecology to Hasidic and Mitnagdic appraisals of nature.

R. Soloveitchik offers many excursions into anthropological and theological underpinnings of Halakhah. See, for example, the examinations of laws of repentance in Pinchas H. Peli, *Soloveitchik on Repentance* (New York, 1984); the analyses of laws of prayer in *Worship of the Heart*, ed. Shalom Carmy (New York, 2003); and the explanations of laws of marriage, parenthood, and filial piety in *Family Redeemed*, ed. David Shatz and Joel B. Wolowelsky (New York, 2000). R. Soloveitchik's philosophy is phenomenological, focusing on the human experience expressed in or created by halakhic observance.

Perhaps the most significant dissenter from the claim that Jewish law expresses Jewish philosophy is the late Israeli philosopher, Yeshayahu Leibowitz, who denies that Judaism puts forward a metaphysics at all and asserts that the religion consists purely of obeying Halakhah. See, for example, *Judaism, Human Values and the Jewish State*, ed. Eliezer Goldman, trans. Eliezer Goldman, Yoram Navon et al. (Cambridge, MA, 1992), chs. 1-6.

For a brief but very valuable exploration of the differences between Aggadah and Halakhah, one that analyzes talmudic discussions of the distinction and articulates the importance of Aggadah, see Yitzchak Blau, *Fresh Fruit & Vintage Wine: The Ethics and Wisdom of the Aggada* (Jersey City, NJ, 2009), xv-xxii, 1-4. Relevant rabbinic sources cited by Blau include *Bava Kamma* 60b, *Sotah* 40a, and *Sifrei Devarim* 49.

For analyses of various halakhic concepts on the part of analytic philo-sophers, see Eli Hirsch, "Identity in the Talmud," *Midwest Studies in Philosophy* 23 (1999): 166-80 and his "Rashi's View of the Open Future: Indeterminateness and Bivalence," *Oxford Studies in Metaphysics* 2 (2006): 111-35; Jed Lewinsohn, "Philosophy *In* Halakhah: The Case of Intentional Action," *The Torah u-Madda Journal* 14 (2007-2008): 97-136, which draws the distinction I mention between philosophy of Halakhah and philosophy in Halakhah; Mark Steiner, "Rabbi Israel Salanter As a Jewish Philosopher," *The Torah u-Madda Journal* 9 (2000): 42-57, esp. 43-45.

2   This section overlaps with material in "'From the Depths I Have Called To You'," in this volume.

3   I do not restrict the category "evil" to cases in which an agent is suffering. Various sorts of conditions that do not involve suffering qualify as well — a comatose state, or sudden death, or just simply being dead. But my discussion will proceed most smoothly by focusing on suffering.

4   This and the theodicies that follow are drawn from talmudic and midrashic sources. For some sources, see the first paragraph and accompanying notes of the section titled "Another Disconnect?," below.

5   The lack of coherence is especially striking, of course, if one adopts a retributivist theodicy.

6   One of R. Joseph Soloveitchik's essays on theodicy, "A Halakhic Approach to Suffering," in *Out of the Whirlwind*, 86-115, gives sharp expression to this disconnect. See the end of "'From the Depths I Have Called to You'," in this volume. The problem, of course, is not, deep down, specifically Jewish. Even within a Christian framework, why should I act to fight evil if I have a theodicy? Christians, however, have been more receptive to soulmaking theodicies.

7   The best known modern explication of a soulmaking theodicy is John Hick's *Evil and the God of Love* (New York, 1978).

8   Human indolence, lack of self-control, and poor judgment often contribute to creating those evils. A flood can be prevented by building proper dams, a fire by installing detection devices, disease and premature death by watching what one ingests. Poverty, which can be a natural evil (e.g. one's house is destroyed in an earthquake), sometimes is brought on by bad choices. If one wants to limit natural evils to cases in which people's action or inaction are not contributing factors, it will not affect my discussion.

9   Ironically, one complaint that critics voice *against* the soulmaking theodicy is that it cannot make sense of moral action. The critics' reasoning is that by removing evil, we are reducing opportunities for free virtuous responses and thereby reducing the total good in the universe. So, by the theist's logic, it is said, we ought not try to eliminate evil, for if we do we will make the universe worse. What this objection overlooks is that the response of those who seek to alleviate the evil is itself a free virtuous response that can serve to justify the evil. Interesting philosophical objections to the soulmaking theodicy remain, but I believe that they can be met. See Clement Dore, "An Examination of the Soulmaking Theodicy," *American Philosophical Quarterly* 7 (1970): 119-30.

10   See R. Nissim of Gerona, *Derashot ha-Ran,* ed. Leon Feldman (Jerusalem, 1977),
     Derashah #10, 174-75; Maharal, *Netivot Olam, Netiv ha-Yissurin,* chap. 1. See also
     Hasdai Crescas, *Or Hashem, Ma'amar* 2, *Kelal* 2, *Perek* 4. (My thanks to R. Yitzchak
     Blau for suggesting these potential precedents.) *Penei Yehoshua*'s comments are
     in his explanation of the passage about *yissurin shel ahavah* in *Berakhot* 5a.

11   The essay "The Bible As a Source of Philosophical Reflection," in this volume,
     suggests ascribing a soulmaking theodicy to the book of Job.

12   There is a superficial resemblance between the problem of the disconnect and
     questions posed by Turnus Rufus to R. Akiva in *Bava Batra* 10a, and likewise
     a superficial resemblance between statements by R. Akiva in that *sugya* and
     soulmaking theodicies. There, Turnus Rufus asks R. Akiva, "If your God loves
     the poor, why doesn't He sustain them?" In replying, R. Akiva suggests, in the
     first stage of discussion, that giving charity saves one from Gehinnom (hell), and
     in the last part of the discussion he asserts that God will be pleased if we aid
     someone whom He has punished. While one can pry out certain pieces of this
     whole discussion and relate them to soulmaking theodicies, the fit is not tight
     enough to warrant calling that discussion a precedent. I thank Shalom Carmy
     for stressing this point.

13   Aaron Segal made this suggestion (in correspondence) in the context of R. Solo-
     veitchik's views, since R. Soloveitchik had a phenomenological orientation.

14   See the references in note 1 to R. Soloveitchik's works. Spero, "Rabbi Joseph
     Dov Soloveitchik and the Philosophy of Halakhah," 49, takes a different
     approach to the issue considered in this paragraph. He argues that, in contrast
     to theodicies, normative statements — in this case, about how to react to
     suffering — are not part of a worldview. On this ground, he rejects Marvin Fox's
     claim that in *Kol Dodi Dofek* we have "one of the most clear and explicit cases in
     which important religious doctrine emerges from a proper understanding of
     the Halakha" and in which "Halakhic norms generate theological principles."
     (See Fox, "The Unity and Structure of Rabbi Joseph B. Soloveitchik's Thought,"
     Tradition 24, 2 [1989]: 52 and 49 respectively.)

15   "If a person sees that tribulations have come upon him, he should search his
     deeds" (*Berakhot* 5a). Maimonides is clear that when adversity strikes the
     community, that is a time for *teshuvah* (repentance) (*Hilkhot Ta'aniyyot,* ch. 1).
     Regarding communal tragedy, the Rabbis may not present explanations other
     than retributivist ones — if the community suffers, the community deserves it. I
     am understanding *hester panim,* the withdrawal of providence, as a providential
     punishment. Another mandated response is prayer, but I leave it out of the
     discussion because it does not pose the same disconnect as the imperative to
     examine one's deeds and repent.

16   See Yaakov Elman, "The Contribution of Rabbinic Thought to a Theology
     of Misfortune," in *Jewish Perspectives on the Experience of Suffering,* 155-212. He
     points out that the Jerusalem Talmud by and large does not offer the alternatives
     that the Talmud Bavli does.

17   This notion may be understood in various ways, two of which are: (a) The
     righteous suffer more in this world to increase reward in the next. This

interpretation was embraced by the Geonim and is rooted in *Kiddushin* 39b and *Berakhot* 61b; (b) The suffering of the righteous cleanses them of or distances them from physicality, as in the interpretations of *yissurin shel ahavah* found in Ran, Maharal and *Penei Yehoshua*. This soulmaking theodicy could be understood as consistent with, or as an example of, a more general idea that the suffering of the righteous gives them an opportunity to display virtue, independently of any reward that they will receive. This is, again, a version of the soulmaking theodicy. For an interesting discussion, see Joel B. Wolowelsky, "A Talmudic Discussion on *Yissurin Shel Ahavah*," *Judaism* 33, 4 (Fall 1984): 465-68.

18   In an attempt to reconcile this statement of Rava with the accepted view that,"Israel is not subject to *mazzal*" (*Shabbat* 156a-b), Tosafot and other commentators explain that a person can override the constellations by righteous deeds. However, in the text in *Mo'ed Katan*, Rava came to his view that length of life, children and sustenance depend not on merit but on *mazzal* based on the fact that of two equally meritorious individuals, R. Hisda and Rabbah, one had a life filled with good or happy things and the other had one filled with hardship. If good deeds override the constellations, they should have had the same fates. Even Tosafot states only that good deeds "*sometimes* can override *mazzal*." See also *Tosafot Ha-Rosh, Rosh ha-Shanah* 18a, s.v. *Rabbah va-Abbayei*, where it appears that *mazzal* can override the merit of Torah study. I thank Yehuda Galinsky for this reference and R. Gedalyah Berger for further discussion of it.

19   This reading is based primarily on God's anger at Job's friends for not speaking properly (42:7). See "The Bible As a Source for Philosophical Reflection," in this volume. It is not necessarily the case that claiming that we do not know the reason for suffering is a rejection of retributivist theodicy. It is logically possible to say that all evils are punishments, but it eludes us why seeming innocents suffer. After all, the problem of evil is often equated with *tzaddik ve-ra lo, rasha ve-tov lo,* why the righteous suffer and the wicked prosper. Or, the retributivist view may be true, and saying "We don't know why" indicates that we don't know that for sure.

20   We must be cautious in citing this rejection, however. Although the specific counterexamples given by the Talmud are cases of death without sin rather than suffering without transgression, the *sugya* ostensibly concludes that there is death without sin *and* there is suffering without transgression. The *sugya* seems to see R. Ammi's view as a package, and to take rejection of one part of R. Ammi's statement as implying rejection of the other. On one interpretation, Tosafot adopts this reading. See *Shabbat* 55b, s.v. *u-shema mina*. On another interpretation, however, Tosafot leaves the proposition about suffering unrefuted. Nahmanides differentiates between death and suffering. See *Torat ha-Adam, Sha'ar ha-Gemul,* in *Kitvei Ramban*, trans. Charles B. Chavel (Jerusalem, 1963), 274. (I thank R. Yitzhak Blau for noting this.) It is good to keep in mind, though, that on Nahmanides' view, most if not nearly all suffering is the result of God consigning all but exceptionally righteous people to the operations of natural law. See David Berger, "Miracles and the Natural Order in Nahmanides," in *Rabbi Moses Nahmanides (Ramban): Explorations in His Religious and Literary Virtuosity*," ed. Isadore Twersky (Cambridge, MA, 1983), 107-28, esp. 113-28.

In the Midrash, R. Ammi's view appears without the refutation. See *Va-yikra Rabbah* 37:1, *Kohelet Rabbah* 5:4. Maimonides, *Guide of the Perplexed*, III:17 and III:24, accepts R. Ammi (contrary to the Babylonian Talmud's conclusion). Maimonides' view of providence is unusual, so his acceptance of the statement must be viewed in these terms. Note that the Talmud's disproofs of the "death" part of the statement could be read technically and narrowly as rejecting R. Ammi's view for just the four cases that are cited as refutation. In any event, R. Ammi's argument seems to be based on a fallacious reading of the verses he cites. The verses state that all sin is punished, not that all death and suffering is punishment for sin. A particularly powerful story that rests on assuming a retributivist theodicy is in *Mekhilta de-Rabbi Yishmael, Nezikin*, at *Mishpatim* 18. With regard to communal tragedy, of course, the dominant explanation is, "Because of our sins we were exiled from our land."

At the end of the day, it does not matter whether certain sources accept R. Ammi. What matters is that other sources propose non-retributivist theodicies.

21 As Aaron Segal noted, however, Maimonides' view in *Hilkhot Ta'aniyyot* 1 is that calling out to God and sounding trumpets leads people to appreciate the retributivist theodicy. See also *Guide* III:36. Thus, for Maimonides, Segal writes, "The normative response is in the service of the apprehension of the theodicy, as opposed to the suggestion, which is perhaps a simpler one, that the normative response comes on the heels of a prior appreciation of the theodicy." In other words, even if one accepts a retributivist theodicy, the relationship between appreciation of the theodicy and the normative response may be presented in different ways.

22 "Out of the Whirlwind," in *Out of the Whirlwind*, 131-32.

23 See the full essay "Out of the Whirlwind."

24 See, for example, the lecture *Kol Dodi Dofek*, translated by Lawrence Kaplan as *Fate and Destiny* (Hoboken, NJ, 1992), 11; and "The Crisis of Human Finitude," in *Out of the Whirlwind*, 152-54 and 176-77, where R. Soloveitchik characterizes Job as originally a "religious philistine." To this list we can add a soulmaking idea explained earlier, that suffering distances one from physicality. R. Soloveitchik would probably reject Maharal's and Ran's views because he stresses that Judaism affirms the "dignity of the body." See, for example, *Family Redeemed*, 73-78.

25 "Redemption, Prayer, and Talmud Torah," *Tradition* 17, 2 (Spring 1978): 65.

26 See "*Aninut* and *Avelut*," in *Out of the Whirlwind*, 5.

27 See especially *Derashot ha-Ran*, 175.

28 See *Fate and Destiny*, 1-17. I am speaking here of the distinction between an *existence* of fate and an *existence* of destiny, as distinct from R. Soloveitchik's better known distinction between a *covenant* of fate and a *covenant* of destiny. One who participates in a *covenant* of fate is required to *act* (and sympathize).

29 Moshe Sokol, "Is There a 'Halakhic' Response to the Problem of Evil?," in *Jewish Studies in Violence*, ed. Roberta Rosenberg Farber and Simcha Fishbane (Lanham, MD, 2007), 230. Besides making the point I made in the previous note, Sokol

also raises the interesting question of why intellectual speculation — reasoning about why God allows evil — could not be the proper response. Trying to make sense of it all is surely an activity that is distinctively human. Perhaps the futility of speculation rules it out as a response.

30   The quotation is from a letter to Dr. Dan Vogel that is quoted in the editors' introduction to *Out of the Whirlwind*, xxxvi.

31   See *Out of the Whirlwind*, 128, 136, 138. This essay, we should note, contains passages that suggest that tribulations *are* punishments

32   We can appreciate this point if we contrast R. Soloveitchik's account of evil with his account of *ta'amei ha-mitzvot* (reasons for the commandments). In the latter account, too, he says that while we cannot fathom God's intentions in giving a *mitzvah*, we can seek meaning in it. In that instance R. Soloveitchik does not insist that the meaning and significance must take a particular form. See "May We Interpret Hukim," in *Man of Faith in the Modern World: Reflections of the Rav, Volume Two*, adapted by Abraham R. Besdin (Hoboken, NJ, 1989), 91-99.

33   Aaron Segal pointed out, however, that if the sufferer is obliged to attribute his or her suffering to a *specific* sin, it would not be clear why the response must take the particular form it does if one rejects the retributivist theodicy.

34   See also Shalom Carmy, "Cops and Robbers," *Tradition* 40, 4 (Winter 2007): 4-6.

35   See Ibid.

36   Once again, I recommend reading Dore, "An Examination."

37   Recall the difference between soulmaking theodies in Ran and Maharal and those in contemporary philosophy.

BEYOND OBEDIENCE:
The Ethical Theory of
Rabbi Walter Wurzburger

Rabbi Dr. Walter Wurzburger (1920-2002) was a vital force in Modern Orthodox thought. As editor of the journal *Tradition*, published by the Rabbinical Council of America, for a quarter of a century, he helped shape the agenda of the Modern Orthodox community and significantly elevated its ideological discourse. On the one hand a close student of R. Joseph B. Soloveitchik, from whom he received his rabbinic ordination, and on the other a Harvard-trained professor of philosophy, he was outstandingly equipped to fuse classic Jewish texts and teachings with the tools, resources and concerns of cutting-edge contemporary philosophy. The result was a body of thought distinguished by its creativity, breadth of learning, interpretive ingenuity and analytical insight.

Wurzburger's most vigorous contributions to a single area were his extensive investigations into the philosophical underpinnings of Jewish ethics. Though occupied with theory, his lucid, incisive, and wide-ranging accounts of this topic carry profound implications for practice. How a Jewish religious community responds to ethical dilemmas and to moral doctrines in the surrounding culture is deeply affected by its understanding of halakhic decision making and of the relationship between Halakhah and general morality. The culmination of these studies was an important book, *Ethics of Responsibility: Pluralistic Approaches To Covenantal Ethics*, to which I devote this essay.[1]

I

The central thesis of the book (and much of its author's writing) is perhaps best expressed in a comment that he attributes to R. Soloveitchik: "Halakhah is not a ceiling, but a floor" (32). As Wurzburger glosses this comment, it means that a halakhic orientation does not amount to legal formalism; the Jewish code of behavior does not reduce to a set of fully articulated rules.

> Jewish piety involves more than meticulous adherence to the various rules and norms of religious law; it also demands the cultivation of an ethical personality...We are commanded to engage in a never-ending quest for moral perfection, which transcends the requirements of an "ethics of obedience"...[The] halakhic system serves merely as the foundation of Jewish piety (3).

Wurzburger argues that, "because mere obedience to a set of formal rules as specified by the Torah is only a necessary but not a sufficient condition of ethical propriety, another source of moral authority must be found" (28). As to what this authority might be, a hint appears in the commentary of Nahmanides. The latter points out that the commandments of "You shall be holy" (Lev. 19:2) and "Do the straight and the good" (Deut. 6:18) beckon us to behave in consonance with ethical ideals even in situations for which the Torah offers no explicit and precise edicts. By taking this stance, Nahmanides "validated the intuitions of a moral conscience formed within the matrix of Torah teachings."[2]

It follows that in Covenantal Ethics — as Wurzburger labels his own account — "intuitive ethical judgments play a major role" (4). Specifically, cases inevitably arise that are not (yet) covered by a formal, explicit rule; these must be adjudicated by reference to "intuited, subjective religious responses to a particular concrete situation" (32). In addition, ethical intuitions must be utilized to propel the Jew beyond what the formal rules require and to act in accord with the demands of *lifnim mi-shurat ha-din* (beyond the strict requirement of the law), *middat hasidut* (the practice of the pious), and cognate supererogatory ideals.[3] Intuitions are the locus of freedom, and individuals bear personal responsibility for decisions based upon them. It is this fusion of objective divine commands with subjective intuitions, obedience with personal judgment, heteronomy with freedom, that creates the distinctive character of Jewish ethics.

Wurzburger is not the only thinker to have advocated such ideas. Thus, the notion that every case a halakhic decisor confronts is resolvable by reference to preexisting rules — i.e., "that everything can be looked up, every moral dilemma resolved by reference to code or canon" — has been declared by R. Aharon Lichtenstein "both palpably naive and patently false."[4] Since the rules inevitably "run out" and some cases do not fit any precedent exactly, it will clearly be up to the individual to determine whether a particular case can be decided by a straight application of precedent, and if not, then to deliver a decision on some auxiliary basis.[5] Furthermore, it is asserted quite often that moral dilemmas not covered by an explicit rule may be adjudicated, in particular, by "moral conscience."[6] Yet, though his position is not completely novel, Wurzburger's articulation of it stands out as virtually unique. For despite his seemingly clear endorsement of ethical intuitions, Wurzburger's approach is less trusting of intuition, ergo more qualified and nuanced, than other views that assign a significant role to ethical judgments in halakhic decision making.

Several classical authors — among them R. Sa'adyah Ga'on, R. Nissim Ga'on, Nahmanides, R. Yosef Albo, and the nineteenth century figure R. Naftali Tzvi Yehudah Berlin (Netziv) — believe in an ethical standard that (1) is valid independently of Halakhah and also (2) can be known independently of Halakhah, a kind of "natural law" or rational ethic (see 17-18, 26-27). The specific "moral" laws of Halakhah, such as the prohibitions against murder and theft, give expression to this ethical standard, according to these authorities. Wurzburger embraces their position while openly resisting the contrary thesis implied by R. Ovadyah mi-Bartenura and R. Abraham Yeshahayu Karelitz (Hazon Ish) (115, note 4).[7] Indeed, Wurzburger echoes the celebrated contention associated with Plato: an action is not right because God commands it, but rather God commands it because it is right (17).[8] And yet, a genuinely distinctive feature of Wurzburger's analysis is its frank and acute awareness of the challenges that today's philosophical climate poses to ethical objectivity. Contemporary philosophers often argue that ethical values cannot be established objectively and/or that values are relative to cultures and historical periods. While such views boast an ancient pedigree, they are now philosophical orthodoxy. Alert to contemporary forms of moral skepticism, subjectivism, relativism and historicism, Wurzburger views ethical intuitions with a questioning eye.[9]

Even though intuitions are divinely implanted, they are, he concedes, "notorious for their dependence upon individual idiosyncrasies, which are due to a host of genetic and environmental factors" (34). The Spartans condoned exposing unfit babies to death by starvation; the United States allowed slavery until about a century and a half ago; and (I would add) it was only in the twentieth century that women gained the right to vote! Intuitions that Westerners maintain about democracy and equality today are not universally held truths hallowed by time but products of a specific culture. It is because intuitions reflect "social, cultural, historical and psychological factors" (23) that contemporary philosophers frequently deny to ethics any objective foundation in reason or nature.

Wurzburger partially joins in this attack on ethical objectivity, though he also partially resists it. He gestures toward disavowal by saying that subjectivism and cultural relativism fail "to do justice to the moral experience, since moral perceptions are seen as universally applicable, without regard to the cultural or social background of the agent whose conduct is being evaluated" (23; see also 7-8). But this, I think, amounts to only small resistance. The fact that someone who issues an ethical judgment perceives it as being objective and as having universal relevance and applicability does not allay the subjectivist's worry that every value judgment is actually not objective, cannot be known to be true and need not apply universally. Elsewhere (e.g., 32, 33, 39) Wurzburger openly uses the word "subjective" to describe the epistemological credentials of intuitions.[10]

Wurzburger's trust in ethical intuition is tempered in yet another way. Notwithstanding his rejection of formalism and his emphasis on natural law, conscience and intuitive ethical judgments, he naturally takes pains to preserve Halakhah's special authority and status. Over against non-Orthodox views, which would sanction deviations from stated halakhic norms when those norms run contrary to the human conscience (6),[11] Wurzburger's language is emphatic: "It would be the height of arrogance to challenge the validity of an explicit divine imperative on the ground that it runs counter to our own ethical intuitions. Indeed, to permit humanistic considerations to override divinely revealed commandments amounts to a desecration of the Divine Name. In the event of conflict with explicit halakhic requirements, all ethical, aesthetic, intellectual or prudential considerations must be set aside" (29; see also 5-6, 87).

Wurzburger does not furnish examples of such conflicts, but among instances that come to mind are the command to destroy the nation of Amalek and laws that restrict whom a *mamzer* may marry. In general, "an ethics formed within the matrix of a halakhic system will differ from the kinds of ethical judgments that reflect the societal norms of a secular culture" (7; also 23, 37).

In the light of certain theological premises that Wurzburger endorses, it makes sense that human intuitions cannot override divine norms. Like R. Samson Raphael Hirsch, Wurzburger regards the promptings of conscience as a form of revelation: "Our ethical intuitions reveal to us divine imperatives stemming from our Covenantal relationship with God" (4). I am not sure how best to square this idea that intuitions are implanted by God with either the doctrine of natural law (that ethics is accessed through reason) or the idea that norms result from social conditioning. Be that as it may, if intuitions gain their credibility only from being divinely implanted, and yet, as is clearly the case, these divinely implanted intuitions are also prone to distortion by human beings, then an express divine command should surely override them. God and Sinai thus would never forfeit their centrality.

Wurzburger's position, as I understand it, is thus unusually complex and nuanced. He combines (1) the allegiance to intuition exemplified by adherents of the view that halakhic commitment must be infused by

308

an independent ethic with (2) the awareness of skeptical challenges that galvanizes many of that view's critics. The latter celebrate human fallibility and question the very possibility of an objective ethic without divine commands.[12] This is bound to be a difficult balancing act. We must turn now to the question of whether the required equilibrium is attainable.

II

It is in truth hard to agree that "The fact that explicit, unambiguous halakhic rules take precedence over the dictates of the human conscience by no means diminishes the role of ethical intuitions in Jewish Covenantal Ethics" (31). On the contrary, Wurzburger's strenuous attempt to limit the nature and role of intuition in halakhic decision making arguably tends to undermine the reliability of intuition and thereby to discredit appeals to natural law, general ethics and conscience altogether.

The existence of conflicts between halakhic rules and ethical intuitions cannot but reduce the halakhically committed Jew's confidence in his or her ability to make sound ethical judgments without explicit divine guidance. For example, the ethical intuitions that often create feelings of discomfort over the command about Amalek or the laws of *mamzerut* are more vivid and firm to people than any that might be invoked in the kind of cases in which Wurzburger wants intuition to play a role. The obvious question is: how can anyone have confidence in personal intuitions in the kinds of cases where Wurzburger thinks intuitions are to be followed, cases where intuitions of different people will surely conflict, if even powerful and widespread human ethical intuitions have already been exposed as faulty because they conflict with the divine command? Would you persist in using a calculator to solve complex multiplication if, by consulting a superior source, you previously have found the calculator to give whoppingly wrong answers even to much simpler-looking questions?

Thus, once it is acknowledged that halakhic laws bind even if they are contrary to ethics, the epistemological force of human intuition, its trustworthiness, is thrust into doubt. Add now to this the contemporary attack on objectivity and the notion that ethics is culture-bound, and the problem, "Why trust intuition?" surely intensifies. Certainly, when we move to socially conditioned judgments pertaining to sexual morality or medical ethics, Orthodox Jews predominantly regard social norms as a subversive force. Hence, the role of independent ethical intuitions in Jewish ethics should be diminished — significantly — by the concessions that Wurzburger, however aptly, makes to their fallibility.[13]

Faced with this difficulty, Wurzburger might reply as follows. Flawed though our intuitions may be, we must do the best we can; and so we must continue to consult general ethical intuition. But this reply papers over a difficulty. For what is "the best we can do," the best procedure to follow? Someone could argue that because Halakhah conflicts often with general ethical intuitions, we do "the best we can" not if we consult general ethical intuitions, but if we ignore them. Let me elaborate.

Consider the following theory, which I believe captures the thinking of many Orthodox Jews.[14] Jews committed to Halakhah, goes this theory, ought to consult intuitions; existing precedents cannot cover all cases, and precedents may often conflict. But the kinds of "intuitions" they ought to consult are not general moral intuitions, such as those of a modern Westernized Jew encumbered by humanistic and liberal sensibilities. Those intuitions are the ones have been exposed as unreliable because they clash with specific halakhic laws; those are the ones that historicism and skepticism undercut. Rather, the only intuitions that count are intuitions that arise from specifically Jewish sources. This approach, I believe, accurately captures Nahmanides' language in his famous comments about "You shall be holy" and "Do the straight and the good"; as Wurzburger puts it in his paraphrase of Nahmanides, the latter appeals to "the intuitions of a moral conscience *formed within the matrix of Torah teachings*" (28, emphasis mine). Nahmanides' model is extrapolation from explicit rules, not appeal to something outside.[15] Ironically, when Wurzburger lists the factors that influence the formation of an individual's ethical perceptions "insofar as Jewish Covenantal Ethics is concerned" (37), he cites (a) the study of specific laws, (b) moral conduct in conformity with Torah norms, (c) Aggadah and biblical narratives, and (d) personal contact with scholars (37-39). Absent from this list is general ethical intuitions, and hence the reader not familiar with other passages might conclude that Wurzburger himself excludes "the ethos of a given society" from the list of legitimate influences (37; see also 7, 23)![16]

Restricting admissible intuitions to those formed from Jewish sources will of course not eradicate the problem of human fallibility. Conflicts may well remain between laws about Amalek, *mamzerim*, slavery and even "Jewishly-formed" intuitions, e.g., between halakhic and aggadic pronouncements. Such clashes would undermine trust even in people's ability to extract correct intuitions from their understanding of Jewish sources. Nevertheless, (a) conflicts between Halakhah and Jewishly-formed intuitions are less prevalent than conflicts between Halakhah and secular morality, and (b) "Jewishly formed" intuitions, one might submit, represent eternal objective truths, while secular intuitions are socially conditioned and relativistic, as Wurzburger so forcefully states. We often have to reject socially-conditioned norms. Hence, social norms have no presumptive favorable status, and even Hirsch's theory of intuition-as-revelation cannot deny that intuition gets ethics terribly wrong. Torah, it will be said, is a bastion against society's values, not a repository of them. In sum, it is not true that we do "the best we can" when we consult general ethical intuitions. We do better, though of course not perfectly, when we consult our Jewishly-formed intuitions. Or so one can argue — and many have.[17]

This is sharply different from Wurzburger's view. "Covenantal Ethics," he writes, "operates with intuitions that represent value judgments arising from specific historic-cultural situations" (7). Covenantal Ethics does embrace socially conditioned norms as legitimate sources of intuition.

What if Wurzburger were simply to shift positions and permit only "Jewishly formed" intuitions? What if he were to exclude general moral intuitions as sources of halakhic decision making and insist that we filter out socially conditioned norms before forming an intuition? The answer is that one of his long-standing and worthy objectives would be undercut. In his seminal essay, "Covenantal Imperatives," which forms the basis of *Ethics of Responsibility*'s account of intuition, Wurzburger opens with the statement that, to be relevant, religion must comment on the agonizing ethical dilemmas of the day — for example, racial strife.[18] When we exclude socially conditioned norms from the range of admissible intuitions, however, all sorts of causes might lose their Jewish ethical underpinnings — ranging from the abolition of slavery (cf. 34) to women's suffrage[19] to civil rights legislation. Jews would have no ethical reason to support any of these causes in their host societies, and no reason to, say, ban slavery or enfranchise women in a Jewish polity. One might try to gain the allegiance of Jews to such causes by reference to Jewish values such as relief of suffering, equality before the law and freedom. Yet surely someone can counter, one, that Judaism contains specific rulings that conflict with these values, and, two, that the technical Halakhah must have already factored in all those considerations and yet overridden them; at the bottom line, the Halakhah allowed slavery and licensed certain forms of discrimination.

Thus far we have focused on the following question: why should we rely on a source — ethical intuition — that leads us astray so often and so drastically? To make matters now still more difficult, Wurzburger needs to reconcile his trust in intuition with the "subjectivity" and relativity-to-historical-situation that he posits.

An especially stark form of this difficulty emerges via the following scenario. Suppose that a generation from now, the moral and political climate in America changes significantly. Most Americans, imagine, call for a repeal of civil rights legislation, a return to slavery, and the disenfranchisement of women. Their views are of course strenuously opposed by the previous generation (i.e., ours), but to no avail. An Orthodox Jew of that future generation is challenged about his moral positions. As a student of Wurzburger's writings, he responds as follows: "Socially conditioned norms are a perfectly legitimate basis for ethical conduct. The norms I accept are those of my society. My society wants slavery and discrimination. The previous one didn't. My norms are just as legitimate as theirs. So I am in no way violating Jewish ethical sensitivities." Would Wurzburger be able to convince him that the previous generation's norms are superior to the present generation's? Is there anything wrong with the younger Jew's argument?[20]

To be sure, Wurzburger labors briefly to dispel the worry that intuitions cannot achieve objectivity; but his rejoinder, in my opinion, does not provide the necessary comfort. Wurzburger notes that "it is only in cases when we cannot have recourse to explicit formal rules for moral guidance that we must rely on intuition" (34-35). But this does not fully engage the issue. The question was not how the parts of Jewish law that involve formal rules and divine commands achieve objectivity (34-35). The question was how *intuitions* achieve objectivity. Furthermore, since many or most of the "explicit formal rules for moral guidance" were formulated by decisors who did not have exact precedents to draw on but had to exercise intuition, the objectivity problem Wurzburger poses has wide application. Wurzburger does state, to be sure, that ethical intuitions are made "objective" by eventually being codified in Halakhah (35). However, this does not explain why they deserve to be made objective and binding on Wurzburger's premises. If a person's intuitions go against those of an earlier authority, why are the later intuitions less valid than the earlier ones? Wurzburger is clearly right that Covenantal Ethics "cannot avoid the difficulties besetting all forms of intuitionist ethics" (34). But unlike a secular ethicist, a Jewish ethicist has the option of not relying on general ethical intuitions. Subjectivity might infuse one's intuitions about Jewish sources, but there will be in total less subjectivity than if we allowed general ethical intuitions as well.

I have argued that Wurzburger needs to supply an epistemology that will lend credibility to ethical intuition, or else Jewish law's extensive appeal to intuition will seem unwarranted and baffling in terms of his theory. His account can only be enriched by an open confrontation with this weighty problem.

III

Since there are manifold instances in which halakhic authorities have appealed to *sekhel* (the intellect) or *sevara* (logic), in the sense of a compelling general ethical arguments, one might think it easy to establish that halakhists admit general ethical intuitions into their decision making. And indeed, for the practical purpose of validating the use of general ethical intuitions in halakhic decisionmaking, perhaps such an appeal to precedents, if accurate, is all that is needed. But to understand philosophically why intuitions are trusted, more is required. The assertion that *sevara* and *sekhel* have a voice in Halakhah became most conspicuous in the medieval and early modern philosophical context, where it fits nicely. That context was largely untroubled by the problems of historicism and skepticism; it placed great faith in human reason, natural law and ethical sense.[21] The problem is how to transplant this trust in *sekhel* and *sevara* to a climate like today's, which harbors deep skepticism about their powers. To put it another way, Jewish sources do not typically call for legislation based on norms that are known to be transient, subjective and culture-relative.[22] And in this respect, any appeal to moral intuition as a historically valid basis of halakhic decision making sits uneasily with an awareness of subjectivist, historicist and skeptical challenges.

The difficulties I have canvassed point the way to two constructive suggestions that must be implemented if we are to philosophically justify using general ethical intuitions as a basis for decision making.

First, for the admittance of general moral intuition into halakhic decision making to constitute "the best we can do," ethical judgments must not be purely subjective. General ethical intuitions require a stronger grounding than Wurzburger provides. Easier said than done, of course. But typically, the subjectivity and relativity of ethics has been wielded against the kind of position Wurzburger favors; his theory will be best served by a firmer rejection of these views and a vigorous defense of particular ethical judgments.

Second, the distrust of intuition that is occasioned by conflicts between Halakhah and morality must be mitigated significantly. One way to achieve this goal is to find some moral dimension of the Amalek or *mamzer* situation that has not been appreciated by those who find the Jewish law contrary to moral intuition; once we appreciate the full situation, our general moral intuitions about the cases would change.[23] Another way to mitigate the conflicts appears in a passing comment by Wurzburger (29). He refers to the role of conscience (or ethical intuition) as a "hermeneutical principle." That is, when a specific *halakhah* clashes with intuition, this should prompt an exploration into whether there are admissible interpretations concerning the scope or applicability of the laws that have been overlooked. Where sufficient ambiguity exists in the law, ethical intuition is not flatly rejected, but on the contrary, is used to interpret the scope of the law. To be sure, a *midrash* reminds us that not all difficult laws can be reinterpreted or suitably restricted: only God can comfort the *mamzer*, we are told, while the Sanhedrin remains that child's "oppressor" *(Lev. Rabbah* 32:10; see also *Eccl. Rabbah* 4:1). Still, we can at least diminish the clashes by a process of interpretation. Emphasizing the technique of interpretation, I think, would yield a more subtle picture of how halakhists have related to ethics than does Wurzburger's emphasis on the point that when a divine command or legal precedent clashes with ethics, we bow to the divine command or legal precedent. And it would also mitigate the charge that intuitions cannot be trusted; no longer do we routinely reject intuitions in the face of divine commands.

Such an appeal to ethical intuitions as a source of interpretation requires an account of how the conversation between social norms and Halakhah has proceeded in the past and may legitimately proceed now. To write that account one must draw upon a much larger fund of historical examples than the book supplies.[24] We need explicit discussion of what examples exist and of whether authorities in these instances were relying on general ethical intuitions or instead Jewishly formed ones. Marvin Fox has suggested that when a moral norm appears to have affected the law, "it is generally the case that the so-called moral norm is itself based on either unimpeachable sources or, at least, sources that serve as authoritative support."[25] Clearly, the question of how general ethical intuitions function in halakhic decision making requires further elucidation.

IV

Another topic that needs to be addressed more fully is authority. This lacuna is especially noticeable when Wurzburger attempts to differentiate his view from that of *Da'at Torah,* generally understood as the position that Torah scholars are to be granted virtually unlimited authority over followers' decisions, based on those scholars' intuitive discernment of what are commonly called "Torah values." *Da'at Torah,* like Covenantal Ethics, appeals to intuitions; *Da'at Torah,* like Covenantal Ethics, posits that there are some "religiously significant issues that cannot be decided on the basis of purely formal halakhic reasoning" (31). Thus, both views hold that "the residual influence of exposure to halakhic categories of thought makes itself felt in areas where the law itself cannot be applied" (33). Where, if anywhere, is the difference?

Wurzburger responds as follows:

Whereas [*Da'at Torah*] purports to represent authoritative, objective religious truth, my notion of Covenantal Imperatives disclaims any pretensions to objectivity. In my view, so long as we are dealing with matters that are not subject to halakhic legislation [he writes elsewhere on the same page: "where no formal halakhic ruling is feasible"], there is no authoritative body to provide guidance and it is incumbent upon individuals to assume *personal* responsibility on the basis of their own purely subjective, intuitive decisions (33).

This point calls out for explanation, for what does Wurzburger mean by "matters that are not subject to halakhic legislation" and "where no formal halakhic ruling is feasible"? To be sure, many cases cannot be decided by straightforward application of an exact precedent. But that does not *ipso facto* exclude them from halakhic legislation, especially given Wurzburger's preceding account. All along, Wurzburger's point has been that Jewish decision making often arises precisely in such instances. The words, "It is incumbent upon individuals to assume personal responsibility on the basis of their own purely subjective, intuitive decisions," appear to imply that once one knows the rules and *aggadot* that are relevant to a given situation, there would be no point in consulting and relying upon a decisor. Any layperson will be permitted to follow his own intuition over that of a learned authority, or not consult such an authority all in those situations. And surely that is not Wurzburger's position. Wurzburger has indicated that exposure to halakhic categories of thought, to *aggadot*, and to other scholars creates sound intuitions (37-38) — and plainly, some individuals will have greater exposure to these elements than others (cf. 6-7, 39).[26]

What is meant, then, by the phrases, "matters that are not subject to halakhic legislation," and, "where no formal halakhic ruling is feasible"? Wurzburger refers to "various sensitive political, social or economic issues" (31), but precisely how is that area delineated, given that many political, social and economic decisions in responsa are not based on precise precedents? These questions cannot be passed over. To some extent Wurzburger is right that advocates of *Da'at Torah* themselves suggest a distinction between formal halakhic decision making (*pesak*) and *Da'at Torah* simply by designating only some decisions as *Da'at Torah* (31). But it is still fair to ask how Wurzburger, on his premises, demarcates those areas that are not subject to formal decision.

There are ways to distinguish advocates and critics of *Da'at Torah* without the critics declaring all putatively *Da'at Torah* decisions to be purely subjective and insusceptible to authority. For example, advocates and critics of *Da'at Torah* might differ — and perhaps this is really the difference in real-world terms — over who counts as an appropriate rabbinic authority, how much weight should be assigned to an authority's possessing formal secular expertise, and how much freedom individuals have in choosing a rabbinic authority.[27]

V

A larger question I would like to raise is where one should look for an understanding of Jewish ethics. Wurzburger sets out a distinction between ritual laws and ethical laws, and, with certain qualifications (12-13), makes clear that his subject is ethics (10, 112; cf. 44). In line with this emphasis, he focuses on materials, both Jewish and non-Jewish, that pertain to interpersonal morality. However, insofar as his main thesis is concerned, the distinction between the ethical and the ritual is diverting. Like other works in Jewish ethics, it tends to marginalize certain sources and topics that should be highlighted.

The underlying reasons that one needs to appeal to intuition in ethics, according to Wurzburger, are that (1) situations arise that are not governed by formal rules, (2) intuition is needed to ascertain that a given instance falls under a given rule, and (3) there can be conflicts between different principles (34). But these reasons apply no less to questions about sacrifices, Shabbat, and family purity than to questions about life-threatening situations and theft. Of course, ethical laws, as we have seen, utilize secular intuitions, which, presumably, ritual decision making does not. But certainly much of the section on intuition (especially 37-39, cited earlier, where Wurzburger lists "Jewish" sources of intuition) could have been written about Shabbat no less than ethics.

Wurzburger would not deny these points. But the result of noticing them should be to shift emphasis or at least expand the range of sources from which to draw support. For example, at one point Wurzburger writes that, "It is only in the area of ethics and not within the domain of ritual law that Judaism mandates going beyond legal requirements" (112). Yet there are certainly examples of special individuals assuming ritual stringencies. Again, Nahmanides, in the very explanation of the requirement to "be holy," and "Do the straight and the good" that is so often cited to support non-formalistic approaches to Jewish ethics, explicitly notes that decision making about the laws of Shabbat resembles decision making about appetites and about interpersonal behavior. Resting on the seventh day, he explains, is analogous to being holy and doing the straight and the good in that it offers general guidance for cases not covered by explicit rules. In principle, therefore, certain cases of decision making concerning Shabbat are no different from cases that require an invocation of being holy or doing the straight and the good.[28]

To define the role of intuitions in halakhic ethics, we need to highlight the nature of halakhic reasoning generally, rather than to explore Jewish ethics in isolation. In other words, a theory of intuition in Jewish ethics will profit from a more general account of how Jewish legal decision making operates. In his introduction to his legal commentary *Milhamot Hashem,* Nahmanides declares that "every student of our Talmud knows that in the disputes of its commentators there are no decisive proofs nor, in the majority of cases, absolute refutations. In this science there are no demonstrative proofs." He is speaking, surely, of all halakhic reasoning.[29] *Mutatis mutandis,* any legal system confronts the problem, "What happens when the rules run out?", and whatever uniqueness Jewish law might possess in other respects, Nahmanides' point that arguments typically fall short of demonstrative proof holds for legal reasoning in any system. Wurzburger finds "legal models" of limited value for understanding Covenantal Ethics (15). Yet, writings of philosophers of law about the nature of legal reasoning are relevant to his concerns and would nicely supplement works on secular ethics that Wurzburger frequently cites.[30]

VI

Thus far I have examined how Wurzburger's opposition to legal formalism manifests itself in his conception of halakhic decision making. However, his insistence that Jewish ethics is concerned with more than legal rules leads him also to a second major theme. Wurzburger distinguishes between act morality and agent morality. Act morality emphasizes what actions a person should perform; agent morality (or "virtue ethics") focuses on what character traits a person should cultivate. Contemporary philosophers frequently call for a diminished emphasis on an "ethics of obligation" and a return to an "ethics of virtue" like that pursued in ancient philosophy.[31] Wurzburger issues a similar call with respect to Jewish ethics.

Wurzburger credits Maimonides with "originality," indeed with "a pioneering breakthrough in Jewish ethics," when the latter attaches great importance to the cultivation of character traits (71-75) and regards the acquisition of desirable traits as a fulfillment of the mitzvah to "walk in His ways" (*imitatio Dei*). In analyzing Maimonides' position, Wurzburger puts the distinction between act morality and agent morality to work in interesting and ingenious ways. For example, *Hilkhot De'ot* (6:3) mandates that we love every Jew, while *Hilkhot Evel* (14:1) obliges us to love only "your brother in Torah and commandments." Wurzburger resolves the discrepancy by stating that in *Hilkhot De'ot,* Maimonides is concerned with keeping people away from callousness and self-cente-redness (agent morality), while in *Hilkhot Evel,* he is concerned with the commandment of loving one's neighbor as oneself (act morality) (73-74). Again, Wurzburger suggests an interesting reason why Maimonides emphasized that people ought not act for the sake of reward: it is because God, whom we are to imitate, acts without ulterior motives (80-81). To resolve an ostensible contradiction in *Hilkhot De'ot,* he explains that traits of character may be cultivated either because they contribute to civilizing the world or because they form the ethics of the pious; in Maimonides' thought, he claims, there is a perpetual dialectic between these two perspectives, paralleling the dialectic between majesty and humility articulated by R. Soloveitchik (82-86).

This approach shows great subtlety and originality, although its stress on Maimonides' distinctiveness is somewhat at cross purposes with Wurzburger's hope of showing that Judaism (and not only a particular thinker) demands the cultivation of an ethical personality.[32] However, the notion implicit in Wurzburger's resolution of the discrepancy between *Hilkot De'ot* and *Hilkhot Evel* — that outside of *Hilkhot De'ot* one finds act morality but not agent morality — is belied by a passage that Wurzburger himself cites. In *Hilkhot Melakhim* 10:12, Maimonides grounds the obligation to give charity to non-Jews in the verse, "His mercy extends to all His creatures" (Ps. 145:9; see 50-51).

It further seems to me that Wurzburger's reading of Maimonides' concept of *imitatio Dei,* while highly attractive for the *Mishneh Torah* code, applies less cogently to the *Guide.*[33] Maimonides' concept of *imitatio Dei* in the *Guide* (I:54) is shaped by a crucial assertion, namely, that the thirteen attributes of God refer only to God's actions and not His state of mind or emotions. God does not have states of mind or emotions. True imitation of God's attributes, therefore, requires both imitating God's actions and imitating the emotionless way in which God acts. Maimonides strongly implies this conclusion.[34] Consequently, the *Guide* would not support a theory of *imitatio Dei* which requires "the cultivation of desirable states of mind, be they intellectual beliefs or emotional dispositions" (69). The point of the *Guide* chapter is the opposite, that one cultivates the absence of an emotional state of mind in exemplifying a divine attribute. For this reason the *Guide* also supports an emphasis on *acts* of *imitatio Dei,* rather than states of mind.[35]

There is, finally, an un-addressed difficulty with the widespread idea of using *imitatio Dei* as a ground for specific duties. As noted in *Midrash ha-Gadol* to Genesis 37:1, there are attributes of God (pride, jealousy, vengefulness, and perpetration of ruses) that should not be imitated. Hence, one might say, people are to imitate only those attributes that they ought to imitate; and this implies, in turn, that we need some other principle or text, different from *imitatio Dei,* that will enlighten us as to which attributes should be imitated. Consequently, I am not sure that *imitatio Dei* can do all the work often demanded of it. The principle adds a dimension to certain interpersonal duties, but does not fully determine what our interpersonal duties are.[36]

VII

A third major theme of Wurzburger's theory is pluralism. "Judaism operates with a pluralistic ethics that incorporates a variety of incommensurable values" (87). Potential conflicts between values are resolved either by means of "casuistry," i.e., formal rules, or else, when formal rules are not decisive, critical reflection and intuition (94).

Now, whereas Wurzburger implies that secular ethical systems are not pluralistic, I would note that some secular ethical and legal systems do operate with a variety of norms and values. Nonetheless, Wurzburger may be right to ascribe "uniqueness" to Judaism because of the range of values that Judaism must and does balance: "Love with justice, universalism with particularism, self-love with altruism, quietism with activism, self-assertion with humility, submissiveness with activity" (100).[37] In this ode to dialectic and multiple values and its accompanying vision of Halakhah as the repository of dialectic, the influence of R. Soloveitchik shines through.

To illustrate the pluralism of Jewish ethics, Wurzburger presents a spectrum of specific "moral dilemmas" that Halakhah addresses. His analyses of halakhic positions are often compelling — as when he argues that rules which govern the body politic differ from those that a person would follow in a purely individual context (94; also see 36-37).[38] In other instances, questions arise about his account. For example, addressing the dilemmas of triage, Wurzburger writes that a rational system of priorities is preferable to random selection: "It still is preferable to make informed judgments than to rely on purely arbitrary methods" (91). Yet halakhists today severely restrict the application of the priorities fixed by the text of the Mishnah (*Horayot* 3:7-8). In many cases they favor a "first come, first served" procedure — exactly the same procedure favored by secular ethicists who advocate randomness — albeit they may not value randomness per se.[39]

I also do not agree that "Ahad Ha-Am misreads R. Akiva's ruling" in the famous case of the two thirst-plagued travelers, one of whom has a flask of water. If they split the available water, they both die; if one of them drinks the entire flask, he lives while his comrade dies. R. Akiva rules in that case that "your life takes precedence over that of your friend" (*Bava Metzi'a* 62a; *Sifra, Behar* 5). Ahad Ha-Am sees this ruling as reflecting formal justice and equal treatment of people, rather than a priority of self over other (99). The denial that the ruling is based on priority of the self is implicit in the writings of halakhists: the owner keeps the flask not because per se a person can give priority to his own interests, but because (a) it makes no sense to split the water if both will die; and (b) by keeping the flask, the owner is disturbing the status quo less than he would by transferring it. On these interpretations, we adjudicate the conflict by using an impartial legal principle — a kind of "least change" principle — and not by positing some sort of prerogative for the self.[40]

Another type of pluralism that Wurzburger invokes is "a variety of visions of the good" (114). "Individuals are free to select whatever ideals are most suitable to their respective personalities" (ibid.). The concept of plural models of character and plural conceptions of the good, so central to modern liberal political theory, has been elaborated and defended in a Jewish context by Moshe Sokol (114).[41]

VIII

Today there is enormous, wonderful productivity in "Jewish ethics" in the sense of practical Jewish law; but extended philosophical treatments of Jewish ethics in an Orthodox framework are far harder to come by.[42] Positions of medieval and modern sages about the existence of an independent standard of ethics and about the distinction between action and character, are widely parroted but rarely wrestled with. On a sociological plane, many Jews who follow Halakhah are occupied only with what acts to perform or refrain from, ignoring the varied questions about ideals and personality formation that so powerfully engaged thinkers like Maimonides and Nahmanides. These questions manifest an aspiration to a higher spirituality, beyond legal obedience and yet embracing it. "Halakhah represents not merely the way of God...It also functions as a way to God" (3). Forcefully and eloquently, Walter Wurzburger reminds his readers of this often neglected truth.

NOTES

1   *Ethics of Responsibility: Pluralistic Approaches to Covenantal Ethics* (Philadelphia, 1994).

2   See Nahmanides' commentaries to the quoted verses. See also the commentary of R. Naftali Tzvi Yehudah Berlin (Netziv; nineteenth century), *Ha'amek Davar* to Ex. 19:6, quoted by Wurzburger, 26.

3   For Nahmanides, the two functions of intuition are to some extent one, since conduct *lifnim mi-shurat ha-din* is called for in cases where existing formal rules do not cover one's situation.

4   Aharon Lichtenstein: "Does Jewish Tradition Recognize An Ethic Independent of Halakha?," originally published in *Modern Jewish Ethics,* ed. Marvin Fox (Columbus, OH, 1975), 107. See also R. Lichtenstein's "*Halakhah va-Halakhim ke-Oshyot Musar: Hirhurim Mahshavtiyyim ve-Hinukhiyyim,*" *Arakhim be-Mivhan Milhamah* (Jerusalem, 1985), 13-24.

5   The main dissenter from this view is Hazon Ish in *Sefer Hazon Ish, Hoshen Mishpat, Likkutim,* 16:1, 465: "There is no law that is not explicit, for everything is explicit in the Torah." For an illuminating discussion of how comprehensive halakhic rules are, see Dov N. Linzer, "*Be-Hesber Shittat ha-Geonim ve-ha-Rambam be-Dina de-Malkhuta Dina,*" *Beit Yitzhak* 26 (1994): 661ff.

6   Those who hold this view often add, however, that we are to follow moral conscience because God and the Halakhah instruct us to follow moral conscience.

7   See R. Ovadyah's celebrated commentary to the Mishnah, at *Avot* 1:1; R. Avraham Yeshayahu Karelitz (d. 1953), *Sefer Hazon Ish,* ed. S. Greineman (Jerusalem, 1954), 21-43. It has been argued, however, that R. Ovadyah mi-Bartenura and Hazon Ish did not deny a valid independent standard; they only denied a valid *knowable* independent standard. See Avi Sagi and Daniel Statman, "*Teluto Shel ha-Musar ba-Dat bi-Mesoret ha-Yahadut,*" in *Bein Dat le-Musar,* ed. Statman and Sagi (Ramat Gan, 1993), 115-44. The authors argue that, in fact, there are almost no examples of Jewish thinkers who denied the existence of a valid independent standard of ethics and embraced "divine command morality." By contrast, there are many thinkers who combined belief in the existence of such a standard with a denial that human beings can know it well enough to issue sound judgments on their own.

      Among contemporary thinkers cited by Wurzburger, R. Aharon Lichtenstein and R. Shubert Spero believe in an independent and knowable ethic, while R. J. David Bleich and Marvin Fox deny the validity of any extra-halakhic standard of ethics or at least the knowability of such a standard (115, n. 4).

8   See Plato, *Euthyphro* 9d-11b. In truth, Plato seems concerned with piety and impiety, which are religiously charged notions, rather than the ostensibly secular notions of right and wrong. Nevertheless, philosophers have generally treated Plato as seeking a definition of the latter terms.

9   For purposes of this essay, I will not try to sort out the many ambiguities in the terms subjectivism, relativism, historicism and skepticism, nor will I try to define the otherwise important distinctions between them. Instead, I will rely on the reader's rough sense of what these views assert and will treat the views as a bloc.

10   See also his "Meta-Halakhic Propositions," *Leo Jung Jubilee Volume,* ed. Menahem Kasher, Norman Lamm and Leonard Rosenfeld (New York, 1962), 211-21. The book's conclusion (110-11) insists that ethical judgments are objective, but the only defenses I find of this claim are on pp. 7-8, 23-24, and 34-35, all of which I take up in this review.

11   Reductions to ethical monotheism fail also because they ignore ritual prescriptions (21-22).

12 For R. Ovadyah mi-Bartenura in his commentary to *Avot* 1:1, even the commonsensical and immensely persuasive teachings of *Pirkei Avot* command credibility only because they were revealed at Sinai. They would not impress us as valid were they arrived at independently. On whether R. Ovadyah is denying the existence of an independent ethic or merely its knowability, see Sagi and Statman, 121-22.

13 Wurzburger speaks of direct divine commands; the difficulty grows when we move beyond these and look at the larger canvas of Halakhah. For instance, R. J. David Bleich maintains that Halakhah would allow the use of data from Nazi experimentations ("Survey of Recent Halakhic Periodical Literature," *Tradition* 26:1 [Fall 1991]: 65-73). Responding to the fact that many people (Jews and non-Jews) find the use of Nazi data morally objectionable, Bleich writes that "such reactions are intuitive and emotional"; but although such reactions "are entirely salutary," nevertheless "the postulates of Halakhah are by no means always identical with intuitive reactions. ... The ability to suspend one's own subjective judgment is a necessary condition and prerequisite for service as a judge and as a rabbinic decisor" (Ibid., 72).

   As I read Wurzburger, he would not disagree with this statement (whatever his view on Nazi experimentation). But if formally halakhic rulings go contrary to intuition often enough, then the very idea that intuitions are to be trusted totters on the brink.

14 I do not refer only to Jews who do not value secular culture. For example, the eminent Jewish philosopher Marvin Fox has also put forward such a thesis. See, *inter alia*, his *The Philosophical Foundations of Jewish Ethics: Some Initial Reflections* (Cincinnati, 1979), 12-20.

15 Although Nahmanides' language accords with this formulation, his ultimate intent may not. If Nahmanides believes that Torah law reflects an independent ethic, then indirectly, extrapolation from the Torah's laws is extrapolation from an independent ethic. But I am trying to see how the argument would go.

16 In conversation, Wurzburger explained to me that in the cited passage he did not intend to exclude general ethical intuitions, but was trying to catalogue only Jewish sources of intuition.

17 This is not to deny that conflicts may exist within the Jewish sources. These will have to be adjudicated; preference will have to be given to one strand over another, and intuitions surely will have to play a role in this process. But without further argument, there is no decisive reason to think that resolving these tensions requires an external standard of conduct. Education, role models and intuitions formed from other halakhic sources, without reference to secular ethics, might serve as the "third verse" that harmonizes the two contradictory ones. Appealing to general ethical intuitions will exacerbate whatever problems an appeal to intuition faces when we confine ourselves to Jewish sources. (I am here trying to say how the argument would go; I am not espousing the position it tries to justify.)

18 See his "Covenantal Imperatives," *Samuel K. Mirsky Memorial Volume*, ed. Gersion Appel (New York, 1970), 3-12.

19 R. Kook and other rabbis held that women's suffrage is contrary to Halakhah. See *Ma'amarei ha-Reayah* (Jerusalem, 1984), 189-91. But cf. R. Ben-Zion Uziel,

Piskei Uziel bi-She'eolot ha-Zeman (Jerusalem, 1978), 228-34, #44 (= *Mishpetei Uziel, Hoshen Mishpat,* # 6).

[20]   On p. 111, Wurzburger states that,

> What is right or wrong at a given time may also be influenced by contingent historical factors…Thus, for example, the standards of sexual morality acceptable in a polygamous civilization would hardly be suitable in a monogamous society. Similarly, a patriarchal society would naturally view filial obligation or the status of women in a different light from what would be considered proper under contemporary circumstances.

This passage suggests that perhaps the young Jew's argument is right in Wurzburger's opinion after all. But the quoted passage clearly does not mean to validate any and every set of cultural mores. Also, the passage on p. 111 is ostensibly at odds with one on p. 24. There, in his effort to protect moral objectivity, Wurzburger writes in a quite different spirit: "Moral perceptions are seen as universally applicable, without regard to the cultural or social background of the agent whose conduct is evaluated."

[21]   I do not deny that some medieval Jewish thinkers believed that ethics is conventional, but it would have to be explored whether they allowed general ethics into halakhic reasoning.

[22]   There are prima facie exceptions; for instance, *Maggid Mishneh* to Maimonides' *Hilkhot Shekhenim* 14:15 (cited by Wurzburger, p. 27). But the general rule holds, and I am not sure that the prima facie exceptions prove to be genuine ones. The writings of Rav Kook on morality are especially provocative as regards the topic of moral relativism.

[23]   For an analysis of this and other responses to the Amalek problem, see Avi Sagi, "The Punishment of Amalek in Jewish Tradition: Coping with the Moral Problem," *Harvard Theological Review* 87(1995): 323-46. Cf. Lichtenstein, "Halakhah va-Halakhim," 23-24.

[24]   There is a vast literature that explores such precedents. Recent contributions include the two volumes of Aaron Kirschenbaum's *Equity in Jewish Law* (Hoboken, NJ and New York, 1991) and several of the essays on "Religious Law and Legal Pluralism" in *Cardozo Law Review* 12, 3-4 (February-March, 1991). (Wurzburger touches on the historical question on pp. 111-13; see also pp. 34-35.) In a review essay of Kirschenbaum's volumes, Samuel Morell — assembling points made by Kirschenbaum himself — makes the interesting observation that "in almost all of the major categories of equity discussed in volume 1, post-talmudic developments curtailed the flexibility which [Kirschenbaum] has so painstakingly documented." See Morell, "The Religious Dimension of Jewish Civil Law," *AJS Review* 18 (1993): 267.

[25]   Fox, 17.

[26]   Also, it is difficult to apply the concept of "taking responsibility" to a situation in which no matter what one chooses, one makes the right decision.

[27]   In some recent defenses of *Da'at Torah,* one finds a frank recognition that each of several conflicting views might lay claim to constituting *Da'at Torah,* along with an assertion that rabbinic infallibility is not an essential component of the

concept. See Berel Wein, "Daas Torah: An Ancient Definition of Authority and Responsibility," *The Jewish Observer* 27:7 (October 1994): 8. Acknowledgment of conflict and fallibility narrows the gap between *Da'at Torah* and its critics, suggesting that the differences will lie in the areas I noted.

[28] Admittedly, though, certain terms denoting supererogatory conduct might appear only or predominantly in the context of "ethical" behavior.

[29] I may have taken some liberty in extending Nahmanides from the topic of talmudic commentary to that of practical halakhic decision making. But his remarks seem to apply to both.

[30] There is a large literature by legal theorists on this topic. For a discussion from a Jewish standpoint, see Martin Golding, "Reasoning and the Authoritative Expansion of the Law," *Studies in Jewish Philosophy,* ed. Norbert Samuelson (Lanham, MD, 1987), 421-62.

[31] See, for example, Alasdair MacIntyre, *After Virtue* (2nd ed., Notre Dame, ID, 1984).

[32] The Maimonidean stress on agent morality is of course not unique; Bahya ibn Pakuda, Nahmanides, the author of *Sefer ha-Hinukh,* and the figures of the Musar movement, to name a few, all prize the cultivation of virtuous traits as the goal of some or all *mitzvot*. However, Wurzburger maintains that for Maimonides, the cultivation of various traits is intrinsically valuable, an end in itself, whereas other thinkers who stressed agent morality arguably viewed character traits as instrumentally valuable, i.e., valuable only insofar as they lead to right acts. Even so, on pp. 77-78, Wurzburger himself seems to retreat from his earlier attribution of uniqueness to Maimonides.

[33] In a footnote, Wurzburger refers to one potential difficulty — that *imitatio Dei* in the *Guide* may be confined to the philosopher-statesman and that the thirteen attributes are not to be imitated by him in the ordinary moral sense (128 note 55; see *Guide* I:54 and III:54). Wurzburger's response to that objection is contained in the concluding paragraphs of his "The Centrality of Virtue-Ethics in Maimonides," in *Of Scholars, Savants, and Saints: Essays in Honor of Arthur Hyman,* ed. Ruth Link-Salinger (New York, 1989), 251-60.

[34] The point that imitation of God requires emotionlessness was made by Eliezer Goldman in his *"Ha-Avodah ha-Meyuhedet be-Massigei ha-Amitot," Bar-Ilan Annual* 6 (1968): 287-313. The crucial supporting passage in the *Guide* appears near the end of I:54, when Maimonides urges the ruler (who practices *imitatio Dei*) not to experience emotion when carrying out the functions of a leader that exemplify the thirteen attributes. Wurzburger would have to argue (1) that I:54 applies not only to leaders (see the previous note) and also (2) that Jews who are not leaders should not strive for the emotionless state aimed for by the ruler. Even if point (1) is granted, point (2) has no corroboration in the texts of the *Guide*.

[35] Though in *Guide* I:54 the imitator has certain *beliefs* about what certain people deserve.

[36] See Leon Roth, *Ha-Dat ve-Erkhei ha-Adam* (Jerusalem and Tel Aviv, 1973), 20-30. In fairness, I would note that in the *Guide* passage cited earlier, Maimonides in effect meets this difficulty by suggesting that the leader imitates *all* of God's attributes. The problem I raise is directed to other conceptions of *imitatio Dei*.

37 Wurzburger notes also that whereas a divine system of ethics *cannot* be inconsistent, a secular system has no such automatic guarantee (88).

38 On this point, see also Moshe Tendler, "*Be'ayot bi-Kedimah be-Hatzalah: ha-Taktziv ha-Tzibburi ve-Dihuy Nefesh Mippenei Nefesh*," *Sefer Kevod ha-Rav*, ed. Moshe Sherman and Yosef Woolf (New York, 1984): 167-69.

39 See *Iggerot Mosheh, Hoshen Mishpat* (Bnei Brak, 1985) II: #73:2, pp. 303-304 and 74:1, p. 312; also Moshe Hershler, in *Halakhah u-Refuah IV*, ed. Hershler (Jerusalem, 1985), 79-84. The topic, and the shift I referred to, is discussed at length in Moshe Sokol, "The Allocation of Scarce Medical Resources: A Philosophical Analysis of the Halakhic Sources," *AJS Review* 15, 1 (Spring 1990): 86-89. Two possible grounds for justifying "first come, first served" halakhically are (a) that the order is determined by providence and (b) that the first-to-come acquires a right to treatment. (One can rationally choose to follow a random procedure, a fact that Maimonides highlights in discussing the reasons for the commandments [*Guide* III:26].)

40 The analysis I sketched is discussed at length in my essay, "As Thyself: The Limits of Altruism in Jewish Ethics," in this volume. Ahad Ha-Am's analysis is found in "*Al Shtei ha-Se'ippim*," in *Al Parashat Derakhim* (Berlin, 1913), IV: 38-55, translated in part as "Jewish and Christian Ethics" in Leon Simon (ed.), *Ahad Ha-am: Essays, Letters, and Memoirs* (Oxford, 1946), 127-32.

41 See Moshe Sokol, "Personal Autonomy and Religious Authority," in *Rabbinic Authority and Personal Autonomy*, ed. Sokol (Northvale, NJ, 1992), 207-16. To be sure, there is a difference between defending pluralism on philosophical grounds and attributing pluralism to particular thinkers. Wurzburger concedes, for example, that Maimonides did not believe in pluralism of this sort, for he ranked intellectual perfection as the highest good. Sokol handles this case differently but notes that there is a paradox in allowing for pluralistic conceptions of the good while maintaining that one good is higher than another (212). This, is a paradox for pluralism in general.

42 An exception is Shubert Spero's *Halakhah, Morality and the Jewish Tradition* (New York and Hoboken, 1983), along with several of the articles cited in this essay.

"AS THYSELF":
The Limits of Altruism in Jewish Ethics

One of the most striking and curious differences between Jewish and non-Jewish systems of ethics lies in their contrasting attitudes toward altruistic self-sacrifice — giving up or risking one's own life for the sake of another. Defining morality as the very antithesis of self-interest, most Western moral theorists prize altruism as *the* ethical virtue *par excellence*.[1] From within a perspective that so exalts altruism, if life is the greatest good of all, then *surrender* of one's life for the sake of another is the ultimate moral act.[2] To be sure, such acts of self-sacrifice cannot be morally *required*; few people could fulfill so stringent a demand. Yet, while not obligatory, acts of altruistic self-sacrifice definitely fall within the category of the "supererogatory" — acts that are beyond the call of duty, and, for that reason, merit great admiration and praise. They are, indeed, the stuff of moral heroism.[3]

In contrast, Jewish tradition contains attitudes toward altruistic sacrifice of life that are strongly negative, reflecting a radically strong imperative to pursue self-interest when one's life is at stake. As is well known, if two people are in danger of dying from lack of water, and one is in possession of a flask, R. Akiva permits the possessor to save his own life by drinking rather than requiring him to hand the flask over to his equally deprived and imperiled comrade.[4] Now what if I, the canteen's possessor, can't bear to bring the canteen to my lips while watching my comrade perish? What if I *prefer* to hand it over? Whereas many non-Jewish ethicists would probably find the very question foolish, rabbinic authorities often deny me this expression of kindness, as they construe R. Akiva's ruling as a *mandate* rather than a mere prerogative. These authorities do not laud altruistic self-sacrifice as an act of *hasidut*; on the contrary, they condemn it as akin to self-murder. And although most authorities permit one to undertake *some* risks to save others from certain or near-certain death — indeed, they *obligate* a person to do so when the risk is small enough, as "you must not stand idly over the blood of your neighbor" (Lev. 19:16) — incurring risks of real magnitude to rescue another is prohibited by important decisors.[5] Of course, we should not ignore those rabbinic figures who regard an individual who risks or even voluntarily gives up his life for another as "saintly" and "pious,"[6] at least in certain circumstances. Still, in light of the inclination of non-Jewish thinkers to take the value of altruism as a given, the frequent opposition to it among some Jewish authorities seems rather odd. The oddity is only enhanced by the facts that Judaism stresses the duty to help others, and especially the duty to rescue, more than secular ethicists do, and that, in other contexts, it encourages supererogatory acts under rubrics like *middat hasidut* and *lifnim mi-shurat ha-din*. The fact that Jewish opinion on altruistic self-sacrifice is so polarized — altruistic self-sacrifice is *either* saintly *or* prohibited — is all the more reason to seek an account of the matter.[7]

What explains the ambivalence within Judaism toward altruistic self-sacrifice? Why, especially, do some rabbinic authorities not share the enthusiasm of secular ethicists? The question carries more than theoretical interest. Certain enterprises vital to society — organ donations by live donors, experimentation on consenting human subjects, medical management of dangerous infectious diseases that threaten the lives of attending health care personnel — depend for their very existence on altruistic sacrifice. These enterprises could not be undertaken if individuals were forbidden to place themselves into dangerous situations for the sake of helping others. Even rescue efforts like those undertaken during the Holocaust presented rabbinic authorities with halakhic problems.[8] In practice, sacrificial acts in medical settings have often been permitted on the grounds that the risk is small enough, and Holocaust rescues may be special because the cause was great enough. But the very fact that questions are raised and some authorities rule stringently about some cases is intriguing and important. The gap between Jewish and non-Jewish evaluations of risk-taking and self-sacrifice is significant and worthy of attention. As society comes to rely more and more on altruistic self-sacrifice, and to admire people who perform such acts, those who need to deal with such issues on the level of practical Halakhah might profit from a theoretical treatment that seeks to understand the differing places of altruism in general ethics and in Jewish tradition. This essay is an attempt to provide such a treatment.[9]

I

The first step in my analysis is to isolate the premises of general ethics which explain why altruistic self-sacrifice is regarded as proper and laudatory within that framework. This task will prove surprisingly difficult. For, despite the routine, indeed reflex-like approval of altruistic self-sacrifice which one finds in writings of ethicists (by which I here will mean thinkers not working out of rabbinic tradition), an enthusiastic attitude to acts of this type is difficult to justify by means of the rules, principles and criteria by which acts are normally judged as right or wrong. In a word, altruistic self-sacrifice is morally problematic.

The duty to promote the welfare of others — often referred to as the duty of "beneficence" — is without question central to ethical life. Nevertheless, it is not the *only* moral duty. Rather, the duty to help others is qualified and constrained by other moral considerations and principles. For suppose, by way of example, that we could save five people by tying down Jones, extracting his serviceable organs (thereby killing him) and finally distributing these organs to the five recipients. If promoting human welfare were our sole moral duty, then slicing up Jones would become obligatory. After all, from an "impartial" standpoint, five lives are more weighty than one (assuming that their social contributions are roughly the same). Yet killing Jones to save five others is self-evidently wrong. Ends do not justify means; ethics cannot be reduced to beneficence alone. Certain acts, killing, for example, are wrong on "deontological" grounds — grounds having to do with their intrinsic nature. Because they are wrong in and of themselves, one must not perform them even to save many other lives.

Now, as the American philosopher Michael Slote has pointed out, all of the explanations that ethicists have given for why killing is wrong should logically apply even if one is taking one's own life. And, indeed, frivolous suicide (suicide without good cause) is frequently conceded to be morally wrong. Nevertheless, when a suicide is prompted by altruistic considerations, the picture changes. Slote presents the point as follows:

> Even if one may not cut up another person to furnish healthy organs that will save the lives of five injured or sick individuals, there is no immediate moral bar to cutting oneself up in order to save five other people. There is no fundamental moral reason why someone should not sacrifice himself to save five people who need organ transplants. ... Although one may not kill another person to prevent five killings, one may kill a person in such a cause if that person is oneself.[10]

Slote is puzzled by his own intuitions. Whatever it is that makes killing one to save five morally wrong should make it just as wrong to kill one when that "one" is oneself as when that one is somebody else. Yet when other lives can be saved, an agent is permitted to do something harmful to himself that he would not be permitted to do to someone else as a means to the same purpose. The self enjoys a peculiar prerogative to violate moral principles for the sake of aiding others. What is called common sense morality — that is, the morality commonly agreed upon in the secular world — permits a person to treat himself in ways that others may not treat him. There is, then, a peculiar asymmetry between self and others with respect to the application of moral principles.

It is easy to multiply examples of this asymmetry. You cannot throw somebody on a grenade to prevent the deaths of others. Yet a person can opt to smother the grenade himself to save those people. You cannot take a kidney from Jones to help Smith, but you can if Jones consents. Again, suppose Jones needs all of a medication if he is to live, and he owns the medication. Five other people each need one-fifth of the medicine, and will all die if Jones exercises his right to the drug. Surely you cannot violate Jones' right to that resource just on the grounds that the others need it. Nonetheless, Jones may freely give the medicine to the others if he so chooses. You cannot place Jones at risk by giving him a potentially harmful drug just on the grounds that many will benefit from the scientific knowledge gleaned from your experiment. But Jones can consent to participate in the experiment. You cannot throw someone into dangerous raging waters and order him to try to save another party drowning there. But a person may *voluntarily* attempt such a rescue.

What these examples show is that altruistic acts of self-sacrifice violate some of the basic principles that ethicists use to evaluate the moral quality of certain acts. In particular, they violate the principle that no person should be harmed as a means toward the end of saving others. The talmudic principle, "We do not set aside one life for another"[11] resonates in secular ethics as well. Yet, altruistic self-sacrifice is regarded as moral heroism. It is no accident that Immanuel Kant, who more than any other philosopher emphasized that people must not be used as a means but only treated as ends in themselves, is one of the few secular philosophers to have found altruistic self-sacrifice morally problematic.[12] Kant is the exception, however. And what we need to understand is why — within common sense morality — people *are* permitted to make exceptions of themselves, to treat themselves in way that others may not, when their goal is the rescue of others. There is sornething special and unique about the way in which (secular) moral rules and principles apply to the self. Why is this so? How is the exception justified?

II

If the prerogative an agent possesses to put himself behind others does not flow from the principles by which we usually assess acts, it must flow from a different source: a fundamental, underived, axiomatic principle of human autonomy. In certain situations moral principles can be overridden by an agent's choices. The permission to sacrifice oneself for the sake of others thus derives, in secular ethics, from a person's right to do with himself as he chooses. By permitting altruistic self-sacrifice, ethicists (and common morality) are respecting human individuality and autonomy.

Unfortunately, this answer is rough and simplistic. In the first place, the principle of autonomy needs to be qualified and restricted. Ordinary morality sets bounds on autonomy — as, for instance, when it interdicts a suicide committed for frivolous reasons. To understand fully the prevailing common sense perspective on self-sacrifice we would need to itemize the circumstances under which a person does and does not enjoy autonomy. But suppose that we could articulate an autonomy principle in its full form, specifying all the circumstances in which self-sacrifice is permitted. Invoking autonomy, I submit, is still not enough to explain common attitudes toward self-sacrifice.

Invoking autonomy explains why self-sacrifice is *permitted* even when sacrifice of others would not be permitted. But there is another fact about common sense morality that must be explained besides the "permissibility" of self-sacrifice. That is the fact that this particular choice is commonly viewed as higher, as especially noble, as supererogatory. Why is this? After all, whether X gives up his life for Y or he doesn't, X is exercising his autonomy. Either way, one person lives and one dies. So the two choices seem equally permissible and equally correct on that score. And we cannot argue that altruistic self-sacrifice better conforms to moral principles than does refusal to surrender oneself. On the contrary, we have seen that such acts might *run counter* to moral principles (specifically, counter to deontological restrictions), whereas refusal to sacrifice oneself will, in those cases, *fit* moral principles. Why, then, is altruistic self-sacrifice looked at as a better or higher choice than its opposite? What transforms it from a neutral option to a preferable one?

I believe that this question must be answered in two parts, corresponding to two very different contexts in which a person might sacrifice himself for others. First, consider the case in which one kills oneself to save five other people. Here it can be argued that since (1) beneficence is a principle of ethics (i.e., one has a duty to promote human welfare), (2) one must be impartial in calculating "welfare," and five lives are "impartially considered" more valuable than one, therefore, the only possible restraint on killing one to save five would be that killing is an inherently wrong act. But once we allow people the autonomy to do away with themselves in these cases, that act is permissible; and, once it is permissible, we can also say it is higher because it promotes human welfare. To take another example, suppose that Y has brought X great benefits in the past, so that X feels deep gratitude to Y and gives this gratitude expression by saving Y at the cost of his own life. Here, by saving Y, X would be implementing a moral principle ("repay debts of gratitude"), so his act is regarded as higher. Likewise, Y may be a person of special standing, a parent of X, for example; X may wish to favor Y because he senses a filial obligation. Once again, X's sacrificial act can be justified by reference to a moral principle. To be sure, this other principle, however we formulate it, would not allow a third party, Z, to kill X in order to save Y if X doesn't *want* to be killed; but, to repeat the point yet again, once we include a principle of autonomy in our moral system, X's choice to give himself up removes the objection that one person is being killed to save another, and X's decision may then be justified by reference to other moral principles (beneficence, gratitude, etc.).

We may call such acts of altruism *calculated*. Calculated altruistic self-sacrifice is self-sacrifice that is motivated by a desire to promote good social consequences or else to recognize something special about the other person. In these cases self-sacrifice is higher than self-preservation because the act of self-sacrifice conforms to other moral principles and fulfills other moral duties, while the usual "deontological" constraints on such acts are removed by the agent's exercise of his autonomy.[13]

However, altruistic self-sacrifice may sometimes be *blind*, rather than calculated. And acts of this type pose a greater problem. Blind altruistic self-sacrifice is based neither on considerations of social consequences, nor on any special standing of the potential beneficiary (e.g., merit, or relationship to benefactor). Suppose X gives himself up for Y where it is clear that Y is no more valuable to society or meritorious than X, i.e., where there is no special calculation that makes Y's life more valuable than X's, and no special moral principle that would ground the self-sacrifice. Is even a blind act of altruistic self-sacrifice regarded as higher than an act of self-preservation would be in the same circumstances? Apparently so. Slote, for example, makes reference to cases in which a person opts "to sacrifice or remain indifferent to one's own pain or harm or failures even when this leads to less good results over all."[14] For example, X might endure a significant harm or loss to himself in order to bring about a modest benefit for someone else. In cases like this, the overall human good, the sum total of human welfare impartially considered, is diminished; and still common sense morality regards the sacrificial act as higher. Surely we often praise sacrificial acts of rescue without having collateral information about the identities of rescuers and the persons being saved. In fact, if two adults risk their lives to save a drowning old man who has outlived his usefulness to society, common sense morality will praise their efforts as higher even if the two lives seem prima facie more valuable than the one they try to save. The question is why this is so, and whether the reflex-like approbation of blind self-sacrifice is correct — or instead reflects confused moral thinking.

III

In approaching this question, I introduce a now widely current distinction: that between evaluating *acts* and evaluating the *agents* who perform them.[15] Perhaps when common sense morality praises altruism, it is not really basing this praise, in the first instance, on the act. Rather, it is praising, in the first instance, the character or motivation of the *agents* who perform such acts. This appraisal, however, in turn affects the way adherents of common sense morality assess the act, creating a "halo" around the act that is altogether unrelated to the principles normally used to evaluate acts. Let me elaborate on this hypothesis.

It is natural to assume that, if you think a certain action is right, then you also think well of the person who performs it (assuming, at least, that you trust he acted out of a sense of rightness); and similarly it is tempting to assume that, if you think a certain action is wrong, you think ill of the person who performs it. But, in truth, judgments about actions and judgments about agents do not coincide this neatly. Suppose you are a strong advocate of capital punishment on the grounds that it deters crime or that it restores a moral balance to the world. Does that necessarily imply that you think well of the character of a person who volunteers to perform an execution? Again, a group of Jews hiding in a World War II bunker might know of a *posek's* opinion that one may suffocate a baby to save the lives of the group by preventing its telltale cries;[16] but the person who actually volunteers to perform this act of *"hatzalat rabbim"* (saving the many), even if motivated by the fact that it is *hatzalat rabbim,* might be suspected of callousness. In the Midrash, R. Joshua ben Levi is chastised by Elijah for persuading a fugitive to give himself up to the Romans so as to prevent reprisals for the community. When R. Joshua protests to Elijah that the act was in accordance with an explicit teaching, Elijah informs him that he should have had someone else do it.[17] Elijah might be saying that a right action, even when motivated by a commitment to do the right, may reflect ill on its doer.[18] King Saul acted wrongly in sparing the animals of the Amalekites (I Samuel, ch. 15), and his doing so certainly reflects poorly on his credentials as a king. But if he spared them out of compassion, that would not necessarily reflect poorly on Saul as a person.[19] Sometimes a person does a right act (e.g., a justified act of violence) but reveals thereby a defect of personality; and sometimes a person does something wrong (refraining from violence when violence is called for) but reveals thereby a good trait of character. Some right acts may be such that no good person would ever perform them; some wrong acts may be such that no bad person would ever perform them. Judgments about actions do not fit hand in glove with judgments about character.

One reason that judgments about actions and judgments about character may be separated has to do with a basic principle about virtue: "Virtues cannot be too finely discriminating."[20] Psychological realities set limits to the repertoire of virtuous agents. If a person is able to bring himself to perform a cruel but justified act — as in the example of the man who volunteers to be an executioner — it reflects poorly on his psychological makeup. A person endowed with compassion, a trait which unquestionably leads to right or permissible actions in one context, may not be able, for psychological reasons, to prevent that trait from manifesting itself in other contexts in which it leads to wrong action. Compassion and kindness cannot be turned on and off to suit moral niceties concerning merit or social consequences.[21]

Equipped with this distinction between judgments about actions and judgments about character, let us return to our question: why does common sense morality praise blind altruistic self-sacrifice, if blind altruistic self-sacrifice does not fit moral principles any better than self-preservation would in the same context, and even goes against the imperative, "promote overall human welfare" generally used in evaluating putative acts of beneficence? The answer I propose is that there is *no* way to explain why the altruistic *act* is higher; indeed, acts of blind altruism are at best, permissible, and if not for our respecting autonomy, they would be *wrong*. Nevertheless, X's act reflects, or at least may reflect, a generous, compassionate, giving and courageous spirit or character. Whereas this sort of character normally promotes the good, impartially considered, and normally produces right acts, it has failed to respond to nuances and complexities which make the altruistic deed contrary to principles of act evaluation in *this* set of circumstances. Because X has a good character, his knowledge that his act detracts from "the good impartially considered" does not help X overcome the psychological difficulties of seeing his friends suffer when he could prevent it. So he acts altruistically. To say that X has done the right thing, or the best thing, here would be to conflate two issues, the evaluation of the act and the evaluation of X's character.

Heroic actions are not *invariably right* just because they are heroic:

We admire the qualities that enable the person who dives in midwinter into the Potomac in an effort to save the victims of a plane crash. And we are grateful that people with such qualities (courage, willingness to risk one's life to help others, etc.) exist. The fact that we (correctly) admire and appreciate such people is, however, no reason for thinking that their heroic actions are inevitably right. Suppose (imagining a different case from the actual one in the Potomac) that the would-be rescuer is almost certain to drown, as well as not to save anyone. ... As Kant points out, the mere fact that an act is self-sacrificial and admirable does not entail that it is good to do, that one ought ideally to do it. ... We need, in short, to disentangle the admirable from the right.[22]

As the author's guarded language in this passage might suggest, it is awkward to call heroic acts *wrong* — even when they are blind to consequences or other factors. But there are also no good grounds for calling them right. Nevertheless, in cases like the one described, common sense morality displays the halo effect; it prizes the acts produced by admirable traits, and calls them "right" or "supererogatory." We do not do this consistently, of course: we don't justify the mass suicide of a cult's members as higher just because these people display the "admirable" trait of devotion or courage. But altruistic acts are so closely connected to traits that lie at the heart of morality — sympathy, compassion, benevolence — that they are endowed with a halo.

To see even more clearly why the *trait* of altruism (as distinct from altruistic acts) is indeed admirable and higher than the alternatives, bear in mind that one who does the "really" right thing in these "blind" cases — i.e., who does not subject oneself to pain, or who does not take his own life for the sake of the other — deserves no special credit for having *refrained* from acting altruistically. Given a natural human aversion to pain and a natural human disposition toward self-preservation, the path which should be, in this case, morally prescribed or at least permitted (viz., refraining) would be too convenient and easy. A person would deserve no moral credit for following it. As Kant noted, a person has a duty to preserve his own life; yet acts of self-preservation, he argues, have no moral worth unless they are performed in a special context, as, for instance, a struggle against despondency and impulses to self-destruction.[23] Virtue is tested best in circumstances that make its exercise psychologically difficult. A person who chooses to endure pain or death to help another is so acting in circumstances that normally dispose against self-sacrifice. The depth of his compassion becomes most manifest in this context of challenge, even if his decision to act altruistically is, at best, neutral when we assess the act itself.

I would not suggest that *all* altruistic acts are expressions or results of an antecedently formed virtuous character. As Aaron Kirschenbaum points out on the basis of studies conducted by psychiatrists concerning kidney donors, an altruistic act sometimes "engenders and nurtures saintliness" (what I call "virtue") rather than "reflects and evidences it."[24] Nor should we deny that sometimes altruistic self-sacrifice reflects nothing more than a noble feeling of compassion which the agent happened to develop in that circumstance, but which may not endure. In all cases of blind altruism, nonetheless, I would argue that praise and admiration are directed, initially, at something other than the act — usually, a character we assume the agent has, but often, a feeling the agent has. Only at a second stage does the evaluation of the agent become transferred to the act.

To sum up, cases of altruistic self-sacrifice pose two questions for moral theory. One, why are such acts permissible? Two, why are they regarded as higher? I have suggested that they are permissible only if we add a principle of autonomy to our ethical principles; if we do not, these acts are often morally wrong. Even if we do add a principle of autonomy, the act itself, in the case of blind altruism, will be no more valuable than refraining from altruism (since both acting and refraining are exercises of autonomy). Our positive evaluation of altruism in these cases is more accurately directed toward the agent's character or motive than toward the act, but there seems to be a halo effect, by which the distinction between act and agent, which ought to be conceptually firm, is instead collapsed.

Perhaps we can best summarize why blind altruism is lauded in general ethics by saying as follows: ordinary morality applauds the *autonomous expression of virtue.*

But now, having recognized this, we can speculate that even the praise lavished on "calculated" altruism is a reaction more to agents than to acts. For, as an empirical matter, even altruistic acts which *could* be justified by calculation are not always, maybe not even typically, the product of moral principles and impartial calculations. Rather, they are the product of spontaneous thought, emotion and action. Empirical studies of rescue efforts during the Holocaust underscore this independence, or potential independence, of altruistic motivation from moral principle. This is not to say that no rescuers acted on moral principles, and most assuredly I do not classify all Holocaust rescue efforts as "blindly" altruistic acts. In a sense, though, many were blind *from the standpoint of the rescuers.* Rescuers had a strong perception of themselves as part of common humanity, and acted *spontaneously* on this perception, as distinct from calculatively. Some selections from a recent study make the point forcefully:

> [The rescuers] apparently made little or no conscious decision [except for arranging logistics]. ... There was no conscious choice for them to make in the traditional sense of assessing options and

choosing the best one...They simply saw no other option available to them...Certain behaviors arise spontaneously, resulting from deep-seated dispositions which form one's central identity. ... The concept of a cost/benefit calculus became meaningless. ... We still find it difficult to disentangle the complex relations between identity (which delineates choices nonconsciously) and simple conscious and perhaps volitional adherence to particular moral values.[25]

I would add that, even when a rescuer acts on moral principles, those principles may not be identical with the moral principles of "ordinary" ethics as philosophers formulate them.

We may take our analysis still a step further. I have already suggested that both blind and calculated altruistic acts are praised because of the agent; and the agents are praised not for implementing moral principles but for being people of a certain sort or having motives of a particular kind. But why not now extend this diagnosis? Suppose we return to our original question: why are sacrificial acts "permissible" in common sense morality if they defy deontological restrictions? Our earlier answer was that common sense morality endorses a principle of autonomy. But now we have another answer available: common sense morality is at least in some measure an *ethics of virtue*, or an *agent-morality*. That is to say, sometimes we will have acts that go against our usual principles of act-evaluation, but will *ignore* the fact these principles are being violated because we are so admiring of the agent. The halo effect, not the autonomy principle, is what accounts *both* for the *permissibility* of self-sacrifice *and* for its being regarded as a higher act. What lends cogency to this interpretation is that the bare formula, "people can sacrifice themselves for altruistic purposes because they have the autonomy to do so" is a vacuous, tautological claim, *à la* Moliere's classic "opium puts people to sleep because it has dormative powers." To say that a person has the autonomy to act contrary to principles of act evaluation is just to *restate* the fact that he is permitted to act against these principles, not to explain it. Hence, linking the "permission" to evaluations of the agent is more informative and more plausible than explaining the permission by means of an autonomy principle alone.

However wide-ranging the halo effect — whether it accounts only for the laudatoriness of blind altruism, or also for the laudatoriness of calculated altruism, or even for the very permissibility of both types of self-sacrifice — in my opinion, there is nothing particularly compelling about halos. On the contrary, the halo effect blurs a distinction that ought to be observed: the distinction between acts and agents. Be that as it may, however, our discussion of secular views on self-sacrifice — which focused on the role of human autonomy in accounting for sacrificial prerogatives, the distinction between blind and calculated altruism, and the distinction between virtuous character (or good feeling) and right action — provides a useful framework within which we may now identify key issues that rabbinic decisors confront when they reason about altruistic self-sacrifice.

IV

Halakhic questions about altruistic self-sacrifice can be raised in many ways and in many contexts. The most important and widely discussed of these are (1) altruistic surrender of precious life-sustaining resources (as in the flask example in *Bava Metzi'a* 62a) and (2) altruistic assumption of risk in such contexts as dangerous rescue missions and organ transplants. Questions also arise about such matters as whether and when one may waive a right to self-defense, and whether and when a person may voluntarily give himself over to terrorists or hostile governments to save the lives of the others in his group.

In the rest of this essay, however, I would like to sketch the bearing of our inquiry into topics (1) and (2) upon philosophical questions about the nature and basis of Jewish ethics as contrasted with other ethical systems. In particular, a very popular and otherwise worthy approach to Jewish ethics needs to be reexamined in light of our analysis of altruism.

It is often said that Jewish ethics is an ethics of virtue and not simply an ethics of action.[26] Evidence for this contention is not hard to assemble. Nahmanides and other Jewish thinkers stress that a telos or goal of *mitzvot* is the development of good *"middot,"* and that certain obligations in Halakhah (e.g., those toward animals) boast no rationale other than to prevent the formation of bad traits and facilitate the development of good ones.[27] In his *Hilkhot Teshuvah,* Maimonides writes that one must repent not only for wrong acts he has performed but also for bad traits of character such as jealousy and acquisitiveness — a passage which, Rabbi Joseph B. Soloveitchik suggests, indicates that transformation of character is a more essential, loftier sort of *teshuvah* than repentance over individual acts.[28] Again, Maimonides states that a person who carries out his interpersonal obligations solely out of a sense of duty ranks lower than the man of virtue — one who is naturally disposed against harming others (*hasid*).[29] According to many authorities the command to emulate God (*imitatio Dei*) is to be explained as a command to develop good character.[30] This imperative to form good character is even thought by some authorities to bear concrete halakhic implications.[31] To continue this catalogue of examples, the notions of a *middat hasidut* or of an act done *lifnim mi-shurat ha-din* — indeed the whole range of supererogatory acts — may be understood as acts which either evince good character, reflect an *aspiration* to good character, or *produce* good character. At the other end of the spectrum, a person who deprives others of benefits by abusing his legal rights manifests a "Sodom-like trait," and the law coerces him not to exercise those rights. According to one explanation, this coercion is for the sake of reforming the bad trait — thereby "helping" the *coerced individual* — rather than for the sake of helping the potential beneficiary.[32] In sum, in Judaism, "moral virtue is not reducible to the disposition to obey rules."[33] The whole of Jewish moralistic literature, spanning classics like Maimonides' *Hilkhot De'ot* and the writings of R. Yisrael Salanter, stands as vivid testimony to Judaism's concern with the inner person and not merely his external acts, with what we ought to *be* and not simply what we ought to *do*.

Yet the real test of how deep Judaism's commitment to virtue runs is not whether it speaks of virtue frequently or encourages people to develop virtue. It is whether, when push comes to shove, and the system must deal with intuitively virtuous acts that are problematic in terms of the system's basic principles for evaluating acts, it is prepared to, first, recognize the virtue and, second, create a halo around these acts. Here a contrast to Christianity is instructive. When Thomas Aquinas confronted the question of whether one may sacrifice his life for others, he took the answer to be obvious: "the highest charity" (a "virtue") is manifested in the act, hence it may be done and is worthy of praise.[34] Aquinas is beginning from a position that assesses acts from the perspective of virtue. He took it for granted that altruism ("charity") is a virtue (which it clearly is), and then derived specific obligations from that virtue — without testing the result against principles of act-evaluation or setting limits to the expression of the virtue. But in Judaism, the notion of virtue has a less secure place. Despite all the evidence we assembled for the importance of virtue and character, Judaism might have no room for permitting a given "admirable" act on the basis of jurisprudential principles. In these circumstances, one might either (1) deny that the act manifests virtue, because virtues must be defined by what is halakhically correct; or else (2) insist that whatever standard of virtue Judaism recognizes besides this one is impotent when it comes into clash with a jurisprudential principle. In other words, the test of how strongly Judaism endorses virtue ethics is whether it acknowledges that an act can be virtuous or noble without being right, or whether it instead allows the creation of halos around jurisprudentially problematic acts that issue from noble motives and good character traits.

V

I would argue that, on approaches that prohibit altruistic self-sacrifice, Judaism is not, in a real, ultimate sense, an ethics of virtue. The legalistic, imperatival character of Judaism creates within it a more explicit and comprehensive mandate to save others than one finds in general ethics. But that very same legalistic, imperatival character also stands in the way of allowing that duty to find unlimited expression. Let me explain, in broad strokes just *how* jurisprudential principles stand in the way.

1. Without my denying the range and complexity of cases and opinions that need to be considered, suffice it to say that the limits *posekim* place on voluntary self-sacrifice (*when* they place limits) issue from jurisprudential principles that run deeply through Halakhah in its treatment of life-for-life scenarios. Consider the case of the "two who are travelling and one has in his possession a flask of water," in which R. Akiva issued his ruling that "your life takes precedence." Contrary to what one would surmise from popular writings, authorities in the main assert that R. Akiva is not expressing a principle of *partiality* toward the self, but rather a principle of *impartiality.* According to one analysis, his ruling implements a "principle of least change." This principle dictates that, when faced with a choice between saving X and saving Y, we should try to save one of them; but we are to choose *whom* to save on the basis of what action will introduce the least change into the *status quo.* If I own the flask, handing it to you would introduce a greater change into the *status quo* than taking it for myself. Hence I am the one to drink. The least change principle yields an objective, impartial determination of who drinks from the flask.[35] And so it is easy to trace a path from the least change principle to a *ban* on altruistic self-sacrifice.[36] Notions of least change or else other foundational jurisprudential principles may provide a rationale for a rule prevalent among halakhists today: that one must not undertake a rescue mission or undergo a hazardous operation to save another if one is thereby incurring a likelihood of death.[37]

Why adopt a least change principle? One explanation — a possibility — proceeds by embedding the principle in a theological framework. Ordinarily, we are required to do our utmost to save others, as in the case of medical care. Halakhah does not ordinarily say that aiding others interferes with God's will. But in dire situations, when someone will die no matter what, we look at matters in terms of God's providential control. He, in this construct, has decreed that one person is without water and will die from thirst. Once God has thus decreed the fate of humans, how can "autonomy" find any home? To transfer the flask would be to defy God's decree. This account of R. Akiva's position would explain why secular theorists will not share his hostility to transfer of the flask: anyone not committed to belief in providence has no cause to accept a least change principle in the strong version just enunciated.

Insofar as considerations of autonomy or virtue would have to counteract the principle of least change if they are to result in a permissible and laudatory act of self-sacrifice, it is not likely they will bear the burden demanded of them. Again, this is not to deny that other accounts of R. Akiva's ruling might not result in a prohibition against self-sacrificial surrender of the flask. (As noted earlier, some *posekim* permit such a transfer.) It is, rather, to emphasize how one plausible account of the ruling, the account in terms of least change, negates the force of any considerations pertaining to autonomy and virtue by providing an impartial method for allocating the resource.

2. In some situations of altruistic risk-taking, Jewish law is committed to a *limited* version of an autonomy principle. Specifically, some *posekim* have devised a three-tiered approach to risk-taking. The tiers are: minimal risk, which *must* be undertaken in rescue situations; moderate risk, which *may* be undertaken as an act of *hasidut*; and significant risk which *must not* be undertaken, on pain of being deemed a "pious fool."[38] Let us consider the middle level, where self-sacrifice is permissible and praiseworthy. One must not be *forced* into an act of rescue that carries this degree of risk; yet one may volunteer to do such an act as a *middat hasidut*. What this suggests is a *type* of autonomy, which we may define as follows: *the agent's choice matters* (or "consent matters"). That is, the agent's choice allows him to assume a level of risk (for the purpose of rescuing others) that he may not push others into assuming in order to save himself — and that others may not impose on *him* to save themselves. This is one area in which Judaism believes in autonomy, and conceivably — though this is highly speculative — it grants autonomy in this sphere because it recognizes the virtue of self-sacrifice in these circumstances.

Yet we must keep all this in perspective. For still and all, this autonomy or expression of virtue is limited to rescue situations in which the risk falls below the "significance" line. It has no relevance when the rescuer is himself courting disaster — even, apparently, when the rescue is almost certain to succeed regardless of whether the rescuer lives or dies in the process. Here again, Jewish law places limits on the expression of virtue, this time in the form of the "significant risk" rule.[39]

3. Let us return now to R. Akiva's ruling in the flask example. As we noted earlier, some authorities do permit transfer of the flask. At first glance, it may seem that these *posekim* are affirming autonomy or permitting the expression of virtue over against jurisprudential principles. However, this conclusion is too hasty. In the first place, the permissive positions may not

analyze R. Akiva's ruling in terms of the least change principle and there-fore, on their interpretation of R. Akiva, there may be no jurisprudential obstacle to the owner transferring the flask if he desires to do so. Moreover, even the *permissive* positions on altruistic self-sacrifice in the flask example are not necessarily grounded in a particularly sharp version of the autonomy principle.

To see this point, let us consider the permissive position developed by R. Kook. A good way to understand R. Kook's approach is to introduce a famous ruling in the Mishnah, *Horayot* 3:7-8:

> A man takes priority over a woman when it comes to saving a life and restoring a lost object. A woman takes priority when it comes to being provided with clothes and redeemed from captivity. If both stand an equal chance of being degraded, the man has priority over the woman.
> A *kohen* takes priority over a *levi*, a *levi* over a *yisrael*, a *yisrael* over a *mamzer*, a *mamzer* over a *netin*(a descendant of a certain Canaanite group that converted to Judaism), a *netin* over a *ger* (convert), a *ger* over a freed slave. When [does this apply]? When all are equal. But in the case of a *mamzer* who is a *talmid hakham* (Torah scholar) and a High Priest who is an ignoramus, the *mamzer* who is a *talmid hakham* takes priority.

Essentially, R. Kook's view is that altruistic surrender of the canteen is permitted, and constitutes *hasidut*, only when it is *calculated*, not when it is blind. The possessor's preference for the life of the other must be justified in terms of an acceptable system of priorities.[40] The system set down in *Horayot*, which is often utilized to establish a hierarchy for redeeming captives as well as for a third party's choosing which of two endangered people to save from, say, drowning (when the risk to the third party is low), is one such acceptable system of priorities.[41] Thus, an *am ha-aretz* could voluntarily surrender his flask to save a *talmid hakham*, but not the other way around. Rav Kook considers — indeed, he highlights this more prominently than the *Horayot* scale — the possibility that an individual may also surrender himself for the sake of the *rabbim*. ("*Rabbim*" can mean, simply, a larger group of people, or can mean "the Jewish collective." We need not examine this question here.) For Rav Kook, then, the possessor of the flask has the prerogative to transfer the flask on a *calculated* basis, but not a *blind* basis.

It is crucial to see that, for R. Kook, scales such as the one in *Horayot* or the "*yahid* vs. *rabbim*" criterion represent perfectly appropriate ways to adjudicate cases in which two people need a resource and one owns it. Contrary to R. Feinstein, Rav Kook believes that such scales apply not only when Z, a third party, is choosing whether to save X or save Y; they also

341

apply, according to Rav Kook, when X owns a resource and must choose whether to save *himself or* save Y. If so, why isn't the owner of the flask *required* to hand it over when his comrade ranks higher than he does on the *Horayot* scale? The reason, says Rav Kook, is that we never take life, or force the possessor of a resource to surrender his life, merely on the basis of our estimate of the relative values of lives.[42] In other words, we would resolve the flask example using the *Horayot* scale or the *"yahid/rabbim"* criterion were it not for the fact that we lack the possessor's consent to do so. We cannot force our application of the scale upon him, against his will. However, once the possessor consents to transfer the flask based on *his own* determination that his comrade ranks higher on the scale of priorities than he does, we follow his calculation. For, by permitting him to follow his calculation, all we are doing is letting him apply a correct principle for choosing whom to save.

Once we understand the structure of Rav Kook's reasoning, we realize that what is central to it is *not* the idea that the possessor of a resource such as the flask has the autonomy to *part with* the resource on the basis of a calculation that "the life of the other is more precious than his own." Rather, what is central is the idea that, even when transferring the flask would make sense in terms of the *Horayot* or *yahid/rabbim* criteria, the owner of the flask has the prerogative *not* to transfer it. Suppose the owner is an ignoramus, his comrade a sage. The owner has the autonomy to *preserve* his life by not applying the *Horayot* criteria. If he elects not to exercise this prerogative, he is then merely applying the normal rule, viz., that one should follow the scale of priorities. Thus, the prerogative of the possessor, in Rav Kook's reasoning, is not so much a *self-sacrificial* prerogative as a *self-protective* prerogative. The *sacrificer's* act is, in a clear sense, correct, since it conforms to the proper system of priorities. And it is a higher choice because ultimately it is the *correct* thing to do; the only reason it is not mandated is that we do not implement our humanly-generated *umdana* (assessment) to force surrender of life. Thus, when R. Kook permits transfer of the flask by an *am ha-aretz* to a *talmid hakham*, he is not introducing a principle of autonomy or virtue that overrides the normal criteria for choosing whom to save. On the contrary, the operating principles of the system — the *Horayot* criteria — remain intact. *Mutatis mutandis*, the same is true when a *yahid* elects to surrender himself for the sake of the *rabbim*, a choice not addressed in *Horayot*.

A similar approach, I think, might be invoked to address another issue — the status of calculated altruism in rescue efforts. Is the permissibility/obligatoriness of a rescue mission affected by the *Horayot* scale? Is it affected by the numbers of people involved? R. Eliezer Waldenberg asks the following: although in general, dangerous transplants are not permitted, might they be permitted when the recipient is a Torah scholar and the donor is not? The case for permissibility is "easier," he says, if the "*rabbim*" are in need of the scholar. Here again, the point R. Kook might have urged — though R. Waldenberg does not develop his argument this way — is that it is not the permission to *act,* i.e., to submit to a transplant, which expresses autonomy, but rather the permission *not* to act on the basis of a defensible system of priorities.[43]

There is another ground for denying that R. Kook and R. Waldenberg are invoking a standard notion of virtue when they permit altruistic self-sacrifice. As we noted earlier, those who have sought to explicate the notion of *middat hasidut* or supererogation generally, have tended to view such acts as a course open only to the spiritual elite. Sages or otherwise special individuals are the ones who should act so as to exemplify *hasidut;* others should refrain lest they exude arrogance. Acts of *hasidut* must cohere with other traits of personality; they must not go along with ignorance or depravity. Such, at least, is the impression one gleans from other contexts in which we encounter a standard of *hasidut.*[44] A picture along these lines tends to wed supererogation to overall character and to see supererogatory acts as natural outgrowths of an agent's character.

I agree that there is a general connection in Judaism between supererogation and character. But a *middat hasidut* in the case of altruistic self-sacrifice behaves, as it were, differently. Think of R. Kook's and R. Waldenberg's qualified approval of calculated altruism (the one for the flask case, the other for transplants). According to R. Kook, could a sage turn the flask over to an *am ha-aretz?* No, because that would violate the *Horayot* system of priorities. Could the *am ha-aretz* turn the flask over to a *talmid hakham?* Of course; that would be an act of *hasidut.* Next, according to R. Waldenberg, could a sage undergo a risky transplant to save an *am ha-aretz?* No. Could the *am ha-aretz* undergo a risky transplant to save a *talmid hakham?* R. Waldenberg implies that in theory this might be allowed. But these consequences create an anomaly: the sage, because he is a sage, cannot perform acts of *hasidut* in these contexts; the *am ha-aretz,* because he is an *am ha-aretz,* may perform such acts and is lauded as a *hasid* for doing so.[45] This approach hardly represents supererogatory self-sacrifice as connected to considerations of the agent's *overall* virtue or character. Hence, it is illegitimate to compare the acts of *hasidut* which are allowed by those views which license altruistic self-sacrifice only on a "calculated" basis, to acts of *hasidut* as they arise in other contexts. The respective notions of "*hasidut*" at work are significantly different.

My discussion of halakhic approaches to altruistic self-sacrifice has been far from exhaustive. I reiterate that not all views prohibit altruistic self-sacrifice, and not all that do will fit the picture I have been sketching. Nevertheless, we can safely state the following. Whether ruling stringently or ruling permissively, authorities tend to arrive at decisions about altruistic self-sacrifice by applying general principles for the protection of life. With the possible exception of the permission to undertake a "middle-level" risk to save another, autonomy and agent-based considerations play little role. What this means, I submit, is that according to those who prohibit altruistic self-sacrifice, Judaism is not, in this regard, an agent-morality; it is an act-morality. Halo effects do not operate.

VI

In closing, I should like to address briefly a few precedents that seem to support the opposite perspective: that there *are* "halo effects" in Halakhah. In my opinion, these precedents are too slender to damage my overall claims, but they are suggestive and deserve to be examined further.

Some relevant materials for treating the tension between judgments about agents and judgments about acts have already been noted. R. Joshua ben Levi, recall, was thought ill of by Elijah for turning over a fugitive, even though this was consonant with the law and constituted an act of *hatzalah* for the larger community. He should have let others carry out the law. Elijah chides him in one variant of the story; the teaching R. Joshua cited, Elijah said, was not a "teaching for the pious" (*mishnat hasidim*). Elijah implies that refraining from carrying out the ruling would here have spoken well of R. Joshua. Arguably, some notion of virtue is entering into the picture, overriding the halakhic principles that make it proper to turn the fugitive over. Someone else should turn him over — not R. Joshua.

The text, then, is suggestive of an ethic of virtue. However, it is open to other interpretations as well. For example, perhaps a leader like R. Joshua would be inspiring acts of exploitation and terror if he showed a readiness to cooperate with the authorities in the case at hand, and that is why someone else should have done it.[46] Also, until we know precisely why the law dictated that the fugitive should be handed over, we cannot assess how dissonant R. Joshua's refraining would have been with jurisprudential principles.

Another text that might call to mind the agent/act distinction is R. Shimon Efrati's responsum regarding suffocating a baby to keep the hiding place of the Jews secret from the Nazis.[47] In one line of reasoning the *posek* adduces for his *hetter* (leniency), the baby might be like a *rodef* (pursuer) and hence may be killed. But isn't it a *mitzvah* "not to have pity for the life of a *rodef*"? If so, what of those who refrained from suffocating the child?

Did they not violate this command? R. Efrati replied that, insofar as this particular *rodef* or quasi-*rodef* (the baby) is not pursuing *intentionally*, those who refrain from killing it have "sanctified the name of heaven." It may be said that, in this case, although killing is the right *act*, refraining, in this case, reflects better *character* (although R. Efrati does not use this framework).[48]

One commentator who seems acutely aware of the act/agent distinction is R. Naftali Tzvi Yehudah Berlin (Netziv). However, he is concerned with the effects of cruel but justified actions (e.g., destroying the *ir ha-nidahat*) on *future acts* by the agent — a *post factum* problem.[49] He does not wrestle with the *ante factum* problem: whether an agent may perform an act of compassion that is contrary to jurisprudential principles because he finds that implementing the halakhah, which calls for harsh action, goes against his grain.

A better known candidate for illustrating halo effects is afforded by instances of Jewish martyrdom, or *kiddush Hashem*. During the Middle Ages, Jews frequently committed suicide in circumstances under which such acts would have appeared to be halakhically proscribed. In fact, medieval Jews killed their children and spouses to prevent apostasy and forced baptism, a step that seemed devoid of halakhic license. Notwithstanding, those who died or killed in these settings were thought of by Ashkenazic authorities as "*kedoshim.*" In a famous responsum, Maharam of Rothenburg dealt with the question of whether atonement is necessary for a man who had killed his wife and children with their consent in order to prevent their being forcibly converted. He acknowledges the difficulty of justifying the act halakhically, but notes that "many great rabbis" had slaughtered their children. Maharam then proceeds to construct an original and striking halakhic justification for the practice, and adds this comment: "Anyone who requires atonement for this is besmirching the name of the pious of old." This man's intentions, he continues, were for good; he killed his loved ones "out of great love for our maker."[50]

Maharam and other authorities, it has been said, were influenced by the hard reality and widespread nature of the problematic killings. A practice so prevalent and familiar could not be illicit; hence the acts, they presumed, must be in consonance with Halakhah. But in our context another possibility must be raised. Might it be that, in addition to being influenced by the widespread character of the killings, authorities sensed that these acts sprang from what intuitively were pious and noble motives, and so halakhic justifications that they constructed were in part (albeit only in part) attempts to align their assessments of the acts with their assessments of the agents? After all, did Maharam really suppose that whatever slender halakhic arguments could be given on behalf of the *kedoshim* after the fact are arguments that they consciously ran through in their minds before taking action? Or did he find that there was, instead, a virtue manifested by their action, albeit not the virtue of trying to conform to halakhic prescriptions? From the perspective of the protagonists, the acts were acts of "blind" martyrdom; but the virtue, the profound love of God which these "blind" acts so plainly revealed, and not just the reality and widespread nature of the killings, provides some rationale for the quest for halakhic warrant. Thus, while Maharam sought to provide *some* halakhic argument to defend the killings, and hence was not *merely* placing a halo around the acts, his responsum may signify more than a routine attempt to rationalize a practice simply because it is prevalent.

All these putative examples of "halo effects" are, in any case, isolated, and they hardly lay the firm foundation one needs to establish halo effects as a general phenomenon in Halakhah.[51] What shall we say, though, in conclusion, about the case of altruistic self-sacrifice? Is there a halo effect here?

One of the few Jewish thinkers to evince sensitivity to the conflicting pulls of virtue and action in this topic is Shubert Spero. His view is this:

> It does not seem to me [Spero is here arguing contrary to Louis Jacobs] "that a man who gives his life for his friend is a saint and would be recognized as such by Judaism." I would think, however, that the rare instances of heroic acts where an individual is carried aloft by a love for God and for Israel personified by his fellow man, and sacrifices his own life to save the other must be classified as an *averah lishmah* – "sin for the sake of God" [*Nazir* 23a]. Normative Jewish morality cannot approve of it. Yet we cannot help but stand back in admiration and wonder at such great love and devotion. It is a case of the splendor of the sentiment eclipsing the logic and bursting through the confines of the system.[52]

Spero even quotes an opinion that R. Akiva himself would not have followed his own ruling in a real-life situation.[53]

It seems to me that, if we follow the stringent rulings, then Spero's analysis is right on target. The virtue is recognized. The person is admired. But the norm remains unaffected. There is no halo.

Spero's remarks are a welcome corrective to anyone who treats practical questions about self-sacrifice as if they were questions about pots and spoons. Altruistic impulses have deep wellsprings in human beings, and the powerful emotional drive in such impulses needs to be understood and engaged. But at the bottom line Jewish law will not budge easily from its commitment to jurisprudential principles. There are few halo effects; more, the very notion that altruistic self-sacrifice might constitute *hasidut* even if the act is wrong is not commonly encountered in halakhic sources, though it does exist, as Spero suggests. If, in secular thought, acts of altruistic self-sacrifice are the stuff of moral heroism, in Jewish thought such acts, given certain halakhic opinions, might be regarded as the stuff of moral tragedy. I mean the tragedy of one who finds that the legal system and theological framework for which he stands prepared, if called for, to surrender his life, leaves little room for him to make that surrender for his fellow, and expects him instead to conquer powerful, spontaneous feelings of sympathy and comradeship. Logic and sentiment could not conflict much more sharply. But at least in one school of thought, in Judaism the logic prevails.

NOTES

I am indebted to David Berger, Shalom Carmy, Charles Raffel, and Jacob J. Schacter for their valuable comments and suggestions.

1   See, for example, Kurt Baier, *The Moral Point of View* (Ithaca, NY, 1961); Thomas Nagel, *The Possibility of Altruism* (Oxford, 1970); G. J. Warnock, *The Object of Morality* (London, 1976); and the essays in David Gauthier (ed.), *Morality and Rational Self-Interest* (Englewood Cliffs, NJ, 1970). To be sure, many philosophers (Hobbes, for example) maintain that morality converges with rational self-interest.

2   This viewpoint may well be influenced by Christianity. When Thomas Aquinas confronted the question of whether one may sacrifice his life for others, he declared that, while not obligatory, "Freely to offer oneself...is an act of the highest charity." See *Summa Theologiae*, trans. R. J. Batten (Cambridge, England, 1975), II:2, question 26, article 5, p. 131. Note also the famous Christian view: "Greater love has no man than to offer his life for his friends" (John 15:13).

3   See especially J. O. Urmson, "Saints and Heroes," in *Moral Concepts*, ed. Joel Feinberg (London, 1969), 60-73. An exception to the positive attitude toward altruistic self-sacrifice in Western thought is Kant, who actually opposes supererogatory acts. See Marcia Baron's sympathetic article, "Kantian Ethics and Supererogation," *The Journal of Philosophy* 84 (1987): 237-62. Cf. n. 12 below.

4   *Bava Metzi'a* 62a; *Sifra, Behar* 5, to Lev. 25:36.

5   Excellent English surveys of Jewish views are found in Aaron Kirschenbaum, "The 'Good Samaritan' in Jewish Law," *Dine Israel* 7 (1976): 7-85; and Basil Herring, *Jewish Ethics and Halakhah for Our Time* (New York, 1989), vol. II, chs. l, 4. See also my "Concepts of Autonomy in Jewish Medical Ethics," in this volume. In Hebrew, see, *inter alia*, Nachum Rakover, "*Hatzalat Nefashot — Hebetim Mishpatiyyim,*" *Hadarom* 50 (Nissan 5740): 242-52.

6   This is the language of R. Yehiel Yaakov Weinberg, *Yad Shaul* (memorial volume for Rabbi Dr. Shaul Weingart), ed. J. J. Weinberg and P. Bieberfeld (Tel Aviv, 1953), 393; *Seridei Esh*, vol. I, 314-15. See also the rulings of R. Kook and R. Waldenberg discussed in section V below and in "Concepts of Autonomy in Jewish Medical Ethics," in this volume.

7   There has been extensive discussion of the contrast between Judaism and Christianity, precipitated mostly by Ahad Haam's (Asher Ginzberg's) essay, "*Al Shtei ha-Se'ippim*," in *Al Parashat Derakhim* (Berlin, 1913), IV, 38-55; translated in part as "Jewish and Christian Ethics" in *Ahad Haam: Essays, Letters, and Memoirs*, ed. Leon Simon (Oxford, 1946), 127-32. Ahad Haam was criticized by Louis Jacobs for neglecting (*inter alia*) rabbinic opinions that license supererogatory self-sacrifice. The debate spilled over onto the pages of the *Jewish Chronicle* when Leon Simon and Raphael Loewe responded to Jacobs. See Jacobs, "'Greater Love Hath No Man'...The Jewish Point of View on Self-Sacrifice," *Contemporary Jewish Ethics*, ed. Menahem Kellner (New York, 1978), 175-83, and the commentary on the *Jewish Chronicle* debate by Jacob Petuchowski, "The Limits of Self-Sacrifice," in *Modern Jewish Ethics: Theory and Practice*, ed. Marvin Fox (Columbus, Ohio, 1975), 103-18. See also Ronald Green, "Jewish Ethics and Beneficence," in *Beneficence and Health Care*, ed. E. Shelp (Dordrecht, 1982), 109-25.

Another area in which Judaism limits altruism is charity: one may not expend more than one-fifth of one's funds on charity. Interestingly, according to one view in *Ketubbot* 50a, the same R. Akiva who ruled that "your life comes first" in the case of the flask of water, is the one who prevented a friend from spending more than a fifth on charity. But the charity restriction, so far as I can see, is not accounted for by the principles that explain R. Akiva's ruling in the flask case. The rationale for the ceiling on charity may be to protect society from having to support a person who donates too much to charity; or its purpose may be to promote self-reliance.

For a widely cited discussion of supererogation in Judaism, with emphasis on its relationship to a higher ethic, see Aharon Lichtenstein, "Does Jewish Tradition Recognize an Ethic Independent of Halakha?" in Fox, 52-88; reprinted in Kellner, 102-23.

8   Among significant Holocaust responsa on self-sacrifice involving Jewish rescuers are R. Ephraim Oshry, *She'elot u-Teshuvot mi-Ma'amakkim* XI:1; R. Mordekhai Yaakov Breisch, *Helkat Ya'akov* XI:143. For a discussion of these and other responsa on this topic see Irving Rosenbaum, *Holocaust and Halakhah* (New York, 1976), ch. 2. I am not here concerned with methodological difficulties pertaining to study of or reliance upon Holocaust responsa.

9   We should exclude from discussion one context in which self-sacrifice is not only permitted in Jewish law but required: halakhically sanctioned wars. By its very nature, war requires individuals to place the interests of the community before their own. "On the battlefield," writes R. Eliezer Waldenberg, "the law that...your life comes first [R. Akiva's rule] does not apply." Considerations of *pikuah nefesh* operate differently during wartime; otherwise, since war entails *pikuah nefesh*, all wars would be forbidden. See *She'elot u-Teshuvot Tzitz Eliezer* XIII: #100:10, p. 206, and R. Avraham Yitzhak Ha-Kohen Kook, *Mishpat Kohen*, #143, end. Interestingly, R. Solomon Luria (*Yam Shel Shlomoh, Bava Kamma* VIII:58) suggested that King Saul committed suicide because he was afraid that the children of Israel would try to save him if he were captured "and many would die," but did not explicitly restrict his ruling to wartime. See also Baruch Brody, "A Historical Introduction to Jewish Casuistry on Suicide and Euthanasia," in *Suicide and Euthanasia*, ed. Baruch Brody (Boston, 1989), 50. See also his discussion of war, 58-59.

10 Michael Slote, "Morality and the Self-Other Asymmetry," *The Journal of Philosophy* 81 (1984): 183. Slote is pessimistic about finding a logical explanation for the asymmetry he discusses, and I do not know whether he would agree with the approach I suggest in sections II and III below.
    The asymmetry between self and other that Slote notices is not the only one that ethics exhibits, nor is it the most widely discussed (indeed, only Slote addresses it). A person is permitted to weigh his own interests more heavily than those of others, even though an outside party will have to weigh that agent's interests *equally* with those of the others. See Samuel Scheffler, *The Rejection of Consequentialism* (Oxford, 1982), particularly chs. 1-3. Bernard Williams, "A Critique of Utilitarianism," in *Utilitarianism: For and Against*, ed. J. J. C. Smart and Bernard Williams (Cambridge, 1973), 116, discusses still another phenomenon, the agent's prerogative (or duty) not to do acts of a certain kind (e.g., killing) even if his choice will lead others to do many more acts of the same kind. Thus, a person cannot kill one innocent individual in order to prevent terrorists from killing ten others. Cf. Scheffler, *Rejection of Consequentialism*, ch. 5, who assails the logic behind this principle of ordinary ethics.

11 *Mishnah Ohalot* 7:6. See also *Sanhedrin* 74a, *Pesahim* 25b, where it is ruled that one must give up one's life rather than kill another.

12 Shalom Carmy has suggested to me, however, that Kant's opposition may be rooted in his requirement that ethical principles be universal. Supererogatory principles cannot be universalized.

13 It is interesting to ask (as was pointed out to me by David Berger) why calculated self-sacrifice is not *obligatory* insofar as it fulfills important moral principles. A standard reply (albeit not by an author sensitive to the calculated/blind distinction) is given by Urmson, "Saints and Heroes," 70: "The basic moral code must not be in part too far beyond the capacity of the ordinary man on ordinary occasions, or a general breakdown of compliance with the moral code would be an inevitable consequence."

14 See Slote, "Morality and the Self-Other Asymmetry," 181.

15 An early relevant paper is James Cargile, "On Consequentialism," *Analysis* 29 (1969): 78-88, though credit for a shift to considerations about virtue is usually justly given to G. E. M. Anscombe's earlier article, "Modern Moral Philosophy," *Philosophy* 33(1958): 1-19.

16 See R. Shimon Efrati, *Mi-Gei ha-Haregah* (Jerusalem, 1960/1961), I, pp. 23-30. I am not here concerned with the cogency of the responsum or the possible influence exerted on the *pesak* by the fact it was written after the event. In section VI below, I touch briefly on the act/agent distinction with regard to the case discussed in this responsum. In the responsum, the death of the infant that resulted from covering its mouth is described as accidental.

17 *Gen. Rabbah* 94:9; the story here is not identical with the version in Mishnah *Terumot* 8:10, and the last line in particular is important. See section VI.

18 As noted in section VI, however, Elijah's criticism may have to do with R. Joshua's position as a leader.

19 Whether Saul actually spared the animals out of compassion is not my concern; indeed, even the rabbinic statement that Saul complained about the morality

of killing the animals (e.g., *Kohelet Rabbah* 7:16) does not entail that he spared them for that reason. On the contrary, the cited *midrash* implies that he was censured, then and there, by a heavenly voice. That forces us to find a different account of why subsequently he and the people spared them.

20 J. L. Mackie, *Ethics: Inventing Right and Wrong* (New York, 1977), 188.

21 See *Berakhot* 7a: "'And I shall be gracious to whom I shall be gracious' — even though he is not fitting." Viewed in terms of merits, X may not deserve my help and attention; but a gracious character who seeks to imitate God will open his hand to X anyway. While in the case of God, lack of discrimination obviously cannot be traced to psychological limitations, human beings who are genuinely gracious, who possess the traits as well as perform the acts, will, due to psychological constraints, fail to discriminate between certain cases. The fact that God does not discriminate between cases may suggest the primacy of virtue over principle. Cf. below, sections IV-VI. On the implications of *Berakhot* 7a, see R. Aharon Lichtenstein, "Sa'od Tis'od Immo," *Sefer Zikkaron le-Avraham Spiegelman* (Jerusalem, 1978), 81-93.

22 Baron, "Kantian Ethics and Supererogation," 253-54.

23 See Kant, *Groundwork of the Metaphysic of Morals,* introduction.

24 See Kirschenbaum, "Good Samaritan," 56-57, n. 212.

25 Kristen R. Monroe, Michael C. Barten, and Ute Klingemann, "Altruism and the Theory of Rational Action: Rescuers of Jews in Nazi Europe," *Ethics* 101(1990): 119-22. See also Samuel Oliner and Pearl Oliner, *The Altruistic Personality* (New York, 1988). Cf. the review of the Oliners' book by James W. Fowler: "The Psychology of Altruism," *First Things* 4 (June/July, 1990): 43-49.

26 A forceful advocate of a Jewish "virtue ethics," at least as an interpretation of Maimonides' thinking, is Walter Wurzburger. See his "The Centrality of Virtue-Ethics in Maimonides," in *Of Scholars, Savants, and their Texts: Studies in Philosophy and Religious Thought: Essays in Honor of Arthur Hyman,* ed. Ruth Link-Salinger (New York, 1989), 251-60; "Imitatio Dei in Maimonides' Sefer Hamitzvot and the Mishneh Torah," in *Tradition and Transition: Essays Presented to Chief Rabbi Sir Immanuel Jakobovits,* ed. Jonathan Sacks (London, 1986), 321-24; "Law As the Basis of a Moral Society," *Tradition* 19 (Spring 1981): 42-54; "The Maimonidean Matrix of Rabbi Joseph B. Soloveitchik's Two-Tiered Ethics," *Gesher* 9 (1984): 118-29. Wurzburger's emphasis is on the connection between virtue and "the ways of the *hasid*." "Virtue ethics" is, of course, associated with ancient Greek ethical theory, while "act (or obligation)-centered ethics" is associated with Kant. Many philosophers today advocate a return to virtue theories. The most heralded of these writers is Alasdair MacIntyre, *After Virtue* (Notre Dame, IN, 1981; 2nd ed., 1984). (For analysis of Wurzburger's book *Ethics of Responsibility,* see my essay, "Beyond Obedience," in this volume.)

27 See Nahmanides' commentary to Deuteronomy 22:6; cf. *Bereshit Rabbah* 44:1. R. J. David Bleich cites many similar approaches in Jewish literature in his "Judaism and Animal Experimentation," *Contemporary Halakhic Problems* (New York, 1989), vol. III, ch. 9. In non-Jewish thought, Aquinas and Kant voice related opinions. It should be noted that Nahmanides does not say whether the value of "virtue" (= good *middot*) is intrinsic or instrumental — that is, whether virtue is good in and of itself, or only because it leads to right action.

Another example of the virtue/act distinction at work is in the question of whether charity is mandated for the sake of the recipients or the sake of the benefactors. On charity generally, see R. Michael Rosensweig, *"Tzedakah ke-Hiyyuv u-ke-Mitzvah," Torah She-be-al Peh* 31(1990): 149-160 and the articles cited in n. 31 below. For another application of virtue considerations, see Maimonides, *Sefer ha-Mitzvot,* negative commandments, #317, where the prohibition against cursing people is explained in terms of its impact on character.

28 *Hilkhot Teshuvah* 7:3; R. Yosef Dov Halevi Soloveitchik, *Al ha-Teshuvah,* ed. Pinchas Peli (Jerusalem, 1974), 191-249; in English, Pinchas H. Peli, *Soloveitchik On Repentance:The Thought and Oral Discourses of Rabbi Joseph B. Soloveitchik* (Jerusalem, 1980), 141-202.

29 *Shemonah Perakim,* ch. 6. Cf., however, *Hilkhot Teshuvah* 7:4.

30 This notion may be traced to *Sifrei* to *Deuteronomy* 11:22: "Just as He is *rahum* (merciful), you too be *rahum;* just as He is *hanun* (kind), you too be *hanun."* Cf. *Sotah* 14a, where *imitatio Dei* is represented as a call to imitate divine actions. So, too, Maimonides in *Guide* I:54 emphasizes actions that imitate God. Since Maimonides believes that God does not have emotions, however, the idea that imitation of God refers to *virtue* in the sense of a complex of behavioral *and* affective dispositions is hard to accept.

31 The context I have in mind is *tzedakah.* See R. Aharon Lichtenstein, *"Sa'od Tis'od Immo";* R. Isser Yehudah Unterman, *"Dargot shel Kedimah be-Hatzalat Nefashot, be-Pidyon Shevuyim, bi-Tzedakah u-be-Halva'ah Lefi ha-Halakhah," Yad Shaul,* 56-61.

32 See R. Aharon Lichtenstein, *"Le-Berur 'Kofin al Middat Sedom'," in Hagut Ivrit be-Amerika,* ed. Menahem Zohari (Tel Aviv, 5732): 362-82; cf. Shmuel Shilo, *"Kofin al Midat Sedom:* Jewish Law's Concept of Abuse of Rights," *Israel Law Review* 15 (1980): 49-78.

33 See Wurzburger, *"Imitatio Dei,"* 322, summarizing his understanding of Maimonides.

34 Aquinas, above, n. 2. It is not clear whether in Judaism the catalogue of virtues is derived from reflection on a philosophical standard of virtue that is independent of the Torah, or instead from the Torah alone. This issue is raised by Maharal in a critique of both Maimonides' and Nahmanides' views on the teleology of *mitzvot.* See his argument in *Tiferet Yisrael,* ch. 6.

For discussion of whether a wrong act may be performed so as to mold character, see R. Norman Lamm, *Halakhot va-Halikhot* (Jerusalem, 1990), 149-56.

35 A major advantage of using the least change principle to explain R. Akiva's position is that it enables us to harmonize R. Akiva's ruling with the ruling that one may not kill another person in order to save oneself (*Sanhedrin* 74a; *Pesahim* 25b). The latter ruling is restricted to cases in which one would be *actively* or, more precisely, *directly,* killing the other; in the case of the flask, the "killing" of the other is not direct. The direct/indirect (or active/passive) distinction is a consequence of the least change principle. (Cf. Tosafot *Sanhedrin* 74b, s.v. *ve-ha.*)

For a different analysis of R. Akiva's position (and that of his adversary, Ben Petura), see Moshe Sokol, "The Allocation of Scarce Medical Resources: A Philosophical Analysis of the Halakhic Sources," *AJS Review* 15

(1990): 63-93, esp. sec. II. Other arguments prohibiting transfer of the flask are given by R. Moshe Sternbuch, *"Be-Inyan Ones be-Lo Ta'aseh u-Pidyon Shevuyim,"* *Yad Shaul*, 386-87; R. Isser Yehudah Unterman, *Shevet mi-Yehudah* (Jerusalem, 1983), 15-16.

36   The least change principle appears in secular ethics in the form of a distinction between active and passive causation of death. Philosophers now frequently charge, however, that this distinction is baseless and unmotivated. See James Rachels, "Active and Passive Euthanasia," *New England Journal of Medicine* 292 (1975): 78-80; Scheffler, *Consequentialism*, ch. 5; and cf., *inter alia*, Christopher Boorse and Roy Sorensen, "Ducking Harm," *The Journal of Philosophy* 85 (1988): 115-34, esp. 124-28, 134. The view that transferring ownership of the flask is too large a change in the status quo, and should therefore be prohibited, would probably sound baffling even to secular ethicists who accept the active/passive distinction. The theological account in the next paragraph bears similarities to one in R. Moshe Feinstein, *Iggerot Mosheh, Yoreh De'ah* II: #174, section 4, pp. 292-93. R. Feinstein's position about third-party rescue marginalizes the hierarchy set down in *Horayot* 3:7-8. See *Iggerot Mosheh, Hoshen Mishpat* II: #74:2, p. 312. His position could be argued for by the least change principle, but he does not invoke it there.

37   See, e.g., R. Ovadiah Yosef, *She'elot u-Teshuvot Yehavveh Da'at*, III: #84.

38   An example of the three-tier approach is Avraham Steinberg, "Mahalat ha-AIDS," *Assia* 12, 3-4(1989): 27-28. Much of the literature is based on attempts to harmonize responsa of Radbaz (R. David ben Zimra) on the subject, especially #1052 and #1582. R. J. David Bleich maintains that, when Radbaz characterizes a person who undertakes high risks as a "pious fool," this is *not* tantamount to a prohibition. See Bleich, "Experimentation on Human Subjects," in *Jewish Bioethics*, ed. Fred Rosner and J. David Bleich, (New York, 1979), 384-85. "Significant" risk is often defined in terms of a "50%" line, but precise quantification is not relevant for my purposes. See also my "Concepts of Autonomy in Jewish Medical Ethics," in this volume.

39   David Berger pointed out to me that even secular ethicists might agree that a doctor cannot operate on a transplant donor when the risk is high. This points us toward two distinctions: the difference between a rescuer's undergoing intrusive risky procedures that affect bodily integrity, and his undertaking rescue efforts from which he may emerge unscathed; and the distinction between a patient's own choice and a third party's right to facilitate implementation of the choice.

40   Rav Kook, *Mishpat Kohen*, #143, pp. 310-12, and #144, sect. 15-16, pp. 339-40. R. Kook's responsum (written as part of an exchange with R. Zalman Pines) contains much back-and-forth reasoning on his part and when I call the position "Rav Kook's," I do so only for convenience, ignoring the tentativeness and hesitancy of his statements. *Sefer Hasidim* emphasizes the need for calculation to an even greater degree. For instance, it rules that if enemies want to kill one of two people, and R. Akiva may therefore die, the other must surrender himself "because the many are in need of R. Akiva." See, in the edition of J. Wistinetzki (Frankfurt, 1924), #252, see also #162, #165; in the edition of Reuven Margulies (Jerusalem, 5733), #698, #674, and #677.

41   For an incisive analysis of the declining role of *Horayot* criteria in contemporary responsa, see Sokol, "Scarce Medical Resources."

42   This is based on Maimonides, *Hilkhot Sanhedrin*, 20:1. The term *"umdana"* (*omed ha-da'at*) in Maimonides' ruling refers to imputation of guilt based on circumstantial evidence; but after quoting Maimonides, Rav Kook goes on to use the term to refer to assessments of other kinds. Cf. *Entziklopedyah Talmudit*, s.v. *umdana*.

43   *She'elot u-Teshuvot Tzitz Eliezer* X:25, sect. 7, p. 130. Cf. IX: 45. I bracket one complication: the rescuer is *creating* a risk for himself, so he is not analogous to the already endangered parties in *Horayot* and the flask case. The responsum of R. Oshry, *She'eolot u-Teshuvot mi-Ma'amakkim* XI:1, generates issues about the role of context, consequences, and the status of the rescuer.

44   See *Entziklopedyah Talmudit*, s.v. *hasid*, and J. David Bleich, "Is There An Ethic Beyond Halakhah?" in *Studies in Jewish Philosophy*, ed. Norbert Samuelson (Lanham, MA, 1987), 527-46. Maimonides, *Mishneh Torah, Hilkhot De'ot* 1:5-6 is most plausibly read as ranking a *hakham* higher than a *hasid*, as I argue in "Maimonides' Moral Philosophy," in this volume.

45   This anomaly is avoided if the *am ha-aretz* is required to save the *talmid hakham*. But such a requirement is too stringent, even though *Sefer Hasidim* comes close to endorsing it in certain cases. See above, n. 38. Cf. R. Waldenberg, X:25, sect. 7, p. 128.

46   On this reading, Elijah used the phrase *"mishnat hasidim"* loosely. Query: would Elijah have criticized R. Joshua if the community consisted entirely of R. Joshuas?

47   See above, n. 16.

48   Unfortunately, the arguments in this responsum are tenuous. The perhaps not unrelated facts that the *pesak* was written after the event; that numerous people must have been bearing horrid psychological wounds when the *posek* was approached; and that the whole setting must have been fraught with pain and terror — all these make substantive practical use of this responsum difficult.

49   Netziv, *Ha'amek Davar* to Exodus 32:29; Numbers 25:12; Deuteronomy 13:18. Cf. Nahmanides' commentary to Deuteronomy 23:10.

50   The citation from Maharam is from *Teshuvot, Pesakim, u-Minhagim*, ed. Y. Z. Kahana (Jerusalem, 1960), II:54. I am indebted to David Berger for pointing out the possible relevance of the Maharam's responsum to the virtue/ act issue. The brief translated sentence is from his *The Jewish-Christian Debate in the High Middle Ages* (Philadelphia, 1978), 26. For a general discussion of halakhically problematic martyrdom and its significance, see Haym Solo-veitchik, "Religious Law and Change: The Medieval Ashkenazic Example," *AJS Review* 12 (1987): 205-21.

       Maimonides' opposition to voluntary martyrdom in *Hilkhot Yesodei ha-Torah* 5:4 is surprising in light of his affinity for virtue ethics. (Cf. his *Iggeret ha-Shemad*, ed. Y. Sheilat [Jerusalem, 1988].) The linkage (or lack of same) between the issues of voluntary martyrdom and altruistic self-sacrifice needs study. I have some suspicion (but no more than that) that Maimonides' disapproval of voluntary martyrdom is related to his explanation of the law against self-incrimination in capital cases, viz. that the law is a guard against people finding licit expression for their death wishes. See *Hilkhot Sanhedrin* 18:6.

Some commentators believe that the story of R. Joshua influenced Maimonides to issue his own strict ruling on surrender of others to hostile forces in *Hilkhot Yesodei ha-Torah* 5:5, contrary to the principle that one normally follows the opinion of R. Yohanan rather than R. Shimon ben Lakish.

51   The "heroes" of Masada provide us with yet another example of halakhically dubious acts that spring from what may be thought of as a virtue. The halakhic problems inhering in the conduct of the heroes of Masada are surveyed by Dov Frimer, "Masada in the Light of Halakha," *Tradition* 12 (1971): 27-43.

52   Shubert Spero, *Morality, Halakha, and Jewish Tradition* (New York, 1983), 227. A contrasting view is stated by R. Nahum L. Rabinovitch in "Halakhah and Other Systems of Ethics: Attitudes and Interactions," in Fox (ed.), *Modern Jewish Ethics*, 88-102. He writes: "There is a considerable body of halakhic opinion that the imperative 'You shall not stand by the blood of your neighbor' is accorded equal status with that of self-preservation, so that one is free to choose to sacrifice his own life to save another's. ... The individual's own ordering of the priorities will of course imply a subjective scale of values that the Halakha accepts as valid though not universally so" (95-96). Apart from the difference between Rabinovitch's and Spero's representation of halakhic opinion, there is all the difference between a "subjective scale of values" (Rabinovitch) and "being carried aloft by love" (Spero).

Unfortunately, space does not allow for discussion of other concepts relevant to our topic, such as *averah lishmah* (mentioned by Spero) and (as Shalom Carmy suggested) "sin so that your fellow may benefit" (*Shabbat* 4a).

53   R. Avraham Kariv, *Mi-Sod Hakhamim* (Jerusalem, 1976), 313.

CONCEPTS OF AUTONOMY
IN JEWISH MEDICAL ETHICS

The principle that human beings must be allowed to exercise their autonomy lies at the very heart of contemporary secular writing about
medical ethics, and it represents perhaps the most distinctive of modern
day contributions to thinking in this area.[1] The ascendance of autonomy,
along with equivalent or cognate ideas of self-determination, privacy,
and liberty, has also considerably impacted upon modern conceptions of
a physician's role. Classically, the obligations of physicians were defined
by the Hippocratic tradition: "I will keep [my patients] from harm and
injustice," "I will use treatment to help the sick according to my ability
and judgment, but never with a view to injury"; and by such formulations
as that adopted by the World Medical Association in Geneva (1948): "The
health of my patient will be my first consideration." By allowing significant
room for patient choice, secular ethicists in recent times relax and qualify
these classic obligations, producing a new conception of a physician's
duties. Physicians no longer have as their sole or even main task the curing
or treatment of patients. Instead they are obligated to bring their patients
into a position from which they, the patients, can make informed and
unencumbered, albeit subjective, determinations of what course to follow.
In consonance with this new professional ethic, physicians might even
assist patients in causing their deaths.[2]

As is well known, Jewish law would seem to provide a sharp counterpoint to modern bioethical discussions, as it offers little by way of
an affirmation of autonomy. "*Ein nafsho shel ha-adam kinyano, ella kinyan
ha-Kadosh Barukh Hu*" — a person's life is not his possession but rather
God's. Promulgated by Maimonides and reiterated by R. David ben Zimra
(Radbaz) in a gloss on another part of the *Mishneh Torah*,[3] this "ownership"
principle appears to deny people the prerogative to make their own life-
and-death decisions. When the disciples of R. Haninah ben Teradyon
beseeched him to open his mouth so that smoke from the flames set by the

Romans would asphyxiate him and thus hasten his death, the sage refused: "Better that He who gave the soul should take it, and a man do himself no injury" (*Avodah Zarah* 18a). God owns us; we are His stewards, His custodians, or His bailees; our bodies are on loan. Whereas an insistence on autonomy has led secular bioethicists to highly rigorous requirements of informed consent, contemporary Jewish rabbinic decisors and medical ethicists have taken a very different path. "Jewish law, unlike common law, does not at all demand that a patient consent to a procedure designed to restore health or to prolong life. On the contrary, Jewish law demands that the patient seek medical advice and that he submit to the ministrations of the physician."[4] Thus, a rabbinic authority presented with a question about forcing treatment on an uncomplying subject declares: "*pashut she-kofin* — it is obvious that we coerce."[5] He cites august authorities in support (R. Jacob Emden, R. David Zvi Hoffman and others) and invokes Radbaz, cited above, as the theoretical basis for not requiring patient consent to treatment.[6] In Jewish sources, the imperative to respect patient choices does not compromise, and certainly does not override, the physician's obligation to save a life.[7]

An especially sharp rejection of autonomy is contained in a passage by Maimonides that deals with rabbinic *takkanot* that were introduced to prevent exposure to health risks:

> The rabbis prohibited many things because of *sakkanat nefashot* (danger to life). And anyone who transgresses these, saying "I'll endanger myself, and what concern is it to others?" or: "What do such things matter to me?" — we inflict *makkat mardut* (rabbinically ordained lashes) upon him.[8]

Here Maimonides rejects the idea that a person may choose risky behavior that concerns only himself, and that a person might make life-threatening decisions based on his or her own subjective assessments of value — the very ideas that run through modern defenses of autonomy. Maimonides's vigorous statement is thus tantamount to a resounding rebuff of the modern perspective.

These sources limit the control a person has over his or her life in Jewish law. And yet, precisely because the Jewish denial of autonomy has become so commonplace in writings on Jewish bioethics, precisely because it is so plain and incontrovertible that Judaism does not leave decisions in patients' hands to the extent that secular ethics does, we should look beyond the commonplace and examine some neglected aspects of Halakhah which suggest greater possibilities for agreement and dialogue. It is time to focus not on the differences between Judaism and secular ethics but on the similarities, specifically the surprisingly large area in which Judaism gives patients a choice. Any simple contrast between Jewish and secular ethics — such as, "secular ethics affirms autonomy, Judaism denies it" — is inaccurate. The gap between Jewish and secular bioethical perspectives is quite real, but it is not as great as might appear. Exaggeration of the gap can only distort, and perhaps cause halakhists to throw out the baby with the bath water by ignoring valid and usable insights of the bioethical community about human choice.[9]

In what follows, I will argue that Judaism *affirms* autonomy in a clear sense. Not all choices that affect life and death are mandated. In certain life-and-death situations a person is permitted to make either of two or more choices. Though some conduct is mandated, there are also "permissible" zones within which patients may choose. Further, within these "permissible zones," the following simple thesis holds: consent matters. That is to say, in some life-and-death situations, *a person has the prerogative to treat himself in ways that others may not.* A person may make decisions to risk or bring about the shortening of his life that others may not make and that they may not impose upon him against his will.[10] Sometimes, therefore, the difference between a permissible intervention or act and an impermissible one in Jewish bioethics is not found in the objective features of the intervention or act but in the volition of the individual. This asymmetry between self and other ("consent matters") is a central component of the concept of autonomy, and Jewish law accepts it in a significant range of cases outside and inside the medical context. Outside that context, Ashkenazi authorities conclude that martyrdom is sometimes optional, albeit supererogatory if chosen.[11] There are sources that permit suicide (but do not necessarily mandate it) under such conditions as (i) a desire for repentance;[12] (ii) a fear of not being able to stand up to torture and hence not being able to fulfill the duty of martyrdom in circumstances where Halakhah mandates martyrdom;[13] (iii) a fear of torture and indignity at the hands of one's enemy[14] or (iv) a desire to save others.[15] Some authorities permit an individual to sacrifice himself to an enemy for the sake of the group even though the group would not be permitted to hand him over without his consent for the same purpose.[16] Whether all these views are universally accepted is not crucial; what is crucial is that they were accepted by important authorities despite the fact they place control over life and death in the individual's hands. Similarly, autonomy exists in halakhic bioethics. Some of the key bioethical areas in which consent matters — and which will occupy us here — are risky medical procedures, decisions about end-stage medical care, and altruistic self-sacrifice as in the case of organ donations.

Besides arguing that autonomy exists in medical Halakhah, however, I maintain, at the same time, that the *roots* of the "consent matters" thesis in Judaism are not identical with the roots of the autonomy principle in secular ethics. Jewish sources do not express the belief of secular ethicists that self-determination per se is a *value*, one that might override life itself. Autonomy is a *fact* of the Jewish legal system, but not a value within it. Halakhists can concede autonomy without blurring the contrast between their own view and that of secular bioethicists, because they need not make autonomy per se a value. Where does autonomy, the person's prerogative to choose in life-and-death situations, come from in Jewish law? I hope to clarify that in due course. I submit that this strategy — finding agreement between Halakhah and secular ethics on the bottom line in some situations, while distinguishing between secular and halakhic paths to that bottom line — will enable us to capture the difference between Jewish and secular ethics vis-à-vis autonomy in a more nuanced and accurate way than slogans and broad generalizations can provide.

AUTONOMY AND THE OWNERSHIP PRINCIPLE

Since the principle of divine ownership of the body is the primary basis for denying that autonomy has a place in Jewish law, we should begin by examining it carefully. In Plato's *Phaedo*, Socrates explains to his friends that he will refuse to take his own life. Our bodies are the possession of the gods, he explains, and one must not destroy the property of another. "Divine ownership" affords a Jewish parallel to Socrates' principle, ostensibly denying people choice and control over life-and-death situations. Accordingly, halakhists have often invoked "ownership" to interdict suicide across a range of cases and to limit, for example, the permissibility of self-sacrifice performed to save the life of another.[17] At the same time, the ownership principle seems to explain why religious norms diverge from secular ones. Secularists, after all, do not endorse the principle of divine ownership.

In truth, however, drawing specific normative conclusions from the "ownership" idea is often a *non sequitur*. What, after all, follows from the fact that God, not we, owns our lives? Only this: *If* God has stipulated that a person may not dispose of His, God's, "possession" in a particular context, *then* one who does so has acted wrongly, as he or she has destroyed another's "possession" without permission. But from this principle nothing follows about whether the owner does or does not give such permission to destroy His property in a particular set of circumstances. To be sure, if we knew that God is an owner who would *never* permit His possession to be destroyed, we would be entitled to draw such a sweeping conclusion. But God is not such an owner. On the contrary, He mandates that people surrender their lives in certain cases — as when Jews must surrender their lives rather than commit the three cardinal transgressions. Hence, although we are duty bound to follow God's preferences with respect to the disposition of our lives, and do not possess the autonomy to oppose God where "He" (i.e., the Halakhah) has said we cannot surrender ourselves, we may not assume in advance that a given situation, such as altruistic self-sacrifice, is *not* a type of "destruction of His possession" that "He" would countenance.[18] (This point is reinforced by the willingness of Ashkenazi authorities to rule that martyrdom is sometimes optional.) Similarly, we should not assume, without topic-specific legal analysis, that God would necessarily want a person to prolong his or her life slightly when that slightly extended life will be one of unmitigated pain. After all, the owner may not want His creatures to die with more agony than necessary. The ownership principle alone cannot tell us whether the law would always rule out shortening life; more to our present point, the ownership principle would not alone tell us whether the owner would allow us to make our own decisions in certain areas — in other words, to exercise autonomy.[19]

Thus, the "ownership" thesis is a way of restating the fact we must obey Jewish law about our bodies; it cannot determine the *content* of what the Halakhah rules in a particular case. The Halakhah has to be determined by jurisprudential reasoning, not an invocation of theology. "Ownership" provides only an argument for obeying God *once* He has spoken.[20] Socrates already recognized the limits of the ownership principle when he qualified his refusal to destroy the gods' possessions. We cannot destroy the gods' possessions, he said, unless the gods have given us a clear sign to do so. Socrates did drink the hemlock, after all, confident that the gods did not oppose self-destruction in that form.

The following statement sums up a common argument that Judaism denies autonomy:

> Judaism restricts the notion of autonomy to actions that are morally indifferent. Where conflicting values arise, each individual is bound to act in accordance with a high standard of normative moral conduct in order to achieve fulfillment. Thus, everyone is duty bound to act according to that standard and to relinquish his temporary wishes.[21]

If we think of autonomy as entailing a permission to disregard God's stated rules concerning care of one's own life — to act contrary to divinely-ordained moral values — then in Jewish law people do not have autonomy.[22] It is tautologically true that a person ought not act against moral values. Equally, no matter how one defines autonomy, no secular ethicist could believe that a person has the moral right to act immorally. But if we define autonomy as permission to choose in either of two ways, even in life-or-death situations, then Judaism may well believe in autonomy. For while God might mandate the choice of life in some cases, and might mandate choice of death in other cases, He might make both choices permissible in still other cases. In this sense of the term autonomy, we need to know whether Judaism places certain life-or-death decisions in our hands, as opposed to mandating one decision or the other. I submit it does.

The ownership principle does have *some* normative implications beyond those contained in the explicit content of God's commands. For example, it provides good reason for people not to disfigure or destroy their bodies for *trivial* reasons. Wanton defacement of another's property is obviously wrong. But the crucial question is what counts as wanton destruction. Beyond the obvious, e.g., gratuitous mutilation just for the fun of it, lies the realm of the unknown and the debatable — until we apply legal reasoning to generate a ruling. The ownership principle might also be a reason for prohibiting us from inflicting harm upon ourselves when legal reasoning about that harm is indecisive. The ownership principle might push toward stringency in a case of *safek* (doubt) about whether a particular act of self-destruction is or is not permissible. I do not think that this last idea is borne out by the practice of halakhists, who issue lenient rulings in some cases. But, the essential point remains: belief in divine ownership is compatible with autonomy in the sense I have specified — there are permissible zones, and in them consent matters.[23]

INFORMED CONSENT
AND RISK/BENEFIT RATIOS

Let us now consider the argument that Judaism denies autonomy because, in sharp contrast to bioethicists, it licenses *kefiyyah* (coercion) to medical treatment. If medical treatment can be coerced, how can there be room for autonomy?[24]

The basic reply to this question is that medical treatment can be coerced only in cases where there is a suitably weighty risk/benefit ratio. If some risk-free procedure (a medication, say) will cure a life-threatening condition, then a patient who refuses the treatment is coerced into accepting it. But where the risk/benefit ratio is more complex, Jewish law does not coerce medical treatment, and the patient may decide how to proceed. In earlier times, medical modalities were simple, the alternatives clear and uncomplicated: take treatment X, or die. In modern times, modalities have proliferated, and alternatives are anything but simple.[25] Already in the Talmud, though, we find Rebbi refusing two medications for eye disease, saying "I cannot endure it," and accepting only a third treatment (*Bava Metzi'a* 85b). Whereas Rebbi, it is true, chose *some* treatment, sometimes no treatment might be as reasonable as treatment.

Let us spell this out more precisely. In some cases, there is great risk if medical treatment is not proffered, while the risks involved are negligible and the likely benefits to life expectancy are enormous. Here Jewish law will coerce the patient to undergo the procedure, and will not grant the patient autonomy.[26] In other cases, the procedure is very risky, while forgoing the procedure does not involve significant risk or benefit. Here, a person is prohibited from undertaking the procedure. Finally, there is a grey area, a "permissible" zone, where uncertainty infects the decision-making. There is such-and-such a percentage of risk if the procedure is not done, such-and-such a likelihood of benefit if the procedure is done, such-and-such a percentage of risk if the procedure is done. Assuming each of the percentages involved is non-negligible, Jewish law leaves the decision in the patient's hands. "Procedures which involve any significant risk features are always discretionary rather than mandatory."[27] So, for example, it is often up to the individual whether to undergo an operation that might leave him dead on the table but holds out the hope of curing him or significantly extending longevity; whether, in other words, he should risk his *hayyei sha'ah* (the anticipated short life span if nothing is done) with the prospect of attaining *hayyei olam* (normal longevity) if a procedure is performed.

Now the halakhic literature concerning these cases focuses on three questions:

(1) The threshold question: What statistical likelihood of benefit or risk would make a procedure mandatory, permitted, or prohibited?[28]

(2) The values question: What counts as a risk and what counts as a benefit for purposes of making our calculations? May a cardiac patient undertake a risky surgery if the alternative is death in six months? If *hayyei sha'ah* can be risked for *hayyei olam*, how long a period does *hayyei sha'ah* entail? Would the cardiac patient be required to live out his life in bed if doctors determined that surgery posed a significant risk but

confinement to bed would gain another fifteen years?[29] What about other types of risks and benefits besides life — for instance, would interference with lifestyle be adequate grounds for declining dialysis in favor of a more hazardous route of surgery?[30] Would horror at the thought of disfigurement be adequate grounds for rejecting a radical removal of a tumor rather than pursuing a path of chemotherapy or less radical surgery, which hold out a somewhat smaller promise of longevity? Would the prospect of feeling better about oneself justify cosmetic surgery, or would the risks always posed by anesthesia outweigh the potential psychological benefits?[31] How weighty are considerations about fertility?[32]

The range of views about such risk/benefit questions is striking. For example, on the one hand, R. Jacob Emden expressed reservations about even so seemingly beneficial a procedure as surgery to remove painful stones, arguing that the risk to life was possibly more important than relief from pain; on the other hand, modern decisors sometimes permit cosmetic surgery on the grounds that it removes psychological *tza'ar* (pain), even though anesthesia poses some risk to life (and cosmetic surgery might constitute *havalah*, wounding).[33]

(3) The authority question: Who determines the risk levels? The doctor? The patient? The rabbi?[34] Some combination? Should risk levels be set by the behavior of people (the willingness of the majority to accept or forego certain procedures) or by statistical studies?[35] What role should a rabbi play in answering factual questions?[36]

These questions about thresholds, values, and authorities may lead to the conclusion that the majority of medical decisions today are in the "permissible" zone. However, we must understand that the fact that a decision is left up to the patient is *not* necessarily tantamount to affirming patient autonomy *as a value*. In order to clarify this point fully, we need to distinguish between two types of autonomy: descriptive and prescriptive.[37]

A person has autonomy in the descriptive sense when he or she makes a decision without impediments to full rationality and authenticity. For example, the person is not being unduly pressured or manipulated or brainwashed by others, he or she is not lacking vital information, he or she is not enduring emotional stress that is clouding judgment, etc. X is autonomous in the descriptive sense (or "psychological" sense, if you will) when X makes a decision that satisfies these conditions.[38] X has autonomy in the prescriptive sense, on the other hand, when X is *permitted* to make his or her own choice and when no one may interfere with that choice.

In bioethical decisions, the prescriptive sense is the central one. A person should be given control over decision-making that affects his or her life. Nevertheless, in contemporary affirmations of autonomy the descriptive and prescriptive senses are intertwined. For bioethicists who affirm the principle of respect for autonomy often limit its application to those cases in which the patient is autonomous in the descriptive sense.

A precedent for such restrictions resides in John Stuart Mill's *On Liberty*. Mill, the archenemy of paternalistic intervention, in a work whose avowed purpose is to reject any interference in decisions that are purely self-regarding, nonetheless allows an exception. People may restrain an unwitting man from crossing an unsafe bridge because he does not desire, after all, to fall into the water. The person's ignorance of the danger makes his choice less than fully autonomous. Mill has here opened floodgates. For one might then allow interference with choice in any case in which people are misassessing facts, judging things poorly because of anxieties and misinformation, and the like.

Theoretically, then, if you pitch the standards for descriptive autonomy high enough, you will end up countenancing broad interference in people's lives. Acknowledgment of autonomy, therefore, does not by itself rule out the interference of others. Now no patient is ever fully rational, and anyone's emotions might cloud their judgment; hence, even choices that are less than fully autonomous must be respected — for otherwise the autonomy principle will lose all applicability. And yet the replacement of "respect patients' choices" with "respect patients' autonomous choices" is highly significant.

Bioethicists understand that respect for patients' autonomy may be compatible with interference in patients' preferences, and therefore they seem willing to belittle the significance of the superficial, stated preferences of patients and to respect only those choices that are descriptively autonomous. But won't this justify widespread refusals to carry out patients' decisions? No. For bioethicists often hold that physicians must not simply reject non-autonomous decisions and then proceed to impose treatment. Rather, they have a duty to bring their patients into a position from which the latter can make decisions in a manner that is *descriptively* autonomous. Bioethicist Jay Katz posits a "duty for conversation":

> Physicians...must assist patients to distinguish unrealistic and too hopeful expectations from more realistic ones. Both parties must make an effort to expose to scrutiny their doubts, fears, distortions, misconceptions, uncertainties, and plain ignorance. Since they can never be fully exposed or clarified, however, nagging questions will always remain about the influence of unconscious, irrational and

just plain unconsidered thoughts and feelings on physician-patient deliberations and final decisions.[39]

Similarly, Tom Beauchamp and James Childress write:

> For the patient's or subject's consent to be a valid authorization for the professional to proceed, it must be based on understanding and must be voluntary. Because of the unequal distribution of knowledge between professionals on the one hand and patients or subjects on the other, the principle of respect for autonomy entails that professionals have a prima facie obligation to disclose information, to ensure understanding and voluntariness, and to foster adequate decision-making.[40]

The aim of all this interaction is to bring the patient into an optimal situation for making decisions. Once those *optimally made* decisions have been expressed, physicians must respect them.

With this in mind, let us return to those cases in which Judaism appears to affirm autonomy — the cases in the "permissible" zone. Halakhah, we saw, allows patients to accept or decline certain risky procedures. Note the irony, however. For a bioethicist who believes in the autonomy principle, a "yes" or "no" from a patient does not close the book. The doctor is still obligated to explore the patient's motives before honoring the decision. Secular bioethicists emphasize the need to enable patients' rationality and authenticity. Jewish bioethicists, in contrast, leave the matter entirely in patient hands *without exploring the concept of descriptive autonomy from a halakhic standpoint and without setting down further conditions that assure that the patient's decision is (descriptively) autonomous*. Basically, in this area, secular bioethicists are *mahmir* (stringent), requiring more of physicians than their Jewish counterparts do.

The source of this contrast may be easy to identify. Jewish law tends to define the "permitted" zone exclusively in terms of the objective probabilities of certain outcomes, whereas secular bioethicists to a great extent define the "permitted" zone in terms of a patient's subjective values. For secular bioethicists, therefore, the patient's expressed choice must reflect his or her "real" self, his or her "real" values. In Judaism, precisely because the values are set more or less objectively, and precisely because there is no strong tradition of autonomy on which to draw, it does not seem crucial that the patient's expressed choice reflect his or her "real" values. What matters, one may surmise, is that the decision be justifi*able*, not that it be justified *in terms of the patient's own authentic preferences*. If autonomy is not a *value* in Judaism, there is little basis for physicians trying to ensure rationality and authenticity.

Indeed, the reasons why Halakhah leaves a "permissible" zone in cases of risky medical interventions may be quite prosaic, having nothing to do with embracing autonomy as a value. In cases of complex risk/benefit ratios, Halakhah has little choice but to leave risky decisions in patient hands. For one thing, there is no unique rational decision in cases of uncertainty. Hence a *posek* would not have a basis for mandating a particular decision. For another, suppose there were some "best" rational course. If rabbis and doctors were to impose as a mandate whatever course they thought was best in these conditions of uncertainty, bereaved family members would regularly scream that by letting rabbis and doctors, rather than patients, make decisions about what the most rational course is, the Halakhah killed their loved one, who may have had different preferences and calculations than the rabbis and doctors. These epistemological and sociological problems suffice to warrant a discretionary area in the case of risky procedures. If so, rationality and authenticity need not be required.

Even if the Halakhah does not have great respect for autonomy per se, the difference between Halakhah and secular ethics in this respect might be one of emphasis, not substance. I sincerely doubt that any halakhic authorities would *fight* the suggestion that physicians should engage patients in conversation or that they should lift cognitive and affective impediments to rational and authentic decision making. To be sure, the fact that halakhists might expand the physicians' role once that expansion is posed does not alter the fact that halakhic writings on informed consent do not emphasize the duty of conversation, as do bioethical writings.[41] But Jewish law does contain elements which, if elaborated, would expand the physicians' role and make it similar to that recommended nowadays in secular ethics.

To begin with, Halakhah, according to many, is willing to incorporate valid ethical insights drawn from other sources, which in this case might oblige physicians and patients to engage in conversation. More specifically, it could be argued that the verse "And thou shalt restore it unto him," (Deut. 22:2) used by some[42] to mandate medical treatment, could be read boldly and broadly as an imperative to restore full human functioning, including the attainment of rationality and authenticity. Further, Halakhah acknowledges that physicians are fallible and that medicine is an uncertain enterprise — which, as Katz (quoted previously) had emphasized, would limit pressuring or manipulation by physicians.[43] Indeed, one writer has argued that the fallibility of physicians is so often cited by rabbinic decisors that it severely limits the range of cases in which coercion is legitimate and gives patients significant decision-making power.[44] Also, Jewish law to some degree recognizes the need to prevent law from becoming a vehicle for suicidal wishes, so an exploration of motive is in place.[45] Furthermore, mental incompetence will limit patient choice. Together, these factors might create a duty of conversation, though I am not aware of any full-scale halakhic expansion of them that would match the scope of bioethical discussions. It seems to me, then, that there is good reason for halakhists to utilize the insights of bioethicists when they explore the notion of "autonomy" as it figures in their "permissible" zone.

Descriptive autonomy is also related to the issue of informedness. In secular law, doctors must apprise patients of potential risks, even those that the doctor feels are not worth caring about and that indeed are objectively silly to worry about.[46] Disclosing risks is important in a framework that treats autonomy as a central value. In a system that does not treat autonomy as a value (and in addition does not always insist on truth-telling[47]), it is not clear whether and why a physician would have to disclose risks whose significance the patient might irrationally exaggerate. Jewish writings on "disclosure" usually deal only with informing terminal patients of their condition, not with disclosure of distant risks in procedures being considered. Perhaps there are real possibilities for a dialogue with bioethicists in this area.[48]

Let me summarize this section, since the argument has been complex. We began by noting that, while Judaism denies patient autonomy in cases that exemplify suitably weighty risk/benefit ratios, nevertheless, where the risk/benefit ratio does not determine a single rational course, Halakhah permits some autonomy. This formulation is misleading, though, because although Halakhah permits *the exercise of preference*, that is not the same as *endorsing a principle of autonomy*. Affirming that "consent matters," is not the same as embracing autonomy as a value. The existence of a permitted zone in Judaism does not entail the affirmation of a principle of autonomy equivalent to the secularist's, unless Judaism also insists on creating conditions of descriptive autonomy for the patient and perhaps requires doctors to disclose risks to patients. Because Judaism does not have a rich tradition of autonomy, it works with a relatively easy-to-satisfy descriptive conception of autonomy in those cases in which it allows patients to exercise their own preferences. At the same time, perhaps Halakhah can appropriate insights of bioethicists about creating descriptive autonomy. Specifically, I have suggested that Judaism has room for greater emphasis on rationality, motives, physician fallibility, and the duty of conversation. Exaggerating the gap between Jewish and secular approaches blinds us to the potential benefit of finding elements of the Jewish tradition that have affinities to secular ideas about descriptive autonomy.[49]

DECISIONS ABOUT END-STAGE MEDICAL CARE

Until fairly recently, halakhic writings on euthanasia did not suggest that patient choice can determine the legal status of an act or omission in end-of-life decisions. The literature, rather, prefers "objective" formulations such as "one is not permitted to actively hasten the death of a *goses* (someone in the penultimate state before death, which is variously defined)," "one is/is not permitted to withdraw medication from a *goses*," "one is/is not permitted to withdraw food from a *goses*," "one is permitted to remove impediments to the dying process," or "one is/is not permitted to pray for the death of a *goses*," and so on. These formulations share the claim that the permission to terminate or not extend life (in particular cases) and the prohibition against doing so (in particular cases) are strictly a function of the type of act or omission that is being considered. The patients' *wishes* do not seem to affect the legal status of the deed.[50]

To begin with the clearest example of this, suppose one rules stringently, prohibiting the withdrawal of food or medication in case X. Quite obviously a patient's wishes must be disregarded here.[51] But think now of the opposite situation. Suppose one rules leniently, permitting one to withdraw medication or food from a terminal patient. What happens if the patient has specifically requested that these not be withdrawn? Is it wrong to withdraw them? Earlier sources are not very helpful on this issue.

Authorities have recently begun to define a role for patients' wishes, however. In a 1968 responsum about heart transplants, R. Moshe Feinstein objects to attempts to prolong life where the only result would be prolongation of pain.[52] R. Feinstein reiterates his stand in two later responsa, dated 1982 and spring 1988; and in a responsum dated in Iyyar 5744 (1984), R. Feinstein writes that, if (a) the treatment cannot cure; (b) it only prolongs life a bit; and (c) the life will be filled with pain, then we inform the patient of these facts *and ask the patient whether he prefers an extension of a pain-filled life to death*. His choice determines whether the treatment is administered.[53] (Does that turn the withdrawal into a violation of "Thou shalt not stand idly by over the blood of your neighbor"?)

Compare this to the view of another eminent *posek*, R.Shlomo Zalman Auerbach:

> It is logical that if the sick person is suffering much physical pain, or even if he is in psychological pain, I believe that we are obliged to give him food and oxygen for breathing against his wishes, but we can withhold treatment that causes pain if he requests it. But if he is pious and will not become despondent, it is desirable to explain to him that

> one moment of repentance in this world is more valuable than all
> of the world to come, as we find in *Sotah* 20a that it is a "privilege"
> (*zekhut*) to suffer seven years rather than die immediately.[54]

As Baruch Brody points out, R. Auerbach here presents no argument
for allowing wishes to be determinative. "It is logical" is all he says by
way of rationale. R. Auerbach is reported to have restricted his ruling to
treatments that themselves cause pain (a condition R. Feinstein did not
impose) and therapies that are not routine. A diabetic who already had one
leg amputated was given permission to reject an amputation of his other
gangrenous leg, where (a) refusing the operation would certainly lead to
death soon; (b) the operation, even if successful, would only extend his
hayyei sha'ah; and (c) the operation would lead to much pain, which is why
the patient refused it. R. Auerbach's permission suggests that the patient's
wish to avoid pain is a legitimate factor in the decision, but only in narrowly
defined circumstances.[55]

Taking patient's wishes into account signals that *in some situations*
patients have the right (or, if you prefer, permission) to determine
values subjectively. Why do they have this right or permission, though?
What is the conceptual basis for making a patient's assessment of pain
determinative? I suggest that in this regard there is a difference between
R. Feinstein and R. Auerbach. Whereas the former quotes the well-known
view that one may pray for the death of someone who is suffering,[56] and
on this basis states that prolonging life when there will be more pain is
not proper, the latter seems to clearly value life over non-life even when
pain is part of that life. Yet for all that, R. Auerbach leaves room for
patients to assess things differently. Thus R. Feinstein's view seems more
straightforward.

More to our present point, it is plausible to read R. Feinstein's Iyyar
5744 responsum in a way that distinguishes his position from that of
secular ethicists who grant autonomy in end-of-life scenarios. Most
fundamentally, his decision to establish a *fact* of autonomy has nothing
to with defending the *value* of autonomy. We are not giving the patient
a choice just because in and of itself choice is a good thing. R. Feinstein
says nothing to that effect. Furthermore, R. Feinstein claims that the default
course is to not administer life-extending treatment where pain will be
prolonged. A physician ought to withhold medicine from this patient
unless the patient requests the medicine. This means that the patient has
the autonomy to extend his or her life as opposed to opting for the default
position of not extending it. This, though, should be contrasted with what
secular ethicists confer in situations where they introduce autonomy,

viz., the autonomy to not extend life, as opposed to a default position of extending it. Even though with either construct the patient is permitted to choose, the difference is subtle but important. For R. Feinstein, patients *in a sense* do not have the autonomous choice to not extend their lives, because not extending their lives is the default option. When secular ethicists speak of autonomy, they have in mind the autonomy to not extend, or even, for some, the autonomy to actively shorten.

On both of these contemporary rabbinic views, patient preference justifies only certain measures and not others: passive withdrawal is permissible, not active euthanasia;[57] withholding medication (or certain categories of procedures) could be permissible while withholding food is not. Clearly, the autonomy implied by both rabbis is subject to constraints pertaining to the type of action or omission that would be performed. When death is soon to come, we respect someone who does not want to endure pain throughout his remaining time, but we do so only within limits that have been set by laws that ban active euthanasia, food withdrawal, etc. The specific features of the acts or omissions we perform still have the heaviest role in determining the legal status of those acts and omissions; patient choice enters only at specific points.[58] Here, too, therefore, halakhists may agree with certain views of bioethicists[59] without damaging fundamentals of the halakhic approach to euthanasia.

ALTRUISTIC SELF-SACRIFICE
AND ALTRUISTIC RISK-TAKING

In contrast to non-Jewish systems of ethics, both Christian and secular, Judaism does not unequivocally laud one's person's giving up his life to save another, nor even risking one's life to save another. Quite the contrary, in some circumstances, such acts sometimes are classified by halakhists as akin to suicide.[60] In " 'As Thyself': The Limits of Altruism in Jewish Ethics," reprinted in this volume, I explored the roots of the contrast between Judaism and other ethical systems over the issue of altruistic self-sacrifice, tracing them to a distinction between evaluating acts and evaluating agents.[61] Jewish opposition to altruistic self-sacrifice would generate problems that go to the heart of the medical enterprise as presently conducted. Organ transplants, especially from the living; experimentation on consenting human subjects; medical management of infectious diseases that threaten the lives of health care personnel — all these activities are vital to contemporary society, and yet all depend for their very existence on altruistic self-sacrifice. Halakhic decisors have essentially two possible options, assuming they do not want a society in which transplants are unavailable, experimentation is outlawed, and health care workers can regularly withdraw from cases for their own safety. The first option is to show that Jewish opposition to altruism does not extend to transplants, experimentation, and the professional duties of health care workers. The second option is to argue for a distinction between performing acts of altruistic self-sacrifice (which might be prohibited) and benefiting from the fruits of such activities on the part of others (which would on the present suggestion be permitted). Depending on the example, authorities have selected one or the other or a mix of these alternatives.[62]

A popular approach is the three-tiered view of risking oneself for the sake of another. The tiers are minimal risk, which must be undertaken; moderate risk, which may be undertaken as an act of special piety (*hasidut*); and significant risk, which should not be undertaken on pain of being regarded as a "pious fool."[63] Now at the middle level, we find a type of autonomy: one must not be forced into an act of altruism that carries this degree of risk, but one may volunteer to undertake it. Consent matters.

Although this point suffices to show that Jewish law endorses a kind of autonomy in situations of altruistic self-sacrifice, it will prove fruitful to scrutinize what we might call "resource" cases. Person X is in danger but possesses a resource — water or medicine — that he or she can use to survive. Person Y also needs the resource, and will die if X does not turn it over.[64] R. Akiva ruled in the classic resource case that, "Your life takes priority over the life of your comrade."

> Two people are traveling, and one of them has (*be-yad ehad mehem*) a flask of water. If both drink, both will die; if one drinks, he will arrive at civilization (or: a town). Ben Petura expounded: better that both drink and die, and neither of them witness the death of his companion. Until R. Akiva came and taught: "And your brother shall live with you" (Lev. 25:36) — your life (*hayyekha*) takes precedence over the life of your comrade (*Bava Metzi'a* 62b; see also *Sifra, Behar* 5, to Lev. 25:36).

Let us assume that the law accords with R. Akiva.[65] R. Akiva did not say whether you are *obligated to* keep the water, in which case transfer of the flask would be prohibited, or whether you are merely permitted to, in which case transfer to the other would be permissible and possibly even supererogatory. There are three positions found in halakhic sources about this question.

1. The possessor of the flask is prohibited to give the water to his comrade. (R. Moshe Feinstein; R. Moshe Sternbuch; R. Isser Yehudah Unterman).[66]

2. The possessor is permitted to give the flask. To do so, moreover, is to exemplify a *middat hasidut* (pious trait). (R. Jacob Jehiel Weinberg, though I have heard some argue that he may have restricted the permission to cases of saving the collective).[67]

3. The possessor is permitted to transfer the flask and to do so is to exemplify a *middat hasidut*, but only when the other's life ranks higher in terms of the Halakhah's own priorities for saving a life when resources are limited. So, for instance, the Mishnah in *Horayot* 3:7-8 implies that a scholar is to be saved before an *am ha-aretz* (ignoramus). An ignoramus could transfer his flask to a scholar, but not the other way around (R. Abraham Isaac Kook). Also, an individual could surrender himself for the *rabbim* (collective).[68]

We may characterize these positions by means of a distinction between calculated altruistic self-sacrifice and blind altruistic self-sacrifice. Calculated altruistic self-sacrifice is self-sacrifice that is motivated by a desire to satisfy some acceptable system of priorities. Blind altruism is altruism that is not motivated in this way. Using these terms we might summarize the positions as follows: both position 1 and position 3 prohibit "blind" altruism; position 1 prohibits even calculated altruism; position 3 allows calculated altruism; position 2 (in unqualified form) permits even blind altruism.

Now I think it is obvious that position 1 leaves no room for autonomy in the resource case. I explained in my article "As Thyself" that this position is arguably grounded in a "least change" principle, according to which dire choices about whom to save are decided in accordance with what course of action will introduce the least change into the *status quo*. That X owns the flask is part of the *status quo*; therefore, X should not transfer the flask. Considerations of autonomy and virtue do not override this least-change principle.[69]

By contrast, positions 2 and 3 agree that Judaism allows for autonomy in the case of altruistic self-sacrifice in the sense delineated before: *consent matters*. However, we should tread carefully in thinking of position 3. Broadly speaking there are two ways to understand this position.

The first is afforded by R. Kook. According to R. Kook's analysis, all cases of altruistic self-sacrifice should theoretically be decided by means of objective hierarchies such as that set down in *Horayot*. However, he explains, such hierarchies never *require* a person to rescue someone else at a time when he himself is in danger. Hierarchies govern only third-party decisions about whom to rescue. If Z has to choose between saving X, a scholar, and saving Y, an ignoramus, he should choose to save X; but if Y himself is choosing between his own life and X's, he cannot be forced to save X. According to R. Kook's reasoning, then, the owner of a resource does not have autonomy to *part with* the resource to save another rather than use it to save himself; instead, the owner of the resource has the prerogative *not* to part with it. He may *preserve* his life by not applying the *Horayot* criteria. If he elects not to exercise this prerogative, he then follows the priorities enunciated in *Horayot*. This logic is analogous to R. Feinstein's logic concerning treatment that will prolong pain, which was a prerogative to extend life rather than to not extend it. Note, also, that the autonomy R. Kook grants does not *automatically* carry over to cases in which a person would be placing himself *into* great risk by attempting a rescue, though we might make this extension. *Horayot* is speaking of two parties who are *already* endangered. In sum, by insisting on calculated altruism, some authorities limit the cases in which one may give up one's life for the sake of another's.[70]

Perhaps there is a different explanation for a permissive ruling in favor of altruistic self-sacrifice, one that views this sacrifice in terms of a "higher" value system. Self-sacrifice is preferable,[71] but Halakhah does not impose this choice because a person is not obligated to follow the "higher" ethic. This "higher ethic" approach is problematic here. It is normally accepted that in Judaism the elite take upon themselves truly supererogatory conduct, but not those lower on a hierarchy.[72] Yet by the nature of calculated altruism, only people who are not of high rank on the priority scale could fulfill this supposedly higher obligation. The *am ha-aretz* can give his resource to the Torah scholar, but the Torah scholar may not be an altruist toward the *am ha-aretz*!! Thus, defending altruistic self-sacrifice in resource cases based on notions of "higher" conduct becomes difficult. (Other cases — such as voluntary martyrdom — may still fit the "higher ethic" analysis.[73])

CONCLUSION

Our inquiry warrants drawing the following conclusions:

1. Contrary to an argument often found in the literature, the principle of divine ownership of our bodies does not logically entail that individuals cannot make their own choices in life-and-death situations. We have identified situations, concentrating on medical ethics, where people are given

choices, and have indicated other situations in which Halakhah allows people to make life-or-death decisions that others cannot impose on them.

2. Autonomy is a fact of the Jewish legal system, not a value within it. In none of the cases we have considered does Jewish law straightforwardly embrace the idea that in giving choices to people we are trying to protect or promote the exercise of liberty, or that liberty outweighs life.

3. We also sought out the roots of autonomy in Jewish law. In the case of hazardous procedures, consent matters because uncertainty about medical outcomes ends up conferring autonomy upon patients, who carry out their own calculations. In the rulings of R. Feinstein on end-of-life decisions, autonomy emerges as the prerogative to extend one's life when the default position is that it not be extended, rather than the other way around. In altruistic self-sacrifice, those who permit blind altruism are conferring the autonomy to surrender life when the default position is not to, while R. Kook's permission of calculated altruism (using the *Horayot* scale) confers a prerogative to preserve one's life when the default position, or at least the preferred position, is to extend the life of the other if the latter ranks higher on the *Horayot* scale. Outside the medical ethics context, there are views on which Halakhah views voluntary martyrdom as acceptable and laudatory. In these and other cases the person has the choice to shorten his or her life.

4. Halakhah might appropriate certain elements of bioethicists' advocacy of autonomy, specifically a physician's duty of "conversation."

So, Halakhah does not deny autonomy entirely. Rather, halakhists can agree that "consent matters" in a range of cases, without their view converging completely with the secularist camp's.

I should like to make two final comments.

First, we must be careful not to allow a grant of autonomy to become a license for fulfilling suicidal wishes. Maimonides argued that confessions are not accepted in capital cases because the person may be confessing out of a suicidal desire, in which case a confession turns out to be unreliable evidence.[74] Limiting the range of cases that fall into the "permitted" zone is an effective way of preventing Halakhah from becoming a vehicle for suicidal urges. Although overall, we have seen, Jewish law allows people to sacrifice themselves for others in a range of circumstances. Maimonides's point about motives reminds us of the dangers of autonomy.

My other closing point is that the contrast between Jewish and secular ethics can be reduced without damage to the integrity of Halakhah because "*the* secular position" is a fiction. Ethicists do not uniformly make autonomy so supreme a value as is implied by proponents of the Jewish/secular contrast.

First of all, there are liberals and there are conservatives. "Liberal" bioethicists assert that the principle of autonomy gives people the right to chart their own course and make their own decisions, provided that others are not harmed by those decisions. Most importantly, this right holds even for unpopular or foolish decisions — ones that are detrimental to the person's own interests. For example, a person with a gangrenous leg must not be forced to undergo necessary surgery if he or she prefers to risk death rather than lose the limb or endure post-operative pain; members of religious sects opposed to blood transfusions must not be forced to receive them; requests not to be resuscitated must be honored; doctors who assist patients in suicide attempts must not be prosecuted; physicians who fail to warn patients of even seemingly insignificant risks must be punished.

But not all secular bioethicists agree with these positions. Quite the contrary, some of the positions mentioned evoke vigorous dissent. Although perhaps all bioethicists give the autonomy principle some weight in medical decision-making, ethicists disagree over how much weight to assign it when it conflicts with other principles. In particular, the principle of beneficence — which is the basis for much "paternalistic" intervention by governments in cases where a person is acting contrary to his or her best interest — sometimes clashes with that of autonomy. In legal terms, there is a "state interest" in preserving the health and welfare of citizens, and this interest must be balanced against the state's interest in preserving freedom and self-determination.[75] Hence, we have laws that require seat belts, laws that control the purchase or sale of drugs or tobacco, laws that outlaw dueling, proposals to outlaw boxing, and laws that restrain suicides. In these cases, too, we must decide whether to limit choice in order to benefit people, overriding their preferences, or — contrariwise — to preserve choice even if people will bring harm upon themselves as a result. Yet many secular ethicists advocate paternalistic policies. Conservative bioethicists will not go along with efforts to make autonomy supreme, and the courts sometimes back them up.

Second, as we have observed previously, bioethicists usually recognize a category of "diminished autonomy." Autonomy is respected only when the decision-maker manifests enough competence and informedness to make rational decisions, both in general and in the particular case. This proviso further reduces the gap between Jewish and secular perspectives by limiting the applications of the autonomy principle in the secular system.

Third, and most vitally for us, we have perhaps misrepresented the position of many liberal bioethicists. A bioethicist's respect for patient's decisions does not necessarily reflect the idea that people have the right to make foolish decisions. Even though some Western societies are thought to be in the grip of the autonomy principle, paternalistic legislation is part and parcel of those societies. *Truly foolish* decisions are *not* automatically respected. For instance, it is not likely that modern bioethicists would permit X to kill Y upon Y's request when Y is bemoaning the loss of his pet snake and therefore finds life no longer worth living. Similarly, it is not likely that they would allow a patient with meningitis to refuse a lifesaving antibiotic because it is too expensive. In many medical contexts, patients' choices are respected not because people have the right to make foolish decisions; they don't always have that right. Rather, regarding certain decisions, for example, decisions how to cope with pain or with an impending or hypothetical comatose state, or decisions that involve a complicated calculus of risks and benefits, there is no objective way to show that decisions to terminate life *are* foolish. More than one course is rationally defensible. In such cases, "the patient's interests" are set by the patient's preferences. It is one thing to refuse a simple pill that could cure a potentially fatal disease, another to refuse treatment that would protract life pointlessly and increase pain.

Halakhah's refusal to permit patients' choices in certain areas reflects the Halakhah's view that in those areas we *can* assign objective values. If secular bioethicists would agree on the value system, they might agree that autonomy may not be exercised in those situations, just as they do in cases where they agree that value judgments can be objectively made. The real issue is the objectivity and bindingness of the Jewish value system, not the right of patients to opt for an objectively detrimental choice over an objectively beneficial one. I agree with Avraham Steinberg that unless there are common, shared values such as those enunciated in religious traditions, there is little hope of resolving complex dilemmas in medicine.[76] But a corollary is that the real contrast between Halakhah and other systems is not that secular ethicists let freedom override objective values while halakhists let other objective values override other freedom. The real contrast is that in crucial cases Jewish law believes in an objective ordering of values, while secular ethics in this area often does not.[77]

NOTES

I thank Edward Reichman for his comments on the manuscript.

[1]   Virtually all of the many books now available on medical ethics place the concept of autonomy and the competing concept of beneficence at center stage. As random examples of, respectively, an extreme and a moderate stress

on autonomy, see H. T. Engelhardt, *The Foundations of Bioethics* (New York, 1986) and Tom L. Beauchamp and James F. Childress, *Principles of Biomedical Ethics* (3rd ed., New York, 1989). Avraham Steinberg advances the theory that insistence on autonomy is "an extreme counterreaction" to the dehumanization which accompanied paternalistic policies. See Avraham Steinberg, "Medical Ethics: Secular and Jewish Approaches," in Fred Rosner, ed., *Medicine and Jewish Law* (Northvale, New Jersey, 1990), 20.

2   For a survey of both moral and legal aspects of informed consent (with emphasis on United States law) see my two-part article, "Autonomy, Beneficence, and Informed Consent: Rethinking the Connections," *Cancer Investigation* 4, 3 and 4, 4 (1986): 257-69, 353-61.

3   See *Mishneh Torah, Hilkhot Rotzeah* 1:4 and Radbaz's comments on *Hilkhot Sanhedrin* 18:6, explaining why confessions are accepted in monetary cases but not capital cases.

4   R. J. David Bleich, "Risks versus Benefits in Treating the Gravely Ill Patient: Ethical and Religious Considerations," in *Jewish Values in Bioethics*, ed. Levi Meier (New York, 1986), 73. R. Bleich, it should be noted, makes this remark in the context of discussing hazardous surgery, an area where he emphasizes that patients *do* have discretion and where informed consent is necessary. My debt to his work on hazardous therapies will become evident later in this essay. His formulation neatly captures contemporary *pesak* with regard to non-hazardous therapies.

5   R. Gedaliah A. Rabinowitz, "Procedure for a Daughter who has Digressed from the Correct Way" (Heb.), in R. Moshe Hershler (ed.), *Halakhah u-Refu'ah*, I (Jerusalem and Chicago, 1980), 336-42. Obviously, coercion must not harm the patient. See R. Moshe Feinstein, *Iggerot Mosheh, Hoshen Mishpat* II: 73:5, 74:3.

6   R. Jacob Emden, *Mor u-Ketzi'ah, Orah Hayyim* 328; Radbaz, Responsa IV:67 (#1139) regarding forcing treatment on Shabbat against a patient's will; R. David Zvi Hoffman, *Melammed le-Ho'il, Yoreh De'ah* #104. To be sure, some Jewish views look negatively upon seeking medical treatment in lieu of trusting God and therefore seem incompatible with coercion (e.g., R. Aha in *Berakhot* 60a [see Rashi]; Nahmanides commentary to Lev. 26:11). See R. Neriyah Gotel, "Medical Treatment: Between Choice and Coercion" (Heb.), *Or Ha-Mizrach* 40, 1 (Tishrei 5752), 59-70; Daniel B. Sinclair "Non-consensual Medical Treatment of Competent Individuals in Jewish Law, with Some Comparative Reference in Anglo-American Law," *Tel-Aviv University Studies in Law* 11 (1992), 227-58, esp. 227-43. Cf. R. Eliezer Waldenberg, Responsa *Tzitz Eliezer* XV:40, XVII:2.

7   This statement will be qualified later. As an aside, a minority of authorities maintain that there is no obligation to stop a suicide and/or that the duty of *hatzalah* (rescue) does not apply if a person does not want to be saved. This position gives a person some degree of autonomy. See *Minhat Hinnukh*, #34; R. Zalman Nehemyah Goldberg, in *Halakhah u-Refu'ah* II, ed. M. Hershler, 146-84; R. Neriyah Gotel, "In The Question of Accepting Medical Treatment" (Heb.), *Or Ha-Mizrach* 40, 2 (Tevet 5752), 167-76.

8   *Hilkhot Rotzeah* 11:4-5. See also *Shulhan Arukh, Hoshen Mishpat*, 427:9-10.

9   Similarly, see Baruch A. Brody, "A Historical Introduction to Jewish Casuistry on Suicide and Euthanasia," in *Suicide and Euthanasia*, ed. B. Brody (Boston, 1989), 39-75. Brody's focus is on the "sanctity of life" doctrine rather than autonomy, though these issues clearly are interconnected. See also Sinclair, "Non-consensual Medical Treatment."

10   The term "shortening" is actually misleading in the end-of-life decisions I will consider, as we shall see. Really the choice in those cases is not extending vs. extending. But I leave the rougher formulation in place for the moment.

11   Contrast Maimonides' prohibition of martyrdom where it is not mandated (*Hilkhot Yesodei ha-Torah* 5:4) with, e.g., the positive view of Tosafot, *Avodah Zarah* 27b, s.v. *yakhol*.

12   R. Jacob Reischer, Responsa *Shevut Ya'akov*, II:111.

13   Tosafot *Avodah Zarah* 18a, s.v. *ve-al*; cf. *Da'at Zekenim* to Gen. 9:5; cf. R. Solomon Luria, *Yam shel Shelomo, Bava Kamma* VIII:58. See Haym Soloveitchik, "Religious Law and Change: The Medieval Ashkenazic Example," *AJS Review* 12 (1987): 205-21.

14   The extensive literature on King Saul's death is of great relevance here. See, for example, R. Ephraim Oshry, Responsa *Mi-Ma'amakkim*, I:45. Often the permission is limited to cases of *hillul ha-Shem*, desecration of the divine name.

15   Luria sees this as Saul's rationale, as do some of the sources quoted in the section on altruism below and "As Thyself" (in this volume). Brody explores all these categories in "A Historical Introduction," 40-62. See also Dov I. Frimer, "Masada In the Light of Halakhah," *Tradition* 12, 1 (Summer 1971), 27-43.

16   A group cannot surrender an unspecified individual to a hostile enemy, arguably because there is no criterion for deciding "whose blood is redder" (R. Yosef Karo, *Kesef Mishneh* to *Hilkhot Yesodei ha-Torah* 5:5); but some authorities might permit a person to surrender himself voluntarily to save the group, even though that individual will also not know whose blood is redder. For possible bases for permitting volunteering, see Rashi, *Pesahim* 50a, s.v. *harugei Lud*; *Sefer Hasidim*, ed. Wistinetski (Frankfurt, 1924), #252, and also see 162, 165; in the Margulies edition (Jerusalem, 5733), #698, 674, 677 (though these last texts may make submission mandatory in some cases); R. Abraham Isaac Kook, *Mishpat Kohen*, #143-44; R. Hayyim Beneveniste, *Sheyarei Keneset ha-Gedolah* to *Yoreh De'ah* 157. The issue of volunteers came up during the Holocaust.

17   For example, see R. Moshe Sternbuch, "Regarding Duress in the Case of Negative Commandments and Redemption of Captives" (Heb.), *Yad Sha'ul* (Memorial Volume for Rabbi Dr. Shmuel Weingart) (Tel Aviv, 1953), 371-90, at 386-87.

18   In fact, in the case of altruistic self-sacrifice, the rescuer who gives up his life would be preserving one of God's *other* possessions.

19   Cf. B.A. Brody, "Morality and Religion Reconsidered," *Readings in the Philosophy of Religion: An Analytic Approach* (Englewood Cliffs, New Jersey, 1974), 592-603, 2nd ed. (1992), 491-503.

20   Radbaz seems not to have made the distinction I've suggested, because in his view the law against self-incrimination in capital cases is explained by

the "ownership" principle. But even Radbaz offers the explanation only as a *"ketzat ta'am,"* and ultimately sees the ruling on confessions as a scriptural decree.

The ownership thesis also cannot be *God's* reason for banning any particular type of choice. If He is not to be arbitrary, He needs to have a reason for differentiating choices He bans and choices He permits.

21   Steinberg, 26.

22   The observation by R. Avram Israel Reisner that "the patient has the autonomy of individual free will, including the autonomy to reject God's commands and seek death" is not true of normative (prescriptive) autonomy but only of descriptive autonomy, affirming the reality of free choice. Cf. R. Reisner, "A Halakhic Ethic of Care for the Terminally Ill," *Conservative Judaism* 43, 3 (Spring 1991): 52-89, at 62.

23   More broadly stated, Jewish Law cannot be derived from its theological principles. To take another example, a person might believe that all suffering is punishment for sin, or, for that matter, a reward for sin ("suffering improves"), but this is no reason to rule that one ought not come to the aid of a sufferer. See my "Does Jewish Law Express Jewish Philosophy?," in this volume.

24   Although I will not examine them, see Gotel's interesting suggestions in "Medical Treatment" and "In the Question." According to some views, he shows, the pious may refuse medical treatment and place their trust in God — thereby exercising their autonomy. See also Sinclair, "Non-consensual Medical Treatment," 227-43.

25   Coercion is applied to a case of *"refu'ah bedukah,"* a therapy of proven worth. See R. Jacob Emden, *Mor u-Ketzi'ah, Orah Hayyim* 328. For clarification of this concept, see R. Gedaliah Rabinowitz, "Insufficiently Tested Medical Procedures" (Heb.), in *Halakhah u-Refu'ah* III, ed. M. Hershler (Jerusalem and Chicago, 1983), 115-18. It is not clear how tested a therapy must be to qualify as *bedukah.* Modern research distinguishes between controlled and uncontrolled studies, blinded and unblinded trials, single-blinded and double-blinded trials, not to mention studies that reach a 95% level of certainty and studies that attain 90%, etc. How do all these categories translate into the halakhic category of *bedukah,* which was devised before the development of probability theory and before modern refinements of the concept of a valid controlled study? Gotel, "in the Question," argues that according to R. Emden the subjective attitude of the patient toward experimental medications is important, and that confers a degree of autonomy upon patients.

26   There are many questions regarding *kefiyyah* of medical treatment. For example, is it rooted in the principle of *kefiyyah al ha-mitzvot* (general religious coercion) or in the principle of *lo ta'amod al dam re'akha*? Can *kefiyyah* be carried out by individuals or only by courts? Must doctors apply coercion even when hospital regulations prohibit it?

27   Bleich, "The Obligation to Heal," 28; *Contemporary Halachic Problems* II (New York, 1983), 83. In "Risks versus Benefits," he claims that Jewish law regarding hazardous procedures is based on the "bailee" analogy.

28 For a digest of views, see R. J. David Bleich, *Contemporary Halachic Problems* II, 82-83; Basil Herring, *Jewish Ethics and Halakhah for Our Time* II (New York, 1989), 28-34.

29 On these questions, see R. Moshe Feinstein, *Halakhah u-Refu'ah*, I, 131-42; *Iggerot Mosheh, Yoreh De'ah* II:58, III:36; and *Hoshen Mishpat* II:73-75. Interestingly, in *Yoreh De'ah* III:36 R. Feinstein explains that in choosing between *hayyei sha'ah* and *hayyei olam* a person "has, in this respect, *ba'alut* (ownership) over his life" (see also his statement in Hershler, *Halakhah u-Refu'ah* I, 137). This of course seems to be *restatement* of the ruling rather than the *basis* for it. For a thoughtful approach to risk-benefit questions, see Fred Rosner, "Risk-Benefit Ratio: Hazardous Surgery and Experimental Therapy" and R. Moshe D. Tendler, "Rabbinic Comment: Risk-Benefit Ratio," both in *Mount Sinai Journal of Medicine*, 51, 1 (January-February 1984), 58-59 and 60-64 respectively.

30 See R. Moshe Meiselman, "Kidney Transplants" (Heb.), in *Halakhah u-Refu'ah* II, ed. M. Hershler (Jerusalem and Chicago, 1981), 114-21.

31 See R. J. D. Bleich, *Contemporary Halachic Problems* II, 80-84. *Avodah Zarah* 27b is a key source about uncertainty; see also R. Jacob Reischer, *Shevut Ya'akov* III:85.

32 See R. Moshe Feinstein in *Halakhah u-Refu'ah* II, ed. M. Hershler, 71-75.

33 See Bleich, *Contemporary Halachic Problems* I (New York, 1977), 119-23. See Emden, *Mor u-Ketzi'ah, Orah Hayyim* 328; Tosafot *Shabbat* 50b, s.v. *bishvil*; Meiri, *Beit ha-Behirah* to *Sanhedrin* 84b; Rama, *Yoreh De'ah* 241:3; R. Jacob Breisch, *Helkat Ya'akov* III:11; R. Moshe Feinstein, *Iggerot Mosheh, Hoshen Mishpat*, II:66.

34 This is an issue in laws of Shabbat and Yom Kippur. See *Orah Hayyim* 328, 618. See note 43, below.

35 See R. Herschel Schachter, "*Eilav hu Nosei et Nafsho*," *Beit Yitzhak* 18 (5746): 104-8. Also see R. Feinstein, *Iggerot Mosheh, Yoreh De'ah* III:36.

36 See Herring, *Jewish Ethics and Halakhah*, 33; he quotes Responsa *Shevut Ya'akov* III:75 (R. Jacob Reischer) requiring (i) a medical opinion by a majority of two to one plus (ii) consultation with the preeminent rabbinical authority of the city.

37 The distinction I will sketch can be found in Laurence Haworth, *Autonomy* (New Haven, 1986) and Gerald Dworkin, *The Theory and Practice of Autonomy* (New York, 1988).

38 See Beauchamp and Childress, *Principles*, 69: "We analyze autonomous action in terms of normal choosers who act (1) intentionally (2) with understanding and (3) without controlling influences that determine the action."

39 Jay Katz, *The Silent World of Doctor and Patient*, (New York, 1984), 152.

40 Beauchamp and Childress, *Principles*, 73.

41 A notable exception is found in Rabbi Dr. David Feldman and Fred Rosner, M.D., eds. *Compendium on Medical Ethics: Jewish Moral, Ethical and Religious Principles in Medical Practice* (New York, 1984), 18-19.

42 E.g., Maimonides, *Commentary to the Mishnah, Nedarim* 4:4. See *Sanhedrin* 73a.

43 Physician fallibility is clearest when *pikuah nefesh* overrides laws of Shabbat and Yom Kippur; see e.g., *Shulhan Arukh, Orah Hayyim* 328, 618. There may

be a distinction between a patient's reliability vis-à-vis food and vis-à-vis medicine. For sources and discussion, see R. S. Wollner, "The Rights and Prerogatives of the Physician" (Heb.), *Ha-Torah ve-ha-Medinah* 7-8 (5716), sect. XI, reprinted in *Be-Tzomet ha-Torah ve-ha-Medinah* ed. R. Y. Shaviv (Jerusalem, 1991), 392-93; Gotel, "In the Question"; Sinclair "Non-consensual Medical Treatment," 243-47.

44 See Gotel, "Medical Treatment."

45 See below my discussion of Maimonides' explanation of why confessions are not accepted in capital cases (*Hilkhot Sanhedrin* 18:6).

46 See my treatment of this subject in part II of my "Autonomy, Beneficence and Informed Consent." There are competing views among secular ethicists about whether "causation" should have to be proved in order for a doctor to be successfully sued or (as some would prefer) prosecuted. If a patient is harmed because risk x materialized during surgery, and the doctor did not divulge risk x, must a plaintiff prove that knowing of risk x would have deterred him or her from having the surgery done? What if a patient was not informed of risk x, but died when risk y, which he or she was told about, materialized?

47 For Jewish sources and discussion concerning truth-telling in medicine, see Basil Herring, *Jewish Ethics and Halakhah for Our Time* I (New York 1984), 47-65.

48 It is interesting to inquire whether coercing a patient to a treatment he has not consented to falls into a category of murder if the patient dies. The decision itself is objectively defensible, though it was not the *patient's* choice.

49 Jewish law contains an explicit license for some foolishness. "The Lord preserves the simple" (Ps. 116:6) permits some assumption of *slight* risks because of a faith in divine providence. See, e.g. *Shabbat* 129b. Conceivably, "the Lord preserves the simple" would allow Jews to undertake some definite but not very high medical risks if those risks are commonly undertaken. (See R. Ya'akov Breisch, *Helkat Ya'akov* III: 11. Cf. *Darkhei Teshuvah* to *Yoreh De'ah* 155:2; R. Eliezer Waldenberg, *Tzitz Eliezer* X:25, XVII:1.) I presume that in all such cases, "consent matters." For example, authorities who permit smoking on the grounds that "the Lord preserves the simple" do not permit it when others will be affected and have not given their permission to the smoker. Here too, consent matters. See R. Moshe Tendler, "In the Law of *ve-Nishmartem*: The Definition of Risk in Halakahah" (Heb.), *Beit Yitzhak* 15 (1981-82): 72.

50 A *locus classicus* for laws governing euthanasia is *Shulhan Arukh, Yoreh De'ah* 339, including the very important glosses of Rama. For further sources and discussion, see Herring *Jewish Ethics*, 67-90. In his extensively documented and insightful study, *Tradition and the Biological Revolution* (Edinburgh, 1989), much of which deals with euthanasia, Daniel B. Sinclair expressly excludes the topic of patient wishes from his purview, maintaining that in Jewish law people cannot dispose of their bodies according to their wishes (p. 4). This conscious omission in a well-researched book testifies to the paucity of literature on this topic. Cf. Sinclair, "Non-consensual Medical Treatment."

51 I will not address here the potential conflict between a physician's ethical commitments and hospital policies. See A. Jeff Ifrah, "The Living Will," *Journal of Halacha and Contemporary Society* 24 (Fall 1992): 121-52, at 139-46.

52 *Iggerot Mosheh, Yoreh De'ah* II: 174. The story of R. Haninah ben Teradyon (*Avodah Zarah* 18a) and the subsequent halakhic literature on "removing impediments" (especially Rama to *Yoreh De'ah* 339:4) are used to support this thesis. If we can remove impediments to the dying process, the argument goes, it is surely not mandated to provide impediments.

53 See Responsa *Iggerot Mosheh, Hoshen Mishpat* II: 73-75, esp. II: 73:1; 74:1; and finally 75:1, which I am here quoting.

54 R. Auerbach, "Treatment of the Dying (*Goses*)," in *Halakhah u-Refu'ah* II, ed. M. Hershler, 131; I've expanded the translation of Brody, "A Historical Introduction," 70. R. Feinstein also addresses the food-drink/medication distinction. See also Abraham S. Abraham, *Nishmat Avraham* (Jerusalem, 1982) to *Yoreh De'ah* 339:4 (pp. 244-46).

55 Abraham S. Abraham, "Treatment of the Dying and the Determination of Death," (Heb.), in *Halakhah u-Refu'ah* II, ed. M. Hershler, 188-90; also in *Nishmat Avraham*, 246. See Brody, "A Historical Introduction," 72.

56 See *Ketubbot* 104a; R. Nissim of Gerondi to *Nedarim* 40a. Cf. R. Eliezer Waldenberg, *Ramat Rahel* #5.

57 Jewish law is not *radically* different from secular thinking in this respect, since many ethicists continue to distinguish between active and passive euthanasia even though the rationale for passive euthanasia might also justify active euthanasia. See, however, the controversial attack on the active/passive distinction in James Rachels, "Active and Passive Euthanasia," *New England Journal of Medicine* 292 (1975): 78-80.

58 Cf. R. Herschel Schachter, "Regarding the Laws of a Dead Person and a *Gavra Ketila*," *Assia* 13, 1-2 (July 1990): 134-35.

59 I am not saying that no secular bioethicists distinguish active from passive.The majority do.

60 Good surveys of Jewish views include Herring, *Jewish Ethics and Halakha* II, ch. 1 and ch. 4, 115-19, and Aaron Kirschenbaum, "The 'Good Samaritan' in Jewish Law," *Dine Israel* 7 (1976): 7-85.

61 There is some overlap between this section and part of the other article, but whereas the other article highlighted stringent views, here I give permissive views greater attention.

62 R. Bleich has shown that Halakhah does not ban all products of wrongful activity. See his "Experimental Procedures and *Pikuah Nefesh*: The Concept of *Refuah Bedukah*," *Tradition* 25, 1 (Fall 1989): 55 and "Utilization of Scientific Data Obtained Through Immoral Experimentation," *Tradition* 26, 1 (Fall 1991): 65-76. He also suggests that according to Jewish law, "a physician has no greater responsibility than any other individual to jeopardize his life on behalf of others." See his "AIDS: A Jewish Perspective," *Tradition* 26, 3 (Spring 1992): 69-70. See also R. Waldenberg, *Tzitz Eliezer* IX:17:5 and XII:57. Cf. David Novak, *Jewish Social Ethics* (New York, 1992), 112-14.

63 See Avraham Steinberg, "The Disease of AIDS" (Heb.), *Assia* 12:3-4 (1989), 18-30, at 27-28. "Significant" risk is often defined in terms of a 50% line. Key sources about taking risks for the sake of another include ostensibly conflicting views of the Babylonian and Jerusalem Talmuds, and some responsa of Rabdaz, esp. #1052 and #1582; see also *Leshonot ha-Rambam* 5:218. For details of these texts and other references, see Herring, *Jewish Ethics and Halakhah* II, 20-28, and Brody, "A Historical Introduction," 52-59. See also R. Waldenberg, *Tzitz Eliezer* IX:45, X:25:7, 18. R. J.D. Bleich has argued that labeling someone a "pious fool" is not tantamount to a prohibition. See his "Experimentation on Human Subjects," in Rosner and Bleich, *Jewish Bioethics*, 384-85.

64 "Rescue" missions might seem more problematic than "resource" cases in that an altruistic rescue mission involves *creating* a risk where one did not exist previously, whereas in the classic resource cases, the possessor of the resource is in danger already. However, most writers explain that many *resource* cases are more problematic: for here one will *certainly* die if he saves the other, whereas in many rescue cases one will be merely *risking* one's life to save another.

65 Although not codified by Maimonides or R. Yosef Karo, and although regarded by some as aggadic rather than halakhic in character, R. Akiva's *hayyekha* principle has become critical in rabbinic decisions about self-endangerment. Interesting grounds for doubting that his decision is normative are found in R. Abraham Isaac Kook, *Mishpat Kohen* (Jerusalem, 5745), #144, sect. 16, p. 340. Explicit rulings in accord with R. Akiva are found in R. Menahem ha-Meiri, *Beit ha-Behirah* to *Bava Metzi'a* 62a and Hazon Ish (R. Avraham Yeshayahu Karelitz), *Hoshen Mishpat, Likkutim* 20. For surveys of the various accounts of R. Akiva's and ben Petura's positions, see S. B. Werner, *Mishpetei Shemuel* (Jerusalem, 1980), 21-61; Shemuel Dichovsky, "*Kidmiyyut va-Adifiyyut be-Hatzalat Nefashot*," *Dine Israel* 7 (1976): 45-66; Moshe Sokol, "The Allocation of Scarce Medical Resources," *AJS Review* 15 (1990): 63-93, sect. I; Aharon Enker, *Hekhreah ve-Tzorekh be-Dinei Oneshim* (Ramat-Gan, 1977), ch. 7.

66 R. Feinstein, *Iggerot Mosheh, Yoreh De'ah* II:174:4, pp. 292-93; R. Sternbuch, in *Yad Sha'ul* (see above, n. 18), 386-87; R. Unterman, *Shevet Yehudah* (Jerusalem, 1983), 15-16.

67 R. Weinberg, in *Yad Sha'ul*, 371-95; *Seridei Esh* I (Jerusalem, 1977), 314-15; cf. Meiri, *Beit ha-Behirah* to *Sanhedrin* 73a.

68 R. Kook, *Mishpat Kohen*, #143, at pp. 310-12 and #144 section 15-16, pp. 339-40. When I call the position "Rav Kook's," I ignore the tentative and hesitant character of his statements. An antecedent of his position may be found in *Sefer Hasidim*, ed. Wistinetski (Frankfurt, 1924), #252, and also see 162, 165; in the Margulies edition (Jerusalem, 5733), #698, 674, 677. See also R. Waldenberg, *Tzitz Eliezer*, X:25:7; cf. IX:45. On the question of risking one's life for the *tzibbur*, see R. Shlomo Dichovsky, "Priorities in the Saving of the Lives of the *Tzibbur*" (Heb.), *Torah she-be-al Peh* 31 (1990): 40-51.

69 Least-change principles are appealing because they can reconcile R. Akiva's ruling with the ruling that one may not actively kill another person in order to save oneself (*Sanhedrin* 74a, *Pesahim* 25b). The least change principle could

be framed as a distinction between active killing and passive withholding of a resource. However, since according to R. Akiva one does something active, namely drink, it is best to find a better way to frame the distinction, such as between direct causation and indirect causation. The indirect causation of drinking involves least change because the person who drinks is the owner. But "indirect causation" has other associations and may still not capture what we need.

70   R. Kook's view may not have a ready practical application. For, as Sokol argues in "The Allocation of Scarce Medical Resources," authors of more recent responsa are reluctant to apply *Horayot* criteria to actual situations. The category of "greater number" (saving the many over the few) is sometimes invoked, however, and this category, not mentioned in *Horayot*, may continue to be applied.

71   Perhaps calculations are needed to justify it, but I am not clear why, given that the key is a higher ethic, and that may apply to blind as well as calculated altruism.

72   See my "As Thyself."

73   Ibid., 270-71.

74   Maimonides argues that a confessor may be confessing out of a suicidal desire, in which case his confessions turn out to be unreliable evidence (*Hilkhot Sanhedrin* 18:6). Now Maimonides also rules that if in a given situation a person is permitted to violate a certain prohibition rather than give up his life, but gives up his life anyway, "he is deserving of death," i. e. has given up a life unnecessarily (*Hilkhot Yesodei ha-Torah* 5:1). A possible explanation of this position, albeit highly speculative and unconfirmed, is that, in line with his point about confessions, Maimonides was aware that people could otherwise act out their death wishes with halakhic license. Limiting the range of cases that fall into the "permitted" zone is an effective way of preventing Halakhah from becoming a vehicle for suicidal urges. The analogy between confessions and martyrdom is of course imperfect. In the case of confessions, the possibility of a suicidal wish undermines the confession's *probative value*, a factor that is not relevant in the case of voluntary martyrdom.

Interestingly, according to the line of reasoning given by Enker, ch. 7, Maimonides probably would not have permitted voluntary surrender by an individual in a case where a group was threatened "give us over some one from among you or we will kill you all." According to Enker, Maimonides rules in accordance with Resh Lakish — not to give over anyone even if the person is specified and all will be killed if he is not given over (unless the person is deserving of death) — based on a principle of not giving in to arbitrary demands of the enemy. By this logic, volunteers should not be accepted, because volunteering gives in to those arbitrary demands. However, in the case where no one is specified, if we highlight the fact that the enemy is merely trying to put the Jews into a "Sophie's Choice" situation, where they must pick one of their own, then a volunteer would actually be thwarting the enemy.

Oddly, Maimonides refers to the law against self-incrimination as a "*gezerat ha-katuv*" or "*gezerat ha-melekh*" (decree of Scripture or decree of the King) even though he has provided a rationale for it. For a proposal to remove this anomaly and others like it see Josef Stern, "On An Alleged Contradiction between Maimonides's *Mishneh Torah* and *The Guide of the Perplexed*" (Heb.), *Shenaton Ha-Mishpat Ha-Ivri* 14-15 (1988-89): 283-98.

75 See R. J. David Bleich, *Time of Death in Jewish Law* (New York, 1991), 107-27; also 79-80. An especially vigorous critique of autonomy is E. Pellegrino and D. C. Thomasma, *For the Patient's Good* (New York, 1988).

76 Steinberg, "Medical Ethics," 27.

77 Postscript (2009): The late Benjamin Freedman, a distinguished bioethicist, explores the concept of autonomy from both a secular and Jewish standpoint in *Duty and Healing: Foundations of a Jewish Bioethic,* ed. Charles Weijer (New York, 1999).

CONCLUDING REFLECTIONS ON RELIGIOUS BELIEF

THE OVEREXAMINED LIFE IS
NOT WORTH LIVING*

I am an Orthodox Jew and have been so all my life. I did not choose Judaism but was born to parents who, while modern in dress, educational ideals, and occupations, were Orthodox; and so my early life was permeated with Jewish observances, while my education took place in schools that combined a secular curriculum with a traditional Jewish one. I attended a yeshiva elementary day school in Monsey, New York, then studied at the high school administered by Yeshiva University in New York City, went next to Yeshiva University for my B.A., and finally culminated my Judaic training by receiving rabbinical ordination at the university's affiliate theological seminary. A few years later I earned a Ph. D in philosophy at Columbia University, specializing in contemporary epistemology. In contrast to two other sorts of institutions — religious schools that eye secular curricula with suspicion and contempt and Jewish universities that are secular in character — Yeshiva University maintains that traditional Jewish study and commitment to the full range of Jewish law must be combined with worldly wisdom and broad exposure to secular culture. Indeed, Yeshiva is unique among Jewish institutions of higher learning by virtue of this driving ideology, which it captures in the slogan "Torah u-Madda" — roughly translated as "Torah and general knowledge." Consequently, when I began to pursue my Ph.D., it was the first time I had been free of a formal commitment to a dual curriculum. Up to the age of twenty-four, every day of my formal education — eighteen years' worth, often eleven hours a day — had included intensive exposure to Jewish sources, with study of Talmud and Jewish law embracing more hours than secular subjects and constituting around eighty percent of Jewish studies after the early grades.

---

*   (2009): This essay was published in an anthology of autobiographical essays by religiously committed professional philosophers. I have included it in this collection because it discusses central issues in religious epistemology and raises questions about the relationship between philosophy and human life, questions that trace back to the ancient philosophy and have sparked renewed interest among philosophers today.

You might now expect the next sentence to read, "And then the roof fell in." But it didn't. Obviously, as time moved on, the demands of professional life and of enlarged domestic responsibilities — not to mention personal deficiencies in motivation and stamina — shoved the idea of six to eight hours of Talmud study a day beyond the pale of realistic possibility. Nonetheless, neither graduate school in philosophy nor a career in the field did much to change my overall religious orientation and practice. I have always belonged to Orthodox synagogues and attended them regularly; for many years, in fact, I've cultivated avocations as the regular Torah reader in my synagogue (this involves chanting the weekly biblical portion) and occasional cantor. (The humorous side of a philosophy professor's leading the climactic prayer for forgiveness on Yom Kippur has not escaped the congregation's notice.) My wife is a rabbi's daughter — a descendant, on both her father's and mother's side, of distinguished Hasidic families. My children, like other American teenagers, are tuned in to entertainment, sports, and politics; but they attend religious schools, pray the prescribed three times a day, study religious texts intensively, and observe the precepts of Jewish law piously and meticulously. We have never tried any other way of life. In a nutshell, my upbringing and lifestyle have been basically uniform, without the on-again, off-again quality described by some of the other contributors to this volume [i.e., the volume of autobiographical essays by religious philosophers in which this article first appeared].

I wish I could boast that my continuance in my religious lifestyle is the result of some grand synthesis of religion and philosophy on the order of that envisaged by Maimonides; or, alternatively, that it testifies to my being a Kierkegaardian knight of faith. But the immediate explanation, I'm afraid, is more prosaic and far from self-congratulatory. I didn't come to religion, I merely managed to hold on to it in conducive circumstances. My familial, educational, and social lives were so much built around Judaism; the social context in New York, with its impressive Orthodox population and its abundance of personalities, synagogues, and houses of study, was so friendly to the status quo; and the atmosphere at my place of work was so congenial to my inherited ways that holding on psychologically was easy. My present academic appointment is at Yeshiva University, where I enjoy the unusual luxury of presenting myself to my students exactly as I am, without having to explain myself or apologize, and where, unlike so many of my Orthodox friends who feel themselves the odd one out in their work environment, I can enjoy a pleasing continuity between my personal and professional lives.

Leaving the fold thus never made an appearance as a serious option, because my very identity was so tied up with my faith and religious practice. And I cherished the "halakhic" way of life (i.e., life in accordance with Halakhah, Jewish law) despite — or maybe because of — its many demands. Religious observances, while multifarious and laden with myriad technicalities, impart structure to daily life, give rhythm to the calendar, inject warmth into family celebrations, and create solidarity during times of sadness and crisis. Most important, the many laws governing routine activities serve, in a classic but pointed phrase, to "sanctify the mundane." Study of Jewish texts, furthermore, excited my mind. These attractions and benefits, on which I shall elaborate later, might have looked different had I found myself in some far-flung and God-forsaken community where everyone around me thought differently and where temptation lurked in every cranny. But in the actual world, given the acute sense of community I enjoyed, there seemed to be (in William James's phrase), no "live options," no real competitors, to my established way of life. On top of that, my personality is somewhat allergic to change — adjustments intimidate me — and so a conservative course in life seemed a foregone result.

Some of my conservatism has also to do with the educational philosophy in which I was reared. In Chaim Potok's novels — Potok, by the way, was a Yeshiva University graduate — protagonists experience powerful tensions between their traditional Jewish upbringing and exposure in later life to broader horizons. And in Potok's novels the characters rebel, or at a minimum undergo profound and wrenching conflict. But rebellion and conflict often emerge precisely when one's early education takes place in an atmosphere that is extreme and denigrates secular studies totally. Open the window, just a bit, later in their lives and expose them to some of the finer things in culture, and those same people who had been conditioned to think of secular studies as vapid, alien, and dangerous sometimes feel they've been cheated, their talents stifled, their true calling unactualized. When one is taught from the outset, as I was, that secular studies are of value and can coexist with Judaism, when one hears this, moreover, trumpeted as ideology, as I did, one might, of course, rebel as conflicts become evident, casting doubt on the ideology's optimism; but another result can be a refusal to see oneself as mired in either-or situations — one hopes for a resolution down the line. That others with comparable backgrounds and training have not held on but have instead felt conflicts to be insuperable doesn't alter *my* realities. In *my* case social identity, psychological boons, the inspiration of role models (more on this later), the power of ideology, and inveterate aversion to change proved a strong enough bond, and I suspect that in the cases of others who turned out differently, psychological and sociological forces were likewise conspiring — albeit to produce a contrasting result.

Birth, upbringing, tradition, education, and community are focal categories in analyses of religious commitment that flow from Jewish law,

Jewish thought, and Jewish experience. There is a definite fit between these analyses and my biography. Indeed, typically, so goes my impression, "born" Orthodox Jews, while they interpret events in light of their belief in divine providence, nonetheless report few or no specific episodes of experiencing God's voice or immediate presence, few or no direct personal revelations, which sustain them in their faith. My own history, stressing as it does contingency over choice, community over individuality, study over personal revelation, is therefore not unusual among my coreligionists and may be quite representative of a large population. (I make no comment here on converts to Judaism, who may represent a contrasting category.)

But how do I feel about this narrative? My preceding description might seem doubly shameful: It testifies to no great spiritual strength, and it amounts to a philosopher's *mea culpa* (or to use the Hebrew, "*al het*"). Philosophy — in the spirit of Bacon's methods and the opening lines of Descartes's *Meditations* — is supposed to root out the prejudices we acquire in our youth and from our peers. If so, why didn't a career spent pursuing truth and rationality dislodge any psychological and social forces that were keeping me in the fold? Why didn't being so aware of the contingency of my upbringing make me worry about the epistemological merits of what I believed? Didn't I violate professional norms?

Naturally, I have been asked these questions often in my life, and from two different points of origin. Nonreligious academics ask — if not by words, then by their glances: "Shouldn't philosophy have affected your lifestyle?" Members of my religious community ask me — again, often by their glances — the reverse: "How can a religious Jew study this stuff and survive spiritually?" Behind such questions lie immense presuppositions and expectations about what effect philosophy "should" have on religious belief. By and large, these presuppositions remain unarticulated and unexamined by the people who make them. Yet they persist, and their tenacity, in large part, is what motivates this anthology [the book of autobiographies in which this essay first appeared] and will make its contents and direction surprising to many.

I am inclined to think that questions about how one can be both religious and a philosopher rest on some misconceptions. These include misconceptions about the state of philosophy today, about the impact of philosophy on life's big questions, and about the urgency of purging prejudice from one's being in order to number oneself among professional philosophers. There are, on the contrary, several ways in which a professional philosopher can shut out philosophy from his or her religious life — with or without conscious rationalization — all the while maintaining professional integrity; and there are also ways in which a philosopher can let philosophy enter religious life without emerging scathed by the intrusion. I don't mean to say that bifurcation is praiseworthy; I do mean to say that the lives of many religiously committed philosophers cannot be understood without first appreciating to the fullest the *potential* that exists for defensible, rationalizable bifurcation. And I would describe my own process of intellectual maturation as a struggle to break down the walls of a bifurcation that I could, if necessary, legitimate intellectually and for a long while did, as a quest for a meaningful way of integrating my professional and personal commitments.

The answers I would have given to the questions at hand (about how I could be a religious philosopher) at certain stages in my career are not identical with the answers I'd have given at other stages. As a result, the reader may detect some contrasts or even inconsistencies among the answers I catalog below. But let me nonetheless lay out the total territory — the several ways in which one could, if so motivated, separate philosophy from life or, alternatively, find it congenial. I now recognize the limitations of these tactics and will explain them in due course. Even so, all have played some role at some point in my own narrative, and there is something to be learned from them, I think.

1. *Specialization*: If a philosopher doesn't want to examine his or her religious beliefs with professional tools, philosophy offers many "safe" fields that constitute neutral ground; they don't need to be connected to religion at all. The age of academic specialization and, to be frank, narrowness has made segregation possible. You can specialize in epistemology, philosophy of language, logic, history of philosophy, philosophy of science, and, yes, *even* metaphysics, and yes, *even* ethics, without the slightest intrusion of religiously sensitive material — unless you want the intrusion, in which case there are numerous ways you can invite it. Many of the problems I address in professional life have nothing immediately to do with religion. A philosopher friend of mine once asked facetiously about a colleague: "How does he reconcile substitutional quantification with Judaism?" His point, here expressed humorously, was that if you specialized in substitutional quantification, you didn't have to grapple with God. Just as mathematicians, scientists, and computer experts can avoid religiously charged questions if they want to, so can a professional philosopher.[1] Some people of my faith do exactly that. They violate no professional norm in the process. If anything, the contrary holds. Professional norms for a time viewed philosophy of religion as "soft" philosophy, unsuitable for the truly serious. Due to my graduate department's particular emphases, I did no work in philosophy of religion for many years, and specializing elsewhere served me for that time as a defense against thinking too hard about my beliefs and lifestyle.

2. *Internalization*: An assumption that lies behind the questions we religious philosophers get asked is that philosophers internalize the conclusions that their intellects draw — and live by them. David Hume taught us otherwise. Hume was fascinated by the divorce between philosophy and practical life. In my study, he said, I come to appreciate that I lack adequate grounds for all sorts of things I take for granted in my life — the regularity of nature, the reality of the physical world; yet when I exit, those intellectual infirmities have not the slightest influence on my belief system. A philosophical skeptic, someone who casts doubt on our grounds for these and other common beliefs (e.g., belief in other sentient creatures, belief in the trustworthiness of memory), cannot *live* his skepticism, Hume holds. (Here Hume is rejecting the contrary view of the ancient skeptics.) Even in his study, in fact, Hume isn't really a skeptic. He doesn't doubt he's putting pen to paper, and doesn't wonder whether the paper will abruptly pop out of existence. That nobody is *really* a skeptic — *even* while philosophizing — becomes clear if you watch what we philosophers do, not what we say. When a philosopher publishes an article called "Why There Are No People" (an actual title!), he invites a joke: Whom does he think he's writing for? Whom will he blame if he gets turned down for tenure?

Think of another specialization in philosophy: ethics. Many philosophers can rehearse arguments to show that ethics is relative, that it is subjective, that it is biologically determined, that it is contingent on tradition and upbringing. And they don't generally know how to rebut all those arguments. Some may actually endorse *intellectually* one or more of these bugaboo theses. But do they internalize them? Do they take leave of ethical behavior or of their particular moral beliefs because of it? Or consider the old conundrum of political philosophy: why must we obey the laws of the state? Philosophers who find no compelling argument for obeying government do not necessarily use this as a license to flout the law or to look sympathetically at those who do. Determinists can be just as ready as everyone else to excoriate wrongdoers, even if they can't articulate a theory of responsibility that is consonant with determinist assumptions. Again, there are philosophers who find ingenious ways to show that death need not concern us; how they weather a gloomy medical prognosis remains to be seen. In the sphere of religion, proofs for the existence of God don't always sway people into belief (the ontological argument of Anselm is notorious for not converting those who think it is sound); intellectual solutions to the problem of evil, however formidable, often fail to soothe the gut-level feeling that a perfect God would not allow evil; and, by the same token, objections to a theistic position don't always translate into abandonment of belief, because other forces shape us. So, even if philosophy were to deliver its conclusions about religion, it would not be astonishing if professionals did not internalize them.

My point so far has been descriptive only; philosophers, I've said, don't *in fact* internalize philosophical arguments. Hume's point, however, was probably normative as well as descriptive. Hume taught us, in effect, that it is a vice to be too rational, to hold out for rigorous arguments in all walks of life. Only a mad person would want to conduct his or her life with complete, Spock-like logicality. We are possessed not of minds alone, but of hearts, emotions, needs, instincts, and habits; and we inhabit social contexts. Obviously, without the use of reason, anarchy enters; still, in most areas of belief and practice, we don't — and shouldn't — let *philosophical* worries get to us. When the subject isn't religion, people joke regularly about the sterotypical philosopher whose head is in the clouds and who worries about intellectual puzzles that no one else gives a thought to — or, to repeat, *should* give a thought to. But then we get to religion, and here I detect a double standard. Suddenly, if our philosophical ruminations don't profoundly impact on our lives, if we live without the two synchronized, we're accused of being hypocrites and irrational. True, Hume was speaking of beliefs everyone shares — "natural beliefs" — and religion, in our age, no longer fills that bill. Also, the beliefs Hume spoke of were irresistible, which religious belief is not. But try to explain *why* his point should work only for universally held and irresistible beliefs. The plain fact is that we allow ourselves a considerable degree of nonrational influence when we engage in the business of forming a metaphysics and a worldview. I shall say more later about what experiences keep one wedded to religious belief.[2]

In my early years in the field, throughout the 1970s, I found it particularly easy to resist internalizing philosophy. The regnant analytic approach to philosophy had curiously distanced itself from real religious life by insisting on putting everything in its characteristic idiom: technical, dry discourse, inaccessible to all but the philosophically trained. A clever student of mine, having sat through a long, complex technical series of arguments and objections I had dutifully presented in logical notation, once put this question to me with only partially mock astonishment: "Do you mean to tell me that the existence of God might depend on the scope of a quantifier?" A certain cynicism set in as one followed the literature. No sooner had one become convinced that — to put it in professional jargon — "(17a) follows from (16d), assuming the correctness of (14)" than a subsequent issue of the same journal appeared where one learned that, "Unfortunately, (12) is not as evident as might appear, vitiating the inference from (18) to (19)." It is not just that the notion grew that every position and argument could be refuted with sufficient ingenuity, so that no individual argument could be cause for panic. After years of thinking and writing in this genre — and enjoying it,

I confess — I got weaned off the habit when it hit me that philosophy had lived for nearly two and a half millennia with hardly anyone — including the greats — expressing ideas that way. When I coedited a text on philosophy of religion in 1982 and searched the literature for accessible articles to reprint, I was amazed at how few pieces could be grasped by the uninitiated. Does all this really have much to do with religious life, I wondered? If you saw somebody trying to resolve a spat with a spouse by putting pen to paper and setting up numbered premises, you'd find it a crazy way to settle things, and maybe would also brand it as a tactic for fleeing the real issues. Only in philosophy does this sort of exactitude win an imprimatur; elsewhere, we find it stultifying, obsessive, and immature. There was no reason to carry this mindset into life in general and religious life in particular. Religious people who look at philosophy sometimes find themselves put off at what strikes them as mind games that have no hold on what it *feels* like to be religious — no existential grip. Worst of all, those thinkers who *were* touching chords in religious people, who were drawing on religion as it is actually lived, were being scoffed at as mere "theologians." The unkindest cut of all, presumably.

In light of this, I wonder whether my extensive exposure to Talmud was what led me to like the philosophy I studied as an undergraduate and to whet my appetite for more. Subtlety, rigor, complexity; dexterity at deciphering difficult texts; the mongering of distinctions and counterexamples — all these are nurtured in both Talmud study and analytic philosophy. Philosophy, in other words, catered to my talmudically trained mind. But beyond that lay something else. In studying Talmud, one was immersed in a world that need have no effect on practical life. Some tractates deal with institutions no longer standing — sacrifices and high courts, for example — and even in tractates that dealt with applicable laws such as Sabbath, holidays, prayer, blessings, dietary laws, mourning, marriage and divorce, the particular discussions and debates in the talmudic text were freighted with fantastic cases (used to clarify legal principles) and with theoretical objections that had no effect on the practical law. In other words, in Talmud you learned to tolerate irrelevance and unreality and to let intellectual gyrations satisfy you for their own sake. Indeed, "study for its own sake" was an ideal to be aimed at; pragmatic irrelevance was to be consciously cultivated. To put it better: the world of Talmud is a world, real, vibrant and woven into the fabric of religious existence, but it is populated by abstract entities, classifications, principles, and situations. The same carefree willingness to forego practical application, to luxuriate instead in the motions of the mind, to move about in an abstract universe — a sine qua non for grappling with Talmud — was also a sine qua non for studying philosophy and truly loving it. "Study for its own sake" is an alluring ideal indeed.

The tactic of saying that philosophy, however passionately pursued, didn't have to affect life served me well for a while. Its utility declined when academic philosophy of religion became conscious of psychological, human dimensions of religion it had previously ignored and related itself to deeper aspects of ordinary life. But the above mentioned obstacles to internalizing philosophy probably played a role at a pivotal stage of my development.

3. *Prejudice*: My questioners assume that philosophers ought to be especially ashamed of the prejudices they acquire from their youth. Now we do indeed take question, criticism, and dialogue more seriously than perhaps any other specialists do. But we all have our prejudices. When is a problem interesting and when is it not? When is a reply to an objection contrived and ad hoc, and when is it intuitively satisfying? Often your answer depends on your training and prior conviction. That is one reason why some people find themselves thoroughly satisfied with arguments that others find preposterous, while their opponents remain insensitive to and unmoved by objections that those people think devastating. Then also there's the (alleged) halo effect some complain about: Work in certain journals is more likely to be admired than work in other journals; work by people in school X is more likely to be appreciated than work by people in school Y; and the like. (The frequent insistence on blind review of submissions to journals and conferences surely concedes some of these worries.) But if philosophers are not immune from prejudices, then might there also be other forms of prejudice? Couldn't atheists be as much a product of their upbringing and environment as theists are? What about personal circumstances, like an unhappy home? Did every *atheist* philosopher I knew have a reasoned argument in hand? Did each of them know how to reply to, say, the clever theistic moves of the renowned analytic philosopher Alvin Plantinga? I saw no reason to accept a double standard.

My ability to live with philosophical assaults on religion was enhanced, not threatened, by the nasty attitude to religion that prevailed while I pursued my doctorate. Although by then few philosophers held any more to logical positivism — the view, once the rage, that religious statements are meaningless — its legacy was palpable, its grip still strong. And this led many departments to regard philosophy of religion as not worth attending to. Nobody in these departments "did" philosophy of religion. The assumption I read into that fact was that there were no interesting controversies in the field because religion had no philosophical merit. All this called to mind Bertrand Russell's complaint that religious motives (along with ethical ones) "have been on the whole a hindrance to the progress of philosophy, and ought now to be consciously thrust aside by those who wish to discover philosophical truth."

That was the party line. But then I'd read something by a good mind sympathetic to religion, and I'd see instantly that the supposedly decisive objections were poorly formulated and easily met; the questions were still open after all. This led me to think that philosophers were just being prejudicial. If more philosophers had deigned at that time to treat religious claims more seriously, it might have led theists to take their objections more seriously. As things were, philosophers seemed to be taking cheap shots and missing; philosophers didn't notice the extent of the partisanship because there were too few believers working in the field. Rumor had it that some journals would never publish an article on religion, let alone one defending it; and I heard speculation that acceptance was easier for hostile than for friendly pieces. (For all I know, both this perception and vehement denials of its accuracy were themselves products of prejudice!) Sure, the pro-theistic philosophers were bringing their own prejudices in too. But knowing that others were culpable took the sting out of any charges of prejudice leveled at the religious.

Some years ago, I was asked to referee a paper in the philosophy of religion that took a pro-theistic stance. After much thinking and weighing, I decided to recommend against acceptance. The author's point seemed insufficiently argued, I felt, and even if it was right, it had been made already in the literature in a different form. My identity as a referee was, of course, unknown to the author. A while later, the editor of the journal sent me, apologetically, a letter that he had received from the paper's author and that the author had insisted I see. The letter angrily took issue with my evaluation — and charged that the referee was obviously biased against theism! I relate this not to commend myself for my objectivity; in truth, the incident only attests to the degree of compartmentalization a philosopher could achieve, and anyway, subscribing to theism does not require accepting *every* argument offered on its behalf. My critic may have thought, though, that only those unsympathetic to religion could criticize a pro-religious paper. If so, at least we agreed that prejudice existed in the academy. Here then was another reason to bracket philosophical anxieties about religious belief: for you never knew when you were being suckered or browbeaten unfairly. (Of course, this response works best when you find a particular argument appealing while your adversary does not, so it necessitates your having an argument to begin with. I think the design argument provides a lovely example for this purpose.)

4. *The state of philosophy*: So far, I haven't touched on how philosophy could actually prove friendly to religion. Over the past ten to twelve years, however [this essay was written in 1994], another response has come into focus as trends have shifted in the philosophical community. We live in an age of ideological pluralism. No methods are privileged; even science

is just one slice of culture, not a supreme judge and jury. In the wake of Thomas Kuhn's *Structure of Scientific Revolutions*, scientific theories are often thought not to be the bastions of objectivity people thought they were.[3] In this atmosphere, religion now claims parity with other views and approaches. Some even argue that religion can set its own standards; let other disciplines and contentions stand before its tribunal, rather than the other way around.[4] Also, it is fashionable in philosophy today to recognize a "social" dimension in the justification of belief. You are justified in doing or believing something provided that the practice or belief is appropriate given your community's standards. If your religious community is your dominant one, then, if your beliefs and actions are justified by *its* standards, they are "justified," given this social account. (I realize the situation gets complex when you belong to *both* a religious *and* an academic community; that's why I stress dominance.)

There's more. When we're dealing with large-scale ways of looking at the world, "methodological conservatism" is now recognized as good rational practice; the mere fact that you already believe something gives you a reason to keep believing it. You can be the most rabid critic of the behaviorism espoused by B. F. Skinner, but surely you don't expect Skinner to suddenly drop his view of human psychology just because someone has posed a strong-sounding objection at some conference. He's too invested in it. If he'd dropped his lifelong belief just because someone came up with an objection, it's not just that you'd be surprised; to a certain degree, you'd think Skinner was irrational. We all begin our inquiries somewhere, with a large complex of presuppositions and convictions. We should be open to change, but all change is gradual. As one philosopher (Gilbert Harman) has put it, we strive to "maximize coherence and minimize change."

Philosophy today also teaches that no theory of the world is perfect — intellectual maturity requires living with objections. As a Yiddish expression neatly puts it: "A person does not die from a question." Finally, philosophers are more open than ever before to the realization that their bread and butter — to wit, arguments — doesn't coerce listeners. Philosophical expositions furnish them with new *perspectives*, not knockdown weapons of persuasion. What someone called the *scorched earth* approach to philosophical argument is giving way to a more accepting attitude to rock-bottom disagreement.

So, to some extent, the very *expectation* that philosophy, as it exists today, would undermine religious life betrays ignorance of what's going on in academic life; it rests on an outmoded stereotype. A lot of pro-traditional recent work in the philosophy of religion plays off of this kind of focus on epistemology and on the nature of philosophical argument. Now I don't want to grant this response more punch than it deserves — there are times when it downright irritates me. I am not terribly gratified at defending my point of view by saying to opponents of religion, "Look, you're in the same boat as regards a lot of things you believe." And I've never seen a good answer to the following challenge: if I can claim immunity from criticism on the grounds that justification is social, that starting points enjoy special protection, and the like, can't *anyone* in *any* community do likewise? If so, do I really want to allow that — to legitimize any and every worldview? Surely there's no *other* philosophical position I'd care to defend just by pointing up the difficulties of proving anything whatsoever or by positing the "basicality" of that belief in my "noetic structure" (these terms are borrowed from Plantinga's recent attempts to reinstate Reformed epistemology). Still, any realistic look at how philosophers assess religion has got to take notice of the contemporary pluralist, "postmodern" consciousness. And that's a key part of the answer to the questions I get asked. Moreover, Alasdair MacIntyre and Charles Taylor, eminent philosophers both, have argued forcefully not only that worldviews and moral commitments must arise in the context of tradition and community, but that religious communities deserve pride of place.

I haven't even introduced yet the fact that natural theology, which attempts to prove basic religious doctrines, is making a vigorous comeback. Top-flight philosophers who have forged their stellar reputations in mainline, "hard" fields like epistemology, metaphysics, philosophy of language, and philosophy of science, are theists and argue proudly for it. Now citing authorities who hold a position is hardly a way to make a philosophical point, particularly when the views of those authorities are hotly disputed. Even so, clearly philosophy isn't the devil it once allegedly was, and a religious philosopher can exude greater tranquility and confidence today than at any other time in recent decades.[5]

5. *The challenge of other fields*: All this leads to another question: Why pick on philosophy? Writing in *The American Scholar* in 1979, Kenneth Seeskin of Northwestern noted: "Such disciplines as science, history and mathematics culminate in a body of accepted beliefs...But it would be hard to find any accepted beliefs that originated with philosophy." True to this assessment, the toughest challenges to religion today, or at least orthodox religion today, come from empirical disciplines: history, archaeology, biblical scholarship, neuropsychology, genetics, artificial intelligence, and the like. When it comes to these challenges, philosophers have a luxury that religiously inclined specialists in those other fields lack: They can profess that they don't know enough about the state of empirical affairs to form an intelligent judgment on whether those fields threaten their views. More important, though, philosophers are also very adept at undermining the credentials of other disciplines; give them a view, and they'll find a way to destroy it.

Confronted with challenges from the empirical world, philosophers might even emerge as cool heads, pleading for restraint and methodological caution. Disagreement between scholars, frequent changes in the ortho-doxies of other fields, foundational issues about the basis for accepted methods — all these, a philosopher might say, promote a rational skepticism about the claims put forward by scholarship, lending succor to the religious position. The people in the other fields, on the other hand, commit professional suicide if they move to the meta level at which they question the very foundations of their disciplines; to steal a quip of Russell's, imagine a tailor running through the streets yelling, "There are no pants! There are no pants!" It is high time for the hackneyed identification of philosophy as *the* nemesis of religion to give way to the indictment of other suspects in other professional associations, and for the potential of philosophy to defuse some of these cultural challenges to become widely recognized.

The notion that there's something *especially* incongruous about being a philosopher and being religious is, then, a holdover from an earlier era. The climate may change back again soon, so in flux is the discipline. But in today's environment, not seeking proof for everything and learning not to capitulate in the face of objections and difficulties can be a mark of sophistication.

Taking all this together, it's clear that a philosopher has multiple routes to either rationalize not bringing philosophy and religion together, or to convince himself or herself that relations between the two domains are congenial, at least compared to the relations between religion and other disciplines.

With the heightened self-awareness that comes with middle age, I re-cognize elements of immaturity and unseemly defensiveness in each of the strategies I've outlined for explaining how one can be a religious philosopher. Some of the responses involve not really dealing with the issue but evading it; this applies to response 1, "specialization"; and response 2, "internalization," though I think it is fundamentally right, at moments strikes me as evasive too. Other responses ask, in effect, "Are you any better?" (This applies to response 3, "prejudice"); or else they amount to complaining "Hey, he or she is doing the same thing." (This applies to response 3 and response 5, "the challenge of other fields.") I've already expressed some discontent with response 4. These moves, then, fall short of being fully satisfying. And so it's natural for me, as time passes, to grow uneasy about making them, and to seek in lieu of them a meaningful integration of two worlds I could keep separate. But how does one do that? What form can integration take?

More on this anon. Bifurcation, however, has other sources, to which I now turn.

So far I've spoken about being religious despite being a philosopher. I haven't yet considered the second half of the problem: being a philosopher while being religious. Here the challenge has been not to justify my religious beliefs in the face of philosophy, but to justify my pursuit of philosophy in light of the religious ideals put forth in my tradition.

If the concept of a religious philosopher strikes you as oxymoronic, then the thought of an Orthodox Jew in academic philosophy must strike you as stranger still. Christianity has a strong philosophical tradition, especially conspicuous in Catholicism. In Catholic schools people are trained on philosophical texts; those texts are part and parcel of the curriculum. But in Orthodox Judaism the most hallowed texts are not philosophical but legal. The corpus of Jewish law is vast and staggering. Its base is the imposing sixty-three tractates of the Talmud, which are written mostly in Aramaic and which deal with topics both relevant and irrelevant to contemporary practice: holidays, divorce, theft, sacrificial offerings, court proceedings, Sabbath observance, ritual purity, oaths, ethics. And the actual text of a talmudic discussion, formidable as it may be, is just the starting point. There are mountains and mountains of legal commentary and codes, and as you get older and more experienced, you are expected to do more and more climbing. The texts themselves are often linguistically terse and conceptually complex, so it is all very challenging. Yet the educational system prizes not erudition alone but cleverness too; the challenge is not merely to master the texts but to create — to ask good questions and devise good solutions. In some circles, Bible study is deemed "soft" by comparison to legal study, and therefore is marginalized or thought of as something that requires formal instruction only in the early stages of education. The test of your mettle, at least in the classical "Lithuanian" approach, is your talmudic ability and facility in the legal codes — study of these, significantly, is referred to by the simple term "learning." The educational curriculum of Orthodoxy is geared to producing, if not legal giants, then professionals of all types who will be competent to deal with legal texts and who every day of their lives will devote time to study in deference to religious duty. God is experienced primarily through His words, through a text, not through philosophical reason and not by personal mystical revelation.

As I explained earlier, Talmud and philosophy are to an extent congenial; the two domains call for similar qualities of mind. And I would be dense not to see how greatly Talmud study both attracted me to philosophy and has helped me in pursuing arguments. Returning the favor, philosophy, I believe, makes my mind sharper when I turn to a talmudic discourse. Creativity is valued in both as well.[6] Having said this, I still have to urge that in Judaism, the personal ideal of Talmud study inhibits assigning other things a significant role in the process of internalizing beliefs and values.

Talmud study is not just part of your training, it is a lifelong commitment, no matter what your profession. As far removed as it may often seem from real life, it is supposed to dominate your time away from work and from domestic responsibility. "This book of the Torah shall not depart from your mouth; you shall meditate upon them [words of Torah] day and night" (Joshua 1:8). "You shall teach them to your children; you shall speak of them — when you dwell in your house and when you travel, when you go to sleep and when you awake" (Deuteronomy 6:7). Torah study is a primary religious experience. God is experienced through the words of Torah scholars, and it is through study that we simultaneously link ourselves to the Jewish collective across time and keep the tradition alive. (The Hebrew word for "tradition," *masorah*, actually derives from the root "to give over." Learning and teaching are inextricably bound.)[7]

Accordingly, many Orthodox professionals — prominent economists, scientists, lawyers, doctors and professors — rise at 5 A.M. to study before services, fit in a lunchtime *shiur* (class) or private study at the workplace, and at night go to the *bet midrash* (study hall) to labor until late. There's no such thing as having mastered an area and earned the right to get on to something else: "One who has learned 100 times cannot be compared to one who has learned 101 times." Pressured by ideals like this, where is there room for philosophy, save at best as a nine-to-five (for professors, one-to-four!) living? In many schools the philosophical works of Sa'adyah Ga'on or Maimonides are studied mainly as diversions when one needs a break from the exhausting activity of Talmud or, at most, as ancillary supplements. So, whereas Christians who want to be exposed to religious texts are likely to turn to philosophical ones, Orthodox Jews are not.

Despite the parallels between Talmud study and philosophy that I noted before, it is, I think, a result of the structure of Jewish education that there are very few Orthodox Jews in university philosophy departments, and in many cases whatever philosophy they do has only a tenuous connection to internal religious life. Your theological needs, many feel, are met by the talmudic text. Therein lies a complete spiritual world. To be sure, some of the key movements in Judaism — medieval rationalism, for example, or, else Kabbalah — arose as reactions against an exclusive preoccupation with Talmud to the detriment of broader spirituality. Philosophy and Kabbalah help Jews put flesh on their belief system, indeed create much of that system. Still, speaking sociologically rather than prescriptively, broad conceptions of spirituality and appreciation of philosophy's potential contribution are far more the exception than the rule.

Time allocation is not the sole issue. Much of Jewish tradition is downright hostile to philosophical pursuits because of their historical association with heresy. I realize that Christianity has its own history of hostility to secular doctrines, the most recent segment of which is the controversy in America over evolution in schools. Still, I have often felt that because Jews need to protect themselves as a tiny people in an intellectually threatening milieu, the conflicts between philosophy and religion — or, for that matter, history and religion or science and religion — were especially threatening to them, those conflicts coming as they did from the outside world. And so Jews needed to band around a common text that was unique to them and could set its own standards rather than answer to an externally imposed one. The few stunning exemplars of philosophy who have been produced from mainstream, legalistic Judaism have sometimes met with suspicion or even enmity. In medieval times, Maimonides sought an integration of law with philosophy, producing, on the one hand, a mammoth and monumental code of law that represented the first ever topically organized assemblage of Jewish law, and, on the other, the *Guide of the Perplexed*, his philosophic magnum opus and a landmark of the Middle Ages. Maimonides (and others) even posited a religious *obligation* to study philosophy; for Maimonides, the "*mitzvah* of Talmud Torah" (commandment to study Torah) *includes* the study of philosophy. Yet Maimonides was perceived by many as overly bold, and his stature as a legal authority made it even more imperative for those who felt threatened by philosophy to limit his influence as a thinker. To this day, Maimonides has been the subject of revisionist biography that seeks — indefensibly, in my opinion — to dismiss the nature and extent of his commitment to philosophy and restore the image of the pure legal scholar, even while academics sometimes go to the other extreme of belittling his commitment to law and Torah study. And so it has been with other legal giants who cast their net wide; their biographies are sometimes mirrors of the biographers. In any case, Jews dedicated to the standard Orthodox curricular emphasis typically have no room in their day for philosophy. Notwithstanding the genius of Maimonides or, to mention a latter-day giant, Rabbi Joseph Soloveitchik, most minds have not proved capacious and quick enough to excel in both or hospitable enough to assign value to both. All of this contributes, of course, to the neglect of philosophy among talmudists. And it ultimately marginalizes the role of philosophy — even *Jewish* philosophy — in the religious lives of many committed and highly educated Jews. I do not think I fully escaped this effect in my education, even with commitment to a dual curriculum and even with an ideology committed to the synthesis of Judaism with general culture. For to a significant extent, the individual must take the initiative in achieving integration.

I have spoken at length about the extent to which being a religious philosopher, especially an Orthodox Jewish philosopher, brings with it or even requires a feeling of bifurcation. And I have also explained that as

I grew older, I became increasingly aware of what was happening and more conscious of the forces that were producing bifurcation. In the wake of this realization, I sought a way of breaking down the walls. Of course, I could reach my goal by fixating on the postmodern consciousness I elaborated on earlier, a consciousness that could grant a license to religious commitment (albeit, as I said before, only as part of a broad license that for parity's sake would then have to be granted to many horrendous worldviews). But in my own life I think I have finally overcome bifurcation in a different way: not by bringing reason and religion together on every point, but by utilizing philosophical methods, categories, and distinctions to clarify my tradition and to reveal layers of richness that would otherwise have eluded me.

To some extent, this means appreciating philosophically interesting material in Judaism on classical philosophical conundra: attributes of God, evil, free will, morality and divine commands, weakness of will, immortality, belief and the will. Analytic training has helped me clarify biblical narratives, comprehend talmudic positions, and sort out arguments by Jewish thinkers from Philo to Maimonides to thinkers of today. In this way, I feel my belief system enriched and deepened. Reciprocally, Jewish knowledge has served to contribute vital suggestions to my personal reflection on current debates in philosophy. Thus, contemporary philosophy both illuminates and is illuminated by religious resources, and I have found groups of kindred spirits with whom to share this endeavor. In the process, I have learned that authoritative thinkers of the tradition have been prepared — within limits — to reinterpret teachings that strike them as philosophically problematic, furnishing both a general method for reconciling philosophy and religion and important reformulations of specific doctrines. Many views held by people at the popular level — for example, that all suffering is punishment for sin — were rejected by major thinkers and indeed by sages of the talmudic period. A commitment informed by the philosophy that has preceded looks quite different from one not thus informed.

When I have not been doing straight philosophy, the issues that have occupied me most in recent years (though often in discussions at conferences and think tanks rather than in writing) are those that grow out of the confrontation between Judaism and modernity. What are the prospects for transposing an ancient system of law to modern circumstances without violating its essence? How does the Jewish political tradition react to contemporary dilemmas inherent in setting up a state in Israel with a quasi-religious character? What is the place of autonomy in Judaism? What is the meaning of idolatry in contemporary society? How does Judaism assess democratic ideals? What can be done to assuage conflicts between modern liberalism and Jewish moral principles? What have the effects of secularism been on Jewish life, and how does Jewish tradition regard the more positive aspects of secularism — technological and medical advances, for example? It is stimulating for me to see, for example, how Ronald Dworkin's or Robert Bork's theories of American law illuminate the nature of Jewish law and the notion of precedent that is so central to it; how theories of reference and approaches to scientific thinking help clarify the nature of belief in God; how communitarian views of political existence clarify Jewish ones, and vice versa; how Jewish and secular systems of medical ethics converse with each other. All the projects I have described reflect the ideal on which I was nurtured, "Torah u-Madda." Secular philosophical tools are brought forth to illuminate an ancient tradition and to appropriate the tradition in a distinctive way; at the same time, philosophical ideas are illuminated and refined by that tradition. Thereby, integration, not bifurcation, has finally become the keynote of my thinking.

And yet, at a deeper level, integration has its limits. Bifurcation is encouraged, and internalization of philosophy frustrated, by still another hard fact of life: things that affect and move us in real life, that give our existence texture and richness, resist philosophical defense and in fact are at odds with a philosophical perspective. I see no way to deny this. Here are a few examples.

Models: Models, to lift yet another of Russell's famous witty phrases, have all the advantages of theft over honest toil. When you have a model, you can content yourself with reasoning as follows: this person is brilliant and erudite, so this person must have figured it all out; since *he's* this way, why need *I* sweat over whether it can be done? I had several major models while growing up, living examples of how religion and culture could be fused. Collectively they saved me from having to carve out an articulate rationale for being religious. Now to a hard-nosed philosopher, citing someone else who does or believes X goes no way toward explaining why believing or doing X is a justified course. Someone has got to have an argument for believing or doing X, and the argument should be what counts, not the charisma or IQ of the people who believe or do X. But in flesh-and-blood life, models shape us, and in the presence of a vivid and impressive one, philosophical grappling pales into irrelevance.

For students of Yeshiva University, no one can surpass R. Joseph B. Soloveitchik, who passed away in the spring of 1993 at the age of ninety, and with whom I studied in the late 1960s and early 1970s. Scion of a great family of talmudists, R. Soloveitchik's analytic brilliance in handling a talmudic text was arguably the greatest in generations, and he ceaselessly inspired thousands of students in America over the past half-century. His powers of exposition were magnificent, and his rare combination of genius, passion, clarity, and flair made it possible for people to sit and listen to him — with rapt attention — for four or five hours on end. But what made him truly unique was that, apart from vast talmudic erudition and astounding creativity, apart from an intense impassioned love for Torah study that infected all around him, R. Soloveitchik was also a philosopher. He received a doctorate from the University of Berlin and was thoroughly conversant with the philosophy, science, and literature of his time. He published relatively few works in religious philosophy (relative, that is, to other theologians), but what he did publish showed, first, wide cultural awareness and, second, a depth of feeling that was unusual to behold in such a rigorous intellect. Here was a man who knew as much European philosophy as anyone I had met (albeit not analytic philosophy) and yet, when all is said and done, was one of the greatest men of faith I had ever seen. R. Soloveitchik indeed had little patience for conflicts between biblical scholarship and religion or between science and religion; he focused instead on the psychological state of the contemporary believer — on how the modern consciousness has left the religious personality lonely and alienated. To belittle or dismiss that which this great mind had embraced seemed inconceivable. Surely his deep spirituality and unwavering faith did not reflect weakness of mind or deficiencies in erudition. The best tribute I know to R. Soloveitchik came from a well-known philosopher who studied Talmud with him nearly five decades ago. This philosopher is no longer Orthodox, but he has remarked many times that, "After having had Soloveitchik, I could not be intimidated by anyone else's intellect."

Nor is R. Soloveitchik the only great Talmudist to be so erudite and reflective. One of his sons-in-law, R. Aharon Lichtenstein, earned a Ph.D. in literature from Harvard and published a book on the Cambridge Platonists, yet chose to spend his life teaching Talmud and now heads a yeshivah in Israel. A master of language and a stimulating thinker, besides being a stunning talmudist, R. Lichtenstein is well versed in general culture, and he has argued eloquently that exposure to culture refines one's spiritual sensibilities and is encouraged by Judaism. I can name other bright minds too — well known scientists, historians, philosophers, linguists, biblical scholars, experts on artificial intelligence, and psychologists — who, if not quite as immersed in Talmud, are people of faith, committed to Torah study and devoted to Halakhah. One little synagogue in my neighborhood boasts the nucleus of a good university: a distinguished physicist, a linguist whose discoveries made *The New York Times*, a prizewinning medieval historian, and several chairs of departments from music to Judaic studies. Knowing of the existence and availability of such people not only eases the burden of being religious in a secular world, it positively inspires. But again, not by furnishing a decisive philosophical argument. On the contrary, I now realize that some models may be what they are because they have not channeled their reflections in the directions in which the challenges lie or else have not been really tough-minded about certain issues. Yet their impact remains.

Intellectual excitement: Teachers and spiritual leaders do not generally influence us by proving points; they do so by exciting our minds, by making texts and concepts come alive. (This was my experience in philosophy too. The late Sidney Morgenbesser, whose philosophical brilliance was astonishing, had an enduring influence on students like me more by making philosophy intensely exhilarating than by pushing particular positions.) As a teacher myself, I can attest that the sheer rigor and imagination of classical Jewish texts is part of what inspires students to study more and more. Amazingly, many gifted young men and women today defer entering law school or medical school — and even starting lucrative jobs in law firms — to study religious subjects for an additional year or two. No material incentive motivates their choice. Large numbers of Jews enroll in adult education programs in non-degree-granting institutions. They study *lishmah*, "for its own sake." While their choice reflects, above all, religious commitment, part of that commitment is sustained by the intellectual invigoration that study provides.

In an earlier period, I went through a similar process of being energized by my tradition. A pivotal figure was an extraordinarily talented rabbi named Norman Lamm, who served the congregation in which I spent my teenage years. R. Lamm attended Yeshiva College, graduating as a chemistry major and a top-flight student of R. Soloveitchik, and then turned to the pulpit. Combining a dynamic delivery, adroit turns of phrase, intellectual substance, and a great feel for homily, he was a mesmerizing master of the sermon; in his hands it became an art form. My father was such a devotee of the sermons that he had the rabbi send him a typed version after each Sabbath, and we reread these with the excitement you experience when you finally get hold of a recording of that song you loved but whose tune you couldn't remember well enough. For a while, I even wanted to have a pulpit myself. Dr. Lamm is now president of Yeshiva University, and as I sit through the soporific tones at other colleges' ceremonies, I prize his oratorical prowess still more. What he provided me with in my teenage years (and thereafter continued to provide through his many writings on Jewish thought and law) was a conviction indispensable to my later life: that Judaism could excite and energize the mind, and that its ideas can be expressed with eloquence and power.

Which counts more: vividness, excitement, and intellectual engagement — or analytic proof? My own vote is for the former (though I perhaps am overdrawing the dichotomy). When a Jewish text comes alive in the hands of its masters, the religion's teachers and preachers, you feel yourself part of a living tradition and indeed in conversation with august authorities in centuries past. It is the experience that counts; these texts touch me at the deepest recesses of self. No, I don't have a full-dress account of where inspiration and excitement shade off into the text-centered fanaticism of a David Koresh. But this is not a reason for me to be wary of religious excitement. As an autobiographical matter, I find the love of Jewish texts more engaging than abstract explorations into their philosophical validity.

Inspiration: Intellectual excitement is one source of my love for my religion; another is the inspired lives of my religion's devotees. Recently I attended a talk given by an Orthodox woman who has been bound to a wheelchair from childhood. She is married — to a blind man — and remarkably, they are raising a family. She spoke about the Jewish concept that "This, too, is for the good." She explained how life had done her good turns by means of *ostensible* "coincidences," which in truth, she felt, were signs of God's intervention. By means of her theology, she had turned adversity into inner strength and advantage. The thought of contesting her "invisible hand" interpretation with philosophical arguments seemed so offensive as to be unthinkable. Anyone who would impugn her perspective would only be reflecting their own lack of spirit. If that evening someone had furnished me on the spot with a dazzling philosophical solution to the problem of evil, that would have done less for me as a person than this single autobiographical expression — which from a philosophical standpoint seemed so simplistic.

There are couples I know, friends and co-worshippers, who have children with Downs syndrome, Tay-Sachs disease, cerebral palsy. Their powers of spirit are extraordinary. On the one hand, they view their circumstances with complete honesty about the initial numbness — the "why me?" reaction — and about the magnitude of the problem of coping. Yet, at the same time, they view their situation as an opportunity God has granted them for moral growth — as a chance to shower love, care, and responsibility on another human being. Survivors of the Holocaust saw their families butchered and brutalized before their eyes, losing parents and siblings and children to the Nazi machine. Of the survivors whom I know, many have drawn from their religious belief the strength, trust, and resolve to persevere and to live productive, well-adjusted lives.

I can hear the voice of the philosopher arraigning me on a fallacy: "In all these instances, what one is admiring is the people who exemplify such spirit; it does not follow, nor is it true, that all such admirers admire also the *content* of the worldviews being expressed. Indeed, insofar as there are no atheists in foxholes, we fully expect religion to be useful as an emotional crutch. So do not confuse evaluating a perspective philosophically with evaluating the experience of seeing or hearing it expressed by someone with a certain kind of history; you mix up focusing on ideas and focusing on people. As long as we keep these objects of evaluation distinct, we can avoid being attracted to 'simple' views of providence while simultaneously admiring greatness of spirit."

I am not convinced that this argument does full justice to the situation. First of all, the mere fact that we admire the people means that we recognize virtues besides philosophical rigor. And in any case, there is a real issue here as to *how* ideas themselves are to be evaluated. Religion provides a coherent view of life, one that galvanizes people to moral action, infuses them with strength of character, and gives them perspective on their own troubles. Life would be poorer without that perspective. Is rigor the only criterion by which to judge a perspective? Or is it appropriate only in certain settings?

I cannot overstate how surprised I am by my own admiration for providence filled interpretations of life. Of all the ideas preached by religion, the one that has brought on it the most ridicule from both philosophers and the person on the street is the notion of Divine providence. God is lampooned as the Father who art in Heaven who distributes lollipops and spankings according to our deeds. When I was a little boy, I took this idea with the utmost literalness: if the New York Yankees blew a double-header, I must have done something really bad. As I grew up, I sought within tradition a different picture of how things operate.

The ridicule to which the simple view is subjected stems from at least six sources. First, in human experience, goods and evils don't get distributed according to the pattern one would expect on the basis of the religious model. Second, the notion that God causes many events in everyday life seems out of step with a scientific worldview. Third, religious ethics becomes infantile and heteronomous; you blindly obey because you'll get zapped if you don't. Fourth, you allegedly become self-centered, imagining that all that happens revolves around you. Fifth, you allegedly become helpless and dependent. Sixth, you become callous toward evil, because all is supposedly for the good.

I discovered in Maimonides a captivating idea: that although there is reward and punishment in the universe, we are living a lower form of spiritual existence if we place this idea at the forefront of consciousness. Maimonides bids us to abandon an anthropocentric perspective even while believing in providence. A description of how he carries out this balancing act is beyond my purposes. But surely there is something inspiring about the idea that trust in God does not require belief that He will supply your material needs, but instead requires a steadfast resolve to do His will no matter what life brings you or — phrasing it differently — to deem His will the "good" of your life. And yet, despite my personal attraction to Maimonides' view, those who *do* see events as directed toward their personal interests often tend to be the most benevolent and the most conscious of evils around them. If strong belief in providence yields a self-centered reading of events, it isn't self-centered in any negative sense. In this worldview lie the seeds of greatness of spirit. It deserves a place in religious life, even if only as part of a perpetual dialectic, the other pole of which is a Maimonidean outlook that transports us beyond our own interests. [See also "Divine Intervention and Religious Sensibilities; in this volume.]

Religious commitment has also had striking effects on the conduct of religious youth. Many young men and women elect to spend their summers caring for others as counselors in an upstate New York camp for special children. Competition for counselor positions there is stiff — eloquent testimony to the value that benevolence and kindness have for these youth. Without question, a secular person could also make altruism and care for others a primary good in life; nevertheless, religious values exert a palpable added impact. Is this impact a philosophical basis for a theistic argument? I doubt it. Is it a reason to value being part of a religious community and to share in its outlook? I think so.

Community: I have just returned from the funeral of a friend, a member of my community, who died abruptly at the age of forty from a heart attack. At the service, people spoke lovingly of his warmth and his selflessness. As is standard at funerals, they related the circumstances to key phrases or ideas in the Talmud, the biblical portion of the week, or the laws governing the season in which his death took place (it was the season for mourning the destruction of the Temple). They compared the situation to others described in the Talmud; they found parallels between him and ancient models. It was all beautiful and moving, and it enabled the hundreds of attendees to begin speaking about, dealing with, and adjusting to a loss that had left them numb and speechless. Yes, of course, people wondered how God could allow a man in his prime, a man without a jealous streak in his body, a man who was incredibly giving, cheerful, and gregarious, to be snatched from a wife and children and mother without warning. And we still wonder. I know enough about Jewish theology to know that Judaism does not believe that if a person died, he or she must have sinned; and the Book of Job tells me that there is no perfect nexus in the world between deed and destiny. Yet apart from this intellectual resolution by means of "texts," I really wonder what the tribute would have been like were it not for the rich evocative imagery and literary gold mines that brought us together in spirit.

Contingency: I mentioned earlier that philosophers are sometimes troubled by the contingency of religious commitments: were we born in a different place, born to parents whose convictions were different, or educated differently, we'd have turned out differently. Consequently, in forming our beliefs, we need to filter out the results of upbringing and engage in purely rational reflection on what to believe. As already noted, this idea is on shaky turf today, since it is widely recognized that our traditions and environments are inescapably parts of what we are. But Judaism takes this still a step further; it *celebrates* contingency by insisting that one's accident of birth imposes special obligations. We are obligated to carry on a tradition. The destruction of European Jewry and its centers of Torah study during World War II has intensified this feeling, creating a powerful sense in the next generation that we must preserve the tradition for which our ancestors died and must not (in theologian Emil Fackenheim's phrase) give Hitler a posthumous victory. The establishment of a Jewish state heightens the Jew's sense of identity and makes turning away from the people of Israel an act of betrayal. To be sure, Judaism comes in many forms, of which Orthodoxy is but one, and I have no need here to digress about the differences between the denominations. But I would be surprised if any Jew of any religious denomination denied that the contingency of his or her Jewishness had an effect on commitment. But contingency, again, is precisely what the philosopher points to as a reason to *abandon* commitment.

Is it really possible to integrate these religious perspectives with a philosophically detached "assessment" of their "epistemological merits"? My point has been: no. My commitment is not rooted in the (naive) notion that reason vindicates my beliefs. It is rooted rather in what Judaism provides me with: intellectual excitement, feeling, caring for others, inspiration, and a total perspective that is evocative and affecting. I have no doubt that people of other faiths and of other denominations in Judaism gain parallel benefits from their commitments. For all I know, secularists find secularism appealing for many of the same reasons I find my religion appealing. But then they can surely respect why I would hold on to a way of life that furnished those benefits. If I love my family, you can't argue me out of it just by telling me that I *could* also learn to love a different family, or would have had I been born into one.

Philosophy has its place among the truly enjoyable, challenging, and edifying endeavors in our culture. But it is not the arbiter of all we think and do. What we do in our study and what we do in the rest of our lives are often not commensurate, because the study is the smaller room in life.

Without question, the essay that has stayed with me the longest is William James' "The Will to Believe." James's argument was that "our passional nature not only lawfully may, but must, decide an option between propositions, whenever it is a genuine option that cannot by its nature be decided on intellectual grounds." Notoriously, James has been accused of giving license to wishful thinking and fanaticism, and I've taken pains to admit both that I don't want to license just any view and that I do not have a principled way of licensing some things and outlawing others. But in choosing between living with this uncertainty about how to draw lines and discarding passional attractions altogether, the former seems the more human and appealing course.

NOTES

Although the one subject on which I fancy myself the world's greatest expert is my own life and outlook, I cannot but acknowledge that I have benefited greatly from comments by Shalom Carmy and Josef Stern on an earlier draft of this narrative.

1   These remarks are de facto, not de jure. On the de jure level, it is well worth pondering Alvin Plantinga's view in his autobiography, written for James Tomberlin and Peter van Inwagen, *Alvin Plantinga* (Dordrechr, Boston, Lancaster, Pa.: Reidel, 1985):

> Serious intellectual work and religious allegiance, I believe, are inevitably intertwined. There is no such thing as serious, substantial, and relatively complete intellectual endeavor that is religiously neutral (p. 13).

This is an attractive position, though one must add, as Plantinga does, that "it isn't always easy to see how to establish it, or how to develop and articulate it in detail." I can certainly think of illustrations of Plantinga's bold claim.

2   There is an issue I need to bracket here. In the case of commonsense belief, we have no evidence against what we believe; whereas, one may argue, we do have evidence against religious belief namely, the existence of evil. My response to this would entail a fuller discussion of evil than I want to undertake here, but it suffices to say that philosophers have articulated well a set of value judgments that could make the existence of evil understandable in a world created by a benevolent God. Moreover, as I say, some religious philosophers do not internalize the problem of evil either.

3   To be sure, Kuhn disavowed certain conclusions and applications people drew.

4   I will cite an example from recent work on theodicy. Atheists argue that, "Since there is unjustified evil, there is no perfect God." Theists can retort that, "You put the argument backward. Since there is a perfect God, all apparent evil is justified evil." Who can prove which starting point is better?

5   In fact, philosophy may never have been the devil until the Enlightenment. Prior to that, philosophers nearly always believed in God and religion, and it was primarily the details of their beliefs (about creation, for example, or divine foreknowledge) that led to association with heresy. The fact is striking that Descartes "solved" the fundamental problem, "what justifies us in our beliefs?" by appealing to a God who guaranteed the reliability of our cognitive faculties.

George Berkeley's philosophy affords yet another instance of a great philosopher utilizing religious belief to solve a major philosophical problem. The separation between philosophy and religion has been rather brief.

6   Though paradoxically a creative and original theory in Talmud gets real standing when one finds some important legal authority who said the same thing. In contrast to academia, having been beaten to the punch is an occasion for delight, not disappointment. There are few better illustrations of how intellectual creativity and autonomy are fused with — as George Schlesinger notes — humility. See Schlesinger, "Truth, Humility, and Philosophers," in *God and the Philosophers*, ed. Thomas V.Morris (New York, 1994), 248-62. Josef Stern has also pointed out that whereas in philosophy a good question about a position will often be taken to refute the position, a good question about a position taken by an eminent authority in Talmud will often be followed up by a modest comment that "The subject needs further examination."

7   For a masterly and fertile articulation of the ideal of Torah study, see Rabbi Aharon Lichtenstein's article "Study," in *Contemporary Jewish Religious Thought*, ed. Arthur Cohen and Paul Mendes-Flohr (New York: Scribners, 1987), 931-38.

INDEX OF BIBLICAL
AND RABBINIC SOURCES

Categories that have many entries or subdivisions (viz., Bible, Talmud, Midrashic literature, Maimonides, Nahmanides, Kook, and Soloveitchik) are listed first, in chronological order. Other sources are then listed alphabetically.

When a statement is quoted or paraphrased in the text of an essay and the source is given in the accompanying endnote, only the text page is cited in this index. By contrast, when a note cites additional information and references not alluded to in the text, the page and number of the note are cited.

Hyphenation in page numbers indicates that the passages are treated as a unit on the relevant page(s).

Bible

Genesis

chap. 1	9
chap. 2	9
2:7	162-63
2:17	8
2:18	174n65
3:5	8
3:6	9
3:11	9
3:22	8
4:9	10
4:10	10
6:2	10, 24n29
6:3	64
6:5	251n36
6:6	4, 15
8:21	271
9:5	377n13
15:13	16
15:14	17, 25n52, 289n69
18:20-33	284n43
18:23-25	11
21:12	7
chap. 22	xvi, 6, 23n22, 24n44, 261-2, 264-67
22:2	7
22:12	15, 265
27:44	18
29:29	17
29:26	18
29:29	17
34:31	10
36:36	281
chaps. 37-50	16
42:21	10, 17
45:5	16
45:8	16
47:9	18
47:29	25n50
50:15	17
50:20	16
50:24	25

Exodus

7:3	15
9:12	15
10:1	15
10:20	15

12:2	19, 25n58	19:2	169n21
12:9	15	22:2	288n63
14:4	15	chaps. 73-74	11
14:8	15	110:3	281n7
14:17	15	111:5	19
17:14-16	267	130:11	257
chap. 19	10	136:1	268
19:6	320n2	*Proverbs*	
21:13	15	3:17	265
Leviticus		*Job*	4, 6, 11
19:2	306	chaps. 1-2	12
19:16	326	4:7	272
19:19	205n44	5:17	13
chap. 26	203n38	chaps. 6-7	14
Numbers		9:22-23	13
27:1-11	10, 284n43	9:30-31	14
Deuteronomy		10:3-4	14
6:7	401	13:15	13
chap. 18	194	19:21	13
18:9	205n51	23:5	13
18:10	205n49	chaps. 38-41	12
18:13	193, 205n51	42:5	12
20:16-17	267	42:7	12, 273, 302n19
21:18-21	270	*Ecclesiastes*	
22:8	15	11:1	186
25:17-19	267		
chap. 28	203n38	**Mishnah**	
28:9	39	*Berakhot*	
Joshua		9:5	272
1:8	401	*Shabbat*	
I Samuel		2:6	288n64
chap. 15	332	*Sotah*	
15:3	7	1:7	288n64
15:11	4	*Horayot*	
23:10-12	22n12	3:7-8	319, 341, 352n26, 371
Isaiah		*Avot*	
51: 12-13	257	1:3	198, 222n13
55:8	11	1:16	36
chaps. 62-63	11	3:15	249
Jeremiah		4:4	34, 35
6:14	277	4:19	288
8:11	277	5:6	288
12:1-2	11	5:23	40
17:7	186	*Ohalot*	
Ezekiel		7:6	349n11
1:10	4		
Habakkuk	11	**Babylonian Talmud**	
Psalms		*Berakhot*	
18:1	268	5a	293, 301n10, 301n15

5b	280
7a	288n63, 350n21
10a	253n53
33b	249n21
60a	376n6
60b	288n50
61b	287n53, 302n17

Shabbat
4a	354
55a-b	294
56a	272
56b	286n48
115b	35
129b	380
133b	105
156a-b	287n54, 302n18

Pesahim
25b	349n11, 351n35, 382n69
50a	377n16
64b	154, 180
113b	205n49

Yoma
22b	7
23a	35
69b	288n63

Sukkah
52a	40

Rosh ha-Shanah
18a	302n18

Mo'ed Katan
28a	204n40, 250n26, 273, 294

Ketubbot
50a	348n7, 381n56

Nazir
23a	346

Sotah
4b	34
40a	299n1
14a	351n30
20a	368

Kiddushin
39b	273, 287n53, 294, 302n17

Bava Kamma
38b	288n64
60b	299n1

Bava Metzi'a
58b	272
62a	xxiii, 319, 326, 337

Bava Batra
10a	108
12a	108

Sanhedrin
56b	24n28
65b	205n49
71a	270
73a	379n42
74a	349n11, 351n35, 382n69

Avodah Zarah
18a	356, 381n52
22a	31
27b	379

Menahot
29b	288n63

Hullin
142a	204nn40-41

Niddah
31a	135n33

Jerusalem Talmud
Shekalim
6:3	180, 201n7

Midrashic literature
Mekhilta de-Rabbi Yishmael
Nezikin, Misphatim
18	286n48, 288-89n64, 303n20

Sifra
Kedoshim 10:11 to Lev. 20:26	40
Behar 5 to Lev. 25:36	319, 326, 370

Sifrei
32 to Deut 6:5	280n4
49 to Deut 11:22	299n1, 351n30

Avot de-Rabbi Natan
5:23	208n72, 222n13

Bereshit Rabbah
7:3	104
9:7	232
39:8	281n6
44:1	350n27
89:2	203n27
94:9	332

Va-Yikra Rabbah
20	288n63
32:10	314
37:1	286n48, 303n20

Kohelet Rabbah
4:1	314
5:4	286n48, 303n20
7:16	7, 350n19

Tanhuma (Buber)
11	26n59

Midrash ha-Gadol
37:1	318

Moses Maimonides (Rambam)
Commentary to the Mishnah
Pesahim 4:9	159, 193
Nedarim 4:4	379n42

Avot
4:4	35
5:6	200n1
5: 7	47n18

Shemonah Perakim (*Eight Chapters* —
introduction to commentary on *Avot*)
	29-30, 32-33, 38,
	46n12, 47n20,
	251n31
Introduction	39
1	30-31
4	30-35, 37, 39-40,
	47n19
5	27
6	28, 39-40, 337
7	31, 89n43
8	184, 202n22, 206n56,
	251n31, 255n79

Mishneh Torah
Hilkhot Yesodei ha-Torah (Laws of
the Foundations of the Torah)
1:1	168n17
1:6	142-43
1:10	89n43
2:2	65, 142-43, 147, 194,
	244
2:10	153
4:12-13	30
4:13	109
5:1	383n74
5:4	255n73, 353-54n50,
	377n11

5:5	354-55n50
7:6	48n50, 89n43

Hilkhot De'ot
(Laws of Character Traits)
1: 4-5	38
1:4	48n44
1:5-6	47n18, 353n44
2:2	34
2:3	34, 35, 47n35
3:1	33, 48n41
4:20	194, 204n42,
	205n47
6:3	317

Hilkhot Talmud Torah
(Laws of the Study of Torah)
1:2, 1:9, 2:1, 3:4,	
3:10, 3:11	207n65
3:12	38

Hilkhot Avodah Zarah
(Laws of Idolatry)
11:8	205n49
11:16	193-94

Hilkhot Teshuvah
(Laws of Repentance)
chap. 4	206n60
5:5	153
7:3	30, 337
7:4	351n29
chap. 8	27
10:1	213
10:2	199, 206n61,
	208n74, 215, 280n4
10:6	280n4

Hilkhot Ta'aniyyot
(Laws of Fasts)
chap. 1	289, 301n15,
	303n21

Hilkhot Ishut
(Laws of Marriage)
15:3	38

Hilkhot Gerushin
(Laws of Divorce)
2:20	241

Hilkhot Shevu'ot
(Laws of Oaths)
13:23	48n41

Hilkhot Nezirut
(Laws of the Nazirite)
10:14	37-38, 47n19

Hilkhot Rotzeah
(Laws of Murder)
   1:4   355
   11:4-5   356
   18:6   354n50, 380n45, 383n74

Hilkhot Shekhenim
(Laws of Neighbors)
   14:15   195

Hilkhot Zekhiyyah u-Mattanah
(Laws of Acquisitions)
   12:17   207n62

Hilkhot Sanhedrin
(Laws of the Sanhedrin)
   18:6   373
   20:1   353n42

Hilkhot Mamrim
(Laws of Rebels)
   6:7   36

Hilkhot Evel
(Laws of Mourning)
   14:1   317

Hilkhot Mattenot Aniyyim
(Laws of Gifts for the Poor)
   10:19   195

Hilkhot Melakhim
(Laws of Kings)
   6:1   268
   6:4   283n33
   10:12   318
   chaps. 11-12 213

Guide of the Perplexed
Since the chapter "Worship, Corporeality and Human Perfection" is devoted entirely to *Guide* III:51-54, the entire span of that article's pages (50-92) is given in the references to III:51 and III:54.
   I:1-2   4
   I:1   41, 62, 63, 73n49, 88n29, 89n34, 90n47, 173n49
   I:2   23n23, 63, 289
   I:14   64
   I:15   45
   I:17   74
   I:21   73

I:24   44
I:31   73
I:32   73
I:33-34   88n27
I:34   27, 231
I:36-37   4
I:36   85n11
I:37   73
I:38   44, 73
I:49   63
I:50-60   139
I:54   44, 49n65, 73, 74, 75, 84n7, 90n48, 318
I:58   139-40, 167n8
I:68   72, 153
I:69   41
I:72   67, 68, 73
II:7   90n50
II:11   43, 68-69
II:12   90n50
II:28   206n54
II:29   179
II:32-48 179
II:33   28
II:36   38
II:39-40 30, 38, 55, 84n8, 172n37
II:48   179, 205n45, 250n25
III:1-8   4, 22n5
III:8-25 54
III:8-12 63
III:8   29, 38, 46n5, 54, 64, 65, 231
III:9   63, 73
III:11-12 70
III:13   84n5
III:17-23 70, 179
III:20   11
III:22-23 4, 90n51
III:24   82, 88n26
III:25-49 56, 57, 59, 60, 61, 85n11, 85n14, 87n25, 88n29
III:25-29 172n37
III:25   54, 60, 84n9, 85n11, 193, 206n54
III:27   27, 30, 38, 54-55, 57, 58, 59, 60, 89n40

III:28	54, 55, 59, 60, 85n10, 89n40, 206n54
III:32	64, 85n11, 205n48
III:33	29
III:34	37, 77, 87n24, 88n39
III:41	253
III:44	82, 85n17
III:48	38
III:49	87n25, 206n54, 206n55
III:50	55
III:51	50-92, 171n33, 179
III:52	56, 61, 65, 83-84n3, 88n26, 244
III:53	39, 43, 61, 83-84n3, 88n31, 172n39
III:54	27, 41-42, 44, 45, 46n3, 49n59, 50-92, 139-40, 148, 169n21, 324n33, 324n35
Letter on Astrology	194, 206n56, 245

Moses Nahmanides (Ramban)

Gen. 1:1	19
Gen. 2:9	23n23, 232
Gen. 6:2	10
Gen. 8:21	286n47
Gen. 12:7	25n52
Gen. 15:14	17, 219, 289n69
Gen. 42:6	17
Lev. 19:2	306, 310, 316, 324n29
Lev. 19:19	205n44
Lev. 26:11	203n30, 205n51, 219, 376n6
Deut. 6:18	306
Deut. 18:9	205n51
Deut. 18:13	205n51
Deut. 22:6	205n44, 337
Deut. 23:10	353
Deut. 30:6	233
Job, 10:3-4	14
Milhamot Hashem, introduction	317
Torat ha-Adam	205n51, 279, 286n48, 302n20
Torat Hashem Temimah	205n51
Teshuvah be-Inyan Emunot ve-De'ot	205n51

R. Abraham Isaac Kook
Arpelei Tohar

40	101
42	96
46	93, 96
47	122
55	101
79	93, 113n26
127	101

Da'at Kohen (Responsa)

#140-42	105, 126-27

Eder ha-Yakar

34-35	113n26
34-62	103
37-38	104, 135n30
38	104
42	104
52	101

Iggerot ha-Reayah
(by volume and letter number)

I: #40	109
I: #44	101, 103
I: #48-49	103
I: #91	103-105, 126
I: #103	123
I: #108	109
I: #134	115n61, 245-46
I: #140	115n65
I: #158	96
I: #311	123
II: #18	132n4
II: #478	135n36, 115n53
II: #493	129
II: #570	109

Ikkevei ha-Tzon

22-23	130
129	107-108

Mishpat Kohen (Responsa)

#143-44	371-72, 377

Olat Reiyah (siddur)

I: 376-77	93
I: 386-87	93
II: 1-3	99

Orot

13-16 ("Ha-Milhamah")	133n13
48-88 ("Orot ha-Tehiyyah")	122
72 ("Keri'ah Gedolah")	111n10

129-30 ("*Le-Milhemet ha-De'ot ve-ha-Emunot*")　97
120-21 ("*Hakham Adif mi-Navi*")　108
135 ("*Erekh ha-Tehiyyah*") 98
152 ("*Yisrael ve-Umot ha-Olam*")　93
Orot ha-Emunah
23-24　106
57　93
60　101
65-66　101
65　99
73　100
83-84　99
Orot ha-Kodesh
(by volume and page)
I: 1-158　96
I: 1-3　102
I: 44　101
I:64　98, 111n11
I: 115　114n42
I: 143　96
I: 145　111n11, 114n42
I: 178　99
I: 208　101
I: 278　96
II: 537　97, 126, 127
II: 538-42　97, 108
II: 563　96
III: 67-68　108
IV: 516-17　115n65
Orot ha-Teshuvah
5:8　93
Orot ha-Torah
Chaps. 2-5　108
3:8　116n75
6:1　108
8:6　116n77
9:6　109
9:12　109
Shemonah Kevatzim
xvii　117n88, 137n61
Tov Ro'i al Massekhet Shabbat
78, 126-28　115n63, 135n32

Other (MHR = *Maamarei ha-Re'ayah*)
"*Al Bamoteinu Halalim*"
(eulogy for fallen soldiers; in *MHR*)　119

"*Al Behirat Nashim*"
(in *MHR*)　120
"*Ha-Torah ve-ha-Tarbut ha-Enoshit*"
(in *MHR*)　103, 106
Hartza'at ha-Rav
(to his *yeshivah*)　116n80, 134n24
Hebrew University address (in *MHR*)　93, 108
"*Merhavim, Merhavim*"
(poem)　100
"*Nedar ba-Kodesh*"
(in *MHR*)　95-96, 127

R. Joseph B. Soloveitchik
Before Hashem You Shall be Purified
135　164
139niv　164
"Catharsis"
44-54　173n53
"Confrontation"　174-75n65, 196
Divrei Hashkafah　25n57
The Emergence of Ethical Man　251n37
Family Redeemed　248n13, 299n1, 303n24
6　232
73-85　256n87
Fate and Destiny (Kol Dodi Dofek)　214, 216, 301n14
1-17　274, 289n64, 296
11　303n24
57-60　174n61
Halakhic Man　xviii
1　139
11　139-40
12　167n7
19　141
25　155
40　141
45-46　175n70
57-58　142, 168n14
63-64　143, 148, 164, 169-70n21
74　168n14
83-84　142, 170n23
87　168n14
110-17　164
128　169-70n19

137   139, 167n11, 170n25, 176nn73-74

139-143(n.4)   141, 173n56, 257-58

144n10   172n40

146n18   139, 172n40

153n80   173n47

161n125   164

161n127   164

The Halakhic Mind   128

85   143

101-102   163, 298n1

"Ha-Yehudi Mashul le-Sefer Torah"   23n21

The Lonely Man of Faith (1992 Doubleday edition)   xviii, 55-57

1-7   99, 121, 156

9   176n74

12-13   155-57, 159, 246n3

17-19   148, 156-59, 162, 246n3

18   246n3

20   175n69

21-22   159, 207n63

26   157

29   159

29-32   148, 157

32   157, 207n63

37-38   13

47-49   159, 171n36

51-52   99, 168n17

81-84   159

85-86   157-58

87-90   154

90   208n68

93-102   163

97-98   163

"Mah Dodekh mi-Dod"

70-71   167n11

75ff   167n10

"Majesty and Humilty"

25-37   196, 244

27-31   176n79

34-37   173n53

36   265

Man of Faith in the Modern World — Reflections of the Rav, Volume II

22-23 ("The First Jewish Grandfather")   168n11

30-31 ("The Symbolism of Blue and White")   174n59

91-99 ("May We Interpret *Hukkim?*")   172n37, 304n32

Out of the Whirlwind   288n61, 295

xxxvi   296

5   296

9-10   298-99n1

86-115   300n6

86   116, 216, 274

101   275

128   296

131-32   295

136   296

138   296

152-54   303n24

176-177   303n24

Ra'ayanot al ha-Tefillah

239-71   280n1

The Rav Speaks

25-33   173n57

69-70   173n54

73-80   174-75n65

78   174n60

"Redemption, Prayer and Talmud Torah"

65   296

Reflections of the Rav

21-27 ("Imitating God")   173n55

26   173n57

26-27   175n72

34 ("The World is not Forsaken")   174n59

71-72 ("Prayer As Dialogue")   172n42

97 ("Mt. Sinai — Their Finest Hour")   173n55

162 ("Engaging the Heart and Teaching the Mind")   172n42

169-77 ("A Stranger and a Resident")   174n63, 174-75n65

Soloveitchik on Repentance   299n1

129-34   168n17

141-202	337
172-73	239, 250n27
180-82	171n37

U-Bikkashtem mi-Sham
(page numbers in *And From There You Shall Seek*) xviii

7	145
12	171n34
13-14	148
19	146
21	171n34
22-23	146
22-27	246n3
24-25	145-46
32	148
41	146, 149
43-44	146
56-57	146, 155, 175n70
94	149
102-103	151-52
106	146
107-110	152, 167n11
119-20	151-52
131-33	148, 173n45
135-56	145
136-37	172n39
143-46	171n30
150	152
153-57n2	171n30, 172n39
157-58n3	171n34
158n4	168n17
162-64n10	145, 149-50, 170n28
169-72n11	145
187n16	148

Worship of the Heart 299n1
Yemei Zikkaron

87-88	173n55

Other rabbinic literature
(Rabbinic titles are self-understood and are omitted from authors' names.)

Isaac Abarbanel
  Commentary to

Deut. 8:17-18	205n46

Nahalot Avot

on *Avot* 1:3	199, 215

Abraham ben David (Ravad)
  Glosses to Maimonides'
  Mishneh Torah

Hilkhot Teshuvah 5:5	230

Joseph Albo
  Sefer ha-Ikkarim

IV:14, 15	24

Hayyim ibn Atar
  Orah Hayyim

Gen. 6:6	24n43

Bahya ibn Pakuda
  Duties of the Heart
  (*Hovot ha-Levavot*)

IV	186
V: 3	82
X: 7	82

Baruch of Shklov
  Sefer Uklidus

Introduction	168n16

Hayyim Benveniste
  Sheyarei Keneset ha-Gedolah

Yoreh De'ah 157	377n16

Naftali Tzvi Yehuda Berlin (Netziv)
  Ha'amek Davar (biblical commentary)

Ex. 19:6	307, 345
Ex. 32:29	345
Num. 25:12	345
Deut. 13:18	345

MordekhaiYaakov Breisch
  Helkat Ya'akov

III:11	379n33, 380n49
XI:143	348n8

Hasdai Crescas
  Or Hashem

2:2:4	296

Eliyahu Dessler
  Mikhtav me-Eliyahu

I:111-18	234
I:116-18	233
I:178	183
I: 188	186
I:197	186

Shimon ben Zemach Duran
Teshuvot Tashbetz I:63 255n73

Jacob Emden
Mor u-Ketzi'ah
Orah Hayyim 328   356, 362,
                        378n25, 379n33

Yehoshua ben Tzvi Hirsch Falk
Penei Yehoshua
Berakhot 5a   293, 296,
                        302n17

Moshe Feinstein
Iggerot Mosheh
Hoshen Mishpat
    II: 66   379n33
    II: 73-75   361-62, 367
    II: 73   319, 376n5
    II: 74   319, 352n36, 367,
                        368, 369, 371
    II: 75   361-62
Yoreh De'ah
    II: 58   361-62
    II: 174   325n39, 367
    III: 36   379n29, 379n35

Levi Gersonides (Ralbag)
Milhamot Hashem
    II:2   230

Judah Halevi
Kuzari
    I:1   90n47
    IV:16   259

Yaakov Hillel
Tamim Tihyeh   205n51

Samson Raphael Hirsch
Commentary to the Torah
    Gen. 6:5   251
    Gen. 8:21   271
    Ps. 22:2   288n63
Nineteen Letters of Ben Uziel
    #18   130

Hoffmann, David Zvi
Melammed le-Ho'il
    Yoreh De'ah #104 356

Isaiah Horowitz
Shenei Luhot ha-Berit
    9b-10a (Jozewow, 1878) 204n44

Yitzhak Hutner
Pahad Yitzhak
    Rosh ha-Shanah   269

Abraham Ibn Ezra
Commentary to
    Deut. 22:8   4

Ibn Gabbai, Meir,
Avodat ha-Kodesh
    II: 17   204n44

Moses Isserles (Rama)
glosses on *Shulkhan Arukh*
    Yoreh De'ah 241:3 379n33
    Yoreh De'ah 339   380n50

Avraham Yeshayau Karelitz (Hazon Ish)
Emunah u-Bittahon
    16-17   207n66
Sefer Hazon Ish
    Hoshen Mishpat,
    Likkutim 16:1   321n5
    Likkutim 20   382n65

Joseph Karo
Kesef Mishneh to Maimonides,
    Mishneh Torah, Hilkhot
    Yesodei ha-Torah 5:5 377n16
Shulhan Arukh
    Orah Hayyim
    328   379n34
    618   379n34
    Yoreh De'ah 339   380n50

Shlomo Luria
Yam Shel Shlomoh
    Bava Kamma VIII:58 348, 377n13,
                          377n15

Maharal (R. Judah Loew of Prague)
Netivot Olam, Netiv
    ha-Yissurin, chap. 1 293, 296,
                          302n17
Tiferet Yisrael, ch. 6 351n34

Meir Leibush Malbim
  Commentary to
    Job 10:3-4   14

Menachem ha-Meiri
  Beit ha-Behirah
    Bava Metzi'a 62a   382n65
    Sanhedrin 73a   382n67
    Sanhedrin 84b   379
    Avodah Zarah 20a   222

Nissim of Gerona (Ran)
  Commentary to
    Nedarim 40a   381
    Derashot ha-Ran #10 293, 296

Ovadyah mi-Bartenura
  Commentary to
    the Mishnah
    Avot 1:1   307, 322n12

Radbaz (R. David ben Zimra)
  to Maimonides, *Mishneh
    Torah, Hilkhot
    Sanhedrin* 18:6   355-56
  Responsa,
    #1052, #1582   352n38, 356

Rashbam
  (R. Shmuel ben Meir)   26n62

Rashi (R. Shlomo Yitzhaki)
  Gen. 1:1   18-19
  Gen. 2:7   162
  Gen. 6:6   24n43
  Berakhot 60a   376n6
  Pesahim 50a   377n16

Jacob Reischer
  Shevut Ya'akov
    II:85   379n31
    II:111   377n12
    III:75   379n36

Aharon Szelensky
  Likkutei Batar Likkutei
    6-11   134n21

Tosafot
  Shabbat 50b,
    s. v. *bishvi*   379n33
  Shabbat 55b,
    s. v. *shema mina*   302n20
  Shabbat 156a-b, s.v.
    ein mazzal le-Yisrael 287n54, 302n18
  Mo'ed Katan 28a, s. v.
    *ela ba-mazala talya
    milta*   287n54, 302n18
  Sanhedrin 74b,
    s. v. *ve-ha*   351n35
  Avodah Zarah 18a,
    s. v. *ve-al*   377n13
  Avodah Zarah 27b,
    s. v. *yakhol*   377n11
  Tosafot ha-Rosh,
    Rosh ha-Shanah 18a,
    s.v. *Abbayei
    ve-Rabbah*   287n54, 302n18

Ben-Zion Uziel
  Mishpetei Uziel
    Hoshen Misphat #36 322n19

Eliezer Waldenberg
  Tzitz Eliezer
    IX: 17   381n62
    IX: 45   382n63, 382n68
    X: 25   342-43, 353n45,
                         380n49, 382n63,
                         382n68
    XII: 57   381n62
    XIII: 100   348n9
    XV: 40   376n7
    XVII: 2   376n7
    XVII: 1   380n49
  Ramat Rahel #5   381n56
  Zohar
    Balak 212b   289n66

Shlomo Wolbe
  Alei Shur, I: 156   255n71

The listing under "Other rabbinic literature"
does not include articles published in
various books and journals.

INDEX OF TOPICS AND NAMES

Names that occur in general acknowledgements (those in the introduction and before the first note in each essay) are not indexed.

Honorifics have been omitted except to identify Sages of the Talmud and Midrash and to explain an acronym (e. g., R. David ben Zimra = Radbaz).

After "*See*" and "*See also* ," a semicolon is used to separate between main entries, whereas a comma is used to separate between a main entry and a subentry that appears under that entry.

A

Aaron, 70, 72

Abarbanel, Isaac, 5, 25n51, 199, 205n46, 208n73, 215-16, 222nn16-17

Abel, 10

Abraham, 6-8, 11, 15, 72, 129, 174n65, 261, 264-66, 282n22, 283nn27-28, 284n43

Abraham, Abraham S., 381nn54-55

R. Abraham ben David (Ravad), 230, 241

Abravanel, Isaac *See* Abarbanel, Isaac

Act-morality vs. agent morality (virtue ethics), 29-30, 317-18

Adam, 8-10, 19, 24n28, 28, 63-64, 162, 232, 284n43
    Adam the first, 154-58, 174n65, 175n69
    Adam the second, 154, 157-60, 174n64, 175n71

Adams, Robert Merrihew, 22n12, 246n3, 253n53, 286n46

Academy for Jewish Philosophy, xiii

active vs. passive taking of life, 352n36, 367-69, 381n57, 381n59, 382-83n69
    See also euthanasia; least change principle

Aggadah, xxv, 95, 108, 116n80, 123-24, 135n33, 274, 291, 298-99n1, 310, 315, 382n65

R. Aha, 376n6

Ahad Haam (Asher Ginzberg), 319, 348n7

Akedah (*Akedat Yitzhak*), xvi, xxi, 7-8, 23n18, 23n22, 261, 264-66, 282nn21-22, 283n27, 283n30, 285n43

R. Akiva, xxviii n28, 129, 205n49, 249n18, 288n59, 301n12, 319, 326, 339-41, 346, 348n7, 348n9, 351n35, 352n40, 370, 382n65, 382-83n69

akrasia, 242-43

Al Qaeda, 261, 266

Albo, Joseph, 24n35, 24n44, 307

Aleksandrov, Shmuel, 103

Alfarabi, 33

Alter, Robert, 24n47

Altmann, Alexander, 48n57, 84n4, 88n33, 88nn36-37, 90n44, 90n54, 203n28, 206n57, 207n62, 284n38

altruism, xxiii, 233, 319, 326-47, 347n3, 348n7, 353n50, 357-59, 369-73, 382n64, 409
    blind vs. calculated, 331-37, 342-43, 371-73, 383n71

See also autonomy; ethics, secular; ethics, virtue ethics; halo effects; Horayot priorities

Amalek, 7, 267-68, 283n32, 308-10, 313, 323n23, 332

Amiel, Moshe, 165n1

Amital, Yehuda, 282n19, 285n45

R. Ammi, 272, 286-87nn48-49, 294, 302-303n20

Anscombe, G.E.M. (Elizabeth), 249n14, 349n15

Anselm, 392

anthropology, xviii, xix-xx, 20, 209-20, 221n3, 223n24

anti-Zionism, 134n26, 219, 223n22

Antigonus of Sokho, 198-99, 208nn72-73, 215, 222n13, 222n17

antinomianism, 57, 59, 65, 77, 82, 87n24, 124

Aquinas, Thomas, 338, 347n2, 350n27, 351n34, 241

Arberry, Arthur J., 92n70

Aristotle and Aristotelianism, xvi, xviii, 21n3, 27, 30-35, 41-42, 46n13, 52, 73, 91n63, 101, 133n7, 147, 149, 171n30, 179, 181, 199, 202n14, 207n65, 215, 220n2, 239. 240, 255n71

asceticism, 32-33, 38, 41, 48n41, 48n44, 48n50

astrology, 193-94, 205nn49-50, 206nn55-56, 230-31, 245, 250n26, 250n29, 273, 294

atheism, xxviii n25, 290n75, 395, 407, 411n4

attributes, affirmative 79-80, 140
See also God, attributes of

attributes, negative 139, 140
See also God, attributes of

Audi, Robert, 247n5

Auerbach, Shlomo Zalman, 367-68

autonomy,
    and altruism, 330-46
    descriptive vs. prescriptive, 362-66, 378n22
    in end-of-life decisions, xxiii, xxiv, 367-69
    in Garden of Eden narrative, 9-11
    and heteronomy, xxii, 306, 408
    and naturalism, xix, 187, 209-11, 217-19

    in risk-taking, xxiv, 331-34, 340, 355-57, 370-73
    in secular ethics, xxiii, 182, 327-32, 356-66, 373-75, 375-76n1, 379n38, 380n46, 384n77
    in self-sacrifice, xxiv, 328-32, 357-60, 370-72
    in Soloveitchik, 143
    See also coercion

Avicenna, 82, 85n16

B

Bacon, Francis, 390

Bahya ibn Pakuda, 82, 186, 203n28, 324n32, 92nn71-72

Baier, Kurt, 347n1

Barbour, Ian, 202n16

Barnes, Jonathan, 22n10

Baron, Marcia, 347n3, 350n22

Barten, Michael C., 350n25

Barth, Karl, 23n23, 165, 176n75

Barukh of Shklov, 168n16

Basinger, David, 201n10, 204n41

Basinger, Randall, 201n10, 204n41

Beauchamp, Tom, 276n1, 364, 379n38, 379n40

Begley, Sharon, 248n10

Ben Azzai, 38

Ben Petura, xxviii n28, 351, 370, 382

Ben Yehuda, Eliezer, 132n4

Bennett, Jonathan, xxvi-xxvii n7

Benveniste, Hayyim, 377n16

Benor, Ehud, 44, 49n62, 201n11, 204n43, 222n11

Ben-Sasson, Yonah, 86n18, 88n26, 114n48, 156, 173n56

Ben-Shlomo, Yosef, 111n10

Berger, David, xxvi n4, 21, 83, 132n6, 133-34n17, 204n44, 246n1, 280, 285n44, 286n46, 286n48, 302, 347, 349n13, 352n39, 353n50

Berger, Gedalyah, 287n54, 302n18

Berger, Yitzhak, 246, 252n46

Bergson, Henri, 95, 128

Berkeley, George, 183, 202n14, 202n20, 412

Berlin, Naftali Tzvi Yehuda (Netziv), 307, 320n2, 345, 353n49

Berman, Lawrence, 22n7, 46n6

Besdin, Abraham R., 165n1, 168n11, 175n65, 304n32
biblical criticism, 103, 114n45, 398, 405, 409
Bin Laden, Osama, 277-78
bittahon, see trust in God
Blau, Yitzchak, 246, 267, 280, 283n31, 284n40, 284n42, 285n46, 286n48, 298, 299n1, 301n10, 302n20
Blau, Yosef, 276-77, 280, 289n68
Bleich, J. David, 321n7, 322n13, 350n27, 352n38, 353n44, 376n4, 378nn27-28, 379n31, 379n33, 381n62, 382n63, 384n75
Blidstein, Gerald J., xxvi n4, 87n24, 133n17, 134n26, 154, 162, 173n51, 176n76, 176n78, 176n90, 246n1
Bodoff, Lippman, 32n18, 282n21
Bok, Hilary, 248n14
Boorse, Christopher, 352n36
Borges, Jose Luis, 236
Breisch, Mordekhai Yaakov, 348n8, 379n33, 380n49
Brody, Baruch A., 348n9, 368, 377n9, 377n15, 377n19, 381nn54-55, 382n63
Brody, Robert, 83
Brunner, Emil, xvii, 165
Buber, Martin, 164, 165
Butterworth, Charles, 46n4, 47n14, 48n49, 251n31
Byrne, Peter, xxviii n23

C
Cain, xvi, 10, 24n28
Calvin, John, 269
Campbell, C.A., 252n46
Cantor, Geoffrey, 246n1
capital punishment, 10, 332
Cargile, James, 349n15
Carmy, Shalom, xv, 23nn21-22, 26nn66-67, 110, 111n8, 112n17, 113n23, 116n66, 116n78, 135n32, 136n41, 165, 170n25, 201n11, 246, 252n46, 280, 282n19, 282n25, 283n27, 283n29, 285nn43-44, 287n50, 287n52, 299n1, 301n12, 304n34, 347, 349n12, 354n52, 411
Cassuto, Umberto, 25n53
Chalmers, David, 247n5

Cherry, Shai, 246n1
Childress, James, 364, 376n1, 379n38, 379n40
Chipman, Jonathan, 223n22
Churchland, Patricia, 248n11
Churchland, Paul, 248n11
Clark, Thomas W., 248n10, 249n15, 250n23
coercion, 169n19, 233, 240, 242-43, 255n73, 338, 356, 360-61, 365, 376nn5-6, 378n25, 378n26, 380n48
cognition,
    halakhic, 142-44, 150-54, 160-61, 167n11, 169n21, 170n29, 172-73n44, 173n48, 274
    metaphysical, 4, 27-28, 42, 62-63, 73
    moral, 27-29, 266, 268
    religious, xvii, 98-102, 107
    scientific, 139-44, 148-54, 160-61, 269n21, 170, 172-73n44, 174n58
    See also cognitive man; cognitive pluralism; ethics and morality; intuition; metaphysics; science
cognitive man (in Soloveitchik), 139-41, 147, 155, 160, 168
cognitive pluralism, 128, 143-44
Cohen, Hermann, 48n55, 137n59, 165, 171n35
Cohen, Jeremy, 24n44
Cohen, Tobias, 246n1
Cohn-Sherbok, Daniel, 201n11
compatibilism, 206n57, 234-37, 240-45, 253-54n55, 255n77, 256n80
Cooper, John, 91n63
Copernicus, 224, 243, 246n1
corporeality, xvi, 63-83, 88n31, 89n39, 89n41, 89n43, 92n73. *See also* asceticism
covenantal ethics, 306, 309-12, 314, 317
creation narrative, 3, 9-10, 18-20, 26n62, 26n66, 94, 99, 101, 104, 118, 156, 248n12, 411n5
Crescas, Hasdai, 296, 301n10
Crick, Francis, 225, 247n6

D
Da'at Torah, 314-15
D'Aquila, Eugene, 247n4
Da Vinci, Leonardo, 142

Darwin and Darwinism, 128, 243, 245, 246n1

David, 22n12, 129

R. David ben Zimra (Radbaz), 352n38, 355-56, 376n3, 377-78n20

Davidson, Herbert, 30, 33, 45, 46n10, 47n21, 48n46, 49n63, 49n65

Delmedigo, Yosef Shlomo, 246n1

Dennett, Daniel, 247n6, 252n49, 254n64

Déscartes, René, 390, 411n5

Dessler, Eliyahu
    on *bittahon*, 186-87, 204n42
    on free will, 185, 232-34, 240, 245, 251n41, 252nn46-47
    on hesed, 187
    on hishttadelut, 186, 203n27, 204n42
    as occasionalist, 183-86
    as philosopher, xiv

determinism, xxi, 203n39, 228-49, 249n20, 250n29, 253nn53-54, 254n56
    See also free will

devekut, 146-47, 149, 152-53, 161, 169n21, 170n29, 173n45

Dichovsky, Shmuel, 382n65, 382n68

Diesendruck, Zvi, 90n52

divine providence, 3-4, 15-18, 42, 51-54, 67-76, 90n53, 90n57, 115n49, 143, 147, 159-60, 168-69nn18-19, 179, 185-90, 193-99, 200n5, 204n44, 205n47, 206n58, 209, 214-15, 229, 249n21, 250n25, 286n48, 293, 301n15, 303n20, 325n39, 340, 380n49, 390, 408-409
    See also interventionism; miracles

Dinah, 10

Dore, Clement, 300n9, 304n36

Dostoevsky, Fyodor, 239

Dressler, Joshua, 255n71

dualism (mind-body), 247n5
    See also materialism

Dworkin, Gerald, 379n37

Dworkin, Ronald, xxiii, 404

E

Eden, Garden of, 4, 6, 8, 10, 11, 19, 20, 28, 115n61, 234

Efrati, Shimon, 345, 349n16

Eichrodt, Walther, 26n60

Eisen, Robert, xxvii n14

Ekstrom, Linda, 248n14

Elihu, 12, 24n40

Elijah, 332, 344, 353n46

Elijah of Vilna (Vilna Gaon), 142-43, 168n16

Eliphaz, 14

Elkanah, 166n4

Elman, Yaakov, 24n36, 110, 115n58, 273, 287n52, 301n16

Elon, Binyamin, 115n63, 135n32

Emden, Jacob, 356, 362, 376n6, 378n25, 379n33

end-of-life decisions, xxiv, 219, 245, 367-69, 377n10
    See also euthanasia

Engel, Joseph, 282n20

Engelhardt, H.T., 376n1

Enker, Aharon, 382n65, 383n74

Esau, 17

Esther, 18, 25n56

ethics, *see* ethics and morality

ethics and morality, 46n7, 219, 398, 403
    act morality vs. agent morality, 317-18, 323n20, 324n32, 328-40, 343-45
    in Bible, 4-11, 15, 17, 26n66
    divine command theory, xxii, 6-8, 23n18, 260-67, 306-14, 321n7, 322n13
    independent of Halakhah, xxi, xxii, xxviii n27, 6, 10, 269, 307-309, 320, 321n7, 322n12, 322n15, 351n34
    and religion, 267-71, 290n74
    secular, xii, xxi, xxiii, 310, 317, 322n17, 329-30, 352n36, 356-58, 365, 373-75
    virtue ethics, xxiii, 29-30, 317, 338, 350n26, 353n50
    See also altruism; evil, response to; free will, value of; intuition, moral; Kook, Abraham Isaac, on morality; Maimonides, on moral cognition; moral relativism; Soloveitchik, Joseph B., on morality

euthanasia, 367-69, 380n50, 381n57

Eve, 8-10, 19, 28, 232, 284n43

evil,
    and moral choice, 8-10, 23n26, 28, 40, 44, 232-33, 241-43, 271, 287, 292

problem of, xv, xxi-xxii, 3, 6, 11-15,
181, 184-85, 189, 203n32, 208n68,
211, 223n18, 258, 269-80, 284n41,
288n61, 289n64, 291-98, 300n3,
303n24, 303-304n29, 304n32, 392,
403, 407-408, 411n2, 411n4
response to, xix, 173n52, 174-
75n65, 211, 216, 223n18, 267,
273-80, 288n61, 289n65, 292-95,
300n6, 300n9, 408-409
See also theodicy
evolution, 20, 26n66, 97, 103-106,
112n20, 115n58, 115n61, 118, 125-26,
135n33, 156, 245, 246n1, 256n92, 401
evolutionary philosophy,
see progressivist philosophy
Exodus, 214, 218, 222n9
Ezekiel, 276

F
Fackenheim, Emil, xxvii n9
Falk, Yaakov Yehoshua ben Tzvi Hirsch
(*Penei Yehoshua*), 293, 296, 302n17
fallibilism, xvii, 102-107
Falwell, Jerry, 272
Farber, Roberta Rosenberg, 290n75
fear of God, 56, 61, 65, 73, 82, 84n3,
85n15, 85n17, 88n26, 99, 143-48, 167n7,
190, 244, 249n21, 263-64, 279, 284n40
Feinberg, Joel, 253n50
Feinstein, Moshe,
altruistic self-sacrifice, 340-41,
352n36, 371, 379n35, 381n54,
382n66
end-of-life decisions, 369-73,
376n5, 379n29, 379nn32-33
Horayot principles, 341-42
Feldman, David, 379n41
Feldman, Seymour, 24n44
Feldman, Tzvi, 26n66, 115n53, 135n36,
256n92, 283n26
fideism, 113n27
Fischer, John Martin, 242, 249n19,
253n54, 254n56, 254n59, 256n81
Fishbane, Michael, 24n30, 303n29
Fishbane, Simcha, 20n75
Forking Paths Principle (Principle of
Alternative Possibilities), 236-43,
253-54n55, 254n60

Foster, J., 247n5
Fowler, James, 350n25
Fox, Marvin, xvi, xxvii n15, 46n6, 92n73,
176n84, 201n11, 301n14, 314, 321n4,
321n7, 322n14, 323n25, 348n7, 354n52
Frank, Daniel, 34, 47n27, 47n31, 48n51,
48n53, 251n40
Frankfurt, Harry, 237, 254nn59-60,
254n63, 352n40, 377n16, 382n68
Freddoso, Alfred J., 202nn14-15, 202n17,
202nn20-23, 203n35
Freedman, Benjamin, 384n77
free will,
in Bible, xv, 9, 15-18, 228
existence of, xi, xii, xix-xx, 184,
189, 206nn56-57, 224-30, 233-35,
244-46, 248n12, 250n20, 250n29,
254n56, 403
nature of, xxi, 227, 229-45, 249n20,
251-52n42
value of, xv, xxi, 15, 185, 189-92,
208n70, 213, 228-33, 252n49
See also akrasia; autonomy;
coercion; determinism;
libertarianism; occasionalism;
restrictivism; theodicy, free-will
Freud, Sigmund, xx, 216-18, 223n19,
244, 256n90
Frimer, Dov, 135n34, 354n51, 377n15

G
Galinsky, Yehuda, 287n54, 302n18
Galston, Miriam, 84n6, 85n9
Gans, David, 246n1
Garb, Jonathan, 117n88
Garden of Eden, *see* Eden, Garden of
Gauthier, David, 347n1
Gellman, Jerome (Yehuda), 23n18,
24n34, 85n17, 112n14, 113n37, 137n60,
171n33, 175n66, 175n68, 190, 192,
195, 201n6, 203n36, 205n47, 206n57,
221n2, 249n21, 261, 281n6, 281nn8-10,
281n14, 283n26
genetics, 174n65, 217, 224-31, 236, 243,
249n16, 307, 398
Gersonides, Levi, xiii, 5, 12-14, 22n6,
24n44, 230-31, 241, 251nn34-35, 255n77
Ginzberg, Asher (Ahad Ha-Am), 319,
348n7

Ginzberg, Louis, 298n1
Glatzer, Nahum, 24n38
God,
  ascribing emotions to, 4, 21-22n3, 36, 43-45, 318, 324n34, 351n30
  attributes of, 21n11, 36, 43-44, 53, 60-61, 74-75, 79-80, 84, 139-40, 148, 167n8, 169n21, 284n37, 284n40, 318, 324nn33-34, 324n36, 403
  goodness of, xx, 12, 196, 200, 215, 266, 268, 271, 283-84n37
  justice of, xx, 6, 11, 197-200, 207n66, 211, 215, 279
  plan for world, 16-18, 25n57, 219, 228, 277, 290n69
  See also attributes, negative; attributes, affirmative; creation narrative; divine providence; fear of God; interventionism; love of God; trust in God
Goldberg, Hillel, 132n3
Goldberg, Zalman Nehemyah, 376n7
Goldenberg, Robert, 24n36
Golding, Martin, 324n30
Goldman, Eliezer, 49n60, 84nn3-4, 84n6, 85n15, 86n18, 86n20, 88n31, 88n33, 89n41, 90n48, 90n53, 90n56, 91n68, 111nn9-10, 112n18, 113n36, 114n48, 116n71, 130, 132n6, 133n13, 136n51, 137nn53-55, 172n39, 200n5, 201nn5-6, 202n16, 202n18, 299n1, 324n34
Goodman, Lenn Evan, 24n42
Gotel, Neryah, 376nn6-7, 378nn24-25, 380nn43-44
gratitude, xx, xxi, 214-16, 220, 222n11, 228, 269-70, 284n40, 295, 331
Green, Arthur, 114n37
Green, Ronald, 23n18, 23n20, 282n21, 348n7
Grossman, Avraham, 286n46

H
hakham, 38-39, 42, 353n44
Halakhah,
  and altruism, 327, 337-47, 348n9, 354n51, 354n52
  and autonomy, xxiv, 355-75
  Kook on, 108, 116n77, 116n80, 123-27, 134nn20-21, 134n23, 137n61

  and medical ethics, xxiii, 326-27, 352nn38-40, 355-58, 360-84
  Soloveitchik on, xviii, 141-45, 150-55, 160-64, 167n9, 167nn10-11, 170n22, 171n30, 173n48, 173n52, 175n65, 175n70, 175n72, 208n68, 274-75, 288n61, 298n1, 299n1, 301n14
  Wurzburger on, xxii, 305-306, 308-12, 314-17, 319-20, 322n13
  See also ethics, independent of Halakhah; halakhic man; humrot; philosophy, of Halakhah; Talmud, study of
halakhic man, 142-45, 147, 160, 165, 167n11, 168n15, 169-70nn20-21, 170n23, 173n45
Halbertal, Moshe, 281n7
Halevi, Yehuda, 100, 110-11n6, 145, 259, 260, 270, 280n4, 351n28
halo effects, xxiii, 332-46, 395
R. Hanina ben Teradyon, 355, 381n52
hard naturalism, xix, xx, 188-92, 195-99, 204n40, 204n42
  See also soft naturalism
Harman, Gilbert, 397
Hart, W.D., 247n5
Hartman, David, xxviii n20, 48n48, 86n18, 168n13
  on adequacy and autonomy, 209, 218-19, 223n24
  on anthropology and metaphysics, xx, 209, 211, 213, 220, 223n24
  on Exodus, 214, 218, 222n9
  vs. Freud, xx, 216, 217, 218
  on holidays, 214
  on interventionism, xx, 210-15, 220
  and Joseph Soloveitchik, 210
  on Maimonides, 87-88n25, 91n68, 201n6, 209, 220-21n2
  on passivism, 219
  religious values according to, xx, 210
  on revelation at Sinai, 212, 214, 218
  on secularization and science, 207n64
  and social action, xx, 218-19
  and teleology of mitzvot, 87-88n25, 91n68
  view of God of, 211

and Yeshayahu Leibowitz, 86n18,
201n6, 207n64
Harvey, John W., 24n37
Harvey, Steven, 84n3, 85n16
Harvey, Warren Zev, 49n58, 55, 57,
85n9, 89n36, 89n38, 89n42, 90n47,
91n58, 167n8, 168-69n19
hasid, 32, 38-40, 337, 353n44
Hasidism, 91n65, 121, 183, 229, 232, 245,
249n21, 250n22, 299n1, 388
Haught, John, 256nn90-91
Haworth, Laurence, 329n37
Hayyim of Volozhin, 152-53, 167n11
Hazon Ish (Avraham Yeshayahu
Karelitz), 207n66, 307, 321n5, 321n7,
382n65
Hegel, George, 23n18, 95, 136n52
Heidegger, Martin, 290n71
Helfgot, Nathaniel, 132n7
Henson, Richard, 221n7
Herman, Barbara, 222n7
Herring, Basil, 347n5, 379n28, 370n36,
380n47, 380n50, 381n60, 382n63
Hershler, Moshe, 325n39
Hertz, J.H., 26n66
Herzog, Isaac Halevi, 127, 135n34
Heschel, Abraham Joshua, xxvii n9
hesed, 39, 42-43, 61, 74, 84n3, 172n39,
187, 279
Hess, Moses, 130
heteronomy, xxii, 9-11, 306, 408
Hezekiah, 205n47
Hick, John, 300n7
Hillel, Yaakov, 205n51
Hirsch, Eli, 300n1
Hirsch, Samson Raphael, 136n52, 165n1,
246n1, 251n36, 286n47, 288n63, 308, 311
Hirschfeld, Hartwig, 90n47, 280n4
R. Hisda, 287n54, 302n18
hishtaddelut, 186, 203n27, 204n42
    See also practical endeavor
Hitler, Adolf, xxviii n25, 290n75, 410
Hobbes, Thomas, 347n1
Hoffman, David Zvi, 246n1, 356, 376n6
holidays, 214, 294, 400
Holocaust, 168n11, 269, 289n64, 327,
335, 348n8, 377n16, 407
holy and profane, *see kodesh* and *hol*
homo religiosus, 139-40, 168n15

Hook, Sidney, 204n42
Horayot priorities, 319, 341-43, 352n36,
353n41, 353n43, 371-73, 383n70
Horowitz, Isaiah, 204n44
humanities, xviii, 162-65, 176n77,
176n90, 245
humrot (halakhic stringencies), 123-27,
134n21, 316, 326-27, 344, 346, 353n45,
360, 364, 367
Hume, David, 11, 24n32, 46n12, 182,
184, 201n13, 202n20, 237-38, 242-43,
253n55, 254n61, 392-93
Hutner, Yitzchak, 269, 284n39
Hyman, Israel G. 115n64, 135n31

I

Ibn Atar, Hayyim (*Orah Hayyim*), 24n43
Ibn Ezra, Abraham, 4, 24n46
Ibn Gabbai, Meir, 204n44
Ibn Gabirol, Solomon, xiv
Ibn Pakuda, Bahya, 82, 186, 203n28,
324n32
Ibn Tibbon, Samuel, 70, 90n49, 90n52,
91n68
idealism, 149-50, 172n40, 172n42, 172-
73n44, 173n48
idolatry, 35, 57, 85n11, 99, 184, 206n55,
255n73, 260, 266, 270, 280-81n6,
281n7, 281n11, 403
Idziak, Janine Marie, 22n15
Ifrah, Jeffrey, 381n51
imitatio Dei, 35-36, 39, 41-45, 47n20,
49n65, 61, 84n7, 146, 148-49, 158,
171n35, 172n37, 175n72, 317-18,
324n34, 324n36, 337, 351n30
individualism, 195-96, 207n65
interventionism, xix, xx, 179-99, 203n38,
210-20
    Hartman on, 209
    Leibowitz on, 180
    Maimonides on, 179-84, 189-90,
    192-99, 204n44, 209
    See also divine providence;
    miracles
intuition, 145, 168n17, 237, 240-42, 395
    moral, xxii, 226, 267-71, 306-20,
    321n3, 322n13, 322nn16-17, 328,
    338, 345
    religious, 101

Isaac, 6-7, 17, 72, 261, 265-66, 282n22
   See also Akedah
ish ha-Elokim (in Soloveitchik), 144-45, 170n25
ish ha-Halakha, see halakhic man
Ish-Shalom, Benjamin, 112n14, 112nn17-18, 120-21, 129-30, 132n2, 133n9, 133n12, 133n15, 134n21, 134nn23, 134n25, 136n45, 136nn50-51, 137n54, 137nn59-60, 282n19
Israel, Land of, xxviii n18, 19-20, 93, 111n7, 117n87, 122-23, 125
Israel, State of, 132n1, 214, 217-19, 258, 267, 271, 282n15, 403
Isserles, R. Moshe (Rama), 379n33, 380n50, 381n52
Ivry, Alfred, 73, 91nn61-62

J
Jacob, 10, 16-18, 25n49, 25n55, 45, 72, 175n65, 281n11
R. Jacob, 273, 294
Jacobs, Louis, 22n16, 23nn21-22, 201n13, 346, 348n7
James, William, xiv, 164, 210, 389, 410
Jeremiah, 279
Job, Book of, 4, 6, 11, 15, 22n6, 24n38, 24n42, 169, 242, 272-73, 278, 288n61, 289n64, 294, 296, 301n11, 302n19, 303n24, 409
Jonah, 21n1
Rabbenu Jonah, 222n9
Jones, Jim, 264
Joseph, 10, 16-18, 25nn48-49, 25nn55-57, 144
R. Joshua ben Levi, 332, 344, 349n18, 353n46, 354n50

K
Kabbalah, xiv, 21, 22n8, 26n64, 97, 102, 112n18, 112n20, 114n37, 121-22, 126, 129-30, 133n7, 133n12, 135n33, 137n55, 153, 204n44, 205n44, 250n25, 401
   See also mysticism
Kamin, Sara, 26n62
Kane, Robert, 252n48, 255n68
Kant and Kantianism xviii, xix, 5, 7, 23n18, 97, 133n96, 128-30, 133n12, 149, 151-54, 161, 170n21, 171n30,

174n58, 208n70, 209, 213, 241, 244, 249n14, 255n75, 329, 334, 347n3, 349n12, 350n23, 350n26
   See also neo-Kantianism
Kaplan, Lawrence, 46n9, 47n37, 48nn39-40, 49n58, 85n12, 88n26, 89n34, 89n36, 90n46, 91n65, 111n8, 112n15, 112n17, 113n23, 115n58, 132n4, 133n16, 136n45, 165-66n1, 167n10, 174n61, 201n6, 221n2, 222n10, 280n1, 288n58, 303n24
Kaplan, Mordecai, 200n3, 226, 248n12
Karelitz, Avraham Yeshayahu (Hazon Ish), 207n66, 307, 321n5, 321n7, 382n65
Kariv, Avraham, 354n53
Karo, Yosef, 377n16, 382n65
Katz, Jacob, 115n64
Katz, Jay, 363, 365, 379n39
Katz, Tovia, 246n1
Katzoff, Charlotte, xxvii
Kellner, Menachem, xxvii n9, 22n16, 249n18, 249n21, 251n34, 254n65, 255n74, 255nn76-77, 256n87, 284n42, 348n7
Kierkegaard, Soren, xvi, xvii, 7, 23nn18-19, 138, 165, 176n75, 260-61, 264-65, 281n6, 281n12, 283n28, 388
Kirschenbaum, Aaron, 323n24, 334, 347n5, 350n24, 381n60
Klein-Braslavy, Sara, 91n61, 22n7
Klingemann, Ute, 350n25
kodesh and *hol*, 95, 107-108, 111n10, 127, 260
Kogan, Barry, 48n48, 89nn36-37, 90n47
Kook, R. Abraham Isaac (*Reayah*)
   on Aggadah and Halakhah, 108, 116n80, 123-24
   on akedah, 264-66
   on altruism, 341-43, 352n40, 371-73, 383
   on autonomy, 342-43, 347n6, 352n40, 371-72
   bases views on anthropological and phenomenological considerations, 97, 127, 221n3
   on biblical criticism, 103, 114n45
   on cognition, 98-102, 107, 112n22, 126, 128

creativity of, 95, 110n4
on creativity, 93, 108, 116n80
dialectical thinking of, 108, 115n49,
    115n51, 121, 132n2, 132n6, 244
discrepancies in, 114-15n48,
    115n61, 119, 134n21, 137n61,
    256n92
on evolution, 20, 97, 103-106,
    122n20, 115n58, 115n61, 118, 125-
    26, 135n33, 245, 246n1, 256n92
as fallibilist, xvii, 102-107
on fear of God, 99, 244, 263-64
fideistic aspects of, 113n27
as halakhic decisor, 105, 123-24,
    126, 137n61, 322n19, 341-43,
    352n40, 353n42, 371-73, 382n65,
    382n68, 383n70
on halakhic scholarship, 108,
    116n77
and Jehuda Halevi, 110-11n6
on harmonization, 101-103, 115n49,
    121, 126
on history, 105, 244
humrot (stringencies) of, 123-25,
    134n21
on idolatry, 260, 266, 280-81n6
as Kabbalist, xiv, 97, 102-103,
    112n18, 112n20, 121-22, 126,
    129-30, 133n7, 133n12, 135n33,
    137n55, 260
on *kodesh* and *hol*, 95, 107-108,
    111n10, 127, 260
on the Land of Israel, 93, 111n7,
    117n87, 122-23, 125
on love of God, 99-100, 244
on materialism, 244
vs. medieval thinkers, 94-97, 100,
    127
messianism of, 124-25, 134n25
on metzitzah, 105, 126-27, 135n33
misrepresentation of, xxviii, 119,
    132n3
as monist, 104, 117n87, 134n24
on morality, 263-68, 323n22
as pantheist, xix, 210
on philosophy, 97, 106, 113n27
post-Kantianism of, 133n12
as progressivist philosopher, xiv,
    xvii, 95, 103, 106-107, 112n18,

115n51, 121-22, 127, 129-30,
    133n12, 135n37, 136n44, 137n55
on *rahavut* and *penimiyut*, 100-102
on religious intuition, xvii, 98-102,
    107
on religious passion, 260, 264
secular disciplines, his personal
    study of, xvii, 95, 107-10,
    116n71, 129-30, 136n51, 137n59,
    137n60
on science, xvii, 20, 26n66, 97-99,
    105-107, 112n15, 120, 125-29,
    133n15, 135n33, 135n37, 244-45
and secular Jews, 119, 122, 132n4
on secular studies, 93-104, 108-10,
    116n77, 118, 127-30
and Soloveitchik, xvi, xvii, 107,
    113n27, 121, 128, 133n11, 244
and truth claims, 95-96, 98, 106,
    110, 113n23, 115n41, 119, 127,
    134n23
on women's suffrage, 120, 124,
    322n19
and World War I, 133n13
on Zionism, 111n7, 118, 121-22,
    124-25
Kook, Zvi Yehuda, xxviii n18, 117n86,
    137n59
Koresh, David, 407
Korn, Eugene, 262, 281n7, 282n16,
    282n18, 282n21, 282n24, 284n42
Kramer, Peter D., 225, 247n7
Krauss, Aviva, 171n29
Kreisel, Howard, xxviii n17, 28, 35,
    46nn5-6, 46n11, 47n30, 48nn46-48,
    49n58, 49n61, 49n64, 89n43, 117n88,
    200n2
Krochmal, Nahman, 110n6
Kuhn, Thomas, 116n70, 128, 136n44,
    224, 246n2, 396, 411n3

L
Lamm, Norman, 262-63, 281n11,
    282n17, 282n20, 288n63, 289n64,
    299n1, 321n10, 351n34, 406
Lampronti, Isaac, 246n1
Landes, Daniel, 113n35, 221n6
Laplace, Pierre, 191, 203n39
Leah, 18

least change principle, xxiii, 320, 339-41, 351n35, 352n36, 371, 382n69

Lehmann, James H., 86n18

Leibniz, Gottfried von Wilhelm, 268, 283n36

Leibowitz, Nehama, 23n23, 24n44, 25n55, 86n18, 256n79

Leibowitz, Yeshayahu, xxviii n23, 23n19, 138, 166n3, 168n12, 180-81, 196, 201n6, 201n8, 206n58, 207n64, 216, 281n13, 299n1

Leiman, Shnayer Z., xxvi n4, 22n16, 134n17, 246n1

Leiner, Jacob, 249n21

Leiner, Mordechai Joseph, 249n21

Lerner, Ralph, 205n48

Levenson, Jon D., 26n60, 282n21, 283n28

R. Levi ben Gershon (Ralbag), see Gersonides

Levine, Hillel, 246n1

R. Levitas, 34

Lewinsohn, Jed, 300n1

Lewis, C.S., 192

Lewis, H.D., 203n33

Lewis, Justin Harley, 117n87

Libertarianism, 235

Libet, Benjamin, 249n15, 250n23, 252n43, 248n10

Lichtenstein, Aharon, xxvi n4, 22n16, 133-34n17, 207n67, 223n23, 245, 246n1, 272, 283n 29, 283n32, 283n35, 284n42, 287n50, 288n63, 290n73, 306, 321n4, 321n7, 323n23, 348n7, 350n21, 351n31, 351n32, 405, 412n7

Lichtenstein, Mosheh, 166n4

Lilla, Mark, 281n15

Linzer, Dov, 255n73, 284n39, 321n5

Lipschitz, Israel, 115n58

lishmah, 195, 198-99, 206n61, 208nn72-73, 215, 223n17, 346, 406

Locke, John, 237, 254n57, 254n59

Loeb, Louis E., 202n20

Loewe, Raphael, 348n7

loneliness, 248n13, 289n65, 295, 405

Lorberbaum, Yair, xvi, xxvi n3, xxvii n15, 92n73

Lorberman, Menachem, xxvi n3

love of God, 52, 56, 61-72, 82, 85n17, 87n25, 88n26, 99-100, 143-48, 167n7, 190, 194-95, 212, 215-16, 222n13, 244, 251n41, 259, 263, 279, 280n4, 284n40, 345-46

Lowe, Yehuda Leib (Maharal), 26n61, 293, 296, 301n10, 302n17, 303n24, 304n37, 351n34

Luria, Solomon, 348n9, 377n13, 377n15

Lustiger, Arnold, 167n4, 176n88

Luther, Martin, 328, 269

Luz, Ehud, 112n18

M

MacIntyre, Alasdaire, 128, 324n31, 350n26

Mackie, J.L., 350n20

Maharal (Yehuda Leib Lowy), 26n61, 293, 296, 301n10, 302n17, 303n24, 304n37, 351n34

Maharam (R. Meir of Rothenberg), 345-46, 353n50

Maimon, Solomon, 116n71, 136n51, 172n42

Maimonides, Moses (R. Moses ben Maimon),
    on acting lishmah, 195, 198-99, 206n61, 208n72, 215
    and Alfarabi, 33
    on anger, 35-36
    and antinomianism, 57, 59, 65, 77, 82, 87n24
    and Aristotle, xvi, 27, 30-35, 41-42, 46n13, 73, 91n63, 133n7, 147, 179, 207n65, 220n2
    on asceticism, 32-33, 38, 41, 48n41, 48n44, 48n50
    and autonomy, 353-54, n50, 356, 373, 377n11, 383n74
    as biblical interpreter, 4-5, 11, 22n5, 28
    on bittahon, 194-97, 408
    as compatibilist, 206n57, 241
    on continent man vs. hasid, 39-40
    contradictions in writings of, xxvii, 30, 42-44, 46n5, 48n41, 49n65, 50-53, 73, 76, 83-84n3, 85n14, 92n73, 119, 139
    on corporeality, 63-66, 72-76, 92n73
    on divine attributes, 61, 80, 139, 169n21

on divine providence, 69-70,
90n57, 189-90, 193-96, 200n5,
250n25, 286n48, 303n20, 408
on doctrine of the mean, 34-40,
44-45, 46n5, 46n13, 47n29, 264
esoteric readings of, 43, 78-83,
92n73. *See also* subentry
contradictions in writings of
on fear of God, 56, 61, 65, 73, 82,
84n3, 85n15, 85n17, 88n26,
147-48, 190, 244, 256n87
on free will, 184, 206n56, 229,
231, 234, 241-42, 245, 251n31,
251n39, 255n73, 255n77, 255n79,
299n1
on *hakham*, 38-39, 42, 353n44
on *hasid*, 32, 38-40, 337, 353n44
on human perfection, 50-53, 56,
63-77
on humility, 34, 47n29
on *imitatio Dei*, 36, 41-44, 47n20,
49n65, 61, 84n7, 148, 171n35,
317-18, 324n34, 324n36, 337,
351n30
on individualism, 195-96, 207n65
on intellectual perfection, 27-31,
42-45, 46n5, 46n11, 49n65,
60-64, 68-69, 71, 76, 88n30, 89n40,
169n19, 325n41
on knowledge of God, 139, 142
on love of God, 52, 56, 61, 65,
67-68, 70, 72, 82, 85n17, 87n25,
88n26, 147-48, 171n33, 190,
194-95, 215-16, 222n13, 280n4
on magic and astrology, 193-94,
205nn49-50, 206nn55-56, 230-31,
245
on medicine, 193, 204n42, 205n47
on messianic era, 213
on moral cognition, xvi, 27-45,
46n11, 48n55, 49n65
on morality, 268, 317-18
on Moses and the Patriarchs, 66-72,
78, 84n7
vs. Nahmanides on nature and
providence, 190-91, 204-205n44
naturalism of, 179, 181, 184, 189-90,
192-95, 200n1, 205n47, 221n2,
250n25

on Nazirite, 32-33, 37-38
and negative theology, 11, 41,
167n8
and Neoplatonism, 73, 133n7,
220n2
on ownership principle, 355
on performance of *mitzvot*, 78-83,
86n20, 91n67
and philosophy, 30, 33, 36-37, 40,
65, 76, 86n19, 143, 169n19, 402
on nature and activities of
philosopher, 47n28, 56-59, 65-
66, 69-71, 74-80, 83, 87nn24-25,
324n33
on phronesis, 36, 43-44
on political activity, 44-45, 53, 67-68,
74, 84n7
and pragmatism, 158-59, 175n68,
193
on prayer, 56, 78-83, 85n16, 88n26,
91n65, 201n11, 222n11
on prophecy, 179
and rationalism, 181-82, 194,
206n55, 280n4
reconciles tradition and
philosophy, xvi, 33-37, 40, 388
on repentance, 337
on scientific study, 169n21, 196
on self-interest, 195-96, 207n65
study of, 401-403
and Sufism, 34-35, 82, 89n42, 90n50
on teleology of *mitzvot*, 28, 36-37,
40, 54-61, 64-66, 76-77, 84n8,
85n11, 85-86n17, 86n19, 87nn24-
25, 88n26, 89n39, 172n37, 205n44,
325n33, 351n27, 351n34
on theodicy, 289n64, 301n15, 303n21
on theory of the soul, 46n12
on World to Come, 213, 222n8
See also Soloveitchik, on
Maimonides; Wurzburger,
on Maimonides
Malbim, Meir Leibush, 14
Malebranche, Nicolas, 183, 202nn19-20
mamzer, 308-10, 313, 341
Manekin, Charles, xxvii n14, xxviii n23,
230, 241, 249n18, 249n21, 250n28,
251n34, 251n35, 251n40, 254n65,
255n74, 255nn76-77, 256n87

martyrdom, 259, 270-71, 280n4, 285nn45-46, 285-86n46, 345-46, 353n50, 357, 359, 372-73, 377n11, 383n74

Marx, Karl, 217

Masada, 354n51

materialism, xx, xxi, 224-32, 244-45, 247n5, 248n9, 248n14, 250n25

mazzal, 302n18, 204n40, 230, 287n54

McCracken, Charles J., 202n20

mean, doctrine of, 31-40, 44-45, 46n5, 46n13, 264

medical treatment, use of, 154, 159, 173n52, 193, 204n42, 205n47, 219

Meier, Menahem, 207n62

R. Meir, 282n20

Meiri, *see* Menahem ha-Meiri

Meiselman, Moshe, 379n30

Menahem ha-Meiri, 222n9, 287n7, 379n33, 382n65, 382n67

Menahem Mendel of Rymanov, 289n67

messianism, 125, 134n25, 218-19

metaphysics,
    and anthropology, xix-xx, 179-83, 209-12
    after Kant, xix, 209
    knowledge of in Maimonides, 4, 27-28, 42, 62-63, 73
    See also anthropology

methodological conservatism, 397-98

metzitzah, 105, 115nn63-64, 126-27, 135n33

Michelangelo, 142

middat hasidut, 306, 327, 338, 340, 343, 371

militant Orthodox, 218

Mill, John Stuart, 253n55, 283-84n37, 284n40, 363

miracles, xix-xx, 4, 154, 179, 180-82, 189, 192-93, 200nn1-2, 201n7, 201n9, 210, 214
    See also divine providence; interventionism

Miriam, 70, 72

Mises, Fabius, 116n71, 136n51

mitzvot,
    performance of , 36-37, 77-83, 86n20, 91n67, 305-7, 389
    teleology of, 28, 36-37, 40, 54-61, 64-66, 76-77, 84n8, 85n11, 85-86n17, 86n19, 87-88nn24-25, 88n26,

89n39, 91n68, 172n37, 205n44, 299n1, 304n32, 324n32, 337, 350n27, 325n33, 351n27, 351n34

Mizrachi movement, 156

Mizrachi, Eliyahu, 26n61

Molière, 336

monism, 95-96, 103-104, 110, 117n87, 134n24

Monroe, Kristen R., 350n25

Moore, Michael, 255n71

morality, *see* ethics and morality

moral relativism, 277-78, 307, 310, 321n9, 323n22

Morgenbesser, Sidney, 252n49, 406

Morell, Samuel, 323n24

Morris, Paul, 23n23

Morris, Thomas, 202n14, 290n71, 412n6

Moses, 26n62, 44, 47n29, 48n50, 53, 66-76, 78-81, 83, 84n7, 89n43, 90n47, 129, 148

R. Moses ben Maimon (Rambam), *see* Maimonides

R. Moses ben Nahman (Ramban), *see* Nahmanides, Moses

Munk, Reinier, 172n40

Mussolini, Benito, xxviii n25, 290n75

mysticism, xvii, 88n32, 91n65, 102-103, 106, 110, 121-22, 133n15, 204, 208n68, 260, 400
    See also Kabbalah

N

Naftali Horowitz of Ropshitz, 289n67

Nagel, Thomas, 347n1

Nahman of Bratzlav, 100, 114n37

Nahmanides, Moses (Moses ben Nahman; Ramban)
    on divine providence, 17, 190, 204n44
    on free will, 17, 25n55, 25n57, 232-33, 245, 289n69, 290n71
    on independent ethic, 10, 306-307, 310, 316-17, 320, 321n3, 322n15, 324n29
    and kabbalah, 26n64, 204-205n44
    vs. Maimonides, 204-205n44
    as philosopher, xiv
    on practical endeavor, 17, 203n30, 205n49, 205n51, 219

on teleology of *mitzvot*, 205n44, 324n32, 337, 350n27, 351n34
on theodicy, 14, 19, 278-79, 286n48, 302n20
on truth of Bible, 19-20
Napoleon, 220, 276, 289n67
Narboni, Moses, 70-71, 90n53, 90n55
naturalism, xix, xx, 18, 69-70, 90n57, 159, 179-200, 200nn1-3, 200-201nn5-6, 201n11, 203n35, 204n40, 204n42, 204n44, 205n43, 206n60, 207n66, 209-11, 215-18, 221n2, 226, 248n9, 248n12
  hard vs. soft, *see* hard naturalism; soft naturalism
Nazis, 236, 271, 278, 290n71, 322n13, 344, 407
Nazirite, 32-33, 37-38
negative theology, 41, 167n8
Neher, Andre, 246n1
Nehorai, Michael, 124-25, 132n4, 134n21, 134n25
Neo-Kantianism, 151-52, 171n30
Neoplatonism, 73, 82, 133n7, 220n2
Netziv, *see* Berlin, Naftali Tzvi Yehuda
Neuberger, Yaakov, 135n33
neuroscience, xx, xxi, 224-31, 243-44, 248nn10-11
Newberg, Andrew, 247n4
Newton, Isaac, 171n34, 248n12
Nieto, David, 246n1
R. Nissim of Gerona (Ran), 293, 296, 301n10, 302n17, 303n24, 303n27, 304n37
Noah, 10
Novak, David, 381n62
Nozick, Robert, 243, 248n8, 251-52n42

O

occasionalism, xix, 182-89, 199, 202nn14-15, 202n17, 202n23, 208n68
Oliner, Pearl, 350n25
Oliner, Samuel, 350n25
Ormsby, Eric L., 47n27, 89n36, 206n57
Oshry, Ephraim, 348n8, 353n43, 377n14
Otto, Rudolf, 12, 24n37
Ovadyah mi-Bartenura, 249n18, 307, 321n7, 322n12
ownership principle, 355, 358-60, 372, 377-78n20, 379n29

P

pantheism, xix, 133n15, 145, 210
passivism, 194, 219-20, 223n22
Patriarchs, 6, 20, 53, 66-72, 74-76, 78-81, 83, 84n7, 270
Peli, Pinchas, 168n17, 250n27, 254n62, 255n69, 299n1, 351n28
Pellegrino, E., 384n75
Penei Yehoshua (Ya'akov Yehoshua ben Tzvi Hirsch Falk), 293, 296, 302n17
penimiyyut and *rahavut*, 100-102
Pereboom, Derek, 253n50, 253n52
Perkins, Robert L., 23n22
Peterson, Michael, 201n13
Pharoah, 233
Philo, 4, 403
Philosophy,
  analytic, xi-xii, xv, xix-xx, xxvii n14, 182, 209, 300n1, 395, 405
  ancient, 5, 224, 317
  in Bible, xvi, 4-21, 21n1
  Christian, xx, 6, 26n66
  Continental, xv, xix
  of Halakhah, xii, xxii, 291-98, 298-99n1
  history of, xiii-xiv, xxvi-xxvii nn6-7, 391
  instrumentalist philosophy of science, 156
  Islamic, 6, 33, 183
  of law, xxii-xxiii, xxvii n12, 317
  medieval, xvi-xvii, 94-97, 100, 102-103, 127, 155, 230, 241, 250n25
  phenomenological, 144, 150, 163-64, 293-94, 299n1, 301n13
  philosophers and thinkers, xiv-xv
  political, xxvi n3, 392
  realism, *see* realism
  relationship between Jewish and non-Jewish, xi-xii, xvi-xviii, 94, 97, 101
  of religion and theology, xi-xii, xv, xxiv, xxvi n1, xxvii, 139, 182, 210, 395-98, 411n2, 411n5, 412n5
  and religious life, 387-411
  Romantic, 5
  of science, 182, 391
  studying vs. doing, xii-xiv, xxvi nn6-7, xxvii n9

Yehuda Halevi on, 259
See also Aristotle and
Aristotelianism; ethics; Kant
and Kantianism; Neoplatonism;
metaphysics; Maimonides,
and philosophy; Maimonides,
on philosopher; progressivist
philosophy; rationalism;
Soloveitchik, Joseph B.,
on philosophy; theodicy
phronesis, 36, 43-44
physicalism, *see* materialism
Pines, Zalman, 352n40
Pines, Shlomo, 22n4, 42-43, 45n2, 48n56,
49n65, 63, 71, 73-74, 83n1, 83-84n3,
84n6, 89nn35-36, 89n43, 90n48,
91nn-60-62, 91n68, 171n33, 172n39,
206n57, 250n30
Plantinga, Alvin, 248n12, 395, 411n1
Plato, 6, 99, 106, 113n30, 241, 255n75,
307, 321n8, 358, 405
Plotinus, xiv
pluralism, xxii, xxviii n21, 319-20,
325n41, 396, 398
See also cognitive pluralism
post-modernism, xxviii n16, 278, 398,
403
post-modern Orthodoxy, 128, 136n44
Potiphar, 18
Potok, Chaim, 389
practical endeavor, 146, 154, 158-59,
175n68, 180, 193, 203n27, 204n42
See also hishtaddelut
prayer, xix, 56, 78-83, 85n16, 88n26,
91n65, 181-82, 185, 188-89, 192, 196-
97, 201n11, 203n33, 204n40, 204n42,
211-12, 217, 222n9, 222n11, 257, 273,
289n64, 294, 297, 299n1, 301n15, 388,
394
Principle of Alternative Possibilities
(PAP), *see* Forking Paths Principle
progressivist philosophy, xiv, xvii,
95, 103, 106-107, 112n18, 115n51,
121-22, 127, 129-30, 133n12, 136n44,
137n55
prophets and prophecy, 4-6, 11, 17-18,
22n15, 31, 38-39, 44, 48n45, 49n64, 52,
55, 64, 72, 79, 91n59, 104, 108, 123-24,
143, 146-48, 160, 168nn18-19, 170-

71n29, 179, 189, 193, 200n1, 206n55,
250n25, 269, 277
Pulgar, Isaac, 230
punishment,
and determinism, 236, 239, 249n16
for sin, 12, 64, 85n11, 179-80, 187,
189-91, 194-99, 204n41, 204n44,
206n56, 208n73, 211, 214-17,
222n13, 222-23nn16-17, 233,
272-73, 287n49, 289n64, 291,
295-97, 301n15, 302-303nn19-20,
304n31, 378n23, 403, 408. *See also*
theodicy, retributivist
utilitarian vs. retributive,
253nn50-51

Q
quantum physics, 235
Quinn, Phillip L., 202n15

R
Rabbah, 287n54, 302n18
Rabin, Yitzchak, 276
Rabinovitch, Nahum L., 25n51, 354n52
Rabinowitz, Gedaliah A., 376n5, 378n25
Rachel, 18, 181n11
Rachels, James, 352n36, 381n57
Radbaz (R. David ben Zimra), 352n38,
355-56, 376n3, 377-78n20
Radbruch, Gustav, 290n71
Raffel, Charles, 90n53, 91n63, 206n58
rahavut and *penimiyut*, 100-102
Rakeffet-Rothkoff, Aharon, 167n6,
176n81
Rakover, Nachum, 347n5
Rama (R. Mosheh Isserles), 379n33,
380n50, 381n52
Rambam, *see* Maimonides
Ramban, *see* Nahmanides
Ran (R. Nissim of Gerona), 293, 296,
301n10, 302n17, 303n24, 303n27,
304n37
Rashbam (R. Shmuel ben Meir), 26n62
Rashi (R. Shlomo Yitzhaki), 18-20,
24n43, 24n45, 26n61, 26n62, 162,
222n9, 376n6, 377n16
rationalism, xvii, 3-9, 22n8, 28, 30, 45,
46n12, 51, 59, 73, 94, 98-100, 106,
113n27, 121, 136n44, 138-39, 171n30,

181-82, 186, 194, 206n55, 210, 241-44, 248n9, 255n75, 259, 260-67, 277, 280n4, 307, 319, 347n1, 362-68, 374-75, 390-99, 401
Rav, 205n49, 273, 294
Rava, 204n40, 250n26, 287n54, 302n18
Ravad (R. Avraham ben David), 230, 241
Ravitzky, Aviezer, xxviii, 113n22, 115n61, 133n15, 134n26, 136n39, 147, 150-52, 161, 170n21, 171n31, 172n37, 172nn40-43, 173n46, 173n48, 173n50, 223n22
Ravizza, Mark, 254n59
Rawidowicz, Simon, 90n53
reactive attitudes, 228, 234-36, 249n17, 253n50, 254n56
realism, xix, 147-51, 153, 159, 172n40, 182, 202n15
Rebecca, 17-18
Reines, Yitzchak Yaakov, 125, 134n21, 165n1
Reischer, Jacob, 377n12, 379n36
Reisner, Avram Yisrael, 378n22
relativism, moral, *see* moral relativism
repentance, 30, 164, 168n18, 238, 252n47, 276, 289n64, 294-95, 296-98, 299n1, 301n15, 337, 357, 368
rescue and rescue missions, xxiii, 36, 326-29, 331, 334-42, 348n8, 352n39, 376n7, 377n18, 382n64
    priorities in, 319, 341-43, 352n36, 353n41, 353n43, 371-73, 383n70
responsibility, 10, 16, 18, 21, 157-59, 174n65, 180, 186-90, 194, 196, 207n64, 210-19, 228-30, 234-42, 247n7, 249n17, 253n53, 254n56, 255n73
    See also evil, response to
restrictivism, 234
reward, 85n11, 179-80, 187, 189-99, 204nn40-41, 204-205n44, 206n56, 208n73, 211, 213-18, 222n13, 222-23nn16-17, 233, 239, 249n16, 271-74, 287n53, 292, 294, 301-302n17, 318, 378n23, 408
risk taking, xxiv, 260, 326-44, 352nn38-39, 353n43, 356-75, 380n46, 380n49, 382nn63-64
Robinson, Howard, 248n9
Robinson, Ira, 49n58, 89n36, 201n6, 221n2

Rorty, Richard, 128
Rosenak, Avinoam 137n61
Rosenbaum, Irving, 348n8
Rosenberg, Shalom, 111n8, 112n14, 112n18, 113n36, 115n61, 116n71, 133n15, 136n51, 137n54, 137n56, 282n19
Rosensweig, Michael, 351n27
Rosner, Fred, 352n38, 376n1, 379n29, 379n41, 382n63
Ross, Tamar, xxviii n16, xxviii n24, 112n15, 112n17, 112n22, 116n67, 133n16, 221n3, 256n86
Roth, Leon, 324n36
Rudavsky, Tamar, 24n44, 91n62
Ruderman, David, 246n1
Russell, Bertrand, 395, 399, 404

S

Sa'adyah Ga'on, 4, 5, 24n42, 28, 250n22, 269, 284n38, 307
Sabbath (Shabbat), 20, 26n62, 123, 134n21, 274-75, 316, 379n34, 379n43, 394, 400, 406
Sacks, Jonathan, 136n40, 170n22, 170n24, 174n58, 350n26
Sagi, Avi, xxviii n23, 167n8, 168n12, 173n47, 176n90, 283n32, 321n7, 322n12, 323n23
Salanter, Israel, xiv, xxvii n12, 338
Samuelson, Norbert, xxvii n10, 324n30, 353n44
Satan, 12-13
Saul, 7, 22n12, 332, 348n9, 349n19, 377nn14-15
Sawyer, Debra, 23n23
Schachter, Herschel, 379n35, 381n58
Scheffler, Samuel, 349n10
Scheler, Max, xvii, 164-65
Schelling, Freidrich Wilhelm Joseph, 95, 116n71, 136n51
Schimmel, Solomon, 234, 239, 242, 252n45, 255n70, 256n82
Schlesinger, George N., 201n13, 412n6
Schlossberger, Eugene, 253n52
Schneerson, Sholom Dov Beer, 223n22
Schopenhauer, Arthur, 128
Schreiber, Aaron, 253n51
Schwartz, Dov, 250n26

Schwartz, Jeffrey M., 248n10
Schwarzschild, Steven S., 48n48
Schweid, Eliezer, 116n71, 136n51, 141, 165n1, 167n11, 168n12
science,
    ethical dimension of, 158-61
    and halakhic man, 139-44, 170n21
    Kook on, xvii, 20, 26n66, 97-99, 105-107, 112n15, 120, 125-29, 133n15, 135n33, 135n37, 244-45
    Kuhn on, 128, 136n44, 224, 396
    in Maimonides, 169n19, 169n21, 196
    medical treatment, use of, 154, 159, 173n52, 193, 204n42, 205n47, 219
    naturalism and, *see* naturalism
    Soloveitchik on, 138-65, 167nn8-9, 167n10, 168n15, 168n17, 169n19, 169n21, 170nn22-23, 170n28, 171n37, 172n37, 172n39, 173n48, 173n56, 174-75n65, 175n72, 176n90, 196, 246n3, 405
    See also miracles; technology; *Torah u-Madda*
Seeskin, Kenneth, xvi, xxvii n9, xxvii n15, 23n17, 24n41, 48n54, 92n73, 201n9, 201n13, 398
Segal, Aaron, xxvii n13, 301n13, 303n21, 304n33
Segal, Atara, 283n36
Seidel, Moshe, 103, 117n86, 125
Seif, Yehuda, 176n80
September 11th (9/11), 257-58, 269, 271, 276, 279, 288n63
Septimus, Bernard, 49n66, 175n66, 206n55
Shapira, Kalonymus, 284n41
Shapira, Meir, 281n11
Shapiro, David, 111n8
Shatz, David, 49n58, 111n8, 112n15, 112n17, 113n23, 132n4, 133n16, 136n45, 170n25, 175n66, 203n31, 205n51, 223n18, 223n20, 248n9, 248n13, 249n19, 251n40, 252n42, 252n46, 254n65, 284n43, 288n58, 299n1, 376n2, 380n46
Shem Tov, 70, 85n11
Shilo, Shmuel, 351n32
R. Shimon bar Yochai, 129
Rabban Shimon ben Gamliel, 40

R. Shimon ben Lakish, 354n50
Shnayer Zalman of Lyadi, 250n22
Shuchat, Raphael, 246n1
Sihon, 15, 233
Simon, Leon, 325n40, 348n7
Sinai, 10-11, 26n62, 129, 212-14, 218, 220, 269, 308, 322n12
Sinclair, Daniel B., 376n6, 377n9, 380n43, 380n50
Singer, David, 167n11, 175n71
Singer, Isaac Bashevis, 234
Skinner, B.F., 242, 248n12, 397
slavery, 307, 310-12
Slifkin, Natan, 246n1
Slote, Michael, xxiii, 328, 331, 349n10, 349n14
social action, xx, 216-19
    See also pragamaticism
Socrates, 5, 22n10, 224, 358-59
Sodom, 6, 11
soft naturalism, xx, 189, 195-97, 203n35, 204n44
    See also hard naturalism
Sokol, Moshe, 132, 167n11, 175n71, 241, 255n77, 296, 303n29, 320, 325n39, 325n41, 351n35, 353n41, 382n65, 383n70
Sokolow, Moshe, 113n35
Solomon, 40
Solomon, Norman, 167n11
Soloveichik, Ahron, 283n32
Soloveitchik, Haym, 286n46, 353n50, 377n13
Soloveitchik, Joseph B. ("The Rav"; RYD = Rav Yosef Dov)
    and Aggadah, 299n1
    on *bittahon*, 208n68
    on cognition, 138-42, 144, 148-54, 156, 158, 160-62, 167n7, 167n11, 169n21, 170nn28-29, 172n44, 173n48, 173n50, 174n58
    on cognitive man, 139-41, 147, 155, 160, 168
    on cognitive pluralism, 128, 143-44
    on community, 156-58, 161, 163-64, 174n65, 196, 207n63
    on creativity, 141, 143-45, 153, 155, 160-61, 168n19, 169n19, 175n72, 274

on devekut, 146-47, 149, 152-53,
    161, 169n21, 173n45
dialectical thought of, 121, 138,
    145, 154, 165, 244, 258
on evil, xxi, 216, 223n18, 258,
    274-75, 277-79, 289n64, 289n65,
    295-96, 303n24, 304n32
on evolution, 156
as fideist, 113n27
on free will, 25n57, 238-39
on Halakhah, 141-45, 150-54, 155,
    160, 163-64, 167n9, 167nn10-11,
    170n22, 171n30, 173n48, 173n52,
    175n65, 175n70, 175n72, 274-75,
    288n61, 298n1, 299n1, 301n14
on halakhic man, 142-45, 147, 160,
    165, 167n11, 168n15, 169-70nn20-
    21, 170n23, 173n45
on *homo religiosus*, 139-40, 168n15
on humanities, xviii, 162-65,
    176n77, 176n90
on idealism, 149-50, 172n40,
    172n42, 172-73n44, 173n48
on identity of knower and known,
    147, 149-50, 152-53, 170n29,
    173n48
on *imitatio Dei*, 146, 149, 158,
    172n37, 175n72
on ish ha-elokim, 144-45, 170n25
and Kook, xvi, xvii, 107, 113n27,
    121, 128, 133n11, 244
and liberal Judaism, 141, 144, 167n11
on love and fear of God, 145, 148,
    167n7
and Maimonides, xviii, 139-40,
    142-43, 145-47, 149, 150, 153,
    156, 158-61, 164, 167n8, 168-
    69nn17-19, 169n21, 171n30,
    172n37, 172n39, 173n50, 337
on majesty and humility, 154-55,
    210, 244
on man-natura vs. man-persona,
    232, 248n13
and medieval tradition, 138, 147,
    153, 155-58, 170n22
on morality, 138-49
and Nahmanides on theodicy, 278-79
on natural consciousness, 145,
    170n28

phenomenology of, 144, 150, 163-64,
    299n1, 301n13
on philosophy, 162-65, 176n90
on physicalism, 232
on practical initiative, 154-56, 159,
    173n56, 214
on prayer, 257, 294, 299n1
on prophecy, 143, 146-48, 160,
    168nn18-19, 170-71n29
on providence, 168-69n19, 214
and realism, 150-51, 153, 159, 172n40
on religious experience, 163
on repentance, 164, 168n18, 238,
    276, 294, 296-97, 299n1, 337
on responsibility, 159, 174n65
on revelational consciousness, 145,
    120n27
as role model, 403-405
on science, 138-61, 167nn8-9,
    167n10, 168n15, 168n17, 169n19,
    169n21, 170nn22-23, 170n28,
    171n37, 172n39, 173n48, 173n56,
    174-75n65, 175n72, 176n90, 196,
    246n3, 405
on teleology of *mitzvot*, 172n37,
    299n1, 304n32
on teleology of nature, 148-49, 153,
    159, 172nn37-38
on theodicy, 216, 223n18, 274, 278,
    288n61, 297, 300n6, 301n14
on Torah study, 141-42, 146, 152,
    155, 168n14
and *Torah u-Madda*, 139, 162, 164-65,
    166n4
on Zionism, 125, 134n26, 156
See also Adam, the first; Adam,
    the second; Wurzburger, Walter,
    on Soloveitchik
Sorensen, Roy, 353n36
Spero, Shubert, 174n65, 247n5, 299n1,
    301n14, 321n7, 325n42, 346-47,
    354n52
Spiegel, Shalom, 283n30
Spinoza, Benedict, xxvi-xxvii n7, 5,
    22n9, 128, 175n66, 201n9, 241
Stalin, Josef, xxviii n25, 290n75
Statman, Daniel, 321n7, 322n12
Steinberg, Avraham, 352n38, 375,
    376n1, 378n21, 382n63, 384n76

Steinberg, Milton, 23n21
Steiner, Mark, xiv, xxvii n12, 300n1
Steinmetz, Devorah, 24n31
Stern, Josef, 47n34, 73, 78, 80, 85n12,
    85n14, 86n18, 86nn21-22, 87n24,
    91n61, 91n65, 241, 255n76, 255n78,
    256n87, 283n32, 384n74, 412n6
Sternbuch, Moshe, 252n35, 371, 377n17,
    382n66
Strauss, Leo, 92n73
Strawson, P.F., 249n17, 253n50
Stump, Eleonore, xxvii n14, 290n71,
    290n74
Sufism, 34-35, 82, 89n42, 90n50
suicide, 259, 286n46, 328, 330, 334, 345,
    348n9, 357-58, 369, 374, 376n7
suicide bombers, 259, 261, 270-71,
    282n15, 285n45
supernaturalism, 204n42, 213, 217
Swetlitz, Marc, 246n1
Swinburne, Richard, 201n13, 247n5
Swirsky, Michael, 223n22
Sykes, David, 23n27
Szelensky, Aharon, 134n21

T
Ta'amei ha-mitzvot, see mitzvot, teleology
    of
Talmud, study of, 152, 160-62, 168n12,
    168n14, 175n71, 387-88, 394, 400-405,
    409
Ta-Shema, Israel, 286n46
Taylor, Charles, 398
technology, xix, 96, 112n15, 133n11,
    154-61, 173n52, 175n65, 175n70,
    176n90, 182n, 202n16, 244, 404
    See also science
Tendler, Moshe, 325n38, 379n29, 380n49
Tennant, F.R., 191-92, 204n41
theism, xix, 179, 184, 200n3, 210, 226,
    300n9, 392, 395-96, 398, 409, 411n4
theodicy, xii, xxi, xxii, 11-15, 181, 185,
    216, 223n18, 272-79, 287n48, 287-
    88n57, 288n61, 289n64, 291, 300nn4-6,
    301n14, 301n15, 303n20, 411n4
    free-will, 292-93
        retributivist, xxii, 12, 273, 287n48,
        289n64, 294, 297-98, 300n5, 301n15,
        302n19, 303nn20-21, 304n33

soulmaking, xxii, 13, 24n40,
    287n57, 292-94, 297-98, 300nn6-7,
    300n9, 301nn11-12, 302n17
Thomasma, D.C., 384n75
Torah u-Madda, xxv, 121, 139, 162, 164-65,
    166n4, 387, 404
Tosafists, 287n54, 302n18, 302n20,
    351n35, 377n11, 377n13, 379n33
triage, see rescue and rescue missions
Trible, Phyllis, 23n22
trust in God (bittahon), xx, 159, 186-87,
    193-97, 204n42, 205n47, 205n51, 207-
    208nn66-68, 218, 220, 223n23, 257,
    376n6, 378n24, 407-408
    See also bittahon
truth claims, 95-96, 98, 106, 110, 113n23,
    115n41, 119, 127, 134n23
Turnus Rufus, 301n12
Twain, Mark, 254n64
Twersky, Meir, 299n1
Twersky, Yitzchak (Isadore), 48n48,
    48n56, 84n3, 162, 175n66, 176n77,
    200n2, 204n44, 206nn54-55, 286n48,
    302n20
Tzadok ha-Kohen of Lublin, 249n21
Tzelofhad, 10, 284n43

U
Unterman, Isser Yehudah, 168n11,
    351n31, 352n35, 371, 382n66
Urbach, Ephraim, 24n36, 249n18
Urmson, J.O., 46n13, 347n3, 349n13
Uziel, Ben-Zion, 127, 322n19

V
Van Inwagen, Peter, 26n66, 252n44,
    252n46, 254n58, 254n64, 411n1
Van Till, Howard, 248n12
Vilna Gaon, see Eliyahu of Vilna
Vogel, Dan, 275, 288n62, 304n30
Von Rad, Gerhard, 26n60

W
Wagner, Steven, 248n9
Waldenberg, Eliezer (Tzitz Eliezer),
    342-43, 347n6, 348n9, 353n45, 376n6,
    380n49, 381n56, 381n62, 382n63,
    382n68
Walzer, Michael, xxvi n3

Warner, Richard, 248n9
Warnock, G.J., 347n1
Watson, Gary, 256n83
Waxman, Kenneth, 25n54
Wein, Berel, 324n27
Weinberg, Yehiel Yaakov, 347n6, 371, 382n67
Weiss, Joseph, 91n65
Weiss, Raymond, 46n4, 46n6, 47n14, 47nn28-29, 47nn36-38, 48n49
Werner, S.B., 382n65
Wettstein, Howard, xxviii n23, 253n53, 286n46
Widerker, David, 254n60
Williams, Bernard, 349n10
Wolbe, Shlomo, 239, 255n71
Wolf, Susan, 254n64, 255nn66-67, 255n77, 256n84
Wolfson, Harry, xxvi-xxvii n7
Wollner, R.S., 380n43
Wolowelsky, Joel B., 25n55, 223n18, 287n53, 288n58, 289n69, 299n1, 302n17
women's rights, 120, 124, 132n1, 307, 311, 322n19, 323n20
Wood, Allen, 256n84
World to Come, 213, 222n8, 285n45, 368
worship of God, 52-68, 72, 77, 79-82, 84n5, 85n11, 86nn17-18, 86n20, 88n26, 90n46, 91n60, 91n68, 180-81, 190, 194-99, 206n58, 211-12, 216, 265, 269-72, 284n37
Wrathall, Mark, xxviii n23
Wurzburger, Walter, 25n55, 134n22, 134n26, 202n16, 284n42, 289n69
on act morality vs. agent morality, 317-18
on covenantal ethics, 306, 309-12, 314, 317
on Da'at Torah, 314-15
on ethical intuition, xxii, 305-13, 316, 321n7, 322n13, 322n16
on ethical subjectivity, xxii, 307-308, 311-13, 323n20
on Halakhah, xxii, 305-306, 308-12, 314-17, 319-20, 322n13
on *imitatio Dei*, 318, 324n33
on Maimonides, 317-18, 324nn32-34, 325n41, 350n26, 351n33
on pluralism, 319-20, 325n41
on rationalism, 182
on ritual law, 316
and Soloveitchik, 136n34, 305, 319
Wyschogrod, Michael, 8-10, 23n24, 23n26

Y
Yaron, Zvi, 111n8, 112n16, 114n45, 114n48, 132n5
R. Yitzhak, 19, 26n62
Yitzhaki, R. Shlomoh, *see* Rashi
R. Yohanan, 354n50
Yosef, Ovadiah, 352n37

Z
Zionism, 111n7, 121-22, 125, 134n26, 156, 219, 223n22
Zevin, Shlomo Y., 116n72
Ziegler, Reuven, 170n25, 223n18, 283n29, 288n58, 299n1
Zimmerman, Dean, xxvii n13
Zimmerman, Michael J., 253n53, 254n63
Zohar, Noam J., xxvi n3

DAVID SHATZ is Professor of Philosophy at Yeshiva University. He has authored, edited, or co-edited thirteen books, dealing with both Jewish and general philosophy. His work in general philosophy focuses on the theory of knowledge, free will, ethics, and the philosophy of religion, while his work in Jewish philosophy addresses a variety of areas, most of them represented in this volume. His books include *Rabbi Abraham Isaac Kook and Jewish Spirituality; Judaism, Science and Moral Responsibility; Peer Review: A Critical Inquiry;* and three anthologies in the philosophy of religion. He is editor of *The Torah u-Madda Journal*, a publication devoted to the interaction between Judaism and general culture, as well as editor of a book series, thus far ten volumes, which present previously unpublished manuscripts of Rabbi Joseph B. Soloveitchik. He earned his Ph.D. with distinction in general philosophy from Columbia University and ordination from the Rabbi Isaac Elchanan Theological Seminary. In recognition of his achievements as a scholar and teacher, he was awarded the Presidential Medallion at Yeshiva University.

Breinigsville, PA USA
14 January 2010
230680BV00004B/1/P

9 781934 843420